All in One®

A Guide cum Practice Book for All Subjects

Maths, English, Hindi & EVS

AF889470

Class 5

Authors

Maths Astha Singhal

English Vaishali Jaiswal

Hindi Richa Shukla

EVS Parneet Kaur

arihant

SUCCESS AND NOTHING LESS

All in One

Published by
ARIHANT PRAKASHAN
(School Division Series)

卐 ADMINISTRATIVE & PRODUCTION OFFICES

Regd. Office

'Ramchhaya' 4577/15, Agarwal Road, Darya Ganj, New Delhi -110002
Tele: 011- 47630600, 43518550; Fax: 011- 23280316

卐 **Head Office**

Kalindi, TP Nagar, Meerut (UP) - 250002, Tel: 0121-7156203, 7156204

卐 SALES & SUPPORT OFFICES

Agra, Ahmedabad, Bengaluru, Bareilly, Chennai, Delhi, Guwahati, Hyderabad, Jaipur, Jhansi, Kolkata, Lucknow, Nagpur & Pune.

PO No : TXT-XX-XXXXXXX-X-XX

Published By Arihant Publications (India) Ltd.

For further information about the books published by Arihant, log on to www.arihantbooks.com or e-mail at info@arihantbooks.com

Follow us on

卐 PRICE ₹445.00

PRODUCTION TEAM

Publishing Managers	Project Head	Cover Designer	Inner Designer	Page Layouting
Mahendra Singh Rawat & Keshav Mohan	Ashwani, Manju, Mohit, Shivam	Bilal Hashmi	Ankit Prajapati	Amit Agarwal

Allinone

EXCLUSIVE FEATURES

1 Quick Summary at the start of each Chapter

2 Solutions/Answers of All NCERT Questions

3 Additional Practice Questions in each Chapter

All in One

Content List

Math Magic (Maths)

Marigold (English)

रिमझिम (हिंदी)

Looking Around (EVS)

Allinone

MATH-MAGIC

(Maths)

CHAPTER 1

THE FISH TALE

Understanding large numbers

- 1 lakh = One hundred thousand (100000), there are five zeroes in it .
- 1 crore = One hundred lakh (10000000), there are seven zeroes in it.

Understanding Speed

The formula to find up the speed of any object for a given distance and time is

$$\text{Speed} = \frac{\text{Distance}}{\text{Time}}$$

From this, find the formula for time as well as distance.

$$\text{Distance} = \text{Speed} \times \text{Time}$$

and $$\text{Time} = \frac{\text{Distance}}{\text{Speed}}$$

Profit or Loss

- Cost price is that price on which the item is bought.
- Selling price is that price on which the item is sold.
- If **cost price** (CP) is greater than **selling price** (SP), then there is loss and if cost price (CP) is less than selling price (SP), then there is profit.

NCERT FOLDER

NCERT Pg 1

Q.1 Do you know any poems about fish?

Ans. * Yes, I know a poem about fish.

Little Fish

One little fish
Swam in his dish.
He blew bubbles
And made a wish.
All he wanted
was another fish
To swim with him
In his little dish.
Another fish
Came one day.
To blow bubbles
While they played.
Two little fish
Blowing bubbles
In the dish.
Swimming around
Singing plish, plish, plish.

** Students can write alternate answer as per their choice.*

Q.2 When you think of fishes what shapes come to your mind?

Ans. * The following shapes of fishes come to my mind when I think about them.

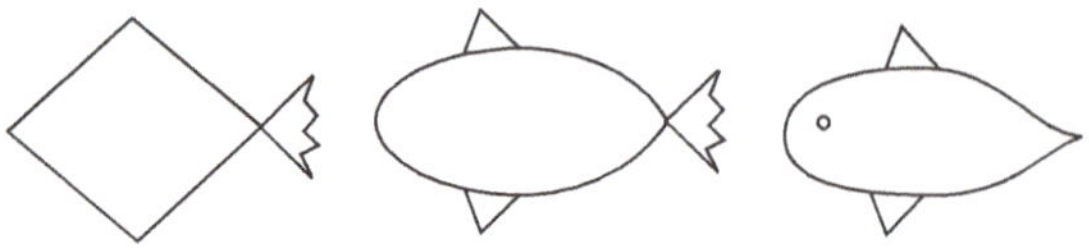

Q.3 Try to use a square and a triangle to draw a fish.

Ans. * A fish can draw by the use of a square and a triangle is given below.

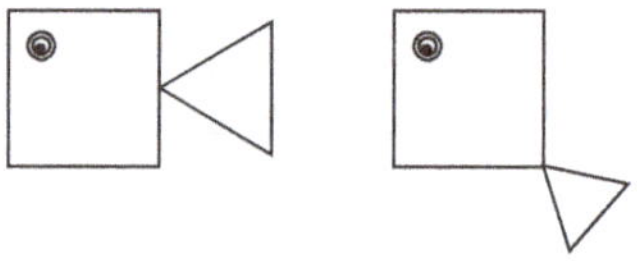

NCERT Pg 2

Q.4 'Meen' means a fish and 'Meenakshi' is a girl whose eyes look like a fish. Can you think of someone who has such eyes?

Draw a face with 'fish eyes'.

Ans. * Following is a face with 'fish eyes'.

Q.5 Fishes can have very different sizes. The smallest fish is about 1 cm long. How long is the biggest fish you can imagine?

Ans. * I can imagine whale shark which is 18 m long.

Q.6 How many times longer is your big fish than the smallest fish?

Ans. * The length of smallest fish is about 1 cm long and longest fish is about 18 m long.

Since, 1 m = 100 cm.

Hence, $18 \text{ m} = 18 \times 100 \text{ cm} = 1800 \text{ cm}$

Hence, the longest fish is 1800 times longer than the smaller fish.

NCERT Pg 3

Q.7 About how many kilograms do you weigh?

Ans. * I weigh about 30 kg.

Q.8 12 children like you put together will weigh about .... kg.

Ans. * Weight of 1 child = 30 kg

Weight of 12 children $= 12 \times 30 = 360$ kg

So, the weight of 12 children like me together will be 360 kg.

Q.9 About how much more does the whale shark weigh than 12 children like you put together?

Ans. * Weight of whale shark = 16000 kg

Weight of 12 children = 360 kg.

Difference in weight

= Weight of whale shark

– Weight of 12 children

= 16000 – 360

= 15640 kg

Hence, the whale shark will weigh 15640 kg more than 12 children like me put together.

'Schools' of Fish! (NCERT Pg 3)

Q.10 Fish like to swim together in the sea in big groups called 'schools' of fish. In their school they feel safe from the bigger fish. Do you feel safe in your school?

Ans. Yes, I feel safe in my school.

NCERT Pg 4-5

Q.11 (i) Jincy used these shapes to make drawings of fish. Now, you also use some shapes to draw the different sea animals shown below.

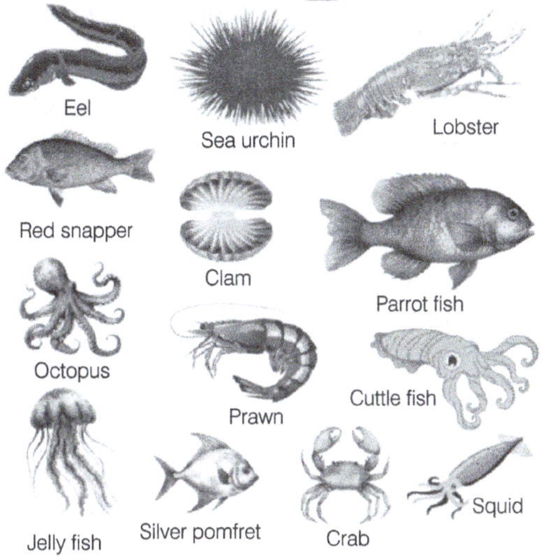

(ii) Which of these sea animals have you seen before?

Ans. (i) Do yourself.

*(ii) I have seen parrot fish and crab before.

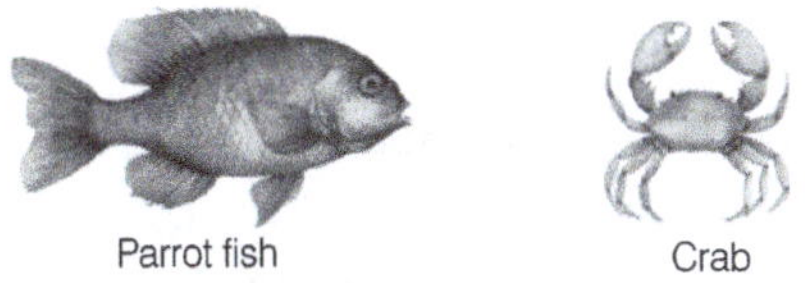

Fishermen in their Boats (NCERT Pg 5-6)

Q.12 How many of you have seen the sea? Where did you see it? Did you see it in a movie or for real? How deep do you think the sea could be? Find out.

Ans. * I have seen the sea and most of my friends have also seen the sea. I have seen the sea at Goa. I have seen the sea in the movies as well as in a real life. I think the depth of the sea is more than thousands of metre.

Q.13 Do you know how to swim? Would you be scared of the high sea waves?

Ans. * No, I do not know how to swim. Yes, I am scared of the high sea waves.

Q.14 Close your eyes and imagine the sea with waves rising high.

Ans. * High sea waves look very fantastic.

Q.15 How high do you think the waves can go?

Ans. * I think that the waves can go more than 40 to 50 m.

Q.16 These log boats do not go very far. If the wind is helpful, they travel about 4 km in one hour.

(i) How long will they take to go a distance of 10 km?

(ii) Guess how far you can go in one hour if you walk fast.

Ans. (i) For 4 km, time take = 1 h

$\therefore$ For 1 km, time will be $= \frac{1}{4}$ h

$\therefore$ 10 km distance, take time $= 10 \times \frac{1}{4}$ h

$= 2\frac{1}{2}$ h

= 2 h and 30 min

(ii) I think if I walk fast, I can cover 2 km to 3 km.

Find Out (NCERT Pg 7)

Q.17 Look at the sun and find out the direction from where it rises.

Ans. I can see the sun is rising from the east direction.

Q.18 From where you are, what interesting things do you see to your east?

Ans. * I can see the orange- red - yellow sky in the east in the morning and the sun is rising from the east.

Q.19 Name two things that are lying to your west.

Ans. * I see a bird sitting in my west and the sky is orange with some red colour in western direction.

What a Catch! (NCERT Pg 7)

Q.20 Look at the different types of boats. Some boats have motors and go further into the sea. Since, they go far out they can catch more fish. These boats travel faster, at the speed of about 20 km in one hour.

(i) How far would the motor boats go in three and a half hours?

(ii) How much time will they take to go 85 km?

Ans. (i) In 1 h, boat goes = 20 km

In 3 h, boat will go = 3×20 km = 60 km

Also, in half hour, boat will go = $\frac{20}{2}$ = 10 km

Hence, in three and a half hours, boat will go $60 + 10 = 70$ km.

(ii) Since, the boat travel at the speed of about 20 km in one hour.

Therefore, the distance travelled by boats in 4 h = $20 \times 4 = 80$ km

The distance of travelled by boats in $\frac{1}{4}$ h

$= 20 \times \frac{1}{4} = 5$ km.

Hence, the total time taken by boat to travel 85 km = 4 h + $\frac{1}{4}$ h = 4 h 15 min

NCERT Pg 9

Q.21 Write a news report about the dangers faced by the fishes in our rivers and seas.

Ans. Big fishing boats, called trawlers, are causing problems for fish and small fisherman.

These trawlers go far from the shore and use large nets to catch a lot of fish , including many baby fish.

Fisherman in the smaller boat, use smaller nets that let baby fish swim away which helps the fish population grow. But these big machine boats catch everything,which leads harms to ocean's fish numbers.

Which Boat Gets How Much? (NCERT Pg 9)

Q.22 In one trip, the log boat brings about 20 kg of fish.But other types of boats bring a bigger catch as given in the table. The table also shows the speed of each type of boat, which is how far each boat goes in one hour. Look at the table and calculate

Type of boats	**Catch of fish in one trip** (in kg)	**Speed of the boat** (how far it goes in one hour)
Log boat	20	4 km per hour
Long tail boat	600	12 km per hour
Motor boat	800	20 km per hour
Machine boat	6000	22 km per hour

(i) About how much fish in all will each type of boat bring in seven trips?

(ii) About how far can a motor boat go in six hours?

(iii) If a long tail boat has to travel 60 km how long will it take?

Ans. (i)

Type of boats	**Catch of fish in one trip** (in kg)	**Catch of fish in 7 trips** (in kg)
Log boat	20	$7 \times 20 = 140$
Long tail boat	600	$7 \times 600 = 4200$
Motor boat	800	$7 \times 800 = 5600$
Machine boat	6000	$7 \times 6000 = 42000$

(ii) Speed of motor boat = 20 km/hr

We know that

distance = Speed × Time

So, distance covered by motor boat in 6 hours = $20 \times 6 = 120$ km

(iii) Speed of long tail boat = 12 km/h

Distance to be covered = 60 km

So, time taken = $\frac{\text{Distance}}{\text{Speed}}$

$= \frac{60}{12} = 5$ h

Hence, it will take 5 h to travel 60 km.

Some Big, Big Numbers! (NCERT Pg 10)

Q.23 In the Class IV Math-Magic you heard of the number 'lakh' which is equal to a hundred thousand. You had read that there are about one lakh brick kilns in our country, where bricks are made.

(i) What other things have you heard of in lakhs?

(ii) Write the number one thousand. Now, write one hundred thousand. So, how many zeroes are there in the number one lakh? Easy, isn't it?

(iii) There are about two lakh boats in our country. Half of them are without a motor. What is the number of boats with a motor? Write it.

(iv) About one fourth of the boats with a motor are big machine boats. How many thousand machine boats are there? Come on, try to do it without writing down.

Ans. *(i) I have heard many things in lakhs out of which few things are mentioned below.

- Population of the city.
- Number of employees in Film-industry.
- Number of shops in the town.

(ii) One thousand = 1000

One-hundred thousand = 100000

There are 5 zeroes in one lakh.

(iii) Total number of boats = 2 lakhs

Number of boats without a motor

$$= \frac{\text{Total number of boats}}{2} = \frac{2}{2} = 1 \text{ lakh}$$

Number of boats with a motor = Total number of boats – Number of boats without a motor

$= 2 - 1 = 1$ lakh

(iv) Number of boats with motor = 1 lakh

Number of machine boats

$$= \frac{\text{Total number of boats with motor}}{4}$$

$$= \frac{100000}{4} = 25000$$

Hence, number of machine boats is 25000.

Q.24 We might wonder about the number of people whose lives are related to fish. In all there are about one hundred lakh fishworkers — who catch fish, clean and sell them, make and repair nets and boats, etc. We also have a name for this big number — 'one hundred lakh' is called a crore.

(i) Where have you heard of a crore? What was the number used for?

(ii) Try writing the number one crore. Don't get lost in all the zeroes!

Ans. *(i) I have heard of a crore in the population of India. The number crore used for the notation of population of India.

(ii) One crore = One hundred lakh = 10000000

There are 7 zeroes in one crore.

The Fish Market (NCERT Pg 11-12)

Q.25 Have you been to a fish market?

Ans. Yes, I have been to a fish market.

Practice Time (NCERT Pg 11-12)

Q.26 Many boats have brought a good catch. The fisherwomen are shouting out their prices to the buyers.

Mini — 'Come here! Come here! Take sardines at ₹ 40 a kg'.

Gracy — 'Never so cheap! Get sword-fish for ₹ 60 a kg'.

Floramma sells prawns for ₹ 150 a kg.

Karuthamma sells squid for ₹ 50 a kg.

Look, Fazila can hardly carry this big kingfish! She says, 'This fish weighs 8 kg. I will sell the whole for ₹ 1200'.

(i) At what price per kg did Fazila sell the kingfish?

(ii) Floramma has sold 10 kg prawns today. How much money did she get for that?

(iii) Gracy sold 6 kg swordfish. Mini has earned as much money as Gracy. How many kg of sardines did Mini sell?

(iv) Basheer has ₹ 100. He spends one-fourth of the money on squid and another three-fourth on prawns.

(a) How many kilograms of squid did he buy?

(b) How many kilograms of prawns did he buy?

Ans. (i) Price of 8 kg kingfish = ₹ 1200

$\therefore$ Price of 1 kg kingfish $= \frac{1200}{8} =$ ₹ 150

Hence, Fazila sold the kingfish at ₹ 150 per kg.

(ii) $\because$ Price of 1 kg prawns = ₹ 150

$\therefore$ Price of 10 kg prawns $= 10 \times 150 =$ ₹ 1500

Hence, Floramma got ₹ 1500 money for 10 kg prawns.

(iii) $\because$ Price of 1 kg swordfish = ₹ 60

$\therefore$ Price of 6 kg swordfish $= 6 \times 60 =$ ₹ 360

$\because$ Money earned by Gracy = Money earned by Mini

$\therefore$ Mini earned ₹ 360.

Price of 1 kg sardines = ₹ 40

Number of sardines sold by Mini $= \frac{360}{40}$

$= 9$ kg

Hence, Mini sold 9 kg sardines.

(iv) (a) Price of 1 kg squid = ₹ 50

Money used for buying squid $= \frac{100}{4}$

= ₹ 25

Amount of squid in ₹ 1 $= \frac{1}{50}$ kg

Amount of squid in ₹ 25 $= 25 \times \frac{1}{50} = \frac{1}{2}$ kg

Hence, Basheer bought $\frac{1}{2}$ kg of squid.

(b) Price of 1 kg prawns = ₹ 150

Money used for buying prawns $= \frac{3}{4} \times 100$

= ₹ 75

Amount of prawns in ₹ 1 $= \frac{1}{150}$ kg

Amount of prawns in ₹ 75 $= 75 \times \frac{1}{150}$

$= \frac{1}{2}$ kg

Hence, Basheer buy half kg of prawns.

Women's 'Meenkar Bank' (NCERT Pg 12-13)

Q.27 The meeting of the Meenkar Bank has just begun. Fazila is the president. Twenty fisherwomen have made their own bank. Each saves ₹ 25 every month and puts it in the bank.

(i) How much money does the group collect each month?

(ii) How much money will be collected in ten years?

Ans. (i) Collection of one woman in bank = ₹ 25

Total number of women = 20

Hence, the total money, the group of 20 women collect $= 20 \times 25$

= ₹ 500

(ii) $\because$ Money collected in 1 month = ₹ 500

$\therefore$ Money collected in 1 year $= 12 \times 500$

= ₹ 6000

Hence, collection of 10 years $= 10 \times 6000$

= ₹ 60000

Practice Time (NCERT Pg 12-13)

Q.28 Gracy needs money to buy a net. Jhansi and her sister want to buy a log boat. So, they take a loan from their bank. They will return it with interest.

(i) Gracy took a loan of ₹ 4000 to buy a net. She paid back ₹ 345 every month for one year. How much money did she pay back to the bank?

(ii) Jhansi and her sister took a loan of ₹ 21000 to buy a log boat. They paid back a total of ₹ 23520 in one year. How much did they pay back every month?

Ans. (i) Amount paid to bank per month = ₹ 345

Total amount paid in a year $= 12 \times 345$

= ₹ 4140

Hence, Gracy paid ₹ 4140 back to the bank.

(ii) Total paid back to bank in a year = ₹ 23520

Amount paid in a month $= \frac{23520}{12} =$ ₹ 1960

Hence, they paid ₹ 1960 back every month.

Why Don't We Start a New Fish-drying Factory? (NCERT Pg 13-15)

Q.29 The women of Meenkar Bank also want to start a factory to dry fish. The Panchayat has given them some land for that. Over the years they have saved ₹ 74000. They find out how much they will need for the factory. Fazila writes the things they need to buy to begin. See the table for the cost of each item and the number of items they want to buy. Find the total cost.

Total cost to set up the factory = _____.

Ans.

Item	Price of each	Number of items	Cost
Bore well for fresh water	₹ 3000	1	1×3000 = ₹ 3000
Bamboo rack for fish drying	₹ 2000	20	20×2000 = ₹ 40000
Cement tank	₹ 1000	4	4×1000 = ₹ 4000
Tray and knife	₹ 300	20	20×300 = ₹ 6000
Bucket	₹ 75	20	20×75 = ₹ 1500

Total cost of set up the factory

$= 3000 + 40000 + 4000 + 6000 + 1500$

= ₹ 54500

Q.30 When fresh fish is dried it becomes $\frac{1}{3}$ its weight. In one month, they plan to dry 6000 kg of fresh fish. How much dried fish will they get in a month?

Ans. Amount of fresh fish in 1 month = 6000 kg

Dry fish in 1 month

$$= \frac{\text{Total amount of fresh fish}}{3} = \frac{6000}{3}$$

= 2000 kg

Q.31 Floramma—Let us first calculate for 6 kg of fresh fish.

We buy fresh fish for	₹ 15 per kg
We sell dried fish for	₹ 70 per kg

(i) We dry 6 kg fresh fish to get _____ kg dried fish.

(ii) For 6 kg fresh, fish we have to pay

$6 \times$ __ = ₹ 90

(iii) We will sell 2 kg dried fish and get

$2 \times$ __ = ₹ __

(iv) So, if we dry 6 kg fresh fish, we will earn

__ – ₹ 90 = ₹ __

(v) But if we dry 6000 kg we can earn ₹ __ $\times$ 1000 = ____ in one month!

(vi) Jhansi—I found that for 6000 kg fish we would need 1500 kg salt every month! Its price is ₹2 per kg.

Monthly Costs -

(a) Salt 1500×2 = ₹ _____

(b) Packing and bus charges = ₹3000

So, the total monthly cost of drying, packing and bus charges = ₹ ______

(vii) Fazila — That sounds very good! Our calculations tell us that every month our Bank will earn ₹ 44000! Check to see if you also get the same answer.

Ans. (i) We dry 6 kg fresh fish to get $= \frac{6}{3} = 2$ kg dried fish.

(ii) For 6 kg fresh fish, we have to pay

$6 \times \underline{15}$ = ₹ 90

(iii) We will sell 2 kg dried fish and get

$2 \times \underline{70}$ = ₹ $\underline{140}$

(iv) So, if we dry 6 kg fresh, fish we will earn

₹ $\underline{140}$ – ₹ 90 = ₹ $\underline{50}$

(v) But if we dry 6000 kg, we can earn

₹ $\underline{50}$ $\times$1000 = ₹ $\underline{50000}$ in one month.

(vi) (a) Salt 1500×2 = ₹ 3000

(b) Total monthly cost = $3000 + 3000$

= ₹ 6000

(vii) Total earning in one month

$= 50000 - 6000$

= ₹ 44000

So, the monthly earning is ₹ 44000 which shows that I found the same answer as Fazila.

PRACTICE QUESTIONS

1. Fill in the blanks
   (i) The length of the boat is measured in ______.
   (ii) A fish has a ______ shape which helps it swim easily in water.
   (iii) The total weight of 5 boxes, each weighing 30 kg, is ______ kg.
   (iv) If the price of one basket of fish is ₹ 500, then 4 baskets will cost ₹ ______ .

2. True or False
   (i) All fish have the same weight.
   (ii) Fish are sold by their lengths, not by their weights.
   (iii) A whale is the largest fish in the world.
   (iv) One lakh is written as 100000.

3. Multiple choice questions
   (i) Which unit is used to measure the weight of fish?
   (a) Metre (b) Litre
   (c) Kilogram (d) Centimetre
   (ii) If 1 kg of fish costs ₹ 120, how much will 3 kg cost?
   (a) ₹ 240 (b) ₹ 360
   (c) ₹ 300 (d) ₹ 150
   (iii) What is the main activity of the fishermen in the story?
   (a) Selling fish (b) Buying fish
   (c) Cooking fish (d) Catching fish

4. Odd-one out
   (i) (a) Kilograms (b) Grams
   (c) Litres (d) Pounds
   (ii) (a) Fishing net (b) Boat
   (c) Fisherman (d) Car

5. Word problems
   (i) A fisherman catches 45 kg of fish in a day. If he sells it at ₹ 200 per kg, how much money does he earn in a day?
   (ii) A basket of fish weight 25 kg. If a fisherman carries 8 such baskets, what is the total weight he carries?

6. Case based questions

   A group of 10 fishermen went to the sea. They caught 500 kg of fish. They sold all the fish at ₹ 100 per kg.

   Based on the above information, answer the following questions.
   (i) How much total money did they earn by selling all the fish?
   (ii) If they shared the money equally among the 10 fishermen, how much did each fisherman get?

ANSWERS & SOLUTIONS

1. (i) Metres (ii) Streamlined
   (iii) 150 (iv) 2000
2. (i) False (ii) False
   (iii) False (iv) True
3. (i) (c) (ii) (b)
   (iii) (d)
4. (i) (c) (ii) (d)
5. (i) Total weight of fishes = 45 kg
   Cost of 1 kg fish = ₹200
   ∴ Earning of fisherman in a day
   = ₹200 × 45 = ₹9000
   So, the fisherman earning ₹ 9000 in a day.
   (ii) Weight of 1 basket of fish = 25 kg
   Weight of 8 basket of fish = 25 × 8
   = 200 kg
   So, the fisherman carries 200 kg fish.
6. (i) Total weight of fish = 500 kg
   Cost of 1 kg fish = ₹100
   ∴ Earning of all fishermen = ₹100 × 500
   = ₹50000
   (ii) Earning of all fishermen = ₹50000
   Number of fishermen = 10
   ∴ Earning of each fisherman = $\frac{50000}{10}$
   = ₹5000

CHAPTER 2 SHAPES AND ANGLES

Some of the common that we shapes observe in daily life are triangles, rectangles, squares, circles etc.

Types of shapes

2D Shapes

These are flat shapes that have length and breadth but no depth such as squares, triangles, circles.

3D shapes

These have length, breadth and height (or depth) such as cubes, spheres and cylinders.

Closed shape

The shape of figure with same starting and ending points, is called a closed shape.

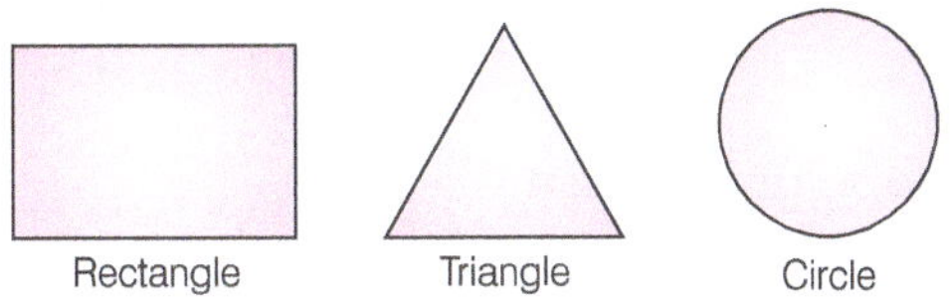

Open shape

The shape of figure with different starting and ending points, is called an open shape.

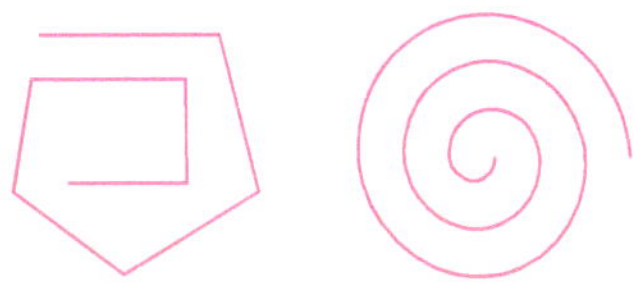

Angle

An angle is formed when two lines or rays meet at a common point (the vertex). Angles measure the amount of rotation between these two lines. Angle is measured in degree (°).

Right angle

The angle which measures 90° is called right angle. It forms a perfect '∟' shape.
e.g. The corners of a square or rectangle are at right angles.

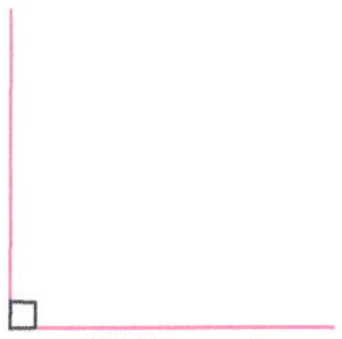

Right angle

Angles in different shapes

- Triangles have three sides and three angles and the sum of the angles in any triangle is always 180°. In an equilateral triangle, all three angles are 60°.
- Rectangles and squares have four right angles.
- Polygons are closed shapes with multiple sides such as pentagon, hexagon etc.

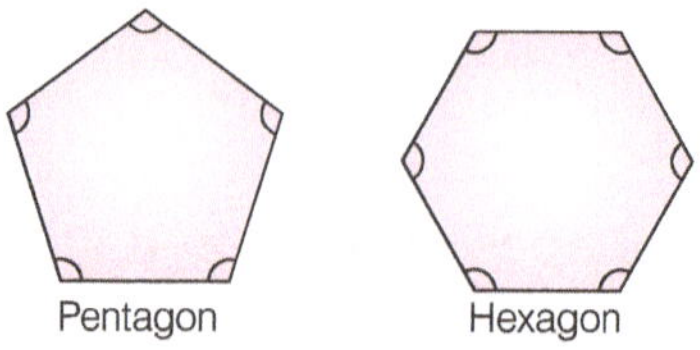

NCERT FOLDER

NCERT Pg 16-17

Q.1 Rohini made this shape.

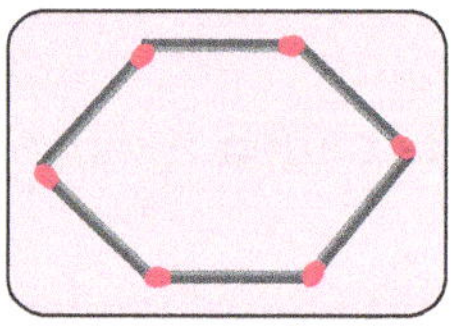

Mohini—Is it a closed shape or an open shape?

Rohini—It is a closed shape.

Mohini—How many sides are there?

Rohini—It has 6 sides.

Mohini made this.

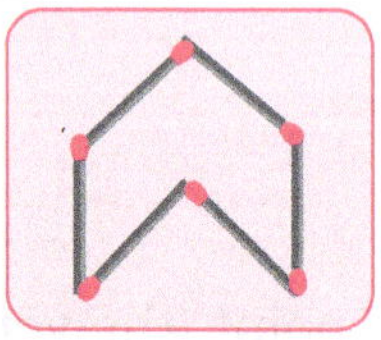

Now, you give the answers.

(i) Is it a closed shape? Does it have 6 sides?

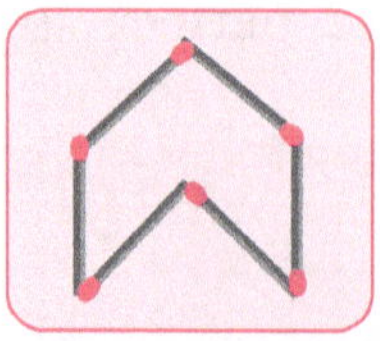

But it is not the same as the one made by Rohini. So, Mohini tried again.

This is what she made.

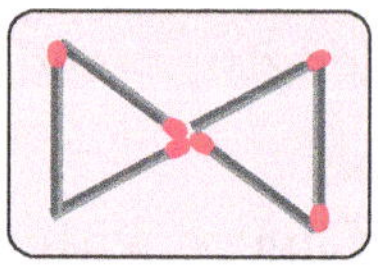

(ii) Is it a closed shape with 6 sides?

(iii) Is it the same as the one made by Rohini?

(iv) Is there some way to say in what way these shapes are different?

Ans. (i) Yes, it is a closed shape and it has 6 sides.

(ii) Yes, it is a closed shape with 6 sides.

(iii) No, it is not the same as the one made by Rohini.

(iv) Yes, in these shapes, the angles between two matchsticks are different.

Q.2 Mohini tried again but got different shapes. Guess and make two more shapes Mohini could have made.

Ans. * Following are the shapes made by Mohini

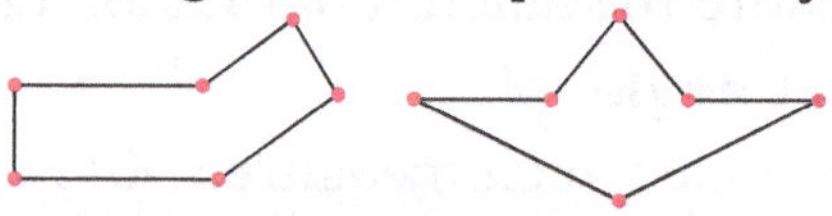

Q.3 Look at the angles marked in these shapes. Can you see the difference?

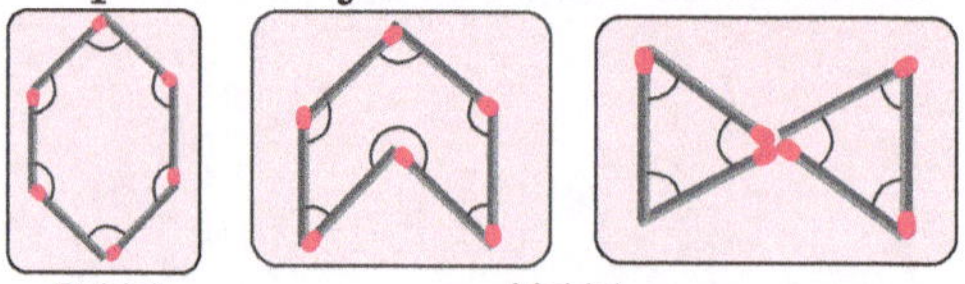

* *Students can write alternate answer as per their choice.*

Ans. Yes, the angles made by matchsticks in these shapes are different. Some are small and some are big.

Practice Time (NCERT Pg 18-19)

Q.4 Look at the shape and answer.

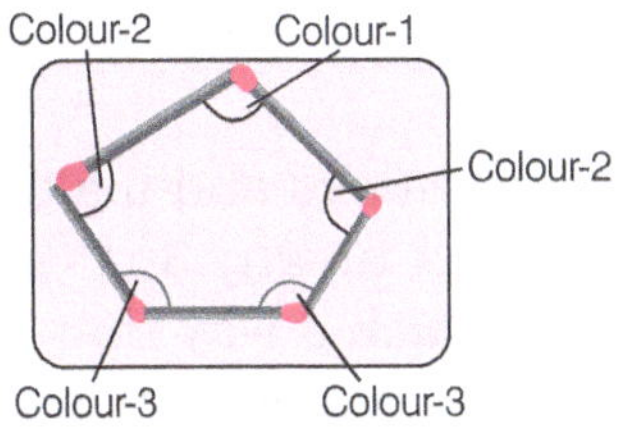

The angle marked as _______ is the biggest angle.

Ans. The angle marked as Colour-1 is the biggest angle.

Q.5

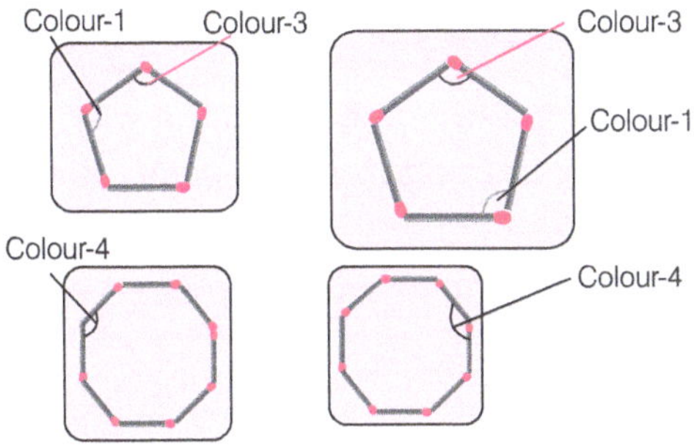

(i) Are the angles marked with Colour-1 equal?

(ii) Are the angles marked with Colour-3 equal?

(iii) Are the angles marked with Colour-4 equal?

Ans. (i) Yes, the angles marked with Colour-1 are equal.

(ii) Yes, the angles marked with Colour-3 are equal.

(iii) Yes, the angles marked with Colour-4 are equal.

Q.6 Four different angles are marked in four colours. Can you find other angles which are the same as the one marked in Colour-5? Mark them as Colour-5. Do this for the other colours.

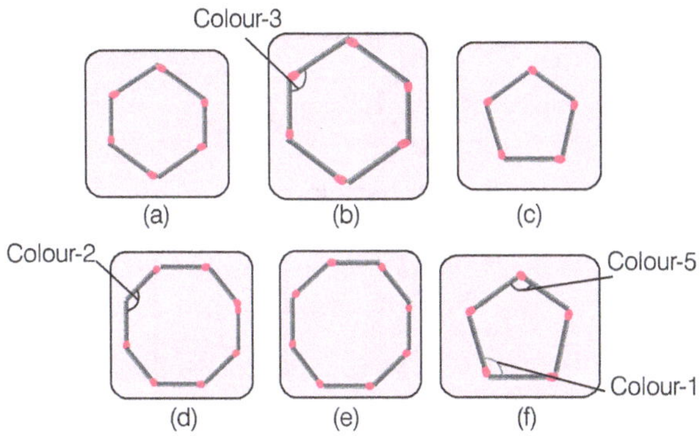

Ans. Yes, the angle marked in Colour-1 is same as the angle marked in Colour-5.

In shapes (a) and (b), all the angles are equal, so all the angles of these shapes marked as Colour-3.

Similarly, in shapes (d) and (e) and shapes (c) and (f), all the angles are equal, so all the angles of these shapes marked as Colour-2 and Colour-5.

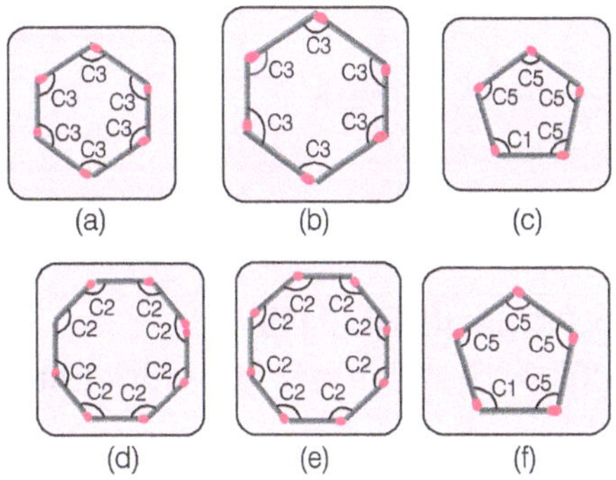

where C1, C2, C3 and C5 stands for Colour-1, Colour-2, Colour-3 and Colour-5.

Q.7 Draw different shapes by changing the angle between the matchsticks in each of these? Try.

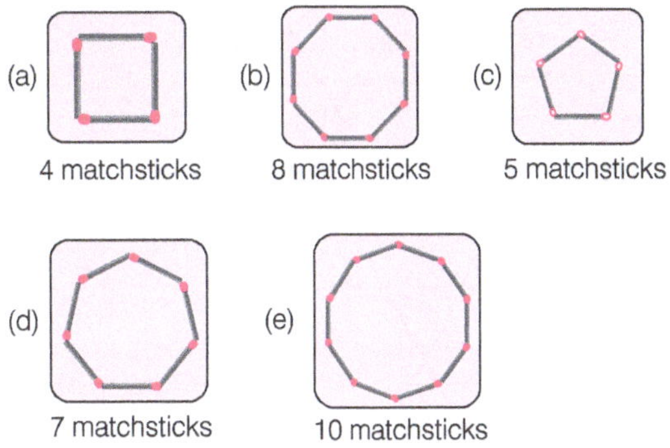

Ans. (a) With 4 matchsticks

(b) With 8 matchsticks

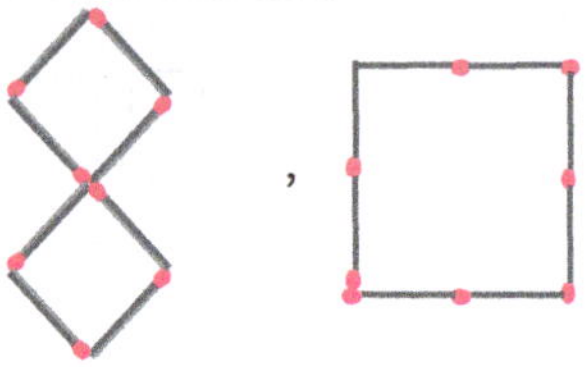

(c) With 5 matchsticks

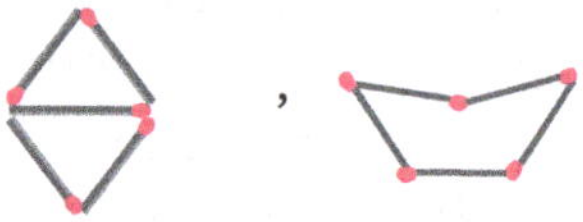

(d) With 7 matchsticks

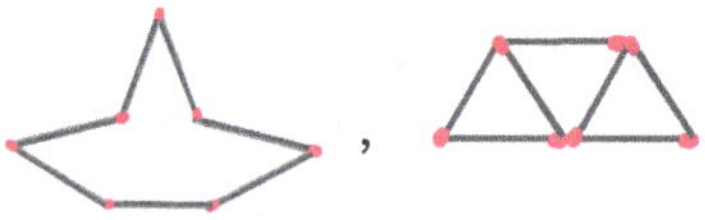

(e) With 10 matchsticks

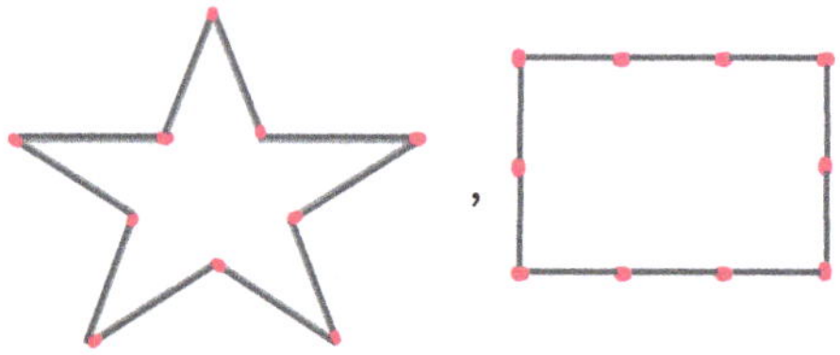

Matchstick Puzzles (NCERT Pg 19)

Q.8 Make 8 triangles using 6 matchsticks. Try!

Ans. Following is the shape with 8 triangles using 6 matchsticks.

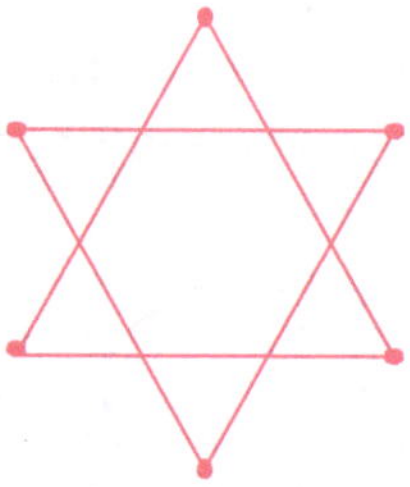

There are 6 small triangles

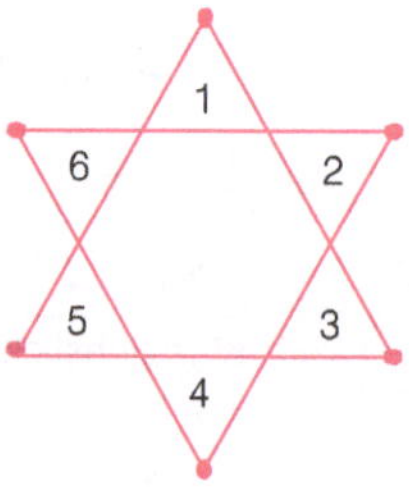

and 2 large triangles

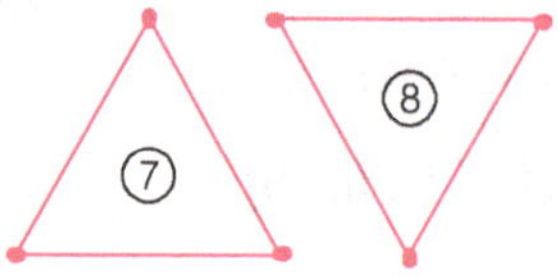

∴ 6 small triangles + 2 large triangle = 8 triangles

Q.9 Take 8 matchsticks and make a fish like this. Now, pick up any 3 matchsticks and put them in such a way that the fish, now starts swimming in the opposite direction. Did it?

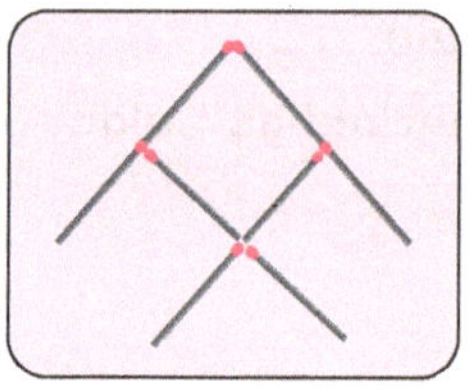

Ans. Following is the fish in such a way that it starts swimming in the opposite direction.

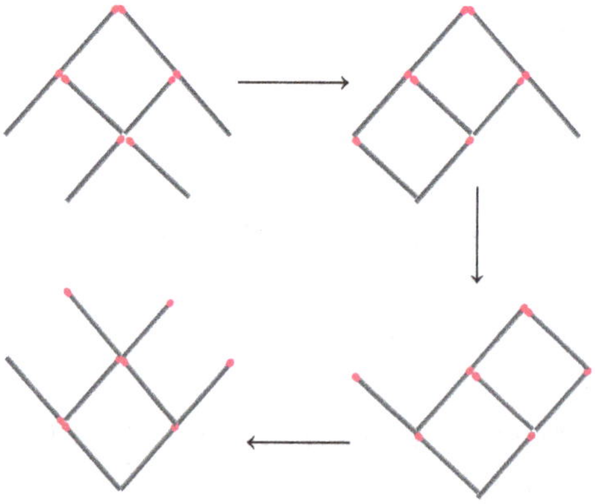

Q.10 Using 10 matchsticks, make this shape. Pick up 5 matchsticks and put them in such a way that you get the shape of a house.

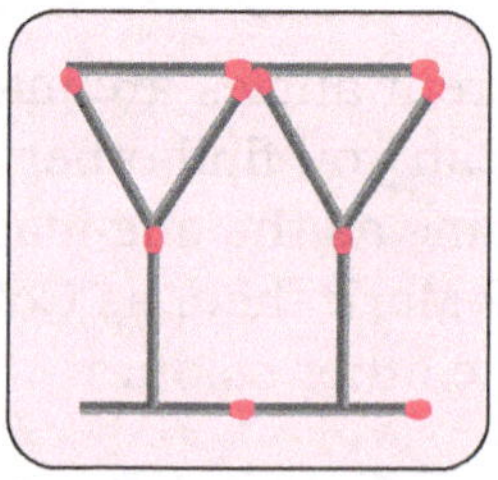

Ans. *

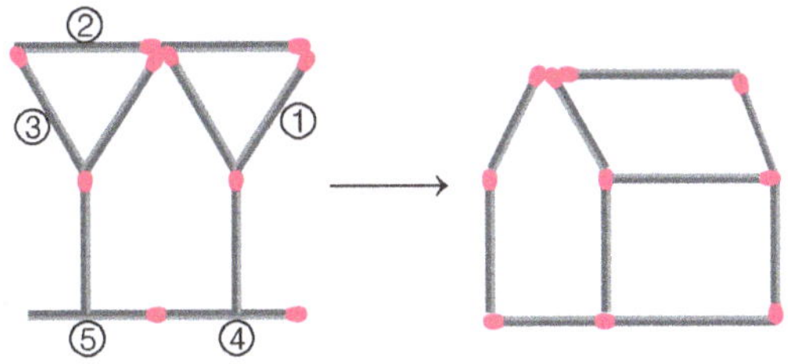

Angle Tester (NCERT Pg 20-21)

Q.11 How do we make equal angles?

Ans. * We can use an angle tester from the geometry box. It is also known as divider.

Q.12 Go around with your tester and draw here those things in which the tester opens like the letter L. Are you sure they all right angles?

Ans. * Yes, all the angles in which the tester looks like the letter L are right angles. Here are some examples given below.

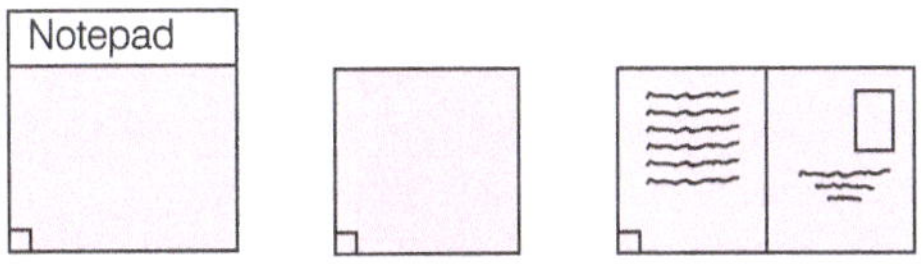

Notepad Square Post card

Practice Time (NCERT Pg 21-22)

Q.13 Look at the angles in the pictures and fill the table.

Ans.

Angle	Right angle	More than a right angle	Less than a right angle
			✓
	✓		
	✓		
		✓	
		✓	

Q.14 Sukhman made this picture with so many angles.

Use colour pencils to mark.

(i) right angles with letter-B.

(ii) angles which are more than a right angle with letter-G.

(iii) angles which are less than a right angle with letter-A.

Ans. * In the above figure,

(i) Letter - B denotes right angles.

(ii) Letter - G denotes angles which are more than a right angle.

(iii) Letter - A denotes angles which are less than a right angle.

Note Students are recommended to use colour pens for making (i.e. black, green and blue).

Q.15 Draw anything of your choice around the angle shown. Also, write what kind of angle it is. The first one is done.

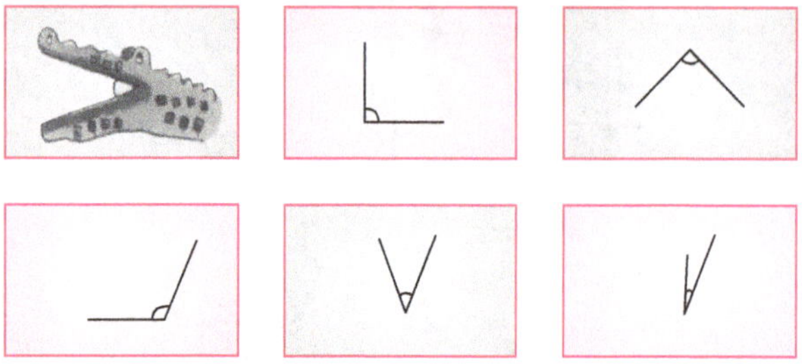

Ans.

Cube
(Right angle)

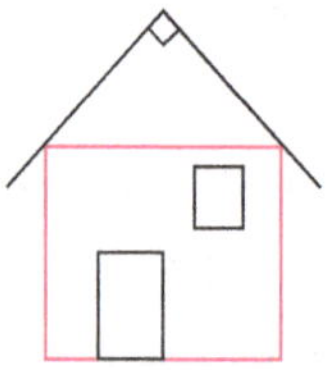

Hut
(Right angle)

Chair
(more than
right angle)

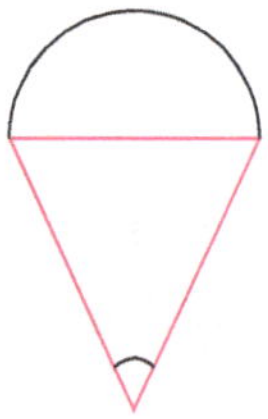

Ice-cream cone
(Acute angle)
(Less than right angle)

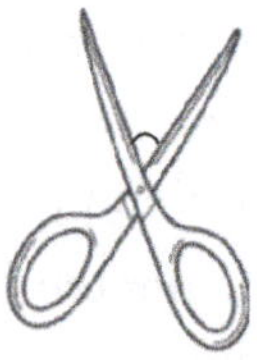

Scissors
(Acute angle)
(Less than right angle)

Activity (NCERT Pg 23)

Q.16 (i) Take a square sheet of paper.

(ii) Fold it in half.

(iii) Fold it once more and press it.

(iv) Open the last fold so that the sheet is folded in half.

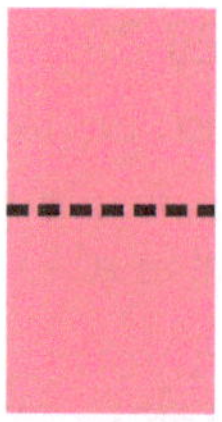

(v) Take one corner and fold it to meet the dotted line.

On the paper, you will find lines making a right angle, an angle less than a right angle and an angle more than a right angle.

Look for each of the angles and mark them with different colours.

Ans. Angles are marked in the following figure.

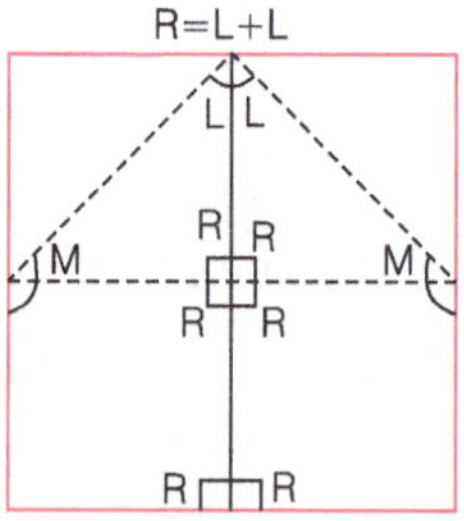

Here, R = Right angle

L = Less than a right angle

M = More than a right angle

Note Students are recommended to use colour pens for making the angles.

Activity-Angles with your body (NCERT Pg 23)

Q.17

Can you make these angles?

(i) A right angle with your hand?

(ii) An angle less than a right angle with your leg?

(iii) An angle more than a right angle with your arm?

(iv) An angle more than a right angle with your body?

Try them out. It's fun! Draw them in your notebook, using stick drawings like these.

Ans. *Yes, we can make these angles.

(i) Right angle 'R' with hand.

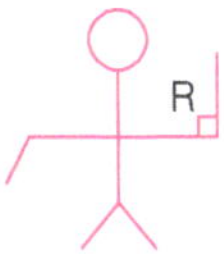

(ii) An angle less than a right angle 'L' with leg.

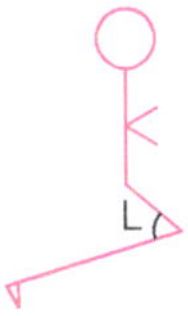

(iii) An angle more than a right angle 'O' with arm.

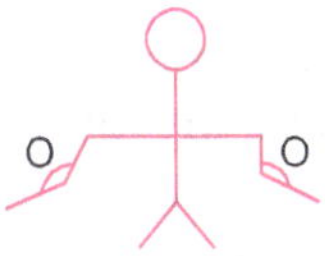

(iv) An angle more than a right angle 'P' with body.

Activity (NCERT Pg 24-25)

Q.18 Collect some leaves from the garden. Colour each leaf and print it. Look at the angles on the leaves.Which of them are more/less than a right angle?

Ans. Do yourself.

Q.19

(i) Look for the birds which have beaks with angles smaller than a right angle.

(ii) In the picture, mark angles between the two branches. Which two branches have the biggest angle?

Ans. (i) Birds denoted by A, B and C have beaks with angles smaller than a right angle.

(ii) Branches P_1 and P_2 have the biggest angle as mentioned in the figure.

Angles in Names (NCERT Pg 25)

Q.20 Write 3 names using straight lines and count the angles.

Ans. *

S. No.	Name	Number of right angles	Number of angles more than a right angle	Number of angles less than a right angle
(i)	LALLAN	3	4	8
(ii)	RIA	8	2	5
(iii)	TEENA	10	2	5

(i) LALLAN

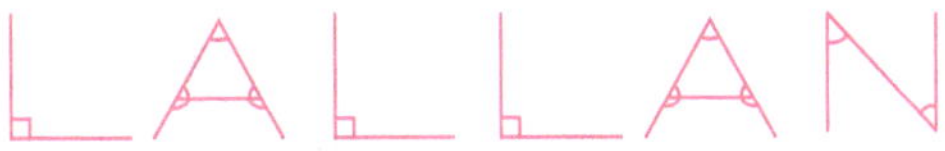

(ii) RIA

(iii) TEENA

Activity (NCERT Pg 25-26)

Q.21 Put 10 Math-Magic books on top of each other. Keep one book slanting to make a slide.

Now, do this with six books.

(i) Roll a ball from the top. From which slide does the ball roll down faster?

(ii) Which slide has the smaller angle?

Ans. (i) If we make a slide by 10 books, the ball rolls down faster.

(ii) Following are the slide made by 10 Math-Magic books and 6 Math-Magic books.

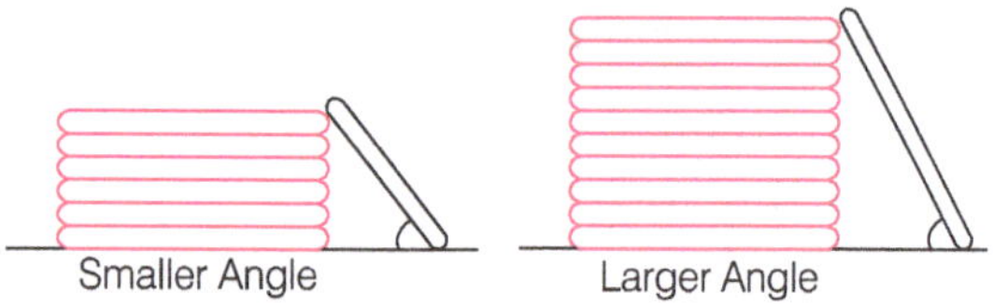

So, the slide made by 6 books has smaller angle.

Q.22

These are two slides in a park.

(i) Which slide has a larger angle?

(ii) Which slide do you think is safer for the little boy? Why?

Ans. (i) The slide on the left side of a boy has a larger angle.

(ii) The slide on the right side of the boy is safer for the little boy because its angle is smaller than the other slide.

Changing Shapes (NCERT Pg 26-27)

Q.23 Things you need — used (or new) matchsticks. Piece of rubber tube used in cycle valves.

- Clean the black end of the matchsticks.

- Cut small pieces of the tube (about 1 cm long).

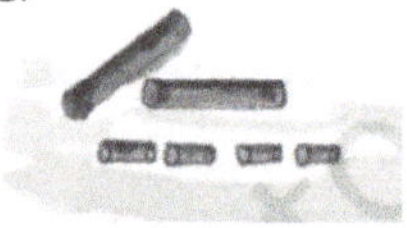

- Push two matchsticks into each end of a tube piece.

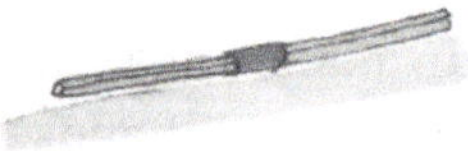

- Add more matchsticks to form a triangle.

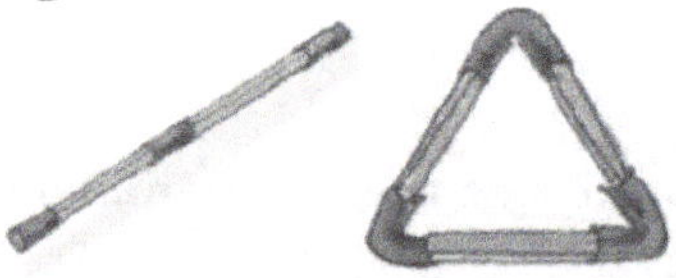

Now, make these 4, 5, 6 sided shapes by tube pieces and matchsticks.

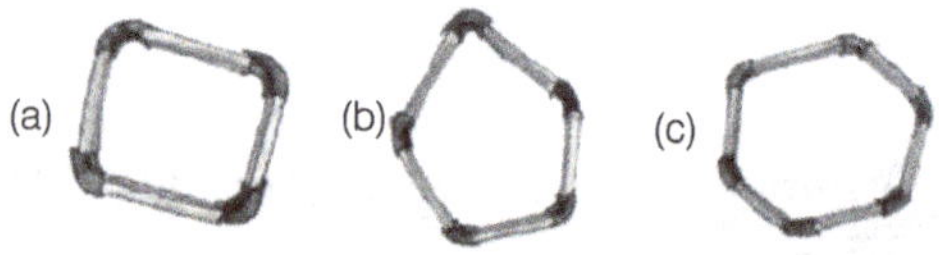

(i) Find out how many angles are there in each of these shapes. Mark them.

(ii) Push each shape downwards with the tip of your finger.

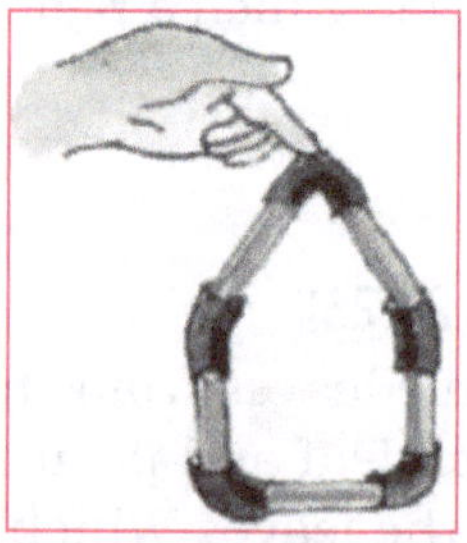

Does the angle change when pushed down by the finger?

Ans. (i)

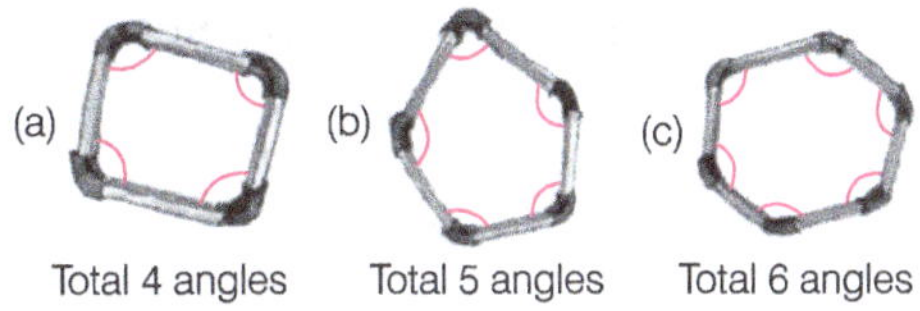

(ii) Yes, the angle changes when pushed down by the finger.

Q.24 Find out and write your results in the table given.

Ans.

Shape	Change in angle Yes/No
	Yes
	Yes
	Yes
	No

Shapes and Towers (NCERT Pg 28)

Q.25 Look for triangles in the pictures below.

(i) From the activity 'Changing Shapes' can you guess why triangles are used in these towers, bridges etc?

(ii) Look around and find out more places where triangles are used.

Ans. *(i) Shapes with a triangular design offer greater stability and strength compared to other shapes. Also, triangular structures take less space than the other shapes.

*(ii) Triangles are used in beams in building like hall, zoo, circus, auditorium and railway bridges.

Angle and Time (NCERT Pg 28-29)

Q.26 There are many times in a day when the hands of a clock make a right angle. Now, you draw some more.

Ans. *

Q.27 Write what kind of angle is made by the hands at these times. Also, write the time.

Ans. *

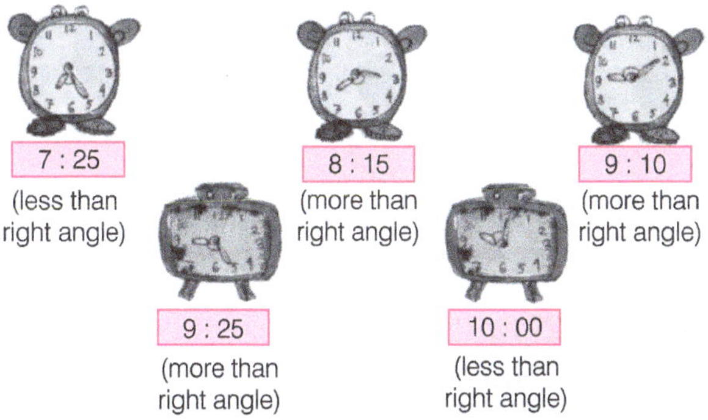

Q.28 Draw the hands of the clock when they make an angle which is less than a right angle. Also, write the time.

Ans. *

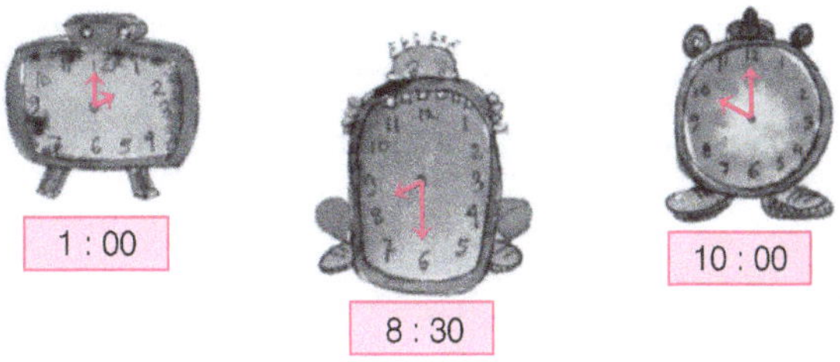

Degree Clock (NCERT Pg 30)

Q.29 In the picture, three points A, B and C are shown.

Draw a line to show from which point Kittu should hit to get the queen.

Ans.

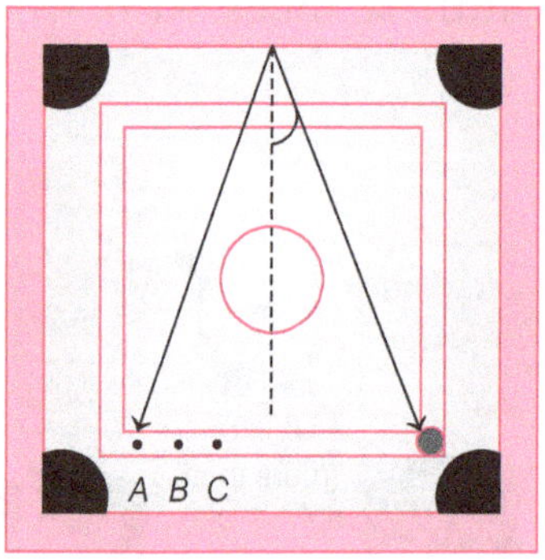

Activity (NCERT Pg 31)

Making a degree clock

- Cut a circle out of paper.

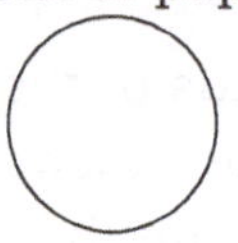

- Fold it into half.

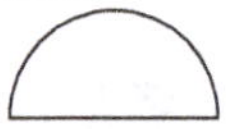

- Fold it once again into a quarter.

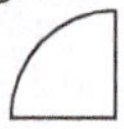

- Fold it once more.

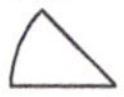

- Open the paper. You will see lines like this.

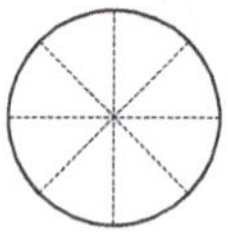

- Now mark 0°, 45°, 90° and 180° as shown.

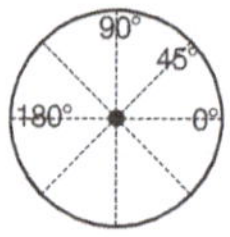

- Paste it on an old card.
- From the centre draw one hand.

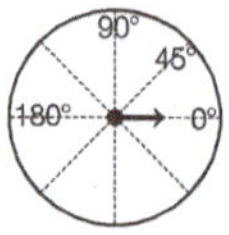

- Make a second hand with a thick paper and fix it to the centre with a drawing pin, so that it is free to move.

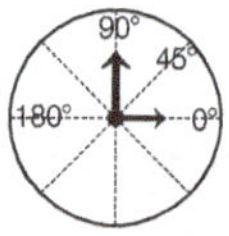

Your degree clock is ready.

Q.30 Use your degree clock to measure the right angle of your pencil box. ______ is the measure of the right angle.

Ans. <u>90°</u> is the measure of the right angle.

Q.31 Can you guess how many degrees is the angle which is

(i) $\frac{1}{2}$ of a right angle ______

(ii) $\frac{1}{3}$ of a right angle ______

(iii) 2 times of a right angle ______

Ans. (i) $\frac{1}{2}$ of a right angle $= \frac{90°}{2} = 45°$

(ii) $\frac{1}{3}$ of a right angle $= \frac{90°}{3} = 30°$

(iii) 2 times of a right angle $= 2 \times 90° = 180°$

Q.32 Measure the angle from where Kittu should hit the striker.

Ans. The measure of angle from where Kittu should hit the striker is 30°.

Angles in a Paper Aeroplane (NCERT Pg 32)

- Take a square sheet of paper.

- Fold it in half and open it.

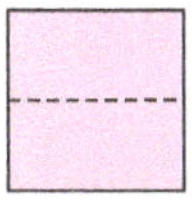

- Fold the corners to the centre. Your paper looks like this.

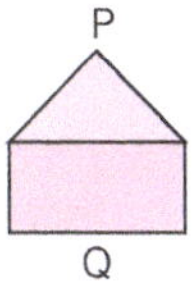

- Fold the green triangle such that P touches Q.

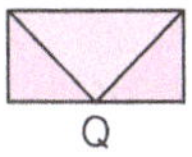

- Fold the top two corners of this rectangle along the dotted lines.

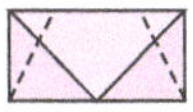

- Your paper will look like this. There is a small triangle in the picture which has to be folded up.

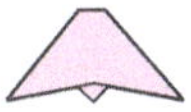

- Turn it over and fold it in half along the dotted line.

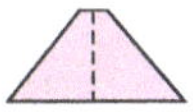

- Now, to make a wing fold the yellow edge over the red edge.

- Turn it and do the same on the other side as well.

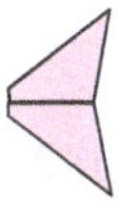

Your plane is ready to fly. How well does it fly?

Q.33 Find the angles of 45° and 90° when you open your plane.

Ans.

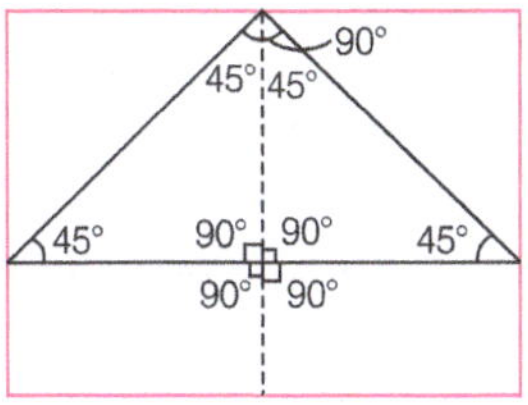

Angles with Yoga (NCERT Pg 33)

Q.34 Rahmat is doing Yoga. These are the pictures of different 'Asanas' he does everyday.

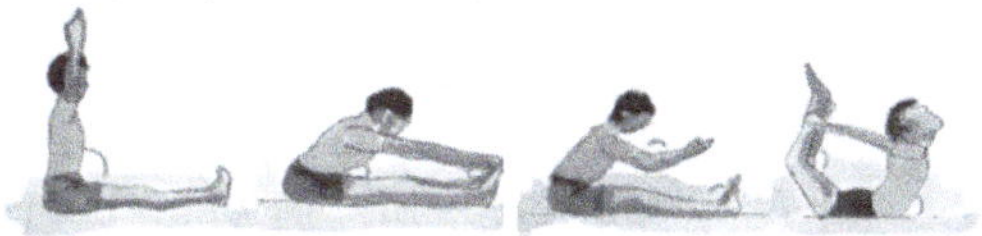

(a) (b) (c) (d)

Estimate the measure of many angles as you can made by different parts of the body while doing 'Asanas'.

Ans.

Pict ure	Angle between body parts	Measures of angle
(a)	Thigh and abdomen	90°
(b)	Thigh and abdomen	less than 90°
(c)	Arm and hand	more than 90°
(d)	Thigh and Leg	more than 90°
(d)	Ground and abdomen	less than 90°

The D Game (NCERT Pg 33)

Q.35 You can play the 'D' game with your friends. You draw an angle. Your friend will guess the measure of that angle. Then, you use your 'D' to measure it. The difference between the measured angle and the guess will be your friend's score. The one with the lowest score will be the winner. Come on, play!

Draw Angle	Guess	Measure	Score

Ans. Do yourself.

PRACTICE QUESTIONS

1. Fill in the blanks.

(i) When two lines meet at a common point, it forms ______ . (an angle/a line)

(ii) A right angle is of ____ degrees. (180/90)

(iii) A triangle has _____ sides and ____ angles. (4, 4/3, 3)

(iv) The angle between two hands of a clock at 8 o'clock is _______ . (more than a right angle/less than a right angle)

2. True or False

(i) A rectangle can have angles less than a right angle.

(ii) $\frac{1}{2}$ of a right angle is 45°.

(iii) The angle between minute hand and hour hand of a clock at 6:15 pm is a right angle.

3. Multiple choice questions

(i) Which of the following angles is less than a right angle?

(a) 45° (b) 90° (c) 120° (d) 180°

(ii) How many angles does a quadrilateral have?

(a) 2 (b) 3 (c) 4 (d) 5

(iii) At which time, the angle between two hands of a clock is less than a right angle?

(a) 8:20 am (b) 9:30 pm
(c) 2:30 pm (d) 11:10 am

4. Odd-one out

(i) (a) Circle (b) Square
(c) Triangle (d) Rectangle

(ii)

(a)

(b)
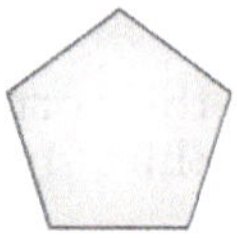

(c)
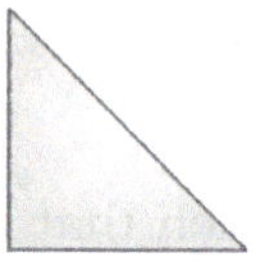

(d)
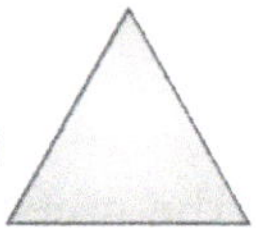

5. Match the columns

	Column A		Column B
(i)	Less than a right angle	(a)	9:00 am
(ii)	Right angle	(b)	1:00 pm
(iii)	More than a right angle	(c)	3:15 pm
(iv)	$\frac{1}{3}$ of a right angle	(d)	6:50 am

6. Write the word 'ELEPHANT' using the straight lines and count the angles.

ANSWERS & SOLUTIONS

1. (i) an angle
(ii) 90
(iii) 3, 3
(iv) more than a right angle

2. (i) False (ii) True
(iii) False

3. (i) (a) (ii) (c)
(iii) (d)

4. (i) (a) (ii) (c)

5. (i) → (c) (ii) → (a)
(iii) → (d) (iv) → (b)

6. The word 'ELEPHANT' using straight lines is written as

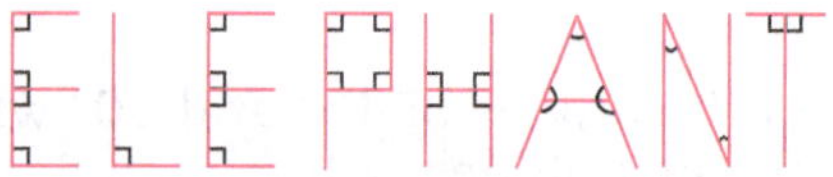

Number of right angles = 19

Number of angles less than a right angle = 5

Number of angles more than a right angle = 2

CHAPTER 3 HOW MANY SQUARES?

Square

A square is a two dimensional shape with four equal sides and four right angles.

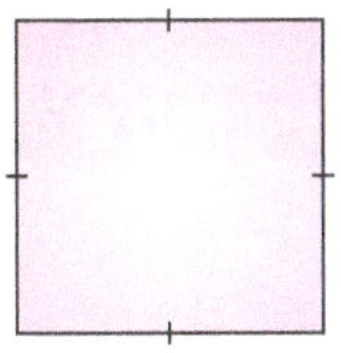

Grids

A grid is a network of squares arranged in rows and columns.
e.g. 3×3 grid means there are 3 rows and 3 columns of squares making a total of 9 squares.

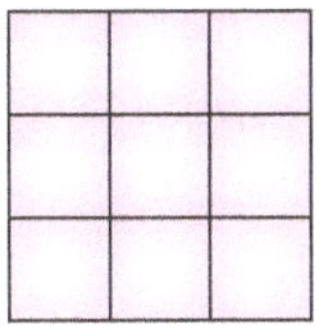

Square numbers

A square number is a number that can be expressed as the product of an integer by itself.

Area and perimeter of a square

The area of a square is calculated by multiplying the length of one side by itself.

Area of a square = Side × Side

The perimeter of square is the total length of its four sides.

Perimeter of a square = 4 × Side

Area and perimeter of a rectangle

The area of a rectangle is calculated by multiplying the length and breadth.

Area of a rectangle = Length × Breadth

Perimeter of the rectangle is the sum of all four sides.

Perimeter of a rectangle = 2 (Length + Breadth)

Area of a complex shapes

For irregular shapes like footprints and palms etc. drawn on a grid, then estimate the area by counting the complete squares inside the shape and adding the more than half filled squares.

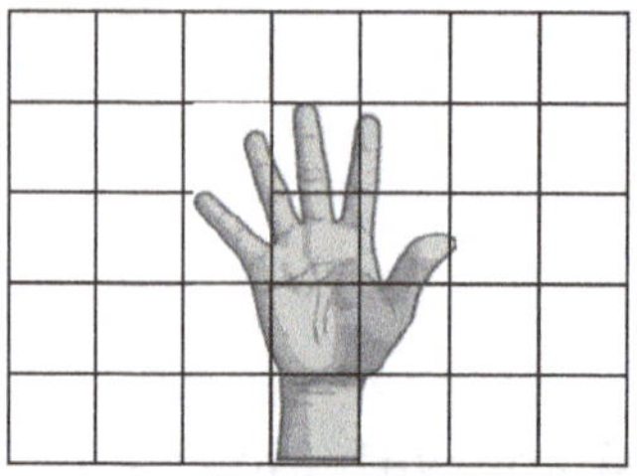

NCERT FOLDER

NCERT Pg 34

Q.1

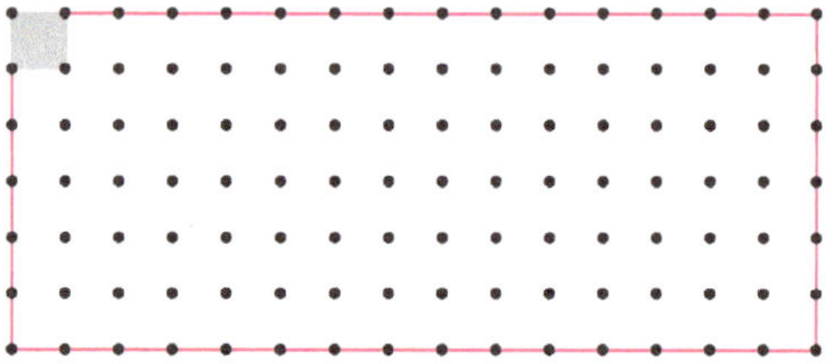

(i) Measure the side of the shaded square on the dotted sheet. Draw here as many rectangles as possible using 12 such squares.

(ii) How many rectangles could you make?

(iii) Which of these rectangles has the longest perimeter?

(iv) Which of these rectangles has the smallest perimeter?

Ans. *(i) The side of the shaded square is 1 cm. The possible rectangles made from 12 identical squares are shown below.

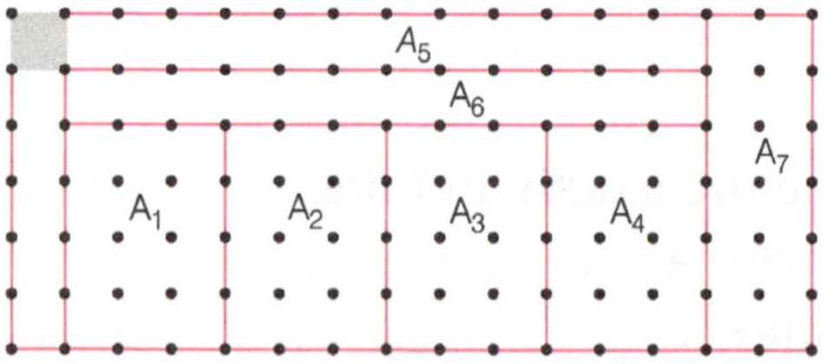

*(ii) There are 7 rectangles.
4 rectangles are of size 3×4,
(A_1, A_2, A_3 and A_4)

2 rectangles are of size 1×12 (A_5 and A_6) and 1 rectangle is of size 2×6 (A_7).
So, the total number of rectangles
$= 4 + 2 + 1 = 7$

(iii) Perimeter of rectangles A_1, A_2, A_3 and A_4.
$= 2(l + b)$ [here, $l = 3$ and $b = 4$]
$= 2(3 + 4) = 2 \times 7 = 14$ cm

Perimeter of rectangles A_5, A_6
$= 2(l + b)$ [here, $l = 1$ and $b = 12$]
$= 2(1 + 12)$
$= 2 \times 13 = 26$ cm

Perimeter of rectangle A_7
$= 2(l + b)$ [here, $l = 2$ and $b = 6$]
$= 2[2 + 6]$
$= 2 \times 8 = 16$ cm

So, the rectangles of size 1×12 (which are A_5 and A_6) have the longest perimeter.

(iv) The rectangles of size 3×4 (which are A_1, A_2, A_3 and A_4) have the smallest perimeter.

* *Students can write alternate answer as per their choice.*

Measure Stamps (NCERT Pg 35)

Q.2

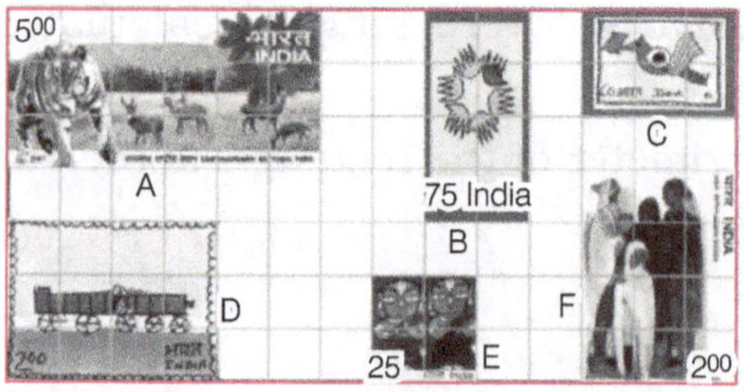

Look at these interesting stamps.

(i) How many squares of one centimetre sides does stamp A cover ?
And stamp B?

(ii) Which stamp has the biggest area?
How many squares of side 1 cm does this stamp cover?
How much is the area of the biggest stamp? ________ square cm.

(iii) Which two stamps have the same area?
How much is the area of each of these stamps?________ square cm.

(iv) The area of the smallest stamp is ______ square cm.
The difference between the area of the smallest and the biggest stamp is ______ square cm.

(v) Collect some old stamps. Place them on the square grid and find their area and perimeter.

Ans. (i) The area of stamp A is $6 \times 3 = 18$ square cm
So, stamp A covers 18 squares.
And, area of stamp B is $4 \times 2 = 8$ square cm
So, stamp B covers 8 squares.

(ii) Stamp A has the biggest area.
$\because$ Area of stamp A = 18 square cm
$\therefore$ Stamp A covers 18 squares of side 1 cm.

(iii) Area of stamp D = 3×4
= 12 square cm
Area of stamp F = 4×3
= 12 square cm
So, stamps D and F have the same area. The area of each of these stamps is 12 square cm.

(iv) Area of stamp E = $2 \times 2 = 4$ square cm
So, the area of the smallest stamp is 4 square cm.
Now, Area of biggest stamp – Area of smallest stamp
= 18 square cm – 4 square cm
= 14 square cm

(v) Do yourself.

Guess (NCERT Pg 36)

Q.3 (i) Which has the bigger area - one of your footprints or the page of this book?

(ii) Which has the smaller area - two five-rupee notes together or a hundred rupee note?

(iii) Look at a 10 rupee-note. Is its area more than hundred square cm?

(iv) Is the area of the blue shape more than the area of the yellow shape? Why?

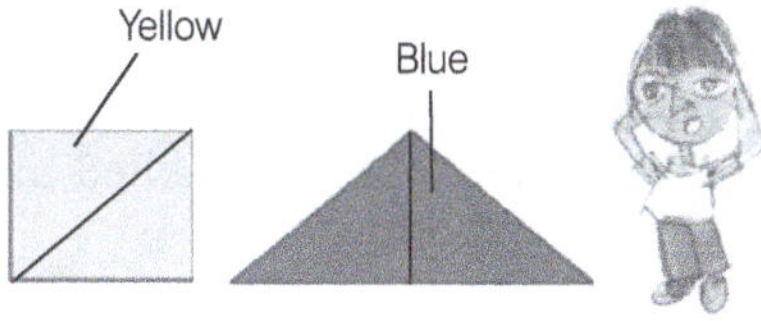

(v) Is the perimeter of the yellow shape more than the perimeter of the blue shape? Why?

Ans. (i) The area of the page of this book has bigger area than one of my footprint.

(ii) A hundred-rupee note has the smaller area.

(iii) No, the area of 10 rupee-note is not more than hundred square cm.

(iv) No, area of blue shape is equal to the area of the yellow shape. We can easily prove it by taking a cutout of these blue shape and yellow shape using a square sheet paper and calculating their areas.

(v) No, the perimeter of yellow shape is less than the perimeter of blue shape. We can easily prove it by measuring their boundaries with the help of ruler or thread.

How Big is My Hand? (NCERT Pg 36-37)

Q.4 Trace your hand on the squared sheet on the NCERT page 37.

(i) How will you decide whose hand is bigger your hand or your friend's hand?

(ii) What is the area of your hand? ________ square cm.

(iii) What is the area of your friend's hand? _______ square cm.

Ans. *(i)

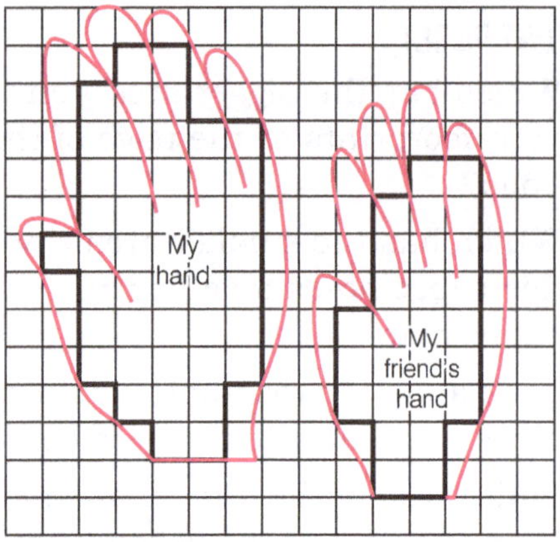

Firstly, trace your hand and your friend's hand on the square sheet paper.

Now, find how many of each type of squares. Suppose, there are like fullfilled, half-filled, more than half-filled and less than half filled square.

Now, neglect the squares that are less than half-filled and consider more than half-filled square as one.

From the figure	My hand	My friend's hand
Total number of complete squares	46	27
Total number of half filled squares	8	6
Total number of more than half filled squares	14	15

*(ii) Area of my hand $= 46 + \frac{8}{2} + 14 = 46 + 4 + 14$

$= 64$ square cm

*(iii) Area of my friend's hand $= 27 + \frac{6}{2} + 15$

$= 27 + 3 + 15$

$= 45$ square cm

Area of my hand is more than area of my friend's hand.

My Footprints (NCERT Pg 37-39)

Q.5 (i) Whose footprint is larger—yours or your friend's?

(ii) How will you decide? Discuss.

(iii) Is the area of both your footprints the same?

Ans. (i) My footprint is larger than my friend's foot print.

(ii) We can decide by finding areas of both footprints on a square sheet of paper after the tracing. The one with larger total area is the bigger footprint.

(iii) Yes, the area of both of my footprints is the same.

Q.6 (i) Guess which animal's footprint will have the same area as yours. Discuss.

(ii) Here are some footprints of animals (in actual sizes). Guess the area of their footprints.

Ans. *(i) A baboon's footprint may be similar in size to mine.

*(ii) Area of hen's footprint = 3 square cm (approx.)

Area of dog's footprint = 12 square cm (approx.)

So, here we can say that dog's footprint has a larger area than the hen's footprint.

Q.7

Make big squares and rectangles like this to find the area faster.

Ans. *Area of A $= \left(7 + 2 \times \frac{1}{2} + 8\right)$ square cm

$= 7 + 1 + 8 = 16$ square cm

Area of B $= \left(7 + 4 \times \frac{1}{2} + 5\right)$ square cm

$= 7 + 2 + 5$

$= 14$ square cm

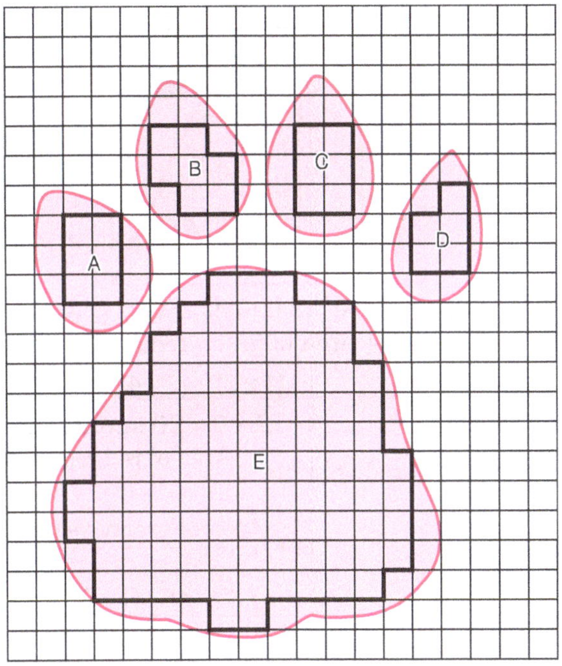

Area of C $= \left(6 + 2 \times \frac{1}{2} + 8\right)$ square cm

$= 6 + 1 + 8$

$= 15$ square cm

Area of D $= \left(5 + 2 \times \frac{1}{2} + 5\right)$ square cm

$= 5 + 1 + 5 = 11$ square cm

Area of E $= \left(101 + 8 \times \frac{1}{2} + 15\right)$ square cm

$= 101 + 4 + 15 = 120$ square cm

Total area of footprints

$= 16 + 14 + 15 + 11 + 120$

$= 176$ square cm

How Many Squares in Me? (NCERT Pg 40)

Q.8 (i) What is the area of this triangle?

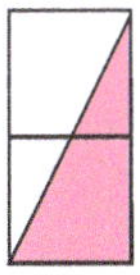

[**Hint** The triangle is half the rectangle of area 2 square cm. So, its area is ______ square cm.]

(ii) Is this shape half of the big rectangle?

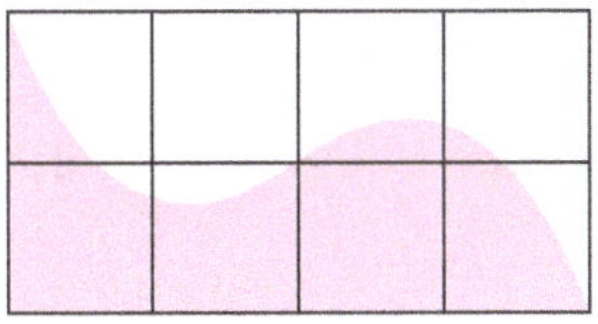

[**Hint** Hmmm... So, its area is ______ square cm.]

Ans. (i) Area of triangle $= \frac{\text{Area of rectangle}}{2}$

$= \frac{2 \text{ square cm}}{2} = \frac{2 \times 1}{2}$

$= 1$ square cm.

(ii) Yes, this shape is half of the big rectangle.

Area of shape $= \frac{\text{Area of rectangle}}{2}$

$= \frac{2 \times 4}{2} = \frac{1}{2} \times 8$

$= 4$ square cm

Q.9 Write the area (in square cm) of the shapes below.

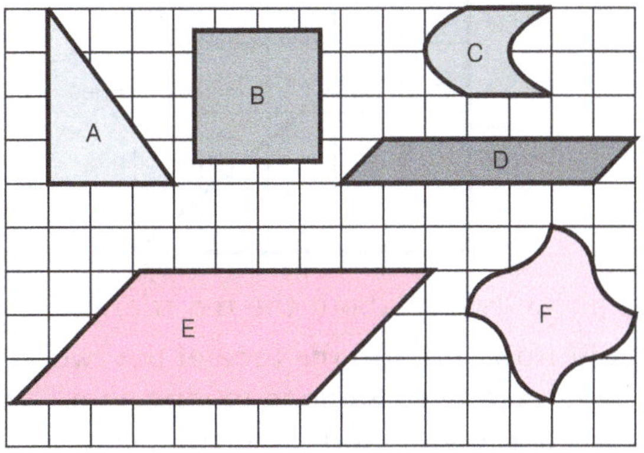

Ans. Area of triangle A = Half of the area of rectangle

$$= \frac{3 \times 4}{2} \text{ cm}^2 = \frac{12}{2} \text{ cm}^2$$

$$= 6 \text{ square cm}$$

Area of square B

= Number of complete squares + Number of half squares + Number of quarter squares

$$= 4 + \frac{1}{2} \times 8 + \frac{1}{4} \times 4$$

$$= 4 + 4 + 1 = 9 \text{ square cm}$$

Area of shape C $= 2 + 0 \times \frac{1}{2} + 2$

$$= 2 + 0 + 2 = 4 \text{ square cm}$$

Area of shape D $= 5 + 2 \times \frac{1}{2} + 0 = 5 + 1$

$$= 6 \text{ square cm}$$

Area of shape E $= 18 + 6 \times \frac{1}{2} + 0 = 18 + 3$

$$= 21 \text{ square cm}$$

Area of shape F $= 4 + 0 \times \frac{1}{2} + 4 = 4 + 0 + 4$

$$= 4 + 4 = 8 \text{ square cm}$$

Try Triangles (NCERT Pg 41-42)

Q.10 (i) The blue triangle is half of the big rectangle. Area of the big rectangle is 20 square cm. So, the area of the blue triangle is _______ square cm.

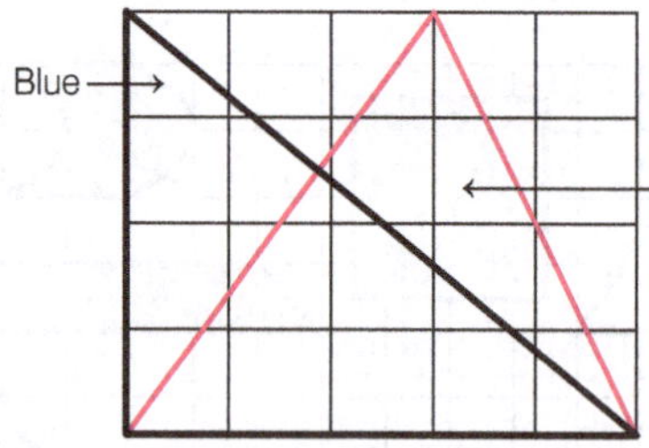

(ii) And what about the red triangle?

(iii) Now you find the area of the two rectangles Sadiq is talking about. What is the area of the red triangle? Explain.

(iv) Help Sadiq in finding some more such triangles. Draw atleast 5 more.

Ans. (i) Area of blue triangle $= \frac{\text{Area of big rectangle}}{2}$

$$= \frac{20 \text{ square cm}}{2}$$

$$= 10 \text{ square cm}$$

(ii) The area of both the red and the blue triangles in this rectangle is same.

So, the area of red triangle is 10 square cm.

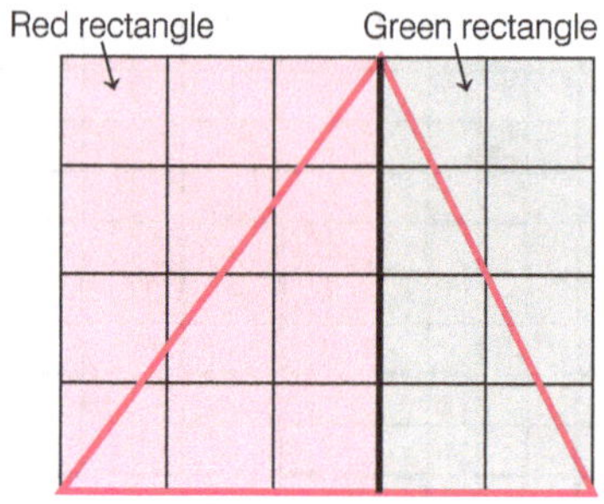

(iii) Area of the big rectangle = Area of red rectangle + Area of green rectangle

$$= (4 \times 3) + (2 \times 4)$$

$$= 12 + 8 = 20 \text{ square cm}$$

Area of red triangle $= \frac{\text{Area of red rectangle}}{2} + \frac{\text{Area of green rectangle}}{2}$

$$= \frac{(3 \times 4)}{2} + \frac{(4 \times 2)}{2}$$

$$= \frac{12}{2} + \frac{8}{2} = 6 + 4$$

$$= 10 \text{ square cm}$$

(iv) Following are the triangles drawn in the picture below which have 10 square cm area.

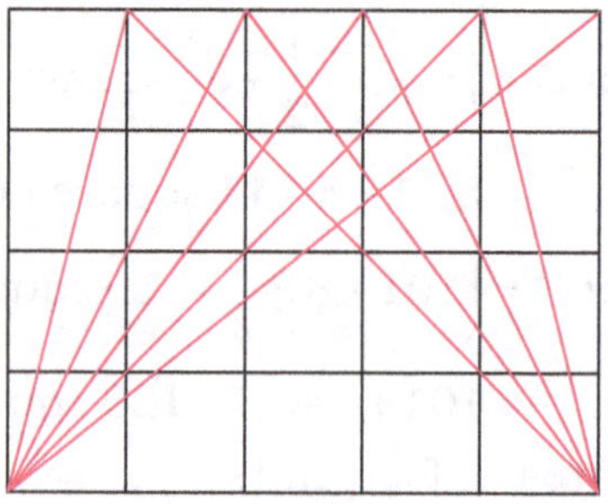

Five triangles having area 10 square cm.

Complete the shape (NCERT Pg 42)

Q.11 Suruchi drew two sides of a shape. She asked Asif to complete the shape with two more sides, so that its area is 10 square cm.

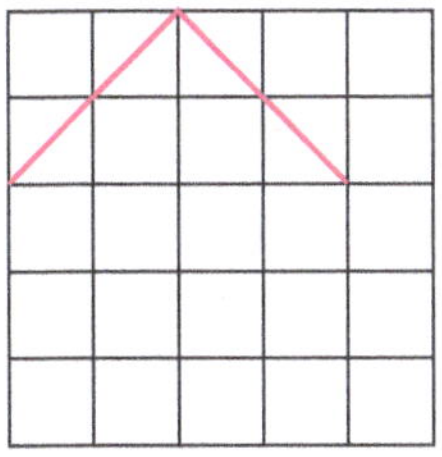

He completed the shape like this.

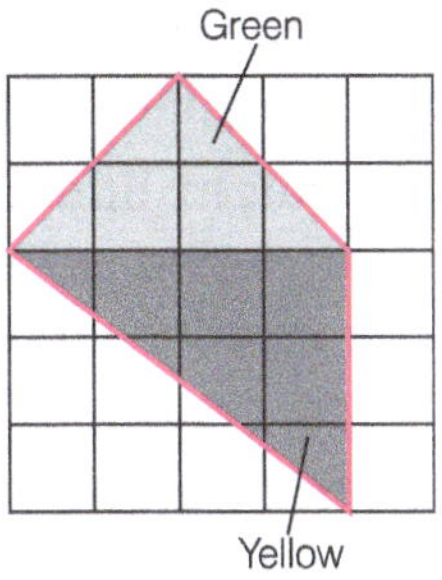

(i) Is he correct? Discuss.

(ii) Explain how the green area is 4 square cm and the yellow area is 6 square cm.

(iii) Is Suruchi correct? How much is the blue area? Explain.

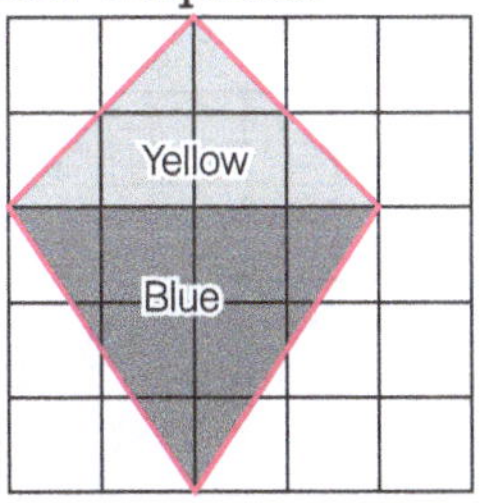

(iv) Can you think of some other ways of completing the shape?

Try some other ways yourself.

Ans. (i) Yes, he is correct.

(ii) Area of green portion

$$= \frac{\text{Area of rectangle measuring } (2 \times 4)}{2}$$

$$= \frac{1}{2} \times 2 \times 4$$

$$= 4 \text{ square cm}$$

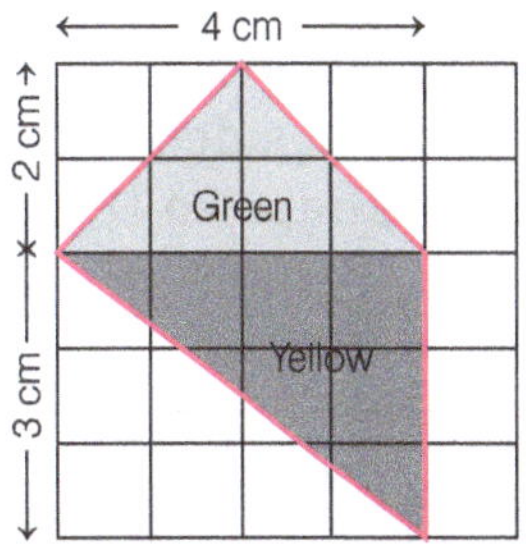

Area of yellow portion

$$= \frac{\text{Area of rectangle measuring } (3 \times 4)}{2}$$

$$= \frac{1}{2} \times 3 \times 4 = 6 \text{ square cm}$$

(iii) Yes, Suruchi is correct.

Explanation

Area of yellow triangle

$$= \frac{\text{Area of rectangle measuring } (4 \times 2)}{2}$$

$$= \frac{1}{2} \times 4 \times 2 = 2 \times 2 = 4 \text{ square cm}$$

Area of blue triangle

$$= \frac{\text{Area of rectangle measuring } (4 \times 3)}{2}$$

$$= \frac{1}{2} \times 4 \times 3 = 2 \times 3 = 6 \text{ square cm}$$

So, the total area

= Area of yellow triangle + Area of blue triangle

$= 4 + 6 = 10$ square cm.

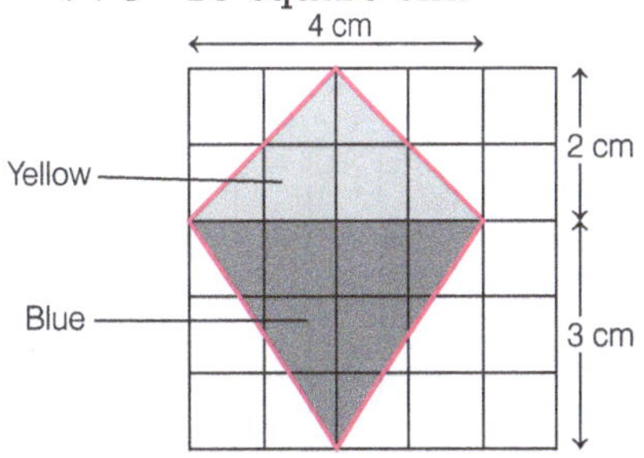

(iv) The area of a triangle is half that of a rectangle with the same height and width. Therefore, we can create a rectangle with 30 square cm. After that, we can draw as many triangles inside it as we can.

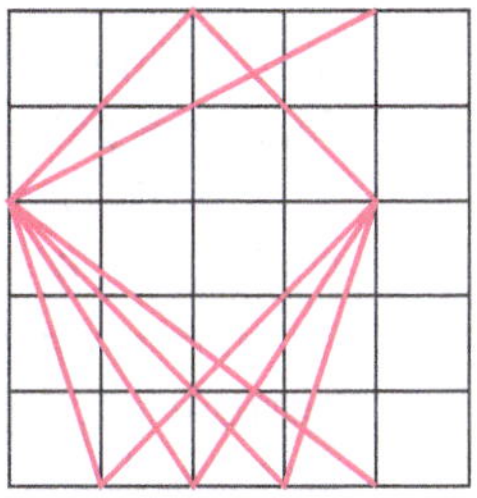

Practice Time (NCERT Pg 43-44)

Q.12 This is one of the sides of a shape. Complete the shape so that its area is 4 square cm.

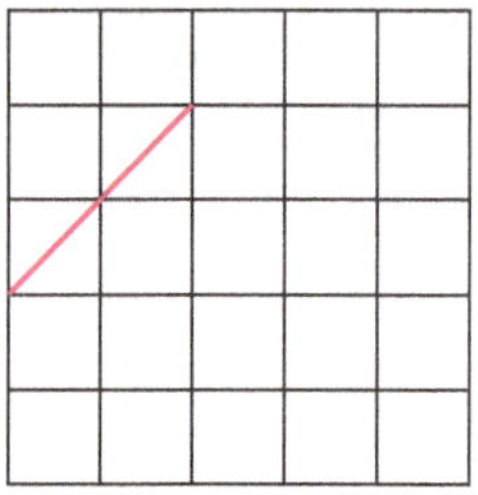

Ans. Following is the required shape with area 4 square cm.

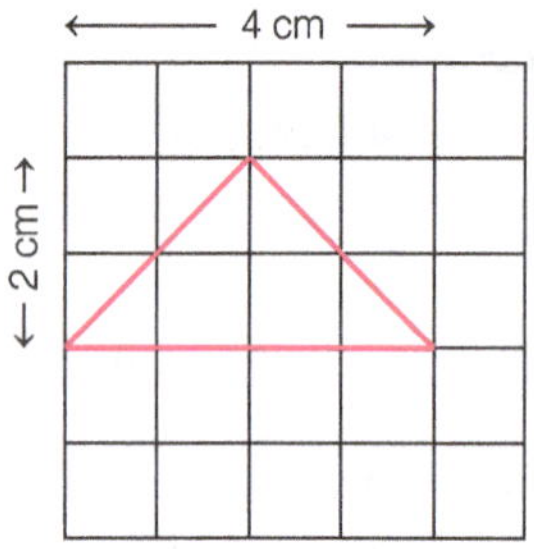

Area of triangle

$$= \frac{\text{Area of rectangle measuring } (2 \times 4)}{2}$$

$$= \frac{1}{2} \times 2 \times 4 = 4 \text{ square cm}$$

Q.13 Two sides of a shape are drawn here. Complete the shape by drawing two more sides so that its area is less than 2 square cm.

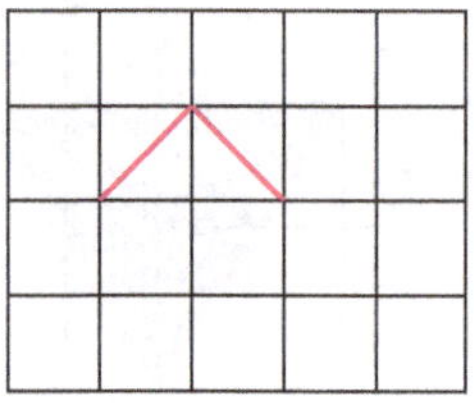

Ans. We get a triangle after drawing two more sides. The area of triangle is 1 square cm. Also, we get a rectangle after a mirror image of triangle drawn below. The area of rectangle is 2 square cm.

Now, draw a point just above side of the bottom vertex of the rectangle and join the given sides with this point.

This will give a shape with area less than 2 square cm.

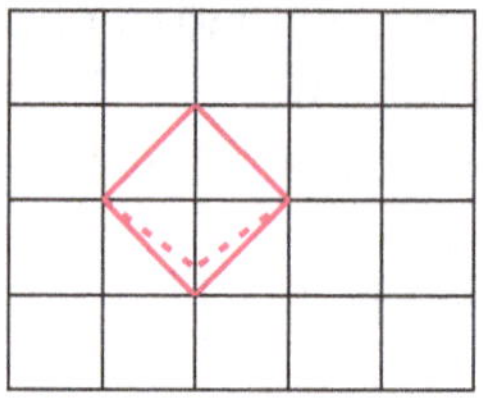

Q.14 Here is a rectangle of area 20 square cm.

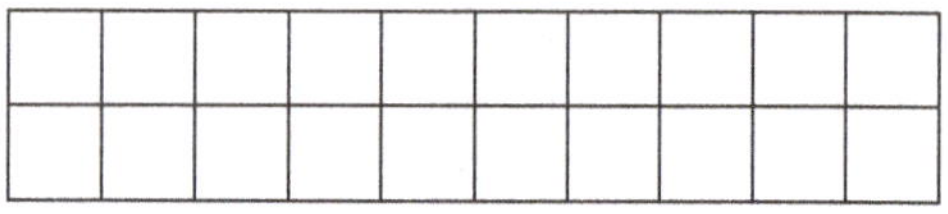

(i) Draw one straight line in this rectangle to divide it into two equal triangles. What is the area of each of the triangles?

(ii) Draw one straight line in this rectangle to divide it into two equal rectangles. What is the area of each of the smaller rectangles?

(iii) Draw two straight lines in this rectangle to divide it into one rectangle and two equal triangles.

(a) What is the area of the rectangle?

(b) What is the area of each of the triangles?

Ans. (i) To divide a rectangle into two equal triangles, a straight line can be drawn as

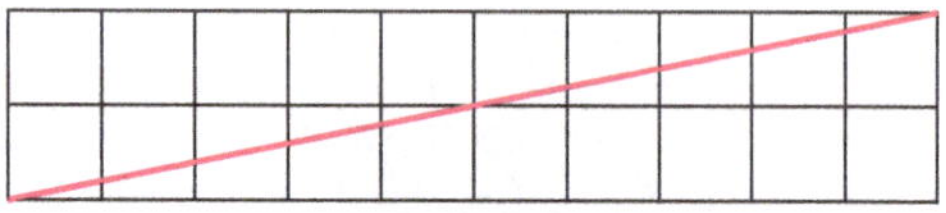

$$\text{Area of each triangle} = \frac{\text{Area of rectangle}}{2}$$

$$= \frac{1}{2} \times 20$$

$$= 10 \text{ square cm}$$

(ii) There are two ways to draw a straight line that is vertically or horizontally to divide it into two equal rectangles ABCD and BEFC.

Vertical line

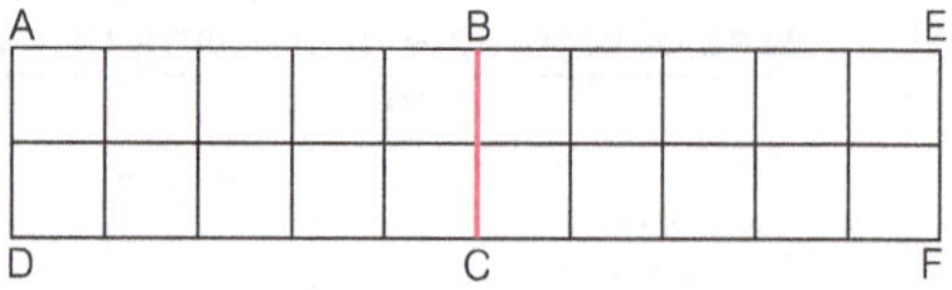

Horizontal line

Area of each smaller rectangle

$= \frac{\text{Area of rectangle}}{2} = \frac{1}{2} \times 20$

= 10 square cm

(iii) Following is the figure in which we divide the big rectangle into two small rectangles and then one rectangle into two triangles.

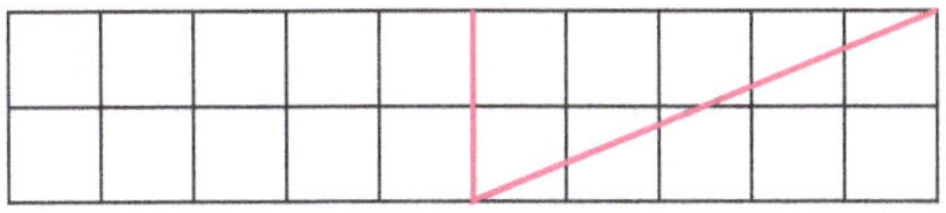

(a) Area of rectangle $= \frac{\text{Area of big rectangle}}{2}$

$= \frac{20}{2} = 10$ square cm

(b) Area of each triangle

$= \frac{\text{Area of smaller rectangle}}{2}$

$= \frac{10}{2} = 5$ square cm

Puzzles with Five Squares (NCERT Pg 44 to 46)

Q.15 Measure the side of a small square on the squared paper on NCERT page 45. Make as many shapes as possible using 5 such square. Three are drawn for you.

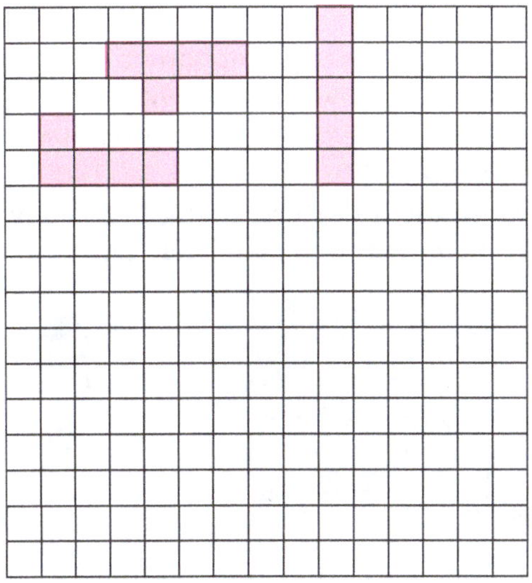

(i) How many different shapes can you draw?

(ii) Which shape has the longest perimeter? How much?

(iii) Which shape has the shortest perimeter? How much?

(iv) What is the area of the shapes? ________ square cm. That's simple!

(v) Did you get all the 12 shapes using 5 squares?

(vi) Try to arrange your 12 shapes in some other way to make a 10×6 rectangle. Could you do not?

Ans. *(i) We can draw 12 different shapes using 5 such squares.

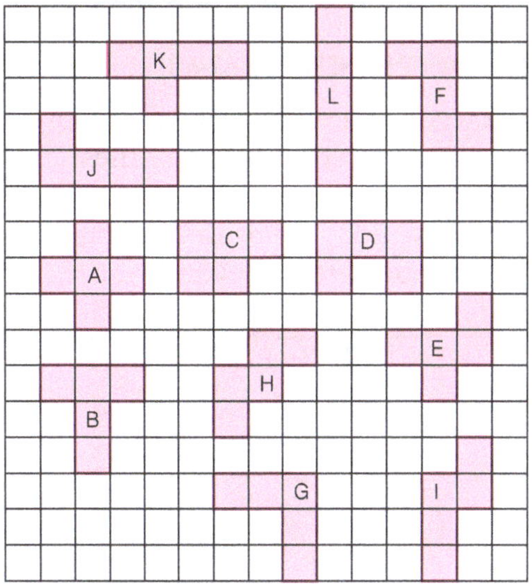

(ii) All the figures have same perimeter which is 12 cm except figure 'C'.

(iii) The perimeter of shape 'C' is 10 cm, so shape 'C' has the shortest perimeter.

(iv) Each shape has 5 squares. So, area of each shape is equal to 5 square cm.

(v) Yes, I got all the 12 shapes using 5 squares.

*(vi) Following is the required 10×6 rectangle made by using 12 shapes.

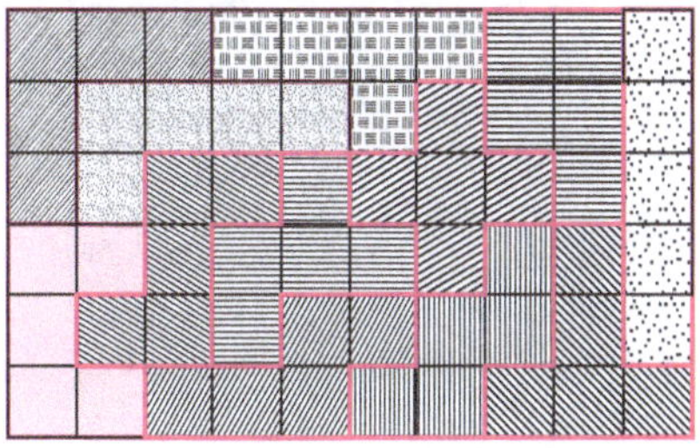

Try Another Puzzle (NCERT Pg 46)

Q.16 You have to make a 5×12 rectangle with these 12 shapes. There are more than 1000 ways to do it. If you can find even one, that's great!

Ans. *The figure given below shows a 5×12 rectangle with 12 shapes.

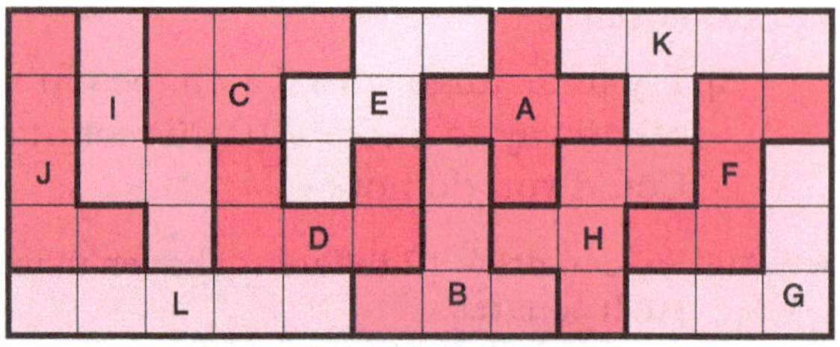

Make Your Own Tile (NCERT Pg 47-49)

Q.17 Ziri went to a shop and was surprised to see the different designs of tiles on the floor. Aren't these beautiful! Can you find the tile which is repeated to make each of these floor patterns? Circle a tile in each pattern.

After looking at the patterns Ziri wanted to make her own yellow tile. You too make a tile this way.

Step I Take a piece of cardboard or thick paper. Draw a  square of side 3 cm on it.

Step II Draw a triangle on any one of the sides of this square. 

Step III Draw another triangle of the same size on another side of the square. 

But this time draw it inside the square.

Step IV Cut this shape from the cardboard. Your tile is ready! 

What is it's area?

Ans. The side of the square is 3 cm.

Since, the triangle of same area is added on one side and removed from another side of square.

So, the area of square tile will remain same.

Therefore, the area of the figure

$= 3 \text{ cm} \times 3 \text{ cm}$

$= 9 \text{ square cm}$

Q.18 Make a pattern using your tile. Trace the shape to repeat it on a page but remember, there must be no gaps between them.

Ziri made a pattern using her yellow tiles. (You know the area of her tile.)

(i) How many tiles has she used?

(ii) What is the area of the floor pattern Ziri has made here?

Ans. *(i) She has used 12 tiles.

(ii) Side of the tile = 3 cm
Number of the tile she used = 12
Area of the floor pattern Ziri has made
$= 12 \times 3 = 36$ square cm

Practice time (NCERT Pg 49)

Q.19 Ziri tried to make some other tiles. She started with a square of 2 cm side and made shapes like these.

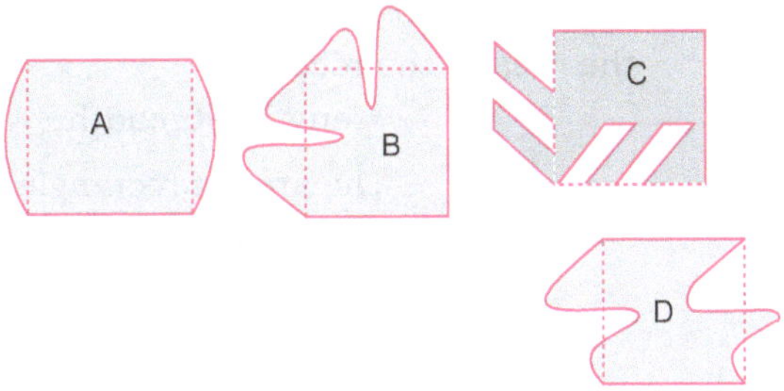

Look at these carefully and find out:

(i) Which of these shapes will tile a floor (without any gaps)? Discuss. What is the area of these shapes?

(ii) Make designs in your copy by tiling those shapes.

(iii) Now you create your own new tiles out of a square. Can you do the same with a triangle? Try doing it.

Ans. (i) Shape C and shape D will tile a floor without any gaps.
Area of these shapes $= 2 \times 2 = 4$ square cm.

*(ii) The designs made by tiling these shapes are given below
Design by tiling the shape C

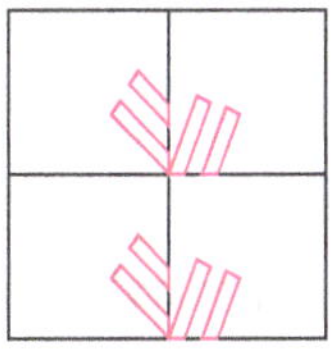

Design by tiling the shape D

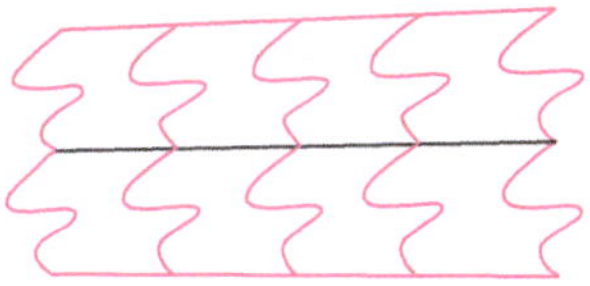

*(iii) Here are some new tiles

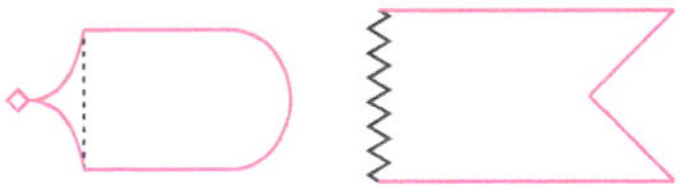

This can also be done using triangle tile as follows

PRACTICE QUESTIONS

1. Fill in the blanks

(i) A square has _______ right angles.

(ii) The opposite sides of a rectangle are _______ to each other.

(iii) The area of a square is calculated by _______ its side length.

(iv) A chessboard has _______ squares in total.

2. Multiple choice questions

(i) What is the perimeter of the square with side length 5 cm?
(a) 20 cm (b) 10 cm
(c) 25 cm (d) 15 cm

(ii) How many squares are there in a 3×3 grid?
(a) 3 (b) 5 (c) 9 (d) 14

(iii) What is the area of square with a side length of 7 cm?
(a) 14 sq cm
(b) 49 sq cm
(c) 21 sq cm
(d) 28 sq cm

(iv) How many right angles are there in a square?
(a) 2 (b) 3 (c) 4 (d) 5

3. Word Problems

(i) A square shaped park has a side length of 50 m. What is its perimeter?

(ii) A chessboard has 64 squares in total. If each square has a side of 2 cm, what is the area of chessboard and each square?

(iii) A rectangle garden has an area of 180 square m and length of the garden is 15 m. What is the breadth of the rectangle garden?

4. Case based questions

Meera wants to tile her kitchen floor, which is shaped like a square. The side length of the floor is 8 m and she uses square tiles that have a side length of 1 m.

Based on the above information, answer the following questions

(i) How many squares tile will Meera need to cover the entire kitchen floor?

(ii) If each tile costs ₹ 25, how much will Meera spend on the tiles?

ANSWERS & SOLUTIONS

1. (i) four (ii) equal (iii) squaring (iv) 64

2. (i) (a) The length of a side of square = 5 cm

We know that the perimeter of a square

$= 4 \times \text{Side} = 4 \times 5 \text{ cm} = 20 \text{ cm}$

(ii) (c) 3×3 grid means there are 3 rows and 3 columns of squares.

Therefore, the total number of squares made by it $= 3 \times 3 = 9$ squares.

(iii) (b) The length of a side of square = 7 cm

$\because$ Area of the square = Side × Side

$\therefore$ The area of a square with side length 7 cm = 7 cm × 7 cm = 49 square cm

(iv) (c) 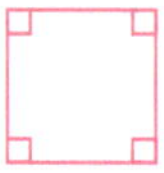

There are 4 right angles in a square.

3. (i) We have, the side length of a square shaped park = 50 m

We know that the perimeter of a square

$= 4 \times \text{Side}$

Therefore, the perimeter of the square shaped park $= 4 \times 50$ [$\because$ Side = 50 m]

$= 200$ m

(ii) $\because$ The area of chessboard

$= 64 \times$ area of each square

$= 64 \times 4$

$= 256$ square cm

Given that the length of a side of each square = 2 cm

$\therefore$ The area of each square

= 2 cm × 2 cm

= 4 square cm

Since, the chessboard has 64 squares in total.

(iii) Given, the area of the rectangle garden

= 180 square m

The length of a side of garden = 15 m

We know that

the area of the rectangle

= length × breadth

$$\Rightarrow \text{Breadth} = \frac{\text{The area of rectangle}}{\text{Length}}$$

$$\therefore \quad \text{Breadth} = \frac{180}{15}$$

$= 12$ m

Hence, the breadth of the rectangle garden is 12 m.

4. Since, the kitchen floor is square shaped.

Given that the side length of the floor

= 8 m

Therefore, the area of the kitchen floor

= 8 m × 8 m

= 64 square m

(i) Since, length of square shaped tile is 1m.

$\therefore$ The area of a tile = 1 square m

$\therefore$ Number of square tiles to cover the entire kitchen floor

$$= \frac{\text{The area of kitchen floor}}{\text{The area of one tile}}$$

$$= \frac{64 \text{ square m}}{1 \text{ square m}}$$

= 64 tiles

Hence, Meera will need 64 tiles to cover the entire kitchen floor.

(ii) Given, the cost of each tile = ₹25

Since, total required tiles = 64

Therefore, the amount, Meera will spend on the tiles

= Total number of tiles × cost of each tile

= 64 × ₹25

= ₹1600

CHAPTER 4 PARTS AND WHOLES

Fraction

A fraction is a way to express that a whole object or quantity has been divided into equal parts. A fraction has two parts : a numerator and a denominator.

The numerator represents how many parts we are considering, while the denominator represents the total number of equal parts the whole is divided into.

Visualizing Fractions

- A shape, like a circle or rectangle, can be divided into equal parts. If a circle is divided into 4 equal parts and one part is shaded, the fraction of the shaded part is $\frac{1}{4}$.

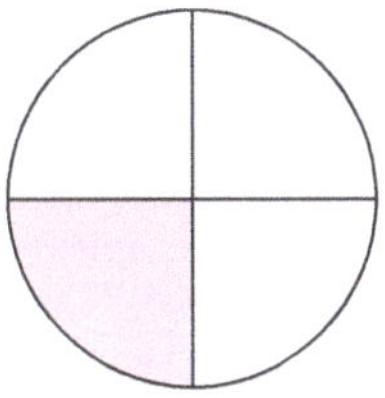

Equal Parts of a Whole

- If a pizza is cut into 4 equal slices, each slice is $\frac{1}{4}$ of the pizza.
- The flag of our country contains 3 equal parts. One third is saffron, one third is white and one third is green.
- If the whole is bigger its part will also be bigger.

Equivalent Fraction

- $\frac{1}{2}$ is equivalent to $\frac{2}{4}$ and $\frac{4}{8}$ because they all represent the same portion of the whole .
- To find equivalent fraction, multiply or divided both the numerator and denominator by the same number .

NCERT FOLDER

Our Flag (NCERT Pg 50-51)

Q.1 (i) You must have seen the flag of our country. Do you know how to draw the flag?

(ii) What is the colour of the middle one-third of the flag?

(iii) Where will you draw the Ashoka chakra?

(iv) How much of the flag will you colour green?

(v) Is the white colour now less than $\frac{1}{3}$ of the flag? Why?

Ans. (i) Yes, I know how to draw the flag.

(ii) The colour of the middle one - third of the flag is white.

(iii) I will draw the Ashoka chakra in the middle of white portion of flag.

(iv) I will colour bottom one- third of the flag with green colour.

(v) The blue Ashok chakra is present in the white colour portion of flag. Hence, the white portion of the flag is little less than $\frac{1}{3}$ of the flag.

Q.2 (i) Now, look at this flag. How much of it is black?

Flag of Afghanistan

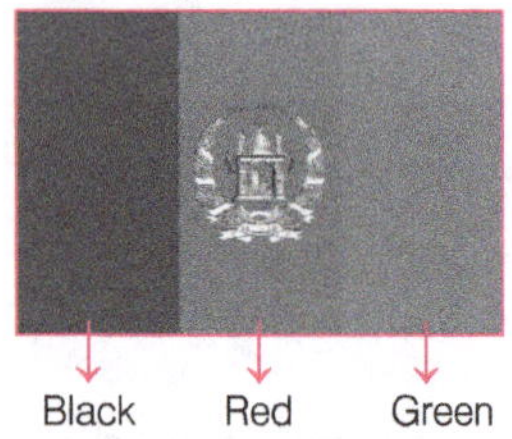

(ii) The green part of the flag can be written as ....

(iii) Is red less than one-third of the flag? Why?

* *Students can write alternate answer as per their choice.*

Ans. (i) One-third of the flag is black.

(ii) The green part of the flag can be written as the one- third of the flag.

(iii) The white emblem is present in the red colour portion. So, red is less than one-third of the flag.

Q.3 This is the flag of Myanmar, our neighbour.

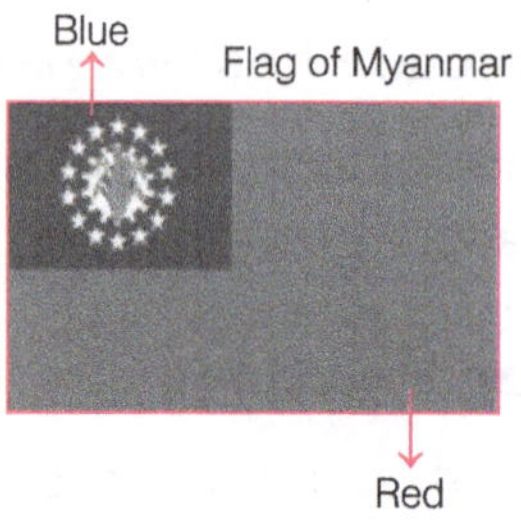

(i) Is blue more than one-fourth of the flag or less?

(ii) Guess how much of the flag is red. Is it more than $\frac{1}{2}$? Is it more than three-fourths?

Ans. (i) The blue colour is little less than one-fourth of the flag.

(ii) Red is more than $\frac{1}{2}$ of the flag.

Yes, it is more than $\frac{1}{2}$.

Yes, it is more than three-fourths.

Find Out

Q.4 Collect as many flags as you can. How many flags have three colours? Are all the coloured parts equal in these flags?

Ans. *Following are some flags

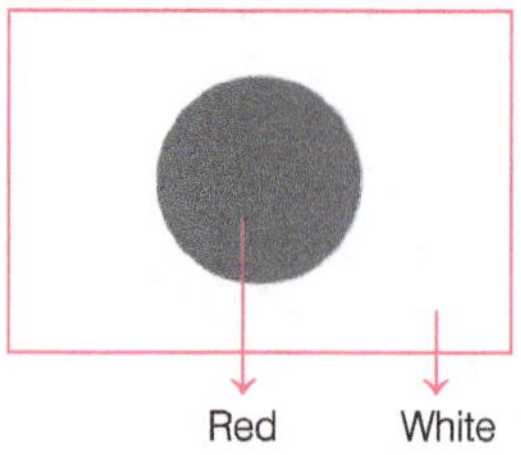

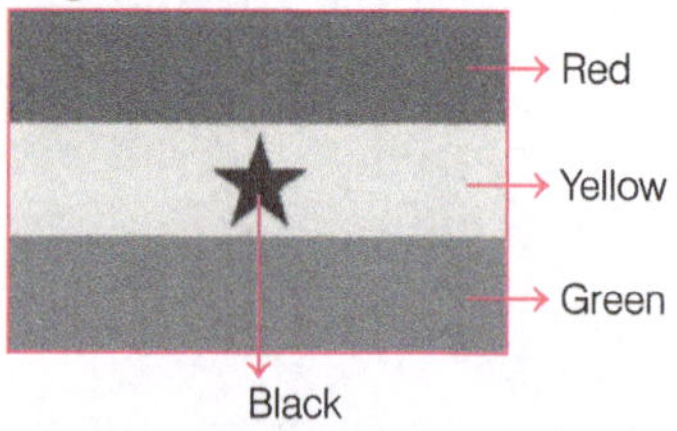

Flag of Italy

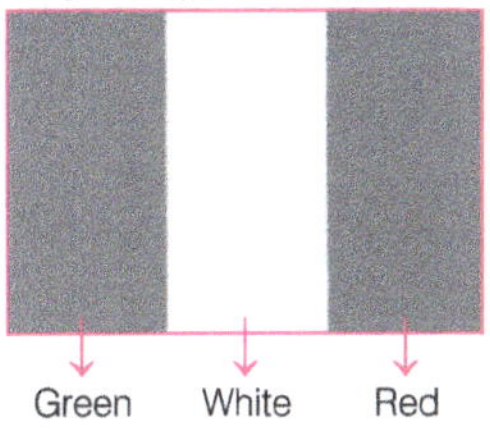

Flag of Germany

In the following flags, Italy and Germany have three colours .

All the coloured parts in Italy and Germany are equal.

Q.5 This is the flag of the Math Çlub in a school in Kerala.

(i) What part of the flag is coloured red? What part is green?

Flag of Math Club in Kerala School

(ii) See this black  logo. Draw it.

(iii) Is there a Math Club in your school? If not, ask your teacher how to set it up. Design a flag for your Math Club. Draw it here.

(a) Have you used the red colour? What part of the flag did you colour red?

(b) What were the other colours you chose?

Ans. (i) Two-fifth part of the flag is in red colour. One-fifth part of the flag is in green colour.

(ii) Here, is the required logo draw below:

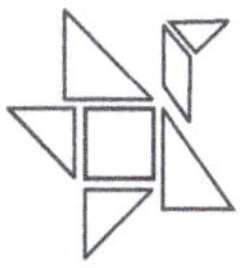

*(iii) No, there is no Math Club in my school. I have requested my teacher to help us in setting up Math Club. I have designed the following flag for the Math Club.

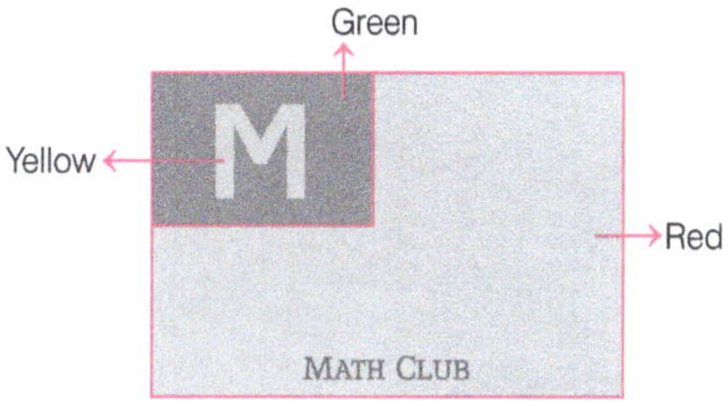

(a) Yes, I have used the red colour.

Red is more than $\frac{1}{2}$ of the flag.

It is more than three-fourths.

(b) I have used green and yellow colours other than red.

Magic Top (NCERT Pg 52)

Q.6 Let us make a magic top. Take a cardboard piece. Draw a circle of radius 3 cm and cut it out. Divide the circle into 8 equal parts. Now, each part is $\frac{1}{8}$ of the circle. Colour $\frac{2}{3}$ red, $\frac{1}{8}$ orange, $\frac{1}{8}$ yellow etc. as shown here. Push a matchstick through the centre of the circle. Your magic top is ready. Spin it fast! What do you see? Can you see all the colours? Write what you see in your notebook.

Ans. When we spin the magic top, we cannot see the all colours exactly as all the colours are overlapping. So, we see only white colours.

Practice time (NCERT Pg 52-54)

A. Chocolate bar

Q.7 Manju had a chocolate. She gave one-fourth of it to Raji, one-third to Sugatha and one-sixth to Sheela. She ate the remaining part.

(i) How many pieces of chocolate did each get? Write here.

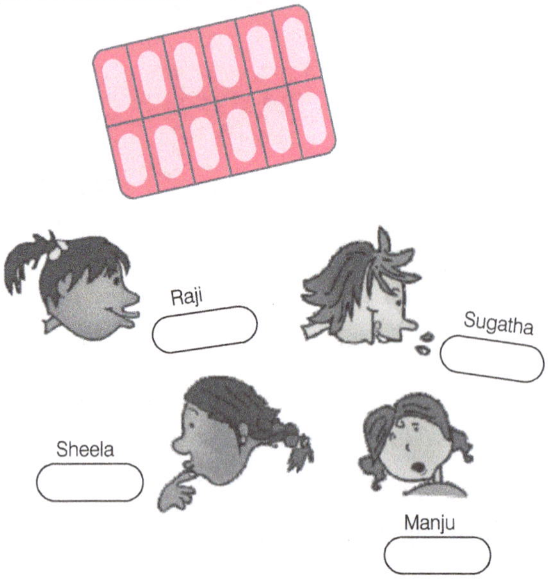

(ii) What part of the chocolate did Manju eat?

Ans. (i) Total number of pieces in chocolates = 12

Raji's share = $\frac{1}{4}$ of the whole = $\frac{1}{4} \times 12 = 3$

Sugatha's share = $\frac{1}{3}$ of the whole = $\frac{1}{3} \times 12 = 4$

Sheela's share = $\frac{1}{6}$ of the whole = $\frac{1}{6} \times 12 = 2$

Manju's share = $12 - (3 + 4 + 2) = 3$

(ii) Manju's share = $\frac{3}{12}$ of the whole

= $\frac{1}{4}$ of the whole

Hence, Manju ate one-fourth of the chocolate.

B. Colour the hats

Q.8 Colour $\frac{1}{3}$ of the hats red. Colour three-fifth hats blue.

(i) How many hats did you colour red?

(ii) How many hats did you colour blue?

(iii) What part of the hats are not coloured?

Ans. (i) Number of total hats = 15

Number of red colour hats = $\frac{1}{3} \times 15 = 5$

So, 5 hats are coloured as red.

(ii) Number of blue colour hats = $\frac{3}{5} \times 15$

$= 3 \times 3 = 9$

So, 9 hats are coloured as blue.

(iii) Number of hats left = $15 - 9 - 5 = 15 - 14$
$= 1$

So, $\frac{1}{15}$ part of hats are not coloured.

C. Equal parts of a triangle

Q.9 The white triangle is divided into three equal parts. Fill each one-third part with a different colour. Can you show that these parts are equal? Think how?

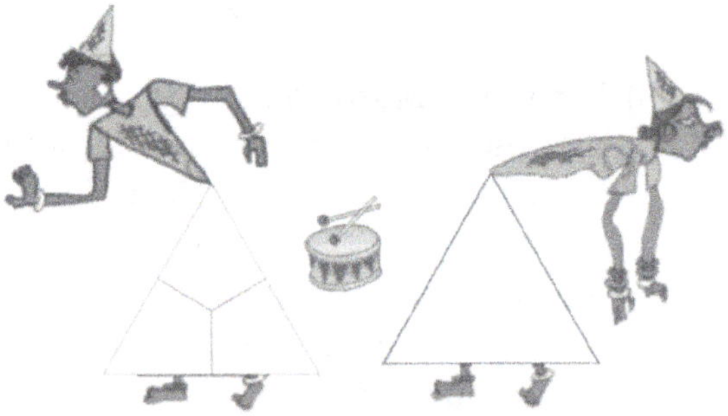

Now, try to make three equal parts of this triangle in a different way. Colour each one-third with a different colour.

Ans. * The triangle is divided into three equal parts. So, each part is one-third of the whole. We can show that these parts are equal using tracing paper.

Firstly, trace each part and then put one part over another. Here, we can observe that they cover each other exactly. Hence, these three parts are equal.

The other way of dividing the given triangle in three equal parts is shown below.

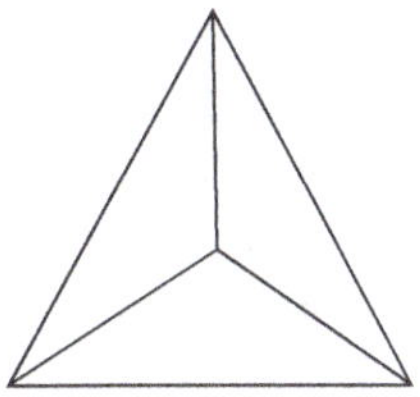

D. Six parts of a rectangle

Q.10 Rani has divided a green rectangle into six equal parts like this.

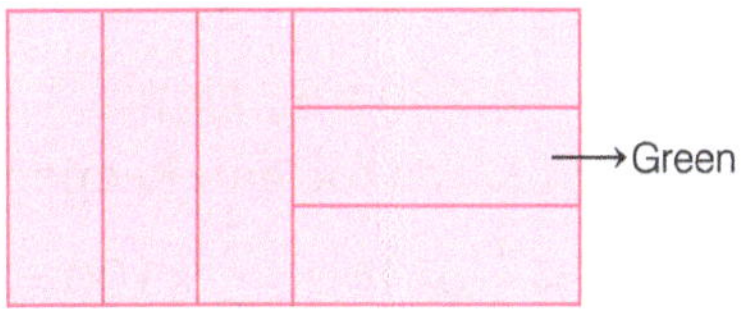

(i) Now, you divide each of these rectangles into six equal parts. Use a different way for each of the three rectangles.

(ii) How will you check that each part is really one-sixth of that rectangle?

(iii) The green rectangle is bigger than the blue one. Can we say that $\frac{1}{6}$ of the green rectangle is bigger than $\frac{1}{6}$ of the blue rectangle?

Ans. (i) * Following are the ways in which we can divide these rectangles into six equal parts.

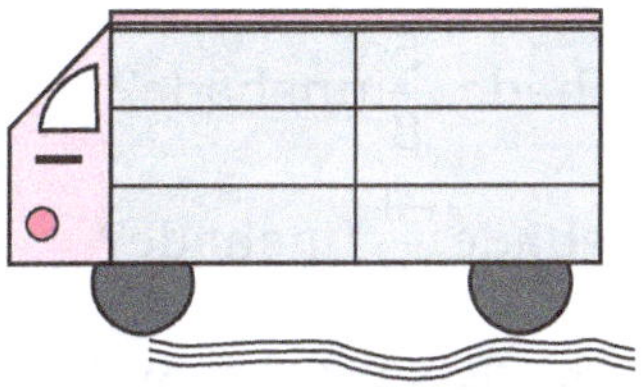

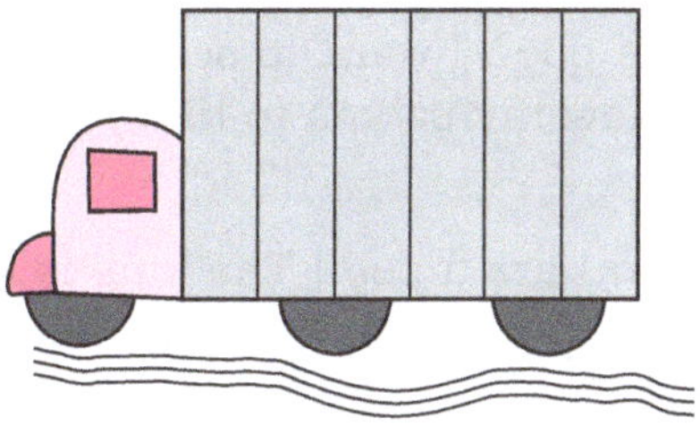

(ii) Using tracing paper, I can check that each part is really one-sixth of that rectangle. Now, one-by-one trace each rectangle on trace paper. After cutting into six parts, place them one over other. If they cover each other completely, it shows that each part is $\frac{1}{6}$ of the whole.

(iii) Yes, if the whole is bigger, then its parts are also bigger. Hence, $\frac{1}{6}$ of the green rectangle is bigger than $\frac{1}{6}$ of the blue rectangle.

Greedy Gatekeepers (NCERT Pg 55-56)

Q.11 Remember Birbal, the clever minister of King Akbar? Do you know how he became a minister?

Birbal was then a young boy living in a village. He was very clever and could write poetry.

He thought he would try his luck in the King's court. So, he took some of his poems and set off for the city.

When he reached the outer gate of the palace, he was stopped by the gatekeeper. "Hey! Stop there! Where are you going?", shouted the gatekeeper.

'I am a poet. I want to see King Akbar and show my poems to him', replied the poet.

'Oh, you are a poet! The king is kind, he will surely give you a prize. I will let you in if you give me $\frac{1}{10}$ of your prize'.

Young Birbal agreed, since he had no other way.

When he went in, the gatekeeper calculated 'If he gets 100 gold coins I will get ___________ gold coins'.

The poet came to a second gatekeeper.

This gatekeeper also said, 'I will let you in if you give me **two-fifth** of your prize'. The poet agreed.

The gatekeeper happily calculated, 'The poet will get at least 100 gold coins, so I will get ___________ gold coins!'

The poet reached the last gate. The gatekeeper said, 'I will allow you to see the king only if you give me **half** of the prize that you get'. The poet had no other way. He agreed and went inside.

The gatekeeper thought, 'Today is a great day. If he gets 100 gold coins I will get _____ gold coins. But if he gets 1000 coins— wow! I will get ______ '.

The king was very happy with the poems and said, 'Your work is very good. You can ask anything as your prize'.

'My Lord, I want 100 slaps'. 'What! 100 slaps? _____'. The king was shocked.

What happened after that? Complete the story. What part of the prize did the poet get?

Ans. * The king wanted to understand why he was asking for 100 slaps. Birbal explained that the gatekeepers at different gates were asking for a share of a prize. As a result, the king punished them with slaps.

The number of slaps for the first gatekeeper at outer gate

$$= \frac{1}{10} \text{ of } 100 = \frac{1}{10} \times 100 = 10 \text{ slaps}$$

Number of slaps for second gatekeeper

$$= \frac{2}{5} \text{ of } 100 = \frac{2}{5} \times 100$$

$$= 2 \times 20 = 40 \text{ slaps}$$

Number of slaps for gatekeeper at last gate

$$= \frac{1}{2} \text{ of } 100 = \frac{1}{2} \times 100 = 50 \text{ slaps}$$

Due to his intelligency, Birbal did not get any slap by the king.

Patterns in Parts (NCERT Pg 57)

Q.12 (i) Make different patterns by shading some squares in the grids B, C, D. What part of the grid did you shade? What part of the grid remained unshade? Write.

A

$\frac{8}{16}$ shade, $\frac{8}{16}$ unshade

(ii) Look at grid A again. Is the grid coloured

(a) $\frac{1}{2}$ shade, $\frac{1}{2}$, unshade?

(b) $\frac{2}{4}$ shade, $\frac{2}{4}$ unshade?

(c) $\frac{3}{8}$ shade, $\frac{5}{8}$ unshade?

(d) $\frac{4}{8}$ shade, $\frac{4}{8}$ unshade?

Choose the wrong answer.

(iii) Draw grids of 16 squares and make patterns with

(a) $\frac{2}{8}$ red, $\frac{1}{2}$ yellow, $\frac{1}{4}$ green

(b) $\frac{3}{16}$ blue, $\frac{5}{16}$ red, $\frac{1}{2}$ yellow

Ans. *(i) (B)

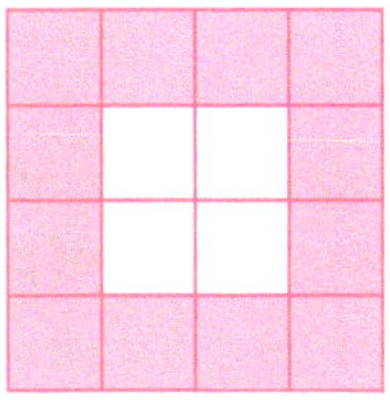

$\frac{12}{16}$ shade, $\frac{4}{16}$ unshade

(C)

$\frac{4}{16}$ shade, $\frac{12}{16}$ unshade

(D)

$\frac{8}{16}$ shade, $\frac{8}{16}$ unshade

(ii) Option (c) is the wrong answer.

(iii) (a) Following is the grid of 16 squares.

Red	Yellow	Yellow	Green
Red	Yellow	Yellow	Green
Red	Yellow	Yellow	Green
Red	Yellow	Yellow	Green

Red squares = $\frac{2}{8} \times 16 = 4$

Yellow squares = $\frac{1}{2} \times 16 = 8$

Green squares = $\frac{1}{4} \times 16 = 4$

(b) Following is the grid of 16 squares.

Red	Blue	Yellow	Yellow
Red	Blue	Yellow	Yellow
Red	Blue	Yellow	Yellow
Red	Blue	Yellow	Yellow

Blue squares = $\frac{3}{16} \times 16 = 3$

Red squares = $\frac{5}{16} \times 16 = 5$

Yellow squares = $\frac{1}{2} \times 16 = 8$

Ramu's Vegetable Field (NCERT Pg 58-59)

Q.13 Ramu's vegetable field has 9 equal parts. What vegetables does he grow?

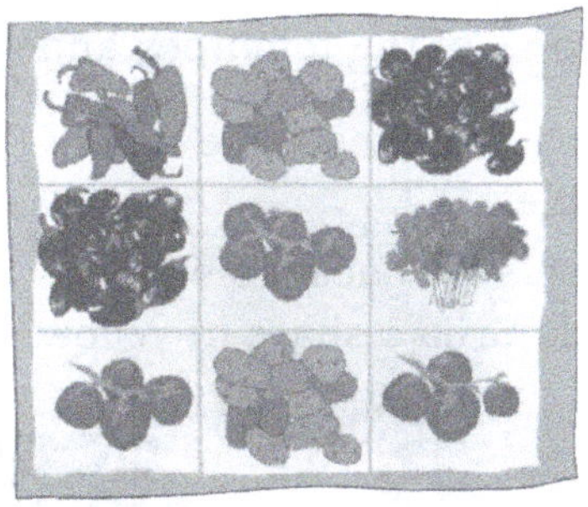

(i) Which vegetable grows in the biggest part of his field? What part?

(ii) On what part of the field does he grow potatoes?

(iii) What part of the field is used to grow spinach? What part is used for brinjals?

(iv) Now, you write some questions by looking at this picture.

Ans. He grows potatoes, brinjals, tomatoes, chilli and spinach.

(i) Since, tomatoes grow in $\frac{1}{3}$ rd part of the field. Hence, tomatoes, grow in the biggest part of his field.

(ii) Total number of parts = 9

He grows potatoes = $\frac{2}{9}$ part

So, he grows potatoes in $\frac{2}{9}$ part of the field.

(iii) Total number of parts = 9

Part used to grow spinach = $\frac{1}{9}$

Part used to grow brinjals = $\frac{2}{9}$

*(iv) Here are some question.

(a) On what part of the field does he grow chillies?

(b) Which two vegetables are grow on equal part of the field?

Q.14 Ramu wanted to give these vegetables to his friends. He gave Aboobacker one-fifth of these tomatoes and $\frac{1}{3}$ of the potatoes. Srija got $\frac{2}{5}$ of the tomatoes and $\frac{3}{6}$ of the potatoes. Nancy got the rest of these vegetables.

(i) Circle Aboobacker's share in blue. Circle Srija's share in yellow.

(ii) How many potatoes and tomatoes did Nancy get?

Ans. (i)

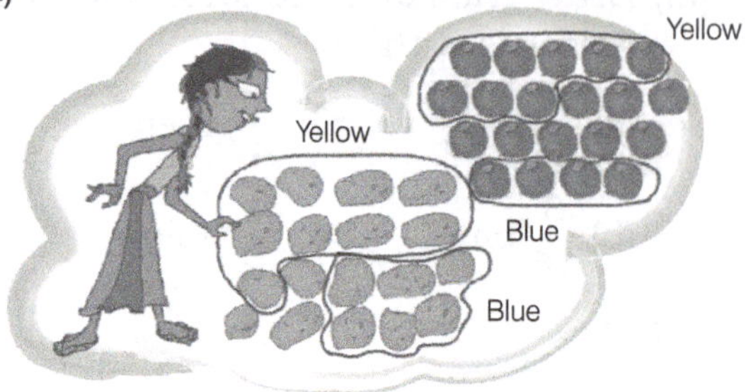

We have, total number of potatoes = 18

∴ Aboobacker's share of potatoes

$= \frac{1}{3}$ of $18 = \frac{1}{3} \times 18 = 6$

and Srija's share of potatoes

$= \frac{3}{6}$ of $18 = \frac{3}{6} \times 18$

$= 3 \times 3 = 9$

We have, total number of tomatoes = 20

∴ Aboobacker's share of tomatoes

$= \frac{1}{5}$ of $20 = \frac{1}{5} \times 20 = 4$

and Srija's share of tomatoes

$= \frac{2}{5}$ of $20 = \frac{2}{5} \times 20 = 2 \times 4 = 8$

(ii) Nancy's share of potatoes = 18 – 6 – 9 = 3

and share of tomatoes = 20 – 4 – 8 = 8

Hence, Nancy got 3 potatoes and 8 tomatoes.

Game : Who Colours the Circle First? (NCERT Pg 60)

Q.15 This game is to be played in groups of 4. Each player has to make a circle as shown. Each one has to make 15 tokens on slips of paper. Write $\frac{1}{2}, \frac{1}{3}, \frac{1}{4}, \frac{1}{6}, \frac{1}{12}, \frac{2}{12}, \frac{3}{12}, \frac{4}{12}, \ldots \frac{11}{12}$ to make your tokens.

Shuffle the tokens and make a pile in the middle of the group. Now, you are ready to start the game.

The first player takes a token from the pile, colours that part of the picture, and puts the token under the pile. The next player does the same, and so on.

The winner is the one who first colours the circle completely.

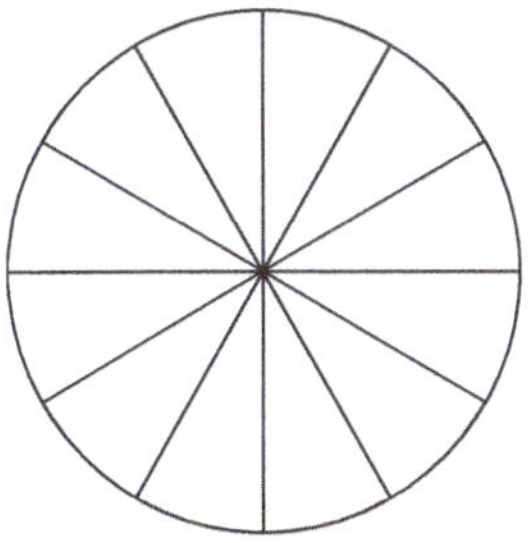

(i) Who won the game?

(ii) What are the winner's tokens?

(iii) Write the tokens you got.

(iv) What part of the circle did you colour?

Ans. *(i) My friend who got $\frac{1}{12}$, $\frac{4}{12}$ and $\frac{7}{12}$ tokens won the game.

(ii) The winner's token are $\frac{1}{12}$, $\frac{4}{12}$, $\frac{7}{12}$.

(iii) I got $\frac{1}{2}$ and $\frac{3}{12}$ tokens.

(iv) I coloured $\frac{1}{2} = \frac{6}{12}$ that is 6 parts first and then $\frac{3}{12}$ that is 3 parts of the circle.

The Card Puzzle (NCERT Pg 60-61)

Q.16

(i) Divide the unshade area in square A into two equal parts. Got the answer? Was that easy?

(ii) Now, do the second question.

Divide the unshade area in square B into three equal parts! That too is easy, is not it?

(iii) Now, see the third question.

Divide the unshade area in square C into four equal parts!!

Is it a bit difficult? Don't worry, take your time.

Only if you have given up, look for the answer.

(iv) Here, comes the last question.

Divide the unshaded area in square D into seven equal parts!!!! The world record for this is 7 seconds. But you can take minutes!

Tired of thinking? Look for the answer on NCERT Pg 68.

So, was that difficult?

Ans. (i) Yes, it was easy and two equal unshade parts as shown below.

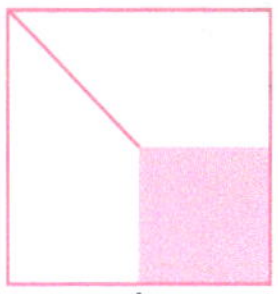

A

(ii) Following is the way to divide the unshaded area in square B into three equal parts.

B

(iii) Following is the way to divide the unshaded area in square B into 4 equal parts.

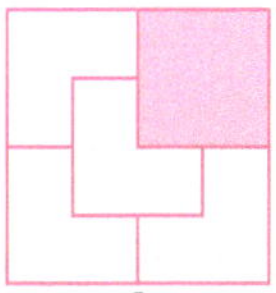

C

(iv) No, it was not difficult. Following is the way to divide the white area in square D into seven equal parts.

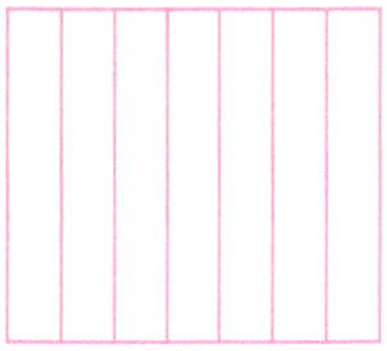

D

Guess and Check (NCERT 61-62)

Q.17 What part of each shape is shaded? First guess the answer, then check.

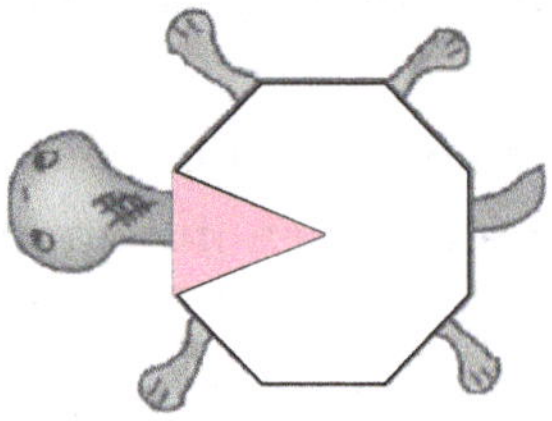

(i)

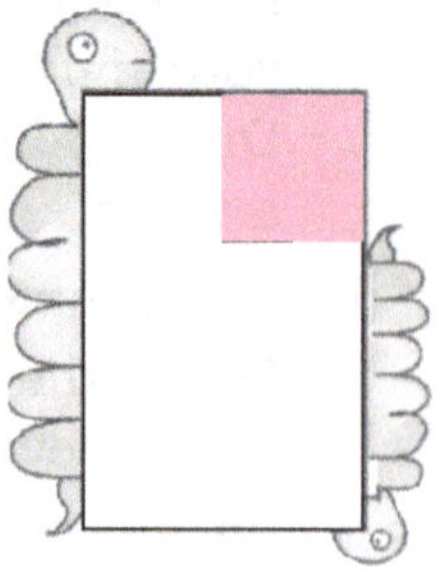

(ii)

(iii)

(iv)

Ans. **Shape (i)** By guessing $= \frac{1}{8}$

By checking $= \frac{1}{8}$

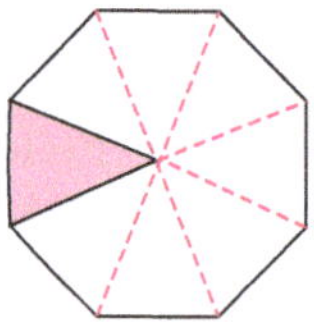

Shape (ii) By guessing $= \frac{1}{6}$

By checking $= \frac{1}{6}$

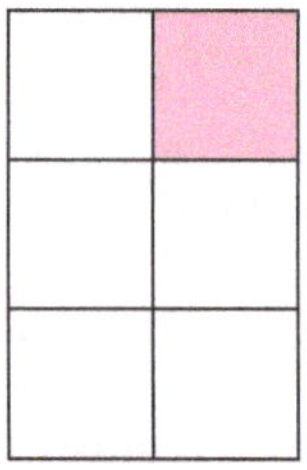

Shape (iii) By guessing $= \frac{2}{9}$

By checking $= \frac{2}{9}$

Shape (iv) By guessing $= \frac{4}{15}$

By checking $= \frac{4}{15}$

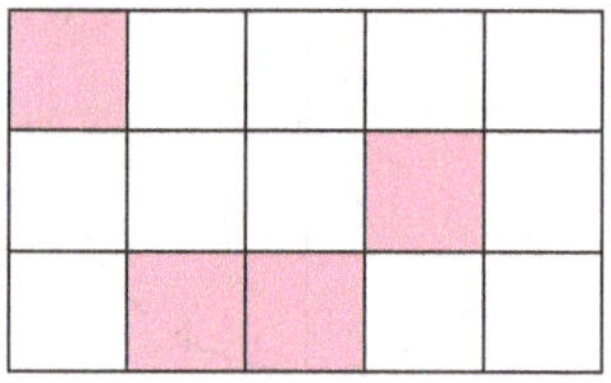

Q.18 Do you remember this picture? Look at the small triangle. What part of the square is it? How will you find this out?

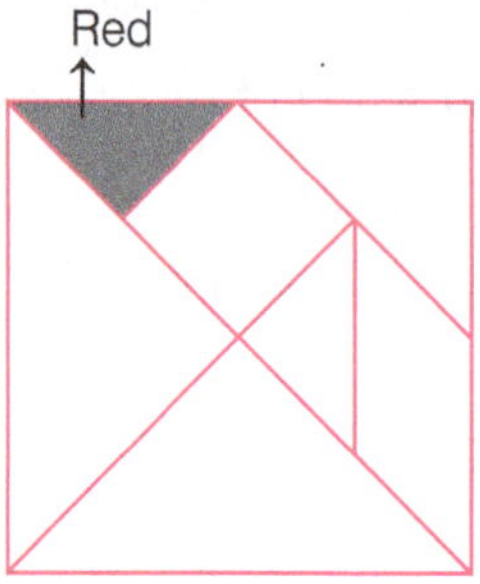

Divide the big triangles and other shapes into small triangles (like the red one). How many small triangles are there altogether?

Ans. Yes, I remember this picture.

The coloured small triangle is $\frac{1}{16}$ part of the square.

Follow these steps to calculate this

Divide the square into small triangles as shown in the figure mentioned below.

The total number of small triangles is 16.

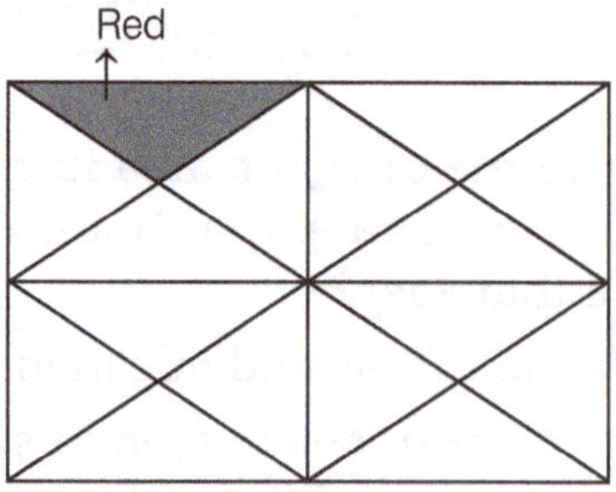

Coloured Parts (NCERT Pg 62)

Q.19 Complete these

(i)

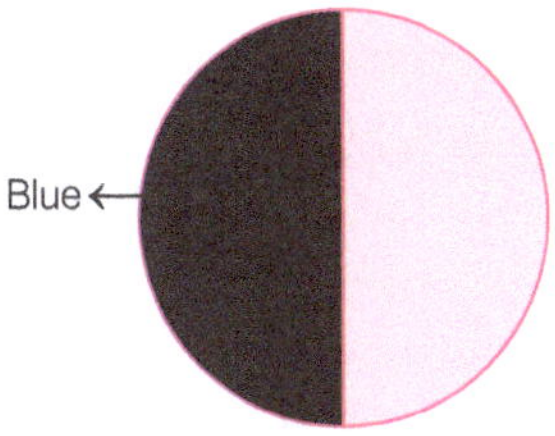

This circle is divided into two equal parts. Out of ________ equal parts one part is coloured blue.

(ii)

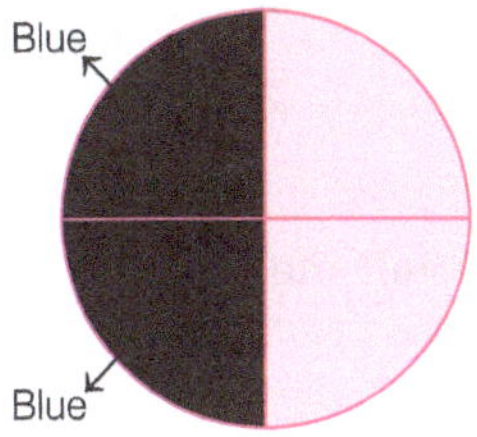

Here, the circle is divided into ________ equal parts. Out of ________ equal parts, ________ parts are coloured blue.

(iii)

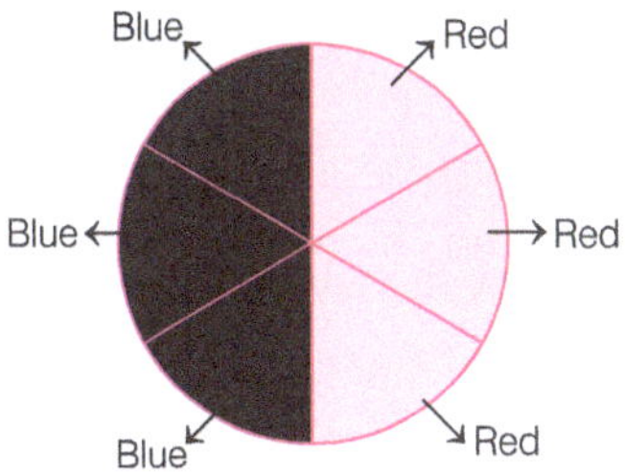

Here, the circle is ________

(iv)

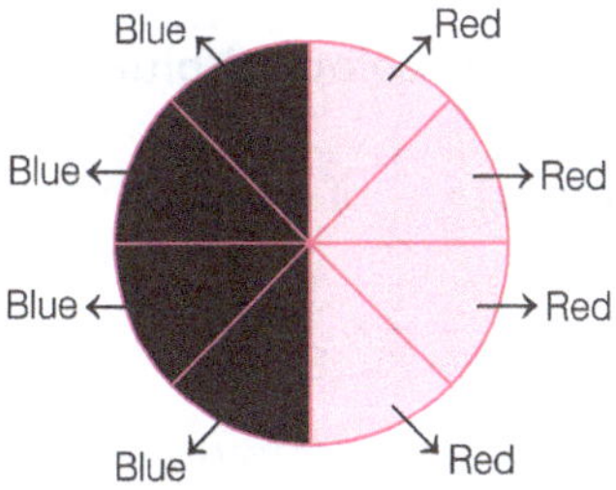

Here the circle is ________

(v) So, we can say that $\frac{1}{2} = \frac{2}{\ } = \frac{\ }{6} = \frac{\ }{8}$

Ans. (i) This circle is divided into two equal parts. Out of 2 equal parts one part is coloured blue.

(ii) Here, the circle is divided into 4 equal parts. Out of 4 equal parts, 2 parts are coloured blue.

(iii) Here, the circle is divided into 6 equal parts. Out of 6 equal parts, 3 are coloured blue and 3 are coloured red.

(iv) Here, the circle is divided into 8 equal parts. Out of 8 equal parts, 4 parts are blue and 4 parts are red coloured.

(v) So, we can say that $\frac{1}{2} = \frac{2}{4} = \frac{3}{6} = \frac{4}{8}$

Cutting the Halwa (NCERT Pg 63-64)

Q.20 Ramesh bought a piece of halwa for his children Ammu and Anu.

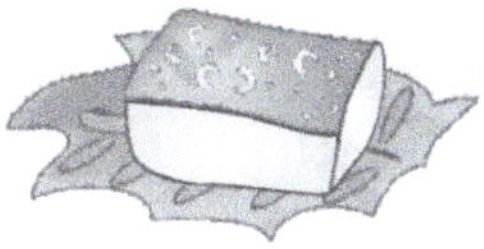

He divided it equally for them.

(i) Each will get ______ part of halwa.

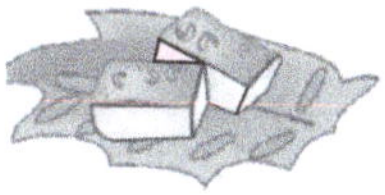

(ii) 'This piece is too big. We can not eat it', they said. So, he divided the pieces into half again. Now, how many pieces will Ammu get?

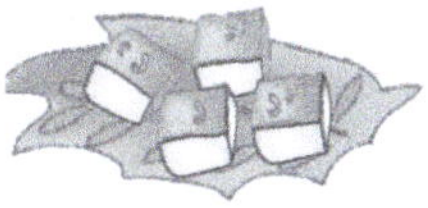

(iii) What part of the halwa is it?

(iv) 'Make it even smaller, Dad' they asked. So, he again cut the halwa into smaller pieces.

'Ok, thank you, Dad.'

(a) Now, how many pieces will each get?

(b) What part of the halwa is each piece now?

(v) If Ramesh had cut the halwa into 6 equal parts how many pieces would each have got? Look at your answers for questions 1 to 4 and write.

$\frac{1}{2}$ = ____ = ____ = ____ = ____ = ____

Ans. (i) Each will get half or $\frac{1}{2}$ part of halwa.

(ii) Ammu get 2 pieces.

(iii) $\frac{2}{4}$ or $\frac{1}{2}$

(iv) (a) Each of them will get 4 pieces.

(b) $\frac{1}{8}$ part

(v) If Ramesh had cut the halwa into 6 equal parts, then each got 3 pieces of halwa.

So, $\frac{1}{2}=\frac{2}{4}=\frac{3}{6}=\frac{4}{8}=\frac{5}{10}=\frac{6}{12}$

Parts of the Strip (NCERT Pg 64)

Q.21 Look at the picture. Write what part of the strip is each green piece. Write the part for a piece of each colour.

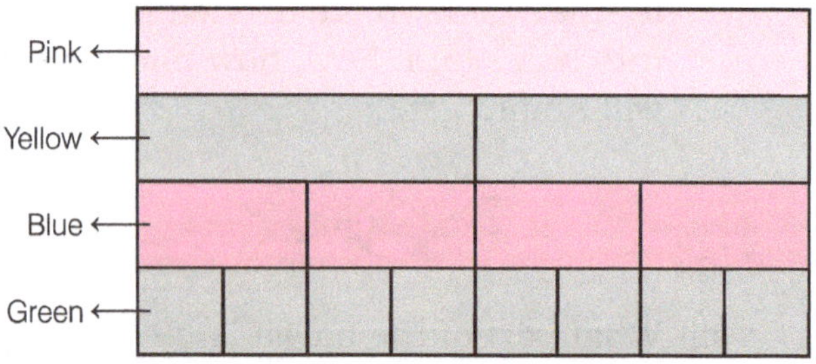

(i) How many one-fourths will make a half?

(ii) How many $\frac{1}{8}$ will make $\frac{1}{4}$?

(iii) How many $\frac{1}{8}$ are in $\frac{1}{2}$?

Ans.

Pink	1							
Yellow	1/2				1/2			
Blue	1/4		1/4		1/4		1/4	
Green	$\frac{1}{8}$	$\frac{1}{8}$	$\frac{1}{8}$	$\frac{1}{8}$	$\frac{1}{8}$	$\frac{1}{8}$	$\frac{1}{8}$	$\frac{1}{8}$

(i) $2\times\frac{1}{4}=\frac{1}{2}$

Hence, two one-fourths will make a half.

(ii) $2\times\frac{1}{8}=\frac{1}{4}$

So, two $\frac{1}{8}$ will make $\frac{1}{4}$.

(iii) $4\times\frac{1}{8}=\frac{1}{2}$

So, Four $\frac{1}{8}$ will make $\frac{1}{2}$.

Patterns (NCERT Pg 64)

Q.22 Look at this square

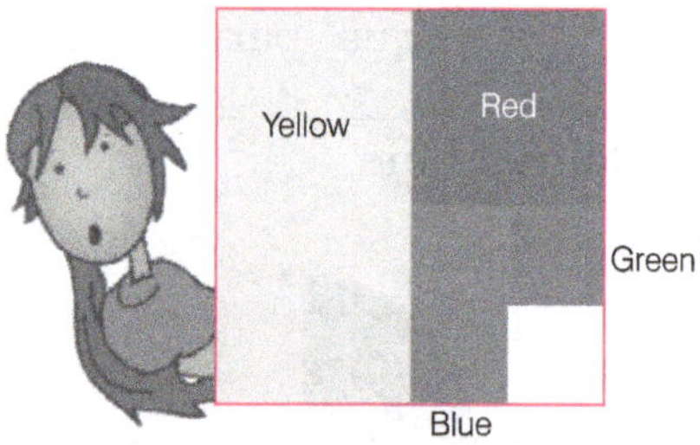

(i) What part is coloured blue?

(ii) What part is green?

Ans. (i) Blue part $=\frac{1}{2}$ of $\frac{1}{4}$

$=\frac{1}{2}\times\frac{1}{4}=\frac{1}{8}$

So, $\frac{1}{8}$ part is coloured blue.

(ii) Green part $=\frac{1}{2}$ of $\frac{1}{8}$

$=\frac{1}{2}\times\frac{1}{8}=\frac{1}{16}$

So, $\frac{1}{16}$ part is coloured green.

Puzzle : Is it Equal ? (NCERT Pg 64)

Q.23 Ammini says half of half and one-third of three-quarters are equal. Do you agree? How will you show this?

Ans. Yes, I agree.

Following is the way to show Ammini is correct.

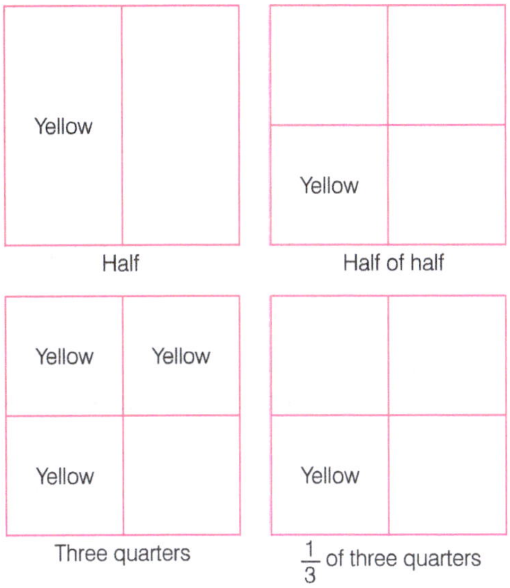

∴ Half of half = One-third of three-fourth

$$\Rightarrow \quad \frac{1}{2}\times\frac{1}{2}=\frac{1}{3}\times\frac{3}{4}\Rightarrow\frac{1}{4}=\frac{1}{4}$$

From a Part to the Whole (NCERT Pg 65)

Q.24 (i) This show $\frac{1}{5}$ petals of a flower.

Complete the flower by drawing the other petals.

(ii) The picture shows one-third of the blades of a fan. Complete the picture by drawing the other blades.

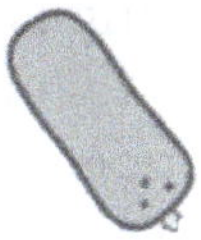

(iii) Half of the blades of another fan are shown here.

Complete the picture by drawing the other half. How many blades have you drawn?

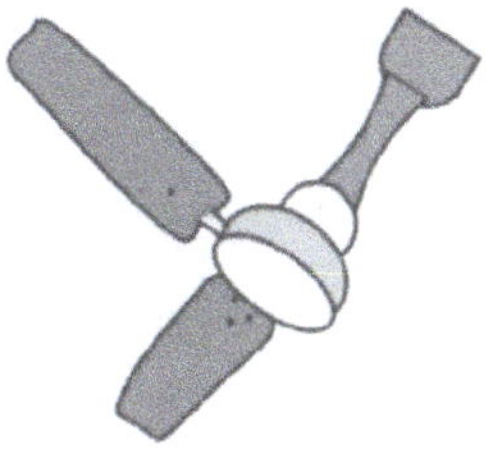

Ans. (i) Here, we have $\frac{1}{5}$ petals of a flower. This shows that a complete flower will have 5 petals like this petal.

$$5\times\frac{1}{5}=1$$

(ii) The complete picture of 3 blades of a fan is given below.

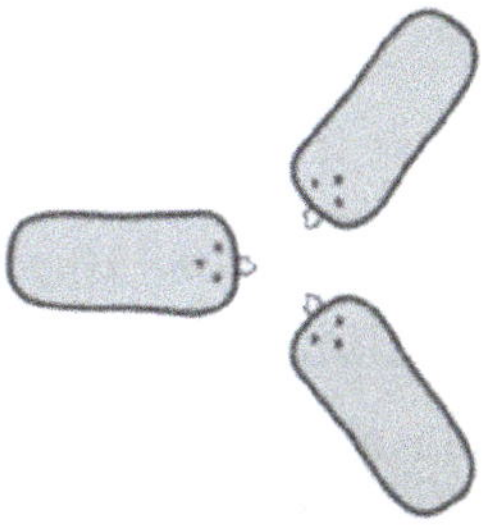

(iii) The complete picture of fan with 4 blades is given below.

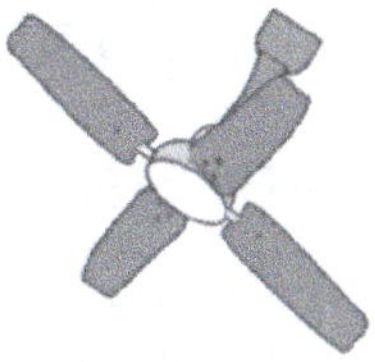

Here, I have drawn two more blades to complete the picture.

Rupees and Paise (NCERT Pg 65)

Q.25 (i) (a) How many  will make one rupee?

(b) Is 50 paise half of one rupee?

(ii) (a) How many  will make one rupee?

(b) 25 paise is ______ part of one rupee.

(iii) 20 paise is ______ part of one rupee.

(iv) (a) How many 10 paise will make one rupee?

(b) So, 10 paise is ______ part of one rupee.

Ans. (i) (a) Two 50 paise coins will make one rupee.

(b) Yes, 50 paise is half of one rupee.

(ii) (a) Four 25 paise coin will make one rupee.

(b) $\because$ One rupee $= 4 \times 25$ paise

$\therefore$ 25 paise $= \dfrac{\text{One rupee}}{4}$

So, 25 paise is $\frac{1}{4}$ part of one rupee.

(iii) $\because$ One rupee $= 5 \times 20$ paise

$\therefore$ 20 paise $= \dfrac{\text{One rupee}}{5}$

So, 20 paise is $\frac{1}{5}$ part of one rupee.

(iv) (a) $\because$ One rupee $= 10 \times 10$ paise

So, ten 10-paise will make one rupee.

(b) $\because$ One rupee $= 10 \times 10$ paise

10 paise $= \dfrac{\text{One rupee}}{10}$

So, 10 paise is $\frac{1}{10}$ part of one rupee.

An Old Woman's Will (NCERT Pg 66-67)

Q.26 Once there lived an old woman. She lived with her three daughters. She was quite rich and had 19 camels. One day she fell ill. The daughters called the doctor. The doctor tried his best but could not save the woman. After her death, the daughters read what she had written in her will.

My eldest daughter will get $\frac{1}{2}$ of my camels.

My second daughter will get $\frac{1}{4}$ of my camels.

My third daughter will get $\frac{1}{5}$ of my camels.

The daughters were really puzzled. 'How can I get $\frac{1}{2}$ of the 19 camels?' asked the eldest daughter.

' Half of 19 is nine and a half. But we can't cut the camel!' The second daughter said.

' That is right. But what will we do now?" asked the third daughter'.

Just, then they saw their aunt coming. The daughters told her their problem.

' Show me the will. I have an idea. You take my camel. So, you have 20 camels. Now, can you divide them as your mother wanted?' the aunt said.

' You want half of the camels, don't you? Take 10 camels' she said to the eldest daughter.

' Take your share', the aunt told the second daughter. She took one-fourth of the camels and got ____ camels.

' You can take one-fifth of the camels', the aunt told the third daughter. She got ____ camels. The daughters were very happy and counted their camels 10 + _____ + _____ = 19.

' The one remaining is mine', said the aunt and took her camel away!

How did this happen? Discuss.

Ans. By adding the aunt's camel, total number of camels $= 19 + 1 = 20$

Eldest daughter's share $= \frac{1}{2}$ of camels

$= \frac{1}{2} \times 20 = 10$

Second daughter's share $= \frac{1}{4}$ of camels

$= \frac{1}{4} \times 20 = 5$

Third daughter's share $= \frac{1}{5}$ of camels

$= \frac{1}{5} \times 20 = 4$

Total camels $= 10 + 5 + 4 = 19$

So, the remaining one camel out of 20 is of aunt. Therefore, she took her camel away.

Note Even though this calculation is not mathematically correct, but it solved the problem for three sisters.

Arun's Time Table (NCERT Pg 67)

Q.27 **Sleeping** One third of a day

Playing One eighth of a day

Studying $\frac{1}{4}$ of a day

(i) How many hours does Arun take for

Sleeping? [ ] hours

Studying? [ ] hours

Playing? [ ] hours

(ii) What part of the day does he use for other activities?

(iii) One day is 24 hours. Then, how will I find out one-third of a day?

Ans. (i) We know that 1 day = 24 hours

Number of hours for sleeping

$= \frac{1}{3} \times 24$

= 8 hours

Number of hours for playing

= One-eighth of a day

$= \frac{1}{8} \times 24$

= 3 hours

Number of hours for studying

$= \frac{1}{4}$ of a day $= \frac{1}{4} \times 24 = 6$ hours

(ii) Arun uses 8 hours for sleeping, 6 hours for studying and 3 hours for playing in a day.

∴ Total time for these three activities

$= 8 + 6 + 3 = 17$ h

Now, time used for other activities

$= 24 - 17 = 7$ h

So, he uses $\frac{7}{24}$ part of the day for other activities.

(iii) Total hours in a day = 24 h

∴ One-third of a day $= \frac{1}{3} \times 24 = 8$ h

School Magazine (NCERT Pg 68)

Q.28 A school has decided to bring out a magazine every quarter of the year. How many magazines will they have in a year? If they want to print it at the end of each quarter of a year, which are the months for printing? Mark the number for those months.

1	2	3	4	5	6	7	8	9	10	11	12

Ans. Total months in a year = 12 months

∴ Quarter of the year $= \frac{1}{4} \times 12 = 3$ months

This implies that they bring out a magazine four times in a year.
It is shown as below.

1	2	(3)	4	5	(6)	7	8	(9)	10	11	(12)

So, they will bring out 4 magazines in a year in the month of March, June, September and December.

Sleeping Beauty! (NCERT Pg 68)

Q.29 Have you heard of Kumbhakarna, the brother of Ravana? He is famous for sleeping for half a year.

Ans. Yes, I have heard about Kumbhakarna.

Q.30 (i) Most people sleep about 8 hours a day. Then, what part of a day is it?

(ii) So, what part of a year do they sleep? A Person 60 yr old must have slept _____ years!!!

Ans. (i) Total hours in a day = 24

$\therefore$ 8 h = $\frac{8}{24}$ part of whole day

= $\frac{1}{3}$ part of whole day

So, 8 h in a day is a $\frac{1}{3}$ rd part of a day.

(ii) They sleep for $\frac{1}{3}$rd of a year.

So, if a person is 60 years old, then $\frac{1}{3}$ of 60 years = $\frac{1}{3} \times 60 = 20$ yr

Hence, he would have slept 20 years.

Keerti's Shopping List (NCERT Pg 69)

Q.31 Look at the price list.

(i) How much does 2 kg of tomato cost?

(ii) How much does $\frac{1}{2}$ kg of tomato cost?

(iii) Kiran wants $2\frac{1}{2}$ kg of tomato. How much will it cost?

(iv) How much does $3\frac{1}{2}$ kg of potato cost?

(v) What is the price of $1\frac{1}{4}$ kg of carrot?

(vi) He bought a gourd of weight $4\frac{3}{4}$ kg and it costs.

(vii) Look at the shopping list in Keerti's hand. How much will she have to pay to buy all of these?

(viii) Make a bill of your own for vegetables you want to buy. Find the total money you will have to pay.

Ans. (i) $\because$ 1 kg of tomato costs = ₹ 12

$\therefore$ 2 kg of tomato costs = 2×12 = ₹ 24

(ii) $\because$ 1 kg of tomato costs = ₹ 12

$\therefore \frac{1}{2}$ kg of tomato cost = $\frac{1}{2} \times 12$ = ₹ 6

(iii) Cost of $2\frac{1}{2}$ kg tomato = cost of 2 kg + cost of $\frac{1}{2}$ kg tomato = ₹ 24 + ₹ 6 = ₹ 30

(iv) Cost of $3\frac{1}{2}$ kg potato = Cost of 3 kg potato + Cost of $\frac{1}{2}$ kg potato

$= 3 \times 10 + 10 \times \frac{1}{2}$

$= 30 + 5$ = ₹ 35

(v) Cost of $1\frac{1}{4}$ kg carrot

= Cost of 1 kg carrot + Cost of $\frac{1}{4}$ kg carrot

$= 18 \times 1 + \frac{1}{4} \times 18 = 18 + 4.50$ = ₹ 22.50

(vi) Cost of $4\frac{3}{4}$ kg gourd = Cost of 4 kg gourd + Cost of $\frac{3}{4}$ kg gourd

$= 4 \times 8 + \frac{3}{4} \times 8 = 32 + 6$ = ₹ 38

(vii)

Item	**Price in ₹ (per kg)**	**Quantity**	**Amount (in ₹)**
Potato	10	$2\frac{1}{4}$ kg	$10 \times 2 + 10 \times \frac{1}{4}$ $= 20 + 2.50$ = ₹ 22.50
Carrot	18	$3\frac{3}{4}$ kg	$18 \times 3 + 18 \times \frac{3}{4}$ $= 54 + 13.50$ = ₹ 67.50
Gourd	8	$1\frac{1}{2}$ kg	$8 \times 1 + 8 \times \frac{1}{2}$ $= 8 + 4$ = ₹ 12
	Total		₹ 22.50 + ₹ 67.50 + ₹ 12 = ₹ 102

*(viii) My own shopping bill of vegetables

Item	Price in ₹ (per kg)	Quantity	Amount (in ₹)
Carrot	18	(1 kg)	$1 \times 18 =$ ₹ 18
Tomato	12	$2\frac{1}{4}$ kg	$2 \times 12 + \frac{1}{4} \times 12$ $= 24 + 3 =$ ₹ 27
Onion	16	$\frac{1}{2}$ kg	$\frac{1}{2} \times 16 =$ ₹ 8
	Total		₹ 18 + ₹ 27 + ₹ 8 = ₹ 53

Practice Time (NCERT Pg 70)

Q.32 Raheem's journey

Raheem has to travel $1\frac{1}{4}$ km to reach school. What distance does he travel to go to school and come back home?

Ans. Total distance travelled by Raheem

$$= 2 \times 1\frac{1}{4} \text{ km} = 2 \times \frac{5}{4} \text{ km}$$

$$= \frac{5}{2} \text{ km or } 2\frac{1}{2} \text{ km}$$

Q.33 What coins?

Latha bought a pencil and a pen for seven and a half rupees. She gave ₹10. The shopkeeper gave back the money in half and quarter rupees. What are the coins she got?

Ans. Price of a pencil and a pen = ₹ 7.5

Money given by Latha to the shopkeeper

= ₹ 10

Shopkeeper gave back the money

= 10 − 7.5 = ₹ 2.5

So, the shopkeeper gave back the money in half and quarter rupees in the following ways.

(i) Two 25 paise coins and four 50 paise coins.

(ii) Eight 25 paise coins and one 50 paise coins.

(iii) Four 25 paise coins and three 50 paise coins.

(iv) Six 25 paise coins and two 50 paise coins.

Q.34 At the railway station

Your attention please. Mangalore Express coming from Mangalore and going to Thiruvananthapuram is now running late by half an hour.
Oh the train is late today.
The right time is a quarter to 7.

(i) What time is the train expected to come today?

(ii) Nazia gets off at a station after $2\frac{1}{2}$ h from this Station. What time will she get off ?

(iii) Shaji will take 5 h to reach Ernakulam by this train. At what time will he reach there?

Ans. (i) Right time is 6 : 45.

The train is 30 min late.

Hence, the expected time = 6:45 + 0:30

= 7:15

So, the train will arrive at quarter past 7.

(ii) Nazia's time after $2\frac{1}{2}$ h = 7:15 + 2:30

= 9:45

So, Nazia will reach at quarter to 10.

(iii) Shaji's time after 5 h = 7:15 + 5:00

= 12:15

So, Shaji will reach at quarter past 12.

PRACTICE QUESTIONS

1. Fill in the blanks
   (i) A fraction represents a part of a ______ .
   (ii) In the fraction $\frac{3}{4}$, the number 3 is called the ______ and 4 is called the ______ .
   (iii) If the whole is smaller, then its parts will be also ______ .
   (iv) One half is written as ______ .

2. Multiple choice questions
   (i) Which of the following fractions is equivalent to $\frac{1}{2}$?

   (a) $\frac{2}{4}$ (b) $\frac{1}{3}$ (c) $\frac{3}{5}$ (d) $\frac{4}{6}$

   (ii) Find the fraction of the shaded part in the given figure.

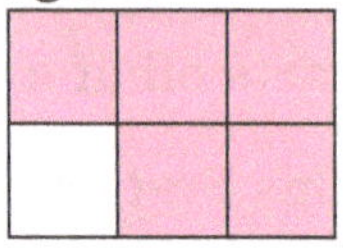

   (a) $\frac{1}{6}$ (b) $\frac{1}{2}$ (c) $\frac{5}{6}$ (d) 1

   (iii) If you divide an object into 5 equal parts, what is each part called?

   (a) One-half (b) One-tenth
   (c) One-third (d) One-fifth

3. Word problems
   (i) Tina cuts a cake into 8 equal slices. If she eats 3 slices, what part of the cake is left?
   (ii) A pizza is cut into 4 equal slices. Rahul eats 3 slices. What part of the pizza has he eaten and what part is left?

4. Case based questions
   Saumya has a chocolate bar that is divided into 8 equal parts. She gives 3 parts to her friend, eats 2 parts herself and saves the rest for later.

   Based on the above information, answer the following questions.
   (i) What part of the chocolate bar did she give to her friend?
   (ii) What part of chocolate bar did Saumya eat herself?

ANSWERS & SOLUTIONS

1. (i) Whole (ii) Numerator, Denominator
   (iii) Smaller (iv) $\frac{1}{2}$

2. (i) (a) (ii) (c) (iii) (d)

3. (i) Total parts of the cake = 8

   Part of cake eaten by Tina = 3

   Number of parts of the cake left
   $= 8 - 3 = 5$

   $\therefore$ Part of the cake is left $= \frac{5}{8}$

   (ii) Total parts of the pizza = 4

   Number of parts that Rahul eats = 3

   $\therefore$ Parts of the pizza that he was eaten $= \frac{3}{4}$

   Number of parts of the pizza left
   $= 4 - 3 = 1$

   $\therefore$ Parts of pizza that is left $= \frac{1}{4}$

4. Total parts of the chocolate = 8

   (i) Number of parts given to her friend = 3

   $\therefore$ Parts of the chocolate given to her friend $= \frac{3}{8}$

   (ii) Number of parts that Saumya eats herself = 2

   $\therefore$ Part of the chocolate that Saumya eats herself $= \frac{2}{8} = \frac{1}{4}$

CHAPTER 5

DOES IT LOOK THE SAME?

Symmetry

Symmetry is the ability to divide an object into two or more identical parts or mirror images that are arranged in an organised way.

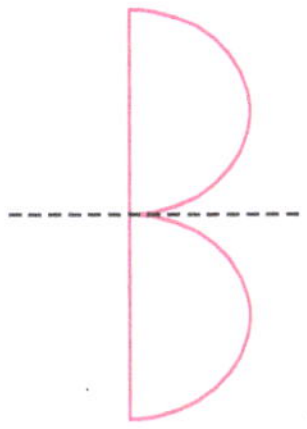

Line of Symmetry

The imaginary line or axis that divides the object into symmetrical halves is called the line of symmetry.

Types of Symmetry

Reflection Symmetry/Mirror Image

This type of symmetry occurs when a line divides an object into two mirror images.

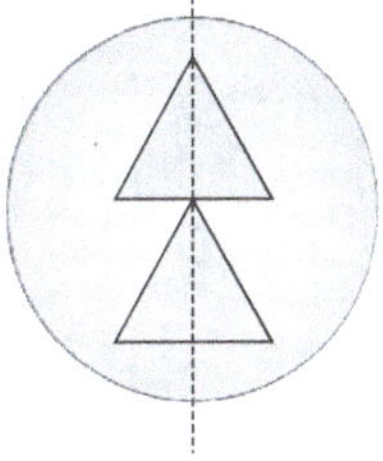

Rotational Symmetry

This type of symmetry occurs when an object can be rotated or turned around a fixed point without changing its shape.

$\frac{1}{4}$th turn of 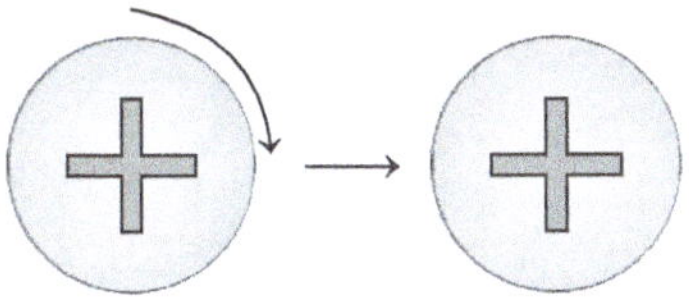

$\frac{1}{6}$th turn of 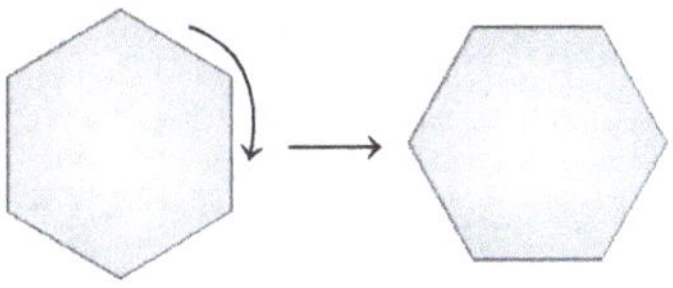

NCERT FOLDER

Make your Pattern (NCERT Pg 71-73)

Q.1

Take a sheet of paper Fold it into half Open the fold and put a drop of colour on the middle line

Fold it twice and press it to spread the colour Open it and see a beautiful pattern

Can you cut this pattern in such a way that you get two similar mirror halves? In how many ways can you do it?

Ans. Yes, I can cut this pattern in two similar mirror halves. It can be done in only one way.

Q.2 Which shapes are divided into two mirror halves by the dotted line?

Ans. Shapes 5, 6, 7, 8, 13 and 15 are divided into mirror halves by the dotted lines.

Mirror Games (NCERT Pg 74-76)

Q.3 (i) Here is a picture of a dog. You can place a mirror on the dotted line. Then, the part of the dog to the right of the line will be hidden behind the mirror. What you will see is like (a).

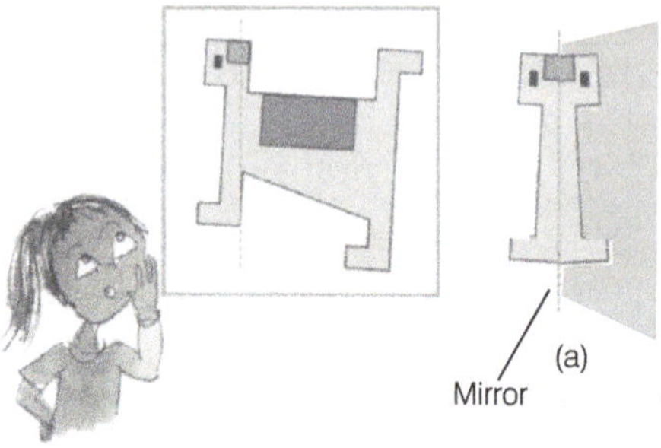

(ii) Look at the figure in the white box. On which of the dotted lines will you keep the mirror so that you get shape (b)? Also tell which part of the picture will be hidden when we keep the mirror on the dotted line.

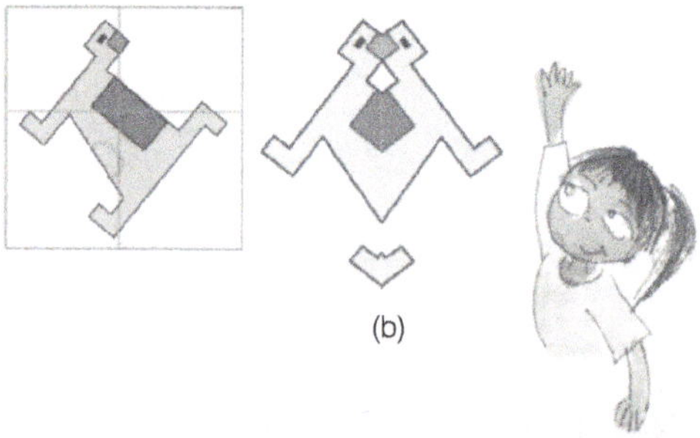

(iii) Now, make a line on the white box to show where you will keep the mirror to get the picture next to it.

(a)

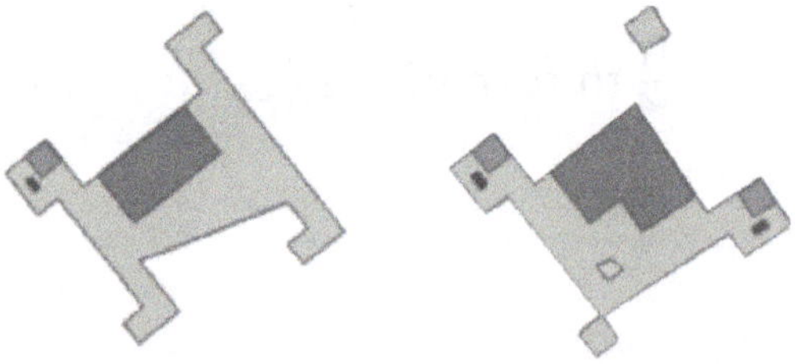

* *Students can write alternate answer as per their choice.*

(b) 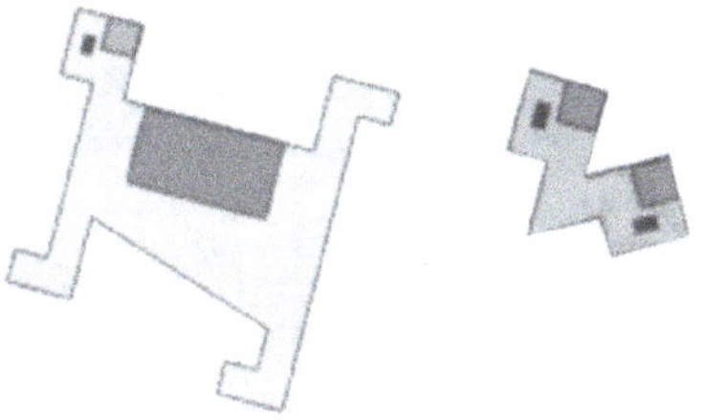

(c) 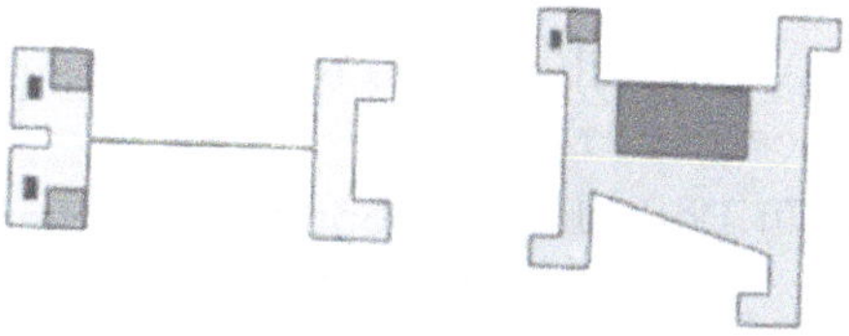

(d) 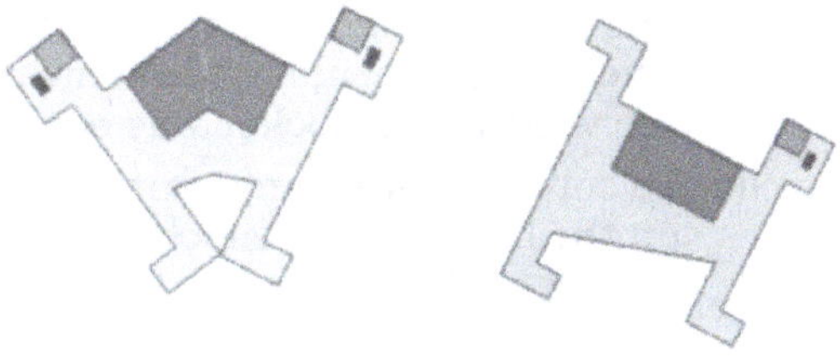

Ans. (i) Yes, we will see like figure (a).

(ii) To get the shape, the mirror needs to be kept on the vertical dotted line.

When the mirror is kept on the dotted line, the part of the picture which is on the right side of the dotted line will be hidden.

(iii) Here, the dotted lines are drawn to obtain the pictures (a), (b), (c) and (d). The position of the mirror is shown by dotted lines.

(a) 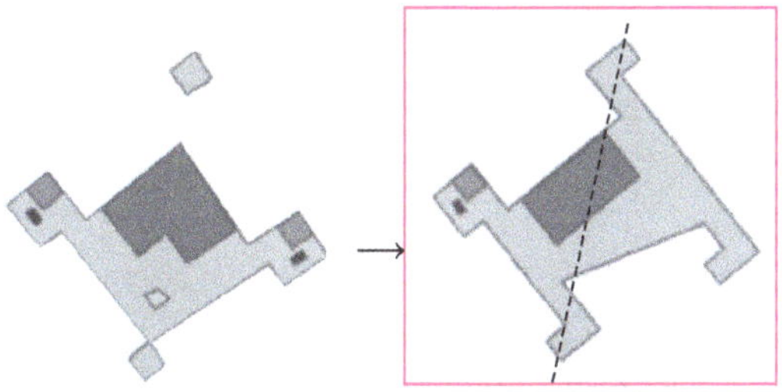

(b) 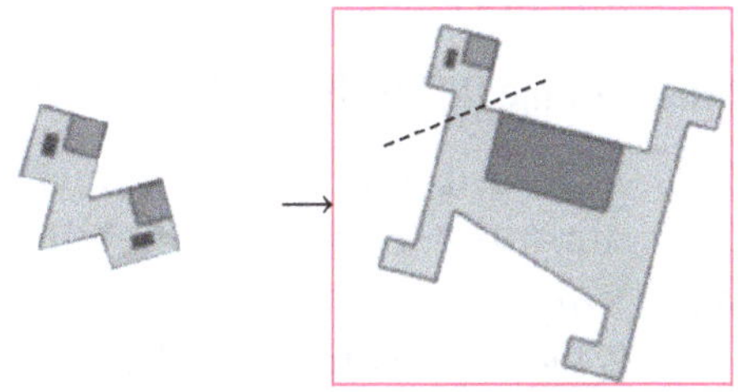

(c) 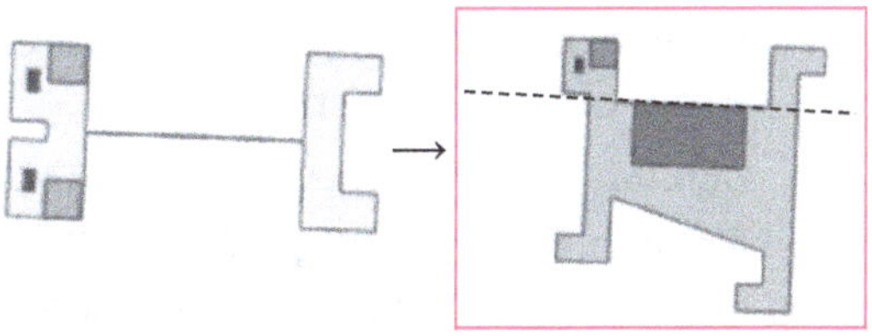

(d) 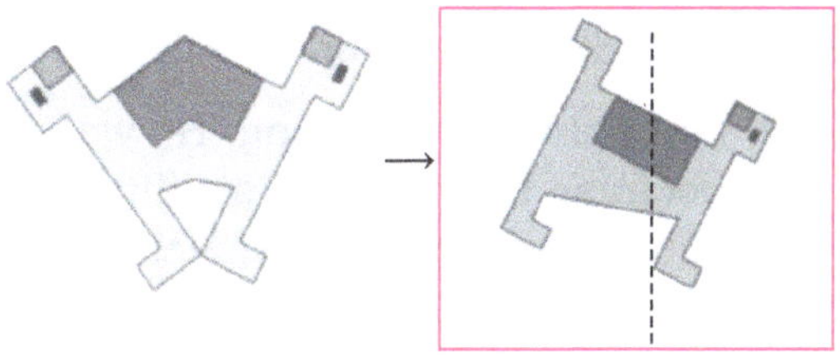

Q.4 Venky has made a shaded and unshaded shape. Make a line on the unshaded box where you will keep a mirror to get that shape. Look at how the line is drawn in the first box to get the picture next to it.

(i) 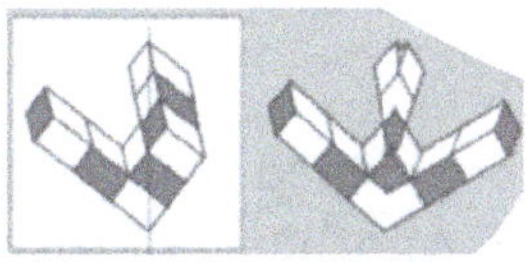

(ii) 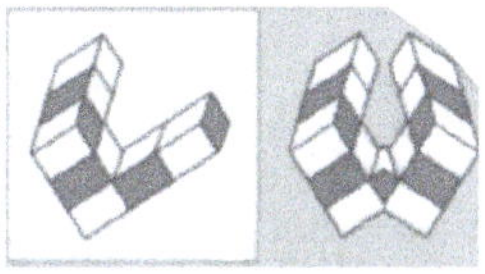

(iii) 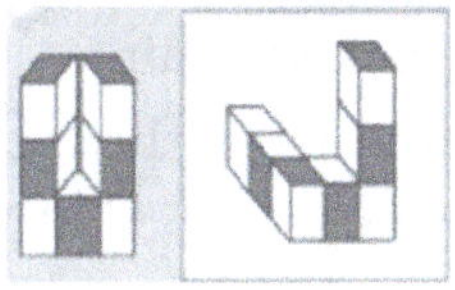

(iv) 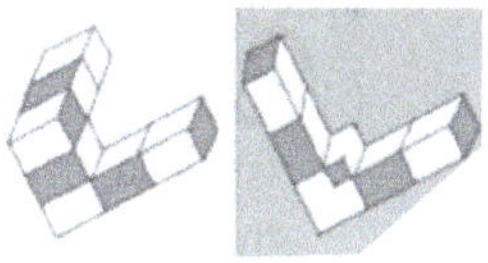

(v) 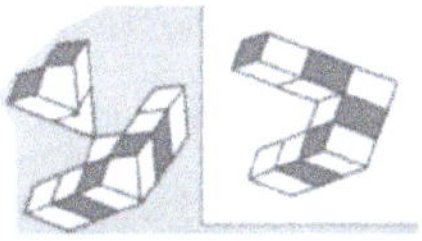

Ans. Dotted lines show the position of mirror.

(ii) 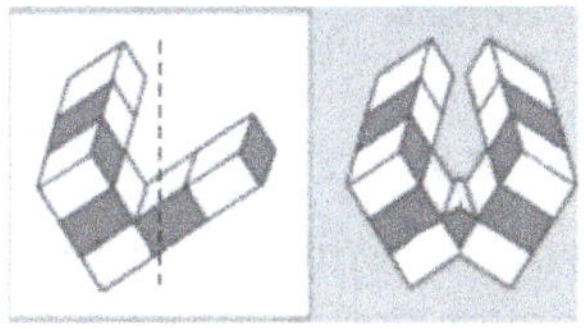

(iii) 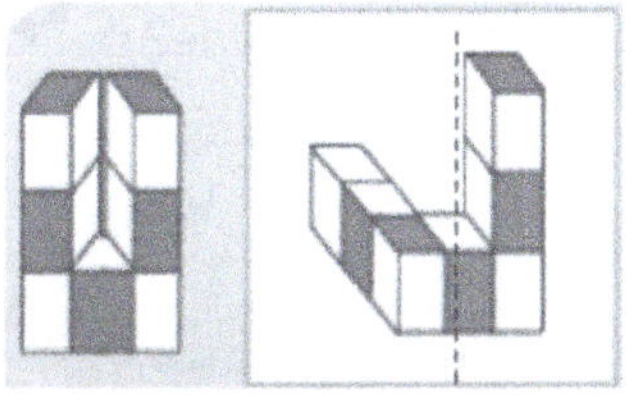

(iv) 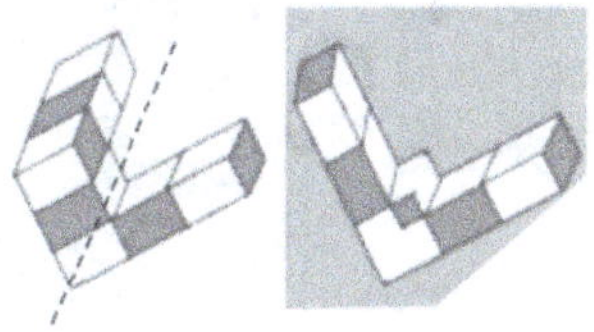

(v) 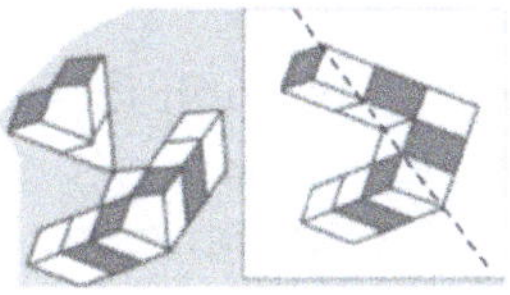

Half a Turn (NCERT Pg 77-78)

Q.5 Once there was a king. He was upset because thieves kept stealing costly jewels from his locker. Here is what the locker looked like.

The locker could be opened by giving its handle half a turn. Another half turn and the locker would be locked again.

(i) The king would often leave the locker open thinking it was locked. Can you guess the reason?

(ii) One day his clever daughter gave him an idea which he liked very much. Now, he never get confused. Can you guess what the idea was?

(iii) The king had many such lockers with different handles. Check if, on giving them half a turn, he can get confused with these too.

What will you do to solve the problem for each of these?

Ans. (i) Both the positions of the locker look like same. So, he often get confuse whether it is locked or open.

(ii) The king's daughter put a dot on the blade when it was open, so it became simple to see whether the locker was open or shut.

(iii) To solve the problem, I put a mark or dot on the blade of these locks. So, it will be simple to check whether the locker was open or closed.

Same after $\frac{1}{2}$ turn? (NCERT Pg 78)

Q.6 Guess which of the shapes below would look the same after half a turn.

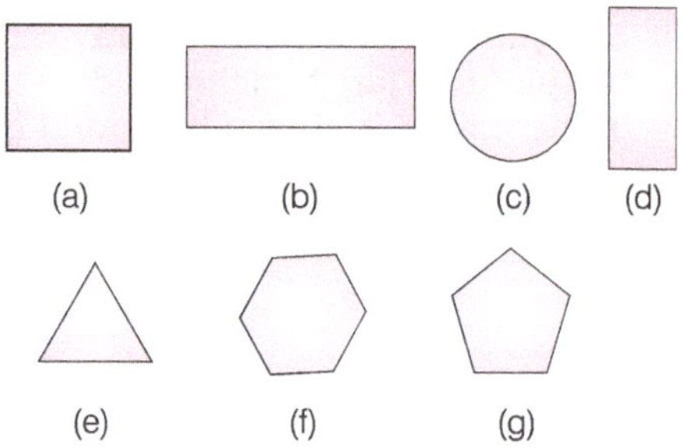

Ans. After half a turn, shapes (a), (b), (c), (d) and (f) will look the same.

Practice Time (NCERT Pg 79-80)

Q.7 Find out which letters in the English alphabet look the same after half a turn.

Ans. English alphabets like H, I, N, O, S, X and Z look the same after half a turn.

Q.8 Which of these English words reads the same on half a turn?

ZOOM, MOW, SWIMS, SIS, NOON

Ans. English words MOW, SWIMS, SIS and NOON read the same on half a turn.

Q.9 Give half a turn to the numbers from 0 to 9. Find which of them still looks the same.

Ans. The numbers from 0 to 9 which still look the same after half a turn are 0, 1 and 8.

Q.10 Think of all 2, 3 and 4 digit numbers which look the same on half a turn.

Example

2-digit numbers 1 1, _____ , _____

3-digit numbers 1 0 1, 1 1 1, _____ , _____ , _____ , _____ , _____ , _____

4-digit numbers 1 0 0 1, 1 1 1 1, _____, _____, _____, _____, _____

Ans. Following are the numbers which look the same on half a turn.

2-digit numbers are 1 1, 8 8

3-digit numbers are 1 0 1, 1 1 1, 1 8 1, 8 0 8, 8 1 8, 8 8 8.

4-digit numbers are 1 0 0 1, 1 1 1 1, 1 8 8 1, 8 0 0 8, 8 1 1 8, 8 8 8 8.

Q.11 Which among the following pictures will look the same on half a turn?

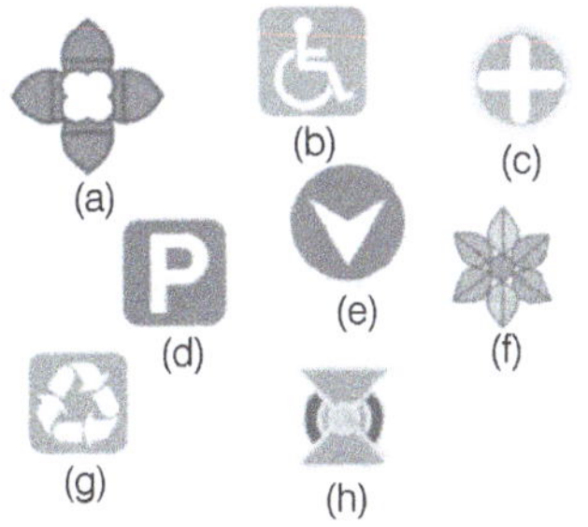

Ans. The pictures (a), (c), (f) and (h) will look the same on half a turn.

Activity Time (NCERT Pg 80-81)

Q.12 (i) Have you ever seen a windmill? What is it used for?

(ii) Does your windmill look the same on $\frac{1}{4}$ of a turn?

(iii) Does it look the same on half a turn? Discuss.

Ans. *(i) Yes, I have seen a windmill. It is used for grinding corn, generating electricity and pumping water etc.

(ii) Yes, it looks the same on $\frac{1}{4}$ of a turn.

(iii) Yes, it looks the same on half a turn. Since, the half a turn is equal to twice of $\frac{1}{4}$ of a turn. So, it looks same on half a turn also.

One-Fourth Turn (NCERT Pg 81-82)

Q.13 (i) Does the fan look the same on $\frac{1}{4}$ turn?

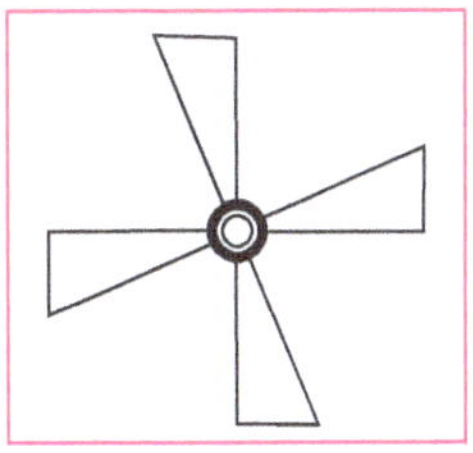

Before turning it

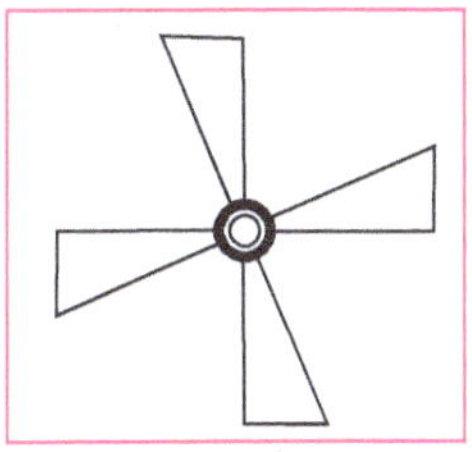

After $\frac{1}{4}$ turn

(ii) Will this fan also look the same after $\frac{1}{4}$ turn? Draw in the blank box.

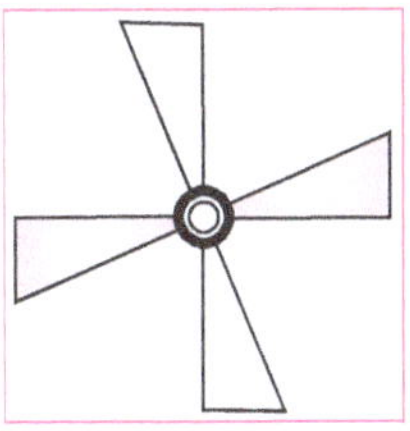

Before turning it

After $\frac{1}{4}$ turn

Ans. (i) Yes, the fan looks the same on $\frac{1}{4}$ turn.

(ii) No, this fan does not look the same after $\frac{1}{4}$ turn.

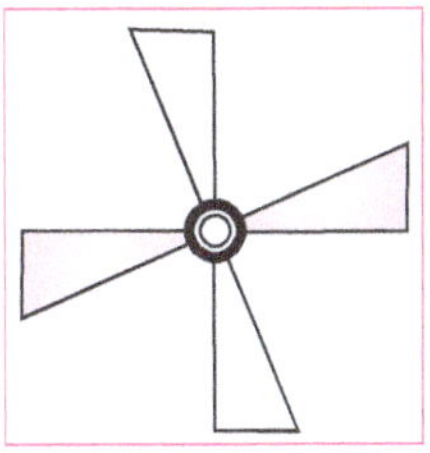

Before turning it

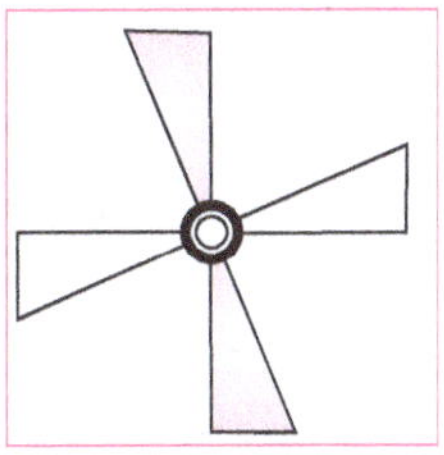

After $\frac{1}{4}$ turn

Practice Time (NCERT Pg 82-84)

Q.14 (i) Among the following shapes, find out which ones would look the same after $\frac{1}{4}$ turn. Put a (✓).

(ii) Put a (×) on the shapes that will not look the same after half a turn.

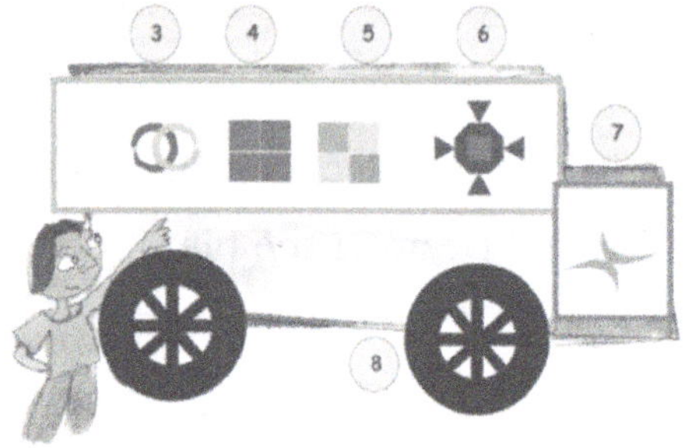

Ans. (i) **On $\frac{1}{4}$ turn**

4. (✓) 6. (✓) 8. (✓)

(ii) **On half turn**

1. (×) 3. (×)

Q.15 Try and change the shapes in such a way that the new shape remains the same on giving it half a turn.

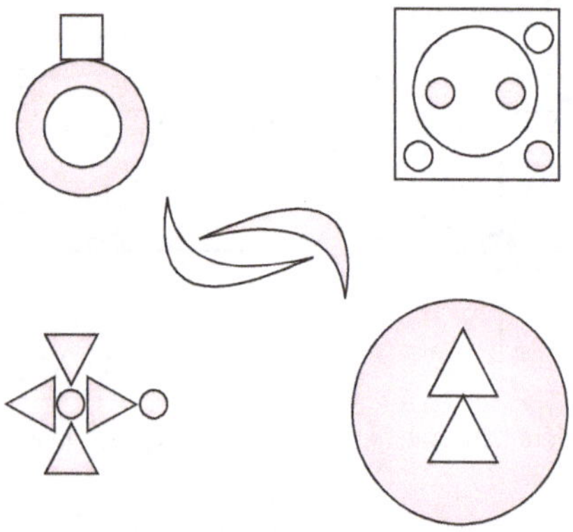

Ans. *New shapes after changing old shapes after giving them half a turn are as follows.

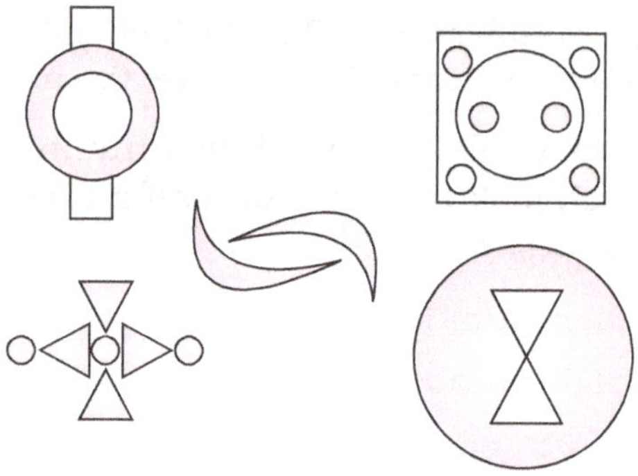

Q.16 (i) Draw what the following shapes would look like on $\frac{1}{4}$ turn and half a turn.

	Shape	**On $\frac{1}{4}$ turn**	**On half turn**
(a)	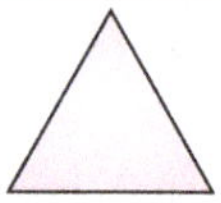		
(b)			
(c)			
(d)	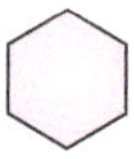		

(ii) Which of the above shapes do not look the same on $\frac{1}{4}$ turn? Which shapes do not look the same on $\frac{1}{2}$ a turn?

Ans. (i)

	Shape	On $\frac{1}{4}$ turn	On half turn
(a)	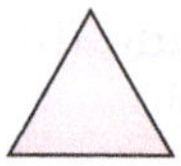	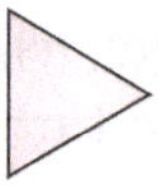	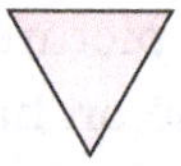
(b)			
(c)			
(d)		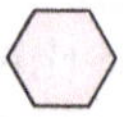	

(ii) From the above shapes, it is clear that shapes (a), (c) and (d) do not look the same on $\frac{1}{4}$ turn and shape (a) does not look the same on $\frac{1}{2}$ a turn.

Q.17 Which fan will look the same on a $\frac{1}{3}$ turn?

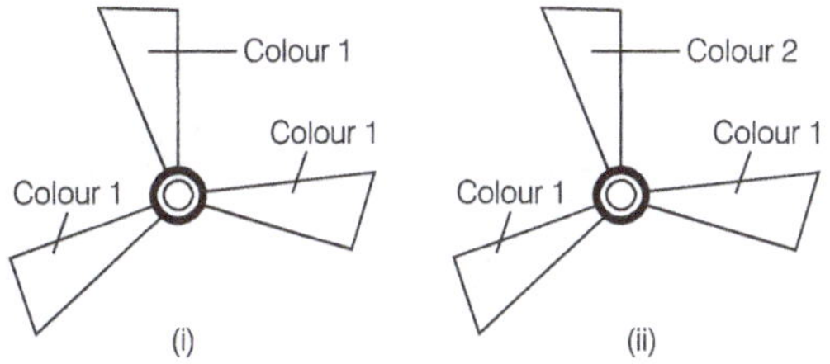

Ans. Fan (i) will look the same on $\frac{1}{3}$ turn.

Q.18 Draw this shape after $\frac{1}{3}$ turn.

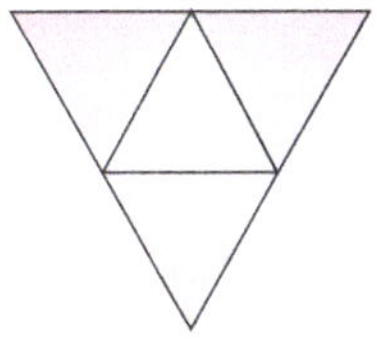

Shape after $\frac{1}{3}$ turn

Ans. The shape after $\frac{1}{3}$ turn is as given below

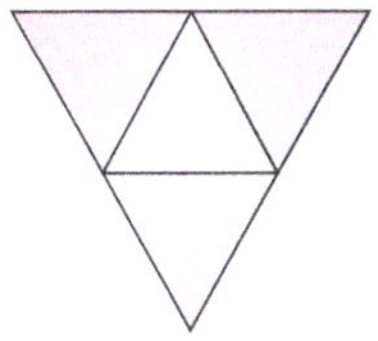

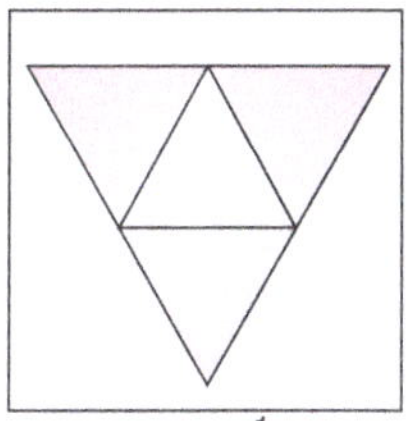

Shape after $\frac{1}{3}$ turn

One-sixth Turn (NCERT Pg 85)

Q.19 Can you see that this shape looks the same on $\frac{1}{6}$ turn?

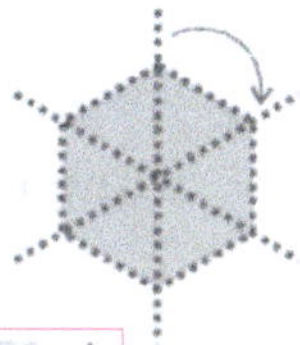

Ans. Yes, the shape looks same on $\frac{1}{6}$ turn.

Practice Time (NCERT Pg 85-86)

Q.20 Look at the following shapes. Draw how they will look on $\frac{1}{3}$ and $\frac{1}{6}$ turn.

	Shape	**On $\frac{1}{3}$ turn**	**On $\frac{1}{6}$ turn**
(a)	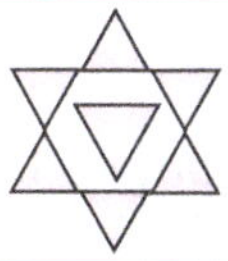		
(b)			
(c)	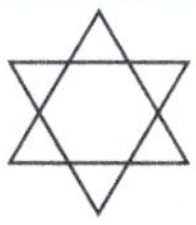		
(d)	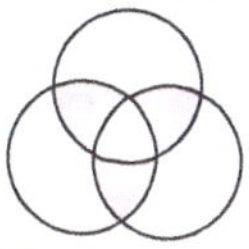		

Ans.

	Shape	On $\frac{1}{3}$ turn	On $\frac{1}{6}$ turn
(a)			
(b)	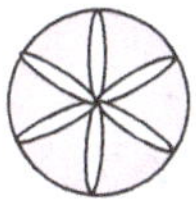	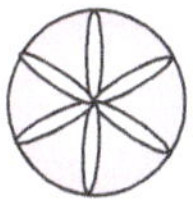	
(c)		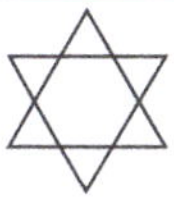	
(d)	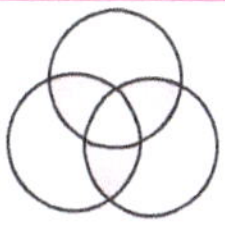	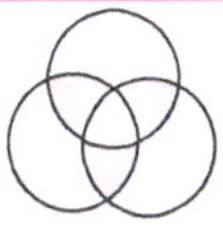	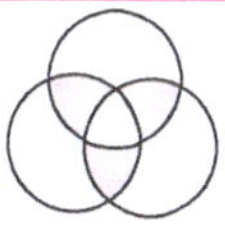

Q.21 Look at the following shapes

(i) Find out which of these figures look the same on $\frac{1}{3}$ turn. Mark them with (✓).

(ii) Which are the ones that will not look the same after $\frac{1}{3}$ turn? Mark them with (✗).

(iii) Try and change the shapes below in such a way that they look the same on $\frac{1}{3}$ turn.

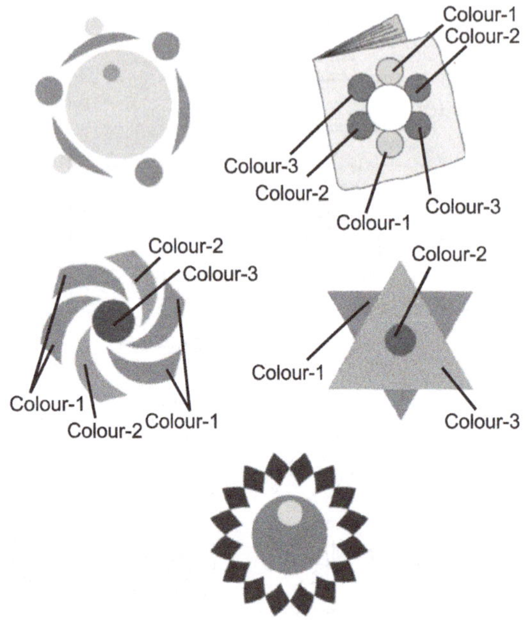

Ans. (i) Following shapes look the same on $\frac{1}{3}$ turn.

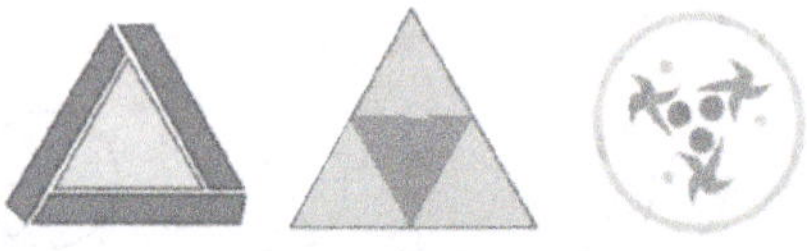

(✓) (✓) (✓)

(ii) Following are the ones that will not look the same after $\frac{1}{3}$ turn.

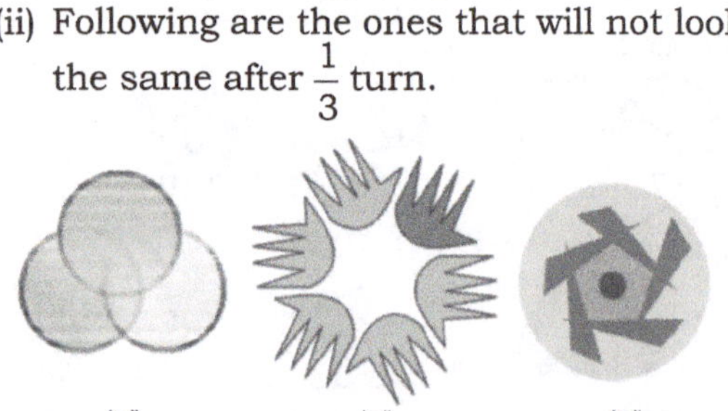

(✗) (✗) (✗)

*(iii) The shapes can be changed as under :

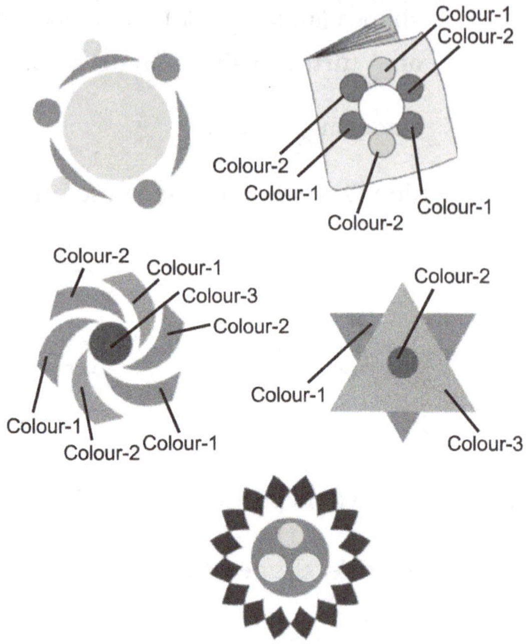

Q.22 Draw some shapes which will look the same after $\frac{1}{3}$ turn.

Ans. *Following are some shapes which will look the same after $\frac{1}{3}$ turn

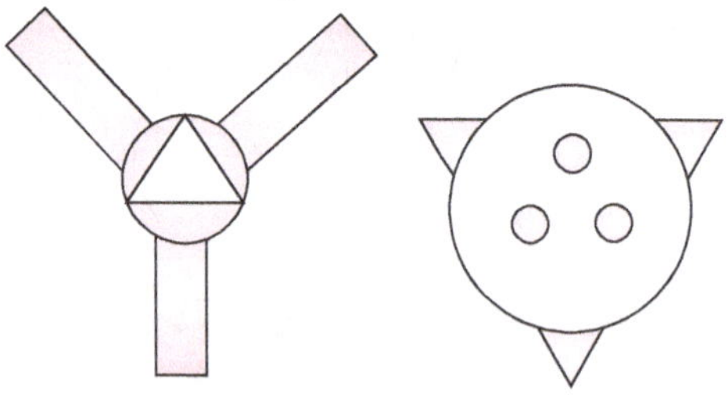

Q.23 Draw some shapes which will look the same after $\frac{1}{6}$ turn.

Ans. *Following shapes will look the same after $\frac{1}{6}$ turn.

PRACTICE QUESTIONS

1. Fill in the blanks.
   (i) When an object is turned around a point without changing its shape, it shows ______ symmetry. (reflection/rotational)
   (ii) A square have ______ lines of symmetry. (2/4)
   (iii) A square shows ______ symmetry after a $\frac{1}{4}$ turn. (rotational/reflection)

2. True or False
   (i) A circle has infinite lines of symmetry.
   (ii) A triangle with all equal sides, looks the same after a $\frac{1}{3}$rd turn.
   (iii) A square looks the same after a half turn.

3. Multiple choice questions
   (i) Which of the following shapes has the highest rotational symmetry?
   (a) Rectangle (b) Circle
   (c) Triangle (d) Hexagon
   (ii) How many times does a square look the same in a full turn?
   (a) 1 time
   (b) 2 times
   (c) 4 times
   (d) 6 times
   (iii) Which shape does not look the same after a half-turn?
   (a) Rectangle
   (b) Circle
   (c) Square
   (d) Triangle

4. Odd-One Out
   (a) Circle
   (b) Square
   (c) Hexagon
   (d) Oval

5. A fan has 3 blades. After $\frac{1}{3}$ turn, it looks the same. How many times will it look the same in a full turn.

ANSWERS & SOLUTIONS

1. (i) rotational
   (ii) 4
   (iii) rotational
2. (i) True
   (ii) True
   (iii) True
3. (i) (b) (ii) (c) (iii) (d)
4. (d)
5.

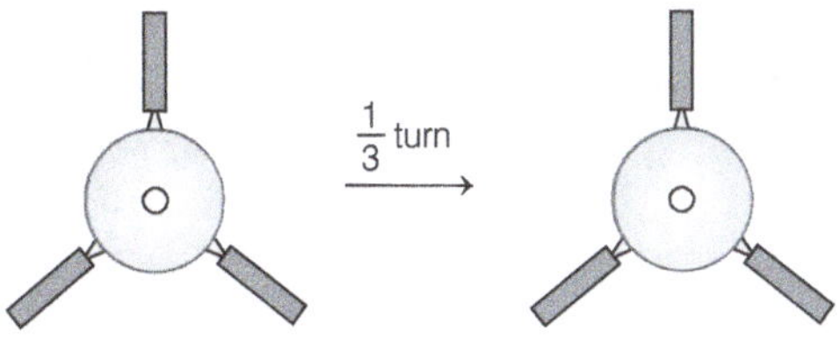

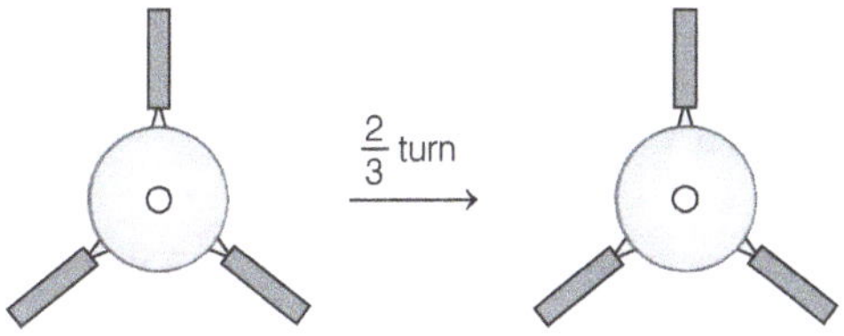

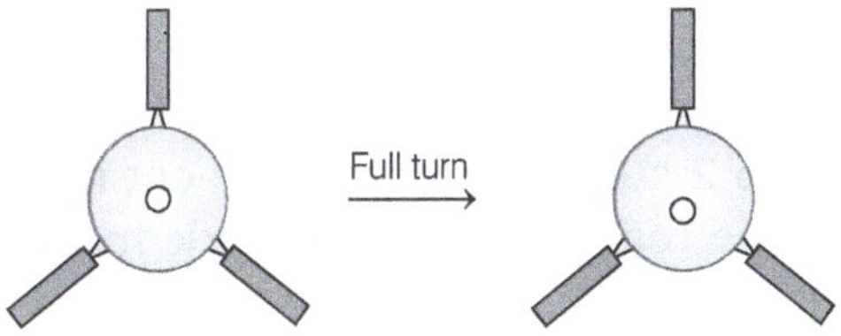

Therefore, a fan having 3 blades looks same 3 times in a full turn.

CHAPTER 6 BE MY MULTIPLE, I'LL BE YOUR FACTOR

Multiples

A multiple of a number is the product obtained by multiplying that number by another natural number. e.g. Multiples of 3 are 3, 6, 9, 12, 15, ...

Common Multiples

Multiples that are common to two or more numbers are known as the common multiple of those numbers.

e.g. Multiples of 3 are 3, 6, 9, 12, 15, ... and multiples of 5 are 5, 10, 15, 20, 25, ...

Here, the common multiples of 3 and 5 are 15, 30, 45, ...

Factors

A factor of a number is a number that divides the given number exactly.

e.g. Factors of 12 are 1, 2, 3, 4, 6 and 12.

Common Factors

The factors that divides the two or more given numbers exactly, are known as the common factors of those numbers. e.g. Common factors of 12 and 18 are 1, 2, 3 and 6.

Relation between Multiples and Factors

If a number A is a multiple of B, then B is a factor of A. e.g. 24 is a multiple of 6 because $6 \times 4 = 24$. Therefore, 6 is a factor of 24.

NCERT FOLDER

The Mouse and the Cat (NCERT Pg 87)

Q.1 The hungry cat is trying to catch Kunjan the mouse. Kunjan is now on the 14th step and it can jump 2 steps at a time. The cat is on the third step. She can jump 3 steps at a time. If the mouse reaches 28, it can hide in the hole. Find out whether the mouse can get away safely!

(i) The steps on which the mouse jumps.

(ii) The steps on which the cat jumps.

(iii) The steps on which both the cat and the mouse jump.

(iv) Can the mouse get away?

* *Students can write alternate answer as per their choice.*

Ans. (i) The mouse jumps on the following steps

$14, 14+2=16, 16+2=18, 18+2=20,$
$20+2=22, 22+2=24, 24+2=26$ and
$26+2=28.$

That is 14, 16, 18, 20, 22, 24, 26, 28.

(ii) The cat jumps on the following steps

$3, 3+3=6, 6+3=9, 9+3=12, 12+3=15,$
$15+3=18, 18+3=21, 21+3=24$ and
$24+3=27.$

That is 3, 6, 9, 12, 15, 18, 21, 24 and 27.

(iii) The steps on which both the cat and mouse jump are 18 and 24.

(iv) Yes, because they do not meet at steps 18 and 24. So, the mouse safely gets away.

Find out (NCERT Pg 87)

Q.2 If the cat starts from the 5th step and jumps five steps at a time and the mouse starts from the 8th step and jumps four steps at a time, can the mouse get away?

Ans. Cat jumps the following steps:

10, 15, [20], 25

The mouse jumps the following steps

12, 16, [20], 24

After 3 jumps, the cat and the mouse reach the step 20. Hence, the mouse will not get away.

Who is Monto Waiting for? (NCERT Pg 88)

Q.3 Monto cat is waiting for somebody. Do you know for whom he is waiting? There is a trick to find out.

			D				X		
1	2	3	4	5	6	7	8	9	10
	M					P			I
11	12	13	14	15	16	17	18	19	20
			O						
21	22	23	24	25	26	27	28	29	30
R			N		U				
31	32	33	34	35	36	37	38	39	40
			B	W			S		
41	42	43	44	45	46	47	48	49	50
	J				H				E
51	52	53	54	55	56	57	58	59	60

Mark with a red dot all the numbers which can be divided by 2.

Mark a yellow dot on the numbers which can be divided by 3 and a blue dot on the numbers which can be divided by 4.

(i) Which are the boxes which have dots of all three colours?

(ii) What are the letters on top of those boxes?

(iii) Write those letters below in order.

[ ]

Ans. (i) Let us mark red with *R*, yellow with *Y* and blue with *B*.

	R	Y	RB(D)		RY		RB(X)	Y	R
1	2	3	4	5	6	7	8	9	10
	RYB(M)		R	Y	RB	P	RY		RB(I)
11	12	13	14	15	16	17	18	19	20
Y	R		RYB(O)		R	Y	RB		RY
21	22	23	24	25	26	27	28	29	30
(R)	RB	Y	R(N)		RYB(U)		R	Y	RB
31	32	33	34	35	36	37	38	39	40
	RY		RB(B)	Y(W)	R		RYB(S)		R
41	42	43	44	45	46	47	48	49	50
Y	RB(J)		RY		RB(H)	Y	R		RYB(E)
51	52	53	54	55	56	57	58	59	60

The boxes which have dots of all three colours are 12, 24, 36, 48 and 60.

(ii) The letters on top of these boxes are M, O, U, S and E.

(iii) [MOUSE]

Hence, Monto cat is waiting for the MOUSE.

Meow Game (NCERT Pg 89)

Q.4 To play this game, everyone stands in a circle. One player calls out 'one'. The next player says 'two' and so on. A player who has to call out 3 or a number which can be divided by 3 has to say 'Meow' instead of the number.

One who forgets to say Meow is out of the game. The last player left is the winner.

(i) Which numbers did you replace with 'Meow' ?

3, 6, 9..................

(ii) Play the game by changing the number to 4. Now, which numbers did you replace with 'Meow'?

(iii) Write any ten multiples of 5.

Ans. (i) The numbers which are multiples of 3 can be replaced with 'Meow' are
3, 6, 9, 12, 15, 18, 21, 24, 27, 30, ...

(ii) The numbers which are replaced with 'Meow' are
4, 8, 12, 16, 20, 24, 28, 32, 36, 40, ...

*(iii) Ten multiples of 5 are
5, 10, 15, 20, 25, 30, 35, 40, 45 and 50.

Dice Game (NCERT Pg 90)

Q.5 Throw two dice together. What are the numbers that turn up on the faces of dice? Make a two-digit number using them. If it is a multiple of any of the numbers written next to the circles, you can write it in that circle. Then, it is your friend's trun. The one who can write more numbers in 10 rounds is the winner.

Hint I have 3 and 2 on my dice. If I make 23, it is not the multiple of any of the numbers. So I will make 32, which is a multiple of 4, and write it in the red circle.

Ans. Do yourself.

Common Multiples (NCERT Pg 91-92)

Q.6 Think of a number. If it is a multiple of 3, write it in the circle 1. If it is a multiple of 5, write it in the circle 2.

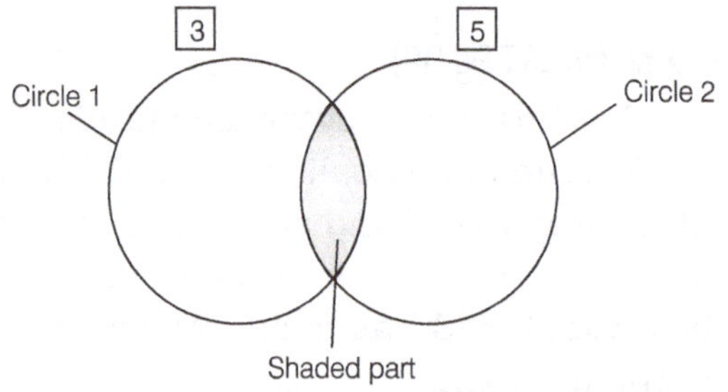

Some numbers are multiples of both 3 and 5. So, we can say that they are common to both 3 and 5.

Think! If you write the multiples common to 3 and 5 in the purple part, then will they still be in both the red and the blue circles?

(i) Where do I write 15? It is a multiple of both 3 and 5.

(ii) Which is the smallest among these common multiples?

(iii) Repeat the game using the numbers 2 and 7. Write the common multiples of 2 and 7.

Ans.

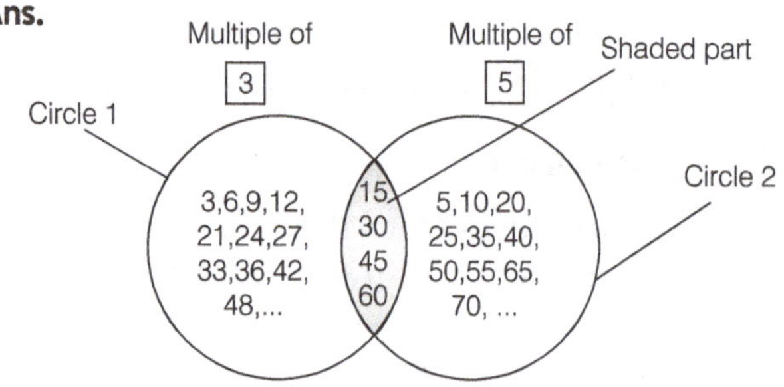

(i) We write 15 in the shaded part.

(ii) The smallest common multiple of 3 and 5 is 15.

(iii) Common multiples of 2 and 7 are 14, 28, 42, 56, 70, ...

Q.7 Repeat the game by putting the multiples of 4, 6 and 5 in the circles.

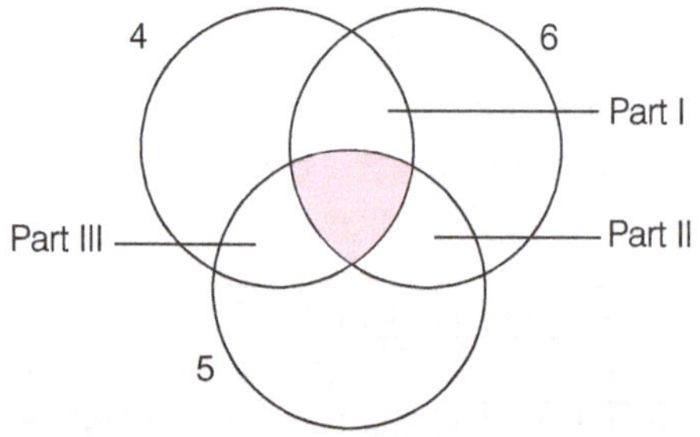

(i) What common multiples of 5 and 6 did you write in the part II?

(ii) What common multiples of 4 and 6 are written in the part I?

(iii) In which part did you write the common multiples of 4,6 and 5?

(iv) What is the smallest common multiple of 4, 6 and 5?

Ans.

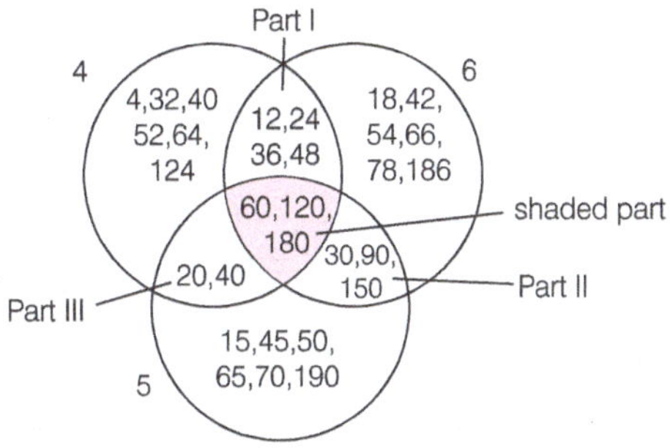

*(i) 30, 90, 150 are in the part II.

*(ii) 12, 24, 36, 48 are in part I.

(iii) The common multiples of 4, 6 and 5 are written in the shaded part.

(iv) The smallest common multiple of 4, 6 and 5 is 60.

Puzzle (NCERT Pg 92-93)

Tamarind seeds

Q.8 Sunita took some tamarind (imli) seeds. She made groups of five with them and found that one seed was left over. She tried making groups of six and groups of four. Each time one seed was left over. What is the smallest number of seeds that Sunita had?

Ans. Multiples of 5 = 5, 10, 15, 20, 25, 30, 35, 40, 45, 50, 55, [60], 65

Multiple of 6 = 6, 12, 18, 24, 30, 42, 48, 54, [60], 66

Multiple of 4 = 4, 8, 12, 16, 20, 24, 28, 32, 36, 40, 44, 48, 52, 56, [60], 64

The smallest common multiple of 5, 6 and 4 is 60.

Since, each time one seed was left over.

∴ The smallest number of seeds that Sunita $= 60 + 1 = 61$

More tamarind Seeds

Q.9 (i) Ammini is arranging 12 tamarind seeds in the form of different rectangles. Try to make more rectangles like this using 12 tamarind seeds. How many different rectangles can you make?

(ii) If there are 15 tamarind seeds, how many rectangles can you make?

Ans. (i) We can make following 3 rectangles using 12 seeds.

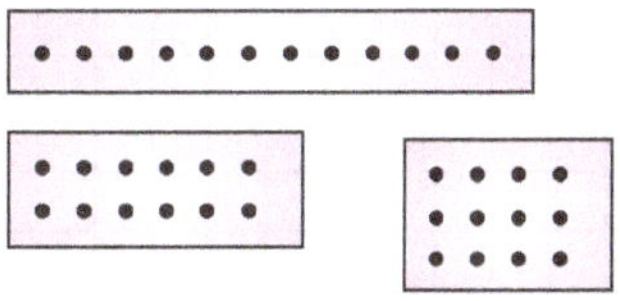

The size of three different rectangles are 1×12, 2×6, 3×4.

(ii) If there are 15 tamarind seeds, we can make 2 rectangles of sizes 1×15 and 3×5.

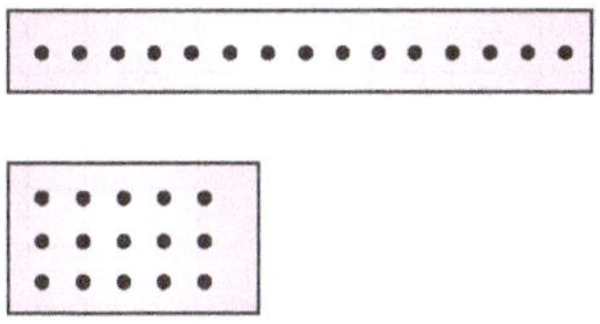

Colouring the Grid (NCERT Pg 93-94)

Q.10 In the grid here, a rectangle made of 20 boxes is drawn. The width of this rectangle is 2 boxes.

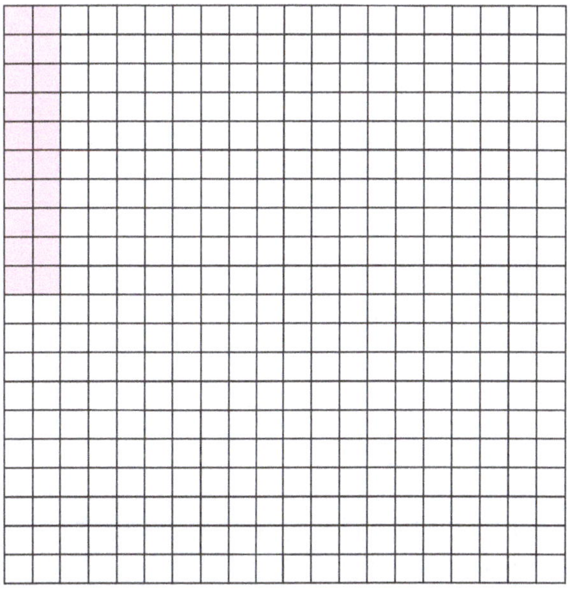

(i) What is its length?

(ii) Shade a rectangle made of 20 boxes in some other way.

(iii) What is the length and width of the rectangle you shade?

(iv) In how many ways can you shade a rectangle of 20 boxes? Shade them all in the grid, and write the length and width of each rectangle you have shaded.

Ans. (i) The length of the rectangle is 10 boxes.

*(ii) It can be shown by following grid

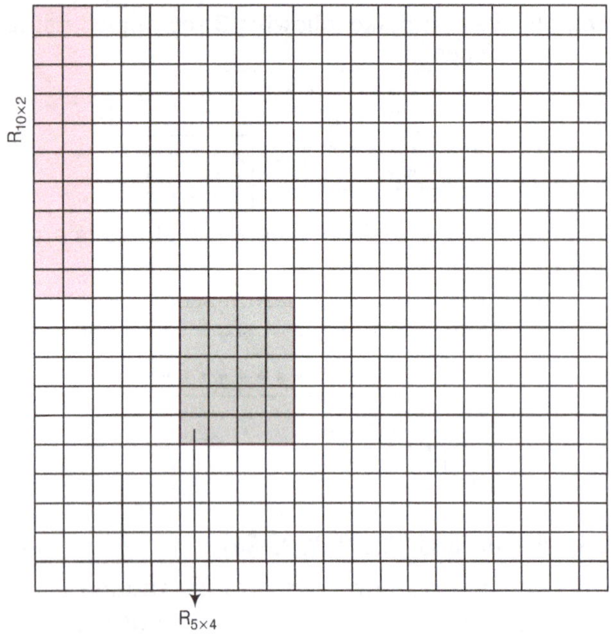

*(iii) The length is 5 boxes and width is 4 boxes.

(iv) We have, three rectangles of 20 boxes in the given grid.

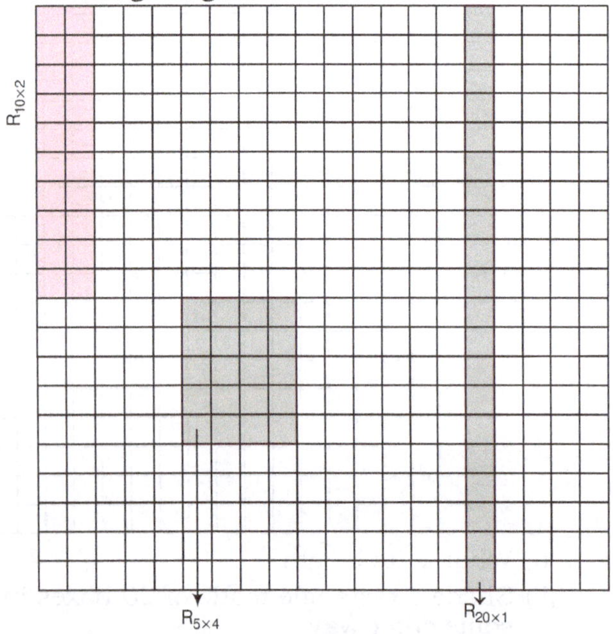

$R_{10\times2}$, length = 10 boxes
width = 2 boxes

$R_{5\times4}$, length = 5 boxes
width = 4 boxes

$R_{20\times1}$, length = 20 boxes
width = 1 box

Bangles (NCERT Pg 94)

Q.11 There are 18 bangles on the rod. Meena is trying to group them. She can put them in groups of 2, 3, 6, 9 and 18 without any bangle being left.

(i) How many groups will she have if she makes groups of 1 bangle each?

(ii) Now, complete the table for different numbers of bangles. For each number see what different groups can be made.

Number of bangles	Different groups we can make
18	1, 2, 3, 6, 9, 18
24	1, 2, ...
5	
9	
7	
2	
10	
1	
20	
13	
21	

Ans. (i) She have 18 groups of 1 bangle each.

(ii) We have completed the table as under.

Number of bangles	Different groups we can make
18	1, 2, 3, 6, 9, 18
24	1, 2, 3, 4, 6, 12, 24
5	1, 5
9	1, 3, 9
7	1, 7
2	1, 2
10	1, 2, 5, 10
1	1
20	1, 2, 4, 5, 10, 20
13	1, 13
21	1, 3, 7, 21

Fill the Chart (NCERT Pg 95-96)

Q.12 Complete the multiplication chart given here.

X	1	2	3	4	5	6	7	8	9	10	11	12
1												
2						12						
3				12			21					
4			12							40		
5				20								
6		12										
7												
8									72			
9												
10												
11						66						
12	12											

Look at the Grey boxes in the chart. These show how we can get 12 by multiplying different numbers.

$12 = 4 \times 3$, so 12 is a multiple of both 4 and 3. 12 is also a multiple of 6 and 2, as well as 12 and 1. We say 1, 2, 3, 4, 6, 12 are factors of 12.

(i) What are the factors of 10? Can you do this from the chart?

(ii) What are the factors of 36?

(iii) Find out all the factors of 36 from the multiplication chart.

(iv) What is the biggest number for which you can find the factors from this chart?

(v) What can you do for numbers bigger than that?

Ans.

X	1	2	3	4	5	6	7	8	9	10	11	12
1	1	2	3	4	5	6	7	8	9	10	11	12
2	2	4	6	8	10	12	14	16	18	20	22	24
3	3	6	9	12	15	18	21	24	27	30	33	36
4	4	8	12	16	20	24	28	32	36	40	44	48
5	5	10	15	20	25	30	35	40	45	50	55	60
6	6	12	18	24	30	36	42	48	54	60	66	72
7	7	14	21	28	35	42	49	56	63	70	77	84
8	8	16	24	32	40	48	56	64	72	80	88	96
9	9	18	27	36	45	54	63	72	81	90	99	108
10	10	20	30	40	50	60	70	80	90	100	110	120
11	11	22	33	44	55	66	77	88	99	110	121	132
12	12	24	36	48	60	72	84	96	108	120	132	144

(i) The factors of 10 are 1, 2, 5 and 10. Yes, we can do this from the chart also.

(ii) The factors of 36 are 1, 2, 3, 4, 6, 9, 12, 18 and 36.

(iii) From the given multiplication chart, we have

$$36 = 3 \times 12$$
$$36 = 4 \times 9$$
$$36 = 6 \times 6$$
$$36 = 9 \times 4$$
$$36 = 12 \times 3$$

So, all the factors of 36 from the given multiplication chart are 3, 4, 6, 9 and 12.

(iv) 144 is the biggest number for which we can find the factors from the chart.

(v) First, we will extend the multiplication chart. Then, complete the chart.

Common Factors (NCERT Pg 96)

Q.13 (i) Write the factors of 25 in the circle 1 and the factors of 35 in the circle 2.

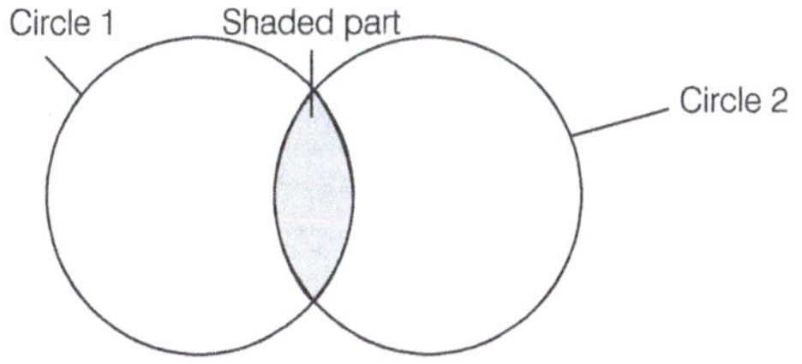

(ii) Which are the factors you have written in the common part (shaded part) of both circles? These are common factors of 25 and 35.

(iii) Write the factors of 40 in the circle 1 and 60 in the circle 2.

(iv) What are the factors written in the common (shaded) part of the circle? Which is the biggest common factor of 40 and 60?

Ans. (i)

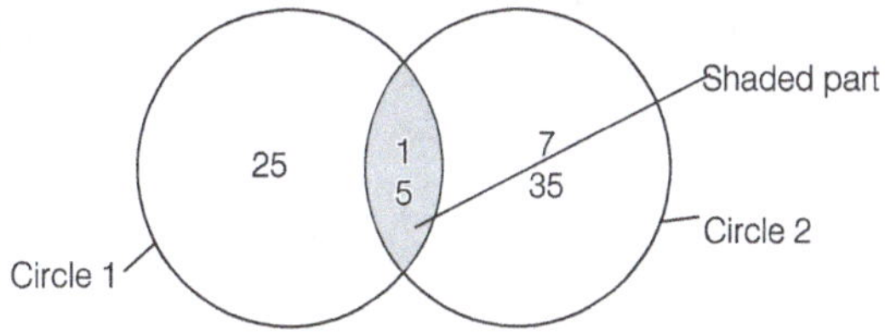

(ii) 1 and 5 are the common factors of 25 and 35 written in the shaded part.

(iii)

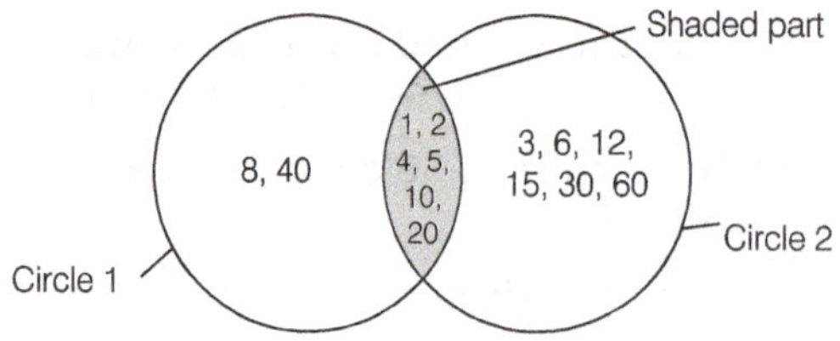

(iv) The factors 1, 2, 4, 5, 10 and 20 are the common factors written in the common (shaded) part of the circle. The biggest common factor of 40 and 60 is 20.

Factor Tree (NCERT Pg 97)

Q.14 Look at the factor tree. Now, can you make another tree like this?

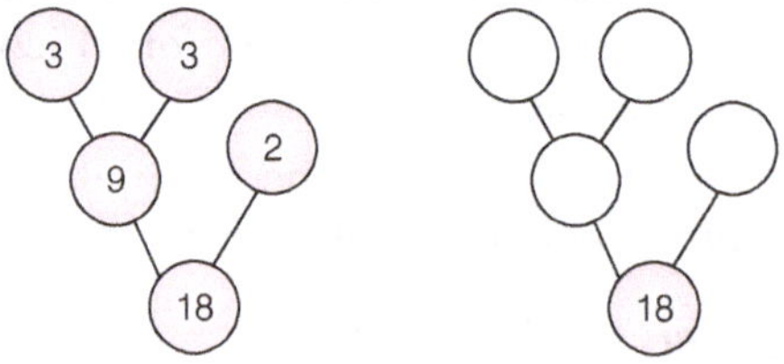

(i) In how many ways can you draw a factor tree for 24? Draw three of them below.

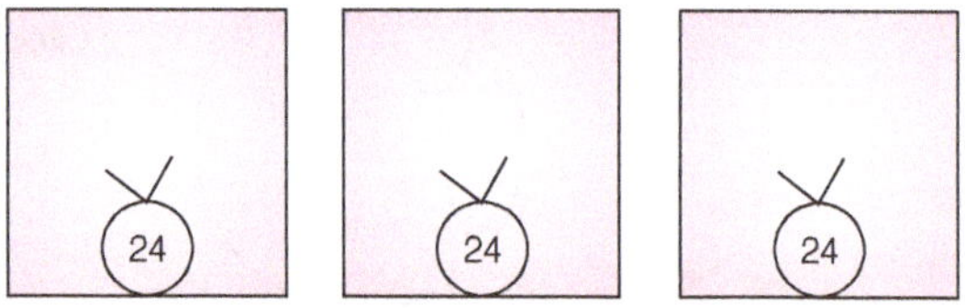

(ii) Try drawing the factor tree using other numbers also.

Ans. Following is the factor tree of 18.

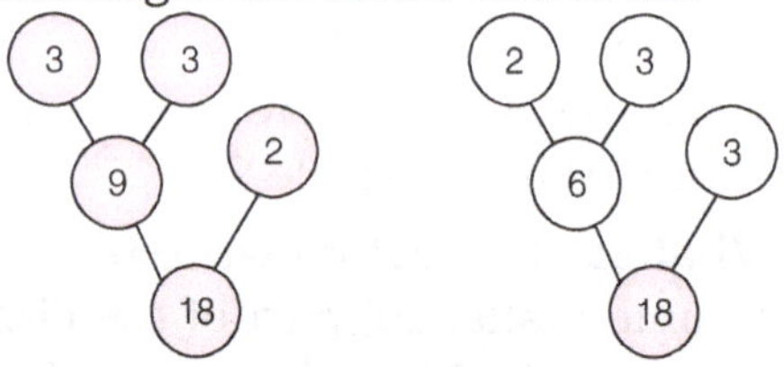

(i) Following are the tree of 24.

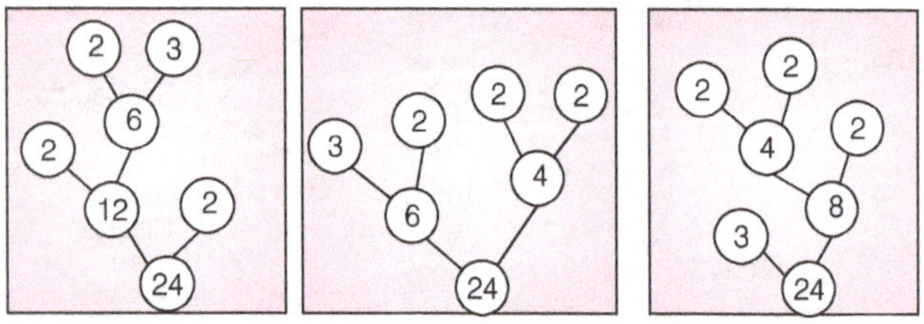

*(ii) Here, we have factors of 16 in different factor trees.

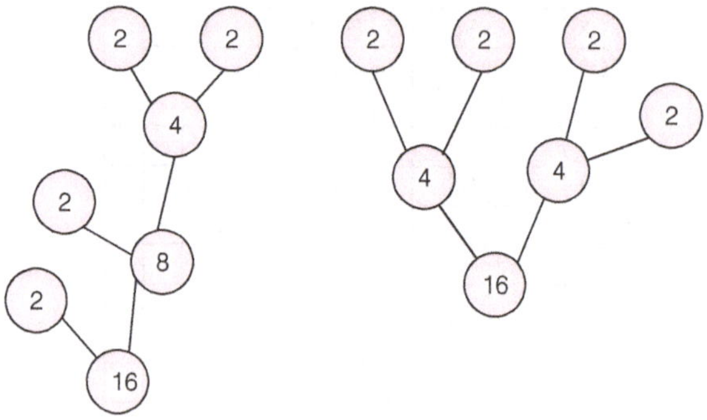

Let us show 48 in factor trees as under

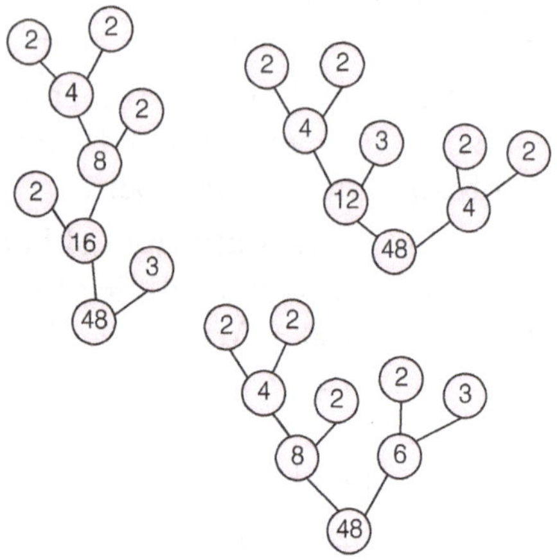

Tiling Problems (NCERT Pg 97-98)

Q.15 There is a garden in Anu's house. In the middle of the garden there is a path. They decided to tile the path using tiles of length 2 feet, 3 feet and 5 feet.

The mason tiled the first row with 2 feet tiles, the second row with 3 feet tiles and the third row with 5 feet tiles. The mason has not cut any of the tiles. Then, what is the shortest length of the path?

Ans. It can be observed that the shortest length of the path is the smallest common multiples of 2, 3 and 5.

Multiples of 2 are 2, 4, 6, 8, 10, 12, 14, 16, 18, 20, 22, 24, 26, 28, [30].

Multiples of 3 are 3, 6, 9, 12, 15, 18, 21, 24, 27, [30].

Multiple of 5 are 5, 10, 15, 20, 25, [30].

Here, 30 is the smallest common multiple.

So, the shortest length of the path is 30 feet.

Q.16 Manoj has made a new house. He wants to lay tiles on the floor. The size of the room is 9 feet × 12 feet. In the market, there are three kinds of square tiles: 1 feet × 1 feet, 2 feet × 2 feet and 3 feet × 3 feet.

Which size of tile should he buy for his room, so that he can lay it without cutting?

Ans. Since, 2 is not a common factor of 9 and 12. So, the tiles of size 2 feet × 2 feet can not be used without cutting them.

However, 1 and 3 are factors of both 9 and 12. Therefore, he should buy tiles of size 1 feet × 1 feet or 3 feet × 3 feet, so he won't have to cut them.

Q.17

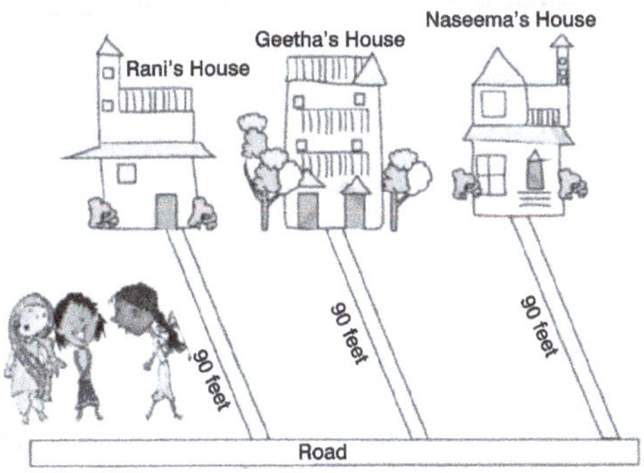

Rani, Geetha and Naseema live near each other. The distance from their houses to the road is 90 feet. They decided to tile the path to the road.

They all bought tiles of different designs and length. Rani bought the shortest tile, Geetha bought the middle sized one and Naseema bought the longest one. If they could tile the path without cutting any of the tiles, what is the size of the tiles each has bought? Suggest 3 different solutions. Explain how you get this answer.

Ans. The distance from their houses to the road is 90 feet.

90 can be factorised as follows

$90 = 1 \times 90$

$90 = 2 \times 45$

$90 = 3 \times 30$

$90 = 5 \times 18$

$90 = 6 \times 15$

$90 = 9 \times 10$

Factors of 90 are 1, 2, 3, 5, 6, 9 etc.

Hence, possible tiles can be as follows

1 feet × 1 feet

2 feet × 2 feet

3 feet × 3 feet

5 feet × 5 feet

6 feet × 6 feet

9 feet × 9 feet etc.

Then, the size of the tiles each has bought are

(i) Rani = 1 feet × 1 feet
Geetha = 2 feet × 2 feet
Naseema = 3 feet × 3 feet

(ii) Rani = 2 feet × 2 feet
Geetha = 3 feet × 3 feet
Naseema = 5 feet × 5 feet

(iii) Rani = 3 feet × 3 feet
Geetha = 5 feet × 5 feet
Naseema = 6 feet × 6 feet

PRACTICE QUESTIONS

1. Fill in the blanks
   (i) A number that divides the another number exactly is called the ______ of the another number.
   (ii) A ______ of a number is the product of the given number and any natural number.
   (iii) The smallest multiple of any number is ______ .
   (iv) The number 1 is a factor of ______ number.

2. True or False
   (i) Every number has a limited number of factors.
   (ii) Multiples of a number can be infinite.
   (iii) The number 0 is a factor of every number.
   (iv) The number 10 is a multiple of both 2 and 5.

3. Multiple choice questions
   (i) What is the smallest factor of any number?
   (a) 0 (b) 1
   (c) 2 (d) The number itself
   (ii) Which of the following is a multiple of 8 ?
   (a) 24 (b) 36 (c) 15 (d) 10
   (iii) The factors of 12 are
   (a) 1, 2, 3, 4, 6, 12 (b) 1, 3, 5, 12
   (c) 2, 4, 6, 8 (d) 1, 2, 9, 12
   (iv) Which of the following is not a factor of 18?
   (a) 1 (b) 9 (c) 3 (d) 5

4. **Odd one out**
   (a) 4 (b) 8 (c) 12 (d) 29

5. **Match the columns**

	Column A		Column B
(i)	Multiple of 5	(a)	1, 2, 4, 8
(ii)	Factors of 8	(b)	3
(iii)	12 is a multiple of	(c)	5, 10, 15, 20
(iv)	Common factor 6 and 9	(d)	2, 3, 4, 6, 12

6. **Word problems**
   (i) 5 cups are sold in a package and 10 plates are sold in a package. If you want to have the same number of each item for a party, what is the least number of packages of each you need to buy?
   (ii) I want to plant 45 sunflower plants, 81 corn plants and 63 tomato plants in my garden. If I put the same number of plants in each row and each row has only one type of plant, what is the greatest number of plants I can put in one row?

ANSWERS & SOLUTIONS

1. (i) Factor (ii) Multiple
   (iii) The number itself (iv) Every
2. (i) True (ii) True (iii) False (iv) True
3. (i) (b) (ii) (a) (iii) (a) (iv) (d)
4. (d)
5. (i) → (c) (ii) → (a) (iii) → (d) (iv) → (b)
6. (i) Multiples of 5 are 5, 10, 15, 20, ...
   Multiples of 10 are 10, 20, 30, 40, ...
   Least common multiple of 5 and 10 is 10. Therefore, you should buy 10 items of each.
   So, you need to buy at least 2 packages of cups and 1 package of plates.
   (ii) To determine the greatest number of plants that can be put in one row, we need to find greatest common factor of 45, 81 and 63.
   Factors of 45 are 1, 3, 5, 9, 15 and 45.
   Factors of 81 are 1, 3, 9, 27 and 81.
   Factors of 63 are 1, 3, 7, 9, 21 and 63.
   Now, common factor of 45, 81 and 63 are 1, 3 and 9.
   Here, greatest common factor is 9.
   Hence, the greatest number of plants that can be put in one row is 9.

CHAPTER 7

CAN YOU SEE THE PATTERN?

Pattern

A pattern is a sequence or arrangement of numbers, shapes or objects that follows a particular rule or set of rules.

e.g. Pattern (i) 2, 4, 6, 8, 10

(Here, the rule is adding '2' each number to get next number).

Pattern (ii) △ ○ △ ○ △ ○

(In this pattern, triangles and circles comes alternatively).

Repeating Patterns

In this pattern, a sequence of numbers, shapes or objects repeats itself.

e.g. △ □ ○ △ □ ○ △ □ ○

Growing Patterns

A pattern where each term in the pattern increases or changes according to a specific rule called growing pattern.

Number Patterns

In such types of patterns, there are only numbers, which follow the specific rule. This follow a particular rule or sequence.

e.g.

- Adding patterns 5, 10, 15, 20, 25
- Subtracting patterns 100, 90, 80, 70, 60
- Multiplying patterns 3, 6, 12, 24, 48
- Dividing patterns 128, 64, 32, 16, 8

NCERT FOLDER

NCERT Pg 99

Q 1

Pattern 1

Pattern 2

Now, you use these two rules to make patterns with this  block. Also, make your own rule.

Ans. In pattern 1, we can see clearly that the rule is one up, one down. Then, repeat this. Therefore, the pattern is

In pattern 2, it is once up, then take a $\frac{1}{4}$ turn every time. The rule is to repeat it with $\frac{1}{4}$ clockwise turn. So, the pattern is

Now, my own rule is ' It is once up, then takes a $\frac{1}{8}$ turn every time. The rule is to repeat it with a $\frac{1}{8}$ clockwise turn.'

** Students can write alternate answer as per their choice.*

Practice Time (NCERT Pg 100-102)

Q.2 What should come next?

(i) 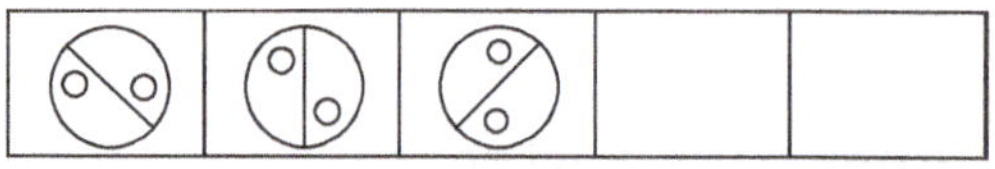

(ii) 

(iii) 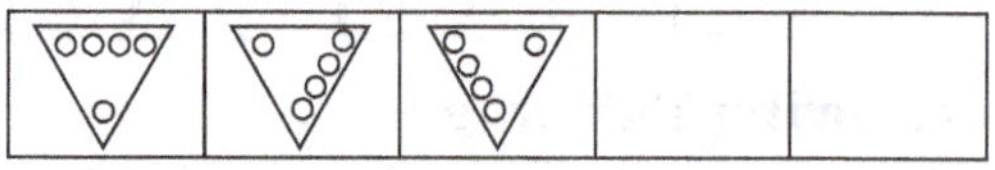

(iv) 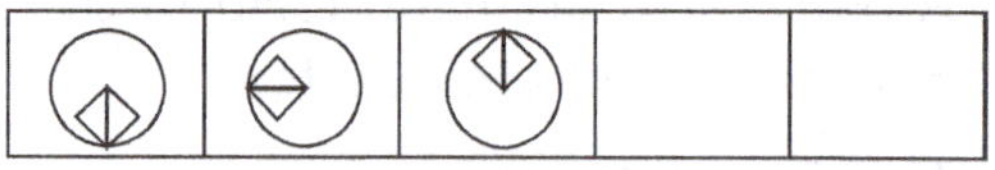

Ans. (i) 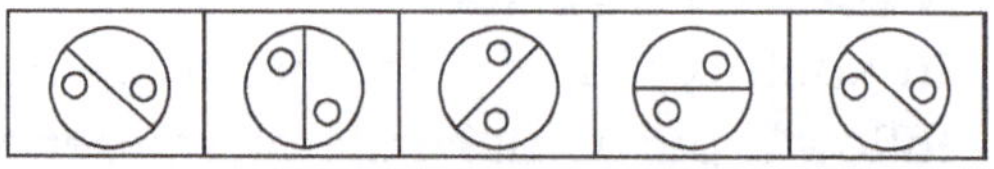

(ii) 

(iii) 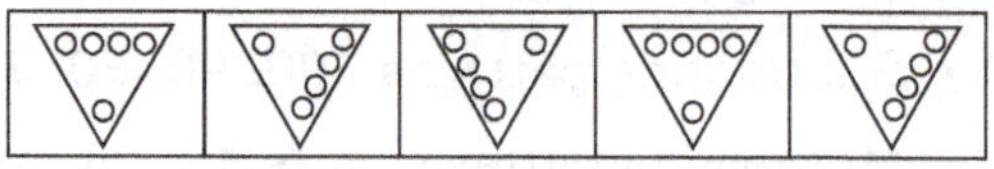

(iv) 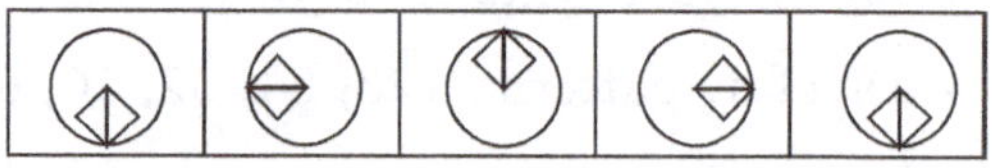

Q.3 See this pattern

(i) 

The rule of the pattern is turning by 45° each time. Which will be the next? Tick (✓) the right one.

 ( )  ( )  ( )

(ii) Using the same rule take it forward till you get back to what you started with.

(a)

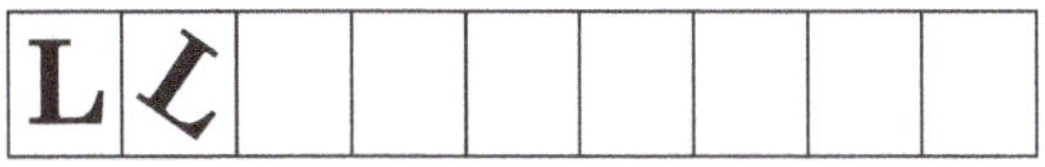

(b)

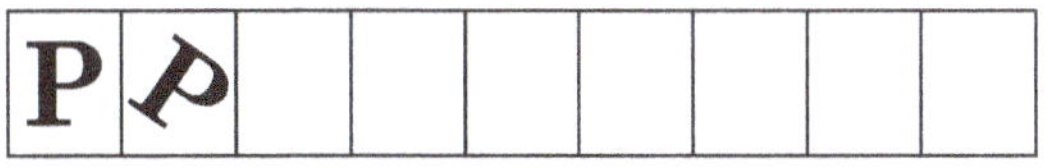

Ans. (i)

( ) ( ) (✓)

(ii) Using the rule, we turn the figure by 45° each time until we get the starting letter

(a)

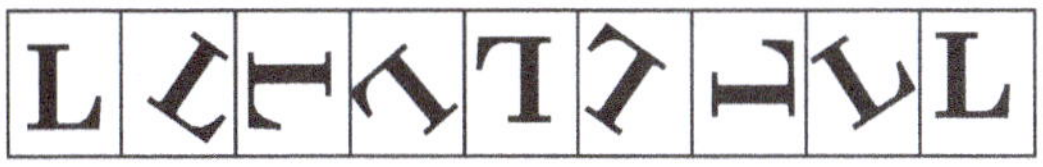

(b)

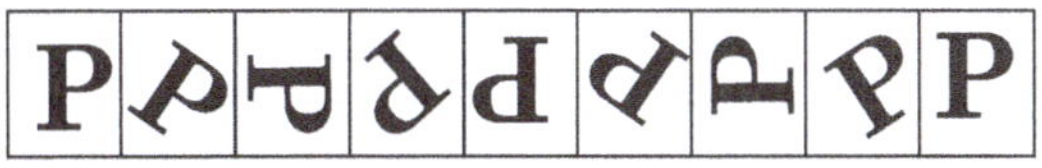

Q.4 Some patterns are given below on the left side of the black line. For each pattern, write the rule. Then, choose what comes next from the right side of the line and tick (✓) it.

(i)

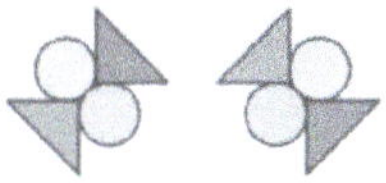
( ) ( )

Rule ____________________

(ii)

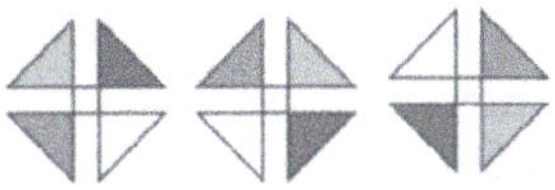

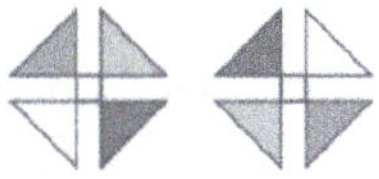
( ) ( )

Rule ____________________

(iii)

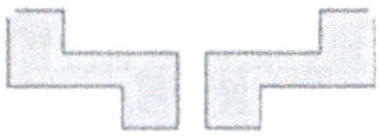
( ) ( )

Rule ____________________

(iv)

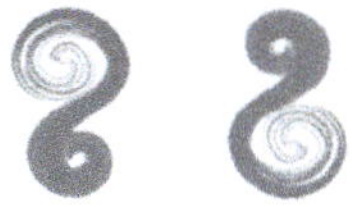
( ) ( )

Rule ____________________

Ans.

(i)

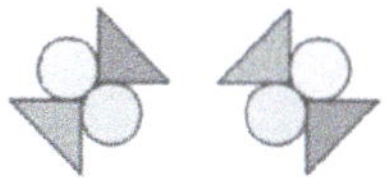
( ) (✓)

Rule The figure is turning by 45° clockwise each time.

(ii)

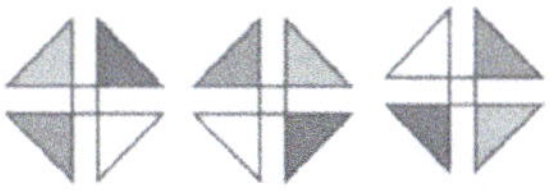

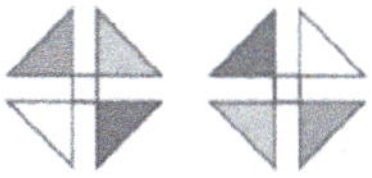
( ) (✓)

Rule The figure is turning by 90° clockwise each time.

(iii)

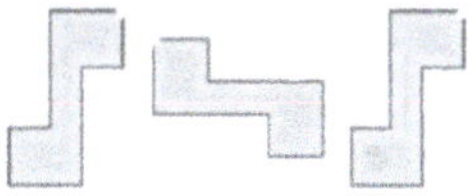

(✓) ( )

Rule The figure is turning alternatively by 90° anti-clockwise and 90° clockwise.

(iv)

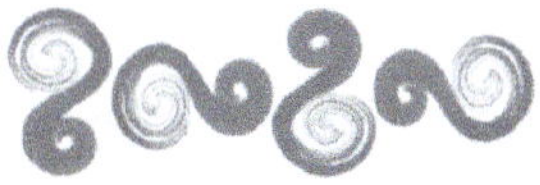

(✓) ( )

Rule The figure is turning by 90° anti-clockwise each time.

Look for a Pattern (NCERT Pg 103)

Q.5 Circle that picture which is breaking the rule. Also, correct it.

(i)

(ii)

(iii)

(iv)

Ans. (i)

Correct figure is 

(ii) 

Correct figure is 

(iii) 

Correct figure is 

(iv) 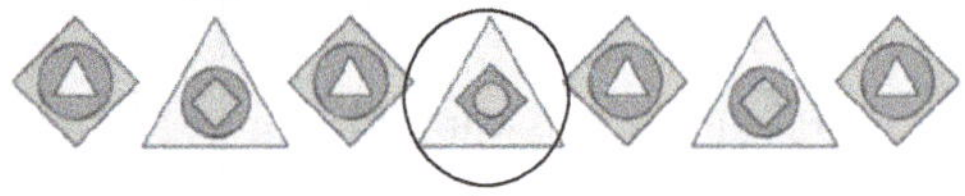

Correct figure is 

Magic Squares (NCERT Pg 103)

Q.6 Do you remember magic triangles? Come now, let's make some magic squares.

(i)

		49
46		
	52	47

Fill this square using all the numbers from 46 to 54.

Rule The total of each line is 150.

(ii)

	25	

Fill this square using all the numbers from 21 to 29.

Rule The total of each side is 75.

Ans. (i) ∵ The total of each line = 150

∴ From the third row

$52 + 47 = 99$ and $150 - 99 = 51$

So, the entry in the blank box of third row is 51.

In first Column

$51 + 46 = 97$ and $150 - 97 = 53$

So, the entry in the blank box of first column is 53.

In first row

$53 + 49 = 102$ and $150 - 102 = 48$

So, the entry in the blank box of first row is 48.

In second column

$52 + 48 = 100$

and $150 - 100 = 50$

So, the entry in the blank box of second column is 50.

In third column

$49 + 47 = 96$

and $150 - 96 = 54$

So, the entry in the blank box of third column is 54.

Row \ Column	I	II	III
I	53	48	49
II	46	50	54
III	51	52	47

*(ii) ∵ The total of each side = 75

As $75 - 25 = 50$

Choose any two numbers from 21 to 29 such that their sum will be equal to 50, in 2nd row, 2nd column and diagonally.

That is $29 + 21 = 50$

$28 + 22 = 50$

$27 + 23 = 50$

$26 + 24 = 50$

In 1st column

$75 - (26 + 22) = 27$

In 1st row

$75 - (26 + 28) = 21$

In 2nd column

$75 - (21 + 25) = 29$

In 3rd column

$75 - (28 + 24) = 23$

26	21	28
27	25	23
22	29	24

Magic Hexagons (NCERT Pg 104)

Q.7 Look at the patterns of numbers in hexagons.

Each side has 2 circles and 1 box.

(i) Look at the number 65 in the box. Which are the circles next to it?

(5) × (13) = [65]

Can you see how the rule works?

( ) × ( ) = [70]

(ii) Use the same rule to fill the hexagons below.

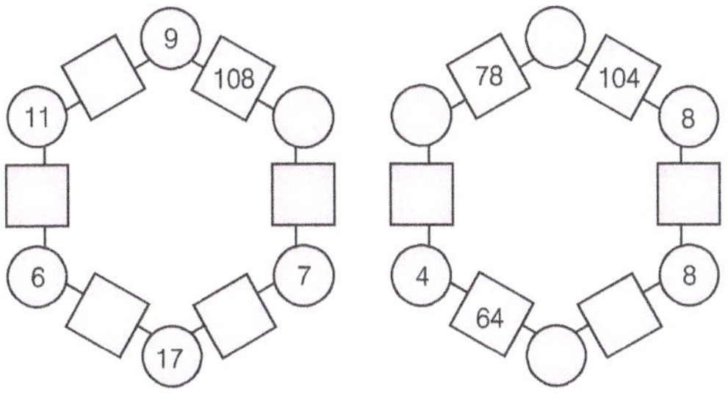

(a) (b)

Ans. (i) Yes, I can see the rule clearly. The number in the box is the product of numbers in adjoining circles.

(14) × (5) = [70]

(ii) (a)

(11) × (9) = [99]

(11) × (6) = [66]

(6) × (17) = [102]

(17) × (7) = [119]

∴ [108] ÷ (9) = (12)

∴ The number in the blank circle will be 12 and 12 × 7 = 84

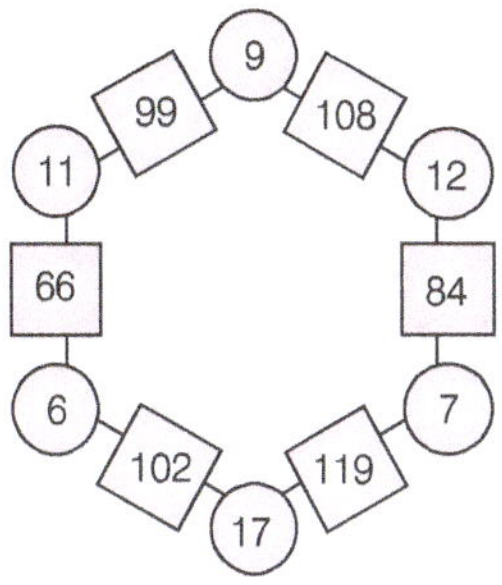

(b)

∵ [104] ÷ (8) = (13)

(8) × (8) = [64]

[64] ÷ (4) = (16)

(16) × (8) = [128]

[78] × (13) = (6)

(6) × (4) = [24]

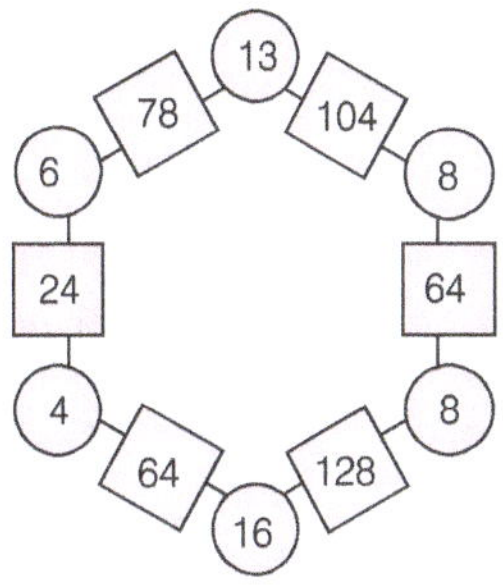

Q.8 You also make your own magic hexagons.

Ans. * Following are some own magic hexagons.

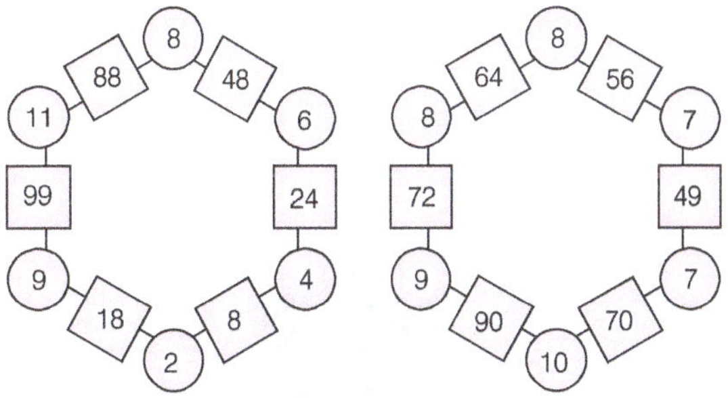

Numbers and Numbers (NCERT Pg 105)

Q.9

24 + 19 + 37 = 37 + 24 + 19

215 + 120 + 600 = 600 + 215 + 120

Are they equal?

Ans. Yes, they are equal.

Q.10 Fill in the blank spaces in the same way.

(i) 14 + ___ + ___ = 34 + 14 + 20

(ii) ___ + 42 + ___ = 65 + ___ + 80

(iii) 200 + 300 + ___ = ___ + 400 + ___

(iv) ___ + ___ + ___ = ___ + ___ + ___

Ans.

(i) 14 + 20 + 34 = 34 + 14 + 20

*(ii) 80 + 42 + 65 = 65 + 42 + 80

*(iii) 200 + 300 + 400 = 300 + 400 + 200

*(iv) 68 + 20 + 84 = 84 + 68 + 20

Q.11 Look at this

48 × 13 = 13 × 48

Check if it is true or not.

Ans. Multiply both the numbers.

$$\begin{array}{r} 48 \\ \times 13 \\ \hline 144 \\ 48\times \\ \hline 624 \\ \hline \end{array} \quad \text{and} \quad \begin{array}{r} 13 \\ \times 48 \\ \hline 104 \\ 52\times \\ \hline 624 \\ \hline \end{array}$$

Hence, it is true

48 × 13 = 13 × 48

Left Right - Same to Same (NCERT Pg 105-106)

Q.12

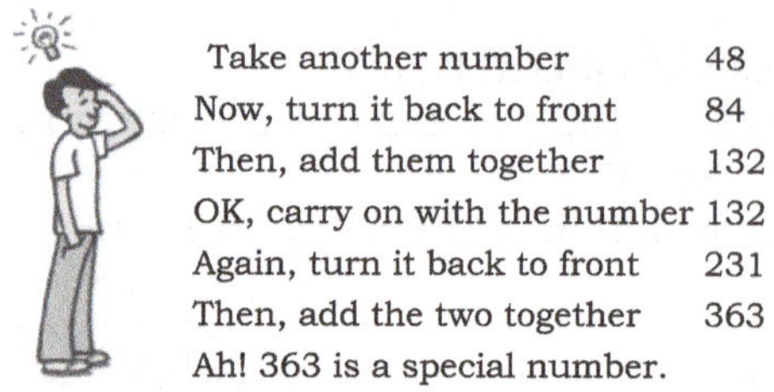

(i) Is 132 a special number? No! Why not?

(ii) Now, you try and change these numbers into special numbers

(a) 28 (b) 132 (c) 273

Ans. (i) No, 132 is not a special number because it is not the same after reversing it.

(ii) (a) Given number = 28

By reversing = 82

By adding them together = 110

110 is not a special number because it is not the same after reversing it.

Now, carry on with the number 110

By reversing = 011

By adding them together = 121

121 is same after reversing it.

∴ 121 is the required special number.

(b) Given number = 132

By reversing = 231

By adding them together = 363

363 is same after reversing it.

∴ 363 is the required special number.

(c) Given number = 273

By reversing = 372

By adding them together = 645

645 is not a special number because it is not the same after reversing it.

Now, carry on with the number 645.

By reversing = 546

By adding them together = 1191

1191 is not a special number as it is not the same after reversing it.

Now, carry on with the number 1191.

By reversing = 1911

By adding them together 3102

It is not a special number.

Now, carry on with the number 3102.

By reversing = 2013

By adding them together = 5115

5115 is same after reversing it.

∴ 5115 is the required special number.

Q.13 Let's use words in a special way.

N O L E M O N S N O M E L O N
S T E P N O T O N P E T S

Did you notice that it reads the same from both sides right to left and left to right?

Now, try and use words in a special way.

Ans. Yes, it reads the same from both sides. Some special words which read the same both ways are:

*(i) A M A N A P L A N A C A N A L P A N A M A

*(ii) A B L E W A S I E R E I S A W E L B A

*(iii) A S A N T A A T N A S A

*(iv) R I S E T O V O T E S I R

*(v) D O O M M O O D

Calendar Magic (NCERT Pg 107)

Q.14 Look at the calendar below.

Let us mark a 3×3 box (9 dates) on the calendar and see some magic.

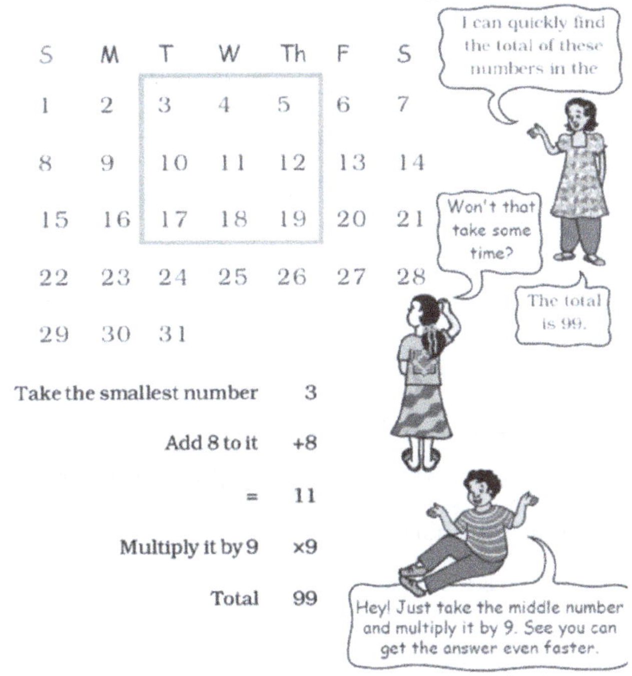

Now, you choose any 3×3 box from a calendar and find the total in the same way. Play this game with your family.

Ans. * We have taken another 3×3 box

8	9	10
15	16	17
22	23	24

Here, smallest number = 8

Add 8 to it $= 8 + 8 = 16$

Multiply it by 9 $= 16 \times 9 = 144$

Now, sum of all 9 numbers in this box

$= 8 + 9 + 10 + 15 + 16 + 17 + 22 + 23 + 24$

$= 144$

To get the answer even faster multiply the middle number by 9 that is $16 \times 9 = 144$

Some more Number Patterns (NCERT Pg 108)

Q.15 (i) Take any number. Now, multiply it by 2, 3, 4........... at every step. Also, add 3 to it at each step. Look at the difference in the answer. Is it the same at every step?

12	×	2	+	3	=	27
12	×	3	+	3	=	39
12	×	4	+	3	=	51
12	×	5	+	3	=	63
12	×		+	3	=	
	×	7	+	3	=	
	×		+	3	=	
	×		+		=	

(ii) Now, try doing it with some other number and also take a different number to add at each step.

Ans. (i)

$12 \times 2 + 3 = 27$

$12 \times 3 + 3 = 39$

$12 \times 4 + 3 = 51$

$12 \times 5 + 3 = 63$

$12 \times 6 + 3 = 75$

$12 \times 7 + 3 = 87$

$12 \times 8 + 3 = 99$

$12 \times 9 + 3 = 111$

We observe that the difference in the answer at each step remains constant and is equal to 12.

*(ii) Now, take another number.

$14 \times 2 + 5 = 33$

$14 \times 3 + 5 = 47$

$14 \times 4 + 5 = 61$

$14 \times 5 + 5 = 75$

$14 \times 6 + 5 = 89$

$14 \times 7 + 5 = 103$

$14 \times 8 + 5 = 117$

$14 \times 9 + 5 = 131$

We observe that the difference in the answer at each step remains constant and is equal to 14.

Q.16 Look at the numbers below. Look for the pattern. Can you take it forward?

$(9 - 1) \div 8 = 1$

$(98 - 2) \div 8 = 12$

$(987 - 3) \div 8 = 123$

$(9876 - 4) \div 8 = ...$

$(98765 - 5) \div 8 = ...$

$(....... - ....) \div 8 = ...$

$(....... - ....) \div 8 = ...$

Ans. $(9 - 1) \div 8 = 1$

$(98 - 2) \div 8 = 12$

$(987 - 3) \div 8 = 123$

$(9876 - 4) \div 8 = \underline{1234}$

$(98765 - 5) \div 8 = \underline{12345}$

$(\underline{987654} - \underline{6}) \div 8 = \underline{123456}$

$(\underline{9876543} - \underline{7}) \div 8 = \underline{1234567}$

Yes, I can take it forward.

Smart Adding (NCERT Pg 109)

Q.17

Did you notice some pattern in the answers?

Ans.

1 + 2 + 3 + 4 + 5 + 6 + 7 + 8 + 9 + 10 = 55

11 + 12 + 13 + 14 + 15 + 16 + 17 + 18 + 19 + 20 = 155

21 + 22 + 23 + 24 + 25 + 26 + 27 + 28 + 29 + 30 = 255

31 + 32 + 33 + 34 + 35 + 36 + 37 + 38 + 39 + 40 = 355

41 + 42 + 43 + 44 + 45 + 46 + 47 + 48 + 49 + 50 = 455

51 + 52 + 53 + 54 + 55 + 56 + 57 + 58 + 59 + 60 = 555

61 + 62 + 63 + 64 + 65 + 66 + 67 + 68 + 69 + 70 = 655

Yes, I have noticed a pattern.

Pattern Multiply by $\frac{10}{2}$ by [first number + last number]

e.g. $21 + 23 + ... + 29 + 30 = \frac{10}{2} \times [21 + 30]$

$= 5 \times 51 = 255$

Fun with Odd Numbers (NCERT Pg 109)

Q.18 Take the first two odd numbers. Now, add them, see what you get.

Now, at every step, add the next odd number.

$1 + 3 = 4 = 2 \times 2$

$1 + 3 + 5 = 9 = 3 \times 3$

$1 + 3 + 5 + 7 = 16 = 4 \times 4$

$1 + 3 + 5 + 7 + 9 = \_\_ = \_\_ \times \_\_$

$1 + 3 + 5 + 7 + 9 + 11 = \_\_ = \_\_ \times \_\_$

$1 + 3 + 5 + 7 + 9 + 11 + 13 = \_\_ = \_\_ \times \_\_$

How far can you go on?

Ans. First we complete the boxes.

$1 + 3 = 4 = 2 \times 2$

$1 + 3 + 5 = 9 = 3 \times 3$

$1 + 3 + 5 + 7 = 16 = 4 \times 4$

$1 + 3 + 5 + 7 + 9 = 25 = 5 \times 5$

$1 + 3 + 5 + 7 + 9 + 11 = 36 = 6 \times 6$

$1 + 3 + 5 + 7 + 9 + 11 + 13 = 49 = 7 \times 7$

This process is never ending.

We observe that when we add the first n odd numbers, then sum is equal to $n \times n$.

Secret Numbers (NCERT Pg 110)

Q.19 Banno and Binod were playing a guessing game by writing clues about a secret number. Each tried to guess the other's secret number from the clues.

(i) **Banno** It is larger than half of 100.

It is more than 6 tens and less than 7 tens.

The tens digit is one more than the ones digit.

Together the digits have a sum of 11.

What is Banno's secret number?

(ii) **Binod** It is smaller than half of 100.

It is more than 4 tens and less than 5 tens.

The tens digit is two more than the ones digit.

Together the digits have a sum of 6.

What is Binod's secret number?

Ans. (i) **From clue (1)**

It is larger than half of 100, it means the number $> \frac{100}{2} = 50$.

From clue (2)

It is more than 6 tens and less than 7 tens means the number is between 60 and 70.

From clue (3)

The tens digit is one more than ones digit means ones digit is $6 - 1 = 5$.

From clue (4)

Together the digits have sum of 11.

That is $6 + 5 = 11$

Hence, the required number is 65.

(ii) **From clue (1)**

Smaller than half of 100 means the number will be less than 50.

From clue (2)

It is more than 4 tens and less than 5 tens means the number lies between 40 and 50.

From clue (3)

The tens digit is two more than the ones digit means ones digit is $4 - 2 = 2$.

From clue (4)

Together the digits have a sum of 6.

That is $4 + 2 = 6$

Hence, the required number is 42.

Q.20 Write a set of clues for a secret number of your own. Then, give it to a friend to guess your secret number.

Ans. * A set of clues to find secret numbers are

(i)
- It is larger than half of 100.
- It is more than 5 tens and less than 6 tens.
- The tens digit is two less than the ones digit.
- Together the digits have a sum of 12.

Answer =57

(ii)
- It is smaller than half of 100.
- It is more than 3 tens and less than 4 tens.

- The tens digit is 1 more than the ones digit.
- Together the digits have a sum of 5.

Answer = 32

Number Surprises (NCERT Pg 110 -111)

Q.21 (i) Ask your friend, write down your age. Add 5 to it. Multiply the sum by 2. Subtract 10 from it. Next divide it by 2. What do you get?

Is your friend surprised?

(ii) Take a number $\square$

Double it $\square \times \boxed{2} = \square$

Multiply by 5 $\square \times \boxed{5} = \square$

Divide your answer by 10

$\square \div \boxed{10} = \square$

(iii) Take a number $\square$

Double it $\square \times \boxed{2} = \square$

Again, double it $\square \times \boxed{2} = \square$

Add the number you took first to the answer $\square + \square = \square$

Now, again double it $\square \times \boxed{2} = \square$

Divide by 10 $\square \div \boxed{10} = \square$

(iv) Look at this pattern of numbers and take it forward.

$1 = 1 \times 1$

$121 = 11 \times 11$

$12321 = 111 \times 111$

$1234321 = ?$

Ans. *(i) Age = 9

Add 5 to it. That is $9 + 5 = 14$

Multiply the sum by 2. That is $14 \times 2 = 28$

Subtract 10 from it. That is $28 - 10 = 18$

Divide it by 2. That is $18 \div 2 = \square$

My friend gets the same answer as his age. So, he is surprised.

*(ii) Let the number be 11.

Double it $\boxed{11} \times \boxed{2} = \boxed{22}$

Multiply by 5 $\boxed{22} \times \boxed{5} = \boxed{110}$

Divide your answer by 10

$\boxed{110} \div \boxed{10} = \boxed{11}$

Oh! I get the same number 11 which I choose.

*(iii) Let a number be 6.

Double it $\boxed{6} \times \boxed{2} = \boxed{12}$

Again, double it $\boxed{12} \times \boxed{2} = \boxed{24}$

Add the number you took first to the answer $\boxed{24} + \boxed{6} = \boxed{30}$

Now, again double it $\boxed{30} \times \boxed{2} = \boxed{60}$

Divide by 10 $\boxed{60} \div \boxed{10} = \boxed{6}$

Result is same as I choose the number.

(iv) $1 = 1 \times 1$

$121 = 11 \times 11$

$12321 = 111 \times 111$

$1234321 = 1111 \times 1111$

Follow the pattern to take it forward.

$123454321 = 11111 \times 11111$

$12345654321 = 111111 \times 111111$

Q.22 Make your own number surprises.

Ans. * Here is my number surprise.

Write your age $\square$

Multiply it by 5 $\square \times 5 = \square$

Add the answer to your age $\square + \square = \square$

Now divide it by 6 $\square \div 6 = \square$

PRACTICE QUESTIONS

1. Fill in the blanks.
   (i) A repeating arrangement of shapes or numbers is called a .... (sequence/pattern)
   (ii) A pattern that repeats itself after a fixed number of steps is called a .... pattern. (repeating/growing)
   (iii) 4, 9, 16, ... , 36.
   (iv) 2, 0, –3, – 7, ...
2. True or False
   (i) Every pattern has a rule that helps us predict the next item in the sequence.
   (ii) An increasing pattern is formed by adding a fixed number at each step.
   (iii) Patterns can only be formed by numbers not shapes.
3. Multiple choice questions
   (i) What is the next number in the pattern 2, 4, 6, 8, ...?
   (a) 10 (b) 12 (c) 9 (d) 11
   (ii) In the pattern 3, 6, 12, 24, what is the rule used to form the pattern?
   (a) Add 3 (b) Multiply by 2
   (c) Subtract 3 (d) Divide by 2
   (iii) Which of the following patterns is made by adding 5 to each number?
   (a) 1, 3, 5, 7 (b) 5, 10, 15, 20
   (c) 2, 4, 8, 16 (d) 10, 30, 50, 70
4. In a pattern, the numbers are increasing by 4. The first number is 5. What will the 5th number in the pattern be?
5. A teacher is arranging chairs in rows. In the first row, there are 3 chairs. In the second row, there are 6 chairs and in the third row there are 9 chairs. How many chairs will be in the fourth row?
6. Case based questions.
   Quilt Design Reena is designing a pattern for a quilt. She decides to use squares and circles in the following order, square, circle, square, circle and so on. She starts with a square, then a circle and continues the pattern.
   Based on the above information, answer the following questions.
   (i) If Reena has completed 8 shapes, what will the 9th shape be?
   (ii) If she continues this pattern, what shape will the 44th shape be?
   (iii) What is the rule of Reena's pattern?

ANSWERS & SOLUTIONS

1. (i) pattern (ii) repeating
   (iii) 25 (iv) –12
2. (i) True (ii) True (iii) False
3. (i) (a) (ii) (b) (iii) (b)
4. Given, first number = 5
   ∵ Number increasing by 4.
   ∴ Pattern is 5, 9, 13, 17, 21, 25, ...
   5th number of the pattern is 21.
5. Number of chairs in first row = 3
   Number of chairs in second row = 6
   Number of chairs in third row = 9
   Therefore, the pattern is 3, 6, 9, ...
   The next number of this pattern
   $= 9 + (9 - 6) = 12$
   Hence, there are 12 chairs in fourth row.
6. ∵ Reena uses squares and circles for designing a pattern. She starts with square, then a circle and continue this pattern.
   So, pattern is
   □ ○ □ ○ □ ○ □ ○ □ ○...
   As we see at odd places, she uses the squares and at even places, she uses the circles.
   (i) ∵ 9 is odd number.
   ∴ The shape at 9th place is □ square.
   (ii) ∵ 44 is even number.
   ∴ The shape at 44th place is ○ circle.
   (iii) The rule that Reena uses in her pattern is at odd places, she uses squares and at even places, she uses circles.

CHAPTER 8 MAPPING YOUR WAY

Map

A map is a representation or drawing of the earth's surface or a part of its area drawn on a flat surface. It shows the rivers, mountains, routes and forests etc.

Directions

Direction is a way or path in which things are move.

There are four cardinal directions;

North, East, South, West

In maps, directions are represented by

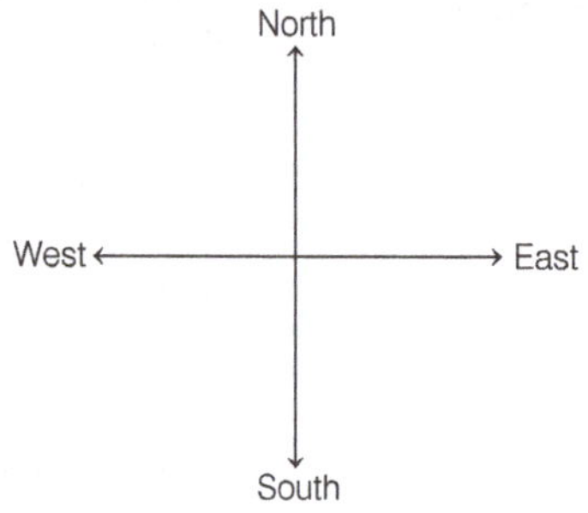

Map Scale

It is difficult to add the exact distance on the map. So, we use the map scale to measure the distance between two points on map.

Map scale is the ratio between a distance on a map and corresponding distance in the real world.

e.g. 1 cm on the map = 10 km on the ground.

NCERT FOLDER

Match the map and the photo (NCERT Pg 113)

Q.1

Map 1

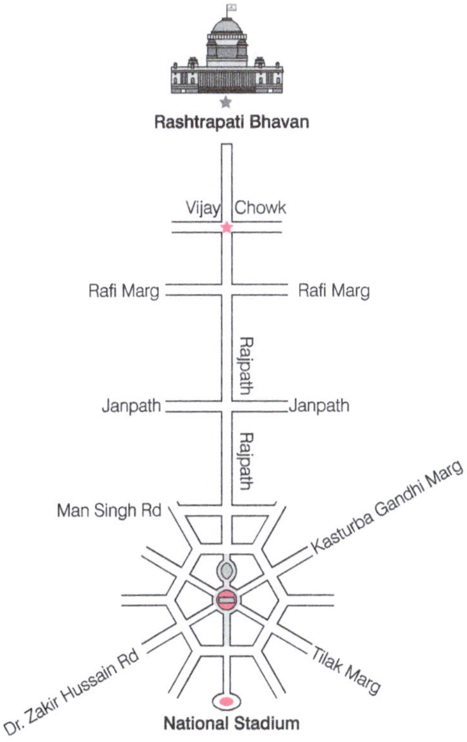

** Students can write alternate answer as per their choice.*

(i) Have you seen a map of a city? Look at Map 1. Match it with the photo and find out where India Gate is. Draw it on the map.

(ii) Some roads are shown in this part of the map. Look for them in the photo.

(iii) Name roads that you will cross on your way from Rashtrapati Bhawan to India Gate.

(iv) Look for the National Stadium in Map 1. Can you see it in the photo?.

Ans. (i) Yes, I have seen a map of a city. After matching the map 1 with the photo, we found the position of India Gate is as follows.

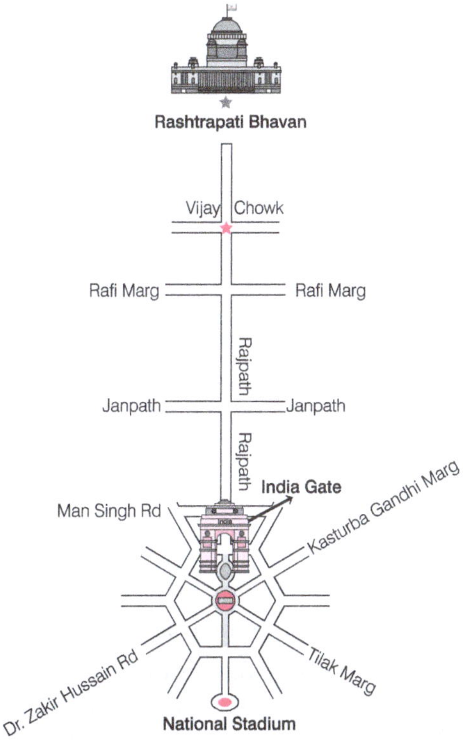

(ii) The roads indicated on the map are clearly visible in the photo.

(iii) The names of the roads crossed on our way from Rashtrapati Bhawan to India Gate are Rafi Marg, Janpath and Man Singh Road.

(iv) The National Stadium is seen in Map 1. But it is not seen in the photo.

The Central Hexagon (NCERT Pg 114)

Q.2 If we 'zoom in' to look more closely at one part of the map, it looks like this.

Map 2

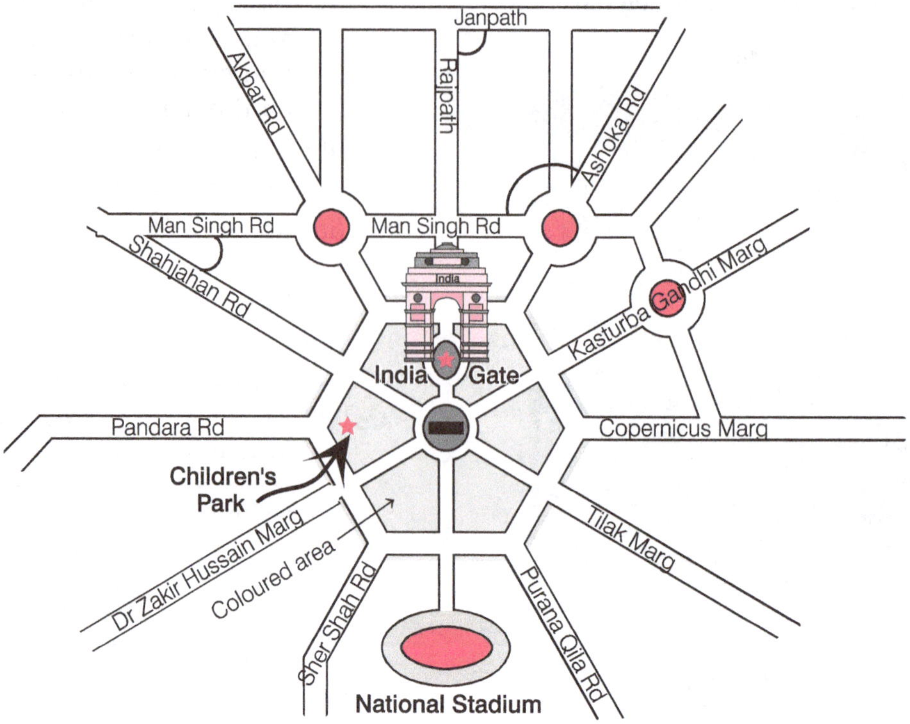

Look at the shape of the coloured area. Have you seen this shape before? How many sides does it have?

Find Out From the Map

(i) If you are walking on Rajpath, then after India Gate on which side would Children's Park be?

(ii) Which of these roads make the biggest angle between them?

(a) Man Singh Road and Shahjahan Road

(b) Ashoka Road and Man Singh Road (the angle away from India Gate)

(c) Janpath and Rajpath

(iii) Which of the above pairs of roads cut at right angles?

Ans. Yes, I have seen this shape before. It has six sides. This place is called the central hexagon.

(i) When we are walking on Rajpath, then after India Gate the Children's Park is on the right side.

(ii) (b) Ashoka Road and Man Singh Road (the angle away from India Gate) make the biggest angle between them.

(iii) Janpath and Rajpath cut at right angles.

Waiting for the Parade (NCERT Pg 115-116)

Q.3 The children look at this map to see the parade route.

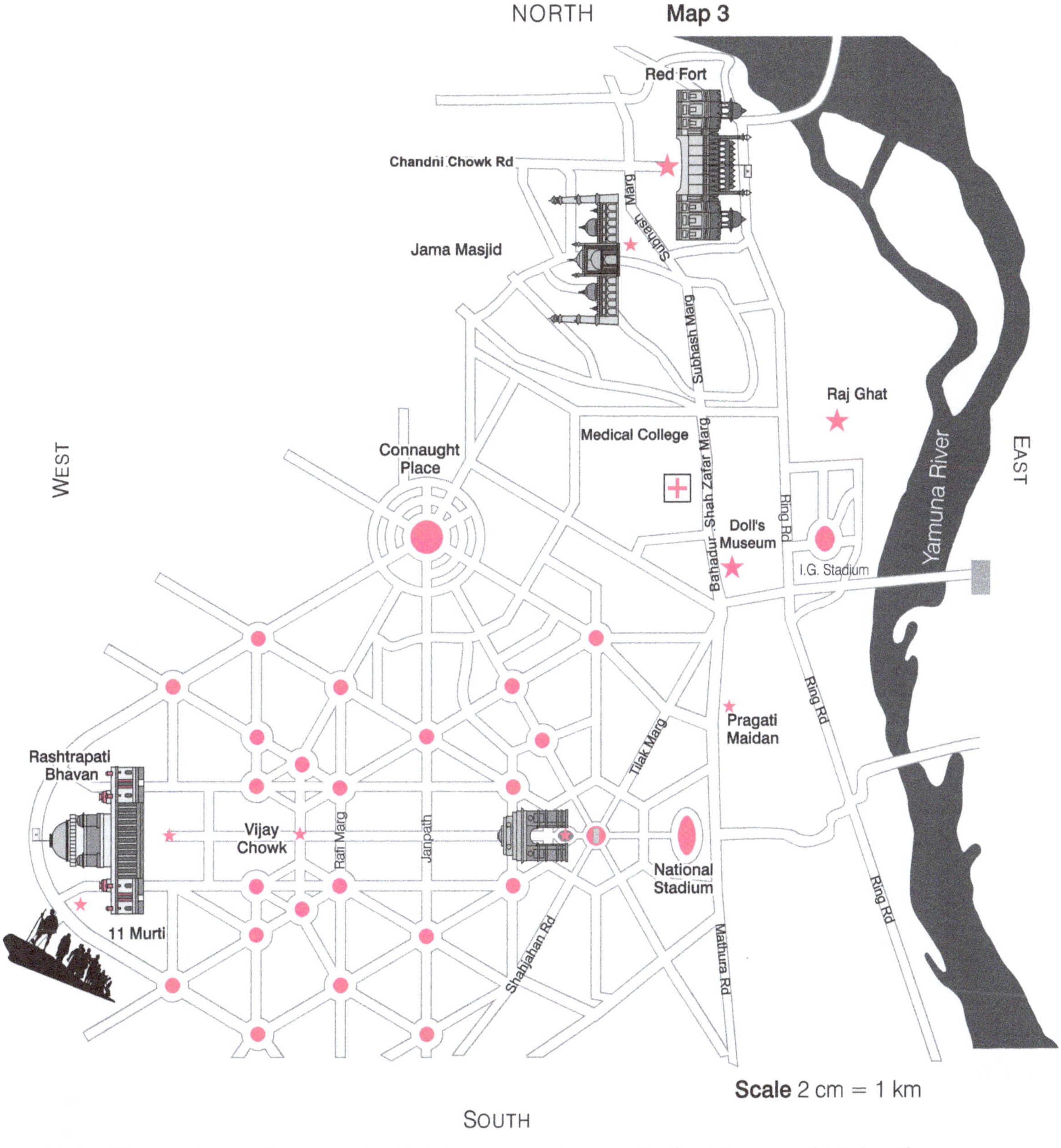

(i) Trace the route of the parade in Map 3 and mark India Gate and Rajpath.

(ii) Look at the map carefully and find out

(a) Which of these is the longest road?

I. B.S. Zafar Marg

II. Subhash Marg

III. Tilak Marg

(b) If Rubia is coming from Jama Masjid to join the parade, guess about how far she will have to walk.

(c) The total route of the parade is about how long?

I. 3 km II. 16 km III. 25 km IV. 8 km

Ans. (i) Route of the parade has been indicated by arrows. In the Map 3, Rajpath is shown by 'R' and India Gate by 'I'.

The children look at this map to see the parade route.

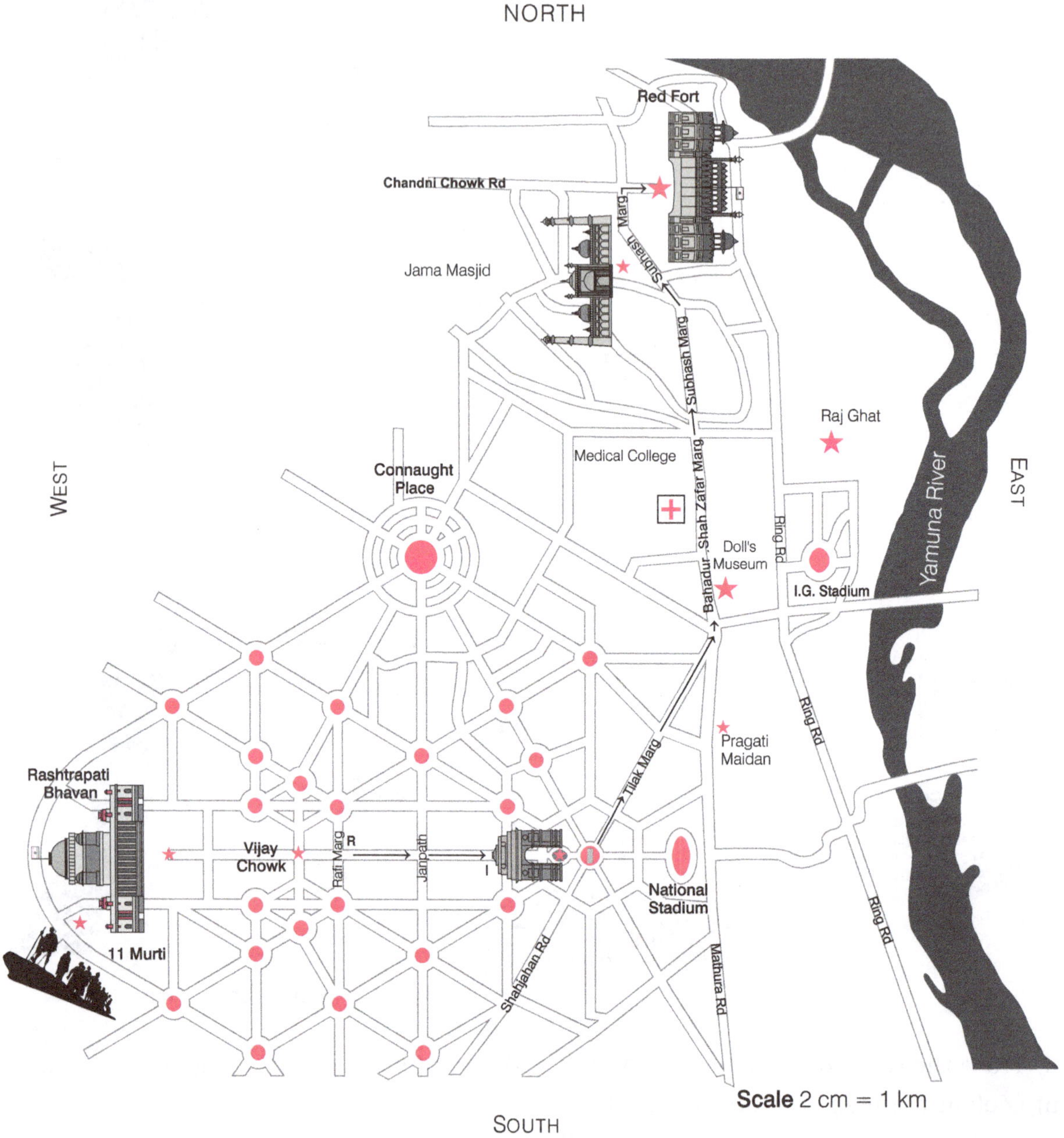

(ii) (a) III Tilak Marg is the longest road.

(b) $\because$ 2 cm = 1 km

So, Rubia has to walk about 1 km to join the parade.

(c) II The total route of the parade is about 16 km long.

Trip of Red Fort (NCERT Pg 117-118)

Q.4

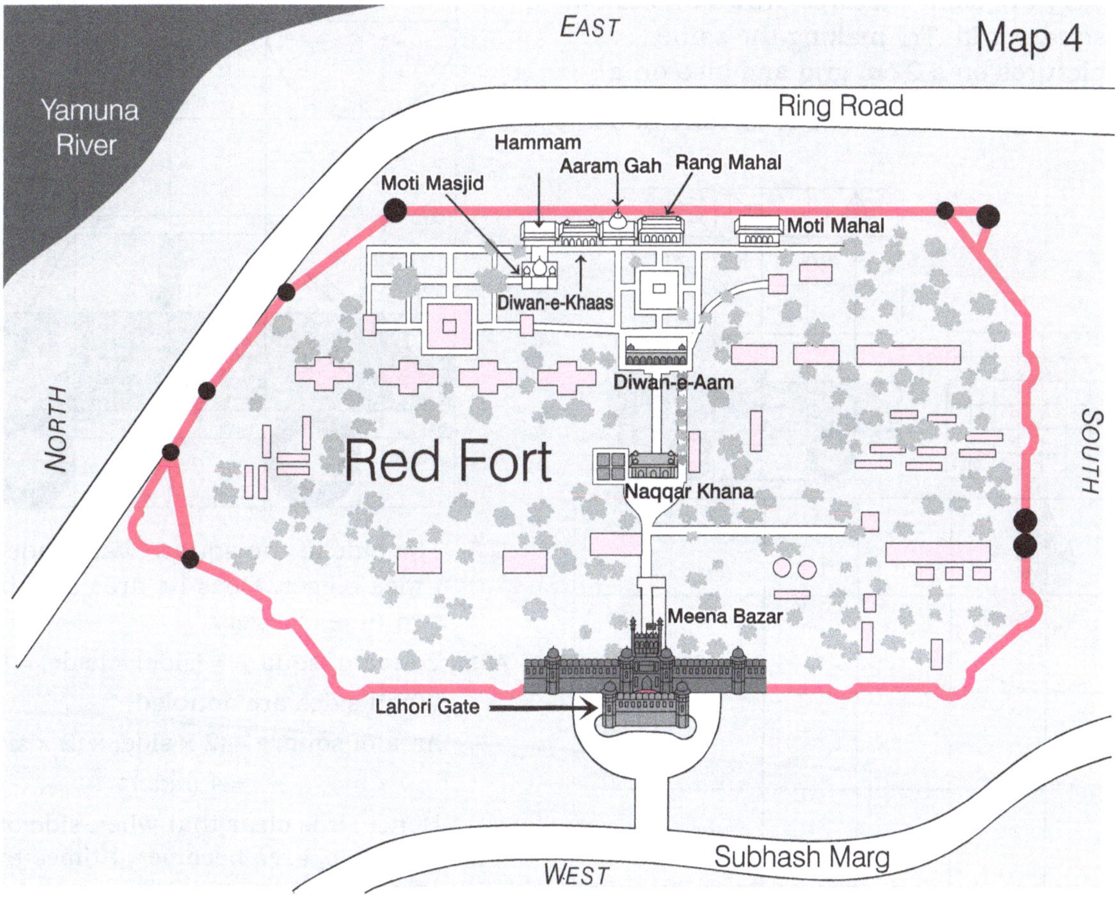

Scale 1 cm = 100 m

Find out from Map 4

(i) Which of these is nearer to river Yamuna? The Diwan-e-Aam or the Diwan-e-Khaas?

(ii) Between which two buildings is Aaram Gah?

(iii) Which buildings do you pass while going from Rang Mahal to the Hammam?

(iv) Which building on this map is farthest from Meena Bazar?

(v) About how far is Lahori Gate from Diwan-e-Khaas?

Ans. (i) The Diwan-e-Khaas is nearer to river Yamuna than the Diwan-e-Aam.

(ii) Aaram Gah is lie between the Diwan-e-Khaas and Rang Mahal.

(iii) We pass Aaram Gah and the Diwan-e-Khaas while going from Rang Mahal to the Hammam.

(iv) Hammam is farthest from Meena Bazar.

(v) $\because$ 1 cm = 100 m

$\therefore$ 6 cm = $6 \times 100 = 600$ m

So, Lahori Gate is about 600 m far from Diwan-e-Khaas.

Make It Bigger, Make It Smaller (NCERT Pg 119)

Q.5 Here are some pictures drawn on a 1 cm square grid. Try making the same pictures on a 2 cm grid and also on a $\frac{1}{2}$ cm grid. One picture is already done.

Ans.

Q.6 The side of the square was made two times bigger. Does its area also become two times bigger?

Ans. $\because$ Area of square = (side) × (side) = $(\text{side})^2$

When sides are doubled,

Area of square = (2 × side) × (2 × side)

$= 4\ (\text{side})^2$

Hence, it is clear that when side of square is double, area becomes 4 times the original.

Now Try This (NCERT Pg 120)

Q.7 This is a part of the parade-route Map 3.

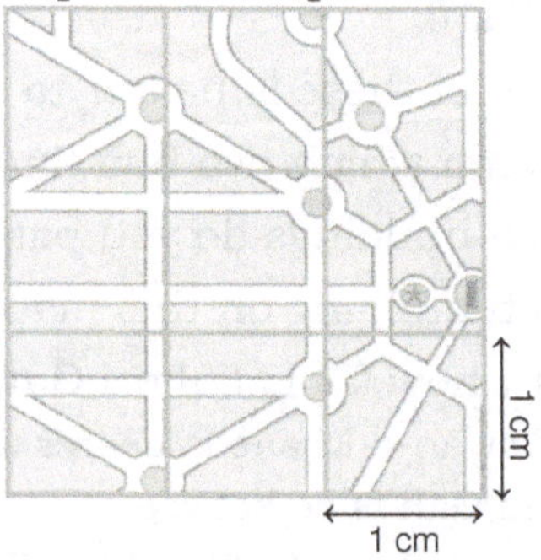

(i) Can you see which part of the route-map it is?

(ii) Now try to make it bigger in this 2 cm grid. Remember that the 'shape' of the map should not change.

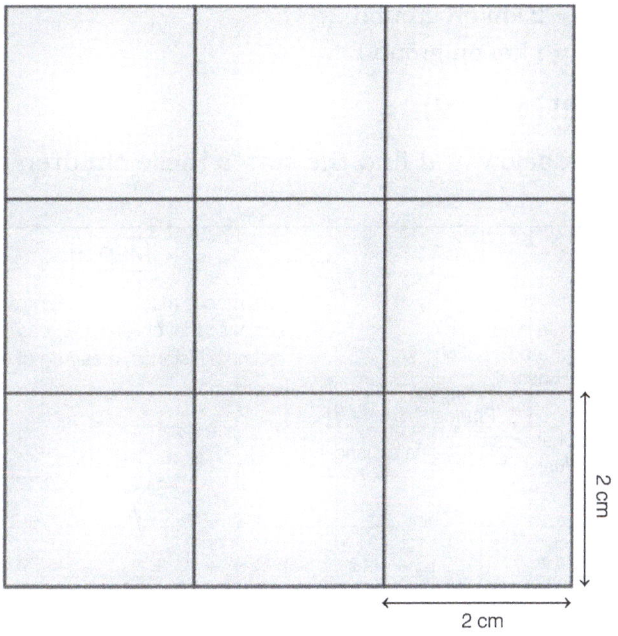

(iii) If the parade route map is smaller and the distance between India Gate and Vijay Chowk becomes 2 cm, what would be its scale?

(a) 1 cm on map = 1 km on ground

(b) $\frac{1}{2}$ cm on map = 1 km on ground

(c) 2 cm on map = 1 km on ground

Ans. (i) It is the route map of Rajpath.

(ii) Following is the map in 2 cm grid

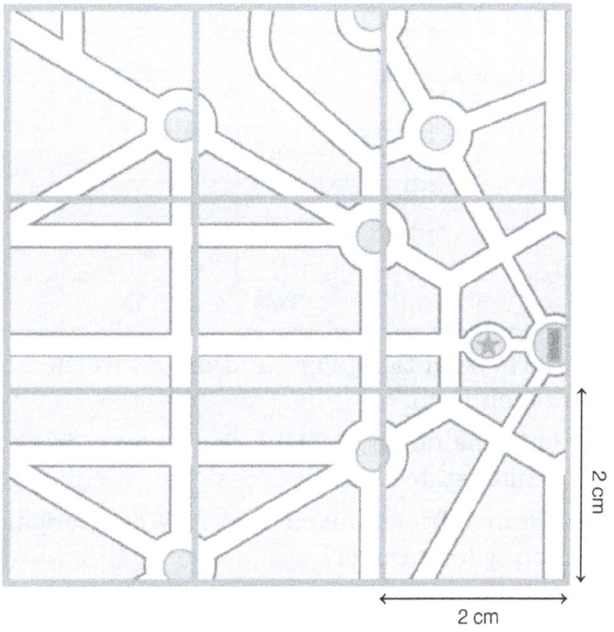

(iii) (c) The distance between Vijay Chowk and India Gate = 2 km [from Map-3]

∵ Distance between Vijay Chowk and India Gate on this map = 2 cm [given]

∴ Scale is 2 cm on map = 2 km on ground

⇒ 1 cm on map = 1 km on ground

Dancers from Different States (NCERT Pg 121-122)

Q.8 Look at the map of India below and find the states these children are talking about. Answer the questions.

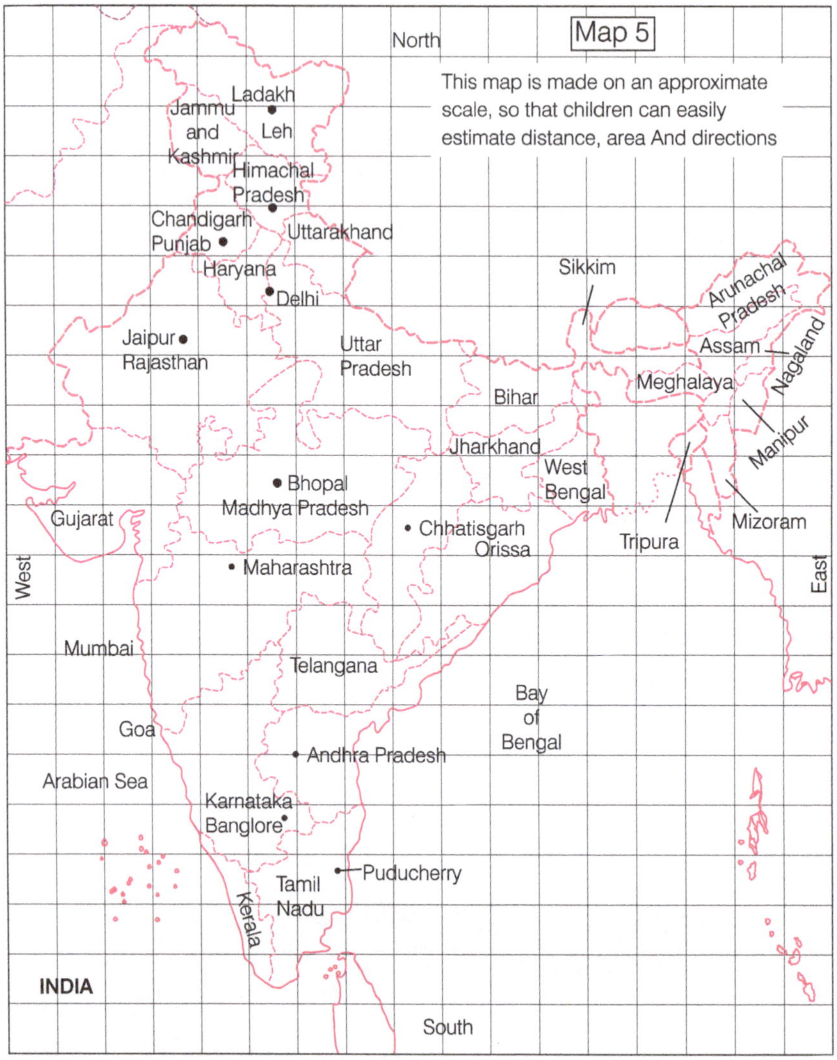

(i) The Karnataka team starts from Bangalore and moves in the north direction. Which states does it cross to reach Delhi?

(ii) Jammu and Kashmir is to the north of Delhi, so the team from there travels towards south to reach Delhi. Which states does it cross?

(iii) Nonu lives in Gujarat. Nonu's friend Javed lives in West Bengal. Nonu wants to visit his friend. In which direction will he travel?

(a) Towards west (b) Towards east (c) Towards south (d) Towards north

(iv) Is there any state which is to the north of Jammu and Kashmir?

(v) Is there any state which is to the west of Gujarat?

(vi) If 1 cm on the map shows 200 km on the ground, use this scale to find out.

(a) About how far is Delhi from Jaipur?

I. 50 km II. 500 km III. 250 km

(b) Estimate, how far is Jaipur from Bhopal?

On the map = ... cm.

On the ground = ... km.

(vii) Look at the map and tell:

(a) Which state is surrounded by four other states?

(b) Which state has the largest area? If its name is not in the map, find it from your teacher or parents.

Explain how you got your answer.

(c) Which state is about 8 times bigger in area than Sikkim?

I. Uttar Pradesh

II. Tripura

III. Maharashtra

IV. Himachal Pradesh

(d) About how many times of Punjab is the area of Rajasthan?

Ans. *(i) Following states they will cross from Bangalore to reach Delhi.

Maharastra, Madhya Pradesh and Uttar Pradesh.

From Madhya Pradesh, the team may also go through Haryana or Rajasthan.

(ii) From Jammu and Kashmir to Delhi, the team crosses following states

Himachal Pradesh, Punjab and Haryana.

(iii) (b) He will travel towards east.

(iv) Yes, Ladakh is the north of Jammu and Kashmir.

(v) No, there is no state which is to the west of Gujarat.

(vi) (a) III 250 km

So, option III is a correct choice.

(b) On the map = <u>2.3 cm</u>

$\because$ 1 cm on the map = 200 km

$\therefore$ 2 cm on the map = 2.3×200

On the ground = <u>460 km</u>

(vii) (a) Telangana

(b) This can be easily observed by looking at the map that Rajasthan has the largest area.

(c) IV Himachal Pradesh

(d) Rajasthan is about 7 times the area of Punjab.

The Sea (NCERT Pg 123)

Q.9 Bala is standing on the sea-coast and looking at the vast sea. The sea looks endless.

(i) Have you seen the sea? In the picture where is the sea? Now, look for the sea in the map of India. What colour is used to show the sea?

(ii) Write the name of those states which have the sea on one side.

(iii) Name one state which does not have the sea on any side.

Ans. (i) Yes, I have seen the sea. In the picture, the sea is in front of Bala. Blue colour is used to show sea on the map.

(ii) Following are the states which have the sea on one side

Gujarat, Maharashtra, Goa, Karnataka, Kerala, Tamil Nadu, Andhra Pradesh, Odisha and West Bengal.

*(iii) The state which does not have the sea on any side is Bihar.

Find out (NCERT Pg 123)

Q.10 Look for different maps. Compare the different scales used in a local area map, a map of India and a world map etc.

Ans. Do yourself.

Distances between Towns (NCERT Pg 124)

Q.11 These are five towns. Find out.

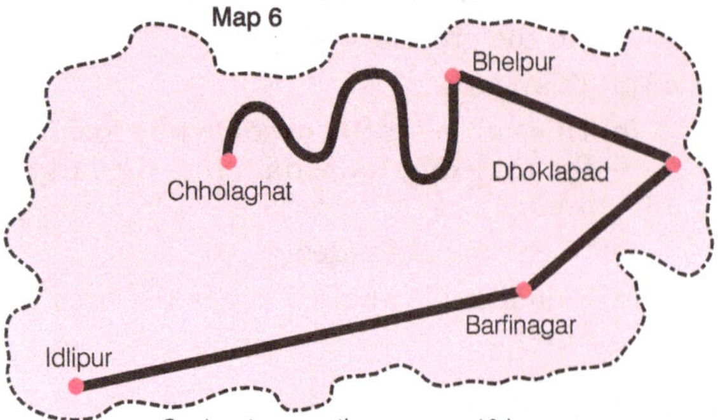

Scale : 1 cm on the paper = 10 km

(i) How many centimetres away is Idlipur from Barfinagar on the map?

(ii) How many kilometres will you have to travel if you go from Idlipur to Barfinagar?

(iii) There is a place called Thukpagram midway between Idlipur and Barfinagar. Mark it with a ' T '.

(iv) A town called Jalebipur is 35 km away from both Chholaghat and Dhoklabad. Where do you think it can be? Mark 'J' for it.

(v) Measure the length of the route between Bhelpur and Chholaghat. (you can use a thread)

Ans. (i) The distance between Idlipur from Barfinagar on the map is 5.2 cm.

(ii) $\because$ 1 cm on the paper = 10 km

$\therefore$ 5.2 cm will be equal to = $5.2 \times 10 = 52$ km

Hence, Idlipur is 52 km away from Barfinagar.

(iii) Thukpagram is denoted by 'T' on the map.

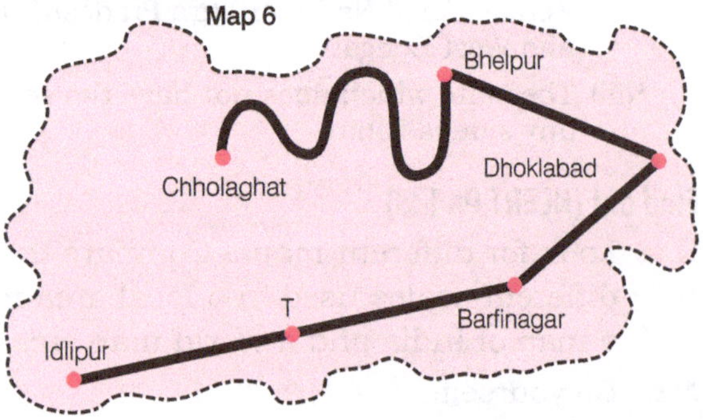

(iv) Jalebipur is denoted by 'J' on the map.

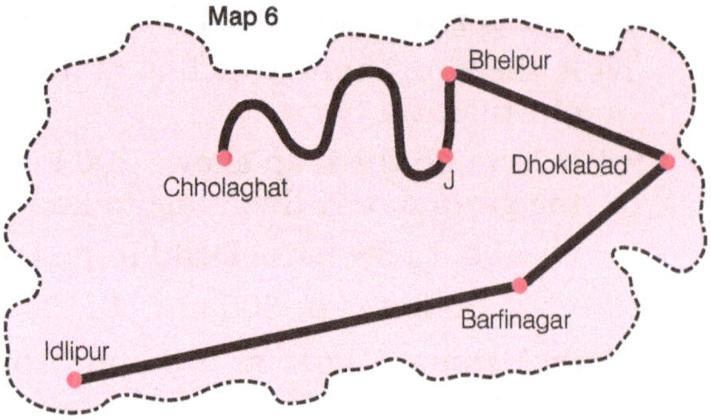

(v) Length of Bhelpur and Chholaghat = 4.3 cm

$\therefore$ Distance = $(4.3) \times 10$ km = 43 km

So, the length of the route between Bhelpur and Chholaghat is 43 km.

Ashi's School (NCERT Pg 124-125)

Q.12 Ashi's school looks like this from the top. Use the squares to find out

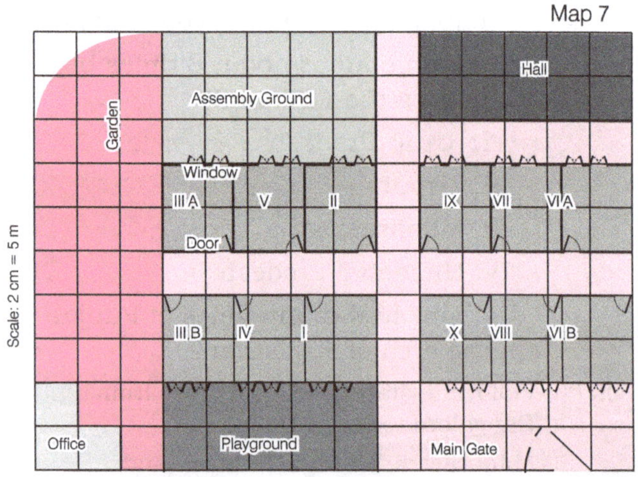

(i) How many times bigger is the area of the Assembly ground than that of the office?

(ii) How much is the length and width of each classroom?

(a) length 5 m, width 4 m

(b) length 2 m, width 1 m

(c) length 12 m, width 10 m

(d) length 5 m, width 5 m

(iii) All the classrooms in Ashi's school look like this.

Map 8

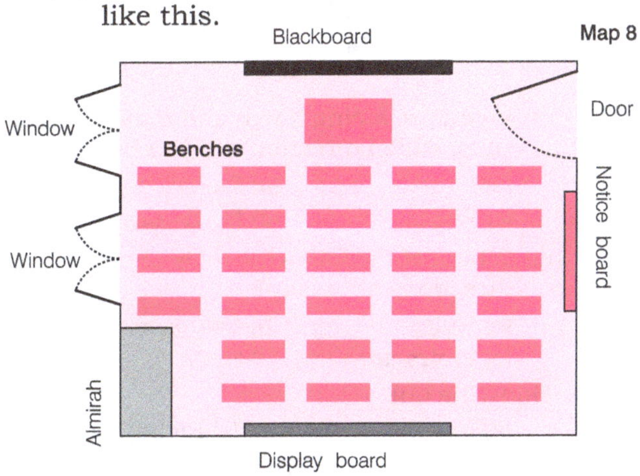

Look carefully and answer.

(a) Which of these is exactly opposite to the blackboard?

Almirah, windows, notice board, display board.

(b) Look at the school-map again. Guess and mark where would these be:

I. Blackboard in III A and VII

II. Almirah in IV and X

III. Notice board in V and VI B

IV. Last seat of middle-row in II

V. Display board in I

(c) Can a child sitting in III A see the playground?

Ans. (i) Area of office = 3 cm^2

Area of assembly ground = 15 cm^2

$$\frac{\text{Area of Assembly ground}}{\text{Area of office}} = \frac{15}{3} = 5$$

Hence, the area of Assembly ground is 5 times bigger than area of office.

(ii) (d) All the classrooms have same area and same size.

$\because$ 2 cm = 5 m [given]

Length of classroom = 2 cm = 5 m

Width of classroom = 2 cm = 5 m

Hence, length and width of each classroom are 5m and 5m, respectively.

(iiii) (a) Display board is exactly opposite to the blackboard.

(b) Things on the map are shown below

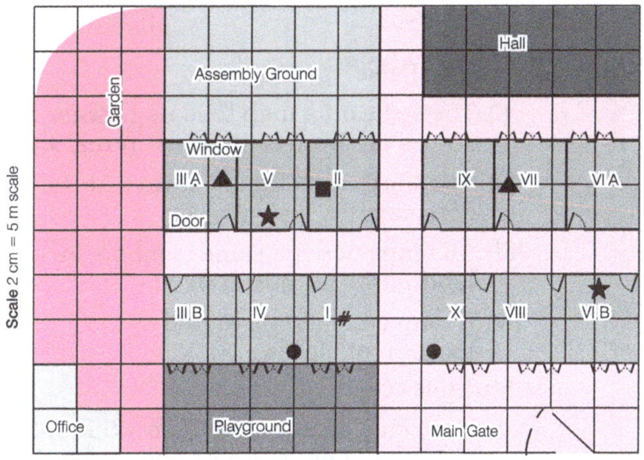

I. Blackboard in III-A and VII is marked by ▲.

II. Almirah in IV and X is marked by ●.

III. Notice board in V and VI-B is marked by ★.

IV. Last seat of middle row in II is marked by ■.

V. Display board in I is marked by #.

(c) No, a child sitting in III-A cannot see the playground.

PRACTICE QUESTIONS

1. Fill in the blanks
   (i) A .... is a drawing that represents a place and routes. (drawing/map)
   (ii) The opposite direction of North is .... (East/South)
   (iii) The scale of a map helps us find the actual .... between two places. (distance/time)
2. True or False
   (i) The scale on a map tells us how far two places are from each other in real world.
   (ii) The North direction is always at the top of a map.
   (iii) All maps use the same symbols for landmarks for hospitals and schools.
   (iv) A map can help us to understand the location of places.
3. Multiple choice questions
   (i) The scale on a map is 1 cm = 5 km. If two cities are 4 cm apart on the map, what is the actual distance between them?
   (a) 10 km (b) 15 km
   (c) 20 km (d) 25 km
   (ii) If you are facing North and make a right turn, which direction will you be facing?
   (a) South (b) East
   (c) West (d) North-East
   (iii) Which of the following tools shows directions on a map?
   (a) Ruler (b) Compass
   (c) Protractor (d) Scale
4. Odd-One out
   (a) North (b) South (c) Right (d) West
5. A map shows a river that is 5 cm away from a mountain. The scale of the map is 1 cm = 1.5 km. What is the real distance between the river and the mountain?
6. You are using a map where the scale is 1 cm = 5 km. You measure the distance between two landmarks as 8 cm. What is the real distance?
7. From the image, the largest distance between A and B is in Map-1 or Map-2.

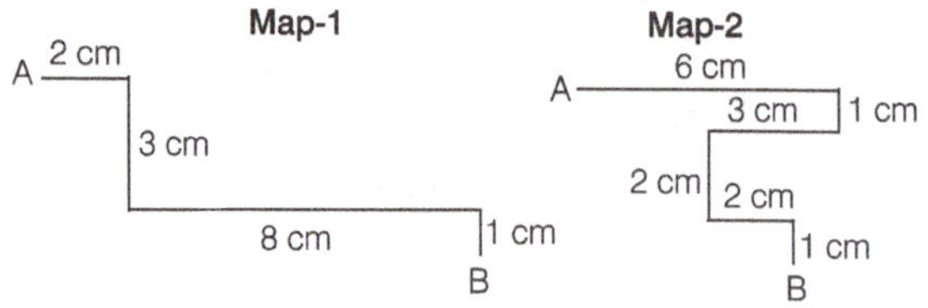

ANSWERS & SOLUTIONS

1. (i) map (ii) South
   (iii) distance
2. (i) False (ii) True
   (iii) True (iv) True
3. (i) (c) (ii) (b)
   (iii) (b)
4. (c)
5. Distance between river and mountain

   = 5 cm

   The scale is 1 cm = 1.5 km

   ∴ The real distance between river and mountain = $5 \times 1.5 = 7.5$ km

   Hence, the real distance between river and mountain is 7.5 km.
6. Scale of the map is

   1 cm = 5 km

   and the distance between two landmarks

   = 8 cm

   The real distance between the two landmarks = $8 \times 5 = 40$ km.
7. Let us first calculate the distance between A and B in Map-1 and Map-2.

   Distance in Map-1

   = 2 cm + 3 cm + 8 cm + 1 cm

   = 14 cm

   Distance in Map-2

   = 6 cm + 1 cm + 3 cm + 2 cm + 2 cm + 1 cm

   = 15 cm

   Hence, from both the distances, we can say that distance in Map-2 is the largest.

CHAPTER 9 BOXES AND SKETCHES

3D shapes (Solid shapes)
Three dimensional shapes are objects that have length, width and height.

Common 3D shapes

- **Cube** A solid shape with six square faces, twelve edges and eight vertices.
- **Cuboid** Similar to a cube but has rectangular faces instead of square ones.
- **Cylinder** A shape with two circular faces and one curved surface.
- **Cone** A shape with a circular base and a pointed top.
- **Sphere** A perfectly round shape like a ball with no edges or vertices.
- **Pyramid** A shape with a polygon base and triangular faces that meet at a point.

Faces, Edges and Vertices

- **Faces** The flat surfaces of a 3D shape. e.g. A cube has 6 faces.
- **Edges** The lines where two faces meet. e.g. A cube has 12 edges.
- **Vertices** The corners where edges meet. e.g. A cube has 8 vertices.

Visualising 3D objects in 2D (sketches)
We cannot draw depth on a flat surface (like a sheet of paper). Sketches are used to represent 3D objects in a way that gives an illusion of depth.

Types of sketches

- **Front view** The shape as seen from the front.
- **Side view** The shape as seen from one of its sides.
- **Top view** The shape as seen from above.

Drawing Cubes and Cuboids

- To drawing a cube, draw a square (front face).
- Draw another square slightly above and to the side (back face).
- Connect the corresponding vertices of the two squares with lines to create the edges.

Similarly, we can draw cuboids on drawing a rectangular (front face).

NCERT FOLDER

Sweet Box (NCERT Pg 126)

Q.1 She (Ramya) made four more shapes. Each is to be folded along the dotted lines. You have to find out which of these can be made into a box.

(a)

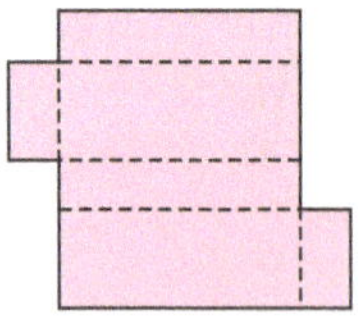

(b)

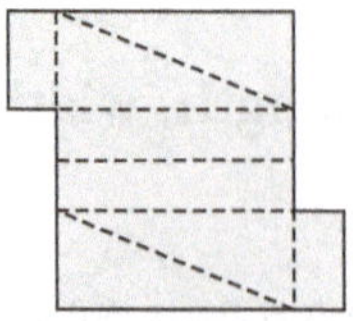

(c)

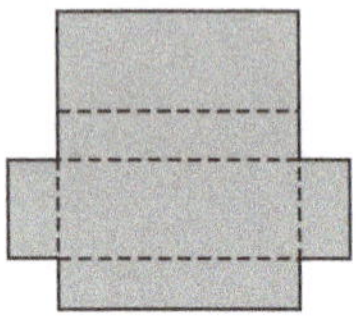

(d)

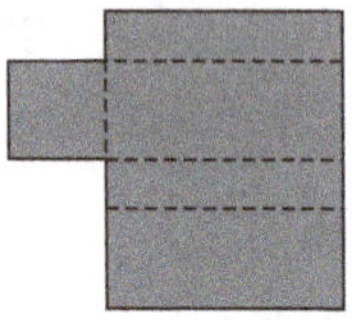

Ans. Here, cut outs of (a) and (c) can be folded along the dotted lines to make a box.

Shapes that Fold into a Cube (NCERT Pg 127)

Q.2 Buddha wants to make a paper cube using a squared sheet. He knows that all the faces of a cube are squares.

He draws two different shapes.

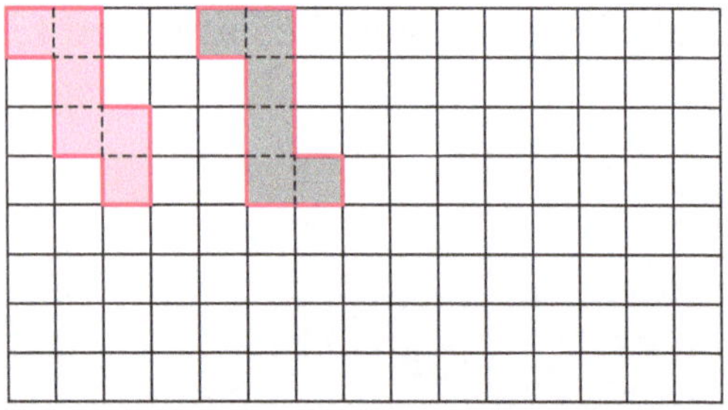

(i) How many faces does the cube have?

(ii) Will both these shapes fold into a cube?

(iii) Draw atleast one more shape which can fold into a cube.

(iv) What will be the area of each face of the cube?

(v) Draw one shape which will not fold into a cube.

(vi) Look around and discuss which things around you look like a cube. List a few.

Ans. (i) A cube has six faces.

(ii) Yes, both these shapes fold into a cube.

*(iii) Following is the another shape which can fold into cube.

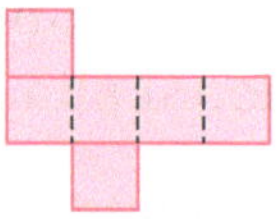

(iv) Area of each face of the cube = Side × Side

= $(\text{Side})^2$

*(v) Here is a shape which will not fold into a cube.

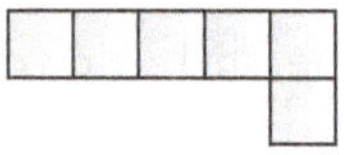

*(vi) Some things like - a die, ice cube, sugar cubes and a chalk box are in the shape of cube.

Shapes for an Open Box (NCERT Pg 127-128)

Q.3 Remember the puzzles with five squares in chapter 3? You saw 12 different shapes made with five squares. If you cut those shapes and fold them, some of those will fold into an open box (box without a top).

(i) Find out which of the other 8 shapes (on NCERT page 46 in chapter 3) can be folded to make an open box.

(ii) Draw more shapes which will not fold to make an open box.

* *Students can write alternate answer as per their choice.*

Ans. (i) Following are the 8 shapes (on NCERT page 46)

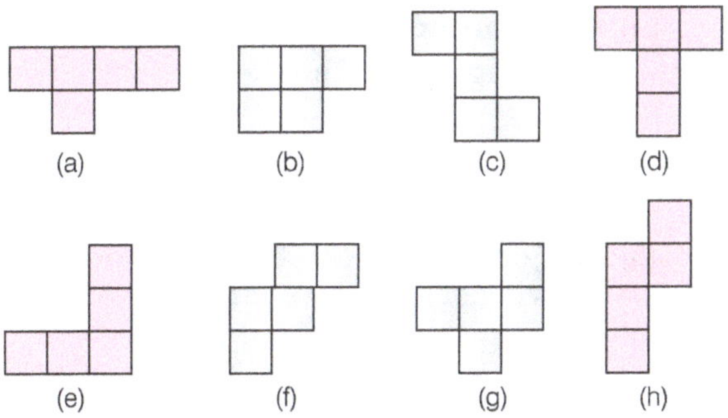

Out of these shapes, (a), (c), (d), (f), (g) and (h) can be folded to make an open box.

(ii) Following are some more shapes which will not fold to make an open box.

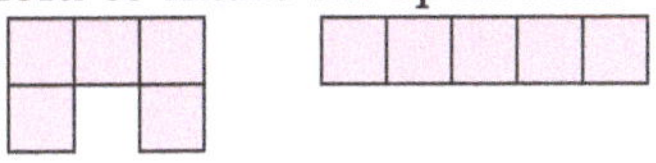

Boxes and Boxes (NCERT Pg 128)

Q.4 All boxes are not cubes. Here are some different kinds of boxes. Match the shape on the left with a box into which it will fold.

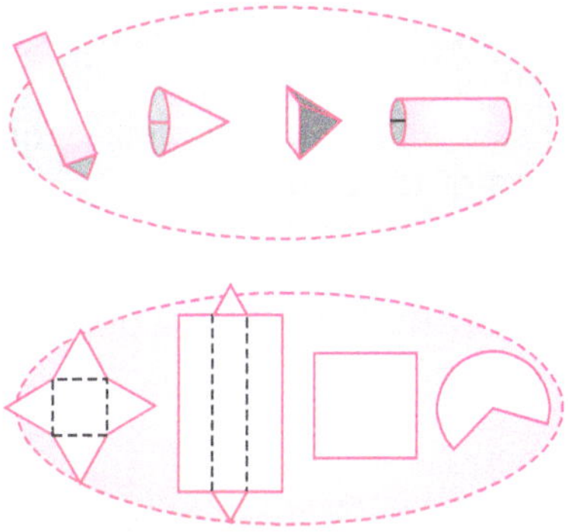

Ans.

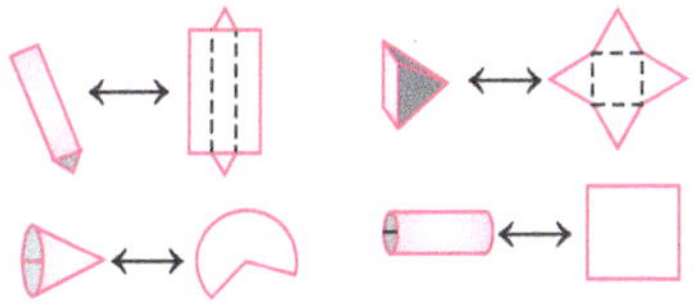

Floor Maps (NCERT Pg 129)

Q.5 For making a house a floor map is first made. Have you ever seen a floor map?

Here is a floor map of Vibha's house. It shows where the windows and the doors are in the house.

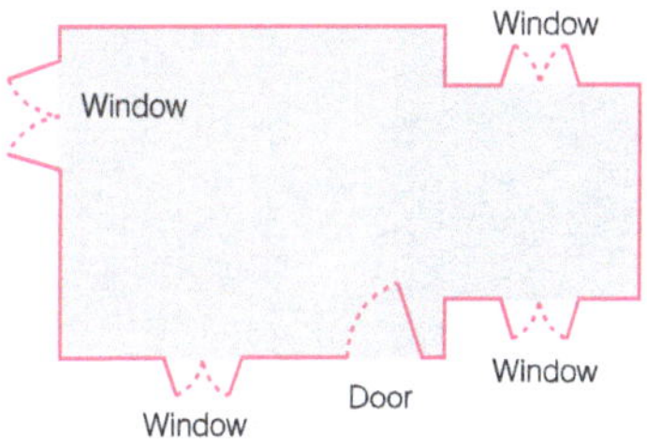

Which is the front side of her house? How many windows are there on the front side?

Ans. The side which contains the door is front side. There are two windows on the front side.

Q.6 From the floor map, we cannot make out what her house really looks like or how high the windows are. So, we look for a special way of drawing the house which is deep to show the length, width and height.

Here are four deep drawings of houses.

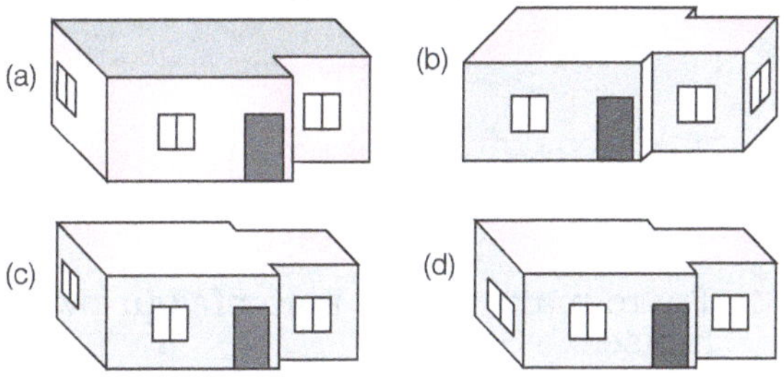

(i) Which one is Vibha's house?

(ii) Why do the other three deep drawings not match the floor map? Discuss.

Ans. (i) Deep drawing (c) is Vibha's house.

(ii) Drawing (a) does not match the floor plan because the back wall is not straight.

Drawing (b) does not match either because there is a window on the far right wall.

In drawing (d), the window on the side wall is in the middle but in the actual plan, it is closer to the corner.

Practice time (NCERT Pg 130)

Q.7 Look at this floor map of a house. Make doors and windows on the deep drawing of this house.

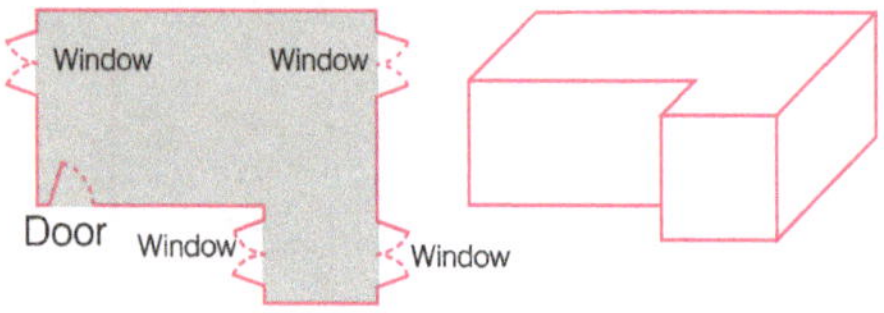

Are there any windows you couldn't show on the deep drawing? Circle them on the floor map.

Ans.

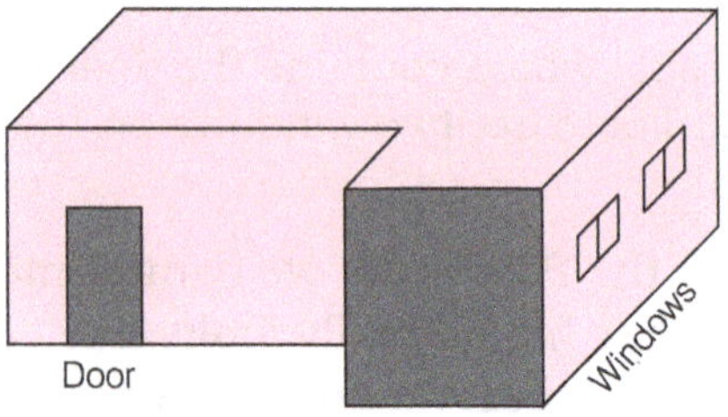

Yes, there are two windows that cannot be seen on the deep drawing, which are encircled in the floor map.

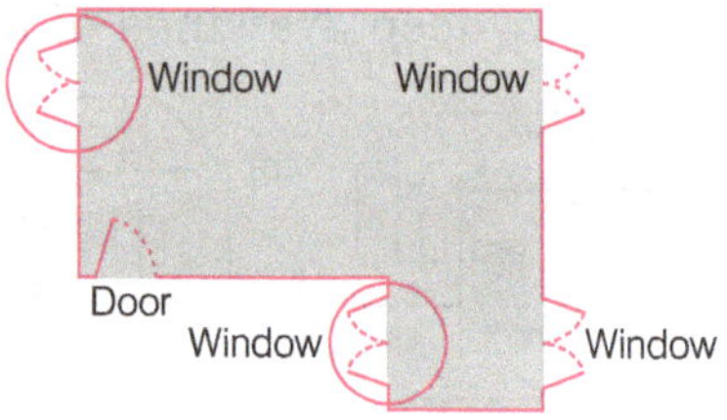

Q.8 Try to make a floor map of your own house.

Ans. Do yourself.

A Deep Drawing of a Cube (NCERT Pg 130)

Q.9 Soumitro and his friends made deep drawings of a cube.
These are their drawings.

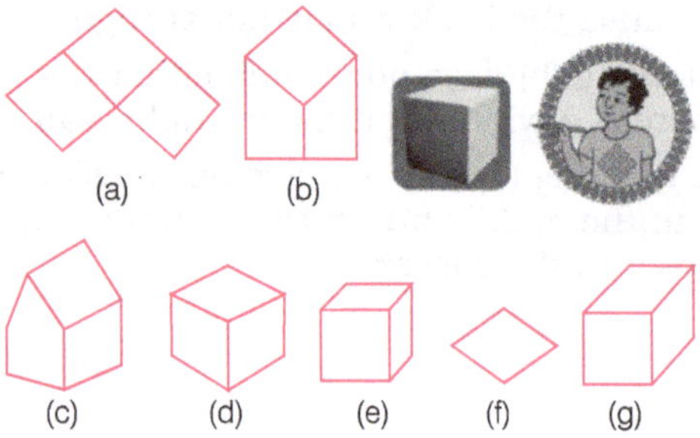

(i) Which of the drawings look correct to you? Discuss.

(ii) Can you add some lines to make drawing (f) into a deep drawing of the cube?

Ans. (i) Drawings (d) and (e) have square faces. So, drawings (d) and (e) are correct.

(ii) Yes, drawing (f) can be made into a deep drawing of cube by adding some lines.

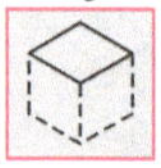

Puzzle (NCERT Pg 131)

Q.10 This cut-out is folded to make a cube.

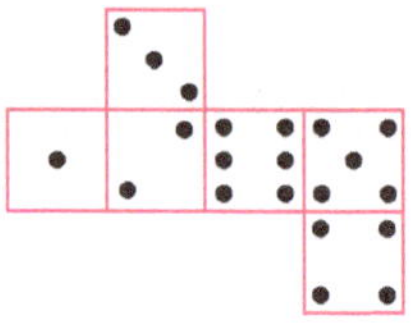

Which of these are the correct deep drawings of that cube?

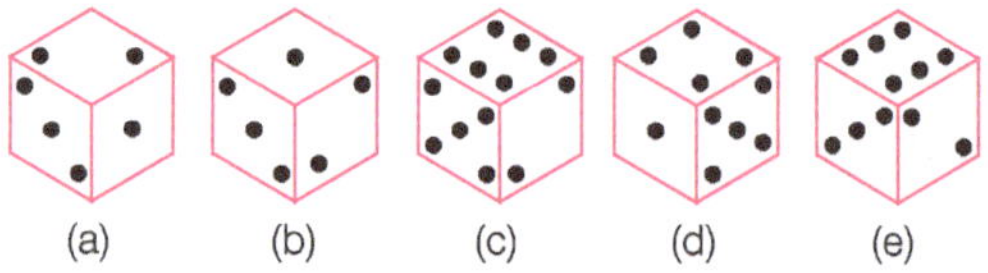

Ans. (a), (d) and (e) are the correct deep drawings of that cube.

A Simple Way to Draw a Cube (NCERT Pg 131)

Q.11 Chanda wants to make a deep drawing of this cube.

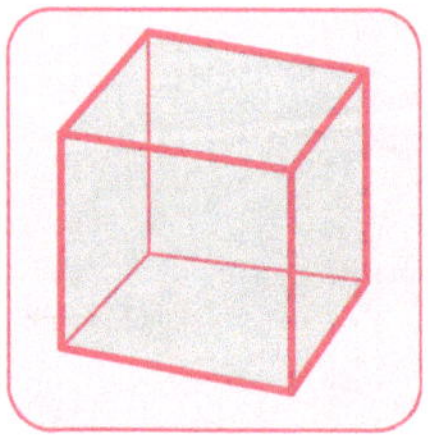

She draws the cube like this.

In the same way, make a deep drawing of a box which looks like this.

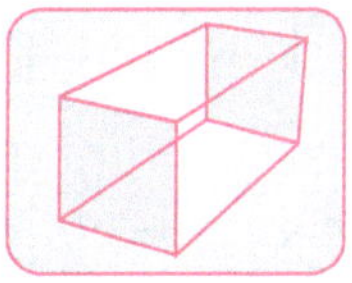

Ans. The deep drawing of the box is shown below.

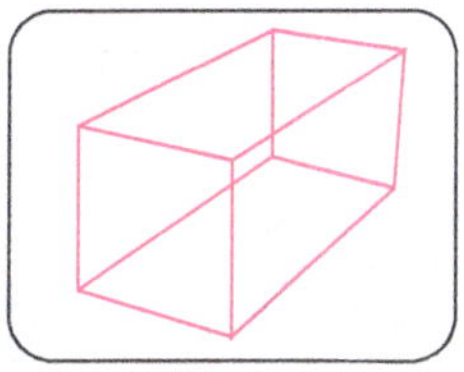

Matchbox Play (NCERT Pg 132-133)

Q.12 Navin,Bhaskar and Pratigya made this bridge using matchboxes.

(i) If you look at the bridge from the top, how will it look? Choose the right drawing below.

(a) 

(b) 

(ii) Look at the photo and try to make a deep drawing of this bridge.

Ans. (i) It looks like the drawing (b) from the top.

(ii) Do yourself.

Practice time (NCERT Pg 133)

Q.13 Make drawings to show how this bridge will look

(i) From the top

(ii) From the front

(iii) From the side

Ans. Following are the drawings of a bridge from different views.

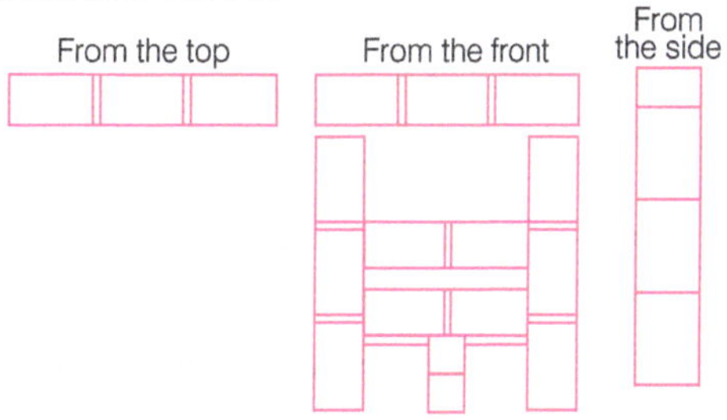

(i) (ii) (iii)

Q.14 Make a matchbox model which looks like this.

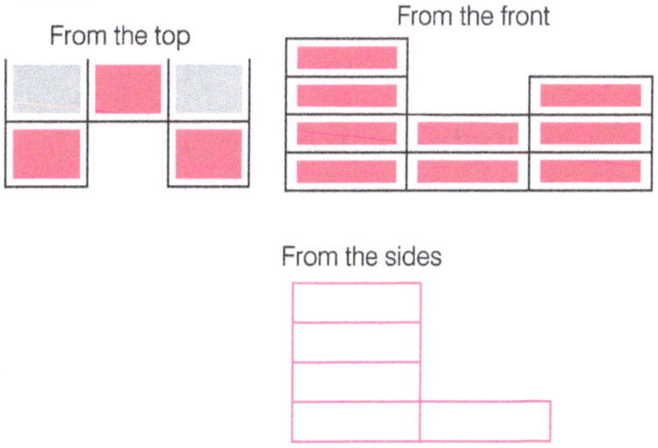

Also, make a deep drawing of the model in your notebook.

Ans. Do yourself.

Q.15 How many cubes are needed to make this interesting model?

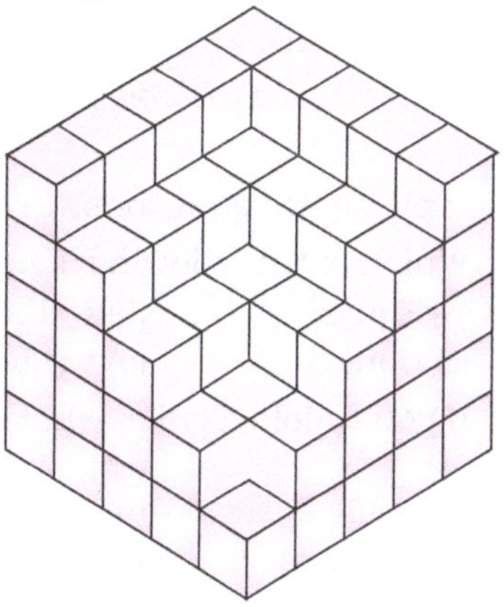

Ans. Number of cubes

Ground floor $(5 \times 5) = 25$

1st floor $(5 \times 5 - 1) = 24$
2nd floor $(5 \times 5 - 4) = 21$
3rd floor $(5 \times 5 - 9) = 16$
Top floor $(5 \times 5 - 16) = 9$
On adding, we get
$25 + 24 + 21 + 16 + 9 = 95$ cubes.
Hence, 95 cubes are needed to make given interesting model.

Q.16 Here are some drawings of the model. Mark the correct top view drawing with T and the correct side view drawing with S.

(a)
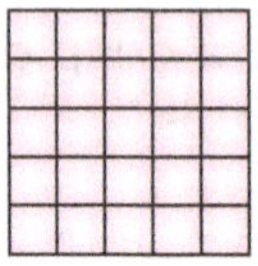

(b)
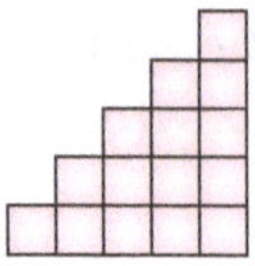

(c)
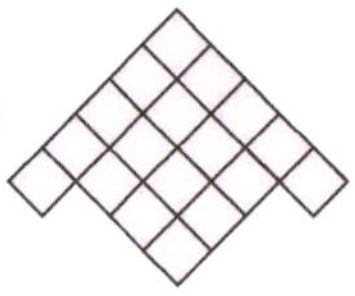

(d)

Ans. Correct top view and correct side view is (a).

PRACTICE QUESTIONS

1. Fill in the blanks.

(i) A .... is a three dimensional object with length, width and height.

(ii) A shape of cylinder has two circular faces and one .... surface.

(iii) A shape with a circular base and a pointed top is called ....

(iv) The .... of a 3D object refers to the flat surfaces that make up the object.

2. True or False.

(i) A cube has all sides of equal length.

(ii) A cuboid and a box are always in different shapes.

(iii) We can not represent 3D shapes on the paper in 2D.

(iv) A sketch of a 3D object can show its depth.

3. Multiple choice questions.

(i) Which of the following is not a 3D shape?
(a) Square (b) Cube
(c) Cone (d) Cylinder

(ii) If you unfold a cube, what would you see?
(a) A circle (b) A net of six squares
(c) A triangle (d) A rectangle

(iii) The length, breadth and height of a box are 3 cm, 4 cm and 5 cm. What is the shape of box?
(a) Cube (b) Cuboid
(c) Square (d) Rectangle

(iv) What shape has 6 square faces, 12 edges and 8 vertices?
(a) Cylinder (b) Cuboid
(c) Cube (d) Cone

4. Case based Questions.

Sanya wants to make a gift box using cardboard. She plans to create a cube shaped box with a side of 6 cm. She draws the net of the cube first.

Based on the above information, answer the following questions.

(i) How many square faces does Sanya's net have for the cube?

(ii) If each square face has a side of 6 cm, what will be the surface area of each face and the total surface area of the cube?

(iii) Sanya uses the net to fold the cardboard into a box. How many edges will the box have after it is folded?

ANSWERS & SOLUTIONS

1. (i) box (ii) curved (iii) cone (iv) faces

2. (i) True (ii) False (iii) False (iv) True

3. (i) (a) (ii) (b) (iii) (b) (iv) (c)

4. (i) 6 square faces

(ii) Surface area $= 6\text{cm} \times 6\text{cm}$
$= 36$ square cm
Since, the cube has 6 square faces.
So, total surface area $= 6 \times 36$
$= 216$ square cm

(iii) 12 edges

CHAPTER 10
TENTHS AND HUNDREDTHS

Decimal point

A decimal point separates the integer part from the fractional part of a number.

e.g. In number 4.5, the decimal points separates 4 (integer part) from 0.5 (fractional part).

Tenths $\left(\frac{1}{10}\right)$

The tenths is the place value of the digit that appears after the decimal.

- $\frac{1}{10}$ is written as 0.1 in decimal form.
- One millimetre = $\frac{1}{10}$ cm or 0.1 cm.

Hundredths $\left(\frac{1}{100}\right)$

The hundredths place is the second position to the right of the decimal point.

- $\frac{1}{100}$ is written as 0.01 in decimal form.
- One centimetre = $\frac{1}{100}$ metre or 0.01 m.

Understanding Decimal place value

Decimal place values continue to the right of the decimal point. Each place to the right represents a smaller fraction of the whole.

How to convert each other?

<table>
<tr><td rowspan="7">Multiply by 10 on each step</td><td rowspan="7">↑</td><td>Millimetre</td><td rowspan="7">↓</td><td rowspan="7">Divide by 10 on each step</td></tr>
<tr><td>Centimetre</td></tr>
<tr><td>Decimetre</td></tr>
<tr><td>Metre</td></tr>
<tr><td>Decametre</td></tr>
<tr><td>Hectometre</td></tr>
<tr><td>Kilometre</td></tr>
</table>

e.g. To convert 6000 m to km, need to divide by 1000 i.e. $6000 \div 1000 = 6$ km

Conversion of different units

- 1 kilogram = 1000 grams
- 1 gram = $\frac{1}{1000}$ kilogram
- 1 kilometre = 1000 metres
- 1 metre = 100 centimetres
- 1 metre = 1000 millimetres
- 1 centimetre = 10 millimetres
- 1 millimetre = $\frac{1}{10}$ centimetre
- 1 millimetre = $\frac{1}{1000}$ metre
- 1 centimetre = $\frac{1}{100}$ metre
- 1 metre = $\frac{1}{1000}$ kilometre
- ₹ 1 = 100 paise
- 1 paise = ₹ $\frac{1}{100}$

NCERT FOLDER

NCERT Pg 134-135

Q.1 What was the length of the smallest pencil you have used?

Ans. * The length of the smallest pencil which I used was 4.2 cm.

Q.2 How long is this pencil ? Guess ____ cm.

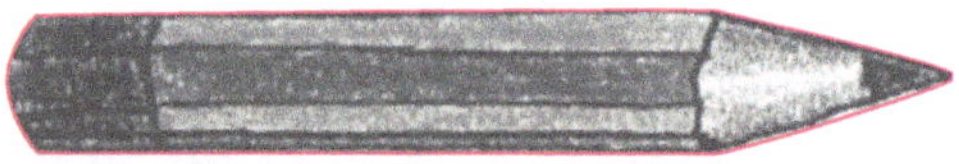

Measure it using a scale. How good is your guess?

Ans. * I guess it is 3.5 cm long. The length of the pencil after measuring it with the help of scale is 3.6 cm. So, my guess is near to the correct value.

Q.3 What is the length of this pencil? ____ mm

What is its length in centimetres?

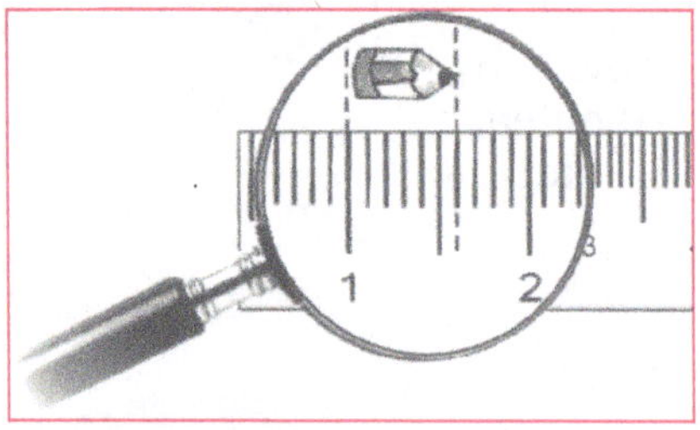

Ans. The length of this pencil is 6 mm. The length in centimetres can be written as 0.6 cm.

** Students can write alternate answer as per their choice.*

Frogs (NCERT Pg 135)

Q.4 Have you seen frogs? Where ? How many different types of frogs have you seen? Are all the frogs of the same length?

Gold frogs This kind of frog is among the smallest in the world. Its length is only 0.9 cm !

Bull frog But this is among the biggest frogs. It is as long as 30.5 cm!

(i) Guess how many gold frogs can sit on your little finger?

(ii) What does 0.9 cm mean? It is the same as _____ millimetres. We can also say this is nine-tenths of a cm. Rights?

(iii) 30.5 cm is the same as ____ cm and _____ millimetre.

(iv) About how many of the big frogs will fit on the 1m scale?

(v) If they sit in a straight line about how many of the small frogs will cover 1m?

Ans. *Yes, I have seen frogs in my garden during the rainy season.

There are different kind of frogs like tree frogs, leopard frogs and hairy frogs. They, also come in different sizes.

*(i) I think five gold frogs can sit on my little finger.

(ii) ∵ 0.1 cm = 1 mm

∴ 0.9 cm = 9 mm

Yes, we can also say this is nine-tenths of a cm.

(iii) 30.5 cm = 30 cm and 5 millimetres

(iv) ∵ 1 m = 100 cm

The length of big frog is 30.5 cm. Therefore, 3 such frogs can fit on a 1 m scale.

(v) 1m = 100 cm = 1000 mm

9)1000(111
−9
10
−9
10
−9
1

So, about 111 small frogs will cover 1 m.

Practice time (NCERT Pg 135-136)

Q.5 Length of the nail is 2 cm and ____ mm or 2. _____ cm.

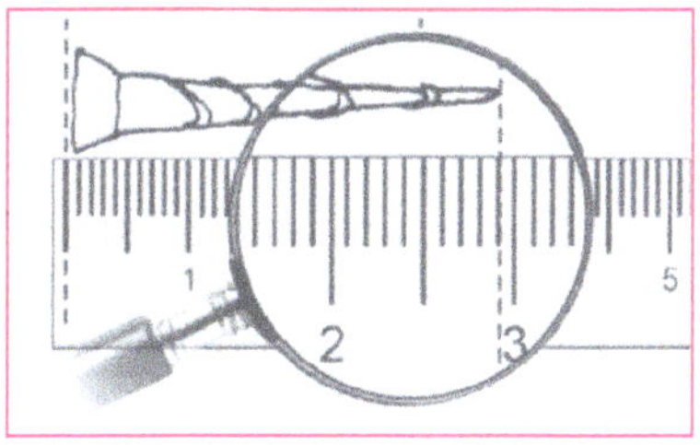

Ans. Length of the nail is 2 cm and 9 mm or 2.9 cm.

Q.6 The length of this lady's finger (bhindi) is ____ cm and ____ mm.

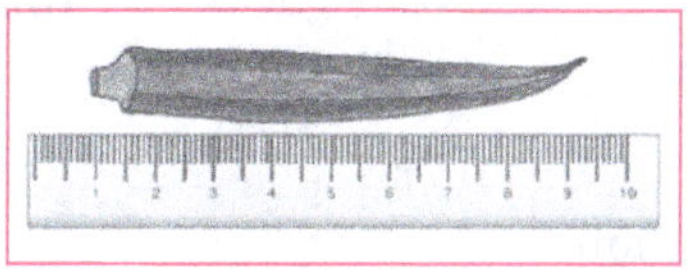

We can also write it as ....cm.

Ans. The length of the lady's finger is 8 cm and 3 mm. It can also be written as 8.3 cm.

Q.7 Using the scale on this page find the difference in length between candle 1 and candle 3.

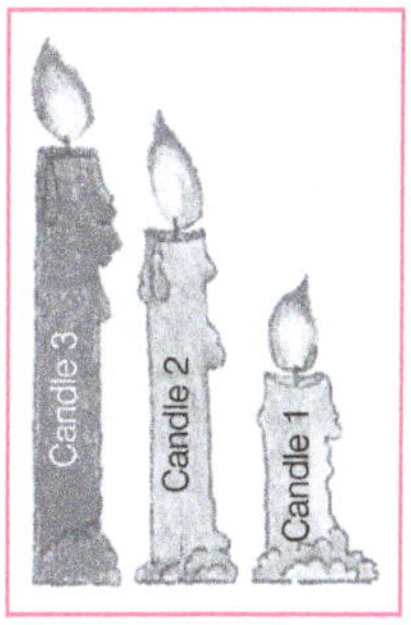

Length of	Length in cm and mm	Length in cm
Candle 1		
Flame 1		
Candle 2		
Flame 2		
Candle 3		
Flame 3		

Ans. *

Length of	Length in cm and mm	Length in cm
Candle 1	2 cm and 8 mm	2.8 cm
Flame 1	1 cm and 3 mm	1.3 cm
Candle 2	4 cm and 9 mm	4.9 cm
Flame 2	1 cm and 7 mm	1.7 cm
Candle 3	6 cm	6 cm
Flame 3	1 cm and 5 mm	1.5 cm

Guess and Colour (NCERT Pg 136)

Q.8 First colour the rods as shown, without measuring! Then check.

Rods of length less than 1 cm — Red

Rods of length between 1 cm and 2 cm — Blue

Rods of length between 2 cm and 3 cm — Green

Rods of length between 3 cm and 4 cm — Orange

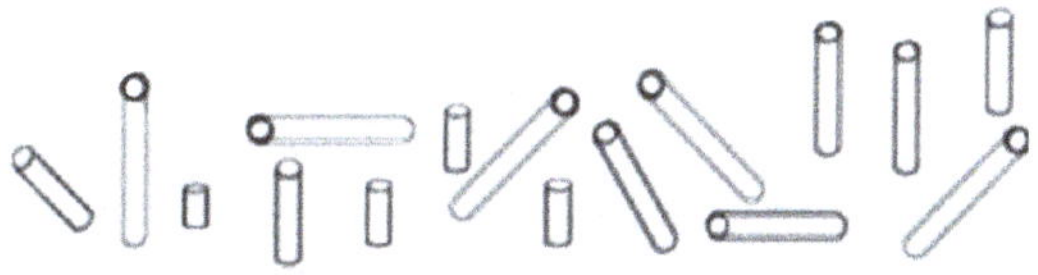

Ans. Do yourself.

Guess, Draw and Measure (NCERT Pg 137)

Q.9 Guess the lengths to draw these things. Ask your friend to draw the same. After you make the drawing use a scale to measure the length. Whose drawing showed a better guess?

Ans. *

Guess its length and draw	Measure of your drawing	Measure of your friends's drawing
An ant of length less than 1 cm	0.8 cm	1.4 cm
Pencil of length about 7 cm	7.2 cm	6.4 cm
A glass 11 cm high with water up to 5 cm	10.5 cm, 4.6 cm	8 cm, 4.5 cm
A bangle of perimeter 20 cm	18.9 cm	20.2 cm
A curly hair of length 16 cm	15 cm	16.6 cm

Our Eyes Get Confused? (NCERT Pg 137)

Q.10 (i) Which line is longer? *A* or *B*? Measure each line and write how long it is in centimetres. How good is your guess?

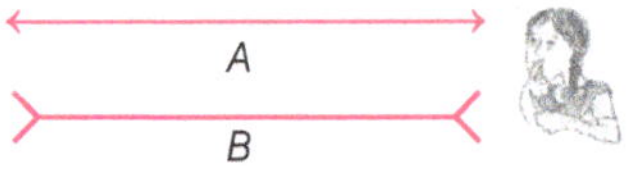

(ii) Which line is longer? *C* or *D* ? Measure each line. How good is your guess?

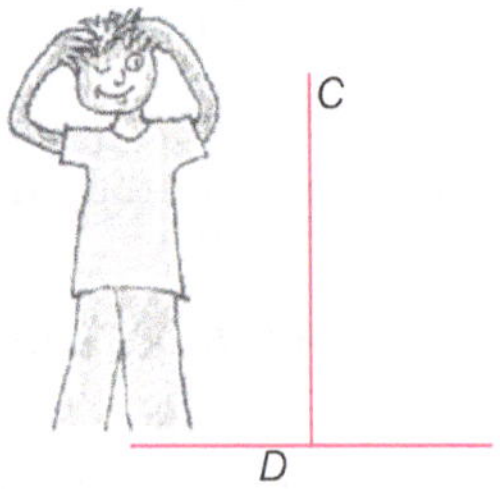

Ans. (i) I think line *A* is longer than line *B*.

A = 4.6 cm, *B* = 4.6 cm

So, my guess was wrong because the length of both lines *A* and *B* are same.

(ii) Line *C* seems to be longer.

On measuring, I found the lengths of line *C* and line *D* as follows

C = 3.2 cm and *D* = 3.2 cm

So, again my guess was wrong because the length of both lines *C* and *D* are equal.

Whose Tail is the Longest (NCERT Pg 138)

Q.11 Guess whose tail is the longest? Now, measure the tails. How good is your guess?

Ans. * According to me the tail of monkey is the longest.

Now, measuring the lengths of tail.

Animals	Length of tail
Lizard	1.6 cm
Rat	1.4 cm
Cat	1.1 cm
Puppy	0.9 cm
Monkey	2.3 cm
Pig	1.2 cm

So, my guess was correct.

Hint Use thread to measure the tails.

The longest Rupee Notes? (NCERT Pg 138)

Q.12 (i) What is the length of a 100 rupee note? Guess.

Now, measure it using a scale.

(ii) Guess the length and width of many other things. Measure and find the difference between your measure and your guess.

Ans. *(i) I guess that it is 16.1 cm long.

After measuring it by using a scale I found it 14.2 cm long.

*(ii)

Size of	Your guess in cm		Your measure in cm	
	Length	Width	Length	Width
100 Rupee note	16.1	7.1	14.2	6.6
10 Rupee note	13.1	6.0	12.3	6.3
20 Rupee note	15.2	6.5	12.9	6.3
5 Rupee note	11.0	6.4	11.7	6.3
Post card	14.1	9.0	14.5	9.5
Math-Magic book	28.2	22.5	28.5	22.0

Difference between my measure and guess is as under.

Size of	Difference in cm	
	Length	Width
100 Rupee note	1.9	0.5
10 Rupee note	0.8	0.3
20 Rupee note	2.3	0.2
5 Rupee note	0.7	0.1
Post card	0.4	0.5
Math-Magic book	0.3	0.5

At the Market (NCERT Pg 138-139)

Q.13

(i) How many paise does a matchbox cost?

(ii) How many matchboxes can be got for ₹ 2.50?

(iii) How many rupees does the soap cost?

(iv) Arun wanted to buy a soap. He has a five-rupee coin, 2 one-rupee coins and 4 half-rupee coins. Write in rupees what money he will get back.

(v) Kannan, take rupees 60 and buy one and half dozen eggs. You can buy pens with the money left.

(a) An egg costs two and a half rupees. How much will one and a half dozen cost?

(b) How many pens can Kannan buy? How much money is left?

(vi) The price of two pens is ₹ ___ . Can she buy two pens?

Ans. (i) 50 paise

(ii) As ₹ 2.50 = 250 paise

$\therefore$ Number of matchboxes $= \frac{250}{50} = 5$

Hence, 5 matchboxes can be got for ₹ 2.50.

(iii) ₹ 8.75

(iv) Total money that Arun has

= (₹ 5 × 1) + (₹ 1 × 2) + (₹ 0.5 × 4)

= ₹ 5 + ₹ 2 + ₹ 2

= ₹ 9

Cost of one soap = ₹ 8.75

Arun wil get back = ₹ 9 – ₹ 8.75

= (900 – 875) paise

= 25 paise = ₹ 0.25

(v) (a) $\because$ Cost of an egg = ₹ 2.50

One and half dozen means 12 + 6

= 18 eggs

$\therefore$ Cost of 18 eggs = 18 × 2.50

= 18 × 2 + 18 × 0.50

= 36 + 9 = ₹ 45

Money left = ₹ (60 – 45) = ₹ 15

(b) $\because$ Cost of pen is ₹ 6.50.

$\therefore$ Cost of 2 pen = 2 × 6.50 = ₹ 13

Kannan can buy 2 pens.

Money left = ₹ (15 – 13) = ₹ 2

(vi) The price of two pens is ₹ 13. Yes, she can buy two pens.

Practice Time - Match these (NCERT Pg 140)

Q.14 Match each Column-I with Column-II and Column-III.

Ans.

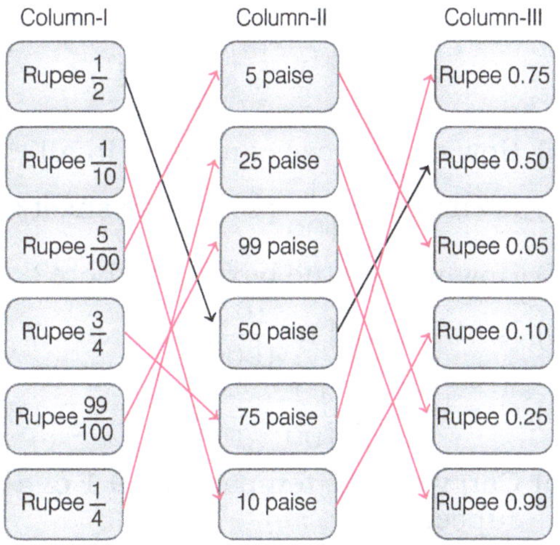

Colourful Design (NCERT Pg 140)

Q.15 Oh, the blue strip is 0.1 of the sheet.

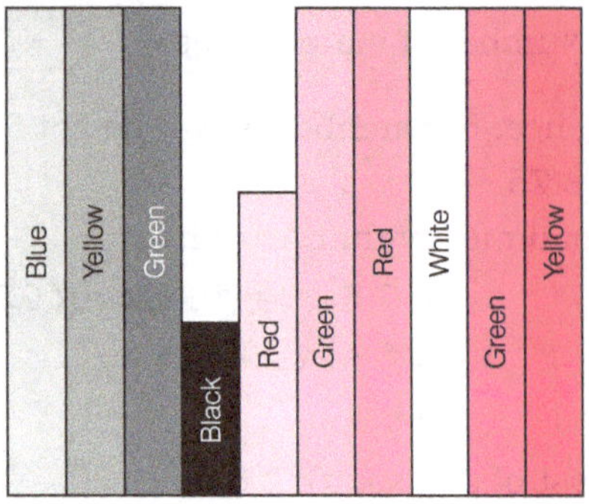

(i) What part of this sheet is coloured blue? ______ / 10

(ii) What part of the sheet is green?

(iii) Which colour covers 0.2 of the sheet?

Ans. (i) $\frac{1}{10}$ part of the sheet is coloured blue.

(ii) $\frac{3}{10}$ part of the sheet is green.

(iii) Yellow part is $= \frac{2}{10} = \frac{1}{5}$ part of sheet = 0.2

Q.16 Look at the second sheet. Each strip is divided into 10 equal boxes.

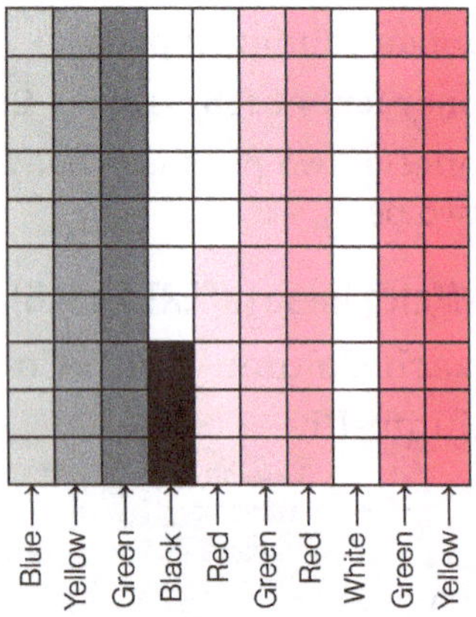

(i) How many boxes are there in all?

(ii) Is each box $\frac{1}{100}$ part of the sheet?

(iii) How many blue boxes are there?

(iv) Is blue equal to $\frac{10}{100}$ of the sheet?

(v) Can we say $\frac{10}{100} = \frac{1}{10} = 0.10 = 0.1$?

(vi) Can we write ten paise as 0.1 of a rupee?

(vii) How many boxes are red? What part of the sheet is this? 15/ _____

Can we also write it as 0.15 of the sheet?

(viii) $\frac{3}{100}$ of the sheet is black. We can say 0. _____ sheet is black.

(ix) How many white boxes are there in the sheet?

(x) What part of the second sheet is white?

Ans. (i) There are $10 \times 10 = 100$ boxes

(ii) Yes, each box is $\frac{1}{100}$ part of the sheet.

(iii) There are 10 blue boxes.

(iv) Yes, blue boxes $= \frac{10}{100} = \frac{1}{10} = 0.1$

(v) Yes

(vi) $\because$ 10 paise $= \frac{10}{100}$ rupee $= \frac{1}{10} = 0.1$ rupee

Hence, we can write 10 paise as 0.1 of a rupee.

(vii) There are 15 red boxes. This is $\frac{15}{100}$.

So, $\frac{15}{100}$ part of the sheet is red.

Yes, $\frac{15}{100}$ can also be written as 0.15 of the sheet.

(viii) $\because \frac{3}{100} = 0.03$

So, we can say 0.03 sheet is black.

(ix) There are 22 white boxes in the sheet.

(x) $\because$ 22 boxes are white out of 100 boxes.

$\therefore \frac{22}{100} = \frac{11}{50}$ part of second sheet is white.

Q.17 (i) Make your designs.

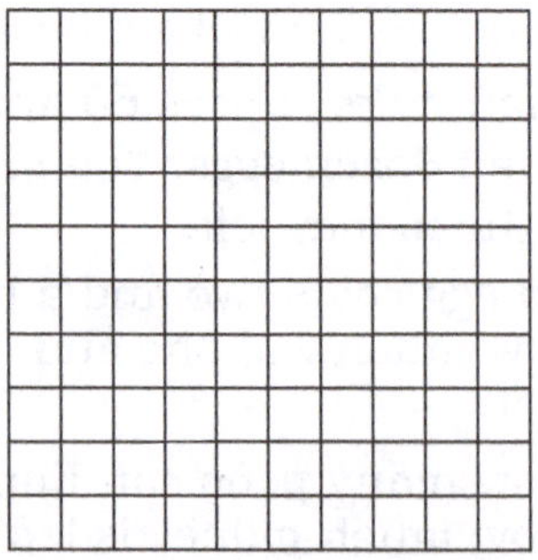

Make a nice design by shading 0.45 part of this square.

(ii)

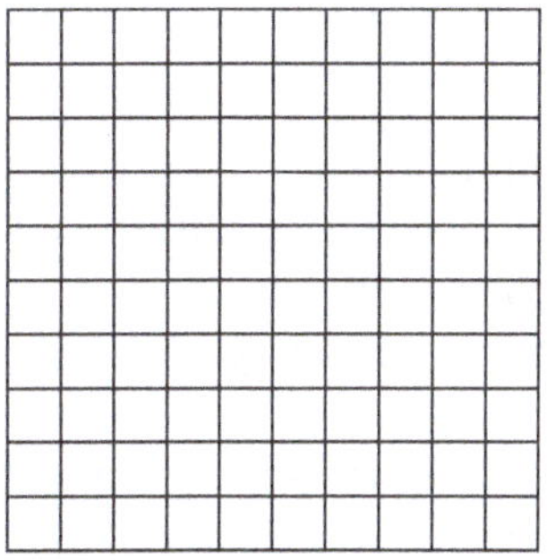

Use four colours. Each colour should cover 0.05 of this square.

Ans. (i) Do yourself.

(ii) Do yourself.

Sports Day (NCERT Pg 141-142)

Q.18 The school at Malappuram has its sports day. The first five children in the long jump are:

Teena jumped 3.50 m, which is 3 m and 50 cm.

(i) But how far did Anu jump?
______ m and ______ cm.

(ii) Who is the winner in the long jump?

(iii) Write the names of the I, II and III winners on this stand.

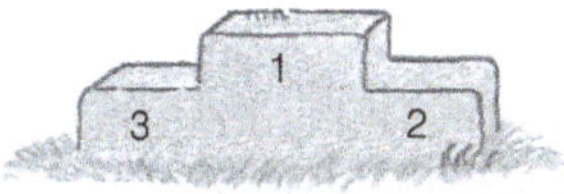

(iv) Do you remember that
1 metre = 100 centimetres?
So, one centimetre is 1/100 of a metre.
We also write 1 cm as _______ m.

Ans. (i) Anu jumped 3.05 m, which is 3 m and 5 cm.

(ii) Rehana is the winner in the long jump.

(iii)

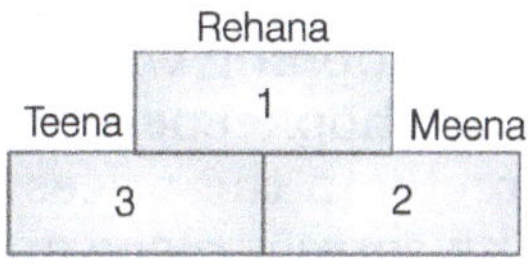

(iv) 1 cm = 0.01 metre

Write in Metres (NCERT Pg 142)

Q.19 (i) 3 metre 45 centimetre ☐ metres

(ii) 99 centimetre ☐ metres

(iii) 1 metre and 5 centimetre ☐ metres

Ans. (i) 3 metres 45 centimetre = 3.45 metres

(ii) 99 centimetre = 0.99 metres

(iii) 1 metre and 5 centimetre = 1.05 metres.

How Big Can You Get? (NCERT Pg 142)

Q.20

After breathing out 1.52 m

On taking a deep breath 1.82 m

(i) Difference in size ☐

(ii) Do this for yourself and find the difference.

Ans. (i) Difference in size = 1.82 m − 1.52 m
= 0.30 m

(ii) Do yourself.

Q.21 You have to grow 45 cm more to reach 2 m height.

What is Dinesh's height in metres?
________ m ________ cm.

Ans. 2 m = 200 cm

∴ 200 cm − 45 cm = 155 cm or 1 m 55 cm.

So, the height of Dinesh is 1m and 55 cm.

Practice Time (NCERT Pg 143-145)

Q.22 Currency from different countries

Have you seen any notes or coins used in any other country?

Shivam Bank has a chart to show us how many Indian ruppees we can get when we change the money of different countries.

Country	Money	Changed into Indian Rupees
Korea	Won	0.04
Sri Lanka	Rupee (LKR)	0.37
Nepal	Rupee (NPR)	0.63
Hong Kong	Dollar (HKD)	5.10
South Africa	Rand	5.18
China	Yuan	5.50
UAE	Dirham	10.80
USA	Dollar	39.70
Germany	Euro	58.30
England	Pound	77.76

(This is the rate on 15-2-2008)

(i) The currency of which country will cost the most in Indian Rupees?

(ii) Mithun's uncle in America had sent him 10 USA dollars as a gift. Mithun used 350 rupees for a school trip. How much money was left with him?

(iii) Majeed's father is working in UAE. He gets 1000 Dirham as salary. Arun's father who is working in Sri Lanka gets 2000 Sri Lankan Rupees. Who gets more Indian rupees as salary?

(iv) Leena's aunty brought a present for her from China. It cost 30 Yuan. Find what is costs in Indian rupees?

(v) Astha wants some Hong Kong Dollars and Won.

(a) How many Won can she change for ₹ 4? For ₹ 400?

(b) How many Hong Kong Dollars can she change for ₹ 508?

Ans. Yes, I have seen notes and coins of the Nepal and Srilanka

(i) The currency of England will cost the most in India Rupees.

(ii) Money received by Mithun = 10 USA dollar

$\because$ 1 USA = ₹ 39.70

$\therefore$ Money received by Mithun = 10×39.70

= ₹ 397 (in ₹)

Money used for school trip = ₹ 350

$\therefore$ Money left with Mithun = ₹ 397 – ₹ 350

= ₹ 47

(iii) Salary of Majeed's father = 1000 Dirham

$\because$ 1 Dirham = ₹ 10.80

$\therefore$ 1000 Dirham = 10.80×1000 = ₹ 10800

Salary of Arun's Father = 2000 Sri Lankan Rupees

$\because$ 1 Rupee (SL) = ₹ 0.37

$\therefore$ 2000 Rupee (SL) = 2000×0.37 = ₹ 740

Hence, Majeed's father gets more Indian rupees as salary.

(iv) $\because$ 1 Yuan = ₹ 5.50

$\therefore$ 30 Yuan = $30 \times 5.50 = 30 \times 5 + 30 \times 0.50$

= ₹ 150 + ₹ 15 = ₹ 165

So, the cost of the present in Indian rupees will be ₹ 165.

(v) (a) $\because$ 1 Won = ₹ 0.04

On multiplying both sides by 100 into the above equation, we get

1 Won $\times 100$ = ₹ 0.04×100

100 Won = ₹ 4

$\therefore$ She can change 100 Won for ₹ 4.

Now, for ₹ 400,

$\because$ ₹ 4 = 100 Won

$\therefore$ ₹ 400 = 100×100 Won = 10000 Won

So, she can change 10000 Won for ₹ 400.

(b) $\because$ 1 (HK) Dollar = ₹5.10

$\therefore$ 1 Indian Rupee = $\frac{1}{5.10}$ (HK) Dollar

$\Rightarrow$ ₹ 508 = $508 \times \frac{1}{5.10}$ (HK) Dollar

= 99.61 (HK) Dollar

So, she will change 99.61 (HK) Dollar for ₹ 508.

Q.23 Kiran went shopping with ₹ 200. Look at the bill. The shopkeeper forgot to put the point correctly in the prices. Put the point in the correct place and find out the total amount of the bill.

Item	Quantity	Price (Rupees)
Soap	1	1250
Green gram	1 kg	5025
Tea	250 gm	2725
Coconut Oil	1 Litre	6000
	Total	________

Ans. The total amount of the bill is 15000.

Q.23 **Which city is cool?**

The temperature in each city was noted at 3 pm on 16 January 2008.

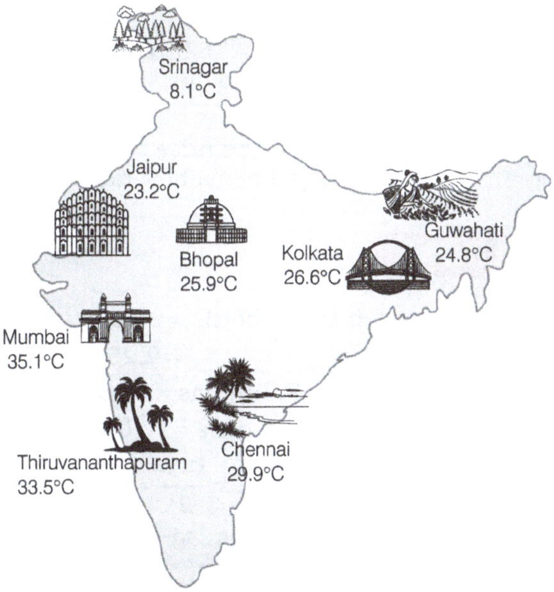

(i) Which place had the highest temperature at 3 pm? Which place is the coolest at that time?

(ii) How much higher is the temperature in Mumbai from that in Srinagar?

(iii) How many degrees will the temperature need to rise for it to reach 40°C in Thiruvananthapuram?

(iv) How much lower is the temperature of Kolkata from that in Chennai?

(v) The temperature in these cities was also noted at 3 am on the same day. Look at the table and answer the question.

City	Temperature at 3 am
Chennai	21.1
Mumbai	19.0
Thiruvananthapuram	21.6
Kolkata	13.1
Bhopal	9.8
Srinagar	1.3
Guwahati	12.8
Jaipur	10.2

(a) Which place had the lowest temperature at 3 am? Imagine yourself to be these describe how it would feel?

(b) What is the difference between the temperatures at 3 pm and 3 am in Chennai? In Bhopal?

Ans. (i) Mumbai has the highest temperature that is 35.1°C at 3 pm.

Srinagar is the coolest at that time with temperature 8.1°C.

(ii) Difference in temperature $= (35.1 - 8.1)^\circ C$

$= 27.0^\circ C$

(iii) Temperature of Thiruvananthapuram

$= 33.5^\circ C$

$\therefore\ 40^\circ C - 33.5^\circ = 6.5^\circ C$

So, 6.5°C temperature need to rise for it to reach 40°C.

(iv) Temperature of Kolkata $= 26.6^\circ C$

Temperature of Chennai $= 29.9^\circ C$

Difference in temperature $= 29.9^\circ C - 26.6^\circ C$

$= 3.3^\circ C$

Hence, the temperature of Kolkata is 3.3°C lower than the temperature of Chennai.

(v) (a) Srinagar had the lowest temperature at 3 am.

The temperature is 1.3°C, making it very cold. It is a good to wear warm cloths and gather around the fire to stay comfortable.

(b) Temperature of Chennai at 3 pm = 29.9°C (from the map)

Temperature of Chennai at 3 am = 21.1°C

Difference in temperature

= 29.9°C − 21.1°C

= 8.8°C

Now, for Bhopal,

Temperature of Bhopal at 3 pm = 25.9°C

Temperature of Bhopal at 3 am = 9.8°C

Difference in temperature = 25.9°C − 9.8°C

= 16.1°C

PRACTICE QUESTIONS

1. Fill in the blanks.

(i) The decimal number .... represents one-tenth. (0.01/0.1)

(ii) If you divide a whole into hundred equal parts each part is .... (0.01/0.001)

(iii) 1 m = ... cm = ... mm.

(iv) 1 paise = ...rupee = ...rupee

$\left(\frac{1}{100}, 0.1 / \frac{1}{100}, 0.01\right)$

2. True or False

(i) The decimal 0.5 represents five hundredths.

(ii) 25 paise is equal to 2.5 rupee.

(iii) The decimal 0.35 has three tenths and five hundredths.

(iv) There are 100 hundredths in a whole.

3. Multiple choice questions

(i) What is the decimal equal to $\frac{3}{10}$?

(a) 0.03 (b) 0.3 (c) 0.33 (d) 0.003

(ii) In the decimal number 0.85, what digit is the tenths place?

(a) 8 (b) 5 (c) 0 (d) 1

(iii) If you add 0.8 and 0.02, what is the result?

(a) 0.802 (b) 0.82 (c) 0.082 (d) 0.10

(iv) 4.50 m is equal to

(a) 4 m and 50 cm (b) 40 m and 5 cm

(c) 40 m and 0.50 cm (d) 0.4 m and 5 cm

4. Odd-One out.

(i) (a) 25 paise (b) 50 paise

(c) 0.25 rupee (d) Rupee $\frac{1}{4}$

(ii) (a) $\frac{10}{100}$ (b) $\frac{1}{10}$ (c) 0.10 (d) 0.01

5. Word problems.

(i) A bottle contains 2.75 litres of juice. If 0.5 litres are poured out, how much juice is left in the bottle?

(ii) Rahul has ₹ 25. The price of two pens is ₹ 10. If he buy 3 pens, how much money is left?

ANSWERS & SOLUTIONS

1. (i) 0.1 (ii) 0.01

(iii) 100, 1000 (iv) $\frac{1}{100}$, 0.01

2. (i) False (ii) False

(iii) True (iv) True

3. (i) (b) (ii) (a)

(iii) (b) (iv) (a)

4. (i) (b) (ii) (d)

5. (i) Juice contains by a bottle = 2.75 litres

Juice poured out = 0.5 litre

Juice left in the bottle = 2.75 − 0.5

= 2.25 litres

(ii) Total money Rahul has = ₹ 25

And price of two pens = ₹ 10

∴ Price of one pen = $\frac{₹10}{2}$ = ₹ 5

Price of 3 pens = ₹ 5 × 3

= ₹ 15

Money left with Rahul = ₹ 25 − ₹ 15

= ₹ 10

CHAPTER 11 AREA AND ITS BOUNDARY

Area

Area is the total space occupied by a shape on a flat surface. Area is measured in square units.

Area of a Rectangle

The area of a rectangle is calculated by multiplying its length and breadth (or width).

$$\text{Area of a rectangle} = \text{Length} \times \text{Breadth}$$

Area of a Square

The area of a square is calculated by multiplying the side of the square by itself.

$$\text{Area of a square} = \text{Side} \times \text{Side}$$

Perimeter Perimeter is the total length of the boundary of a shape. Perimeter is measured in linear units like centimetres (cm), metres (m) etc.

Perimeter of a Rectangle

The perimeter of a rectangle is the sum of all its sides. Since, opposite sides of a rectangle are equal.

$$\text{Perimeter of rectangle} = 2 \times (\text{Length} + \text{Breadth})$$

Perimeter of Square

The perimeter of square is the sum of all four sides. Since, all sides are equal, it can be calculated as 4 times the length of one side.

$$\text{Perimeter of square} = 4 \times \text{Side}$$

Difference between Area and Perimeter

Area measures the total space inside a shape, while perimeter measures the distance around the shape.

Estimating Area with Square Grids

In some cases, it's not possible to use formulas to calculate the area, especially for irregular shapes. In such cases, estimate the area using square grids.

- Place the shape on a grid where each square represents 1 square unit. (e.g. 1 square cm).
- Count the number of full squares inside the shape.
- If there are any partial squares, estimate how many full squares they form together.

NCERT FOLDER

Whose Slice is Bigger? (NCERT Pg 146-147)

Q.1 Parth and Gini bought aam paapad (dried mango slice) from a shop. Their pieces looked like these. Both could not make out whose piece was bigger.

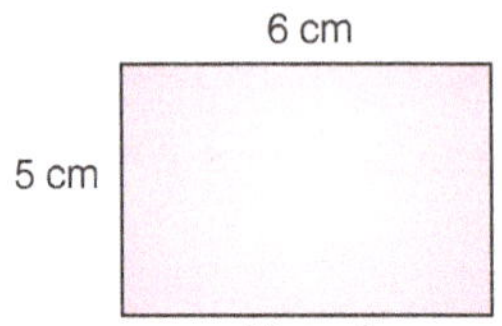

Piece *A*

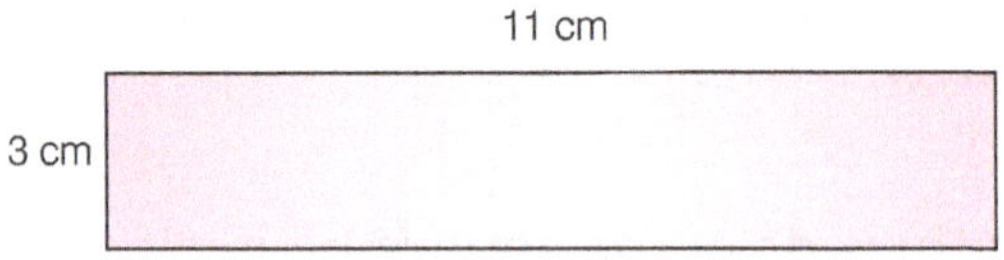

Piece *B*

(i) Suggest some ways to find out whose piece is bigger. Discuss.

(ii) Altogether how many squares can be arranged on piece *A*?

(iii) The area of piece *A* = ____ square cm

(iv) In the same way, find the area of piece *B*.

(v) Who had the bigger piece? How much bigger?

Ans. (i) Following are some ideas to show that whose piece is bigger.

Idea I

First cut the piece *B* into three parts as shown below

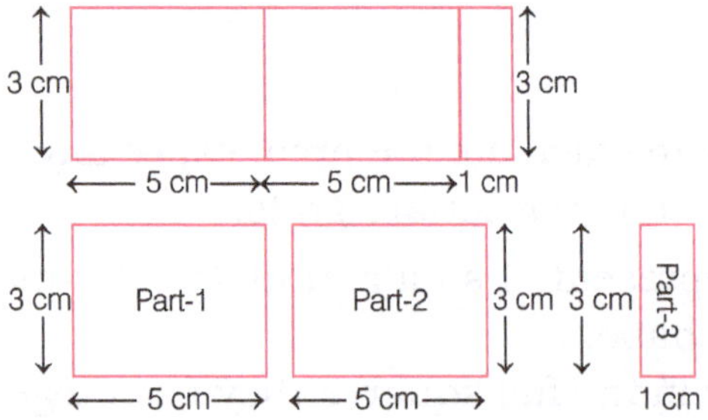

Now, put Part-1 and Part-2 on the top of piece *A*.

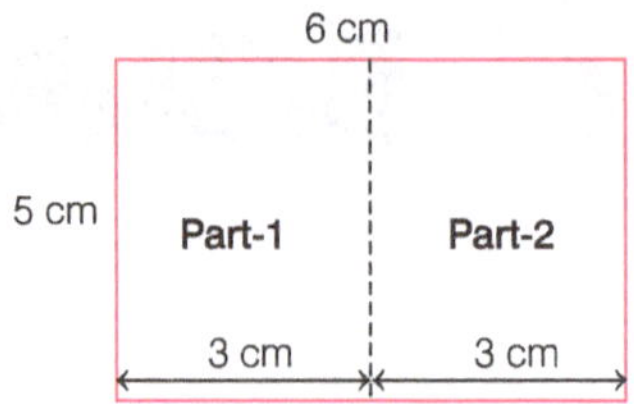

Piece *A*

Conclusion You will notice that they completely cover piece *A*. However, part 3 is still remaining which indicates that piece *B* is larger than piece *A*.

Idea II

We can divide pieces *A* and *B* into 1 cm squares as follows.

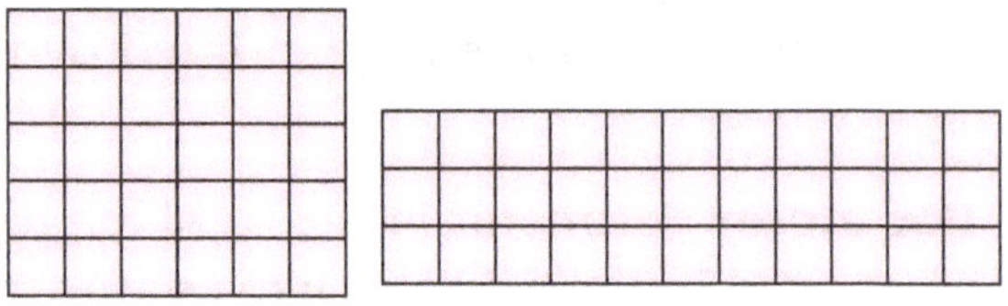
Piece *A* Piece *B*

Let's count how many small boxes are in each piece. Piece *A* has 30 boxes and piece *B* has 33 boxes. This means piece *B* is bigger than piece *A*.

(ii) 30 squares can be arranged on piece *A*.

(iii) Piece *A* can be divided into 30 boxes of side 1 cm.
So, the area of piece *A* = 30 square cm.

(iv) Piece *B* can be divided into 33 boxes of 1 cm.
So, the area of piece *B* = 33 square cm.

(v) Piece *B* is bigger by (33 – 30) = 3 square cm.

Cover with Stamps (NCERT Pg 147-148)

Q.2 This stamp has an area of 4 square cm. Guess how many such stamps will cover this big rectangle.

* *Students can write alternate answer as per their choice.*

Check your guess

(i) Measure the coloured rectangle. It is ______ cm long.

(ii) How many stamps can be placed along its length?

(iii) How wide is the rectangle?

(iv) How many stamps can be placed along its width?

(v) How many stamps are needed to cover the rectangle?

(vi) How close was your earlier guess? Discuss.

(vii) What is the area of the rectangle?

(viii) What is the perimeter of the rectangle?

Ans. *My guess is 20 stamps.

(i) It is 14 cm long.

(ii) 7 stamps can be placed along its length.

(iii) The width of the rectangle is 8 cm.

(iv) 4 stamps can be placed along its width.

(v) 28 stamps are needed to cover the rectangle.

(vi) It was pretty close.

(vii) Area of rectangle $= 14 \times 8 = 112$ square cm.

(viii) Perimeter of the rectangle = Sum of all of its sides

$= 14$ cm $+ 8$ cm $+ 14$ cm $+ 8$ cm $= 44$ cm

So, the perimeter of the rectangle is 44 cm.

Practice Time (NCERT Pg 148-149)

Q.3 Arbaz plans to tile his kitchen floor with green square tiles. Each side of the tile is 10 cm. His kitchen is 220 cm in length and 180 cm wide. How many tiles will he need?

Ans. Area of floor = Length × Breadth

$= 220$ cm $\times 180$ cm

$= 39600$ square cm

Area of tile = Side × Side

$= 10$ cm $\times 10$ cm $= 100$ square cm

$\therefore$ Total number of tiles required to cover the floor $= \dfrac{\text{Area of floor}}{\text{Area of one tile}} = \dfrac{39600}{100} = 396$

So, he will need 396 tiles to cover his kitchen floor.

Q.4 The fencing of a square garden is 20 m in length. How long is one side of the garden?

Ans. $\because$ Fencing of a square garden = Perimeter of square garden

$\therefore$ Perimeter of square garden = 20 m

$\Rightarrow 4 \times \text{Side} = 20$ m

$\text{Side} = \dfrac{20}{4}$ m $= 5$ m

$\therefore$ Length of each side is 5 m.

Q.5 A thin wire 20 centimetres long is formed into a rectangle. If the width of this rectangle is 4 centimetres, what is its length?

Ans. Let l be the length of rectangle.

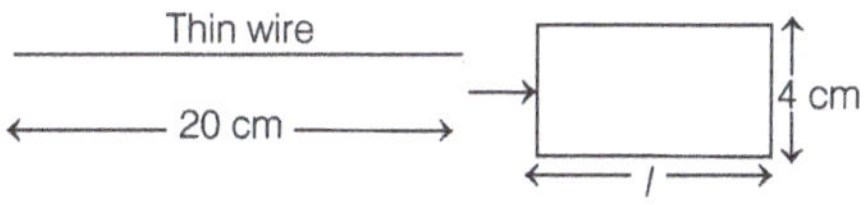

$\because$ The rectangle is formed with the help of 20 cm long thin wire.

$\therefore$ Length of wire = Perimeter of rectangle

$\Rightarrow \quad 20 = 2\,[l + b] \Rightarrow 20 = 2[l + 4]$

$\Rightarrow \quad l + 4 = \dfrac{20}{2} = 10 \Rightarrow l = 10 - 4$

$\Rightarrow \quad l = 6$ cm

So, the length of the rectangle is 6 cm.

Q.6 A square carrom board has a perimeter of 320 cm. How much is its area?

Ans. $\because$ Perimeter of square carrom board $= 320$ cm

$\therefore \quad 4 \times \text{Side} = 320$ cm

$\Rightarrow \quad \text{Side} = \dfrac{320}{4}$ cm $= 80$ cm

Now, area of square carrom board

= Side × Side

$= 80$ cm $\times 80$ cm $= 6400$ square cm

So, the area of a square carrom board is 6400 square cm.

Q.7 How many tiles like the triangle given, here will fit in the white design?
Area of design = ______ square cm

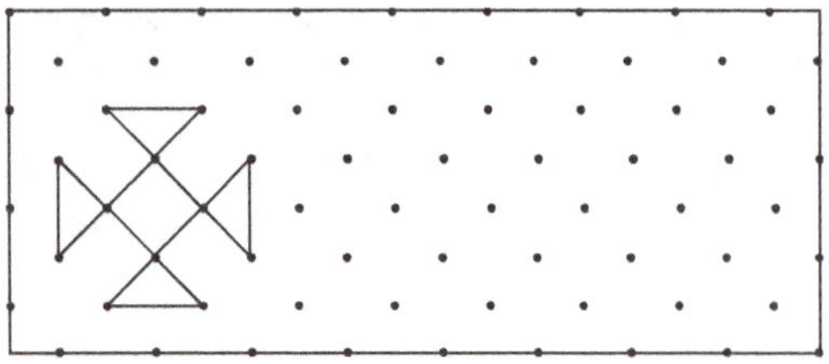

 This triangle is half of the cm square.

Ans. In the given design, 6 triangle tiles are needed.

Area of design = 6 × [Half of area of square]

$$= 6 \times \left[\frac{1}{2} \text{square cm}\right] = 3 \text{ square cm}$$

So, the area of design is 3 square cm.

Q.8 Make your own designs of area 4 and 6 square cm.

Ans. * Since, two triangles make 1 square cm. Therefore, for design of 4 square cm, we need $4 \times 2 = 8$ triangles.

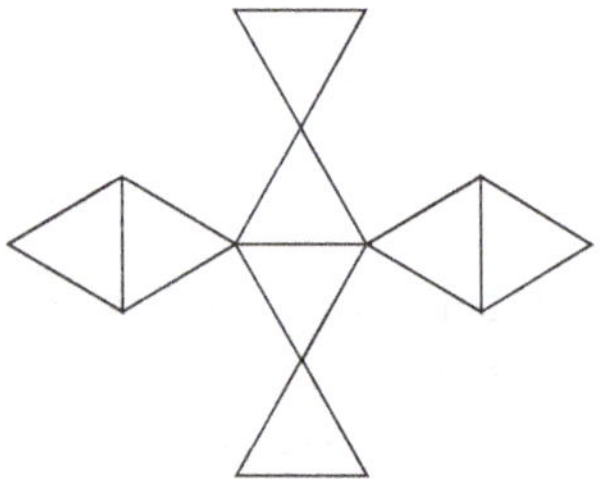

For design of area 6 square cm, we need $6 \times 2 = 12$ triangles

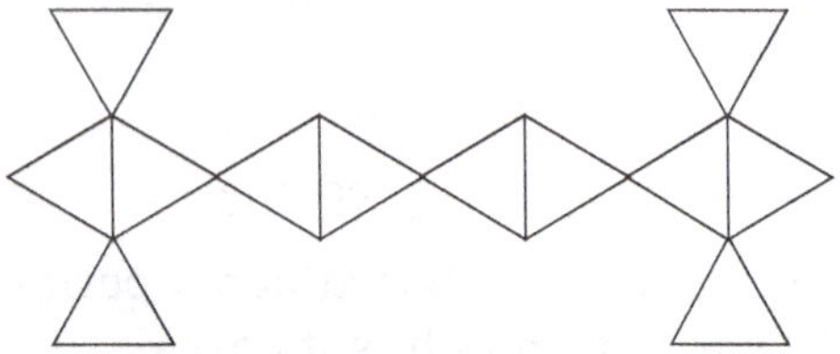

Q.9 Sanya, Aarushi, Manav and Kabir made greeting cards. Complete the table for their cards.

Whose card	Length	Width	Perimeter	Area
Sanya	10 cm	8 cm		
Manav	11 cm		44 cm	
Aarushi		8 cm		80 square cm
Kabir			40 cm	100 square cm

Ans. For Sanya

Given, length = 10 cm and width = 8 cm

∴ Perimeter = 2 [Length + Width]

$= 2[10 + 8] = 2 \times 18 = 36$ cm

Area = Length × Width

$= 10 \text{ cm} \times 8 \text{ cm} = 80$ square cm

For Manav

Given, length = 11 cm

Perimeter = 44 cm

⇒ 2 [Length + Width] = 44 cm

$$\Rightarrow \quad 11 + \text{width} = \frac{44}{2} \text{ cm} = 22 \text{ cm}$$

∵ Width = 22 cm − 11 cm = 11 cm

∴ Area = Length × Width

$= 11 \times 11 = 121$ square cm.

For Aarushi

Given, width = 8 cm

Area = 80 square cm

⇒ Length × Width = 80 square cm

$$\Rightarrow \text{Length} = \frac{80}{8} \text{ cm} = 10 \text{ cm}$$

and perimeter = 2 [Length + Width]

= 2[10 cm + 8 cm]

$= 2 \times 18$ cm = 36 cm

For Kabir

Given, perimeter = 40 cm

⇒ 2[Length + Width] = 40 cm

$$\Rightarrow \text{Length} + \text{Width} = \frac{40}{2} \text{ cm}$$

⇒ Length + Width = 20 cm ...(i)

and area = 100 square cm

⇒ Length × Width = 100 square cm ...(ii)

Therefore, the only length = 10 cm and width = 10 cm satisfy Eqs. (i) and (ii).

Whose card	Length	Width	Perimeter	Area
Sanya	10 cm	8 cm	36 cm	80 cm^2
Manav	11 cm	11 cm	44 cm	121 cm^2
Aarushi	10 cm	8 cm	36 cm	80 cm^2
Kabir	10 cm	10 cm	40 cm	100 cm^2

My Belt is Longest! (NCERT Pg 149-150)

Q.10 Take a thick paper sheet of length 14 cm and width 9 cm. You can also use an old postcard.

(i) What is its area? What is its perimeter?

(ii) Now, cut strips of equal sizes out of it.

Ans. (i) Area of sheet = Length × Width

$$= 14 \text{ cm} \times 9 \text{ cm} = 126 \text{ cm}^2$$

Perimeter of sheet = 2 (Length + Width)

$$= 2(14 + 9) = 46 \text{ cm}$$

*(ii) Let us cut the sheet in strips of width 1 cm. We can have 9 strips of width 1 cm.

Q.11 Using tape join the strips, end to end, to make a belt.

(i) How long is your belt?

(ii) What is its perimeter?

(iii) Whose belt is the longest in the class?

Ans. *(i) Strips of width 1 cm.

Here, we get 9 strips of width 1 cm.

Now, length

$$= 14 + 14 + 14 + 14 + 14 + 14 + 14 + 14 + 14$$

$$= 9 \times 14 = 126 \text{ cm}$$

*(ii) Length of belt = 126 cm

Width of belt = 1 cm

Perimeter = 2 (Length + Width)

$$= 2(126 + 1) \text{ cm} = 254 \text{ cm}$$

*(iii) My friend's belt is longest having width of 0.5 cm.

Discuss (NCERT Pg 150)

Q.12 (i) Why did some of your friends get longer belts than others?

(ii) Is the area of your belt the same as the area of the postcard? Why or why not?

(iii) What will you do to get a longer belt next time?

Ans. (i) Because the width of their belts are smaller than that of the other's belts.

*(ii) Yes, the area is same because postcard was not wasted in cutting.

(iii) Next time, I shall get the longer belt by ensuring that the width of my belt should be narrower than the others.

Puzzle-Pass through a Postcard (NCERT Pg 150)

Q.13 Can you think of how to cut a postcard so that you can pass through it? (See photo.) If you have tried hard enough and still not got it... look for the answer somewhere ahead.

Ans. *Pass through a postcard.

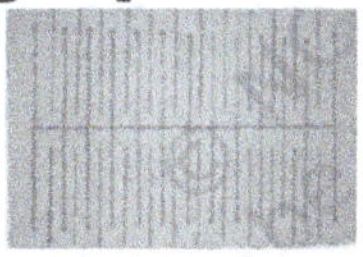

Draw lines on a postcard like above figure.

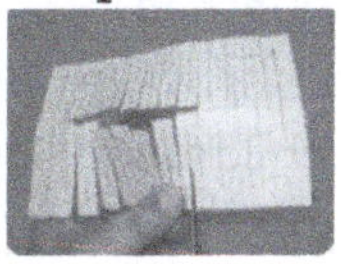

Cut the postcard only on the lines.

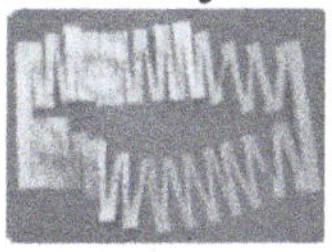

Now, you can pass through it.

People people Everywhere (NCERT Pg 151-152)

Q.14 With four Math-Magic books in a line, you can get the length of around one metre 9 cm. You can play this game in a ground. Make two squares of one square metre each.

Divide your class in two teams. Ready to play!

(i) How many of you can sit in one square metre?

(ii) How many of you can stand in it?

(iii) Which team could make more children stand in their square? How many?

(iv) Which team could make more children sit in their square? How many?

Ans. *(i) Three

*(ii) Six

*(iii) Team *A*. They are six in numbers.

*(iv) Team *A*. They are four in numbers.

Q.15 Measure the length of the floor of your classroom in metres. Also, measure the width.

(i) What is the area of the floor of your classroom in square metres?

(ii) How many children are there in your class?

(iii) How many children can sit in one square metre?

(iv) If you want to move around easily, then how many children do you think should be there in one square metre?

Ans. * Length = 5 m

Width = 4 m

(i) Area = Length × Width = 5 m × 4 m

= 20 square m

(ii) 60 children

(iii) Number of children in 1 square m

$= \frac{\text{Total children}}{\text{Area of floor}} = \frac{60}{20} = 3$

So, 1 children can sit in one square metre.

(iv) To move around easily, I think 2 children should be in one square metre space.

Q.16 Can you imagine how big a square of side 1 km is! It has an area of _______ square km. Guess how many people can live on that.

Ans. * Area = 1 km × 1 km = 1 square km

I think 550 people can live on that.

Share the Land (NCERT Pg 152-153)

Q.17 Nasreena is a farmer who wants to divide her land equally among her three children - Chumki, Jhumri and Imran. She wants to divide the land, so that each piece of land has one tree. Her land looks like this.

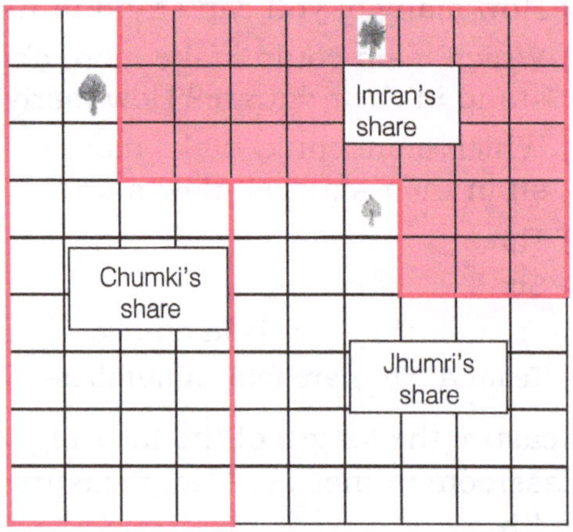

(i) Can you divide the land equally? Show how you will divide it. Remember each person has to get a tree. Colour each person's piece of land differently.

(ii) If each square on this page is equal to 1 square metre of land, how much land will each of her children get?

______ square m

Ans. (i) Yes, I can divide the 1 and equally.

Total number of boxes = 90

Number of children = 3

So, each children will get $= \frac{90}{3} = 30$ boxes

(ii) Each children has 30 boxes. Also, each square is of 1 square metre of land.

$1 \times 30 = 30$ square metres land each of her children will get.

Q.18 Chumki, Jhumri and Imran need wire to make a fence.

(i) Who will need the longest wire for fencing?

(ii) How much wire in all will the three need?

Ans. (i) Perimeter of Chumki's land

$= (9 + 4 + 6 + 2 + 3 + 2)$ m = 26 m

Perimeter of Jhumri's land

$= (6 + 6 + 4 + 3 + 2 + 3)$ m= 24 m

Perimeter of Imran's land

$= (3 + 5 + 8 + 3 + 5 + 2)$ m

= 26 m

It can be easily observed that Chumki and Imran need the longest wire for fencing.

(ii) Total wire needed = 26 m + 24 m + 26 m

= 76 m

So, they need 76 m wire.

Practice time (NCERT Pg 153-154)

Q.19 Look at the table. If you were to write the area of each of these which column would you choose? Make a (✓).

Ans.

	Square cm	Square metre	Square km
Handkerchief	✓		
Sari		✓	
Page of your book	✓		
School land		✓	
Total land of a city			✓
Door of your classroom		✓	
Chair seat	✓		
Blackboard		✓	
Indian flag	✓		
Land over which a river flows			✓

Q.20 Draw a square of 9 square cm. Write A on it. Draw another square with double the side. Write B on it

(i) The perimeter of square A is ______ cm.

(ii) The side of square B is _______ cm.

(iii) The area of square B is ______ square cm.

(iv) The area of square B is _______ times the area of square A.

(v) The perimeter of square B is _____ cm.

(vi) The perimeter of square B is ________ times the perimeter of square A.

Ans.

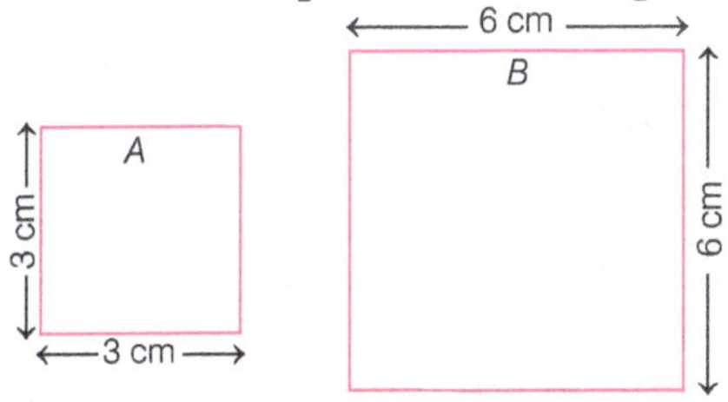

(i) Perimeter of square A
$= 3\text{ cm} + 3\text{ cm} + 3\text{ cm} + 3\text{ cm} = 12\text{ cm}$

(ii) The side of square B is 6 cm.

(iii) Area of square B = Side × Side
$= 6\text{ cm} \times 6\text{ cm} = 36$ square cm

(iv) Area of square A = Side × Side
$= 3\text{ cm} \times 3\text{ cm} = 9$ square cm

and area of square B
= 36 square cm = 4 × (9 square cm)
= 4 × (Area of square A)

The area of square B is 4 times the area of square A.

(v) Perimeter of square B
$= 6\text{ cm} + 6\text{ cm} + 6\text{ cm} + 6\text{ cm} = 24\text{ cm}$

(vi) ∵ Perimeter of square $B = 24$ cm
$= 2 \times (12\text{ cm}) = 2 \times$ (Perimeter of square A)

The perimeter of square B is 2 times the perimeter of square A.

Thread Play (NCERT Pg 155)

Q.21 Take a 15 cm long thread. Make different shapes by joining its ends on this sheet.

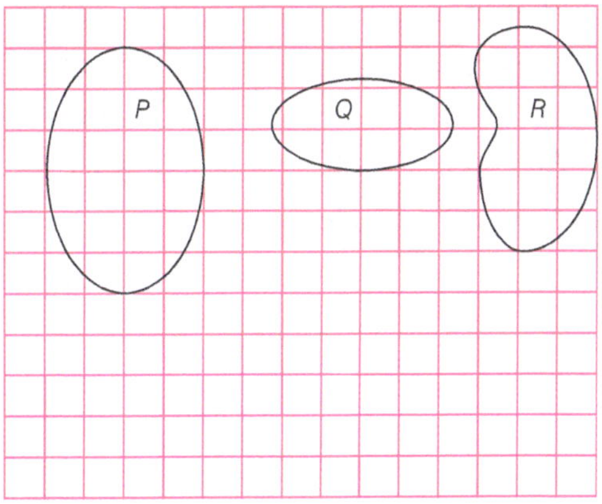

(i) Which shape has the biggest area? How much? What is the perimeter of this shape?

(ii) Which shape has the smallest area? How much? What is the perimeter of this shape?

(iii) Also, make a triangle, a square, a rectangle and a circle. Find which shape has biggest area and which has the smallest.

Ans. (i) **For shape *P***

Area $= 8 + \frac{1}{2} \times 4 + 8 = 8 + 2 + 8 = 18$ square cm

For shape *Q*

Area $= 3 + \frac{1}{2} \times 0 + 5 = 3 + 0 + 5 = 8$ square cm

For shape *R*

Area $= 5 + \frac{1}{2} \times 2 + 6 = 5 + 1 + 6 = 12$ square cm

Hence, shape P has the biggest area.

Perimeter of shape P is 15 cm.

(ii) Shape Q has the smallest area which is equal to 8 cm^2.

Perimeter of shape $Q = 15$ cm

(iii)

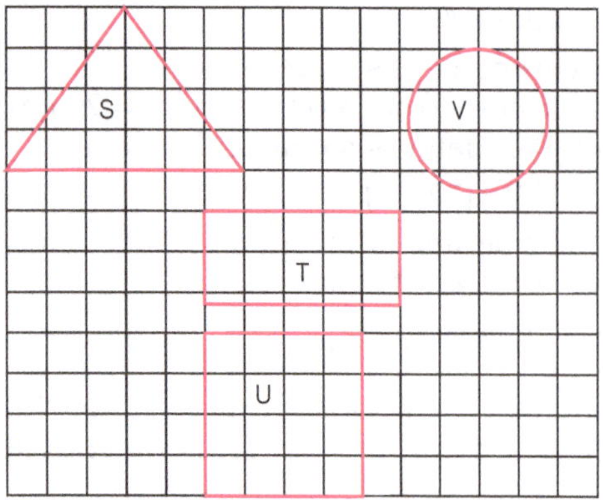

Area of triangle S $= 6 + 4 \times \frac{1}{2} + 2 = 6 + 2 + 2$

$= 10$ square cm

Area of square U $= 4 \times 4 = 16$ square cm

Area of rectangle T $= 10 + \frac{1}{2} \times 5$

$= 10 + 2.5 = 12.5$ square cm

Area of circle V $= 4 + 2 + 4 \times \frac{1}{2}$

$= 4 + 2 + 2 = 8$ square cm

So, square has biggest area and circle has smallest area (roughly).

Save the Birds (NCERT Pg 156-157)

Q.22 There are two beautiful lakes near a village. People come for boating and picnics in both the lakes. The village Panchayat is worried that with the noise of the boats the birds will stop coming. The Panchayat wants motor boats in only one lake. The other lake will be saved for the birds to make their nests.

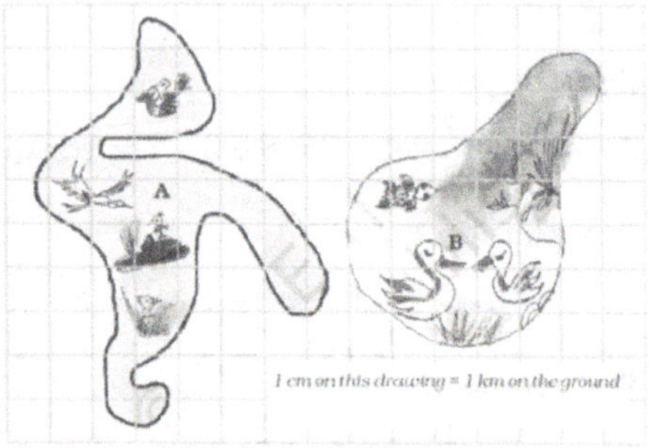

(i) How many cm is the length of the boundary of lake A in the drawing? _______ (use thread to find out).

(ii) What is the length of the boundary of lake B in the drawing?

(iii) How many kilometres long is the actual boundary of lake A?

(iv) How many kilometres long is the actual boundary of lake B?

(v) A longer boundary around the lake will help more birds to lay their eggs. So, which lake should be kept for birds? Which lake should be used for boats?

(vi) Find the area of lake B on the drawing in square cm. What is its actual area in square km?

Ans. (i) 33 cm

(ii) 26 cm

(iii) $\because$ 1 cm on drawing = 1 km on ground

$\therefore$ 33 cm on drawing $= (33 \times 1)$ km $= 33$ km

Thus, the actual length of boundary of lake A is 33 km.

(iv) $\because$ 1 cm on drawing = 1 km on ground

$\therefore$ 26 cm on drawing $= (26 \times 1)$ km $= 26$ km

Thus, the actual length of boundary of lake B is 26 km.

(v) Clearly, lake A has a longer edge than lake B. This makes lake A good for birds and lake B better for boats.

(vi) Area of lake B $= 15 + \frac{1}{2} \times 3 + 8$

$= 15 + 1.5 + 8 = 24.5$ square cm

$\because$ 1 cm on drawing = 1 km on ground

$\therefore$ 24.5 cm $= (24.5 \times 1)$ km $= 24.5$ km

Thus, the actual area of lake B is 24.5 square km.

King's Story (NCERT Pg 157-158)

Q.23 The king was very happy with carpenters Cheggu and Anar. They had made a very big and beautiful bed for him. So, as gifts the king wanted to give some land to Cheggu and some gold to Anar. Cheggu was happy. He took 100 metres of wire and tried to make different rectangles. He made a 10 m × 40 m rectangle. Its area was 400 square metres. So, he next made a 30 m × 20 m rectangle.

(i) What is its area? Is it more than the first rectangle?

(ii) What other rectangles can he make with 100 metres of wire? Discuss which of these rectangles will have the biggest area.

Ans. (i) Area of 30 m × 20 m rectangle

$= 30 \text{ m} \times 20 \text{ m} = 600$ square m

which is clearly more than the area of first rectangle.

*(ii) Following are the rectangles which can be made with 100 metres.

Rectangle with length 20 m and width 30 m.

Area $= 20 \text{ m} \times 30 \text{ m} = 600$ square m

Rectangle with length 45 m and width 5 m

Area $= 45\text{m} \times 5\text{m} = 225$ square m

Rectangle with length 25 m and width 25 m.

Area $= 25 \text{ m} \times 25 \text{ m} = 625$ square m

and so on.

The rectangle having length = Breadth or a square will have the biggest area.

Q.24 Cheggu's wife asked him to make a circle with the wire. She knew it had an area of 800 square metres. Why did Cheggu not choose a rectangle? Explain.

Ans. Cheggu did not choose a rectangle because none of the rectangle will have an area of 800 square metres.

Q.25 Anar also tried many different ways to make a boundary for 800 square metres of land. He made rectangles A, B and C of different sizes. Find out the length of the boundary of each. How much gold wire will he get for these rectangles?

A. 

Gold wire for A = ____ metres

B. 

Gold wire for B = ____ metres

C. 

Gold wire for C = ____ metres

But, then Anar made an even longer rectangle.... See how long!.

D.

8000 m × 0.1 m

So, he will get ___ metres of gold wire!!

Ans. Rectangle A

Perimeter of rectangle A

$= 2 \text{ (Length + Width)}$

$= 2(40 + 20) \text{ m} = 120 \text{ m}$

Thus, gold wire for A = 120 metres

Rectangle B 

Perimeter of rectangle B

$= 2 \text{ (Length + Width)}$

$= 2\ (80 + 10) \text{ m} = 180 \text{ m}$

Thus, gold wire for B = 180 metres.

Rectangle C

Perimeter of rectangle C

$= 2 \text{ (Length + Width)}$

$= 2(800 + 1) \text{ m} = 1602 \text{ m}$

Thus, gold wire for C = 1602 metres.

Rectangle D

8000 m × 0.1 m

Perimeter of rectangle D

$= 2 \text{ (Length + Width)}$

$= 2(8000 + 0.1) \text{ m}$

$= 2 \times 8000.1 \text{ m} = 16000.2 \text{ m}$

So, he will get 16000.2 metres of gold wires for rectangle D.

Q.26 Do you understand why the king fainted!!!

Ans. The king fainted because he has no idea how to arrange so much gold.

Q.27 Can you make a rectangle with a still longer boundary? I made a rectangle 1 cm wide and 80000 m long. Imagine how long that boundary will be !!! With that much gold wire I can become the king!

Ans. Yes, a rectangle with a longer boundary can be made.

Boundary of rectangle 1 cm $= \dfrac{1}{100 \text{ m}}$

$= 0.01 \text{ m}$

Length = 80000 m

$\therefore$ Perimeter $= 2 \text{ (Length + Width)}$

$= 2(80000 + 0.01) \text{ m}$

$= 2 \times (80000.01) \text{ m}$

$= 160000.02 \text{ m}$

PRACTICE QUESTIONS

1. True or False
   (i) The area of a rectangle is calculated by adding its length and width.
   (ii) A square is a special type of rectangle where all sides are equal.
   (iii) The area of a shape can never be a negative number.

2. Multiple choice questions
   (i) Which of the following is the unit used to measure area?
   (a) Metre (b) Kilometre
   (c) Square metre (d) Centimetre
   (ii) If a square has a side length of 4 cm, what is its area?
   (a) 8 square cm (b) 12 square cm
   (c) 16 square cm (d) 20 square cm
   (iii) What is the length of the rectangle whose perimeter is 10 cm and width is 3 cm?
   (a) 2 cm (b) 6 cm
   (c) 4 cm (d) 5 cm

3. Odd-One out
   (i) (a) Square metre (b) Square centimetre
   (c) Square kilometre (d) Metre
   (ii) (a) Rectangle (b) Circle
   (c) Square (d) Triangle

4. Word problems
   (i) A rectangular garden has a length of 10 metres and a width of 6 metres. What is the area and perimeter of the garden?
   (ii) Tarun wants to cover his rectangular table. Which has an area of 36 square feet. If the length of the table is 9 feet, what is the width of the table?

ANSWERS & SOLUTIONS

1. (i) False (ii) True
   (iii) True

2. (i) (c)
   (ii) (c) Area of square = Side × Side
   $= 4 \text{ cm} \times 4 \text{ cm}$ [$\because$ Side = 4 cm]
   $= 16$ square cm
   (iii) (a) We have,
   Perimeter of rectangle = 10 cm
   Width of rectangle = 3 cm
   We know that
   perimeter of rectangle
   $= 2 \times$ (Length + Width)
   $\Rightarrow \quad 10 = 2 \times (\text{Length} + 3 \text{ cm})$
   $\therefore$ Length $= \frac{10}{2} - 3 = 2$ cm

3. (i) (d) (ii) (b)

4. (i) We have,
   length of the rectangular garden = 10 m
   and width of the rectangular garden = 6 m
   We know that
   the area of rectangle = Length × Width
   $\therefore$ The area of rectangular garden
   $= 10 \text{ m} \times 6 \text{ m}$
   $= 60$ square metres
   $\because$ Perimeter of rectangle
   $= 2$ (Length + Width)
   $\therefore$ The perimeter of rectangular garden
   $= 2 (10 \text{ m} + 6 \text{ m})$
   $= 32$ m
   (ii) We have,
   the area of Tarun's rectangular table
   = 36 square feet
   Length of the table = 9 feet
   $\because$ Area of rectangle = Length × Width
   $\Rightarrow$ 36 square feet = 9 feet × width
   $\Rightarrow$ Width $= \frac{36}{9}$ feet
   $= 4$ feet
   Hence, the width of the table is 4 feet.

CHAPTER 12 SMART CHARTS

Data

Data is a collection of facts or informations. Data can be numbers, words, measurements or observations and it helps us understand and analyse things around us.

e.g. The number of students in a class.

- The favourite fruits of students.
- The temperature of a city on different days.

Organising data in a table

Before drawing charts, data is often organised into a table. A table helps present the data in an orderly way, making it easier to understand.

e.g. We can organise the data that is number of students and their favourite colours into table.

Colour	Number of students
Red	5
Blue	7
Green	4

Tally marks

Tally marks are simple lines used to represent and count data. Every fifth mark is drawn diagonally across the previous four lines to form a group of five.

Chapati chart

A chapati chart shows the data in circular graph. e.g. The following chapati represents the number of students in class with their favourite sports:

Cricket - 45, Tennis - 13, Hockey - 12, Golf - 5, Basketball - 25

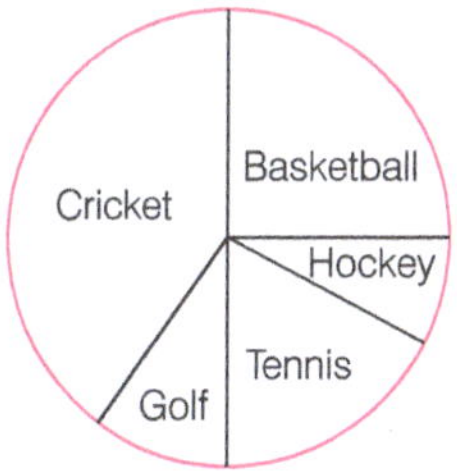

Bar chart

A bar chart is a chart that uses rectangle bars to represent data. The length of each bar corresponds to the quantity of the data.

Family tree

A family tree is a graphical or visual representation of our ancestors.

NCERT FOLDER

Chi-Chi, Meow- Meow (NCERT Pg 159)

Q.1 Yamini did a project 'Animals and Birds'. She asked each child of her class about one favourite pet animal. She used **tally marks** to record each answer. e.g. If someone said 'cat', she put one line | in front of 'cats'. When someone said 'cat' again, she added a line. So ⌐ means two cats and ⧄ means 5 cats. In all 24 children said 'cat' was their favourite animal. Help Yamini complete the table.

Animal	Tally Marks	Number
Cats	⧄⧄⧄⧄□	24
Dogs	⧄⧄⧄⧄⧄⧄⌐	
Rabbits	⧄⧄	
Cows	⧄⧄⧄⧄⌐	
Parrots	⧄⊓	
Goats	⧄⧄⧄⧄	
Squirrel	⧄⧄⧄	

(i) Look at the tally marks and write the number for each animal in the table. How many children in all did Yamini talk to?

(ii) Which is the most favourite pet animal in this table?

(iii) Which pet will you like to have? What will you name it? Which other animals can be kept at home? Discuss.

Ans. Following is the completed table

Animal	Tally Marks	Number
Cats	⧄⧄⧄⧄□	24
Dogs	⧄⧄⧄⧄⧄⧄⌐	32
Rabbits	⧄⧄	10
Cows	⧄⧄⧄⧄⌐	22
Parrots	⧄⊓	8
Goats	⧄⧄⧄⧄	20
Squirrel	⧄⧄⧄	15
	Total	131

(i) We have completed the table above.
Yamini talked to 131 children.

(ii) Dog is the most favourite pet animal in this table.

*(iii) I like dog. I would name it 'Maggie'. Cats, parrots and rabbits are the other animals that can be kept at home.

Making Tally Marks on the Road (NCERT Pg 160-161)

Q.2 Sumita stood on the road for half an hour and counted the number of vehicles passing by. She made a tally mark for each vehicle. This helped her in counting quickly the total number of vehicles in each group.

Vehicle	Tally Marks	Number
Cycle	⧄⧄⧄⧄⧄⊓	
Car	⧄⧄⌐	
Auto rickshaw	⧄⧄⧄⊓	
Bus	⧄⧄⧄	
Cycle rickshaw	⧄⧄⧄⧄□	
Truck	⧄|	

(i) Write the number of each vehicle in the table.

(ii) How many vehicles in all did Sumita see on the road in half an hour?

(iii) Number of auto rickshaws is thrice the number of trucks — True/False?

(iv) Make tally marks for 7 more buses and 2 more trucks.

Ans. (i) Following is the complete table

Vehicle	Tally Marks	Number
Cycle	⧄⧄⧄⧄⧄⊓	28
Car	⧄⧄⌐	12
Auto rickshaw	⧄⧄⧄⊓	18
Bus	⧄⧄⧄	15
Cycle rickshaw	⧄⧄⧄⧄□	24
Truck	⧄|	6
	Total	103

** Students can write alternate answer as per their choice.*

(ii) Total number of vehicles seen by Sumita on the road in half an hour is 103.

(iii) True, number of auto rickshaws
$= 18 = 3 \times 6$
$= 3 \times$ (total number of trucks)

(iv) Tally marks for 7 more buses

 = 22

Tally marks for 2 more trucks

 = 8

Try Yourself (NCERT Pg 161)

Q.3 Take a round in your colony. Find out how many types of trees you can see there. Do you know their names? You can make drawings. Use tally marks to note the number of different trees!

Ans. * I found six types of trees which are Neem, Peepal, Ashoka, Mango, Babool, Banyan.

Following is the tally marks table

Tree Name	Tally Marks	Number
Neem	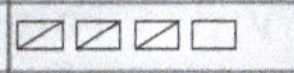	19
Peepal		7
Ashoka		9
Mango		20
Babool	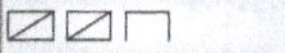	13
Banyan		12
	Total	80

Helping Hands (NCERT Pg 162-163)

Q.4 In the EVS period, the teacher asked children whether they help their parents at home. There were different answers. Children named the work in which they help their parents the most. The teacher collected their answers and made a table.

Help most in house work	Number of children
Going to the market	47
Washing utensils	15
Washing clothes	3
Making, serving food	25
Cleaning the house	10
Total children who said they help their parents	

Ans.

Help most in house work	Number of children
Going to the market	47
Washing utensils	15
Washing clothes	3
Making, serving food	25
Cleaning the house	10
Total children who said they help their parents	100

Q.5 You can fill the chapati chart to show the numbers given in the table.

Look and find out

Children who help in making or serving food are

(a) one-third of the total children

(b) half of the total children

(c) one-fourth of the total children

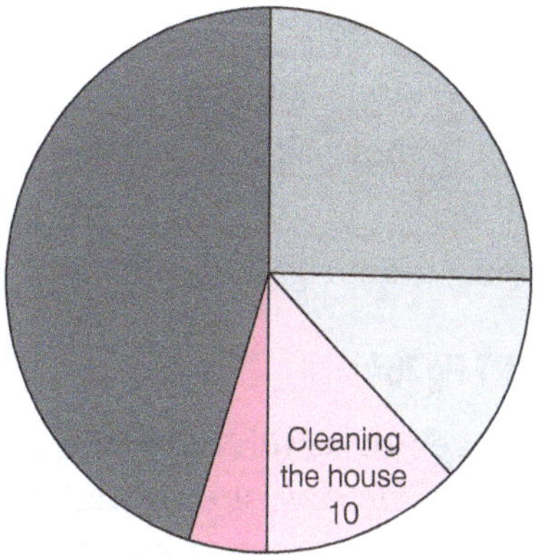

Ans. (c) one-fourth of the total children

Chapati Chart

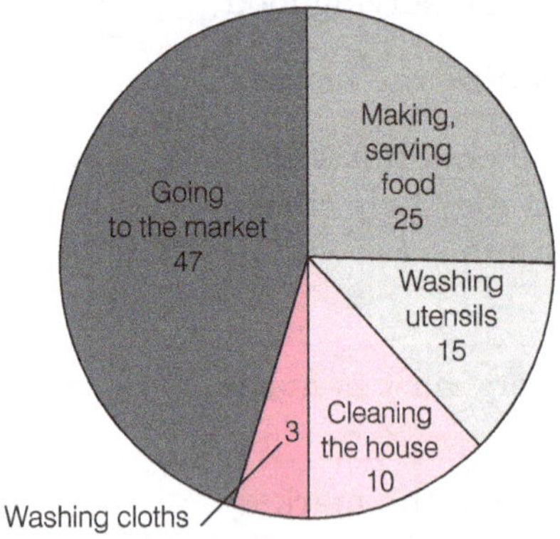

Q.6 Practice time-After school

Ask 10 of your friends about what they like to do most after school.

What they like to do after school	Number of friends
Watching TV	
Playing football	
Reading story books	

Ans. *

What they like to do after school	Number of friends
Watching TV	2
Playing football	4
Reading story books	1
Doing homework	1
Cycling	1
Playing indoor games	1

Ad Mad!! (NCERT Pg 164)

Q.7 Ragini loves to watch cartoons on television. One day she thought of counting the number of ads during the breaks. She found that in each break there were 14 advertisements. In 10 of those ads there were children as actors.

(i) Why do you think that children are used in so many ads?

(ii) Use tally marks to count the number of ads during a short break in a programme.

Were there ads during the news programme?

Ans. (i) Children are often used in ads because kids naturally attract attention, they can create warm and happy feeling and also parents might trust products more if they see happy children using them.

(ii) Tally marks used to count the number of ads during a short break in a programme are as follows.

∵ There were 14 advertisements.

∴ 

Yes, there were ads during news programme.

Try Yourself (NCERT Pg 164)

Q.8 (i) Next time when you watch your favourite TV programme, count the number of advertisements during each break. Use tally marks. Put a dot below the tally when you find children in any advertisement.

(ii) Compare with your friends. Do you get different answers?

Ans. *(i) A tally mark table is shown below. One dot represents advertisement with child.

Break	Tally Marks	Number of ads
First	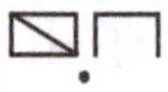	8
Second		11
Third		9
Fourth		12

*(ii) I got different answers after comparing with friends. This might happen because they are not watching the same programme on the TV.

Hot and Cold (NCERT Pg 165)

Q.9 Have you seen the weather report on TV or in a newspaper? These are two bar charts. These show the highest temperature (in degrees Celsius) in four cities, on two different days. The cities are Delhi, Shimla, Bangalore and Jaisalmer.

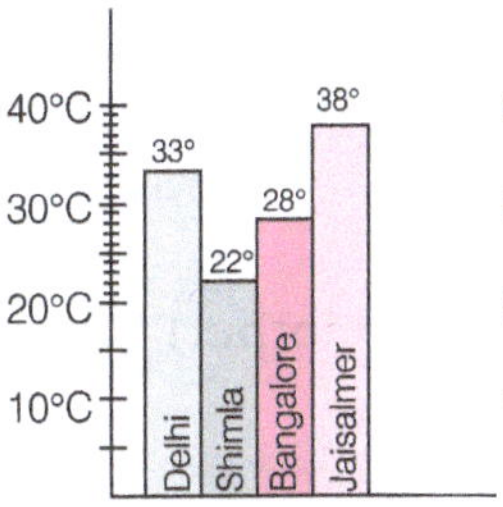

1 June

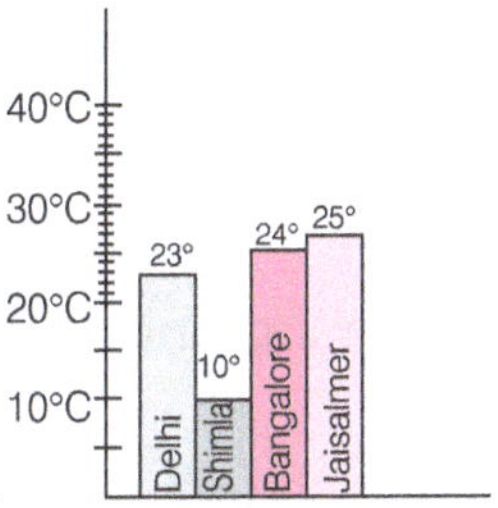

1 December

Find out from the bar chart–

(i) Which city is the hottest on 1 June?

(ii) Which city is the coldest on 1 December?

(iii) Which city shows little change in temperature on the two days, 1 June and 1 December.

Ans. (i) Jaisalmer is the hottest city on 1 June.

(ii) Shimla is the coldest city on 1 December.

(iii) Temperature of Bangalore city on 1 June = 28°C

and on 1 December = 24°C

Change in temperature = 28°C – 24°C = 4°C

So, Bangalore city shows little change in temperature on 1 June and 1 December.

Try Yourself (NCERT Pg 165)

Q.10 On any one day, choose any three cities and record their temperature from the TV or newspaper.

Make a bar chart in your notebook and ask your friends a few questions about it. See if they understand your chart!

Ans. *Let us draw the bar chart showing the highest temperature (in °C) in three cities which are Delhi, Jammu and Bangalore.

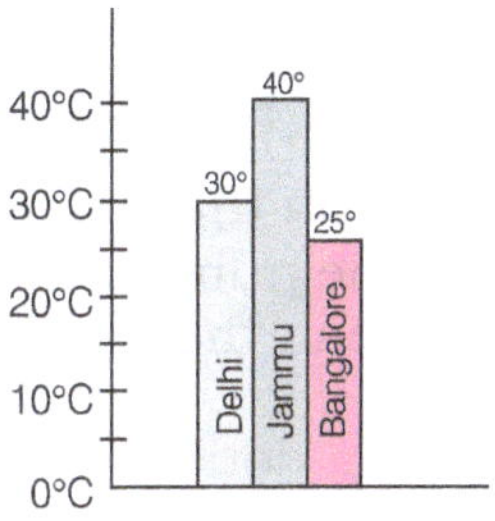

1 May

Questions for my friends :

(i) Which city has lowest temperature on 1 May?

(ii) Which city has highest temperature on 1 May?

(iii) What is the difference between the temperature of city Delhi and Bangalore on 1 May?

Ans.

(i) Bangalore (ii) Jammu

(iii) Temperature of Delhi on 1 May = 30°C

Temperature of Bangalore on 1 May = 25°C

Difference in the temperature = 30°C – 25°C = 5°C

All of my friends answered correctly. So, they understand the chart.

Rabbits in Australia (NCERT Pg 166)

Q.11 Earlier there were no rabbits in Australia. Rabbits were brought to Australia around the year 1780. At that time, there were no animals in Australia which ate rabbits. So, the rabbits began to multiply at a very fast rate. Imagine what they did to the crops!

The table shows how rabbits grew every year.

Time	Number of rabbits
Start	10
1 year	18
2 year	32
3 year	58
4 year	108
5 year	
6 year	

(i) After each year, the number of rabbits was

(a) a little less than double the number of rabbits in the last year.

(b) double the number in the last year.

(c) 8 more than the number in the last year.

(d) more than double the number of rabbits in the last year.

(ii) At the end of year 6, the number of rabbits was close to

(a) 400 (b) 6000 (c) 800

(iii) After which year did the number of rabbits cross 1000?

Ans. (i) (a) A little less than double the number of rabbits in the last year.

(ii) (a) 400

(iii) After the year 1788, the number of rabbits crosses 1000.

Family Tree (NCERT Pg 167-168)

Q.12 Madhav got confused. He couldn't imagine his mother's grandmother's mother! So, Madhav's mother made a family tree for him.

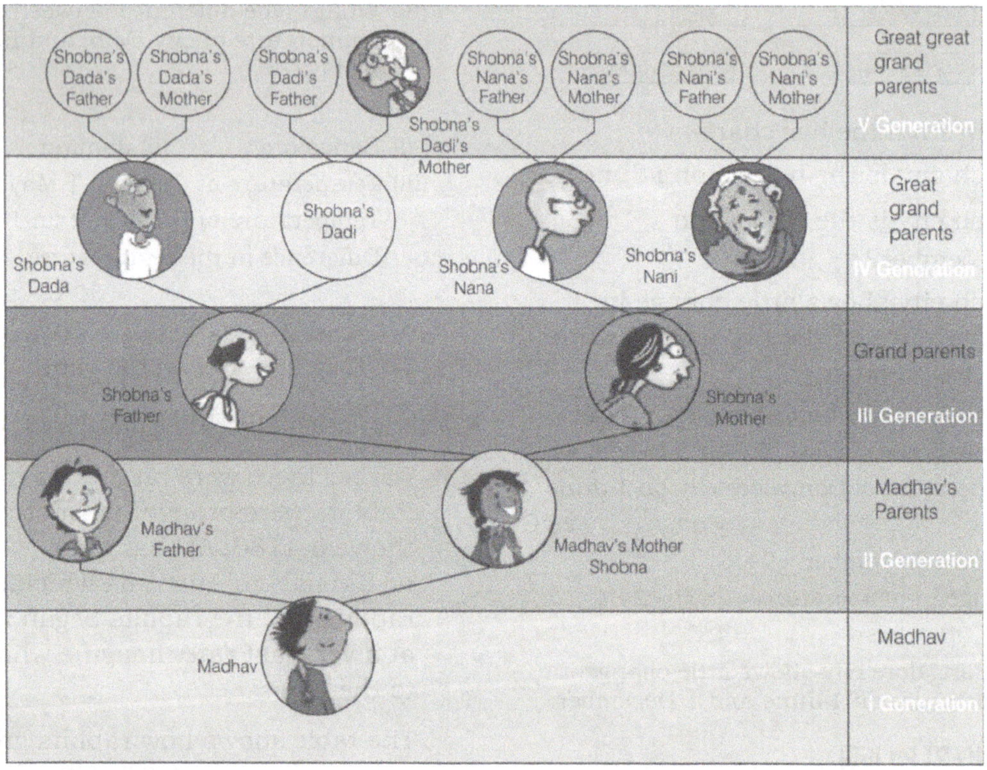

(i) How many grand parents in all does Shobna have?

(ii) How many great, great grand parents in all does Madhav have?

(iii) How many elders will be in the VII generation of his family?

(iv) If he takes his family tree forward, in which generation will he find 128 elders?

Ans. (i) Shobna has four grand parents.

(ii) Madhav has eight great, great grand parents in all.

(iii) $\because$ In VI generation $= 8 \times 2 = 16$

$\therefore$ In VII generation $= 16 \times 2 = 32$

So, there are 32 elders in the VII generation of his family.

(iv) VIII generation → $32 \times 2 = 64$

IX generation → $64 \times 2 = 128$

Thus, in the IX generation, the number of elders in Madhav's family will be 128.

Growth Chart of a Plant (NCERT Pg 168-169)

Q.13 Amit sowed a few seeds of moong dal in the ground. The height of the plant grew to 1.4 cm in the first four days. After that, it started growing faster. Amit measured the height of plant after every four days and put a dot on the chart. e.g. If you look at the dot marked on the fourth day, you can see on the left side scale that it is 1.4 cm high.

Now, look at the height of each dot in cm and check from the table if he has marked the dots correctly.

Day	**Length of the plant** (in cm)
0	0
4	1.4
8	5.3
12	9.5
16	10.2
20	10.9

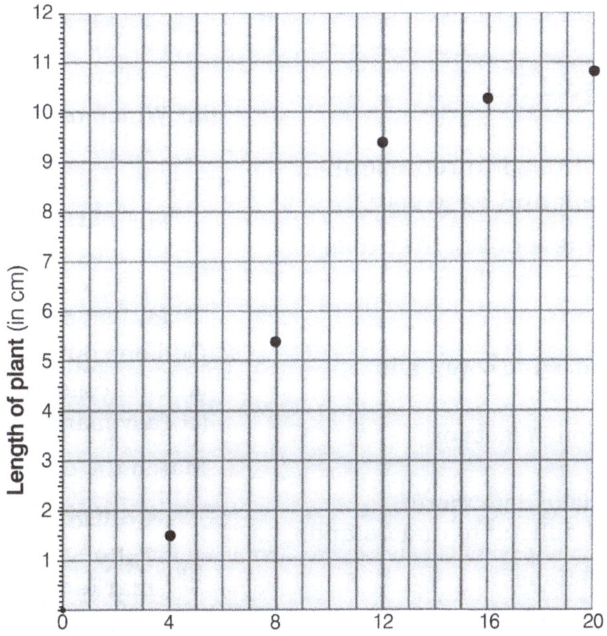

Find out from the growth chart

(i) Between which days did the length of the plant change the most?

(a) 0-4 (b) 4-8 (c) 8-12 (d) 12-16 (e) 16-20

(ii) What could be the length of this plant on the 14th day? Guess.

(a) 8.7cm (b) 9.9 cm (c) 10.2 cm (d) 10.5 cm

(iii) Will the plant keep growing all the time? What will be its length on the 100th day? Make a guess!

Ans. Here,

Day	Length of the plant (in cm)
0	0
4	1.4
8	5.3
12	9.5
16	10.2
20	10.9

Yes, he has marked the dots correctly on the growth chart.

(i) (c) 8-12

(ii) (c) 9.9 cm

*(iii) No, I think its length would be about (16-17) cm on 100th day.

PRACTICE QUESTIONS

1. Fill in the blanks

(i) A chart is a visual representation of ______ .

(ii) Tally marks are used to represent ______ in a quick and easy way.

(iii) A ______ graph is a chart that uses bars to represent the data.

2. True or False

(i) Tally marks are used to count and represent data.

(ii) Data is a collection of facts or information.

(iii) Charts help to make data more complicated and difficult to understand.

3. Multiple choice questions

(i) What is the main purpose of using tally marks?

(a) To represent words
(b) To count and represent data
(c) To create artwork
(d) To show time

(ii) How many tally marks are in a complete group?

(a) Two (b) Five
(c) Three (d) Four

(iii) Which of the following helps to visualise and interpre

t data more easily?

(a) Charts and graphs
(b) Long paragraphs
(c) Random numbers
(d) Text documents

4. Odd one out

(a) Data collection (b) Bar graph
(c) Tally marks (d) Drawing

5. Match the columns

	Column A		Column B
(i)	Tally marks	(a)	shows parts of a whole
(ii)	Chapati chart	(b)	used for counting and organising data
(iii)	Data table	(c)	represents quantities using vertical bars
(iv)	Bar chart	(d)	organises data in rows and columns for clarity

6. Word problems

(i) A survey was conducted in a park to find out the number of people who preferred different types of sports. The results are

Type of games	Number of people
Football	10
Basketball	15
Cricket	12
Tennis	13

If you were to represent this data in a chapati chart, what fraction of chapati chart would represent basketball?

(ii) Write the number of children by seeing the tally marks which show the mode of transport different children use

Mode of transport	Tally Marks	Number of children
Car		
Bus		
Cycle		
Walk		

7. Case based questions

Class Party Preferences

To plan a class party, the teacher asked students about their preferred party activities. The result were

Games : 20 students

Music : 10 students

Dance : 15 students

Food : 25 students

Based on the above information, answer the following questions.

(i) Draw the bar chart for the given information.

(ii) Which activity received the highest preference?

(iii) If a tally chart is created for these preferences, how many groups of five would there be for games?

ANSWERS & SOLUTIONS

1. (i) data (ii) numbers (iii) bar

2. (i) True (ii) True (iii) False

3. (i) (b) (ii) (b) (iii) (a)

4. (d)

5. (i) → (b) (ii) → (a)

(iii) → (d) (iv) → (c)

6. (i) Chapati chart for the given table is

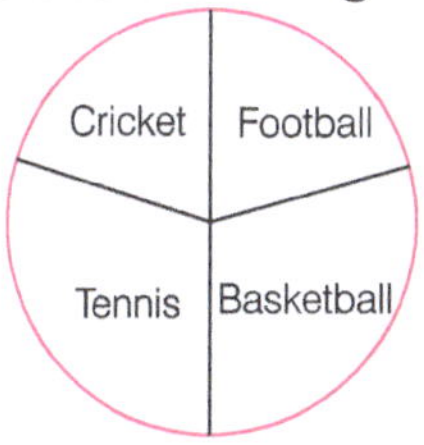

Total number of people

$= 10 + 15 + 12 + 13 = 50$

Number of people who prefered basketball = 15

Fraction for basketball $= \frac{15}{50} = \frac{3}{10}$

(ii) Complete table for given information is given below.

Mode of transport	Tally Marks	Number of children
Car		16
Bus		20
Cycle		24
Walk		23

7. (i) Bar chart for the given information is given below.

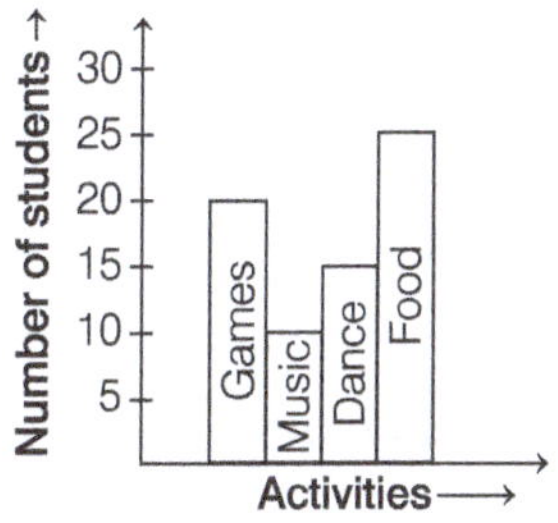

(ii) The activity received the highest preference is food.

(ii) There will be five groups of tally marks for games

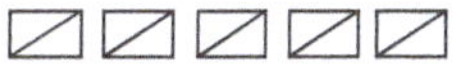

CHAPTER 13

WAYS TO MULTIPLY AND DIVIDE

Multiplication as Repeated Addition

Multiplication can be understood as repeated addition. e.g. Multiplying 3 by 4 means adding 3 four times.

$$3 \times 4 = 3 + 3 + 3 + 3 = 12$$

Different Methods to multiply

(a) The Standard Algorithm (Long multiplication)

It involves multiplying the digits of the numbers systematically and adding the products. e.g. Multiply 32 by 14,

	30	2
10	10×30 **300**	10×2 **20**
4	4×30 **120**	4×2 **8**

Now, $300 + 120 + 20 + 8 = 448$

Thus, $32 \times 14 = 448$

(b) Distributive Property

The distributive property helps break a number into smaller parts and multiply them separately.

e.g. $32 \times 14 = 32 \times (10 + 4)$

$= 32 \times 10 + 32 \times 4$

$= 320 + 128$

$= 448$

Division

Division is the process of sharing on grouping . It is the inverse operation of multiplication.

Division as Repeated Subtraction

To divide 12 by 3 you repeatedly subtract 3 from 12 until you reach 0.

$12 - 3 = 9$, $9 - 3 = 6$, $6 - 3 = 3$, $3 - 3 = 0$

Division by Grouping

This means forming groups of a certain size and counting how many groups can be

made. e.g. If you have 24 pencils and want to group them in sets of 6, you can divide 24 by 6 that is $24 \div 6 = 4$, form 4 groups of 6 pencils.
When dividing , sometimes a number cannot be divided exactly, leaving a remainder . The remainder is the number left over after dividing .

$$\text{Dividend} = (\text{Quotient} \times \text{Divisor}) + \text{Remainder}$$

Division with zero

Any number divided by zero is undefined . Not possible to divide by zero.

e.g. $0 \div 5 = 0$ and $5 \div 0 =$ undefined .

Relationship between Multiplication and Division

Multiplication and division are closely related.
e.g. If $4 \times 5 = 20$, then $20 \div 4 = 5$ and $20 \div 5 = 4$

Word Problems Involving Multiplication and Division

In real life contexts, use multiplication and division such as calculating the total cost of multiple items, distributing objects equally, or finding out how many times one number fits into another.

NCERT FOLDER

Maniratnam-The Cashier (NCERT Pg 170-171)

Q.1 Maniratnam is the cashier of king Jayan. His job is to find out the salary of all the people who work for the king. This chart shows how much salary each person gets in a day.

Person	Salary in a day
Minister	₹ 195
Horse rider	₹ 76
Cook	₹ 65

(i) Maniratnam wanted to calculate the salary of the cook for the month of January.

He wrote–

	60	5
30	60×30 **1800**	5×30 **150**
1	60×1 **60**	5×1 **5**

Rupees $1800 + 150 + 60 + 5 =$ ₹ ______

(ii) Maniratnam's daughter Bela has learnt another method to multiply. She wrote like this and showed it to Bhanu, her brother.

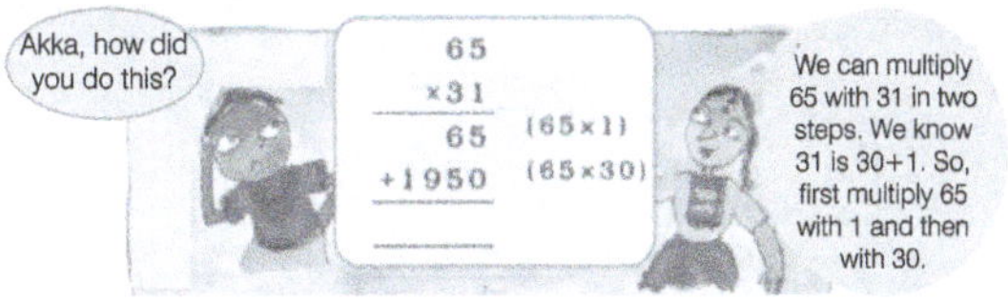

* *Students can write alternate answer as per their choice.*

(iii) Now, Bhanu tried to find the salary of a minister for the month of January. He wanted to multiply 195×31.

Ans. (i) Rupees 1800 + 150 + 60 + 5 = ₹ 2015.

(ii)

```
   6 5
 × 3 1
 -----
   6 5   (65×1)
+1 9 5 0 (65×30)
 -------
 2 0 1 5
```

(iii)

```
   1 9 5
   × 3 1
  ------
   1 9 5 (195×1)
+ 5 8 5 0 (195×30)
  -------
  6 0 4 5
```

Practice Time (NCERT Pg 171)

Q.2 Use Bela's method to multiply these numbers.

(a) 32×46 (b) 67×18

```
    3 2                 6 7
  × 4 6               × 1 8
  -----               -----
  1 9 2 (32×6)        - - -   (67×8)
+ - - - - (32×40)    + 6 7 0  (67×...)
  -----               -----
```

Ans. (a)

```
    3 2
  × 4 6
  -----
  1 9 2 (32×6)
+1 2 8 0 (32×40)
 -------
 1 4 7 2
```

(b)

```
    6 7
  × 1 8
  -----
  5 3 6 (67×8)
+ 6 7 0 (67×10)
  -----
 1 2 0 6
```

Q.3 Do these in your notebook using Bela's method .

(i) 47×19

(ii) 188×91

(iii) 63×57

(iv) 225×22

(v) 360×12

(vi) 163×42

Ans. (i)

```
    4 7
  × 1 9
  -----
  4 2 3  (47×9)
+ 4 7 0  (47×10)
  -----
  8 9 3
```

(ii)

```
    1 8 8
    × 9 1
  -------
    1 8 8  (188×1)
+ 1 6 9 2 0 (188×90)
  ---------
  1 7 1 0 8
```

(iii)

```
    6 3
  × 5 7
  -----
  4 4 1  (63×7)
+ 3 1 5 0 (63×50)
  -------
  3 5 9 1
```

(iv)

```
    2 2 5
    × 2 2
  -------
    4 5 0  (225×2)
+ 4 5 0 0  (225×20)
  -------
  4 9 5 0
```

(v)

```
    3 6 0
    × 1 2
  -------
    7 2 0  (360×2)
+ 3 6 0 0  (360×10)
  -------
  4 3 2 0
```

(vi)

```
    1 6 3
    × 4 2
  -------
    3 2 6  (163×2)
+ 6 5 2 0  (163×40)
  -------
  6 8 4 6
```

Shantaram a Special Cook (NCERT Pg 172)

Q.4 (i) Shantaram is a special cook who comes only on party days. Last year he was called for only 28 days. For each day he has to be paid ₹ 165. Find out how much money he will get in all.

(ii) If he is called for all days of the year, how much salary will he get?

```
      1 6 5
    × 3 6 5
    -------
      - - -   (165 × 5)
    - - - -   (165 × 60)
  + 4 9 5 0 0 (165 × 300)
  -----------
  -----------
```

(iii) Find the salaries of the minister and horse rider for 1 year.

Ans. (i) Amount paid for a day = ₹ 165

Number of days worked = 28

∴
```
      1 6 5
      × 2 8
    -------
    1 3 2 0   (165 × 8)
  + 3 3 0 0   (165 × 20)
  ---------
    4 6 2 0
```

Hence, he will get ₹ 4620.

(ii) ∵ Days in 1 year = 365

∴
```
      1 6 5
    × 3 6 5
    -------
      8 2 5   (165 × 5)
    9 9 0 0   (165 × 60)
 + 4 9 5 0 0  (165 × 300)
 -----------
   6 0 2 2 5
```

(iii) **For minister**

Minister's salary for 1 day = ₹ 195

Number of days in 1 year = 365

∴
```
      1 9 5
    × 3 6 5
    -------
      9 7 5   (195 × 5)
  1 1 7 0 0   (195 × 60)
+ 5 8 5 0 0   (195 × 300)
-----------
  7 1 1 7 5
```

∴ Salary of minister for 1 year = ₹ 71175

For Horse rider

Horse rider's salary for 1 day = ₹76

Number of days in 1 year = 365

∴
```
      3 6 5
      × 7 6
    -------
    2 1 9 0   (365 × 6)
+ 2 5 5 5 0   (365 × 70)
-----------
  2 7 7 4 0
```

∴ Salary of horse rider for 1 year

= ₹ 27740

Years and Years (NCERT Pg 172-173)

Q.5 Sohan drinks 8 glasses of water everyday.

(i) How many glasses will he drink in one month?

(ii) How many glasses will he drink in one year?

(iii) If 125 people living in a colony drink 8 glasses of water in a day, how much water will they drink in a year?

(iv) Can you guess how many glasses of drinking water are used in a day in your colony?

Ans. The number of glasses of water Sohan drinks everyday = 8

(i) ∵ Number of days in a month = 30 days

∴
```
   3 0
   × 8
 -----
 2 4 0
```

So, he will drink 240 glasses in one month.

(ii) ∵ Number of days in one year = 365 days

∴
```
   3 6 5
     × 8
 -------
 2 9 2 0
```

So, he will drink 2920 glasses in one year.

(iii) Number of people in the colony = 125

∵
```
   1 2 5
     × 8
 -------
 1 0 0 0
```

So, they will drink 1000 glasses of water in a day.

Number of days in a year = 365

∴ Number of glasses of water in a year

= 1000 × 365 = 365000

Hence, 365000 glasses of water they will drink in a year.

*(iv) Number of people in my colony = 250

$\therefore$ Number of glasses of drinking water is used in a day by my colony = $250 \times 8 = 2000$

Q.6 (i) If Soha's heart beats 72 times in one minute, how many times does it beat in one hour?

(ii) Find out how many times it beats in one day.

(iii) Count your own heart beats to find out how many times your heart beats in one week.

(iv) Guess how many times it beats in one year.

Ans. (i) The number of times Soha's heart beats in one minute = 72

$\because$ 1 h = 60 min

$\therefore$ The number of times Soha's heart beats in 60 min = $72 \times 60 = 4320$

So, Soha's heart beats 4320 times in one hour.

(ii) $\because$ Number of hours in a day = 24

$\therefore$ Heart beats in a day = 24×4320

$$\begin{array}{rl} 4320 & \\ \times\ 24 & \\ \hline 17280 & (4320 \times 4) \\ +\ 86400 & (4320 \times 20) \\ \hline 103680 & \end{array}$$

So, it beats 103680 times in one day.

*(iii) When I counted my heart beats is 70 times in one minute.

$\therefore$ Number of heart beats in one hour

$= 70 \times 60$ [$\because$ 1 hour = 60 minutes]

= 4200 times

Now, number of heart beats in one day

$= 4200 \times 24$ [$\because$ 1 day = 24 hours]

= 100800 times.

$\therefore$ Number of heart beats in one week

$= 100800 \times 7$ [$\because$ 1 week = 7 days]

$$\begin{array}{r} 100800 \\ \times\ 7 \\ \hline 705600 \end{array}$$

That means if my heart beats 70 times in one minute, then it will beats 705600 times in one week.

*(iv) Number of days in one year = 365

$\therefore$ Heart beats in one year = 100800×365

= 36792000

So, I guess it will beat 36792000 times in one year.

Q.7 A baby elephant drinks around 12 L of milk every day. How much milk will it drink in two years?

Ans. $\because$ Number of days in 1 year = 365

$\therefore$ Number of days in 2 years = 2×365

= 730 days

$\because$ Quantity of milk the baby elephant drinks in 1 day = 12 L

$\therefore$ Quantity of milk the baby elephant drinks in 2 Year = 12×730

$$\begin{array}{rl} 730 & \\ \times\ 12 & \\ \hline 1460 & (730 \times 2) \\ +\ 7300 & (730 \times 10) \\ \hline 8760 & \end{array}$$

So, a baby elephant drinks 8760 L of milk in 2 years.

Q.8 A baby blue whale drinks around 200 L of milk in one day. Just imagine how much milk that is! Find out in how many days your family would use 200 L milk. How much milk would the baby blue whale drink in eight months?

Ans. *Amount of milk consumed by a baby blue whale in a day = 200 L

$\because$ My family uses 2 L milk in a day.

$\therefore$ We will consume 200 L milk in

$(200 \div 2)$ days = 100 days

$\because$ Baby blue whale consume 200 L milk in a day.

$\therefore$ Amount of milk consumed by a baby blue whale in 1 month = 30×200

= 6000 L

$\Rightarrow$ Amount of milk consumed by a baby blue whale in 8 months = 8×6000 L

= 48000 L

So, 48000 L milk will be consumed by the baby blue whale in eight months.

Karunya-The Landlord (NCERT Pg 173-175)

Q.9 Karunya bought three fields.

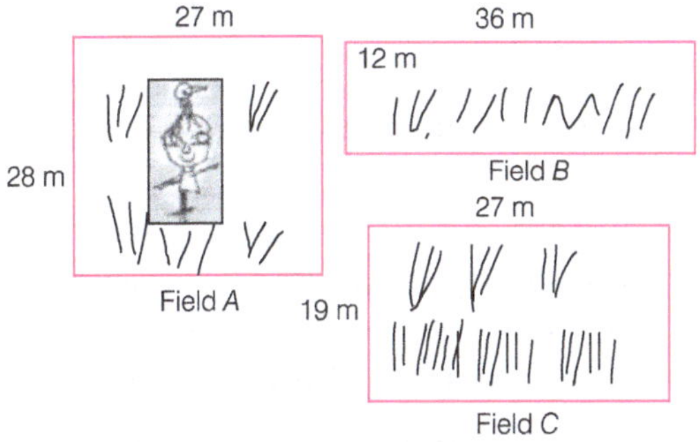

(i) Find the area of all the three fields.

Field A .... square metre.

Field B .... square metre.

Field C .... square metre.

(ii) He bought field A at the rate of ₹ 95 for a square metre, field B at ₹ 110 for a square metre and field C at ₹ 120 for a square metre. Find the cost of all three fields.

(iii) Did he spend more than a lakh of rupees?

Ans. (i) Area of field A

$= \text{Length} \times \text{Width} = 28 \times 27$

$= 756$ square metre

$$\begin{array}{rl} 28 & \\ \times\ 27 & \\ \hline 196 & (28 \times 7) \\ +\ 560 & (28 \times 20) \\ \hline 756 & \end{array}$$

Area of field B

$= \text{Length} \times \text{Width} = 36 \times 12$

$= 432$ square metre

$$\begin{array}{rl} 36 & \\ \times\ 12 & \\ \hline 72 & (36 \times 2) \\ +\ 360 & (36 \times 10) \\ \hline 432 & \end{array}$$

Area of field C

$= \text{Length} \times \text{Width} = 27 \times 19$

$= 513$ square metre

$$\begin{array}{rl} 27 & \\ \times\ 19 & \\ \hline 243 & (27 \times 9) \\ +\ 270 & (27 \times 10) \\ \hline 513 & \end{array}$$

$\therefore$ Area of field $A = 756$ square metre

Area of field $B = 432$ square metre

Area of field $C = 513$ square metre

(ii) **Cost of field *A***

Cost of 1 square metre of field $A =$ ₹ 95

$\therefore$ Cost of 756 square metre of field A

$= 756 \times 95$

$=$ ₹ 71820

$$\begin{array}{rl} 756 & \\ \times\ 95 & \\ \hline 3780 & (756 \times 5) \\ +\ 68040 & (756 \times 90) \\ \hline 71820 & \end{array}$$

Hence, the cost of field A is ₹ 71820.

Cost of field *B*

Cost of 1 square metre of field $B =$ ₹ 110

$\therefore$ Cost of 432 square metre of field B

$= 432 \times 110$

$=$ ₹ 47520

$$\begin{array}{rl} 432 & \\ \times\ 110 & \\ \hline 000 & (432 \times 0) \\ 4320 & (432 \times 10) \\ +\ 43200 & (432 \times 100) \\ \hline 47520 & \end{array}$$

Hence, the cost of field B is ₹ 47520.

Cost of field *C*

Cost of 1 square metre of field $C =$ ₹ 120

$\therefore$ Cost of 513 square metre of field C

$= 513 \times 120$

$=$ ₹ 61560

$$\begin{array}{rl} 513 & \\ \times\ 120 & \\ \hline 000 & (513 \times 0) \\ 10260 & (513 \times 20) \\ +\ 51300 & (513 \times 100) \\ \hline 61560 & \end{array}$$

Hence, the cost of field C is ₹ 61560.

Now, cost of all the three fields

= ₹ 71820 + ₹ 47520 + 61560

= ₹ 180900

(iii) Yes, he spent more than a lakh of rupees.

Q.10 Thulasi and her husband work on Karunya's farm. The Government has said that farm workers should be paid at least ₹ 71 for one day's work. But he pays ₹ 55 to Thulasi and ₹ 58 to her husband.

(i) If Thulasi works for 49 days, how much money does she get?

(ii) If her husband works for 42 days, how much money does he get?

(iii) Find the money they earn together.

(iv) Does he not give them the minimum wage?

(v) Why does he pay less to Thulasi and more to her husband? Discuss.

Ans. (i) **For Thulasi**

∵ One day's wages = ₹ 55

∴ 49 day's wages = 55×49

= 2695

$$\begin{array}{rl} 55 & \\ \times\ 49 & \\ \hline 495 & (55 \times 9) \\ +\ 2200 & (55 \times 40) \\ \hline 2695 & \end{array}$$

(ii) **For Thulasi's husband**

∵ One day's wages = ₹ 58

∴ 42 day's wages = 58×42

= ₹ 2436

$$\begin{array}{rl} 58 & \\ \times\ 42 & \\ \hline 116 & (58 \times 2) \\ 2320 & (58 \times 40) \\ \hline 2436 & \end{array}$$

(iii) Total amount they earned together

= ₹ 2695 + ₹ 2436 = ₹ 5131

Hence, they earned ₹ 5131 together.

(iv) No, he did not give them the minimum wage.

*(v) Gender bias, job roles might be the reasons for paying less to Thulasi as compare to her husband. It's important to talk about these issues because everyone should be treated fairly and paid equally for their hard work, regardless of gender . Fair wages help families thrive and support a good community.

Q.11 I saw this in the newspaper.

Governments of different states have said that farmworkers should not be paid less than this salary for a day's work.

State	Salary for one day
Haryana	₹ 135
Rajasthan	₹ 73
Madhya Pradesh	₹ 97
Orissa	₹ 75

The table shows the amounts fixed by four states.

(i) For farm work which state has fixed the highest amount? Which state has fixed the lowest?

(ii) Bhairon Singh is a worker in Rajasthan. If he works for 8 weeks on the farm, how much will he earn?

(iii) Neelam is a worker in Haryana. If she works for $2\frac{1}{2}$ months on the farm, how much will she earn?

(iv) How much more will a farm worker in Madhya Pradesh get than a worker in Orissa after working for 9 weeks?

Ans. (i) Haryana state fixed the highest amount of ₹ 135 and Rajasthan state fixed the lowest amount of ₹ 73 for farmwork.

(ii) ∵ Payment for a day in Rajasthan = ₹ 73

∴ Payment for a week = ₹ 73×7

[∵ 1 week = 7 days]

= ₹ 511

Now, Bhairon Singh earning for working in the farm for 8 weeks = 8×511 = ₹ 4088

$$\begin{array}{r} 511 \\ \times\ 8 \\ \hline 4088 \end{array}$$

So, he will earn ₹ 4088.

(iii) Number of days in $2\frac{1}{2}$ months

$= 30 \times 2 + 15$

$= 75$ days

One day's wages in Haryana = ₹ 135

∴ 135 day's wage in Haryana = 135×75

= ₹ 10125

$$\begin{array}{r} 135 \\ \times 75 \\ \hline 675 \\ +9450 \\ \hline 10125 \end{array}$$

So, Neelam will earn ₹ 10125.

(iv) One day's wages in Madhya Pradesh = ₹ 97

∵ Wages for 7 days = 7×97

= ₹ 679 (1 week)

∴ Wages for 9 weeks = 9 × ₹ 679

= ₹ 6111

For Orissa

One day's wage = ₹ 75

∵ Wages for 7 day's = 7 × 75 = ₹ 525

∴ Wages for 9 weeks = 9 × 525 = ₹ 4725

Difference in wage = 6111 − 4725 = ₹ 1386

So, the workers in Madhya Pradesh will get ₹ 1386 more wage than a worker in Orissa.

Farmers in Vidarbha (Maharashtra) (NCERT Pg 175-177)

Q.12 Vidarbha is facing a very serious problem. There was no rain and crops failed. Many farmers were unhappy. Some farmers even ended their own lives. A newspaper reporter went around the area and spoke to the people. He wrote these two reports.

I. **Satish's Story**

Satish is a 13 year old boy. His father had taken a loan for farming. But the crops failed. Now, Satish's mother has to pay ₹ 5000 every month for the loan.

Satish started working, he looked after 17 goats of the village.

He earns ₹ 1 everyday for one goat.

(i) How much will he earn in one month?

(ii) Does he earn enough to help pay the loan every month?

(iii) How much will he earn in one year?

II. **Kamla Bai's Story**

To help farmers the State Government gave cows. Kamla Bai Gudhe also got a cow. The cost of the cow was ₹ 17500. She had to pay ₹ 5500 and the government spent the rest of the money.

(i) How much did the government spend on the cow?

(ii) If 9 people from her village got cows, how much did the government spend in all ?

(iii) But Kamla Bai was not to happy. She had to spend ₹ 85 everyday on the cow. She made some money by selling the milk. But still she wanted to sell the cow. If Kamla Bai spends ₹ 85 a day, find out how much she will spend in one month.

(iv) The cow gives 8 litres of milk everyday. How much will it give in one month?

(v) (a) If the milk is sold at ₹ 9 per litre, how much money will Kamla Bai make in one month?

(b) The money spent on keeping the cow was ₹ ______ .

(c) Money earned by selling the milk ₹ ______ .

(d) Which is more - money spent on the cow or money earned from it ? How much?.

(vi) Find out how much do you pay for 1 litre of milk.

(vii) Explain why she wanted to sell the cow.

Ans. I. (i) ∵ He earns ₹ 1 everyday for one goat.

∴ He will earn ₹ 1×17

= ₹ 17 everyday for 17 goats.

Number of days in one month = 30

∴ Earning in 30 days = 30 × ₹ 17 = ₹ 510

⇒ So, he will earn ₹ 510 in one month.

$$\begin{array}{r} 30 \\ \times 17 \\ \hline 210 \\ 300 \\ \hline 510 \end{array}$$

(ii) No, it is not enough.

(iii) ∵ Number of months in one year = 12

∴ His earning in one year = 12 × 510 = ₹ 6120

$$\begin{array}{r} 510 \\ \times 12 \\ \hline 1020 \\ +5100 \\ \hline 6120 \end{array}$$

So, he will earn ₹ 6120 in one year.

II. (i) Cost of the cow = ₹ 17500

Amount paid by Kamla Bai = ₹ 5500

∴ Total amount spent by government

= ₹ 17500 – ₹ 5500 = ₹ 12000

So, the government spend ₹ 12000 on the cow.

(ii) ∵ The amount paid by the government for 1 cow = ₹ 12000

∴ The amount paid for 9 cows = 9 × ₹ 12000 = ₹ 108000

So, the government will spend ₹ 108000 for 9 cows.

(iii) ∵ Amount spent by Kamla Bai in 1 day = ₹ 85

Number of days in one month = 30

∴ Amount spend by Kamla Bai in 30 days

= 30 × 85 = ₹ 2550

$$\begin{array}{r} 85 \\ \times 30 \\ \hline 00 \\ +2550 \\ \hline 2550 \end{array}$$

Hence, Kamla Bai spent ₹ 2550 in a month.

(iv) Quantity of milk given by cow in a day

= 8 litres

∵ Number of day in one month = 30

∴ Quantity of milk given by cow in one month = 30 × 8 = 240 litres

So, the cow gave 240 litres of milk in one month.

(v) (a) ∵ Amount for one litre milk = ₹ 9

∴ Amount for 240 litres milk = 9 × 240 = ₹ 2160

So, Kamla Bai will earn ₹ 2160 in one month.

(b) The money spent on keeping the cow was ₹ 2550.

(c) Money earned by selling the milk is ₹ 2160.

(d) ∵ Money spent on the cow = ₹ 2550

and money earned from it = ₹ 2160

∵ 2550 > 2160

∴ Money spent on cow was more than the money earned.

Difference of money = 2550 – 2160 = ₹ 390

Hence, the difference of money is ₹ 390.

*(vi) I will pay ₹ 9 for 1 litre of milk.

(vii) Since, the money spent on the cow is more than the money earned. So, she wanted to sell the cow.

Practice Time (NCERT Pg 177)

Q.13 Sukhi works on a farm. He is paid ₹ 98 for one day. If he works for 52 days, how much will he earn?

Ans. ∵ Payment for one day = ₹ 98

∴ Payment for 52 days = 52 × 98 = ₹ 5096

$$\begin{array}{r} 98 \\ \times 52 \\ \hline 196 \\ +4900 \\ \hline 5096 \end{array}$$

So, Sukhi will earn ₹ 5096.

Q.14 Hariya took a loan to build his house. He has to pay back ₹ 2750 every month for two years. How much will he pay back in 2 years?

Ans. Amount of loan that is to be paid every month = ₹ 2750

∴ Amount of loan in 1 year = 12 × 2750 = ₹ 33000

Amount of loan that is to be paid in 2 years = 2 × 33000 = ₹ 66000

So, Hariya will pay ₹ 66000 back in 2 years.

Q.15 Ratiram is a milk seller in the city. He sells 13 litres of milk everyday at ₹ 23 per litre. How much does he earn?

Ans. ∵ Selling price of 1 litre of milk = ₹ 23

∴ Selling price of 13 litres of milk $= 13 \times 23$

= ₹ 299

$$\begin{array}{r} 23 \\ \times 13 \\ \hline 69 \\ +230 \\ \hline 299 \\ \hline \end{array}$$

So, Ratiram will earn ₹ 299.

Q.16 A farmer sells 1 litre of milk for ₹ 11. In one month he sells 210 litres of milk. How much does he earn in a month?

Ans. ∵ Selling price of 1 litres of milk = ₹ 11

∴ Selling price of 210 litres of milk

$= 210 \times 11 =$ ₹ 2310

$$\begin{array}{r} 210 \\ \times 11 \\ \hline 210 \\ +2100 \\ \hline 2310 \\ \hline \end{array}$$

So, farmer will earn ₹ 2310 in a month.

Q.17 A company sells 1 litre of packed water for ₹ 12. A shopkeeper buys 240 litres of packed water. How much does he pay?

Ans. ∵ Selling price of 1 litre of packed water

= ₹ 12

∴ Amount spent by the shopkeeper for 240 litres = ₹ 12×240 = ₹ 2880

$$\begin{array}{r} 240 \\ \times 12 \\ \hline 480 \\ +2400 \\ \hline 2880 \\ \hline \end{array}$$

So, he paid ₹ 2880 for 240 litres.

Fun with Multiplication (NCERT Pg 178-179)

Q.18 Look for the pattern and take this forward.

$(0 \times 9) + 1 = 1$

$(1 \times 9) + 2 = 11$

$(12 \times 9) + 3 = 111$

$(123 \times 9) + 4 =$ ______

$(1234 \times 9) + 5 =$ ______

$(12345 \times 9) + 6 =$ ______

Ans. $(0 \times 9) + 1 = 1$

$(1 \times 9) + 2 = 11$

$(12 \times 9) + 3 = 111$

$(123 \times 9) + 4 = \underline{1111}$

$(1234 \times 9) + 5 = \underline{11111}$

$(12345 \times 9) + 6 = \underline{111111}$

Q.19 Each letter *a*, *b*, *c* here stands for a number.

$$\begin{array}{r} aaa \\ \times aaa \\ \hline aaa \\ aaa0 \\ aaa00 \\ \hline abcba \\ \hline \end{array}$$

Take $a = 1$, then find what the numbers *b* and *c* will be.

Ans. If a = 1, then

$$\begin{array}{r} 111 \\ \times 111 \\ \hline 111 \\ 1110 \\ +11100 \\ \hline 12321 \\ \hline \end{array}$$

On comparing, we will get

$b = 2$

and $c = 3$.

Q.20 (i) Tricks with your age.

Write your age ______

Multiply it by 7 ______

Again multiply the answer by 13 ______

Multiply again that answer by 11 ______

(ii) Look at your last answer.

Can you find your age in that answer?

How many times does your age show in the answer?

(iii) Try this trick with other people.

Ans. *(i) Write your age = 11

Multiply it by 7 = $11 \times 7 = 77$

Again, multiply the answer by 13

$= 77 \times 13 = 1001$

$$\begin{array}{r} 77 \\ \times 13 \\ \hline 231 \\ 770 \\ \hline 1001 \end{array}$$

Multiply again that answer by 11

$$\begin{array}{r} 1001 \\ \times 11 \\ \hline 1001 \\ 10010 \\ \hline 11011 \end{array}$$

(ii) In the answer $\boxed{11}\,0\,\boxed{11}$, I found my age two times, that is 11 occurs twice in 11011.

(iii) Do yourself.

Q.21 (i) Going round and round!

142857	142857	142857	142857	142857
× 1	× 2	× 3	× 4	× 5
______	______	______	______	______

(ii) Do you find a pattern in all these answers? Discuss this with your friends.

Ans. (i)

142857	142857	142857	142857	142857
× 1	× 2	× 3	× 4	× 5
142857	285714	428571	571428	714285

(ii) No, I did not find any pattern in the answer.

Division (NCERT Pg 179)

Q.22 Dolma took a loan from a friend to buy a moped for ₹ 9588. She has to pay it back in equal amounts every month for six months.

(i) How much will she have to pay every month? She asked her children to calculate.

Her daughter did it this way

$$\begin{array}{r} 500 + 500 + 500 + 90 + 8 \\ 6\overline{)\,9588} \\ -3000 \\ \hline 6588 \\ -3000 \\ \hline 3588 \\ -3000 \\ \hline 588 \\ -540 \\ \hline 48 \\ -48 \\ \hline \times \end{array}$$

Her son started this way. Now, you complete it.

$$\begin{array}{r} 1000 + \quad\quad\quad \\ 6\overline{)\,9588} \\ -6000 \\ \hline \_\_\_\_ \\ \_\_\_\_ \\ \_\_\_\_ \\ \times \end{array}$$

(ii) Will both of them get the same answer? Discuss.

Ans. (i) Let us complete the solution started by her son.

$$\begin{array}{r} 1000 + 500 + 90 + 8 \\ 6\overline{)\,9588} \\ -6000 \\ \hline 3588 \\ -3000 \\ \hline 588 \\ -540 \\ \hline 48 \\ -48 \\ \hline \times \end{array}$$

∴ Daughter's answer

$= 500 + 500 + 500 + 90 + 8$

$= 1598$

and Son's answer $= 1000 + 500 + 90 + 8$

$= 1598$

∴ Dolma has to pay ₹ 1598 for every month for 6 months.

(ii) Yes, both of them got the same answer.

Practice Time (NCERT Pg 180)

Q.23 Try to solve these using as few steps as you can.

(a) $4228 \div 4$ (b) $770 \div 22$

(c) $9872 \div 8$ (d) $672 \div 21$

(e) $772 \div 7$ (f) $639 \div 13$

Ans. (a) $4228 \div 4$

```
     1000 + 50 + 7
   ______________
 4 ) 4228
    -4000
      228
     -200
       28
      -28
        ×
```

$\therefore\ 4228 \div 4 = 1000 + 50 + 7 = 1057$

(b) $770 \div 22$

```
      30+5
   22)770
     -660
      110
     -110
        ×
```

$\therefore\ 770 \div 22 = 30 + 5 = 35$

(c) $9872 \div 8$

```
     1000 + 200 + 30 + 4
   ____________________
 8 ) 9872
    -8000
     1872
    -1600
      272
     -240
       32
      -32
        ×
```

$\therefore\ 9872 \div 8 = 1000 + 200 + 30 + 4 = 1234$

(d) $672 \div 21$

```
       30 + 2
    _________
 21 ) 672
     -630
       42
      -42
        ×
```

$\therefore\ 672 \div 21 = 30 + 2 = 32$

(e) $772 \div 7$

```
      110
    _______
 7 ) 772
    -770
       2
```

$\therefore 772 \div 7 = 110 \times 7 + 2$

Here, 7 does not divide 772 exactly.

Remainder = 2

(f) $639 \div 13$

```
       40 + 9
    _________
 13 ) 639
     -520
      119
     -117
        2
```

$\therefore 639 \div 13 = 49 \times 13 + 2$

Here, 13 does not divide 639 exactly.

Remainder = 2

How Many Times? (NCERT Pg 180)

Q.24 976 children are going on a picnic. They will be taken in mini buses. If 25 children can go in one bus, how many buses do they need? Two children have solved it. Check if they have made a mistake–correct it. Discuss.

First solution

```
       5 + 10 + 10 + 10 + 4
    ______________________
 25 ) 976
     -125
      851
     -250
      601
     -250
      351
     -250
      101
     -100
        ×
```

Ans. We need 39 buses.

Second solution

```
       20 + 10 + 9 + 1
    __________________
 25 ) 976
     -500
      476
     -250
      226
     -215
       11
```

Ans. We need 40 buses.

Ans. For the first solution, there is a calculation error in the last step. It should be

$$\begin{array}{r} 101 \\ -100 \\ \hline 1 \end{array}$$

So, it should be 1 in the place of X.

For the second solution, there is a error in last step. It should be

$$\begin{array}{r} 226 \\ -225 \\ \hline 001 \end{array}$$

So, instead of 215, it should be 225.

Following is the correct solution

$$\begin{array}{r|l} & 20 + 10 + 9 \\ 25 & 976 \\ & -500 \\ \hline & 476 \\ & -250 \\ \hline & 226 \\ & -225 \\ \hline & 1 \end{array}$$

If they can fit the extra child on one of the 39 buses, then they will need 39 buses. If not, they will need 40 buses. But they cannot take a separate bus for one child. So, they need only 39 buses.

How Much Petrol? (NCERT Pg 181)

Q.25 Isha has ₹1000 with her. She wants to buy petrol. One litre of petrol costs ₹ 47. How many litres can she buy?

Money with Isha = ₹ 1000

Cost of 1 L = ₹ 47

(i) Litres of petrol she can buy

= ₹ 1000 ÷ ₹ 47 = ?

Isha can buy _____ litres of petrol.

(ii) If Isha comes to your city. How much petrol can she buy with the same money?

Ans. (i) Money with Isha = ₹ 1000

Cost of 1 L = ₹ 47

∴ Litres of petrol she can buy

$1000 \div 47 = 47 \times 21 + 13$

Quotient = 21

Remainder = 13

$$\begin{array}{r|l} & 20 + 1 \\ 47 & 1000 \\ & -940 \\ \hline & 60 \\ & -47 \\ \hline & 13 \end{array}$$

So, she can buy $21\frac{13}{47}$ L.

*(ii) In my city, cost of 1 L = ₹ 50

∴ $1000 \div 50 = 20$ L

$$\begin{array}{r|l} & 20 \\ 50 & 1000 \\ & -1000 \\ \hline & \times \end{array}$$

So, she can buy 20 L of petrol will ₹ 1000.

Children's Day (NCERT Pg 181)

Q.26 Children are happy today. They are celebrating Children's Day. Each child will be given 4 coloured pencils from school. The school has got 969 pencils. To find out how many children can get pencils the teacher asks them to divide.

Iru's way

$$\begin{array}{r|l} & 100 + \\ 4 & 969 \\ & -400 \\ \hline & \\ \hline \end{array}$$

Sreeni's way

$$\begin{array}{r|l} & 200 + \\ 4 & 969 \\ & - \\ \hline & \\ \hline \end{array}$$

Complete Iru's and Sreeni's way of division. What is the answer you get?

Ans. Iru's way of division,

$$\begin{array}{r|l} & 100 + 100 + 40 + 2 \\ 4 & 969 \\ & -400 \\ \hline & 569 \\ & -400 \\ \hline & 169 \\ & -160 \\ \hline & 9 \\ & -8 \\ \hline & 1 \end{array}$$

∴ Quotient = 100 + 100 + 40 + 2 = 242

and remainder = 1

Sreeni's way of division,

```
      200 + 40 + 2
4 ) 9 6 9
  - 8 0 0
    1 6 9
  - 1 6 0
        9
      - 8
        1
      - 8
        1
```

∴ Quotient = 200 + 40 + 2 = 242

and remainder = 1

Practice Time (NCERT Pg 183)

Q.27 576 books are to be one packed in boxes. If one box has 24 books, how many boxes are needed?

Ans. Total number of books = 576

Number of books in one box = 24

So, the number of boxes needed for packing them is 576 ÷ 24.

```
      24
24 ) 5 7 6
   - 4 8
     9 6
   - 9 6
       ×
```

So, the required number of boxes are 24.

Q.28 836 people are watching a movie in a hall. If the hall has 44 rows, how many people can sit in 1 row?

Ans. Total number of people watching a movie = 836

Total number of rows = 44

∴ Number of people sitting in 1 row = 836 ÷ 44

```
      19
44 ) 8 3 6
   - 4 4
     3 9 6
   - 3 9 6
         ×
```

So, the required number of rows are 19.

Q.29 A gardener bought 458 apple trees. He wants to plant 15 trees in each row. How many rows can he plant? How many trees would be left over?

Ans. Total number of apple trees = 458

Total number of trees in one row = 15

∴ Number of rows can he plant = 458 ÷ 15

```
      30
15 ) 4 5 8
   - 4 5
       8
     - 0
       8
```

∴ Quotient = 30 and remainder = 8

Hence, required number of rows = 30

and number of trees left over = 8

Brain Teaser (NCERT Pg 183)

Q.30 Shyamli bought a battery. She read on it 'Life: 2000 hours'. She uses it throughout the day and the night. How many days will the battery run?

Ans. Life of battery = 2000 hours

She uses it through the day and the night i.e. 24 hours.

∴ Number of days the battery will run = 2000 ÷ 24

```
      83
24 ) 2 0 0 0
   - 1 9 2
       8 0
     - 7 2
         8
```

So, the battery will run $83\frac{8}{24}$ or $83\frac{1}{3}$ days.

In the other words, we can say that the battery will run 83 complete days and $\frac{1}{3}$ day.

More with Multiplication and Division (NCERT Pg 183)

Q.31 A tank is full of 300 L of water. How much water will be filled in 25 tanks? If 15 buckets can be filled with one tank of water, how many buckets in all can be filled with the water in 25 tanks?

Ans. $\because$ Capacity of one tank = 300 L

$\therefore$ Capacity of 25 tanks = 25×300

= 7500 L of water

Now, 1 tank can fill 15 buckets.

So, 25 tank can fill $(25 \times 15) = 375$ buckets.

Q.32 There are 28 laddoos in 1 kg. How many laddoos will be there in 12 kg? If 16 laddoos can be packed in 1 box, how many boxes are needed to pack all these laddoos?

Ans. $\because$ Number of laddoos in 1 kg = 28

$\therefore$ Number of laddoos in 12 kg = 28×12

= 336 laddoos

Number of laddoos in 1 box = 16

$\therefore$ Number of boxes required = $336 \div 16$

$$\begin{array}{r|l} & 20+1 \\ 16 & 336 \\ & -320 \\ \hline & 16 \\ & -16 \\ \hline & \times \end{array}$$

So, the required number of boxes are 21.

Q.33 There are 26 rooms in a school. Each room has 4 plants. If each plant needs 2 cups of water, how much water do we need for all the plants?

Ans. Number of rooms in the school = 26

Number of plant in 1 room = 4

$\therefore$ Total number of plant = 4×26

= 104

$\because$ Each plant required 2 cup of water.

$\therefore$ 104 plants required = 104×2

= 208 cups of water

So, we need 208 cups of water for all the plants.

Make the Best Story Problem (NCERT Pg 184-185)

Q.34 Each line gives a story. You have to choose the question which makes the best story problem. The first one is already marked.

(i) A shopkeeper has 50 boxes. There are 48 fruits in one box.

Tick the one question which matches with the given problem.

(a) How much will the shopkeeper pay in all?

(b) How many fruits are there in all?

(c) How many more boxes will he need?

Explain why (a) and (c) are not good choices.

(ii) 352 children from a school went on a camping trip. Each tent had a group of 4 children.

(a) How many children did each tent have?

(b) How many tents do they need?

(c) How many children in all are in the school?

(iii) A shopkeeper has 204 eggs. He puts them in egg trays. Each tray has 12 eggs.

(a) How many more eggs will he need?

(b) How many fresh eggs does he sell?

(c) How many egg trays does he need?

(iv) The cost of one book is ₹ 47. Sonu buys 23 books.

(a) How much money does she have?

(b) How much money does she pay for the books?

(c) What is the cost of 47 books?

Ans. (i) Option (b) is the best story problem.

Since, the price is not given in the story. So, option (a) is not a good choice.

Since, the total number of boxes are already given in the question. So, option (c) cannot be the best story problem.

(ii) Option (b) is the best story problem.

Since, the number of children for each tent and total number of children in the school are already given in the question, so options (a) and (c) are not good choices.

(iii) Option (c) is the best story problem.

Since, total number of eggs are already given, so option (a) can not be best choice.

Also, there is no data on number of fresh or spoiled eggs. Hence, option (b) can not be good choice.

(iv) Option (b) is the best story problem.

Since, there is no information regarding the money she has, so option (a) can not be the best story problem.

Since, the number of books bought by Sonu is 23, not 47.

So, option (c) is not a good choice.

Practice Time (NCERT Pg 186)

Q.35 Do these divisions. Check your results by multiplication.

(a) $438 \div 9$ (b) $3480 \div 12$

(c) $450 \div 7$ (d) $900 \div 10$

(e) $678 \div 6$ (f) $2475 \div 11$

Ans. (a) $438 \div 9$

$$\begin{array}{r|l} & 40 + 8 = 48 \\ 9 & 438 \\ & -360 \\ & 78 \\ & -72 \\ & 6 \end{array}$$

Quotient = 48

Remainder = 6

Verification

Dividend = Quotient × Divisor + Remainder

$= 48 \times 9 + 6$

$= 432 + 6$

$= 438$ (Dividend)

(b) $3480 \div 12$

$$\begin{array}{r|l} & 200 + 90 = 290 \\ 12 & 3480 \\ & -2400 \\ & 1080 \\ & -1080 \\ & \times \end{array}$$

Verification

Dividend = Quotient × Divisor + Remainder

$= 290 \times 12 + 0$

$= 3480$ (Dividend)

(c) $450 \div 7$

$$\begin{array}{r|l} & 60 + 4 = 64 \\ 7 & 450 \\ & -420 \\ & 30 \\ & -28 \\ & 2 \end{array}$$

Verification

Dividend = Quotient × Divisor + Remainder

$= 64 \times 7 + 2$

$= 448 + 2 = 450$ (Dividend)

(d) $900 \div 10$

$$\begin{array}{r|l} & 90 \\ 10 & 900 \\ & -900 \\ & \times \end{array}$$

Verification

Dividend = Quotient × Divisor + Remainder

$= 90 \times 10 + 0$

$= 900$ (Dividend)

(e) $678 \div 6$

$$\begin{array}{r|l} & 100 + 10 + 3 = 113 \\ 6 & 678 \\ & -600 \\ & 78 \\ & -60 \\ & 18 \\ & -18 \\ & \times \end{array}$$

Verification

Dividend = Quotient × Divisor + Remainder

$= 6 \times 113 + 0 = 678$ (Dividend)

(f) $2475 \div 11$

$$\begin{array}{r|l} & 200 + 20 + 5 = 225 \\ 11 & 2475 \\ & -2200 \\ & 275 \\ & -220 \\ & 55 \\ & -55 \\ & \times \end{array}$$

Verification

Dividend = Quotient × Divisor + Remainder

$= 225 \times 11 + 0$

$= 2475$ (Dividend)

Q.36 Solve the given sums and shade the answers in the grid given below. See what you find.

(a) 21×16 (b) 15×7 (c) 93×2
(d) 17×5 (e) 10×10 (f) 26×26
(g) 77×10 (h) 50×10 (i) 11×11
(j) 59×7 (k) 31×19 (l) 85×30
(m) 64×42 (n) $3200 \div 40$ (o) 19×3
(p) $248 \div 8$ (q) $432 \div 18$ (r) $729 \div 9$
(s) $825 \div 5$ (t) $221 \div 13$ (u) $576 \div 12$
(v) $288 \div 4$ (w) $869 \div 11$ (x) $847 \div 7$
(y) $981 \div 3$ (z) $475 \div 19$

545	110	434	642	709	623	919	341	12	168
984	16	561	608	236	413	529	62	259	905
709	907	367	632	336	121	492	178	431	25
166	806	584	186	100	589	72	717	248	676
624	82	105	24	165	17	85	770	327	500
247	997	485	2688	81	80	48	901	126	121
742	427	756	531	79	2550	347	1001	314	57
945	1000	687	854	1200	31	124	3126	918	53
109	799	845	1999	864	955	123	1234	678	56
549	459	614	1864	834	559	900	1111	268	171

Ans. (a) 21×16

$$\begin{array}{r} 21 \\ \times 16 \\ \hline 126 \\ +210 \\ \hline 336 \\ \hline \end{array}$$

(b) 15×7

$$\begin{array}{r} 15 \\ \times 7 \\ \hline 105 \\ \hline \end{array}$$

(c) 93×2

$$\begin{array}{r} 93 \\ \times 2 \\ \hline 186 \\ \hline \end{array}$$

(d) 17×5

$$\begin{array}{r} 17 \\ \times 5 \\ \hline 85 \\ \hline \end{array}$$

(e) 10×10

$$\begin{array}{r} 10 \\ \times 10 \\ \hline 00 \\ +100 \\ \hline 100 \\ \hline \end{array}$$

(f) 26×26

$$\begin{array}{r} 26 \\ \times 26 \\ \hline 156 \\ +520 \\ \hline 676 \\ \hline \end{array}$$

(g) 77×10

$$\begin{array}{r} 77 \\ \times 10 \\ \hline 00 \\ +770 \\ \hline 770 \\ \hline \end{array}$$

(h) 50×10

$$\begin{array}{r} 50 \\ \times 10 \\ \hline 00 \\ +500 \\ \hline 500 \\ \hline \end{array}$$

(i) 11×11

$$\begin{array}{r} 11 \\ \times 11 \\ \hline 11 \\ +110 \\ \hline 121 \\ \hline \end{array}$$

(j) 59×7

$$\begin{array}{r} 59 \\ \times\ 7 \\ \hline 413 \\ \hline \end{array}$$

(k) 31×19

$$\begin{array}{r} 31 \\ \times\ 19 \\ \hline 279 \\ +\ 310 \\ \hline 589 \\ \hline \end{array}$$

(l) 85×30

$$\begin{array}{r} 85 \\ \times\ 30 \\ \hline 00 \\ +\ 2550 \\ \hline 2550 \\ \hline \end{array}$$

(m) 64×42

$$\begin{array}{r} 64 \\ \times\ 42 \\ \hline 128 \\ +\ 2560 \\ \hline 2688 \\ \hline \end{array}$$

(n) $3200 \div 40 = 80$

$$\begin{array}{r} 80 \\ 40\,\overline{)\ 3200} \\ -\ 3200 \\ \hline \times \\ \hline \end{array}$$

(o) 19×3

$$\begin{array}{r} 19 \\ \times\ 3 \\ \hline 57 \\ \hline \end{array}$$

(p) $248 \div 8 = 31$

$$\begin{array}{r} 30 + 1 \\ 8\,\overline{)\ 248} \\ -\ 240 \\ \hline 8 \\ -\ 8 \\ \hline \times \\ \hline \end{array}$$

(q) $432 \div 18 = 24$

$$\begin{array}{r} 20 + 4 \\ 18\,\overline{)\ 432} \\ -\ 360 \\ \hline 72 \\ -\ 72 \\ \hline \times \\ \hline \end{array}$$

(r) $729 \div 9 = 81$

$$\begin{array}{r} 80 + 1 \\ 9\,\overline{)\ 729} \\ -\ 720 \\ \hline 9 \\ -\ 9 \\ \hline \times \\ \hline \end{array}$$

(s) $825 \div 5 = 165$

$$\begin{array}{r} 100 + 60 + 5 \\ 5\,\overline{)\ 825} \\ -\ 500 \\ \hline 325 \\ -\ 300 \\ \hline 25 \\ -\ 25 \\ \hline \times \\ \hline \end{array}$$

(t) $221 \div 13 = 17$

$$\begin{array}{r} 10 + 7 \\ 13\,\overline{)\ 221} \\ -\ 130 \\ \hline 91 \\ -\ 91 \\ \hline \times \\ \hline \end{array}$$

(u) $576 \div 12 = 48$

$$\begin{array}{r} 40 + 8 \\ 12\,\overline{)\ 576} \\ -\ 480 \\ \hline 96 \\ -\ 96 \\ \hline \times \\ \hline \end{array}$$

(v) $288 \div 4 = 72$

$$\begin{array}{r} 70 + 2 \\ 4\,\overline{)\ 288} \\ -\ 280 \\ \hline 8 \\ -\ 8 \\ \hline \times \\ \hline \end{array}$$

(w) $869 \div 11 = 79$

$$\begin{array}{r} 70 + 9 \\ 11\,\overline{)\ 869} \\ -\ 770 \\ \hline 99 \\ -\ 99 \\ \hline \times \\ \hline \end{array}$$

(x) $847 \div 7 = 121$

```
      100 + 20 + 1
   7) 8 4 7
     -7 0 0
      1 4 7
     -1 4 0
          7
         -7
          ×
```

(y) $981 \div 3 = 327$

```
      300 + 20 + 7
   3) 9 8 1
     -9 0 0
        8 1
       -6 0
        2 1
       -2 1
          ×
```

(z) $475 \div 19 = 25$

```
        20 + 5
   19) 4 7 5
      -3 8 0
         9 5
        -9 5
           ×
```

We can shade the answers in the grid.

545	110	434	642	709	623	919	341	12	168
984	16	561	608	236	413	529	62	259	905
709	907	367	632	336	121	492	178	431	25
166	806	584	186	100	589	72	717	248	676
624	82	105	24	165	17	85	770	327	500
247	997	485	2688	81	80	48	901	126	121
742	427	756	531	79	2550	347	1001	314	57
945	1000	687	854	1200	31	124	3126	918	53
109	799	845	1999	864	955	123	1234	678	56
549	459	614	1864	834	559	900	1111	268	171

PRACTICE QUESTIONS

1. Fill in the blanks.

(i) Multiplication is repeated ________ of a number.

(ii) Division is the process of splitting a number into ________ parts.

(iii) The result of multiplication is called the ________ .

(iv) In division,the number being divided is called the ________ .

2. True or False

(i) Multiplication is the inverse of division.

(ii) In division, the remainder is always larger than the divisor.

(iii) The product of two numbers is always greater than either number.

(iv) 10 multiplied by 0 is10.

(v) The division of any number by 1 gives the number itself.

3. Multiple choice questions

(i) In the division $75 \div 5$, what is the remainder?

(a) 0 (b) 5
(c) 3 (d) 1

(ii) Which of the following is a correct multiplication fact ?

(a) $6 \times 7 = 42$ (b) $5 \times 8 = 50$
(c) $9 \times 9 = 91$ (d) $4 \times 6 = 20$

(iii) If you divide 100 by 4 , what do you get?

(a) 20 (b) 25
(c) 30 (d) 40

4. Match the Columns

	Column A		Column B
(i)	Dividend	(a)	The answer in multiplication
(ii)	Product	(b)	The number being divided
(iii)	Quotient	(c)	The number use multiply by
(iv)	Multiplies	(d)	The result in division
(v)	Divisor	(e)	The number we divide by

5. Odd-One Out

(i) (a) Remainder (b) Quotient (c) Difference (d) Dividend

(ii) (a) 4×5 (b) 45×25 (c) 10×10 (d) $250 \div 10$

6. Word problems

(i) If one packet contains 12 candies, how many candies are their in 7 such packets?

(ii) Riya has 36 apples and she wants to share them equally among 4 friends. How many apples will each friend get?

(iii) A shopkeeper has 150 pens . He Packs them equally into 5 boxes. How many pens are there in each box ? If each pens costs 10 rupees, what is the total cost of the pens in one box ?

7. Case based questions

Sports Event

Arjun is organising a sports events .He has 48 students and wants to divide them into 6 equal teams for the event.

Based on the above information, answer the following questions.

(i) How many students will be in each team?

(ii) If each student gets 2 chocolates as a reward. How many chocolates does Arjun need in total?

(iii) During the event,each team,plays 4 matches. How many matches will be played in∴ total?

ANSWERS & SOLUTIONS

1. (i) addition (ii) equal (iii) product (iv) dividend

2. (i) True (ii) False (iii) False (iv) False (v) True

3. (i) (a) (ii) (a) (iii) (b)

4. (i) → (b) (ii) → (a) (iii) → (d) (iv) → (c) (v) → (e)

5. (i) (c) (ii) (d)

6. (i) Number of candies in one packet = 12

So, the number of candies in 7 packets

$= 12 \times 7 = 84$

(ii) Total number of apples = 36

Total number of friends = 4

∴ Number of apples each friend get $= 36 \div 4$

$$\begin{array}{r|l} & 9 \\ 4 & 36 \\ & 36 \\ \hline & \times \end{array}$$

So, each friend get 9 apples.

(iii) Total number of pens = 150

Total number of boxes = 5

∴ Number of pens in each box $= 150 \div 5$

$$\begin{array}{r|l} & 30 \\ 5 & 150 \\ & 150 \\ \hline & \times \end{array}$$

So, number of pens in each box = 30

Also, given cost of each pen = ₹ 10

∴ Cost of the pens in one box

$= 30 \times 10 =$ ₹ 300

7. (i) Total number of students = 48

Total number of teams = 6

∴ Number of students in each team

$= 48 \div 6$

$$\begin{array}{r|l} & 8 \\ 6 & 48 \\ & 48 \\ \hline & \times \end{array}$$

So, number of students in each team = 8

(ii) Number of chocolates each student get as reward = 2

∴ Number of chocolates Arjun need

$= 48 \times 2 = 96$

(iii) Total number of teams = 6

Number of matches each team plays = 4

∴ Total number of matches $= 6 \times 4$

$= 24$

CHAPTER 14 HOW BIG? HOW HEAVY?

Volume

Volume refers to the amount of the space an object occupies. In simple terms, volume tells us how big or small an object is.

$$\text{Volume of box} = \text{Length} \times \text{Breadth} \times \text{Height}$$

Volume is usually measured in cubic units such as cm^3, m^3 etc.

Capacity

Capacity is the amount that a container or space can hold. It is a measure of how much fluid can fit inside a container.

Weight and Mass

Weight (or mass) is the measure of how heavy or light an object is.

The weight of an object is usually measured in grams (g) and kilograms (kg).

$$1 \text{ kilogram} = 1000 \text{ grams (g)}$$

Unit of measurement

- Length is measured in centimetres (cm), metres (m) etc.
- Volume is measured in cubic units like cm^3 or m^3.
- Capacity is measured in millilitres (mL) and litres (L).
- Weight is measured in grams (g) and kilograms (kg).

NCERT FOLDER

Your Measuring Glass (NCERT Pg 188)

Q.1 Make a guess. Do you think the volume of 10 five-rupee coins will be more than that of 10 marbles?

Ans. * Yes, I think the volume of 10 five- rupee coins will be little more than that of 10 marbles.

Q.2 Guess the volume of each of these

(i) A ball is nearly............marbles.

(ii) An eraser is nearly............marbles.

(iii) A lemon is nearly............marbles.

(iv) A pencil is nearly............marbles.

(v) A potato is nearly............marbles.

Ans. *(i) A ball is nearly 8 marbles.

(ii) An eraser is nearly 2 marbles.

(iii) A lemon is nearly 4 marbles.

(iv) A pencil is nearly 1 marbles.

(v) A potato is nearly 15 marbles.

* *Students can write alternate answer as per their choice.*

Q.3 Now make your own measuring glass using 35 marbles. Take a glass of water and mark the level of water as '0'. Then, put in 5 marbles and mark the level of water as 5M.

Again, drop 5 marbles and mark the level of water as 10 M. Likewise make the markings for 15 M, 20 M, 25 M, 30 M and 35 M.

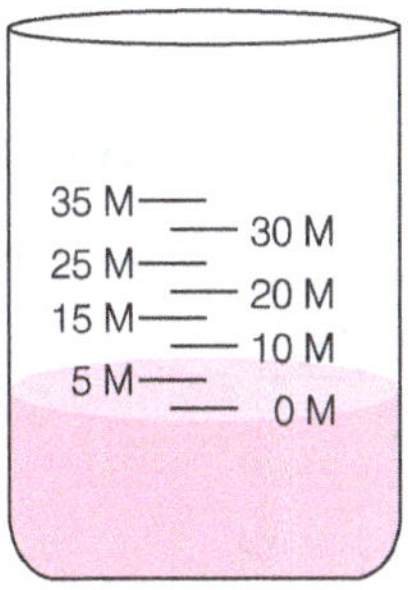

Now, put each thing in the measuring glass and check your guess. Try with different things like a matchbox, a stone, etc. and fill the table.

Name of the things	Its volume (nearly how many marbles ?)

Ans. Do yourself.

Which has More Volume? (NCERT Pg 189 - 190)

Q.4 Use your measuring bottle to find out

(i) What is the volume of 6 marbles? _________ mL

(ii) What is the volume of 16 one-rupee coins? ________ mL.

(iii) The volume of 24 marbles is ______ mL.

(iv) The volume of 32 one-rupee coins? _________ mL

(v) Mollie puts some five-rupee coins in the measuring bottle. How many coins has she put in it:

(a) If 30 mL water is pushed up?

(b) If 60 mL water is pushed up ?

Ans. *(i) 60 mL

*(ii) 32 mL

*(iii) 240 mL $\left[\because 24 \times \frac{60}{6} = 240\right]$

*(iv) 64 mL $\left[\because 32 \times \frac{32}{16} = 64\right]$

(v) (a) 27 coins $\left[\because 30 \times \frac{9}{10} = 27\right]$

(b) 54 coins $\left[\because 60 \times \frac{9}{10} = 54\right]$

Q.5 First guess and then use your measuring bottle to find out the volume in mL of some other things.

Thing	Its volume (in mL)

Ans. Do yourself.

Q.6 Guess how many litres of water your body will push up?

Ans. *28 litres of water.

How Many Can Fit In? (NCERT Pg 190-191)

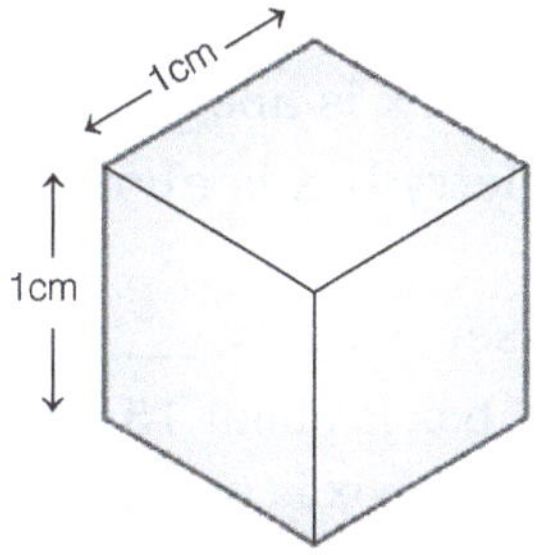

Q.7 (i) This is a cube whose sides are of 1 cm each. See, your Math-Magic book is 1 cm high. So guess how many such centimetre cubes will take the same space as your Math-Magic book?

(ii)

If all these cubes are arranged in one line, then how long will that line be? ________ cm

Ans. *(i) My Math- Magic book is about 26 cm long.

So, 26 cm cubes will fit along its length.

And its width is about 20 cm, so 20 cubes will fit along its width.

∴ Total number of cubes will fit in Math-Magic book = $1 \times 26 \times 20 = 520$ cubes.

So, total 520 cm cubes will fit on the Math-Magic book.

(ii) 520 cm

Practice time (NCERT Pg 191)

Q.8 A stage (platform) is made with 5 Math-Magic books. The volume of this stage is the same as _______ cm cubes.

Ans. * ∵ 520 cubes will fit on the 1 Math- Magic book.

∴ The volume of a stage with 5 Math-Magic book will be $= 5 \times 520$

$= 2600$ cm cubes .

Q.9 Guess the volume of these things in cm cubes.

(i) A matchbox is about ______ cm cubes.

(ii) A geometry box is about ________ cm cubes.

(iii) An eraser is about _______ cm cubes.

Ans. *(i) A matchbox is about 15 cm cubes.

(ii) A geometry box is about 96 cm cubes.

(iii) An eraser is about 4 cm cubes.

Q.10 How will you check your guess? Discuss.

Ans. ***For matchbox**

Volume = Length × Breadth × Height

$= 5 \text{ cm} \times 3 \text{ cm} \times 1 \text{ cm} = 15 \text{ cm}^3$

For geometry box

Volume = Length × Breadth × Height

$= 16 \text{ cm} \times 6 \text{ cm} \times 1 \text{ cm} = 96 \text{ cm}^3$

For eraser

Volume = Length × Breadth × Height

$= 2 \text{ cm} \times 2 \text{ cm} \times 1 \text{ cm} = 4 \text{ cm}^3$

Matchbox Play (NCERT Pg 191-192)

Q.11 Tanu is making a stage with matchboxes. She first puts 14 matchboxes like this in the first layer.

She makes 4 such layers and her stage looks like this.

(i) She used ______ matchboxes to make this stage.

(ii) The volume of one matchbox is the same as10 cm cubes.

Then, the volume of this stage is same as _____ cm cubes .

(iii) If all these cubes are arranged in a line, how long will that line be? ________ cm.

(iv) Which has more volume _______ your Math-Magic book or Tanu's platform?

Ans. (i) ∵ Number of matchboxes used in 1 layer = 14

∴ Number of matchboxes used in 4 layer $= 4 \times 14 = 56$

So, she used 56 matchboxes to make this stage.

(ii) ∵ Volume of one matchboxe = 10 cm^3

∴ Volume of 56 matchboxes = 56×10

= 560 cm cubes.

So, the volume of this stage will be 560 cm^3.

(iii) 560 cm long.

*(iv) Tanu's platform has more volume.

Q.12 With your friends, collect many empty matchboxes of the same size. Measure the sides and write here.

My matchbox ________ cm wide.

It is ______ cm long.

It is _______ cm high

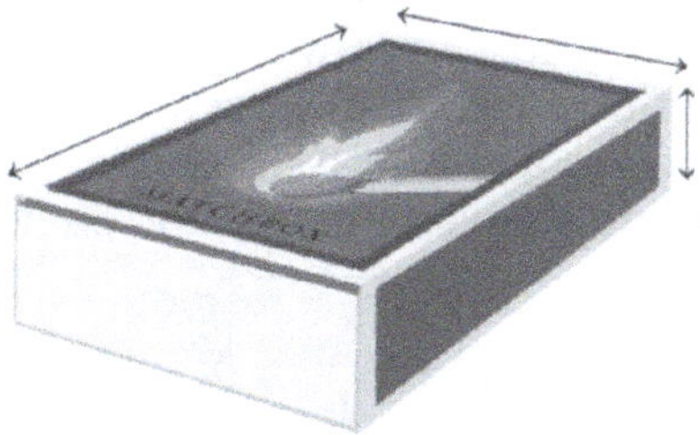

Ans. *My matchbox is 3 cm wide.

It is 5 cm long.

It is 1 cm high.

Q.13 (i) Use 56 matchboxes to make platforms of different heights.

Fill this table.

	How high is it ?	How long is it ?	How wide is it ?
Platform 1			
Platform 2			
Platform 3			

The volume of each platform is equal to _______ matchboxes.

(ii) Make deep drawings of the platforms you have made.

Ans. *(i)

	How high is it ?	How long is it ?	How wide is it ?
Platform 1	2 cm	35 cm	12 cm
Platform 2	4 cm	70 cm	3 cm
Platform 3	1 cm	40 cm	21 cm

The volume of each platform is equal to 56 matchboxes.

(ii) Following are the deep drawings of the above platform :

Platform 1

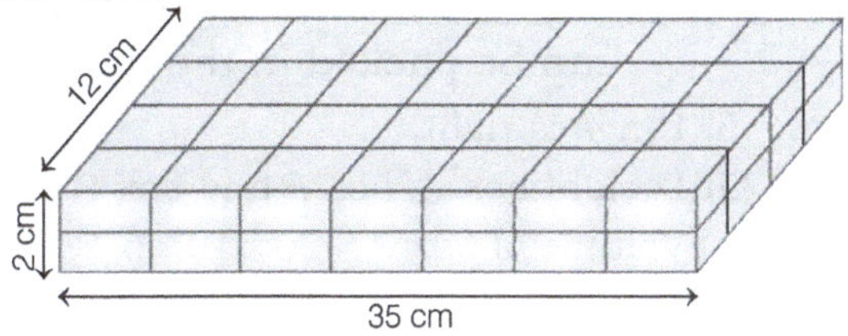

$l = 35$ cm , $h = 2$ cm , $b = 12$ cm

Platform 2

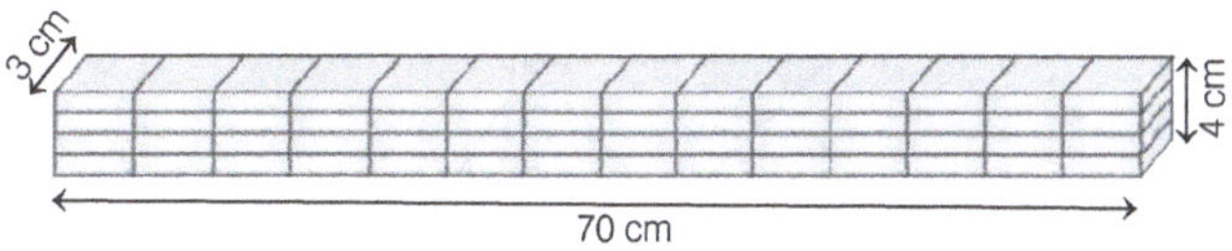

$l = 70$ cm , $b = 3$ cm , $h = 4$ cm

Platform 3

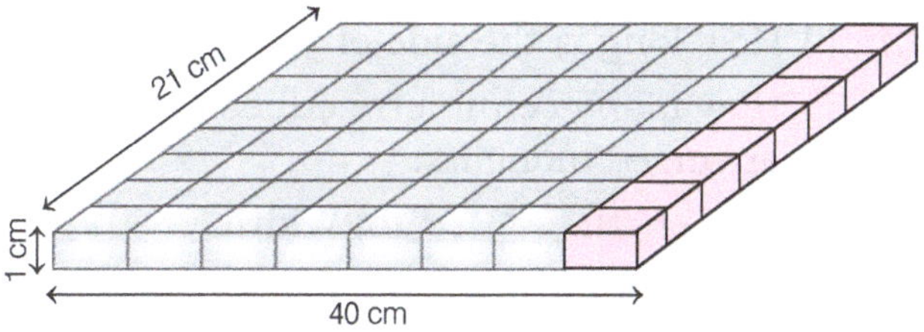

$l = 40$ cm , $b = 21$ cm , $h = 1$ cm

Practice time (NCERT Pg 193)

Q.14 Mohan arranged his matchboxes like this.

(i) How many matchboxes did he use to make it? What is its volume in matchboxes?--------- matchboxes.

(ii) Collect empty matchboxes. Arrange them in an interesting way. Make a deep drawing of it.

Ans. (i) Number of matchboxes used by Mohan

$= 16 + 9 + 4 + 1$

$= 30$

The volume is 30 matchboxes.

*(ii) From 6 matchboxes.

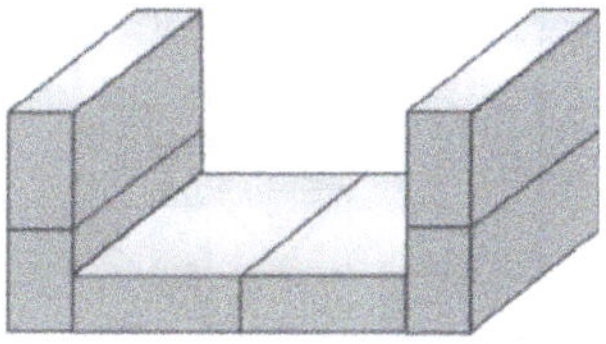

How Big is Your Cube? (NCERT Pg 194-195)

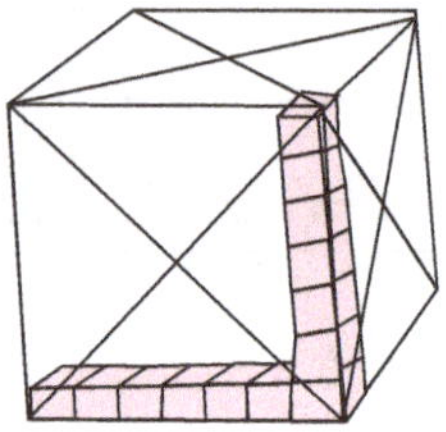

Q.15 (i) How long is the side of your cube?

(ii) How many centimetre cubes can be arranged along its:

(a) Length ______ (b) Width ________

(c) Height ______

(iii) Answer Thimpu's questions

(a) To make the first layer on the table how many cm cubes will I use?

(b) How many such layers will I need to make a paper cube?

(iv) So the total cm cubes = ________

(v) The volume of the paper cube is same as ________ cm cubes.

Ans. (i) 7 cm

(ii) (a) Length = 7 cm (b) Width = 7 cm

(c) Height = 7 cm

(iii) (a) $\because 7 \times 7 \times 1 = 49$

So, he will use 49 cm cubes.

(b) 7 such layers.

(iv) $\because 7 \times 7 \times 7 = 343$ cm

So, the total is 343 cm cubes.

(v) 343 cm cubes.

Q.16 Anan made a big cube having double the side of your paper cube.

How many of the your paper cubes will fit in it? Try doing it by collecting all the cubes made in your class.

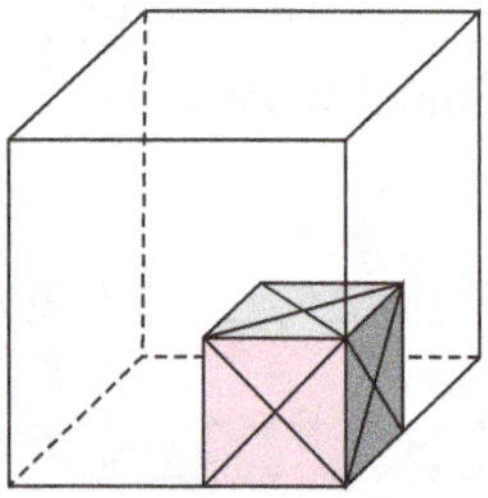

Ans. Side of Anan's cube $= 2 \times 7 = 14$ cm

We have arranged $2 \times 2 = 4$ paper cubes in first layer and 2 such layers of 4 paper cubes made.

$\therefore$ We can arrange $4 \times 2 = 8$ cubes

Packing Cubes (NCERT Pg 195-196)

Q.17 Ganesh and Dinga want to pack 4000 centimetre cubes in boxes. These are to be sent to a school. There are three different boxes available for packing.

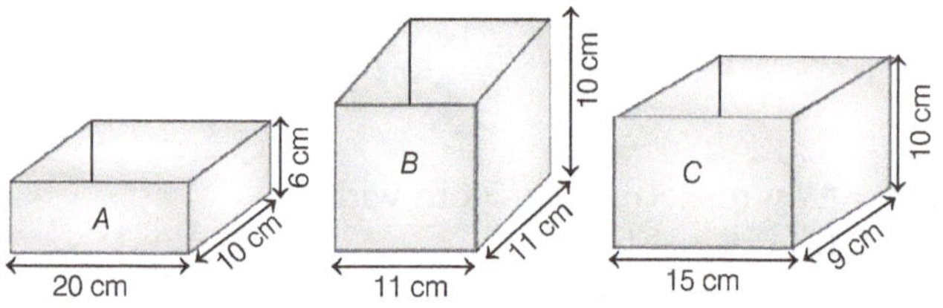

(i) What is your guess? Who is right?

(ii) How can Ganesh and Dinga test their guesses before packing the cubes in the boxes? Discuss with your friend.

(iii) Use Ganesh's method and write

(a) ______ centimetre cubes can be arranged in box *B*.

(b) ______ centimeter cubes can be arranged in box *C*.

(c) So _______ centimetre cubes in all can be packed in the three boxes.

Ans. (i) Dinga is right.

(ii) Look at box *A*, box *B* and box *C*

Volume of box $A = 20 \times 10 \times 6$

$= 1200$ cm cubes

Volume of box $B = 11 \times 11 \times 10$

$= 1210$ cm cubes

Volume of box $C = 15 \times 9 \times 10$

$= 1350$ cm cubes

Adding the volume of all these three boxes, we get

Total volume $= 1200 + 1210 + 1350$

$= 3760$ cm cubes

$\because 3760 < 4000$

This is less than 4000 cm cubes and hence Dinga is right.

(iii) (a) Now, look at box *B*. In the first layer, we can arrange $11 \times 11 = 121$ cubes.

And 10 such layers can be packed.

So, in box *B*, we can arrange $121 \times 10 = 1210$ cubes.

(b) Again, look at box *C*. In the first layer, we can arrange $15 \times 9 = 135$ cubes.

And 10 such layers can be packed.

So, in box *C*, we can arrange $135 \times 10 = 1350$ cubes.

(c) Look at box *A*. In the first layer, we can arrange $20 \times 10 = 200$ cubes.

And 6 such layers can be packed.

So, in box *A*, we can arrange $200 \times 6 = 1200$ cubes.

Therefore, total cm cubes packed in all three boxes

$= 1200 + 1210 + 1350 = 3760$ cubes

Which Pipe Fills More? (NCERT Pg 196)

Q.18 Collect some old postcards. You can also use thick paper of size 14 cm × 9 cm.

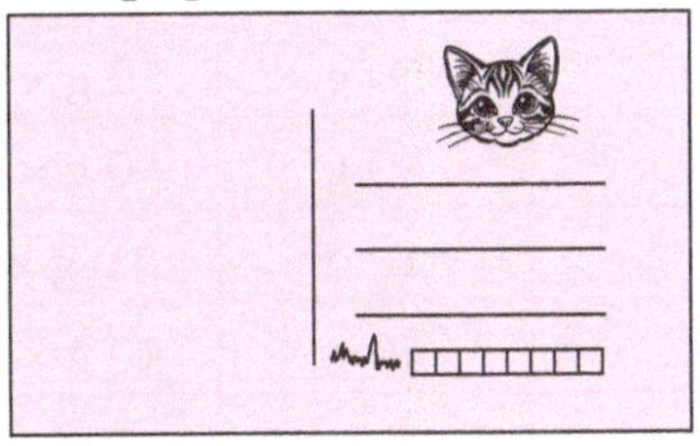

Fold the postcard along the width to make pipe-1. Join the ends with cello tape.

Take another postcard and fold it along the length to make pipe-2. Join the ends with tape. Guess which pipe can take more sand inside it. Hold it on a plate and pour sand to check your guess. Was your guess correct? Discuss.

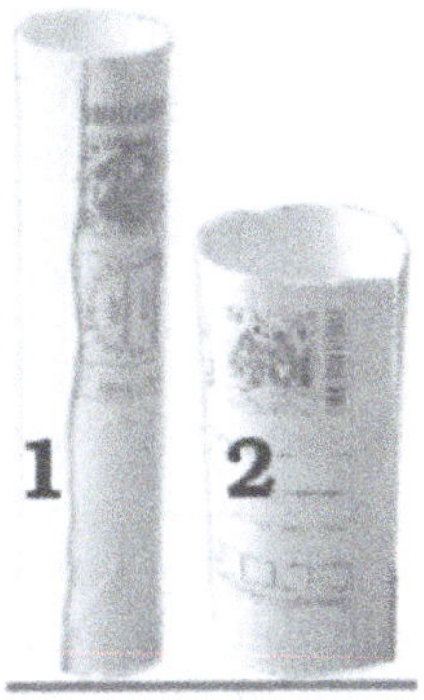

Ans. Pipe 2 can take more sand.

When I checked my answer was correct.

Q.19 Now do the same with other pipes shown here. To make the triangle-shaped pipe-3, draw two lines on the postcard. Fold the postcard along the lines. Join the ends with tape.

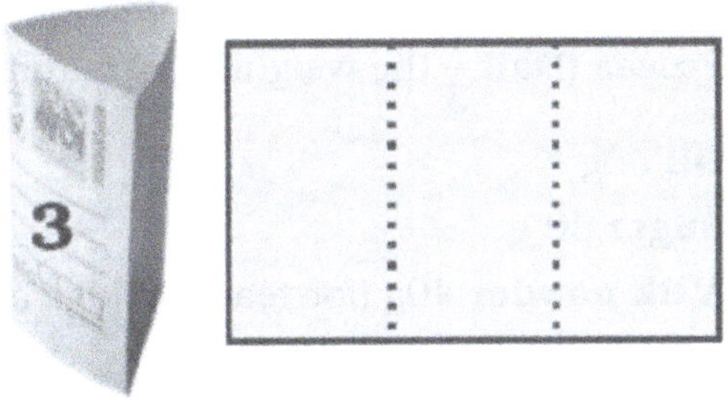

Now make the square-shaped pipe-4.

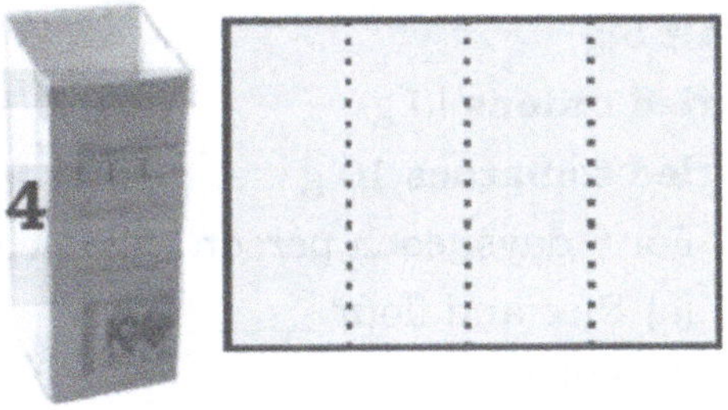

Find out which pipe can take.the most sand inside it. So which pipe has the most volume?

Ans. Pipe-4 can take more sand.

Square-shaped pipe-4 has more volume.

Trek to Gangotri (NCERT Pg 197-198)

Q.20 The students of Class XII are going on a trek to Gangotri. They have to pack their bags for six days and keep them light. They also have to take things that do not take too much space. So, they will look for things that have both less volume and less weight. After all, they will carry their own bags while climbing the mountains! They even dry the onions and tomatoes to make them light. One kg of onions or tomatoes becomes 100 g when the water inside dries up.

The list of food each person will need for one day:

Rice 100g

Flour (Atta) 100 g

Pulses (Dal) $\frac{1}{3}$ the weight of rice and flour

Oil 50g

Sugar 50 g

Milk powder 40g (for tea, porridge and hot drink)

Tea Around 10g

Dalia 40g for breakfast.

Salt 5 g

Dried onions 10 g

Dried tomatoes 10 g

(i) For 6 days, each person will need

(a) Rice and flour ______ g

(b) Pulses ______ g

(c) Dried onions ______ g

(ii) How much of fresh tomatoes should be dried for 10 people?

(iii) What is the total weight of food (for 6 days) in each person's bag?

Ans. (i) (a) For 1 day, each person will need

rice = 100 g and flour = 100 g

$\therefore$ For 6 days, each person will need

rice and flour $= 6 \times (100 + 100)$ g = 1200 g

(b) For 1 day, each person will need

Pulses (Dal) is $\frac{1}{3}$ the weight of rice and flour.

$\therefore$ For 6 days, each person will need

Pulses (Dal) $= \frac{1200}{3}$ g = 400 g

(c) $\because$ Dried onion for 1 day = 10 g.

$\therefore$ Dried onion for 6 days $= 6 \times 10$ g = 60 g

(ii) $\because$ Dried tomatoes need for 1 people for 1 day = 10 g.

$\therefore$ Dried tomatoes need for 6 days for 10 people $= 6 \times 10 \times 10$ g = 600 g

$\because$ 1 kg or 1000 g dried tomatoes becomes 100 g when it dried.

$\therefore$ 600 g dried tomatoes need $= 600 \times \frac{1000}{100}$

$= 6000$ g

So, 6000g or 6 kg fresh tomatoes should be dried for 6 days for 10 people.

(iii) List of food for 6 days

Food	For 1 day	For 6 days
Rice	100 g	6×100 g = 600 g
Flour	100 g	6×100 g = 600 g
Pulse (Dal)	$\frac{200}{3}$ g	$\frac{200}{3}$ g $\times 6 = 400$ g
Oil	50 g	50 g $\times$ 6 = 300 g
Sugar	50 g	50 g $\times$ 6 = 300 g
Milk powder	40 g	40 g $\times$ 6 = 240 g
Tea	10 g	10 g $\times$ 6 = 60 g
Dalia	40 g	40 g $\times$ 6 = 240 g
Salt	5 g	5 g $\times$ 6 = 30 g
Dried onion	10 g	10 g $\times$ 6 = 60 g
Dried tomatoes	10 g	10 g $\times$ 6 = 60 g
		Total = 2890 g

So, the total weight of food for 6 days in each person's bag is 2890 g or 2 kg 890 g.

How Heavy am I? (NCERT Pg 198-199)

Q.21 Do you remember the story of how Vaidika's daughter found the weight of an elephant? (Math-Magic Class IV NCERT Page 143)

Can you guess the weight of the heaviest animal on this earth? No, it's not me. I weigh only 5000 kg!

(i) It is the Blue Whale. Its weight is around 35 times more than me. So, how many thousand kg does it weigh?

(ii) Guess how many children of your weight will be equal to the weight of an elephant of 5000 kg.

(iii) At birth, a baby elephant weighs around 90 kg. How much did you weigh when you were born? Find out. How many times is a baby elephant heavier than you were at birth?

(iv) If a grown up elephant eats 136 kg of food in a day, then it will eat around _______ kg in a month. Guess about how much it will eat in a year.

Ans. (i) Weight of elephant = 5000 kg

$\because$ Weight of blue whale is 35 times more than an elephant.

$\therefore$ Weight of blue whale $= 36 \times 5000$ kg

$= 180000$ kg

So, the weight of blue whale is 180 thousand kilogram.

*(ii) The weight of one children be 50 kg.

$\therefore$ Number of children which will be equal to the weight of an elephant

$$= \frac{5000 \text{ kg}}{50 \text{ kg}} = 100 \text{ children}$$

*(iii) Baby elephant's weight = 90 kg

My weight was 3 kg at the time of birth.

So, $90 \div 3 = 30$

Therefore, baby elephant is 30 times heavier than me at the time of birth.

(iv) Quantity of food eaten by elephant in a day = 136 kg

$\because$ Number of days in a month = 30

$\therefore$ Quantity of food eaten by elephant in 30 days $= 136 \times 30 = 4080$ kg

Now, number of month in a year = 12

$\therefore$ Quantity of food eaten by elephant in a year $= 4080 \times 12 = 48960$ kg

Shahid Saves the Bank! (NCERT Pg 199-200)

Q.22 Shahid works in a bank. He sits at the cash counter. Whenever there are too many coins he does not count them. He just weighs them.

Weighing is so much easier. The weight of a 5-rupee coin is 9 g. Tell me the weight of the sack and I will tell you the number of coins in it.

(i)

Can you hold these coins and say which is the heaviest?

(ii) My bag of 5-rupee coins weighs 9 kg. So, how many coins does it have? One kg is equal to 1000g, so 9 kg is equal to 9000 g. If one coin weighs 9g, then the bag weighing 9000 g has $9000 \div 9 =$ ______ coins in it. Easy!

(iii) How many coins are there in a sack of 5 rupee coins if it weighs

(a) 18 kg ? (b) 54 kg ?

(c) 4500 g ? (d) 2 kg and 250 g ?

(e) 1 kg and 125 g ?

(iv) 2250 g can also be written as 2 kg and 250 g. Can you explain why?

(v) A 2 rupee coin weighs 6 g. What is the weight of a sack with

(a) 2200 coins ? _____ kg _____ g

(b) 3000 coins ? _____ kg

(vi) If 100 one rupee coins weigh 485 g, then how much will 10000 coins weigh? ______ kg _____ g

Ans. (i)  is the heaviest.

(ii) $9000 \div 9 = 1000$

(iii) (a) 18 kg

$\because$ 1 kg = 1000 g

$\therefore$ 18 kg $= 18 \times 1000$ g $= 18000$ g

$\because$ Weight of 1 coins = 9 g

$\therefore$ Number of coins in 18000 g $= \dfrac{18000}{9}$

$= 2000$ coins

So, there are 2000 coins in a sack of 5 rupee coins if it weighs 18 kg.

(b) 54 kg

54 kg $= 54 \times 1000$ g $= 54000$ g

$\because$ Weight of 1 coin = 9 g

$\therefore$ Number of coins in 54000 g $= \dfrac{54000}{9}$

$= 6000$ coins

So, there are 6000 coins in a sack of 5 rupee coins if it weighs 54 kg.

(c) 4500 g

$\because$ Weight of 1 coin = 9 g

$\therefore$ Number of coins in 4500 g $= \dfrac{4500}{9}$

$= 500$ coins

So, there are 500 coins in a sack of 5 rupee coins if it weighs 4500 g.

(d) 2 kg and 250 g

2 kg and 250 g = 2000 g + 250 g = 2250 g

$\because$ Weight of 1 coin = 9 g

$\therefore$ Number of coins in 2250 g $= \dfrac{2250}{9}$

$= 250$ coins

So, there are 250 coins in a sack of 5 rupee coins if it weighs 2250 g or 2 kg and 250 g.

(e) 1 kg and 125 g

1 kg and 125 g = 1000 g + 125 g = 1125 g

$\because$ Weight of one coin = 9 g

$\therefore$ Number of coins in 1125 g $= \dfrac{1125}{9}$

$= 125$ coins

So, there are 125 coins in a sack of 5 rupee coins if it weighs 1125 g or 1 kg and 125 g.

(iv) $\because$ 1 kg = 1000 g

$\therefore$ 2 kg $= 2 \times 1000$ g = 2000 g

$\Rightarrow$ 2 kg and 250 g = 2000 g + 250 g = 2250 g

So, 2250 g can also be written as 2 kg and 250 g.

(v) (a) $\because$ Weight of one 2 rupee coin = 6 g

$\therefore$ Weight of 2200 coins $= 2200 \times 6$ g

= 13200 g

= (13000 + 200) g

= 13000 g + 200 g

= 13 kg 200 g

[$\because$ 1000 g = 1 kg]

So, the weight of a sack with 2200 coins of 2 rupee is 13200 g or 13 kg 200 g.

(b) $\because$ Weight of one 2 rupee coin = 6 g

$\therefore$ Weight of 3000 coins $= 3000 \times 6$ g

= 18000 g

= 18 kg

So, the weight of a sack with 3000 coins of 2 rupee is 18 kg.

(vi) $\because$ Weight of 100 one-rupee coins = 485 g

$\therefore$ Weight of 10000 coins weight of

$= 100 \times 100$ one-rupee coins

$= 100 \times 485$ g = 48500 g

= 48000 g + 500 g

= 48 kg and 500 g

Find out and discuss (NCERT Pg 200)

Q.23 (i) How do people who cannot see make out different notes and coins?

(**Hint** Look for a shape ▲, ■, ●, ▬ etc. on notes of ₹ 20, 50, 100, 500 etc. and feel it)

(ii) What should we look for to check if a 100-rupee note is real or fake?

Ans. (i) Each note has a different shape embossed for recognisation. So, blind people identify them by touch.

(ii) We may check the following things

(a) The shape, size and thickness of the paper.

(b) The printing style and ink used.

(c) The watermark (the white area with Gandhi's picture).

(d) The words 'भारत' and 'RBI' on the shiny security thread.

PRACTICE QUESTIONS

1. Fill in the blanks
   (i) A _______ is used to measure the weight of an object. (weighing machine/scale)
   (ii) The unit used to measure weight in the metric system is ______ .
   (kilogram/metre)
   (iii) Volume is the amount of _______ a 3D object takes up.
   (space/weight)
   (iv) The unit used for measuring liquid capacity is _______ .
   (litre/metre)
2. True or False
   (i) The mass of an object is the same everywhere.
   (ii) The weight of a person is measured in metres.
   (iii) 500 g is equal to 0.5 kg.
   (iv) Volume can be measured in litres for liquids.
3. Multiple choice questions
   (i) 3.5 kg is equal to
   (a) 2500 g (b) 3000 g
   (c) 3500 g (d) 4500 g
   (ii) A container holds 2 L of water. If another container can hold 500 mL more water, what is the capacity of new container?
   (a) 2.5 L (b) 2.2 L
   (c) 3 L (d) 2.7 L
   (iii) If 10 coins weigh 18 gram, then the weight of 225 coins is
   (a) 400 gram (b) 380 gram
   (c) 405 gram (d) 409 gram
4. Odd one out
   (i) (a) Length (b) Width
   (c) Volume (d) Height
   (ii) (a) Metre (b) Kilogram
   (c) Millilitre (d) Centimetre
5. Word problems.
   (i) A water tank has a length of 5 m, a breadth of 4 m and a height of 2 m. What is the volume of the tank?
   (ii) A jug can hold 1.5 L of water. How much water can 4 such jugs hold together?

ANSWERS & SOLUTIONS

1. (i) weighing machine
   (ii) kilogram
   (iii) space
   (iv) litre
2. (i) True
   (ii) False
   (iii) True
   (iv) True
3. (i) (c) (ii) (a)
   (iii) (c)
4. (i) (c)
5. (i) Length of tank = 5 m
   Breadth of tank = 4 m
   and height of tank = 2 m
   ∴ Volume of tank
   = Length × Breadth × Height
   = 5 m × 4 m × 2 m
   = 40 m cubes
   (ii) ∵ Capacity of 1 jug = 1.5 L
   ∴ Capacity of 4 jugs = 1.5 × 4 = 6 L
   Hence, 4 such jugs can hold 6 L water.

Marigold

(English)

CHAPTER 1 ICE-CREAM MAN

Summary of the Poem The poem describes children's love for ice-cream in hot summers. The ice-cream man visits on his cart under a round umbrella. He has many flavours of ice-cream. He also has chilled and colourful frosty-fizz to drink. The ice-cream man becomes a means of happiness for everyone.

Stanza-wise Explanation

Stanza 1

When summer's in the city,
And brick's a blaze of heat,
The Ice-cream Man with his little cart
Goes trundling down the street.

Word-Meaning *Blaze - To shine brightly; Cart - A vehicle with three or four wheels; Trundling - To move slowly*

Exp. The poet describes a hot summer day. It is very difficult to bear the heat of the Sun. The ice-cream man comes with his small ice-cream cart to give relief from the heat. He goes round the street to give the tasty creamy ice-cream to everyone.

Stanza 2

Beneath his round umbrella,
Oh, what a joyful sight,
To see him fill the cones with mounds
Of cooling brown and white:

Word-Meaning *Beneath - Under; Mounds - A small heap or hill, here, scoops of ice-cream.*

Exp. The ice-cream man stands under a round umbrella. He brings a lot of joy and happiness for children. Everyone gets excited when they see him filling the cones with cool and creamy, brown and white scoops of ice-cream.

Stanza 3

Vanilla, chocolate, strawberry,
Or chilly things to drink
From bottles full of frosty-fizz,
Green, orange, white or pink.

Word-Meaning *Chilly - Very cold; Frosty-fizz - A drink made with crushed ice, making a bubbling sound.*

Exp. The ice-cream man has vanilla, chocolate and strawberry flavour of ice-cream. He also brings with him chilled frosty-fizz to drink. It is available in many colours like green, orange, pink and white.

Stanza 4

His cart might be a flower bed,
Of roses and sweet peas,
The way the children cluster round
As thick as honeybees.

Word-Meaning *Sweet peas - A kind of flowers; Cluster - To make a group or gather together.*

Exp. Ice-cream man's cart is like a bed of roses and sweet peas. The children are always gathered round his cart like honeybees. They all are excited to eat the sweet and creamy ice-cream.

NCERT FOLDER

Reading is Fun (NCERT Page 4)

Q.1 In which season is ice-cream popular?

Ans. Ice-cream is popular in the summer season.

Q.2 Who feels joyful on seeing the ice-cream man?

Ans. Children feel joyful on seeing the ice-cream man.

Q.3 Name the different flavours of ice-cream the ice-cream man has in his cart.

Ans. The ice-cream man has vanilla, chocolate and strawberry flavours of ice-cream in his cart.

Q.4 What are the two things that the ice-cream man is selling?

Ans. The ice-cream man is selling creamy ice-cream and chilled frosty-fizz.

Q.5 What is the ice-cream cart compared to in the poem?

Ans. The ice-cream cart is compared to a flower-bed of roses and sweet peas.

Let's Write (Page 4 and 5)

Having an ice cream on a hot summer day is exciting and enjoyable.

Q.1 Write about some of the exciting and enjoyable things that one can do in the winter season.

Ans.
- Building a blanket fort
- Eating ground nuts and popcorn
- Going out on picnics
- Enjoying bonfire
- Playing in the warmth of the Sun
- Sitting in the warmth of a blanket and watching movies.

Q.2 List as many summer activities as you can.

Ans.
- Swimming
- Having ice-cream and cold drinks
- Sipping on coconut water
- Going to hill stations
- Going to beaches

Q.3 Now group these into indoor and outdoor activities.

Indoor Activities	Outdoor Activities
Building a blanket fort	Enjoying bonfire
Sitting in the warmth of a blanket and watching movies	Playing in the warmth of the Sun
Having ice-creams and cold drinks	Going out on picnics
	Swimming
	Going to hill stations
	Going to beaches

Say Aloud (NCERT Page 5)

Circle the words where you get a zzzzz sound. One is done for you.

honeybees

price	prize	maze	face
rice	rise	blaze	fizz
lazy	lacy	busy	racy
raise	rays	race	ace
chase	this	these	frosty

Ans. prize, maze, rise, blaze, fizz, lazy, busy, rise, raise, rays, chase, these

Let's Listen (NCERT Page 6)

Q.1 Listen and tell the sounds of these words in the poem produce.

- Cart - trull .... trulll
- Drink - seeee .... seeee

Can you make these sounds?

Ans. Do it yourself

Q.2 What are some of the different sounds you hear when the ice-cream man comes?

Ans.
- I hear the ringing of the bell of the ice-cream cart.
- I hear the voice of ice-cream man calling children out.
- I hear the joyful sound of children's laughter.
- I hear the clink of coins.
- I hear the sound of children slurping or licking the creamy ice-cream.

Find Out and Write a Report (NCERT Page 6)

Here is a report on Uncle Lal's farm.

Father took me to visit Uncle Lal's dairy farm.

I saw all of Uncle Lal's cows. he has fifty cows. They eat grass in the big green farms. In the evening the farmers bring them to the barn to be milked. Uncle Lal sells his milk in the city.

When writting a report, remember to do these things

- Think of a good title. Write it correctly.
- Keep to your subject.
- Tell things in the right order.
- Make your paper look neat.

In groups of four, write a report on different brands of ice-creams available in your area.

You may use the following clues.

- Start with a short introduction which contains the topic.
- Then list the ice-cream brands available in your area.
- Next, say which are the common flavours of ice-cream in each of the brands.
- Under each brand, find out which flavours are being sold the most. Also find out their prices.
- Finally, write which do you think is the most popular ice-cream.

Ans. **Ice Cream Bonanza**

Everyone enjoys a scoop of creamy chilled ice-cream in the summer. There are many ice-cream shops in my area. Some of the most popular brands are NIC ice-cream, Amul ice-cream, Havmor and Baskin Robbins. They have a variety of flavours for everyone to enjoy. Baskin Robbins is popular for its Gold Medal Ribbon ice-cream. Amul has the best cornettos and brick ice-creams. NIC has unique flavours like coconut. Havmor is famous for its chocolate lollipop ice-cream and brownie sundae ice-cream. All these ice-creams range between ₹ 25-85. Among all of these, cornettos are the most favourite of all children as well as adults.

Word Building (NCERT Page 7 and 8)

Q.1 Colour the boxes that have rhyming words.

city cart	heat street	blows goes	do go
hard yard	bowl doll	cow so	label table
sky my	play obey	race face	write night

Ans.

city cart	heat street	blows goes	do go
hard yard	bowl doll	cow so	label table
sky my	play obey	race face	write night

Q.2 What do the following words describe in the poem?

Joyful ________

Little ________

Round ________

What are the describing words used in the poem for the following?

________ mounds

________ flavour

________ cluster

Ans.
- Joyful sight
  Little cart
  Round umbrella
- Cooling, brown and white mounds
  Vanilla, chocolate, strawberry flavour
  Thick cluster

Fun Time (NCERT Page 8 and 9)

Q.1 Colour the boxes with the colours of the flavours mentioned in each.

chocolate	vanilla	orange	black currant
strawberry	raspberry	butter-scotch	pista

Ans. Do it yourself

Q.2 Draw and colour your dream ice-cream.

Describe it using interesting describing words – the colours, the flavours, the size, how it looks, tastes, feels, etc.

Ans. Note : You can draw the ice cream of your choice.

Here is the ice cream of my dreams. It is a huge cone shaped cornetto and looks like a birthday cap. It has layers of white vanilla and chocolate. It is creamy with a generous sprinkling of nuts. It has an exotic taste, a mixture of several flavours in one.

Q.3 Have you ever eaten kulfi, the ice cream from North India?

The following sentences describe how it is served but they are not in the correct order. Write the correct number before each sentence.

1.  ____ He scoops out the *kulfi* on a plate.

2.  ____ Then he pours some sweet syrup over it and serves it.

3.  ____ The *kulfiwala* takes the *kulfi* mould out of the pitcher.

4.  ____ He arranges some *falooda* around it.

Ans.
1. The kulfiwala takes the kulfi mould out of the pitcher.
2. He scoops out the kulfi on a plate.
3. He arranges some falooda around it.
4. Then he pours some sweet syrup over it and serves it.

PRACTICE QUESTIONS

Multiple Choice Questions

1. Which season is mentioned in the poem?
   (a) Winter (b) Spring
   (c) Summer (d) Autumn
2. What does the ice-cream man have?
   (a) A cart (b) A shop (c) A stand (d) A store
3. What does he offer to children?
   (a) Ice-cream cones (b) Fizzy drinks
   (c) Both (a) and (b) (d) None of these

Ans. 1. (c), 2. (a), 3. (c)

Extract Based Questions

Read the extract given below and answer the questions that follow.

Vanilla, chocolate, strawberry,
Or chilly things to drink
From bottles full of frosty-fizz,
Green, orange, white, or pink.

His cart might be a flower bed,
Of roses and sweet peas,
The way the children cluster round
As thick as honeybees.

1. How many flavours is the ice-cream man selling? Can you name them?

Ans. The Ice-cream Man is selling three flavours of ice-cream. They are vanilla, chocolate and strawberry.

2. What is ice-cream man's cart compared to?

Ans. Ice-cream man's cart is compared to a flower bed.

3. Select the option which describes the meaning of the word 'cluster'.
   (a) Make a round (b) Gather around
   (c) Buy ice-cream (d) Together

Ans. (b) Gather around

Answer the Following Questions

1. What kind of umbrella does the ice-cream man have?

Ans. The ice-cream man has a round umbrella.

2. What does the ice-cream man fill the cones with?

Ans. The ice cream man fills the cones with cooling brown and white mounds.

3. Where does the ice-cream man go with his cart?

Ans. The ice-cream man goes trundling down the street with his cart.

4. What is cold, sweet and creamy to eat?

Ans. Ice-cream is cold, sweet and creamy to eat.

Let's Write

1. Your father took you to a zoo. You have to write a report on different animals you saw and what they were doing in the zoo.

While writing a report, remember to do these things.

- Think of a good title. Write it correctly.
- Keep to your subject
- Tell things in the right order.
- Make your format look neat.

You may use the following clues.

- Start with a short introduction of the topic.
- List all the animals you saw and what they were doing.
- Say what did you like about the zoo.
- What shocked you the most?
- Would you visit the zoo again?

Ans. **My Fun Visit to the Zoo** Father took me to visit the city zoo. It was a pleasant day and all the animals and birds looked splendid. The zoo was full of green plants and many big trees. I saw a lion first. The lion was bigger than I imagined. Then came the lazy hippopotamus resting as always.
I was scared to see a big python snake. For the first time, I saw the difference between a leopard and a tiger. Many peacocks were also there. I saw one dancing with its beautiful wings. The zoo was very vibrant.
I would love to visit it again.

CHAPTER 2

WONDERFUL WASTE!

Summary of the Chapter

Once, the Maharaja of Travancore decided to give a grand dinner party in his palace. In the afternoon, he went into the kitchen to check the dishes prepared for the party. There, he saw a pile of vegetable scraps. He asked his cook about it. The cook replied that he was going to throw them away. The Maharaja told him to find a way to use the scraps wisely.

The cook got puzzled after hearing his commands. Suddenly, an excellent idea came to his mind. He took the bits, cleaned them and cut them into long strips. He put them in a pot and placed it on the fire to cook them. He added many ingredients like grounded coconut, green chillies, garlic, curd and some salt. When the dish was prepared, he decorated it with coconut oil and curry leaves. He served this dish at the dinner party and named it Avial.

Avial became famous in Kerala and is one of the main dishes in traditional Kerala feast. The interesting thing to note is that it was made out of a basket of waste.

WORD-MEANING

Grand - Very big; Survey - To check; Feast - a larger dinner; Scraps - Left over material; Sternly - Strictly, In a fix - Confused, Flash across the mind - An idea that suddenly comes to the mind; Ground - Crushed; Whipped - To beat or mix thoroughly; Tempting - Yummy; Lo and behold - To look with surprise; Traditional feast - Hearty meal served on a special occasion.

NCERT FOLDER

Reading is Fun (NCERT Page 12)

Q.1 What were the preparations in the palace for?

Ans. The preparations in the palace were for a grand feast.

Q.2 Why did the Maharaja go into the kitchen in the afternoon?

Ans. The Maharaja went into the kitchen in the afternoon to survey the dishes that were being prepared for the feast.

Q.3. What had the cook planned to do with the vegetable scraps?

Ans. The cook had planned to throw the vegetable scraps as they were waste.

Q.4 Ingredients are the things that are used to make a dish. Circle the ingredients of avail in the box below.

chillies	groundnut	wood	vegetable scraps
coconut	roasted peanuts	curd	pot
garlic	broken bangles	basket	curry leaves

Ans. chillies, vegetable scraps, coconut, curd, garlic, curry leaves

Q.5 State whether the following are True or False.

(i) The king had ordered a dinner in the palace.

Ans. True

(ii) No one had heard of or tasted avial before.

Ans. True

(iii) The cook had planned to make another dish using the vegetable scraps.

Ans. False

Q.1 A recipe is a list of directions to prepare a dish. The following sentences are not in order for preparing avial. Number them in the correct order.

- [ ] Grind some coconut, green chillies and garlic.
- [ ] Cut the vegetable scraps into long strips.
- [1] Wash and clean the mix of vegetable bits.
- [ ] Decorate with curry leaves.
- [ ] Whip some curd and mix it in.
- [ ] Pour some coconut oil on top.
- [ ] Avial is ready.

Ans. 3, 2, 1, 6, 4, 5, 7

Q.2 Given in the box are some things that children do after they reach home from school. Choose five things that you do when you reach home from school. Write them in order.

> pack school bag, put away school bag, have lunch, read a story book, chat with mummy about school, sleep for a while, wash up, do the home work, watch TV, go to play, change out of school uniform

Ans. First, I put away school bag.
Then, I change out of school uniform.
Next, I have lunch.
After that, I do the homework.
Finally, I watch TV.

Hint You can choose any other activities that you do from the box and write them in a similar order.

Let's Talk (NCERT Page 14)

The Maharaja was a wise man and ordered the cook to use the vegetable scraps instead of throwing them away.

- Name some of the things which are thrown away at home or in school.

Ans. **At school** Used empty pens, paper, cuttings, empty markers, projects, etc.

At home Vegetable peels, fruit peels, leftover food, etc.

Hint You can observe your surroundings and write the things that you see being thrown away as waste both at school and at home.

- Sit in groups of four and think of interesting ways in which they can be made useful.

Ans. Do it Yourself

- Put up your findings on the class board.

Ans. Do it Yourself

Word Building (NCERT Page 14)

Pair work

Q.1 Some words have more than one meaning.

For example, **point**

Meanings **noun** a dot in print or writing, full stop, decimal, the number you score in a game

verb to show or call attention to something

Look up the following words in the dictionary. They may have more than one meaning. List these meanings.

- ground
- scrap
- tempting
- survey
- sternly

Ans. Ground

- **Noun** The surface of the earth or an area which is used for a particular purpose.
- **Verb** Past tense of grind which means to crush.

Survey

- **Noun** Detailed investigation
- **Verb** look carefully

Scrap

- **Noun** Waste material
- **Verb** Get rid of something or cancel it

Sternly As an adverb which means in a serious and severe manner.

Tempting As an adjective which means alluring, tantalising.

Q.2 Make new words by adding/dropping a few letters from the root word. Some are done for you.

Ans.

	–ed	–ing	–er	–est
pound	pounded	pounding	✗	✗
try	tried	trying	✗	✗
large	✗	✗	larger	largest
new	✗	✗	newer	newest
tasty	tasted	tasting	tastier	tastiest
wise	✗	✗	wiser	wisest
stare	stared	staring	✗	✗
clean	cleaned	cleaning	cleaner	cleanest

Find Out (NCERT Page 15)

Q.1 Name food that is made in your home

(i) for a feast/ festival.

(ii) when you are unwell.

(iii) everyday.

Share the information with your friends.

Ans. (i) Sweet dishes, kheer, several vegetables, Dahi-vada, etc.

(ii) Khichri and Daliya.

(iii) Chapatis, vegetables, pulse, rice, curd and salad.

Q.2 Avial is a dish made in Kerala.

Do you have a similar dish in your state made from a mix of many vegetables?

- What is it called?
- Note down the ingredients used to make it.
- Write down the recipe.
- Present attractively and display on the class board. You can draw and stick pictures too.

Ans. Do it Yourself

Bamboo Curry

Summary Bamboo curry is a Santhal folk tale wherein a new goes to his in-laws house. His mother-law cooked a curry for the groom and he liked it very much. When he asked his mother-in-law about it, she pointed to the bamboo door. Next day, when he was leaving he took the bamboo door as he knew his villages did not have any bamboo. At his home, he asked his wife to cook with the bamboo door and even tried to help her. However, the bamboo was very hard. Later when his in-laws came to the house, his mother-in-law told him that the curry was made of bamboo shoot and not bamboo door.

Let's Write (NCERT Page 18)

Q.1 Complete the sentences meaningfully.

(i) The bridegroom left with the door of his in-laws' house because it was made of ________ and there was no bamboo in his ________.

Ans. bamboo, village

(ii) The bridegroom was unable to have bamboo curry in the end because ________

Ans. the curry is made of bamboo shoots, not a bamboo door.

Q.2 Word hunt

Fill in the blanks with words from the story.

(i) The bridegroom went to visit his ________.

(ii) The mother-in-law pointed ________ ________ the bamboo door.

(iii) He stayed the night ________ his in-laws.

(iv) He carried the ________ ________ back with him.

(v) The curry was made ________ bamboo shoots.

Ans. (i) in-laws (ii) at the (iii) with (iv) bamboo door (v) from

Say Aloud (NCERT Page 18)

im-pa-tient (im-pay-shnt)
de-li-cious (di-li-shius)
bo-iled
cho-pped
bam-boo
Be-gan

Ans. Do it Yourself

PRACTICE QUESTIONS

Multiple Choice Questions

1. What did Maharaja order for in his palace?
   (a) Grand dinner (b) Grand lunch
   (c) Grand breakfast (d) Grand supper
2. What did the Maharaja find in the kitchen?
   (a) A pile of clothes
   (b) A pile of vegetable scraps
   (c) A pile of waste paper
   (d) A pile of vegetable peels
3. What was the cook's reaction when the Maharaja told him to use the scraps?
   (a) Threatened (b) Irritated
   (c) Confused (d) Shocked
4. What did the cook finally decide to do with the vegetable scraps?
   (a) Created a new dish (b) Threw them away
   (c) Made a compost (d) None of the above
5. What was the name of the new dish made by the cook?
   (a) Avail (b) Avial
   (c) Kulfi (d) Stew

Ans. 1. (a), 2. (b), 3. (c), 4. (a), 5. (b)

Extract Based Questions

A tempting smell started coming from the pot. Now he whipped some curd and added it to the curry. He also poured a few spoonfuls of coconut oil and decorated the dish with curry leaves.

Lo and behold! The new dish was ready. The cook served this new dish to the guests that evening. Everyone was eager to know the name of the new dish. The cook thought and thought.

1. Why was the tempting smell coming from the pot?

Ans. Tempting smell was coming from the pot because of the new dish that the cook was trying to make.

2. What is the most appropriate synonym of the word tempting?

(a) Exciting (b) Inviting
(c) Foul (d) None of the above

Ans. (b) Inviting

3. What was the cook thinking?

Ans. The cook was thinking of a name for the new dish.

4. Complete the sentence.

He also poured a few spoonfuls of coconut oil and ____________________.

Ans. decorated the dish with curry leaves.

5. Who did the cook serve this dish to?

Ans. The cook served this dish to the guests at the dinner party.

Answer the Following Questions

1. What did the king ask the cook to do with vegetable scraps?

Ans. The king asked the cook to use the vegetable scraps instead of throwing them away.

2. How did the cook prepare the vegetable bits for the new dish?

Ans. The cook took the vegetable bits, washed them and cleaned them properly. Then, he cut them into long strips.

3. What did the cook garnish the dish with?

Ans. The cook garnished the new dish with curry leaves.

4. Do you think the king made a wise decision by telling the cook not to throw away the scraps?

Ans. Yes, the king made a wise decision by rebuking the cook because the vegetable scraps would have otherwise gone into the dustbin. Maharaja taught him a good lesson for lifetime when he asked him to use the scraps instead of throwing them away. The cook created a new dish which is now famous all over Kerala.

5. How is avial used in Kerala? Is it still popular?

Ans. Avial is a very famous dish all over Kerala. It is made out of mixed vegetables along with flavourful ingredients. It is one of the dishes served in a traditional Kerala feast. It is still very popular and is served at all special occasions.

CHAPTER 1 TEAMWORK

Summary of the poem The poem describes the importance of working together as a team. When we work together, our dreams can come true. Together, we can also share the joys of our results. Everyone in a team has a common goal. Thus, a strong team can make anything possible.

Stanza-wise Explanation

Stanza 1

Teamwork, teamwork,
Together we can make our dream work.
Then we'll share the joy of what we've done,
Teamwork, everyone!

Exp. Teamwork is done together by a group of people. Dreams can be achieved easily if there's a group of people helping each other and working together. A team also shares the happiness of the work they have done together.

Stanza 2

It'' fun to shoot the basketball through the hoop,
But if nobody passes then nobody shoots.
And the relay race just can't go on,
If nobody wants to pass the baton.

Word-Meaning *Shoot - To pass through; Hoop - A wooden or iron ring; Baton - Short tube or stick.*

Exp. All the sports and games also need teamwork. In basketball, if no one passes the ball, the goal will not be shot. In relay races, the same thing happens. If one person does not pass the baton to another person, the game will not continue.

Stanza 3

We're the parts that make up the whole,
And we've got our eyes on a common goal.
Sometimes it can be a big plus,
When a you or a me becomes an us!

Word-Meaning *Whole - Complete; Goal - Aim, target.*

Exp. In teamwork, everyone plays an important part. If the team does not stand together, the work becomes difficult. All the members have the same goal. This teamwork can bring big success.

NCERT FOLDER

Let's Read (NCERT Page 22)

Complete the following sentences.

Q.1 If nobody passes the ball in a basketball game, then you can't ________ .

Ans. shoot the ball through the hoop.

Q.2 In a relay race, if no one passes the baton, then ________.

Ans. the race cannot go on.

Think and Write (NCERT Page 22)

Q.1 Name the team members needed for the following.

(i) To play cricket we need

Ans. Batsmen, bowlers, fielders, and coaches

(ii) To make a film we need

Ans. Director, actors, producer, actresses, crew members, etc.

(iii) To run a good school we need

Ans. Principal, vice principal, teachers, students and administration

(iv) To run a restaurant we need

Ans. Cooks, servers, managers, etc.

Q.2 Complete the sets of rhyming words. One has been done for you.

Words from the poem	Your own words
team	beam
plus	
done	
hoop	
shoot	
goal	
joy	

Ans.

Words from the poem	Your own words
team	beam
plus	bus
done	won
hoop	loop
shoot	boot
goal	whole
joy	toy

Q.3 Read the poem.

For want of a Nail

For want of a nail the shoe was lost,
For want of a shoe the horse was lost,
For want of a horse the rider was lost,
For want of a rider the battle was lost,
For want of a battle the kingdom was lost,
And all for the want of a horseshoe naill!

[traditional rhyme]

Now form questions for the answers given in the speech bubbles.

Ans.

Now make three more questions and answers from the poem, *Teamwork*.

Q.1 How can we make our dreams work?

Ans. We can make our dreams work by doing teamwork.

Q.2 How can the relay race go on?

Ans. The relay race can go on when someone passes the baton.

Q.3 Who has eyes on a common goal?

Ans. Everyone in the team has eyes on a common goal.

Picture Composition

Look at the picture and answer the questions in one sentence, using the word clues given in the box.

plumber painter mason electrician labourer carpenter gardener

Q.1 Who is laying the bricks?

Ans. Mason is laying the bricks.

Q.2 Who is holding the ladder?

Ans. A labourer is holding the ladder.

Q.3 Who is the man on the ladder?

Ans. The man on the ladder is electrician.

Q.4 Who is making the door?

Ans. A carpenter is making the door.

Q.5 Who is painting the wall?

Ans. A painter is painting the wall.

Now make up a story about the picture. Give names to the people. Write the story showing the importance of teamwork.

Ans. It's almost festive season and Mr. Malhotra wanted to renovate his house before Diwali.

He was worried how this work would be completed in time. He engaged a team of people to the work. Everyone was supposed to do different things but they had to work together. Hiran Babu, the mason, started laying bricks. Onkar, the carpenter is making the new door.

Shiraj, who is a labourer, is holding the ladder for Aman, the electrician. He is busy with new electrical fittings. Now, the plumber's work was left. Mr. Malhotra called Raghu, the plumber, to help him with plumbing tasks. After everything was almost finished, he wanted to repaint the house.

Ashu Jain, the painter came to help him and the renovation of house was finished before Diwali. He happily celebrated Diwali in his renovated home.

Let's Talk (NCERT Page 25)

Q.1 In groups of five, discuss what you enjoy doing alone and what you like doing in a group.

Now prepare a list as shown below.

Things I like doing alone	Things I like doing in a group

Ans. Do it yourself.

Hint :

In column 1	In column 2
You can mention activities like reading a book, listening to music, studying, praying, etc.	You can mention activities like going to a park, playing video games, having lunch, etc.

Q.2 In your family, what activities are done individually and as a group?

My mother decides ______________

My father decides ______________

I decide ______________

We decide ______________

Ans. Do it yourself.

Hint : Mention the activities that are decided by your mother, father and you individually. For example, I decide the time to study and play. In the last line, write the things that you decide together.

Q.3 In a group, mime an activity (picnic, fair/mela, cricket match, etc.) which you enjoy. The rest of the class should guess the activity and say whether it is done in a group/alone.

Ans. Do it Yourself

Let's Write (NCERT Page 26)

Q.1 In the puzzle find the words given in the column. Notice that these words are formed by joining two words. One is done for you.

Find some more such words

sometime	a	c	h	g	m	k	e	v	e	r	y	o	n	e	m	f	s
everyone	b	c	d	e	g	l	n	m	p	r	s	u	v	x	n	l	s
basketball	a	b	t	e	a	m	w	o	r	k	f	g	i	l	o	w	u
nobody	s	m	b	c	e	g	l	m	p	r	s	u	v	x	b	t	n
teamwork	k	b	s	o	m	e	t	i	m	e	u	g	v	n	o	r	d
baton	e	m	b	c	m	w	m	p	r	q	x	z	w	r	d	q	a
	t	q	w	b	a	b	s	t	a	n	d	b	y	c	y	p	y
	b	a	c	a	d	e	f	g	h	l	j	k	l	m	p	s	r
	a	m	b	t	e	t	m	e	c	a	n	p	o	t	x	b	t
	l	f	g	o	h	c	n	p	t	y	s	u	w	d	a	x	f
	l	z	w	n	x	y	v	h	a	n	d	s	o	m	e	u	s

Ans.

sometime	a	c	h	g	m	k	e	v	e	r	y	o	n	e	m	f	s
everyone	b	c	d	e	g	l	n	m	p	r	s	u	v	x	n	l	s
basketball	a	b	t	e	a	m	w	o	r	k	f	g	i	l	o	w	u
nobody	s	m	b	c	e	g	l	m	p	r	s	u	v	x	b	t	n
teamwork	k	b	s	o	m	e	t	i	m	e	u	g	v	n	o	r	d
stand by	e	m	b	c	m	w	m	p	r	q	x	z	w	r	d	q	a
sunday	t	q	w	b	a	b	s	t	a	n	d	b	y	c	y	p	y
handsome	b	a	c	a	d	e	f	g	h	l	j	k	l	m	p	s	r
	a	m	b	t	e	t	m	e	c	a	n	p	o	t	x	b	t
	l	f	g	o	h	c	n	p	t	y	s	u	w	d	a	x	f
	l	z	w	n	x	y	v	h	a	n	d	s	o	m	e	u	s

Ans. More words: handsome, sunday, standby

Q.2 Let's write a poem.

I have a kite but need a friend to fly it with,
I know a song but need someone to hear it,
I have a ball but need someone to catch it,
I ______________
I ______________
I ______________
I ______________

Ans. I have three sandwiches but I need someone to share them with.

I have a dance act but I need my friends to do it with.

I have a ball but I need someone to play catch with me.

I am sitting on a see-saw but I need my sister to sit on the second seat.

Fun Time (NCERT Page 27)

Make groups of ten and present one of the following activities in class.

Skit song dance painting a chart for class make paper bags from old newspaper

Ans. Do it yourself.

Say Aloud (NCERT Page 27)

- We sometimes use short forms for some words. For example, we use I'm for I am and I've for I have. These shortened words are called contractions.
- The mark(') is an apostrophe which shows where the letters are left out. Now read together.

we will — we'll,	Cannot — can't,
we have — we've	you have — you've
there is — there's	what have — what've
we are — we're	they are — they're

Q.1 Write the contractions for the following phrases.

- has not ____________
- have not ____________
- do not ____________
- are not ____________

Ans. • hasn't • haven't • don't • aren't

Q.2 Write the full forms for the following.

- weren't ____________
- she'll ____________
- wasn't ____________
- who's ____________

Ans. • were not • she will • was not • who is

PRACTICE QUESTIONS

Multiple Choice Questions

1. What can we do together?
   (a) Make a dream work
   (b) Fight
   (c) Break our work
   (d) Shoot the basketball
2. When can't nobody shoot the basketball?
   (a) When nobody passes the baton
   (b) When nobody passes the ball
   (c) When nobody is playing
   (d) None of the above
3. Where have we got our eyes?
   (a) On a common goal
   (b) On a different goal
   (c) On working together
   (d) None of the above

Ans. 1. (a), 2. (b), 3. (a)

Extract Based Questions

It's fun to shoot the basketball through the hoop,
But if nobody passes then nobody shoots.
And the relay race just can't go on,
If nobody wants to pass the baton.
We're the parts that make up the whole,
And we've got our eyes on a common goal.
Sometimes it can be a big plus,
When a you or a me becomes an us!

1. What is fun to shoot through the hoop?

Ans. Basketball is fun to shoot through the hoop.

2. When can't the relay race go on?

Ans. The relay race can't go on when nobody passes the baton.

3. Complete the following sentence appropriately.

Sometimes it can be a big plus, ________________________.

Ans. when a you or a me becomes an us!

4. What is the most appropriate synonym of the word 'goal'?

(a) Target (b) Game
(c) Aim (d) Both (a) and (c)

Ans. (d) Both (a) and (c)

Answer the Following Questions

1. What is teamwork?

Ans. Teamwork is working together harmoniously in a group. It means that everyone is a part of the same team and are working to achieve a common goal.

2. What can we share when we do teamwork?

Ans. We can share the happiness of our results, the joy of what we have achieved through teamwork.

3. Does every individual in the team have some role to play? What do you think?

Ans. Yes, every individual in the team has some role to play. When all the people have different things to do, they work together harmoniously. This helps in making a team strong.

A strong team can handle any situation and do any activity easily when working together.

4. List some activities that require teamwork.

Ans. Some activities that require teamwork are

- Playing games
- Group projects
- Organising an event
- Having a party

5. What do you learn from the poem? Give an explained answer.

Ans. The poem teaches us the value of teamwork. It makes us learn the importance of working together in a team. The poem highlights that teamwork can help you realise your dreams and help you achieve success. In a team, everyone works towards a common goal.

Everyone in a team plays an important role and work is done smoothly if team members cooperate with each other. Teamwork means combined effort of a group.

Let's Write

1. Have you ever been a part of the team? If yes, what was the event? Was it a sports activity or a celebration/event? What role did you play? What was the result of the teamwork?

Ans. Yes, I have been a part of a team many times. I have been a part of group projects, group events and games. I had been a part of the cricket/Volleyball team for many years. I also like to participate in dance programmes wherein our school encourages team work in group performances. In all these projects, I had an important role to play just like all other people in the team. As a result of this, we all not only became good friends but also have successfully won many competitions. We have also received much appreciation from people.

CHAPTER 2 FLYING TOGETHER

Summary of the Chapter

A flock of geese lived on a tall tree in a very deep forest. One of the geese was an old wise bird. He was worried about a creeper growing on the ground at the foot of the tree. He told the other geese to cut it and destroy it otherwise a hunter could climb up the tree and kill them. They forgot the old bird's advice. Soon, the creeper became strong and thick.

In the absence of geese, one day a hunter climbed the tree with the help of the creeper and spread his net. The geese got trapped as soon as they flew into the tree.

The old wise bird reminded them of his advice and then, thought of a plan to help them. He told the birds that when the hunter comes, they should pretend to be dead. The hunter would throw them down after seeing them dead. As soon as the hunter throws the last bird, they can fly together and escape the trap. All the birds followed the plan, flapped their wings and flew away, saving themselves.

WORD-MEANING

Spread out - to cover a large area; Flock - Group; Wise - Intelligent; Creeper - A plant that grows with the support of a tree by climbing around it; Destroy - To kill or break down; Pity - Feeling sorrow; Tender - Soft; Winding up - Wrapping closely around something; Trapped - To catch; Struggled - Tried hard; Fuss - Worry/excitement; Pretend - To act falsely; Muttered - To speak in a low voice; Flapped - to move the wings.

NCERT FOLDER

Let's Read (NCERT Page 33)

Q.1 Where did the geese live?

Ans. The geese lived in the leafy branches of a tall tree in the forest.

Q.2 Why did the old bird advise the other birds to destroy the creeper?

Ans. The old bird advised the other birds to destroy the creeper because when the creeper starts growing thick and strong, a hunter can climb up and kill the birds.

Q.3 Why did the geese cry, 'Help Help'?

Ans. The geese cried for help because they got trapped inside the net that the hunter set for them.

Q.4 What did the hunter do when he thought that the geese were dead?

Ans. The hunter threw them on the ground one by one when he thought that the geese were dead.

Q.5 Why did the geese pretend to be dead?

Ans. The geese pretended to be dead because of the advice of the old wise geese. They knew that the hunter would throw them on the ground, seeing them dead. This way they could escape the trap.

Q.6 Describe one incident when you got into trouble because you did not do your work on time.

Ans. I had my exams starting in a week. My mom was scolding me to study and prepare on time. But I kept ignoring her advice.
I thought there was still a lot of time left.

I kept delaying the preparation and I did not study. One day before the exam, I started to panic. I had a lot of syllabus to finish but very little time. My mom told me that if I had listened to her, this would not have happened. The next day, I went to give the exam. It did not go well. When my results came, I scored very less marks. I was ashamed. I learnt that it is important to follow the advice of your elders and do work on time.

Hint : You can frame your own answer using the following clues

- Not prepared in advance for a quiz/school function/event
- Did not listen to parents
- Kept delaying the preparation
- Ashamed at the result
- Learnt a lesson

State whether the following statements are True or False.

Q.1 The tree was the house of a flock of parrots.

Ans. False

Q.2 The wise old bird wanted the creeper to be destroyed.

Ans. True

Q.3 The hunter climbed the tree with the help of a ladder.

Ans. False

Q.4 When caught in the net the foolish birds began to weep.

Ans. True

Q.5 The wise old bird helped them to escape.

Ans. True

Let's Listen (NCERT Page 35)

Read the story from NCERT Page number 34.

Q.1 Why do you think the dove helped the ant?

Ans. The dove helped the ant because she was friendly and took pity on the ant's life.

Q.2 How do you think the ant felt on finding the leaf?

Ans. The ant must have felt thankful and relieved on finding the leaf.

Q.3 Have you ever been in trouble like the ant? Did anyone help you?

Ans. No, thankfully I have not been in any trouble like that of the ant from the story.

Hint : Students can write yes and describe the problem as well as who helped them.

Let's Talk (NCERT Page 35)

Q.1 Work in pairs.

- Ask your friend questions about all the things he does.
- Use question words such as where, what, how, who, when, why. One is done for you.

Anu : I watch TV in the evening.

Amit : When do you watch TV?

Anu : I play games.

Ans. Amit : What do you play?

Anu : I collect stamps.

Ans. Amit : What do you collect?

Anu : I play in the ground.

Ans. Amit : Where do you play?

Anu : On Sunday I go shopping.

Ans. Amit : When do you go shopping

Q.2 Answer these questions about yourself.

(i) What is your name?

(ii) What languages do you speak?

(iii) How old are you?

(iv) Which is your favourite food?

(v) Where did you go yesterday?

(vi) Which country do you belong to?

(vii) When do you go to sleep?

(viii) Why do you drink milk?

Ans. Do it yourself.

Q.3 In groups of five, discuss what you would do if you were caught in the following situations.

- Your friend falls in the play field and is hurt ....
- You are trapped in a fire .... .
- You are stuck in traffic jam .... .

Ans.
- I will help him by lifting him up. I will give him first aid and take him to the medical room.
- I will try to be calm and call for help. I will look around for water or a fire extinguisher.
- I will be patient and wait for the traffic jam to clear.

Let's Write (NCERT Page 36)

Q.1 The words in the clouds describe something or someone in the story. Name them in the blanks provided.

Make sentences of your own with the words given in the clouds.

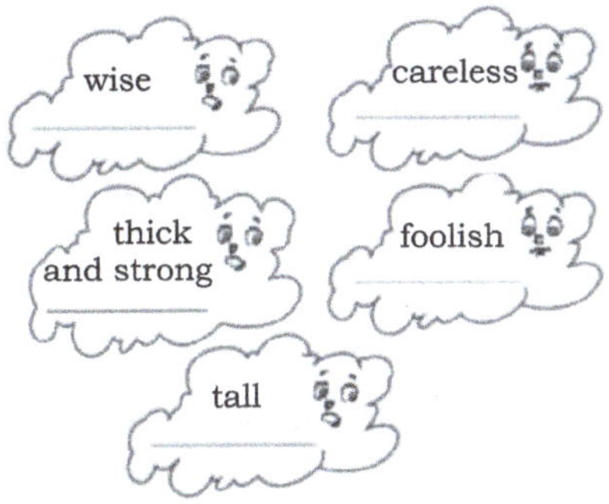

Ans. Wise - old bird

Careless - geese

Thick and strong - creeper

Foolish - geese

Tall - tree

Sentences

- Amit is a very wise boy.
- Sheetija is careless with money.
- My money plant has grown thick and strong.
- Neena is very foolish as she did not understand the story.
- The tree in front of my house is growing very tall.

Q.2 Here are some answers about the given picture.

(i) The colour of the ant is black.

(ii) It lives on land.

(iii) It has two long antennae.

(iv) It crawls on the ground.

(v) It eats sugar.

Now frame questions for the above answers.

Ans. (i) What is the colour of the ant?

(ii) Where does the ant live?

(iii) How many antennae does the ant have?

(iv) How does the ant move? / Where does the ant move?

(v) What does the ant eat?

Q.3 Fill in the blanks with prepositions such as to, at, off, on, in, into, with. One has been done for you.

(i) This tree was the home <u>of</u> a flock of wild geese.

(ii) He noticed the creeper ___ the foot of the tree.

(iii) "It would be a pity ____ destroy it now".

(iv) As they flew ____ the tree they were trapped.

(v) The boy ran ____ the dog.

(vi) The frogs jumped ____ the well.

(vii) The girl was thrilled ____ see her new bicycle.

(viii) The birds were caught ___ the net.

(ix) The children walked ____ the bridge.

Ans. (ii) at (iii) to (iv) into (v) with (vi) into (vii) to (viii) in (ix) over

Q.4 Complete the paragraph with suitable words from the box.

around	across	with	along	to
after	next to	into	from	

One day, as I was walking _________ the bank of the river, I saw my friend running ______ the field. He was calling my name and waving ________ me. I stopped and waited. _________ sometime he reached where I was standing.

He said, 'I went all _______ the town looking for you. I have some exciting news to share ________ you. Do you remember the old house _________ the neem tree? Guess who is moving that house? Janak Das, the great magician. Now we can learn lots of magic tricks ________him'.

Ans. along, across, to, After, around, with, next to, from

Q.5 Fill in the blanks with question words. For example, where do you live?

(i) _________ do you play?

(ii) ________ do you get up?

(iii) ________ do you have for breakfast?

(iv) ________ do you go to school?

(v) ________ do you like the best in the school - games, art or music?

(vi) ________ is your birthday?

(vii) ________ do you want for your birthday?

Ans. (i) What (ii) When (iii) What (iv) How (v) What (vi) When (vii) What

Q.6 Reference to context.

1. "Well there's no hurry, the creeper is very small, it would be a pity to destroy it now."

2. "So this is where the wild geese live."

Who said this? __________

To whom it was said? __________

When was it said? __________

Ans. 1. • The old wise Geese
- The other Geese
- When the old Geese suggested to destroy the creeper.

2. • Hunter
- Himself
- When he found the tree where the Geese lived.

- Draw pictures of the speakers of the above lines.

Ans. Do it yourself

Fun Time (NCERT Page 40)

Q.1 Proverbs are short, wise sayings. For example—Look before you leap. This means that we should think carefully before we take any action. Here are some popular English proverbs.

Read them aloud together and discuss what each could mean.

(i) Old is gold.

(ii) As you sow so shall you reap.

(iii) Unity is strength.

(iv) United we stand divided we fall.

(v) A friend in need is a friend in deed.

Ans. (i) Old things have more value than new ones.

(ii) Whatever we do, either good or bad, we will always get its results. If we do good, the results will be good. If we do bad, the results would be the same. We will have to bear the consequences of our actions.

(iii) When we are together, we are more powerful than a single person.

(iv) We can achieve success when we do teamwork or when we work together. If we get divided, we will not be successful.

(v) A friend who helps you when you are in any problem is your true friend. Somebody who is there with you during bad times, he is your real friend.

Q.2 Look at this proverb: All's well that ends well.

(i) Discuss what it means. Can you think of events/happenings in life where this proverb can be used?

Ans. (i) This proverb means that we can forget about the bitter process or difficulties we faced, if the end result of something is good. We can think about many situation when the proverb can be used. During examinations, we work hard and get good results. While studying, we do a lot of hard work and face many problems. However, when the results come out to be good, we are very happy.

(ii) Write down your story or the event. Then read the paragraph to your neighbour.

Ans. Once upon a time, in a small village, there lived a poor farmer named Ajay. He was known for his hard work and kindness towards others but he always seemed to face one misfortune after another. One day, as Ajay was working on his farm when a terrible storm struck the village. Heavy rains poured down, flooding his fields and ruining his crops. Sad, Ajay thought he would never recover from it. However, a passerby named Radhe, a wise old man known for his positive outlook on life, witnessed Ajay's struggles. He told Ajay to sow his fields again with another crop that needed a lot of water.

Ajay though doubtful, reworked on his crops. This time, he sow rice crops. He had to do a lot of work and many people questioned his decision. However, Ajay persisted. After 3 months, Ajay's hard work paid off. His crops were beautiful and gave him so much crop that he earned a lot of money and even gave some crop to charity. This made Ajay realise that all's well that ends well.

The Clap Word Game

Q.3 Let's play the clap word game.

Where the word produces one sound, clap once, as in 'creep'. Clap twice if the word can be broken up into two syllables as in cree-per, and thrice as in to-mo-rrow.

creeper	struggled	tomorrow	geese
throw	foolish	possible	noticed
carefully	flapped	returned	evening
trapped	surprise		

Ans. Do it yourself. Take help from your teacher.

PRACTICE QUESTIONS

Multiple Choice Questions

1. The tall tree was the home of _______ .
   (a) wild geese (b) wild fox
   (c) the hunter (d) birds

2. What was there at the foot of the tree?
   (a) A small creeper (b) A big plant
   (c) A hunter (d) None of these

3. What is the most appropriate meaning of the word 'creeper'?
   (a) A plant that grows by itself
   (b) A plant that grows with the support of a tree
   (c) A plant that grows climbing up the tree
   (d) A small plant

4. What did the hunter set on the tree for the geese?
   (a) A net (b) A trap
   (c) A nest (d) None of these

Ans. 1. (a), 2. (a), 3. (c), 4. (a)

Answer the Following Questions

1. What did the old wise bird advise the geese about the creeper?

Ans. The old wise bird advised the geese to destroy the creeper before it become too thick and strong.

2. Do you think the geese were wise to ignore the advice of the old wise geese? Why or why not?

Ans. No, the geese were not wise to ignore the wise bird's advise because eventually the creeper helped the hunter to trap them.

3. How did the hunter use the strong and thick creeper?

Ans. The hunter used the strong and thick creeper to climb the tall tree.

4. Did the geese get trapped in the hunter's net? What was their feeling?

Ans. Yes, the geese were trapped in the hunter's net. They felt terrible and wanted help.

5. What plan did the old wise geese make to save all the birds?

Ans. The old wise bird planned for the geese to act dead.

Seeing then dead, the hunter would throw them down. When the last bird is thrown down, all of the birds can fly away together.

Let's Write!

1. Write a speech about 'All is well that ends well' on the basis of your understanding of the story.

Ans. All is well that ends well explores the concept that the conclusion of a journey or endeavor is what ultimately defines its success or failure. Although life itself may sometimes be full of hardships and struggles, the final outcome is what truly matters. In our life, we may encounter numerous obstacles that make it seem as if nothing will ever be well. Yet, it is important to keep moving forward and maintain hope, for it is the ending that defines the journey. The saying teaches us the value of hope, perseverance, and personal growth.

CHAPTER 1 MY SHADOW

Summary of the poem The poem 'My Shadow' is about a child who is curious about his shadow. The child notices that the shadow follows him everywhere and copies everything he does.

Stanza-wise Explanation

Stanza 1

I have a little shadow that goes in and out with me.
And what can be the use of him is more than I can see.
He is very, very like me from the heels up to the head;
And I see him jump before me, When I jump into my bed.

Exp. The child in the poem talks about his shadow which follows him everywhere. He says that his shadow is just like him from his head to his heels. He sees it jump into the bed before he can.

Stanza 2

The funniest thing about him is the way he likes to grow
Not at all like proper children, which is always very slow;
For he sometimes shoots up taller like an India-rubber ball,
And he sometimes gets so little that There's none of him at all.

Exp. The child continues to observe his shadow. He finds the way his shadow grows quickly to be funny. He says that his shadow suddenly becomes tall, shooting up like an India-rubber ball. It is not like the normal children who grow slowly. Sometimes, it becomes so small that he can't even see it.

Stanza 3

One morning, very early, before the sun I was up,
I rose and found the shining dew on every buttercup;
But my lazy little shadow, like an arrant sleepyhead.
Had stayed at home behind me and was Fast asleep in bed.

Word-Meaning *Buttercup - A yellow flower; Arrant - Bad; Sleepyhead - Completely inattentive, India-rubber ball - A ball that bounces very high.*

Exp. The child wakes up very early one morning. He finds dew on the flowers but no sign of his shadow. He thinks that his shadow is lazy like a bad sleepyhead. He says that his shadow has stayed at home and is sleeping while he is outside.

NCERT FOLDER

Let's Read (NCERT Page 44)

Q.1 Who do you think your shadow looks like?

Ans. I think my shadow looks like me.

Q.2 Why do you think your shadow jumps into bed before you can?

Ans. I think my shadow jumps into bed before me because the light in my room is behind me when I face my bed. This way, my shadow reaches the bed before I do.

Q.3 What time of the day do you think it is when your shadow is the tallest? Why?

- Morning
- Afternoon
- Night

Ans. Our shadow is the tallest in the morning. It is because the sun rays come from far away at the time of sunrise.

Q.4 Read the lines from the poem and answer the following.

He is very very like me.

From the heels up to the head!

(i) Who does he refer to?

Ans. 'He' refers to the shadow.

(ii) Who does 'me' refer to?

Ans. 'Me' refers to the poet.

(iii) Why are he and me alike?

Ans. 'He' and 'Me' are alike because 'He' is the shadow of 'Me'.

Let's Talk (NCERT Page 44)

Work in pairs and discuss the following.

What would you do if

- a dog chases you?

Ans. I will scream and run very fast.

- you have forgotten your homework copy at home?

Ans. I will inform my teacher and apologise for my mistake.

- you are alone in a room and lights go out?

Ans. I will look for a torch or call someone for help.

Fun time (NCERT Page 45)

- Shine a torch behind your hand and see its shadow on the wall.
- Move the torch a little away from your hand and see the shadow on the wall.

Do you find a difference in the size of the hand on the wall?

Ans. Hint : You can do the activity and notice the change. Yes, I can find a difference in the size of the hand on the wall.

Working Together (NCERT Page 45)

Q.1 Work in groups of five.

- Make a large hand on a plain sheet.
- Mark the names of fingers, thumb and palm on the hand. Use the hints given in the box.

Ans. Do it yourself

Q.2 Do the actions as given below, and observe which part, or fingers, of your hand is being used.

point at a door	bounce a ball
scratch your chin	twist your ear
comb your hair	draw with a pencil
touch a flower	

Ans. Do it yourself

Let's Write (NCERT Page 46)

Q.1 Fill in the blanks using one of the words given in brackets.

(i) Where is the child ________ parents have come to school? (who/whose/which)

(ii) I saw many houses ________ were quite spacious. (which/whose/who).

(iii) Mathematics, ________ is my favourite subject, is so interesting. (who/which/that)

(iv) The poem ________ you read out, is so lovely. (whose/which/that)

(v) I know the street ________ he lives on. (whose/ that/which)

(vi) I like reading books ________ have pictures in it. (that/who/which)

(vii) The old lady ______________ I met in your house is my neighbour. (whom /that/which)

Ans. (i) whose, (ii) which, (iii) which, (iv) that, (v) which, (vi) which, (vii) whom

Q.2 Complete this description by answering the questions below.

Write a few lines on Mithoo and his little dog named Shadow.

Ans. Mithoo has a little dog named Shadow. She is called 'Shadow' because she follows Mithoo everywhere. Just like his shadow, she never leaves him alone. She is white in colour and very friendly. Mithoo and Shadow play together everyday after school. Shadow likes to eat biscuits and to chew on bones.

Say Aloud (NCERT Page 47)

shoes	shadow	fish	bush
ship	sheep	dish	wash
shell	shade	wish	brush

When the sun shines, I can see
My shadow right in front of me
When I walk, my shadow walks!
When I hop, my shadow hops!
When I jump, my shadow jumps
And when I stop, my shadow stops!

–Louise Binder Scott

Ans. Do it yourself.

PRACTICE QUESTIONS

Multiple Choice Questions

1. What does the child's shadow do?
   (a) Follows the child everywhere
   (b) Hides from the child
   (c) Plays with the child
   (d) Disappears when the child is happy

2. What does the shadow do in the poem?
   (a) It helps him find his way home
   (b) It protects him from danger
   (c) It copies all his actions
   (d) None of the above

3. How does the child describe his shadow's appearance?
   (a) Different from him (b) Smaller than him
   (c) Exactly like him (d) Always changing

Ans. 1. (a), 2. (c), 3. (c)

Extract Based Questions

Read the extract given below and answer the questions that follow.

For he sometimes shoots up taller like an India-rubber ball,
And he sometimes gets so little that
There's none of him at all.

1. What does 'he sometimes shoots up taller like an India-rubber ball' mean?

Ans. It means the shadow sometimes grows tall quickly.

2. Find the synonym of the word 'small' from the given lines.

Ans. Little

3. Who is 'he' in the given lines?
   (a) The child
   (b) A friend
   (c) The shadow
   (d) The poet

Ans. (c) The shadow

4. Complete the sentence.

   Sometimes the shadow gets so little that ____________________.

Ans. there's none of him at all.

Fill in the Blanks

1. The child's shadow grows________like an India-rubber ball.
2. The shadow is_______and stays in bed.
3. The child gets up_________ in the morning.
4. The shadow is _________from proper children.

Ans. 1. quickly, 2. lazy, 3. early, 4. different

True or False

1. The child finds the shadow scary.
2. The shadow can only get smaller but not taller.
3. The shadow jumps into the bed before the child.
4. The shadow is a sleepyhead according to the child.

Ans. 1. False 2. False
3. True 4. True

Answer the Following Questions

1. What is the funniest thing about the child's shadow?

Ans. The funniest thing about the child's shadow is how it grows and shrinks quickly.

2. How does the shadow grow compared to proper children?

Ans. The shadow grows much faster than proper children, sometimes shooting up taller like an India-rubber ball.

3. When did the child get up in the morning?

Ans. The child got up very early, before the sun.

4. What was the child's shadow doing according to him, when he got up?

Ans. The child's shadow was still fast asleep in his bed according to him.

Let's Write

1. Complete the following description using the given hints.
   - Orange colour
   - My pet cat named Fluffy
   - Loves to climb up things
   - Playful
   - Sleeps on my lap

   My cat is named Fluffy. He...

Ans. My cat is named Fluffy. He is a big, orange cat with soft fur. Fluffy loves to climb up things. He can jump really high and often sits on top of the refrigerator or the bookshelf.

Sometimes, he even tries to climb up the curtains! Fluffy is a very playful cat and loves to chase his toy mouse. He is also very cuddly and loves to sleep on my lap.

CHAPTER 2 ROBINSON CRUSOE DISCOVERS A FOOTPRINT

Summary of the Chapter

Robinson Crusoe is a man living alone on an island because his ship had been destroyed by the sea. One day, he found a mysterious footprint on the sand near his boat. He searched the area but couldn't find any other footprints. After thinking about it for sometime, Robinson Crusoe realised that the footprint was not his and that someone else might be living on the island.

He thought it could be one of the savages of the mainland who had wandered out to the sea, in a small boat. This filled him with fear and he spent many days hiding and praying for his protection.

After a few days, Robinson Crusoe became bolder because he did not see anyone. He decided to investigate the footprint further. After taking a closer look, he found that the footprint was larger than his own and that the island was indeed inhabited by someone else.

WORD-MEANING

Shore - The land at the edge of a sea; Destroyed - Damaged; Amazed - Surprised; Savages - Wild or uncontrolled person; Mainland - The main part of a country or continent, which does not include the islands; Bolder - To be fearless; Inhabited - Occupied by someone.

NCERT FOLDER

Let's Read (NCERT Page 52)

Q.1 What made Robinson Crusoe think that the print on the ground was a footprint?

Ans. Robinson Crusoe was sure because the print had toes and heel. It looked just like a human foot.

Q.2 Why was Robinson afraid when he looked at the bushes and trees?

Ans. Robinson was afraid when he looked at the bushes and trees because he mistook them to be a man following him.

Q.3 Why did Robinson pray when he saw the footprint?

Ans. Robinson prayed when he saw the footprint because he was frightened. He thought it was the footprint of a savage who could kill him.

Q.4 Choose the correct answer.

(i) Robinson ran back to his home, as fast as he could because he
(a) was racing.
(b) was afraid.
(c) was in a hurry to go home.

Ans. (b) was afraid.

(ii) He could not sleep because
(a) there was an animal outside his cave.
(b) he thought savages had come from the mainland.
(c) his bed was uncomfortable.

Ans. (b) he thought savages had come from the mainland.

(iii) Why was Robinson Crusoe sure that it was not his footprint?
(a) It didn't look like a human footprint.
(b) It looked smaller than his.
(c) He had not come to this part of the beach in a long time.

Ans. (c) He had not come to this part of the beach in a long time.

(iv) Where was Robinson Crusoe?
(a) On a boat.
(b) In a town.
(c) Alone on an island.
(d) On an aeroplane.

Ans. (c) Alone on an island.

Let's Talk (NCERT Page 53)

Q.1 How would you feel if you saw unknown footprints outside your front door?

Ans. If I saw unknown footprints outside my front door, I would be surprised and tell my parents about it.

Q.2 If you were alone at home and suddenly someone knocked at your door, what would you do?

Ans. First, I would ask who it is and if they are a family member, I will open the door.

If they are a stranger, I would first ask for their name and their reason for the visit, keeping the door shut. Then, I would request them to come at another time when my parents are at home.

Let's Write (NCERT Page 53)

Q.1 The words in the sentences are jumbled. Write them in order. One is done for you.

(i) alone was not Robinson an island on

Ans. Robinson was not alone on an island.

(ii) was island the inhabited

Ans. The island was inhabited.

(iii) footprint to someone this belonged

Ans. This footprint belonged to someone.

(iv) I around me looked

Ans. I looked around me.

(v) I went the towards footprint large

Ans. I went towards the large footprint.

(vi) was afraid I now

Ans. I was now afraid.

Q.2 Fill in the blanks with the correct word.

and but because so

(i) I was frightened __________ curious.

(ii) I decided to go to the beach __________ I went along the water's edge.

(iii) I ran as fast as I could __________ I was frightened.

(iv) I was very tired __________ confused.

Ans. (i) but (ii) so (iii) because (iv) and

Q.3 Write a story on strange footprints.

- Where did you see the footprints?
- What sort of a day was it?
- Did you see them at night?
- What happened when you followed the footprints?
- What did you see?
- What happened then?

Ans. One day, when I was alone at home with my grandmother, she had prepared fruit chaat for me. She told me to close the kitchen window and come to the dining table to eat. When I went to close the window, I saw small footprints in the kitchen. When I followed the footprints, I found that a cat had entered the kitchen and spilled all the milk on the floor. It got scared seeing me and ran out of the window.

Q.4 Use the joining words given below and join the sentences in Column A and B.

or and so but because

	A	B
(i)	I can sing well.	I forgot to post it.
(ii)	She wore a raincoat.	It was raining.
(iii)	We may go to Shimla.	He was late to school.
(iv)	He wanted a book for his birthday.	We may go to Darjeeling.
(v)	He missed the school bus.	He wanted a football for his birthday.
(vi)	I wrote the letter.	I can't dance at all.
e.g., I wrote the letter but I forgot to post it.		

Ans. (i) I can sing well but I can't dance at all.

(ii) She wore a raincoat because it was raining.

(iii) We may go to Shimla or Darjeeling.

(iv) He wanted a book and a football for his birthday.

(v) He missed the school bus so he was late to school.

(vi) I wrote the letter but I forgot to post it.

Fun Time (NCERT Page 55)

Q.1 Look at the footprint shown here.

Hint : This is the footprint of the first man on the moon. His name was _______ .

Ans. Neil Armstrong

Q.2 Let's create a pyramid!

Use the following clues.

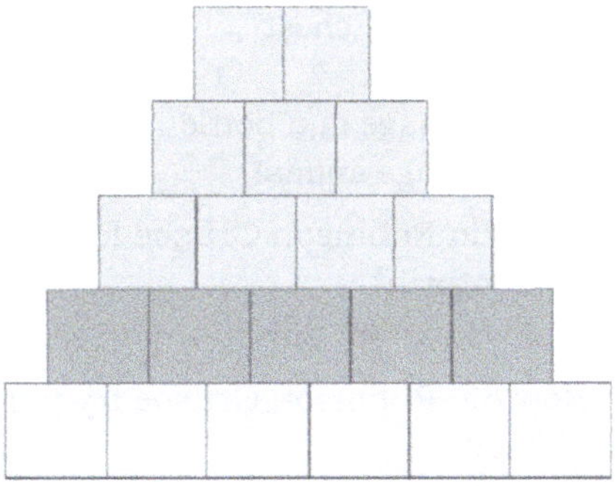

(i) A two letter word beginning with B.

(ii) A three letter word beginning with C.

(iii) A four letter word beginning with D.

(iv) A five letter word beginning with E.

(v) A six letter word beginning with F.

Ans. (i) Be (ii) Cat (iii) Door
(iv) Exact (v) Fabric

Let's Work in Pairs (NCERT Page 56)

Have a conversation with your partner based on the picture below. You can start as

Hunter 1 : "Look at the footprints in the mud!"

Hunter 2 : ____________________

Ans. **Hunter 1** : Of course! This looks like a big lion's footprint.

Hunter 2 : But, how is it possible? There are no lions in this jungle.

Hunter 1: Let us run and get away from here before we see one.

Hunter 2 : Yes! We must run as fast as we can!

Hunter 1: But where is the map? Do you know the way out of this jungle?

Hunter 2: No! I thought you had the map. Now we are in big trouble.

PRACTICE QUESTIONS

Multiple Choice Questions

1. What did Robinson Crusoe find on the sand near his boat?
   (a) A treasure chest
   (b) A footprint
   (c) A message in a bottle
   (d) A strange animal
2. How did Robinson Crusoe feel when he saw the footprint?
   (a) Excited (b) Curious (c) Scared (d) Happy
3. How did Robinson Crusoe try to protect himself?
   (a) He built a fort
   (b) He hid in his cave
   (c) He became friends with the savages
   (d) He fought with the savages

Ans. 1. (b), 2. (c), 3. (b)

Extract Based Questions

I did not sleep that night. The more I thought about what I had seen, the more afraid I became. I thought it could be one of the savages of the mainland who had wandered out to the sea, in a small boat.

1. Who is 'I' in the given lines?

Ans. 'I' in the given lines refers to Robinson Crusoe.

2. Why couldn't he sleep?

Ans. He couldn't sleep because he was afraid that the footprint he found on the shore was of another man. He thought that one of the savages had come to the island and could kill him.

3. What does the word 'savages' mean in the given extract?
   (a) wild animals (b) violent people
   (c) tigers (d) None of the above

Ans. (b) violent people

4. What is the synonym of the word 'afraid'?

Ans. Frightened

Fill in the Blanks

1. Robinson Crusoe____________the area for other footprints.
2. Robinson Crusoe was____________of the savages.
3. Robinson Crusoe________in his cave.

Ans. 1. searched, 2. afraid, 3. hid

True or False

1. Robinson Crusoe thought the footprint could be a ghost's.
2. Robinson Crusoe was no longer afraid after measuring the footprint.
3. Robinson Crusoe hid in his cave to protect himself.

Ans. 1. False, 2. False, 3. True

Answer the Following Questions

1. How did Robinson Crusoe feel when he saw the footprint?

Ans. Robinson Crusoe felt surprised and scared when he saw the footprint.

2. Why was Robinson Crusoe afraid of the footprint?

Ans. Robinson Crusoe was afraid of the footprint because it meant that someone else might be living on the island.
He thought that one of the savages had wandered off from the mainland to the island.

3. What did Robinson Crusoe do to protect himself from the unknown danger?

Ans. Robinson Crusoe protected himself by hiding in his cave and avoiding going out to the shore.

4. What did Robinson Crusoe do after hiding and praying for a while?

Ans. After hiding and praying for a while, he felt bolder and decided to investigate the footprint again.

CHAPTER 1 CRYING

Summary of the Poem The poem talks about finding happiness after crying. The poem suggests crying your heart out, until your pillow is soaked with tears. This way you can cry out all the sadness and feel truly happy.

Stanza-wise Explanation

Stanza 1

Crying only a little bit is no use.
You must cry until your pillow is soaked!
Then you can jump in the shower and splash-splash-splash!

Word-Meaning *Soaked - Completely wet; Shower - Bath; Splash - To make the water fly all around.*

Exp. In these lines, the speaker says that crying a little is not helpful. To feel happy, we must cry out all our sadness completely. We must cry until our pillow becomes wet with tears. After this, we can jump into the shower and wash the tears away.

Stanza 2

Then you can throw open your window and, "Ha, ha! ha ha!"
And if people say, "Hey, what's going on up there?"
"Ha ha!" sing back, "Happiness was hiding in the last tear!
I wept it! Ha ha!"

Word-Meaning *Wept - Shed tears; Throw open - To open.*

Exp. After crying a lot and washing off the sadness, we can open our windows and laugh. If we catch people's attention, we can just tell them that we are happy now. We can sing our happiness that was hiding in the last tear and after crying the last tear, we will happy again.

NCERT FOLDER

Let's Read (NCERT Page 60)

Q.1 According to the poet, should you cry a little or should you cry a lot?

Ans. According to the poet, you should cry a lot.

Q.2 What can you do after crying a lot?

Ans. After crying a lot, you can laugh and be happy.

Q.3 (i) Read the first two lines of the poem. Is the mood

happy? sad? angry? jealous? upset?

Ans. sad

(ii) In the last few lines the mood of the poet has changed. What is it now?

very happy angry cheerful sad jealous

Ans. Very happy

Q.4 Are these sentences right or wrong?

(i) The poet says you must not cry much.

(ii) The poet says that you should cry till your pillow is soaked.

(iii) The poet says that after crying you should open the window and laugh so that people will see that you are happy.

(iv) The poet says that you should open the window and show people that you are crying.

Ans. (i) wrong (ii) right (iii) right (iv) wrong

Let's Talk (NCERT Page 61)

Q.1 Where do you cry? What are the things that make you cry?

Ans. I cry on my bed. I cry when I get hurt while playing, when I lose something that was important or when my teacher scolds me.

Q.2 Can you cry when you are happy?

Ans. Yes, we can sometimes cry when we are happy.

Q.3 Which are the things that make you happy? In what ways do you show your happiness?

Ans. Playing with my friends and eating my favourite food makes me happy. I show my happiness by laughing and singing.

Say Aloud (NCERT Page 61)

dash	bash	splash	cash	trash
steer	tear	clear	deer	dear
shower	power	tower	flower	mower
poked	croaked	soaked	stroked	joked
wept	kept	crept	leapt	slept

Ans. Do it yourself.

Word Building (NCERT Page 61)

The word happiness ends in ness and comes from the word happy. Write three words that end in the same way. Which words do they come from?

Ans. Cheerful	**ness**	:	Cheerfulness
Lonely	**ness**	:	loneliness
Sad	**ness**	:	sadness

Let's Write (NCERT Page 62)

Q.1 Fill in the blanks with the exact word.

(i) The tourists were amazed to see the beautiful Taj Mahal. (amazed, shocked, worried)

(ii) The lights went out suddenly. I was alone and frightened. (worried, shocked, frightened)

(iii) He has been ill for a long time and his parents were worried. (unhappy, worried, angry)

(iv) The shopkeeper was shocked when he saw his safe wide open with all his money missing. (unhappy, shocked, angry)

Creative Writing (NCERT Page 62)

Narrate an incident when you have experienced happiness, excitement, surprise. You can use the following clues.

With whom....

When did it happen...

Why...

Where...

Ans. One day, my friends and family surprised me with a birthday party. It happened on the evening of my birthday.They had decorated my room with balloons and ribbons. They had also put up a banner that said 'Happy Birthday.' When I came home from school, I was surprised to see all my friends and family waiting for me. They shouted "Surprise!" and I was so excited! We played games, ate cake, and had a lot of fun. It was the best birthday party I have ever had!

PRACTICE QUESTIONS

Multiple Choice Questions

1. Which two moods are mentioned in the poem?
   (a) Sad and gloomy
   (b) Nervous and sad
   (c) Sad and happy
   (d) Happy and delighted
2. Choose the synonym of 'soaked'
   (a) Completely wet (b) Dried
   (c) Dehydrated (d) Waterless
3. Where was the happiness hiding?
   (a) In the bed (b) In the last tear
   (c) In the shower (d) In the splash
4. Which is not the meaning of 'wept'?
   (a) Shed (b) Cried
   (c) Laughed (d) Sobbed

Ans. 1. (c), 2. (a), 3. (b), 4. (c)

Extract Based Questions

Read the following extract and answer the questions that follow.

Then you can throw open your window
and, "Ha, ha! ha ha!"

And if people say, "Hey, what's going on
up there?"

"Ha ha!" sing back, "Happiness was hiding
in the last tear!

I wept it! Ha ha!"

1. Why should you 'throw open your window' and laugh?

Ans. We should throw open the window and laugh to show people that we are happy again.

2. What should we say when people ask questions?

Ans. We should tell them that we have found happiness. It was hiding in the last tear.

3. Find the verbs in the last two lines of the given extract.

Ans. sing, hiding, wept

Answer the Following Questions

1. What is the mood of the first two lines of the poem?

Ans. The mood of the first two lines is sad.

2. What is the central idea of the poem crying?

Ans. The central idea of the poem 'Crying' revolves around crying and finding hapiness. It begins by telling if people cry only for a little bit, that will not help them at all. It says that it won't be of any use because when you cry a little, you don't let it all out.

3. List any two things that the poet has suggested to do after crying? (DIKSHA)

Ans. The poet has suggested the following two things to do after crying a lot
   (i) Jump into the shower and splash.
   (ii) Open you window and laugh aloud.

Let's Write

1. Have you ever cried because of something other than an injury. Write a dairy entry about why you cried and how you got over it.

   You may follow the format given below

   Date

   Day

   Time

   Dear Diary

Ans. 22nd October, 20XX

Monday 9:00p.m.

Dear Dairy

Today was a sad day. My best friend was leaving the school and the town because her father got transferred to another city. Even though she had told me about it a month ago, the reality hit me today when I had to bid her my goodbye.
I just couldn't stop crying. I cried till my eyes burned, even though she promised to keep in touch. Even now, the thought makes me want to cry but I know that we will still be best friends.

Mona

CHAPTER 2

MY ELDER BROTHER

Summary of the Chapter

This is a short play which tells a story about two brothers, Munna and Bhaiya. They were very different from each other. They stayed together in a hostel away from home. Munna was nine years old and loved playing outdoors. Bhaiya was fourteen years old and a disciplined student who studied for long hours everyday. As Bhaiya was older, he felt responsible and he was strict with Munna about his studies. Munna being the younger brother, listened to his elder brother and followed his advice.

By following the timetable made by Bhaiya, Munna was able to pass all his classes. However, Bhaiya was not very good at studies, so he failed twice. This made Munna feel too proud of himself. He thought that he could pass easily and did not need to study hard.

One day, Bhaiya found Munna running after a kite and scolded him for becoming too careless. Bhaiya told him that even though they had only one year gap class-wise, he would still remain five years older than him. He explained to him that knowledge was not only gained through studies, but also through experience.

Bhaiya also told Munna that their parents were not educated but still knew more than them as they had more experience in life. Therefore, one should always respect their elders and listen to their advice.

To sum up, this story highlights the importance of listening to our elders as they have more knowledge and experience than us. They may scold us sometimes, but it is always for our own good.

WORD-MEANING

Turning pale - To get scared; Foundation - Base of something; Schedule - Timetable; Tremendous effort - Great amount of effort; Hard earned money - Money that is earned with hard work; Idling away - To do nothing; Mastered - To gain expertise; Examiner - Someone who tests you in an exam; Punctuality - The quality of being on time; Ashamed - Feeling guilty of one's actions; Wisdom - Learning, knowledge; Rush - To hurry; Responsibility - duty; Firmly - Strongly; Prefer - To like something more; Sobbing - To cry while taking sharp breaths; Dawn - Beginning of the day, early morning; Flurry - A sudden outburst, rush.

NCERT FOLDER

Reading is Fun (NCERT Page 71)

Q.1 What are the things that Munna liked to do?

Ans. Munna liked to play different games with his friends. He also liked flying kites.

Q.2 What did Bhaiya do all day?

Ans. Bhaiya studied for long hours and practised writing everyday. He sometimes wrote the same words and sentences twenty times to learn them.

Q.3 Why was Munna not happy with the timetable that Bhaiya made for him?

Ans. Munna was not happy with the timetable that Bhaiya made because it did not have any time for playing.

Q.4 How do you think Munna felt when his brother was so strict with him? Why was Bhaiya so strict with him?

Ans. Munna felt unhappy and disappointed when his brother was strict with him. Bhaiya was strict with him because he knew Munna did not like studying. He only liked playing games and flying kites. Being his elder brother, Bhaiya felt responsible towards him and cared for his studies.

Q.5 Whose character do you like more — Munna's or Bhaiya's? Why?

Ans. I like the character of Bhaiya more as he is very hardworking and responsible.

He is caring towards his younger brother and strict, when needed. He is also very wise. He understands the value of his father's hard earned money and teaches his brother to respect the elders.

Let's Talk (NCERT Page 71)

Q.1 Do you have a timetable at school?

How many periods are there for the following subjects and activities in one week?

English ____, Hindi ____, Maths ____. Science ____, Social studies ____. Games ____, Art ____, Craft ____, Music ____. Dance ____, Any other activity? ____

Ans. English - 5, Hindi - 5, Maths - 5, Science - 5, Social studies - 5, Games - 1, Art - 1, Craft - 1, Music - 1, Dance - 1, Computer science -1

Q.2 Now make a timetable for yourself including your study time and your play time.

Ans. Do it yourself.

Creative Writing (NCERT Page 72 and 73)

The format of a letter is given to you. (See NCERT page 72 for the letter format)

Q.1 After reading the letter, answer the following questions.

(i) Who has written the letter? __________

Ans. Pratap

(ii) To whom has the letter been written? __________

Ans. His mother

(iii) Where is the writer of the letter? __________

Ans. In a hostel, in Kolkata.

(iv) What is the name of his hostel? __________

Ans. Krishna Boy's Hostel

(v) On which date was this letter written?__________

Ans. 10th July, 2000

Q.2 Now, write a letter to your friend or relative in another city telling him/her about activities/events in your school. Follow the same pattern as the above letter.

Ans. Arya Nagar, Aurobindo Marg

CR Park

New Delhi

15th September, 2008

Dear Ravi,

How are you doing? I hope everything is going well with you.

I'm writing to tell you about all the fun activities and events we've been having at school lately. Last week, we had a sports day where we competed in races and games like, jumping and throwing. I won the sack race! It was amazing!

We also had a science exhibition where we displayed our projects. I made a volcano with baking soda, vinegar and some red food colour for the lava. It was really exciting to see it blow up!

Next week, we're going on a school trip to the National Rail Museum. I'm really looking forward to seeing this interesting museum.

I hope you are having a great time too. I can't wait to hear about what you have been up to!

Your best friend,

Kunal

Comprehension (NCERT Page 74)

Read the passage given on page 74 of NCERT Textbook.

Q.1 Why did Oliver live in the orphanage?

Ans. Oliver lived in the orphanage because he had no family or home.

Q.2 Who was Mr Bumble?

Ans. Mr. Bumble was the owner of the orphanage.

Q.3 What meals were the boys given?

Ans. The boys were given only some watery soup.

Q.4 What did Oliver say to Mr Bumble?

Ans. Oliver said to Mr. Bumble that he wanted some extra soup.

Q.5 The boys were given three meals a day. Then why were they always hungry?

(i) Because the soup they were given was never enough.

(ii) Because they worked very hard all day long.

(iii) Because the older boys drank up their soup.

Ans. (i) Because the soup they were given was never enough.

Q.6 Find the words from the passage that mean the same as

(i) very hungry (para 2) ....

Ans. starving

(ii) to vanish (para 3) ....

Ans. disappeared

Q.7 'All the boys assembled in the cold stone hall.' Here the word 'assembled' means

(i) moved away (ii) collected

(iii) worked together

Ans. (ii) collected

Q.8 From the word 'assembled' remove the last two letters. Add one letter to make a word which means a time at the school when the whole school gathers.

assemb ____

Ans. assembly

Q.9 Give a suitable title to the passage.

Ans. Oliver's struggle/ Brave Oliver

Let's Write (NCERT Page 75 and 76)

Q.1 To learn means to understand or to gain knowledge.

To teach means to show how or to explain.

Complete the following sentences using the correct form of teach or learn.

learn	learns	learned	has learned
teach	teaches	taught	has taught

(i) Will you __________ me chess?

(ii) Mr Sharma _________ Class VIII.

(iii) The students have ___________ about 'road safety'.

(iv) My sister has ___________ me how to ride a horse.

(v) I have ___________ some of the customs of India.

(vi) I ________ how to cycle when I was just four years old.

Ans. (i) teach (ii) teaches (iii) learned (iv) taught (v) learned (vi) learned

Q.2 Choose the correct word and complete the paragraph.

All the class V students of our school (a)_____ (were/was) gathering in front of the Principal's office. They (b)____ (were/was) going for the inter-school race. The bus (c)______ (arrive/ arrived) and they (d)______ (leave/left) for the stadium. The runners were (e)____(taking/ taken) to the starting point. The runners (f)___(take/took) their positions. Sir (g)____ (blow / blew) the whistle. One student of our school (h)____ (run/ran) fast and (i)_____ (come/ came) first. Everyone (j)____ (do/did) their best and our school (k)____ (won/ wins) the trophy. Everyone (l)_____ (feel/ felt/ fell) joyous.

Ans. (a) - were, (b) - were, (c) - arrived, (d) - left, (e) - taken, (f) - took, (g) - blew, (h) - ran, (i) - came, (j) - did, (k) - won, (l) - felt

Q.3 Read the following sentences.

- Bhaiya has been studying in the same class for two years. (for a period of time)
- Munna was flying kites since morning. (from a time in the past till the present)

Fill in the blanks using 'for or 'since'.

(i) I have lived in this house ______ I was a baby.

(ii) This big jar has been in our family_____ many years.

(iii) The old banyan tree in the village has been there________ the last 200 years.

(iv) Nobody has seen him ______ yesterday.

Ans. (i) since (ii) for (iii) for (iv) since

Project Work (NCERT Page 76)

Choose a story that you like.

In groups of four, write down dialogues for the story and make in into a short play. You may then present it in the class.

Ans. Do it yourself.

PRACTICE QUESTIONS

Multiple Choice Questions

1. What is the main difference between the two brothers?
   (a) Their height (b) Their age
   (c) Their interests (d) Their appearance
2. Why does the elder brother scold the younger brother?
   (a) Because the younger brother is always late
   (b) Because the younger brother is messy
   (c) Because the younger brother doesn't study hard
   (d) Because the younger brother is disrespectful
3. What does the elder brother teach the younger brother?
   (a) The importance of education
   (b) The value of hard work
   (c) The respect for elders
   (d) All of the above
4. The story of 'My Elder Brother' is based on the famous story of Hindi __________.
   (a) Balidan
   (b) Poos Ki Raat
   (c) Bade Bhai Saheb
   (d) Satyagrah

5. Who said, 'I prefer to study a book.'?
   (a) Munna (b) Bhaiya
   (c) Villagers (d) Kite
6. Who said, 'Now I can play games with my friends and fly kites.'?
   (a) Munna (b) Bhaiya
   (c) Villagers (d) Friends

Ans. 1. (c), 2. (c), 3. (d), 4. (c), 5. (b), 6. (a)

Extract Based Questions

Munna Oh Bhaisaheb! This is scary. I don't think I want to go to the 9th class now, but I will still complete my day's homework so that I get no punishment in class.

Bhaiya Just today, we were asked to write a short essay on the topic of in four pages! And imagine, can something be written on four pages and still be short? It's all so mixed up!

1. What does Munna find 'scary' according to the given extract?

Ans. Munna finds 9th class scary according to the given extract.

2. What was Bhaiya's assignment for the day? Was he happy about it?

Ans. Bhaiya's assignment for the day was to write a short essay on the topic of 'Punctuality' in four pages and he was not happy about it.

3. Why did Munna decide to do his homework?

Ans. Munna decided to do his homework because he did not want to get punished.

4. Find the antonym of the word 'reward' from the extract.

Ans. Punishment

Answer the Following Questions

1. What are some differences between the personalities of the two brothers based on the chapter 'My Elder Brother'?

Ans. The two brothers are very different from each other. The older brother 'Bhaiya', is hardworking and likes to spend his time studying. On the other hand, the younger brother 'Munna' likes to play with his friends and fly kites. The older brother is also more careful and responsible, but the younger brother becomes careless sometimes.

2. Why does Munna feel too proud of himself?

Ans. Munna feels too proud of himself because he easily passes and tops his class.

3. What lesson does Munna learn at the end of the story?

Ans. Munna learns the importance of respecting his elders and listening to their advice. He also realises that even though his elder brother may not be good at studies, he is still more experienced than him. He understands that his elder brother is strict with him because he cares for him deeply.

Let's Write

1. For some reason, Bhaiya decided to complete his schooling from school of open learning and went home. Munna is now in 9th class and has realised the wisdom in his brother's advice. Write a letter from Munna to Bhaiya telling him about it.

   Start with the following

   Dear Bhaiya

   How are you?......

Ans. Dear Bhaiya,

How are you? I am doing fine here. I miss you a lot. I have written this letter to tell you that you were write. Remember you had told me that class 9th was difficult. I realise the truth of it now after the first unit tests. Just like every years, I did not study much and played a lot, thinking I would be able to score good marks. However, it was not the case. I had not scored apt at all.

Now, I have decided to make a time table which include study as well as play time. Hoping that I would score good next time.

Give my love to ma and papa.

Yours lovingly

Munna

CHAPTER 1 RIP VAN WINKLE

Summary of the Chapter

Rip Van Winkle was a simple and good-natured man. He lived in a little village at the foothills of the Kaatskill mountains. He was a kind and helpful neighbour. Everyone in the village liked him. He also played many games with the children and told them long stories. However, Rip had a problem. He avoided all work and was very lazy. He spent most of his time with his dog named Wolf and walked away into the forest with him to avoid work.

One day, while walking with his dog he reached the highest part of the mountain and decided to rest there. After a while, he met a short, old man, with thick hair and a grizzled beard. He was carrying a barrel and kept calling Rip's name asking for his help to carry the barrel. Rip helped him and they reached a place where some more odd looking men were playing a game called ninepins. They all had a serious look on their faces and made no sound. Seeing Rip, they all stopped playing and stared at him. They made him drink the liquid from the barrel which put him into a deep sleep.

After waking up, Rip looked around for his dog but couldn't find him anywhere. He decided to go back to his village. On reaching the village, Rip could not recognise anyone and everyone looked at him with surprise. He touched his face and realised his beard had grown a foot long and was white in colour. Then, an old woman finally recognised him and asked him where he had been for the past twenty years.

WORD-MEANING

Foothills - The lower part of a mountain or hill range; Good Natured - Being kind and friendly; Fences - A line of wooden or metal pillars joined by wires to separate a land; Companion - Partner or friend; Grizzled - Having grey or white hair; Echoed - Repeated a sound or noise;
Contents - Things that are inside somethings; Barrel - A wooden vessel made for storing liquids; Fixed gaze - Looking at something continuously; Trembling - Shivering or shaking with fear; Muttered - To say something quietly; Descend - Move down or go downwards; Astonishment - Great surprise or wonder.

NCERT FOLDER

Fun with New Words (NCERT Page 83)

Q.1 Circle the correct meaning of the given words. You may need to use the dictionary.

idled away	wasted	rested	admired
constant	coffee	construct	steady
companion	dog	stranger	pariner
realise	to understand	to set free	real
descend	to not send	to be decent	to move down
barrel	a wooden container	a musical instrument	a bag
contents	to be happy	the ingredients	the index of a book

Ans. Idled away - wasted
constant - steady
companion - partner
realise - to understand
descend - to move down
barrel - a wooden container
contents - the ingredients

Q.2 Match the words in the box with their meanings. You may take the help of a dictionary.

grizzled astonished foothills
stroked familiar

near the lower part of a mountain ______
with grey hair ______
to rub gently ______
to be very suprised ______
known to you ______

Ans. foothills, grizzled, stroked, astonished, familiar

Let's Read (NCERT Page 83)

Q.1 Say whether the following sentences are True or False.

(i) Rip was kind to children.
(ii) Rip was a hardworking man.
(iii) The short old man on the mountain was his constant companion.
(iv) Rip helped the old man on the mountains because he wanted to have a drink from the barrel.
(v) Rip was away for twenty years because he was asleep on the mountains.
(vi) The drink from the barrel made him fall asleep for twenty years.
(vii) Nobody recognised Rip when he came back because he had reached the wrong village.

Ans. (i) True (ii) False (iii) False (iv) False (v) True (vi) True (vii) False

Q.2 Complete the following sentences.

(i) Rip's village was situated __________.
Ans. at the foothills of Kaatskill village.

(ii) The children of the village loved him because __________________.
Ans. he played with them, taught them how to fly kites and told stories.

(iii) __________________ was his constant companion.
Ans. His dog named Wolf

(iv) The villagers stared at him because__________.
Ans. they could not recognise him.

(v) The old woman who recognised Rip was____________.

Ans. his neighbour

Let's Write (NCERT Page 84)

Work in groups of four.

Q.1 What were the strange things about the men on the mountains?

Ans. (i) They were all odd looking.

(ii) They all had a serious look on their faces.

(iii) They were all dressed in the same way and had beards of various shapes and colours.

(iv) They were playing a game but were absolutely silent.

Q.2 What kind of a man was Rip Van Winkle?

(i) He was a kind neighbour.

Ans. (ii) He loved children and played with them.

(iii) He was always ready to help.

(iv) He was very lazy.

Vocabulary Building (NCERT Page 85)

Q.1 Pick out the names of the games mentioned in the story.

flying kites chess ninepins shooting marbles mountain-climbing shooting skipping hopping

Ans. (i) Flying kites

(ii) Shooting marbles

(iii) Ninepins

Q.2 Sometimes we join two words to make a describing word. For example, Rip was a good-natured man, everybody liked him.

Here are some more describing words. Use them to complete the given paragraph.

long-sleeved, high-heeled, well-dressed open-mouthed, sweet-looking, odd-looking part-time

Mrs Das has a __________ job in a clothes shop. Yesterday, an __________ woman walked into the shop. She was wearing __________shoes. A __________ dog was with her. "I want a __________ shirt for my dog, please,"□she said. "For your dog?" asked Mrs Das, __________ in surprise. "Yes", replied the woman. "I want him to be __________ for my next party."

Ans. part-time, odd-looking, high-heeled, sweet-looking, long-sleeved, open-mouthed, well-dressed.

Q.3 Silent letters

What is common in the following groups of words?

(i) knee, knife, knot, know

(ii) neighbour, daughter, fight, straight

(iii) honest, honour, hour, heir

Try and make more silent letter words.

gnat : __________ . __________

tong**ue** : __________ . __________

cha**l**k : __________ . __________

whis**t**le : __________ . __________

Ans. (i) Silent letter 'k'.

(ii) Silent letter 'gh'.

(iii) Silent letter 'h'.

More Silent Letter Words

gnat	-	gnaw, gnash
tongue	-	fatigue, plague
chalk	-	walk, talk
whistle	-	nestle, listen

Q.4 Read the two paragraphs given below.

My mother is always **awake** before anyone else in the family. I usually **wake up** after 6 O'clock. I loll around **lazily** for a few minutes. The I **get up** and get dressed for school.

At bedtime, I read a story book. When I feel tired I **lie down** and go to sleep very **quickly**. I fall asleep in no time at all!

(i) Now find the opposites of the following words from the paragraphs and complete the table.

awake	fall asleep
wake up	____________
get up	____________
lazily	____________

Ans. wake up - fall asleep
get up - lie down
lazily - quickly

(ii) Fill in the blanks using the words in the previous questions.

(a) ________ and ________ quickly! You will be late for school.

(b) Shh! The baby is ________ . Don't make a sound, or she will ________ .

(c) Are you still ________? You should be ________ now or you will not be able to ________ in the morning for school.

Ans. (a) Wake up, get up (b) asleep, wake up
(c) awake, asleep, get up

Let's Talk (NCERT Page 87)

Q.1 Lots of things must have happened in the village when Rip was away. Imagine you are the neighbour who greets Rip after 20 years. One student should act as Rip. Tell Rip about all that had happened in the village after he left.

(Talk about what happened to his family, to his friends, to the other villagers, to the children he played with, the changes in the village... etc. Your teacher will guide you.) You may start this way.

Guess what happened on the day you left. When you didn't come home in the evening, your wife...

Ans. Do it yourself.

Q.2 Read the speech bubbles. Who walks to school most often? Put them in order.

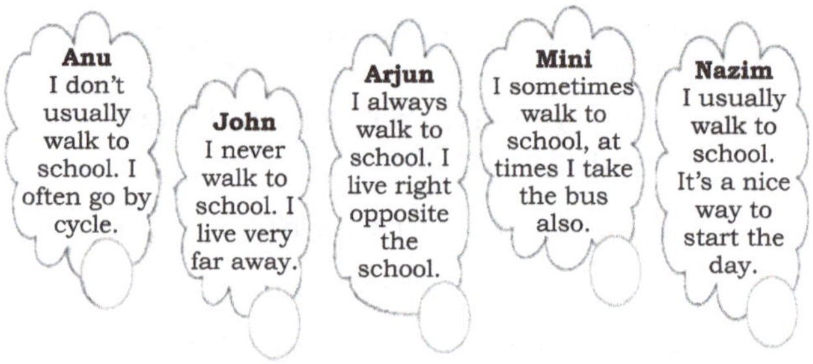

Ans. 1. **Arjun** I always walk to school. I live right opposite the school.
2. **Nazim** I usually walk to school. It's a nice way to start the day.
3. **Mini** I sometimes walk to school, at times I take the bus also.
4. **Anu** I don't usually walk to school. I often go by cycle.
5. **John** I never walk to school. I live very far away.

Creative Writing (NCERT Page 88)

Q.1 Write about yourself using the following expressions (do you play in the park, go to bed late, fuss over food, study hard, etc.?)

always	frequently	usually
often	sometimes	rarely

For example : I always do my work neatly.

Ans. (i) I frequently visit my friend.
(ii) I always study hard.
(iii) I usually play in the park with my ball.
(iv) I sometimes fuss over food.

(v) I rarely go to bed late because I like to sleep on time.

Q.2 Use the following clues to complete the following exercise.

play	stop	buy	learn	see	meet
learn	be	eat	go	travel	start
read	visit				

(i) Write three new things you have done in the last three years.

Ans. (a) I have started learning a new language.

(b) I have visited Jaipur.

(c) I have started playing badminton.

(ii) Write three things you have not done in the last three years.

Ans. (a) I have not played my guitar since I left the music club.

(b) I have not eaten eggs.

(c) I have not met any famous people.

PRACTICE QUESTIONS

Multiple Choice Questions

1. The only problem with ____________ was that he was very lazy.
   (a) villagers (b) Rip
   (c) wolf (d) children

2. Who thought, "Surely, I have not slept here all night".
   (a) Villagers (b) Rip Van Winkle
   (c) Dwarf (d) Wolf

3. Who said, "Rip Van Winkle, Rip Van Winkle!"?
   (a) A short old man (b) Wolf
   (c) Villagers (d) None of these

4. The story of "Rip Van Winkle" is adapted from ____________________ .
   (a) Adventures of Rip
   (b) Rip Van Winkle
   (c) Rip and the Mountain
   (d) The Legend of Rip Van Winkle

Ans. 1. (b), 2. (b), 3. (a), 4. (d)

Answer the Following Questions

1. Describe Rip Van Winkle's personality in a few lines.

Ans. Rip Van Winkle was a kind and helpful man who loved playing with the children. However, he was very lazy and avoided all kinds of work.

2. Where did Rip Van Winkle go while walking with his dog?

Ans. Rip Van Winkle went to the highest part of the mountain while walking with his dog.

3. What happened after Rip Van Winkle drank the liquid from the barrel?

Ans. After Rip Van Winkle drank the liquid from the barrel, he went into deep sleep.

4. Why did the children like Rip? (DIKSHA)

Ans. Children liked Rip because he played with them, he taught them to fly kites and shoot marbles, and told them long stories.

Let's Write!

1. We know that the village had changed. Can you think of ways in which the village might have changed?

Ans. The villages must have changed significantly. The children would have grown up. There might have been more buildings like cinema, schools, hospital, college, etc. in the village. There also might be electronic and vehicles in the city. Further, the dressing style of the times must have also changed significantly.

CHAPTER 1 CLASS DISCUSSION

Summary of the poem During a class discussion, the teacher and the students were sharing their opinions. There was only one girl named Jane, who was not participating in the discussion. Her teacher noticed her and asked her about it. Jane said that there are many people in the world who are quiet by nature and do not like to talk much, just like her.

Stanza-wise Explanation

Stanza 1

"In the class discussion Jane, you hardly said a word.
We all aired our opinions but from you we barely heard.
You sat and stared in silence surrounded by the chatter,
Now tell me Jane, and please be plain, is there anything the matter?"

Word-Meaning *Aired - Expressed; Opinion - View or idea; Chatter - Talking informally; Plain - Honest, clear.*

Exp. In these lines, the teacher tells Jane that during the class discussion, she did not participate. All her classmates were sharing their opinions but she kept quiet. She asks Jane to be honest and to tell her if something was troubling her.

Stanza 2

Jane looked up and then she spoke,
Her voice was clear and low:
"There are many people in this world
Who are rather quiet you know!"

Word-Meaning *Rather - preferably.*

Exp. *Jane looks at her teacher and speaks with a clear and low voice. She says that there are many people in this world who are quiet by choice. She explains that she was quiet because she did not like talking much and did not wish to be a part of the chatter.*

NCERT FOLDER

Let's Read (NCERT Page 92)

Q.1 What activity was going on in the class?

Ans. There was a discussion going on in the class.

Q.2 Who was the quiet one in the class?

Ans. Jane was the quiet one in the class.

Q.3 Why was she quiet?

(i) She was afraid to air her opinions.

(ii) She hated the noise.

(iii) She didn't like the activity.

(iv) She was quiet by nature.

Ans. (iv) She was quiet by nature.

Q.4 How do you interact in class during discussions? Do you participate or remain quiet?

Ans. I generally participate in discussions in class as I feel that I get new ideas from different people.

Think and Write (NCERT Page 92)

Q.1 Choose two friends in your class who are very different from each other. Use the clues in the box to describe their nature. You may also add your own words to describe them.

naughty, lively, sharing, careless, studious, quiet, friendly, helpful, regular, cheerful

Ans. I have two good friends in class, Harsh and Ria. They are very different from each other. Harsh is very naughty and sometimes a little careless too. He likes to jump around in the class when the teacher is away. He also likes to laugh a lot. On the other hand, my friend Ria is quiet and studious. She is very friendly but does not like to talk much. She is helpful and always helps me with my maths homework.

Let's Talk (NCERT Page 93)

Q.1 What is a Discussion?

To discuss means to talk together or decide something. When you do this, you are taking part in a discussion.

Read the sentences below. They tell us what happens in a discussion.

- In a discussion each person gives his ideas one by one.
- Some tell why something should be done. Others may tell how.
- Participants ask questions and answer them.
- Many ideas are given. Everyone helps to decide which ideas are the best.

Note the points you might discuss before palnning a visit to the park.

(i) Choose a day and time.

(ii) What things to bring to play?

(iii) Assign duties.

(iv) Things to eat.

Look at the picture in the poem. Imagine and write what the discussion in the class is about.

Ans. Do it yourself.

Q.2 Fill in the grid given below by assigning qualities to each person. Some clues are given here to help you.

Clues

- Sangeeta lends her pencil to her partner.
- Nirav is also called a chatterbox.
- Pranav recently saved a cat from drowning in the lake.
- Megha is just the opposite of Nirav.
- Mithila always teases everyone.
- Ritu is always seen with a book in hand.

Ans.

	brave	naughty	quiet	talkative	generous	studious
Nirav				✓		
Pranav	✓					
Megha			✓			
Mithila		✓				
Ritu						✓
Sangeeta					✓	

Let's Read and Do (NCERT Page 94)

- Children who show exceptional bravery are honoured with the bravery award to recognise their presence of mind.
- In 1957, the Indian Council of Child Welfare started these National Bravery Awards.
- Brave children are awarded cash prizes, free school education and a certificate from the Prime Minister of India. They ride on an elephant in the Republic Day parade.

- Harsh Srivastava, a 12 year old boy, and his 15 year old sister rescued a child from the attack of a raging bull.
- Yumnan Jayadeo Singh, 11 years old, jumped into the flooded river, and saved a three year-old from drowning. The act of bravery was recognised because he saved the life of an infant.

Find one story of bravery about a child. You can search for the story by talking to older people or watching a TV programme or from a film.

- Write down the story. Also mention its source.
- Narrate the story to the class
- Which story did you like the best? Write down your reasons.

Ans. The given story of a brave girl was taken from news sources like The Times.

A class 10 student, who sells flowers and puja items at the Bateshwar Ghat in Agra district, rescued four youths from drowning in the treacherous waters of Yamuna river as they were being pulled into the deep side during Ganesh Visarjan (immersion). As the youths from Firozabad ventured into the waters while immersing a Ganesh idol on Tuesday evening, they found themselves struggling against the strong currents.

As onlookers raised an alarm, Mohini Goswami, a student, jumped into the river without hesitation to save them. Her exceptional swimming skills, honed since childhood, enabled her to reach the panicked youths and bring them safely to shore.

Write a Notice (NCERT Page 95)

A notice tells who when, where, and what.

The girls and boys of Class V wrote notices for the bulletin board.

Q.1 Read Sheela's notice. Discuss the questions that follow.

Notice

The Drama Committee will meet in the classroom on Monday, at 2 O'clock We'll plan a play for our Annual Day.

Will each one of you please bring a play?

SHEELA

- Who was to meet?
- When were they to meet?
- Where were they to meet?
- What were they to do?

Ans.
- The Drama committee was to meet.
- They were to meet on Monday at 2 o'clock.
- They were to meet in the classroom.
- They were to plan a play for the annual day.

Q.2 Write a notice about a library committee or a football match.

Ans.

XYZ School

Notice

The Library Committee of Class V will meet in the school library on Wednesday in the third period. We shall discuss and make a list of English books and magazines to be added to the library. Please come prepared with your suggestions.

ROHAN
Class Prefect

or

XYZ School
Notice
Football Match

This is to inform you that there will be an Inter-school football match between our school and ABC School on 5th September, 20xx, at 11:00 am, in the school's football ground. All the students are invited to watch the match and requested to be seated by 10:30 am. Please bring your own water bottles and maintain discipline during the match.

PARAG
Sports Captain

PRACTICE QUESTIONS

Multiple Choice Questions

1. How did Jane sound when she spoke?
   (a) Loud and angry
   (b) Clear and low
   (c) Low and sweet
   (d) Happy and low
2. What did Jane say about the people in the world?
   (a) They are very talkative
   (b) They are rather quiet
   (c) They are always angry
   (d) They are always happy
3. What was the teacher worried about?
   (a) Jane's understanding of the lesson
   (b) Jane's behaviour during the discussion
   (c) Jane's absence from the class
   (d) Jane's handwriting

Ans. 1. (b), 2. (b), 3. (b)

Answer the Following Questions

1. Who sat and stared in silence?

Ans. Jane sat and stared in silence.

2. Why do you think Jane was quiet in the class?

Ans. Jane was quiet in the class because she was quiet by nature.

3. What did the teacher do when she saw that Jane was not participating in the discussion?

Ans. When the teacher saw that Jane was not participating in the discussion, she asked Jane to share her views too.

4. What is the central idea of the poem 'Class Discussion'?

Ans. The central idea of the poem is that people can be talkative as well as quiet. Not everyone likes to speak all the time. Some people prefer silence.

Let's Write!

1. Do you know any person who does not like to talk much? Is he/she your friend? Write about the person in about 70 words.

Ans. Yes, I know a person who likes to talk very less. She is a close friend of mine and also my neighbour. Because she talks, she does not have many friends. However, to me, she is a smart and a kind person. She is very good at studies, loves reading and has many hobbies. Because of her, I also started to like reading and developed hobbies. We both bond over art and crafts which make us both very happy. We also love to bake and often do so together. She may be quiet but she is amazing.

CHAPTER 2 THE TALKATIVE BARBER

Summary of the Chapter

This is a story of a barber who lived in the city of Cashgar. He was very talkative. The Sultan once called him to shave his head. The barber kept talking instead of shaving him which made the Sultan very angry. The barber still did not stop and told the Sultan that he was the youngest of seven brothers. He was the only one who talked less. He further started telling the Sultan about the defects his brother's had.

This made the Sultan impatient and he ordered to pay the barber three pieces of gold and to send him away. However, the barber argued that he came to his house on Sultan's request and would not leave until he had shaved his head. The Sultan asked him to hurry as he was getting late for the feast that he had arranged for his friends. To this, the barber replied that he too had invited some of his friends and had made no arrangements for them.

To get rid of him as quickly as possible, Sultan offered him the food that was prepared for the feast and asked him to leave. The barber still did not stop talking or leave. He wished to check the food first. He demanded that there should be fruits for dessert with the food that he received from the Sultan. So, the Sultan gave the barber the fruits too, as he wanted him to leave. After this, the barber started to shave the Sultan's head, but soon started talking again.

WORD-MEANING

Narrated - Told; Ancient - Very old; Chatterer - One who talks too much; Hump-backed - Someone with a bent posture or a curved back; Defect - fault; Sparing with words - Someone who doesn't talk much; Patience - The quality of being able to stay calm; Quit - To leave; Fine speeches - Words or talks that are of good quality but of no use; Hastily - In a hurry; Considered - Understood; Opinion - Idea; Fed up - tired of; Impatiently - Waiting for something to happen quickly; Generous - Giving more than expected.

NCERT FOLDER

Let's Read (NCERT Page 101)

Q.1 How many brothers did the Barber have?

Ans. The Barber had six brothers.

Q.2 Why was the Sultan in a hurry?

Ans. The Sultan was in a hurry because he had invited some of his friends for a feast at noon.

Q.3 Why did the Barber take so long to shave the Sultan?

Ans. The barber took so long to shave the Sultan as he was too talkative and kept talking to the Sultan instead of doing his job.

Q.4 Write True or False.

(i) The Barber was shaving the Sultan's beard. ________

(ii) The Sultan gave him three gold coins. ________

(iii) The Barber refused to leave the Sultan's palace. ________

(iv) There were seven brothers altogether in the Sultan's family. ________

Ans. (i) False (ii) True (iii) True (iv) False

Q.5 Why did the Barber want a lot of food?

Ans. The Barber wanted a lot of food because he had invited a few of his friends to his house. He had not prepared anything for them.

Let's Talk (NCERT Page 102)

Q.1 Did the Sultan enjoy the Barber's talk? Why do you say so?

Ans. No, the Sultan did not enjoy the Barber's talk. We can say so because he gave him all the food prepared for his feast and the fruits which the barber had asked for, in order to get rid of him.

Q.2 Which part of the story did you find the funniest?

Ans. I think the funniest part of the story was the one where the barber left to check the dishes and left the Sultan's head half-shaved.

Q.3 What are the things the Sultan gave to the Barber?

Ans. The Sultan gave the Barber three pieces of gold, all the food prepared for his feast and the fruits.

Q.4 Do you think the Sultan was really very generous? Why do you say so?

Ans. I would say that the Sultan is generous. We may say so because he offered the Barber all the food prepared for his feast, the fruits and three pieces of gold just to shave his head.

He could have easily ordered him to go away and called another barber to shave his head.

Word Building (NCERT Page 102)

Q.1 Study the words in the first column and see the changes in them in the second column. The words in Column II are the opposites of the words in Column I.

I	II
important	unimportant
pattent	impatient
pleasure	displeasure

Now write the opposites of the following using un-, im-, dis-

(i) believe - ________
(ii) shaved - ________
(iii) perfect - ________
(iv) satisfy - ________
(v) polite - ________
(vi) respect - ________
(vii) pure - ________
(viii) expected - ________
(ix) obedient - ________

Ans. disbelieve, unshaved, imperfect, dissatisfy, impolite, disrespect, impure, unexpected, disobedient

Q.2 Fill in the blanks by adding un-, im- or dis- to the words given in the box.

tidy	patient	kind	like
able	appear	possible	

(i) The teacher got upset with Rani because her work was _______ .

(ii) The dog was _______ to climb the tree to chase the cat.

(iii) I _______ hot milk, I like it cold.

(iv) It is _______ to cross the road during peak traffic hours.

(v) The magician waved his magic wand and made the rabbit _______ .

(vi) The passengers became _______ when the train was late again.

(vii) It is very _______ to make fun of another person's weaknesses.

Ans. (i) untidy (ii) unable
(iii) dislike (iv) impossible
(v) disappear (vi) impatient
(vii) unkind

Q.3 Notice the highlighted words in the sentence given below.

You ordered me to come, **so** I will not quit your house **till** I have shaved you. **While** he was shaving me, he could not stop talking.

Now use the joining words given in the box to fill in the blanks.

if	or	till	where	unless	so	while

(i) Please wait with me _______ the bus arrives.

(ii) Do you like football _______ cricket?

(iii) My father packed my lunch _______ my mother combed my hair.

(iv) We will reach on time _______ we go by the car.

(v) Your speech cannot be heard by the audience _______ you use a powerful mike.

(vi) It was a beautiful day _______ they decided to go for a picnic.

(vii) We went to the zoo _______ we saw many animals.

Ans. (i) till (ii) or (iii) while
(iv) if (v) unless (vi) so
(vii) where

Word Fun (NCERT Page 104)

Q.1 Look at the words in the box.

sit, drink, play, yell, dance, sing, serve, run, enjoy, buy, wave, shout, ride, greet, win, cheer, compete

(i) feast? _______

(ii) race? _______

(iii) cricket match? _______

(iv) cinema? _______

(v) fair? _______

(vi) party? _______

Ans. (i) drink, serve, greet
(ii) run, win, compete
(iii) cheer, yell, shout
(iv) enjoy, sit
(v) ride, buy, play, wave
(vi) dance, sing

Let's Write (NCERT Page 104)

How does your father/uncle shave his face every day?

He lathers his face with shaving cream, then he uses his razor. He runs it over his face, in even strokes.

After this, he washes his face and wipes it to get rid of the lather.

Now describe two of the following processes.

(i) How to send a letter/e-mail.

(ii) How to make a salad.

(iii) How to prepare a garden bed to grow flowers.

(iv) How to paint a mural or a wall picture.

Ans. (i) How to send a letter/e-mail.

To send an e-mail

I. The first step is to open the browser, type the mailing website for example gmail.com, rediffmail.com.

II. A web page will appear where you need to put your email id and password in the given box respectively.

III. After logging in a new web page will appear. Click on the COMPOSE button.

IV. A new dialogue box will appear where you need to mention the mailing id in the first box. (to whom you wanted to send the mail)

V. In the next box write the subject or your email or letter.

VI. Now write the body of a letter or email.

VII. After mentioning the purpose, end it with the greetings or regards.

VIII. Last step is to click on the SEND button and your email or letter will be sent

(ii) How to make a salad:

I. Gather the ingredients required: onion, carrot, cucumber, tomato etc.

II. Take a bowl and collect all the ingredients in it, wash them properly.

III. Peel all the ingredients except tomato.

IV. Cut them into small pieces with help of your guardian.

V. Mix all the ingredients in a bowl, add a pinch of salt.

VI. Squeeze a slice of lemon (optional). And your salad is ready to serve.

(iii) How to prepare a garden bed to grow flowers.

I. Remove all the wild shrubs and clear the empty piece of land.

II. Add manure and compost for about 10-12 inches.

III. Remember that the soil must be moist while you are applying the manure and compost.

IV. After the preparation of the garden bed, do apply environment-friendly pesticides to protect your plants from insects which can harm the garden bed.

V. Now sow the flower seeds and look after them.

VI. Water them from time to time.

VII. At last your garden is prepared.

(iv) How to paint a mural or a wall picture.

I. Prepare the wall: Make sure the wall is clean and free of moisture damage, cracks, mould, dirt, wax, oil, or grease.

II. Choose your favourite colours according to what you are going to draw on the wall.

III. Cover the things so that the stuff won't get dirty.

IV. Draw your design on the wall with the help of pencil or chalk to get a perfect painting.

V. Use various colours and brushes to bring out the best, after completing your painting add black outline to highlight the painting.

VI. At the last step, let your painting dry and add a finishing coat over it. Your beautiful wall painting is ready.

PRACTICE QUESTIONS

Multiple Choice Questions

1. When are you going to stop __________ and begin to do your work?
   (a) dancing
   (b) singing
   (c) talking
   (d) cooking
2. Who said to whom, "Please show me the food so that I may judge if it is enough for my five friends?"
   (a) The Barber to The Sultan
   (b) The Sultan to The Barber
   (c) The Guard to The Barber
   (d) The Writer to The Chef
3. Who said, "I never knew that you were so generous?"
   (a) The Friends
   (b) The Writer
   (c) The Sultan
   (d) The Barber
4. What is the meaning of the word "dessert"?
   (a) To look at something
   (b) A sweet dish
   (c) A place full of sand
   (d) A fault
5. The story 'The Talkative Barber' has been taken from __________ .
   (a) The Arabian Nights
   (b) The Aesop's Tale
   (c) The Panchtantra
   (d) Satyagrih
6. Who narrated the story, 'The Talkative Barber' to whom?
   (a) The Queen to The Sultan
   (b) The Sultan to The Queen
   (c) The Sultan to The Courtiers
   (d) The Queen to The Courtiers

Ans. 1. (c), 2. (a), 3. (d), 4. (b), 5. (a), 6. (a)

Answer the Following Questions

1. What were the names of the Barber's brothers?

Ans. The names of the Barber's brothers are Bacbone (buk-bon), Bakbarea (buk-buria), Bakbac (buk-buk), Alcouz (ul-kooz), Alnaschee (ul-nashi) and Schacabac (shaka-bak).

2. Why did the Sultan call the Barber?

Ans. The Sultan called the Barber because he wanted to shave his head.

3. Did the Barber stop talking after receiving the food? What did he do next

Ans. No, the Barber did not stop talking after receiving the food. He again started talking to the Sultan.

Let's Write!

1. You love to hear people talk and often find yourself thinking about writing a poem on it.

   Write the poem. The start of the poem is given to help you.

   In a crowd, their voices rise, Like songs that dance beneath the skies.

Ans. In a crowd, their voices rise,
Like songs that dance beneath the skies.

With tales that twirl and laughter bright,
They fill the air with pure delight.

Words like rivers, flowing free,
Sharing dreams and mystery.

Though silence sometimes calls our name,
Their chatter sparks the wildest flame.

So here's to those who love to share,
With open hearts and vibrant flair.

In every story, a thread we find,
Connecting us all, heart and mind.

Unit 7

CHAPTER 1

TOPSY TURVY LAND

Summary of the poem It is an interesting poem about a very strange land called Topsy-Turvy land. It says that in the land of Topsy-Turvy, everything is upside down. It is a strange and funny land where things are very different from the normal.

Stanza-wise Explanation

Stanza 1

The people walk upon their heads,
The sea is made of sand,
The children go to school by night,
In Topsy-turvy Land.

Word-Meaning *Topsy-Turvy* - *Upside down*

Exp. In these lines, the poet talks about what happens at the Topsy-Turvy Land. The poet describes people in this land walking on their heads instead of their legs. There is sand in the sea instead of water. The children go to school at night and not in the morning.

Stanza 2

The front-door step is at the back,
You're walking when you stand,
You wear your hat upon your feet,
In Topsy-turvy Land.

Word-Meaning *Steps* - *Stairs.*

Exp. As everything is different in the Topsy-Turvy land, the door step is found at the back of the house instead of the front. When you try to walk, you stand in one place and don't move ahead. People wear hats on their feet instead of their heads.

Stanza 3

And buses on the sea you'll meet,
While pleasure boats are planned,
To travel up and down the streets
Of Topsy-turvy Land.

Word-Meaning *Pleasure* - *Fun or enjoyment.*

Exp. Opposite from our world, the buses in the Topsy-Turvy land are found in the sea and the boats are found on roads.

Stanza 4

You pay for what you never get,
I think it must be grand,
For when you go you're coming back,
In Topsy-turvy Land.

Exp. The poet finds it very impressive that in Topsy-Turvy land, you never get what you pay for. When you try to go somewhere, you start coming back to where you started from.

NCERT FOLDER

Reading is Fun (NCERT Page 108)

Q.1 When do children go to school in Topsy-turvy Land?

Ans. Children go to school at night in the Topsy-turvy Land.

Q.2 In the poem, if buses travel on the sea, then where do the boats travel? How should it rightly be?

Ans. In the poem, buses travel an the sea and boats sail on the road. In the real world, buses travel on the road and boats sail in the sea.

Q.3 The Topsy Turvy land is very different from our land. Let's draw a comparison by filling in sentences wherever needed.

Topsy-turvy Land	Our land
(i) People walk on their heads.	(i) **People walk on their legs.**
(ii) **The buses run in the sea.**	(ii) The buses run on land.
(iii) They wear their hats on feet.	(iii) **They wear their hats on their heads.**
(iv) **Boats travel on the streets.**	(iv) Boats sail in the sea.
(v) People pay for what they don't get.	(v) **People get what they pay for.**

Let's Talk (NCERT Page 109)

Q.1 The words in the sentences are jumbled here. Rearrange them to make meaningful sentences. Words that begin with a capital letter are the first word of the sentence.

(i) Renu naughty is a girl.
(ii) untidy room Her always is.
(iii) mother Her advises her clean to it.
(iv) never listens She her mother to.
(v) kind of What child a you are?

Ans. (i) Renu is a naughty girl.
(ii) Her room is always untidy.
(iii) Her mother advises her to clean it.
(iv) She never listens to her mother.
(v) What kind of a child are you?

Q.2 Can you tell of some things that go topsy -turvy at home and there is disorder?

Ans. Yes, I can tell you of some things that go topsy turvy at home. There is disorder when I search for my clothes in my almirah as I cannot find what I want to wear.

Hint : You can write about other such disorders.

Let's Write (NCERT Page 110)

Q.1 Write five things that you do at home to make your home look neat and clean.

Ans. (i) I collect my toys and keep them in the box.
(ii) I keep my shoes in the shoe rack after returning from school.
(iii) I put my books properly on the study table.
(iv) I always make my bed.
(v) Once a week I replace the bedsheet and pillow covers.

Q.2 Let's imagine a topsy-turvy scene and describe it in the lines below.

Ans. One day when I entered my house, I saw my pet dog was dancing, a parrot was cooking and my cat was serving tea. Watching this upside down scene, I was surprised. When I went to the kitchen to have some water, I saw the gas stove becoming a fountain and candles blinking. I was amazed to see this Topsy- Turvy scene.

Q.3 Two stories got mixed up. Sort them out and write them in the appropriate boxes.

- We thought the lion had eaten someone.
- Suddenly the kite lifted him off the ground and took him over the treetops.
- He saw a shoe in the lion's cage.
- Finally, the kite brought him back to the park.
- Our class had gone to the zoo.
- Puran was flying the brand new kite in the park.
- Some children stood and screamed, and some ran to the Director of the zoo.
- Puran was frightened and excited.
- The lion had not eaten anyone, because the shoe was one of the lion's toys.

(i) The Magic Kite

(ii) Who Did the Lion Eat?

Ans. (i) **The Magic Kite**

Puran was flying the brand new kite in the park. Suddenly, the kite lifted him off the ground and took him over the treetops. Puran was frightened and excited. Finally, the kite brought him back to the park.

(ii) **Who Did the Lion Eat?**

Our class had gone to the zoo. We saw a shoe in the lion's cage. We thought the lion had eaten someone. Some children stood and screamed, and some ran to the Director of the zoo.

The lion had not eaten anyone, because the shoe was one of the lion's toys.

PRACTICE QUESTIONS

Multiple Choice Questions

1. Choose the proper place where boats should run.
   (a) Sand (b) Road (c) Sea (d) Front door
2. Read the following line of the poem and identify the nouns in it.
   "The people walk upon their heads"
   (a) people, heads (b) walk
   (c) their (d) upon
3. Who goes to school by night in Topsy-turvy land?
   (a) People (b) Bus-driver
   (c) Children (d) Sailor
4. Where do the boats run in Topsy-turvy land?
   (a) Sand (b) Street
   (c) Sea (d) Feet
5. Read the following lines of the poem and find out the meaning of "topsy-turvy".
   "The children go to school by night, In Topsy-turvy Land"
   (a) Straight (b) Flat
   (c) Upside down (d) Round

Ans. 1. (c), 2. (a), 3. (c), 4. (b), 5. (c)

Answer the Following Questions

1. What are some unusual things about the way people live in Topsy Turvy Land?

Ans. There are many unusual things about the way people live in the Topsy Turvy Land. The people walk on their heads and wear the hat on their feet.

2. When do children go to school in Topsy Turvy land?

Ans. The children go to school in the Topsy Turvy Land at night.

3. What does the poet find 'grand' about the Topsy-turvy land

Ans. The fact that when people have to pay for things they did not get is what is grand about the Topsy Turvy Land.

Let's Write!

1. Suppose you enter the Topsy Turvy Land, how would you feel? What new things would you see except for those mentioned in the poem?

Ans. If I enter the Topsy Turvy Land, I would feel very weird as the place would be very different than what I usually see. I would feel strange and would take time to get used to it. The new things that I would see would include how the vehicles work. There would be wheels on boats and the buses would not have any wheels. The houses will be built on the water and not on land. People would say good night in the morning and good morning at night. Further, the price of things would be same.

CHAPTER 2 GULLIVER'S TRAVELS

Summary of the Chapter

This story is about Gulliver who was a sailor. He went on several voyages. In this story, he talks about one of his voyages where he got stuck in the land of giants. One day, the captain of Gulliver's ship sent him and some more men to check for water on the land they had discovered. After exploring for some time they found that there was no sign of water or people on that land. When Gulliver reached the shore to return to the ship with his companions, he found them rowing away quickly.

They were being chased by a giant but he couldn't catch them. Gulliver was left behind all alone. Gulliver looked for a place to hide and quickly climbed up a steep hill with barley and corn fields. There he saw another giant who was as big as the one he saw on the sea shore. The giant made a loud call and seven more monsters like him joined him in the field. He realised they were all farmers. He called all his friends and observed Gulliver.

The giant farmer took Gulliver to his house and placed him on a very large dining table. There he got some food to eat with the farmer's family. He also saw a giant cat and a baby, who almost dropped him on the floor. Later on, he slept peacefully on a huge bed and dreamed of his family.

WORD-MEANING

Sailors - A person who works and sails on a ship or boat; Giants - Very big and strong people; Discovered - To find something; Vessels - Big pots for storing something, large boats; Barren - Land with no vegetation; Crew - All the people who work on a ship; Rowing - Moving the boat forward; Bellowing - Very loud noise; Inhabitants - Occupants; Astonishment - Great surprise; Crumbled - Broken into very small pieces; Grab - To suddenly catch or hold something; Reapers - People who harvest a crop; Reaping hook - A tool used by farmers for cutting the crop.

NCERT FOLDER

Reading is Fun (NCERT Page 116)

Q.1 Why did the captain send the men to the land?

Ans. The captain sent the men to the land in the search of water.

Q.2 Why did the men rush back to the ship?

Ans. The men rushed back to the ship because they were unable to find water. They did not find anyone on the land and were being chased by a giant.

Q.3 Choose the correct answer.

(i) The giant carried a reaping hook because

(a) he was fighting with the other giants.
(b) he was going to reap the corn.
(c) he wanted to frighten Gulliver.

(ii) They put Gulliver on the ground to look at him because

(a) they had never seen a human before.
(b) they thought he was a doll.
(c) they had never seen such a tiny man.

(iii) Gulliver was

(a) a farmer. (b) a sailor.
(c) a dwarf. (d) a giant.

Ans. (i) (b) (ii) (c) (iii) (b)

Q.4 Name the creature to whom you would look like Gulliver. The creature is now extinct.

The word begins with the letter D ____________ .

Ans. The word begins with the letter D is Dinosaurs. They were huge in size and are extinct now.

Q.5 From the text, write the sentence that tells you the following.

(i) The giant reapers were fascinated by Gulliver.

(ii) Gulliver was a learned man.

(iii) The farmer's son thought Gulliver was a toy.

(iv) The farmer's wife was a kind-hearted woman.

Ans. (i) They all sat on the ground to take a good look at me.

(ii) I tried to speak to them loudly in several languages.

(iii) On seeing me, the child grabbed me from the table and put my head into his head.

(iv) I would have broken my neck if the mother had not held her apron under me. Later, she put me on her own bed and covered me with a clean white handkerchief.

Let's Talk (NCERT Page 117)

Q.1 Read the following sentences carefully.

The giant farmer's voice was as loud as a bellowing trumpet.

or

The giant farmer's voice was as loud as thunder.

When something is very cold, we say it is as cold as ice.

This is because ice is very very cold.

Now complete the following. Use the words given in the box.

red slow black gentle warm strong sweet light white

as light as a feather
as slow as a tortoise
as sweet as honey
as white as snow
as strong as an ox
as black as night
as red as a rose
as warm as a toast
as gentle as a breeze

Use the above expressions to complete the following sentences.

(i) The old man's hair is as white as snow.

(ii) His feet were as cold as ice.

(iii) The newspaper boy was as slow as a tortoise in delivering the papers.

(iv) I felt as light as a feather after exercising.

Create your own comparisons for the following. Work in pairs.

as tall as a tower
as fast as a leopard
as high as a mountain
as angry as a bull
as tiny as an ant or a mosquito
as brave as a soldier

Q.2 There are many reasons why something happens.
For example

	Event	Reasons
1.	Guliver could not climb the fence because	every slep was six feet high,
		he saw one of the giants coming towards him.
		he ran to hide himself.

All the three are reasons why Gulliver was unable to climb the fence.

Q.3 Now look at the pictures and discuss in groups why the following events happened. You may find more than one reason for each of them.

Ans. (i) **Play cancelled**

- The play was cancelled because the play members did not reach the hall.
- The play was cancelled as the lead actor of the play was not prepared.

(ii) **Walking in the moonlight**

- Mr. and Mrs. Kumar were walking at night after having dinner.
- Mr. and Mrs. Kumar were walking to get some vegetables at night.

Let's Write (NCERT Page 120)

Look at the following examples.

- I was trying to climb over the fence when the giant saw me.
- The farmer's wife was stroking the cat when her one year-old son entered.

Both the actions were in the past.

When the first one was going on in the past, the second one happened.

Q.1 Match the following and write complete sentences in the lines below.

	What was happening?	What happened?
(i)	I was writing a letter.	the lights went out
(ii)	Paul was looking out of the window	the bell rang
(iii)	*He was looking for his dog.	he noticed a lovely butterfly
(iv)	*I was just completing the last answer.	he fell off the ladder.
(v)	The man was painting the wall.	I met Arun.
(vi)	Amit was doing his homework.	my pen ran out.
(vii)	My mother was cooking dinner.	ma'am said, "Stop writing"

(i) I was writing a letter when ____________

(ii) ____________

(iii) *When I met Arun, he was looking for his dog.

(iv) * ______________________________

(v) ______________________________

(vi) ______________________________

(vii) ______________________________

Ans. (i) I was writing a letter when my pen ran out.

(ii) Paul was looking out of the window when he noticed a lovely butterfly.

(iii) *When I met Arun, he was looking for his dog.

(iv) *I was just about to complete the last answer when ma'am said "stop writing".

(v) The man was painting the wall when he fell off the ladder.

(vi) Amit was doing his homework when the lights went out.

(vii) My mother was cooking dinner when the bell rang.

*Please note that sometimes the order of the sentences changes.

Q.2 Now complete the following suitably.

(i) I was sitting in a taxi yesterday when ______________ .

(ii) He was cleaning out his cupboard when ______________ .

(iii) __________ a dog ran out onto the road.

(iv) ______________ the teacher walked into the room.

Ans. (i) I saw a flower boy at the signal.

(ii) he came across his old books.

(iii) a dog ran out onto the road.

(iv) the teacher walked into the room.

Q.3 When we compare two things/people, we add or to -er more the describing word.

(Please refer to the theory given in NCERT on page number-121)

Now complete the following in the same way using the words easy or strong

(i) Skipping is ______________.

Jumping is ______________ than skipping.

Walking is the ______________ of all.

(ii) The dog is ______________.

The horse is ______________.

The elephant is ______________.

Ans. (i) Skipping is easy

Jumping is easier than skipping.

Walking is the easiest of all.

(ii) The dog is strong.

The horse is stronger.

The elephant is the strongest.

Now complete the following in the same way using the words juicy or exciting . The order may vary according to your choice.

Ans.

apple orange sugarcane	is juicy is juicier is the juiciest
rock climbing skiing river rafting	is exciting is more exciting is the most exciting.

Q.4 Correct the use of the describing words in the following sentences.

(i) This is the simpler problem of them all.

(ii) Which is the lightest of the two parcels?

(iii) He is cleverer than I am.

(iv) I like this the best of the two.

(v) The flood became badder as the rain increased.

Ans. (i) This is the simplest problem of all.

(ii) Which is the lighter parcel?

(iii) He is cleverer than me.

(iv) I like this better.

(v) The flood became worse as the rain increased.

Q.5 Punctuate the following sentences using capital letters, full stops (.) commas (,) question marks (?) apostrophe (') exclamation mark (!) wherever necessary.

dear samir,

i am sending you a photograph of my newest pet frisky is a bulldog and a very playful puppy by next summer he should be old enough to go with us on our long walks i m sure you are looking forward to seeing him I know you will like him

warm regards

sanju

Ans. Dear Samir

I am sending you a photograph of my newest pet. Frisky is a bulldog and a very playful puppy.

By next summer he should be old enough to go with us on our long-walks. I'm sure you're looking forward to seeing him. I know you'll like him.

Warm regards,

Sanju

Q.6 Punctuate the following sentences

(i) next wednesday my sister mita is going to join the state bank of india

(ii) the dog wags its tail when its pleased but a cat waves its tail when its angry

(iii) when I went fishing I caught an old shoe a plastic bag and a bad cold

(iv) she fed the baby washed the dishes put the lights off and went to sleep

(v) wasn't tim born on the 26th of january 1989

(vi) oh no the bus has gone

Ans. (i) Next Wednesday my sister, Mita, is going to join the State Bank of India.

(ii) The dog wags its tail when it's pleased, but a cat waves its tail when it's angry.

(iii) When I went fishing I caught an old shoe, a plastic bag and a bad cold.

(iv) She fed the baby, washed the dishes, put the lights off and went to sleep.

(v) Wasn't Tim born on the 26th of January, 1989?

(vi) Oh, no! The bus has gone.

Let's Find Out (NCERT Page 123)

Fill in the blanks.

(i) A giant tree	Red wood trees of California
(ii) A giant bird	Ostrich
(iii) A giant land animal	Elephant
(iv) A giant water creature	Blue whale
(v) A giant reptile	Crocodile
(vi) A giant aeroplane	Antonov AN-225

Find out some interesting facts about each of these giants and share them with class.

Ans. Do it yourself.

Creative Writing (NCERT Page 128)

You woke up one morning and found yourself in the land of dwarfs!

Write a paragraph describing your experiences there and how you got back home finally.

You may begin like this.

Everything around me looked different.

Ans. Everything around me looked different. There were ant-like humans and trees that looked like tiny plants. When they saw me, they started making noise, probably talking among themselves as if they had come across the strangest thing in the world. I tried to speak with them but they were not able to understand my language. The buildings looked like matchboxes.

After spending time with me they realised that I was not going to harm them. They gave me enough food in small plates. They helped me to reach home by making a wooden boat. With the help of a boat I reached home safely. It was really a pleasure having such an unusual experience of living with tiny people.

PRACTICE QUESTIONS

Multiple Choice Questions

1. Gulliver ran ______________ he can.
   (a) as high as (b) as fast as
   (c) as tall as (d) None of these
2. Who ordered to find water on the new-found land?
   (a) Gulliver (b) Huge creature
   (c) Sailors (d) Captain
3. Who said, "I shouted so loudly that the baby dropped me" ?
   (a) Sailors (b) Captain
   (c) Gulliver (d) Huge creature

Ans. 1. (b), 2. (d), 3. (c)

Answer the Following Questions

1. Why did the giant chase Gulliver's companions?

Ans. The giant chased Gulliver's companions because he had never seen such tiny creatures.

2. What did Gulliver do when he found himself alone on the island?

Ans. When Gulliver found himself alone on the island, he turned back quickly and climbed up a steep hill with fields of barley on either side.

3. Why did the farmer put Gulliver on the ground? (DIKSHA)

Ans. The farmer put Gulliver on the ground so that other giants can look at him.

4. How did the farmer treat Gulliver after taking him home? (DIKSHA)

Ans. The farmer treated Gulliver with kindness at his home. He gave Gulliver food and a place to sleep.

5. How did Gulliver feel when he saw the giants?

Ans. Gulliver was scared as well as curious when he saw the Giant.

Let's Write!

1. Imagine you are Gulliver. Write a letter to your family telling them about the farmers on the Gaint land.

Ans. Dear Family,

How are you all? I am hoping to return soon. My journey had been long and I have been stuck on an island of Giants. They so big and I look like an ant infront of them. However, their size doesn't matter. What matters is that they all are kind and generous.

When they found me, they were curious but soon one of them took me home. They could have killed me for I looked very different from them. But they didn't. They gave me food and even saved me from trouble. They also prepared a place for me to sleep comfortably.

I had told them about you people. They like me and I like them too. For me, they are trying to find someone who could take me home.

I hope they can do so as soon as possible so that I can also bring you here to meet them.

Yours lovingly

Gulliver

CHAPTER 1 NOBODY'S FRIEND

Summary of the Poem This poem talks about two different types of children. Two children in the poem do not like to share their toys or sweets with the other children. As a result, they have no friends. On the other hand, the speaker offers to share her things and be a friend. Therefore, the poem highlights the importance of sharing and kindness in building friendships.

Stanza-wise Explanation

Stanza 1

She had some sweets that she wouldn't share,
She had a book that she wouldn't lend,
She wouldn't let anyone play with her doll,
She's nobody's friend!

Word-Meaning *Lend - To give something to someone for some time.*

Exp. In these lines, the poet talks about a girl who had sweets but she didn't like to share them with others. She also had a book and a doll which she never shared with anyone. This is why she had no friends.

Stanza 2

He had some toffee, and ate every bit,
He had a tricycle he wouldn't lend,
He never let anyone play with his train, He's nobody's friend!

Word-Meaning *Tricycle - A cycle with three wheels.*

Exp. These lines talk about a boy who doesn't like sharing his sweets or lending his tricycle. He kept them to himself. He also had a train, but he never let anyone else play with it. As a result, he does not have a friend.

Stanza 3

But I'll share all of my sweets with you,
My ball and my books and my games I will lend,
Here's half my apple and half my cake — I'm your friend!

Exp. In these lines, the speaker offers to be a friend and share her things with anyone who wishes to be her friend. She says that they will share her sweets, toys and even her food. This shows that she is generous and willing to be a good friend.

NCERT FOLDER

Reading Is Fun (NCERT Page 128)

Q.1 What are the things the girl does not want to share?

Ans. The girl does not want to share her sweets, book and doll with anyone.

Q.2 Did the boy share his toffee and tricycle with others?

Ans. No, he did not share his toffee and tricycle with others.

Q.3 Why are the two children nobody's friends?

Ans. The two children are nobody's friends because they are selfish in nature. They don't like to share anything with others.

Q.4 What does the child in the last stanza want to share?

Ans. The child in the last stanza wanted to share all the things like sweets, balls, books, games and food with others.

Let's Talk (NCERT Page 128)

1. Do you like to share your favourite food or toys with others? Why?

Ans. Yes, I like to share my favourite food and toys with others because they are my friends. We eat and play together.

2. Who is your best friend? Can you describe him/her?

Ans. Do it yourself.

3. Suppose you and your friends were very thirsty and there was only one glass of water. What would you do?

Ans. If there is one glass of water, I will surely share half a glass of water with my friend.

4. If you had a bat, could you play cricket by yourself?

Ans. No, I will not be able to play cricket alone. I would need other players to play with. Cricket is a team game.

Word Building (NCERT Page 128)

Q.1 Can you find more words ending with-less friendless, homeless,

Ans. hopeless, endless, speechless

Q.2 Can you write the opposite of

(i) lend b ______________ w

Ans. borrow

(ii) nobody s ______________ y

Ans. somebody

What are no Words (NCERT Page 129)

Q.1 Several words mean 'no'. The word 'never' is one. It means at no time or not ever.

Here are some other no words read them

nobody no no where

no one none nothing

Q.2 Read the given sentences and underline the word no in each.

(i) Nobody is at home.
(ii) Ram has no book.
(iii) Can no one help him?
(iv) Was Gopal nowhere around?
(v) None of the two boys came.
(vi) There is nothing to do.
(vii) I have no coat.
(viii) Radha is never late.

Ans. (i) Nobody is at home.
(ii) Ram has no book.
(iii) Can no one help him?
(iv) Was Gopal nowhere around?
(v) None of the two boys came.
(vi) There is nothing to do.
(vii) I have no coat.
(viii) Radha is never late.

Say Aloud (NCERT Page 130)

Nobody everybody somebody
cycle bicycle tricycle share
care stare hair pair stair

Q.2 Now write words that rhyme with
train, friend

Ans. **train** rain, grain, pain

Friend send, bend, spend

Let's Write (NCERT Page No. 130)

Here is a short story.

Once a lion lay fast asleep in a forest. Some mice were playing hide and seek near him. One mouse got trapped under the lion's paw. The lion woke up, laughed loudly and let the mouse go!

After some days the mouse heard the lion's roar. He saw that the lion lay in great pain as he was tied with many ropes. The mouse used his sharp teeth and cut the rope.

"You are a true friend," said the lion.

- From Aesop's Fables

A friend in need is a friend indeed.

What does this mean?

(i) We must be there for friends in trouble.

Ans. Only a good friend will be with us when we are in trouble.

(ii) In a short paragraph write how you can be a good friend.

Ans. **A good friend**

Having a friend whom you can trust, rely on and share everything with, is a blessing. A good friend will always give you advice for your betterment. You can share any secret with your friends and they will never disclose it. You can share happy and sad moments with them. They will help you when in trouble and celebrate your achievements. A true friend always cares for you.

PRACTICE QUESTIONS

Multiple Choice Questions

1. Read the following line of the poem and identify the verb in it.

"She had some sweets that she wouldn't share"

(a) some (b) sweets
(c) share (d) she

2. Which of the following things doesn't belong to the girl?

(a) Book (b) Wweets
(c) Doll (d) Tricycle

3. Who is a friend?

(a) The one who doesn't share sweets
(b) The one who doesn't lend doll
(c) The one who doesn't give his tricycle
(d) The one who shares everything

Ans. 1. (c), 2. (d), 3. (d)

Answer the Following Questions

1. What are the two types of children described in the poem?

Ans. The two types of children described in the poem. The first type is of selfish children who do not share anything with others and thus, have no friends. The second type is a kind girl who shares her things with her friends.

2. Why do the two children in the poem not have any friends?

Ans. The two children in the poem do not have any friend because they do not share their things with anyone.

3. How is the speaker different from the other two children?

Ans. The speaker is different from the two children because she would share her things with her friends.

Let's Write!

1. We often hear our elders telling us that sharing is caring. Write a paragraph on it.

Ans. Sharing is often seen as a simple act of kindness, but in reality, it is so much more than that. Sharing is caring because it shows empathy, fosters trust and builds strong relationships. When we share with others, we show that we care about their well-being and happiness. Whether it is sharing a meal with a friend in need or our feelings, the act of sharing sends a powerful message that we are there for each other in good times and bad. Sharing also fosters trust between individuals. When we share our resources, time and energy with others, we are building a foundation of trust that can lead to deeper connections. Furthermore, sharing can build strong relationships that last a lifetime. By being generous with what we have, we are creating opportunities for deeper conversations, shared memories, and mutual support. In a world that can often feel disconnected and divided, sharing is a powerful way to bridge the gap between individuals and create a sense of community. In conclusion, sharing is caring because it is an act of kindness that goes beyond simply giving and receiving. It is a powerful tool that can foster empathy, build trust, and create strong relationships.

CHAPTER 2 THE LITTLE BULLY

Summary of the Chapter

This is a story about a boy named Hari. He was strong and liked to tease other children in school. He pinched them very hard and pricked them with a pin. All the children hated him because of this.

One day, Hari's whole class went for a picnic at the seaside. Nobody sat with Hari and everyone stayed away from him. Hari got angry and when they reached the seaside, he went into a corner, near a rocky pool and sat alone.

Suddenly, a monster crab came out of the rocky pool and pinched him. Hari cried loudly but nobody came to help him. Then, a lobster, some shrimps and prawns too crawled out of the pool and pinched Hari. His lunch rolled and fell, which distracted the creatures. Hari cried and ran to save his life. He realised his mistake because he was in a lot of pain due to the pinching. He made a promise to himself that he would never pinch anyone again.

WORD-MEANING

Bruise - Injury to the body; Horrid - Terrible; Hoarse - Rough; Nipped - Pinched; Pricking - To cause somebody pain with a sharp point; Telling tales - To tell other people things about someone which are not true; Queer - Strange; Champion - Someone who wins a first prize in a competition; Shan't - Short form of 'shall not'; Jolly well - Used for someone's anger.

NCERT FOLDER

Reading is Fun (NCERT Page 135)

Now that you have read and understood the lesson, can you answer these questions? You can put a (✓) on the right answer.

Q.1 Why did all the children hate Hari?

(i) Because he would not talk to anyone.

(ii) Because he always pinched them.

(iii) Because he loved stealing their food.

Ans. (ii) Because he always pinched them.

Q.2 "Nobody took Hari's hand. Nobody went near him. Nobody played with him." This shows that Hari had

(i) many friends (ii) few friends

(iii) no friends

Ans. (iii) no friends

Q.3 Which of the following actions would make a friendly person? Write them down.

- Respecting other people.
- Eating a small child's tiffin.
- Calling people rude names.
- Pushing a smaller boy and making him cry.
- Being helpful to everyone.
- Helping your classmates in school.
- Mocking at friends and hurting their feelings.
- Protecting a weaker person.

Ans. Actions which would make a friendly person

- Respecting other people.
- Being helpful to everyone
- Helping your classmates in school.
- Protecting a weaker person.

Vocabulary (NCERT Page 136)

Q.1 Find out words which are opposites or are closest to being the opposites of the words given below. Then write down the opposites in the grid.

Down	**Across**
1. smile	3. quiet
2. happy	5. punish
4. strong	

Ans.

Q.2 Hari was pinched till he was black and blue. 'Black and blue' means

(i) Hari fell down in pain.

(ii) there were bruises on his body.

(iii) Hari painted himself in colours.

(iv) Hari had a black and blue shirt.

Ans. (ii) there were bruises on his body.

Q.3 I shan't pinch anyone anymore'. Shan't means

(i) shall (ii) should

(iii) shall not (iv) will not

Ans. (iii) shall not

Q.4 Give the full forms of

(i) won't (ii) weren't

(iii) wouldn't (iv) couldn't

Ans. (i) will not (ii) were not

(iii) would not (iv) could not

Q.5 A girl was sitting quietly beside him. Hari leapt to his feet, crying loudly. The words quietly and loudly tell us how an action is being done.

Find five more words ending in -ly which denote how something is done.

Ans. (i) bravely (ii) safely

(iii) pleasantly (iv) eagerly

(v) heavily

Q.6 Add -ly to the following words.

clear	merry	weary	double
dreary	briht	bad	fond

Ans. clear	-	clearly
merry	-	merrily
weary	-	wearily
double	-	doubly
dreary	-	drearily
bright	-	brightly
bad	-	badly
fond	-	fondly

Now can you make sentences with these words?

Ans. 1. The mountains were **clearly** visible from the seventh floor.

2. The children played **merrily** in the park.
3. Ketan put the bundle of sticks **wearily** on the floor.
4. You might feel **doubly** hungry for breakfast after a morning swim.
5. The dresses I liked are **drearily** the same with the women standing next to me.
6. On Sunday, the sky was clear and the Sun shone **brightly**.
7. Shipra spoke to me **badly**.
8. Ravi **fondly** ate his favourite cupcakes.

Fun With Sounds (NCERT Page 138)

Q.1 Let's practise with P and F

pleased	pricked	pinched	punished
fat	fruit	fell	forgotten
palm	pair	proud	parade
farm	fare	frown	fish

Q.2 Complete the blanks with rhyming words of the following and practice aloud.

(i) bruise	cruise
(ii) carriage	marriage
(iii) prawn	drawn
(iv) creatures	features
(v) teachers	preachers
(vi) vowed	cowed

Let's Practise Some Writing (NCERT Page 139)

Q.1 How did the seaside creatures, the crab, the lobster etc. teach Hari a lesson? Write in a few lines.

Ans. On the picnic day when Hari was all alone in the sandy corner, he was about to have his favourite lunch. Some seaside creatures crawled out of the rocky pool nearby and started pinching Hari. This gave him bruises of black and blue colour and he cried in pain. He realised how it hurts when someone is pinched. He decided not to pinch anyone from that moment.

Q.2 Read these sentences carefully.

I ate an apple.

A boy is standing under the tree.

The sun rises in the east.

A and an do not point out any definite or particular person or thing whereas, the is used when we speak of some particular person or thing. A, an and the are called articles. Remember an is used before words beginning with a vowel a, e, i, o, u.

Now fill in the blanks with appropriate articles.

(i) Hari was ________ unpopular boy.

(ii) The boys and girls went to ________ seaside for a picnic.

(iii) He saw ________ big crab coming towards him.

(iv) I found ________ empty bottle, floating in the water.

(v) ________ sea creatures ate his food.

Ans. (i) an (ii) the (iii) a (iv) an (v) The

Q.3 A crab has a hard shell whereas a frog does not have one. There are many animals that protect themselves from their enemies with their outer cover/shells/quills.

In the box given below are the names of some animals. Encircle the ones that can protect themselves with their hard cover.

crocodile	snail	lizard	snake
turtle	tortoise	gorilla	frog
hedgehog	porcupine		

Ans. Crocodile, snail, turtle, tortoise, hedgehog, porcupine

Now paste/draw the picture of any one animal. Write five lines about it.

Ans. Do it yourself.

Q.4 Can you tell the difference between a turtle and a tortoise? Write a few lines.

Ans. 1. Tortoises live on land while turtles live mostly in water.

2. A tortoise has a heavier shell compared to a turtle.

3. Tortoises usually have a long life from 80-150 years while turtles live from 20-40 years.

4. Tortoises eat only plants but turtles eat both plants and smaller fish.

5. Tortoise's feet are bent, short and hard while turtles have net-like feet with long claws.

Q.5 Describe what is happening in the picture. Use is/are and ing to make your sentences. Clues are given in the box.

swing sit climb lick slid kick

For example, Krishna is swinging.

(i) Mary ________ up the slide.

(ii) Hari ________ and boxing her.

(iii) Little Bitto ________ a lollipop.

(iv) Rita ________ down the slide.

Ans. (i) is climbing (ii) is kicking

(iii) is licking (iv) is sliding

Q.6 Imagine what the children will do in the playground tomorrow. You can take some hints from the words given in the box.
e.g. John will play kabbadi tomorrow.

play football jump race
badminton run

Ans. 1. Aditya will play cricket tomorrow.

2. Rahul and his team will play football.

3. Deepti will jump with Sneha.

4. Sonal and Akriti will compete with each other in the race.

5. Rahul and Shobit will play badminton tomorrow.

6. Harsh and Ayush will run together.

Let's be Creative and Talk (NCERT Page 142)

Work in groups of four. See the picture of a shipwreck at the bottom of the ocean. Suppose you went deep-sea diving. What would you find?

Think of all the words that come to your mind, then build a paragraph. Share your story with other groups.

Hint for writing the story

Ans. There were so many creatures like octopuses, sea horses and starfish that I have only seen in books or videos. I felt afraid and at the same time excited to touch some of them. I also found things like pearls, gems, nets, shoes, etc. Then I came across a big box filled with precious stones of many colours. I picked them all up and took them to my parents.

PRACTICE QUESTIONS

Multiple Choice Questions

1. They tried pinching him back, but that was no good because he could always pinch ____________ .
   (a) hardest (b) hard
   (c) harder (d) None of these

2. Who said, "Ah, here is my good cousin." ?
   (a) Crab (b) Lobster
   (c) Shrimps (d) Prawns

3. Complete the following
   "Nobody took Hari's hand as he had ______ ."
   (a) many friends
   (b) few friends
   (c) no friends
   (d) None of the above

4. Who pinched hard with great pincer-like claws?
   (a) Crab (b) Lobster
   (c) Shrimps (d) Prawns

5. Which is the characteristic of a friendly person?
   (a) Mocking your friends
   (b) Disrespecting your neighbours
   (c) Helping your classmates
   (d) Eating a small child's tiffin

Ans. 1. (c), 2. (a), 3. (c), 4. (a), 5. (c)

Answer the Following Questions

1. "Good morning! I am so pleased to meet a boy like you." Who said these lines?

Ans. The monster crab said these lines to Hari.

2. How many friends did Hari have?

Ans. Hari had no friends.

3. What happened to Hari when he went to the seaside?

Ans. When Hari went to the seaside, he was pinched by the sea creatures.

4. How did Hari feel after he was pinched by the sea creatures?

Ans. Hari felt bad when he was pinched by the sea creatures. He was in pain too.

5. What lesson did Hari learn from this experience?

Ans. Hari learned that he had hurt his classmates by pinching them.

Let's Write!

1. Write a story that begins with "I found out that my friend, Jasmine was bullied again. I rushed to..."

Ans. I found out that my friend, Jasmine was bullied again. I rushed to her side, my heart full of worry and anger. As I approached her, I could see the hurt in her eyes. I asked her if she was okay. Jasmine shook her head. She said, a group of older girls had cornered her in the school garden, taunting and pushing her around. I assured Jasmine that she didn't deserve to be treated that way, and that I would always have her back.

We walked to the principal's office together, and I helped Jasmine report the incident. The principal promised to take action and ensure that we would be safe at school. The principal punished the girls who bullied Jasmine. Such punishment is essential to stop bullying.

CHAPTER 1 SING A SONG OF PEOPLE

Summary of Poem This poem talks about how people in the city are always in a hurry. No matter where they are, they can always be seen rushing. This poem reminds us that there are many different kinds of people that we see in the city. We never get to know them because they are always in a hurry.

Stanza-wise Explanation

Stanza 1

Sing a song of people
Walking fast or slow;
People in the city,
Up and down they go.

Exp. This poem is like a song that talks about the busy lives of people living in the city. They are always in a hurry as they walk around the city.

Stanza 2

People on the side walk,
People on the bus;
People passing, passing,
In back and front of us.

Word-Meaning *Sidewalk - Footpath or pavement*

Exp. In these lines the poem tells us that there are many people on the road. Some are walking on the pavement and others are taking the bus. Wherever the speaker looks, there are people moving.

Stanza 3

People on the subway
Underneath the ground;
People riding taxis
Round and round and round.

Word-Meaning *Subway - Underground passage for people to cross the road, Underneath - Below*

Exp. Some people take the underground subway and some ride taxis to get around the city.

Stanza 4

People with their hats on,
Going in the doors;
People with umbrellas
When it rains and pours.

Word-Meaning *Pours - Heavy rains; steady flow of water*

Exp. The speaker also notices people dressed differently. Some are wearing hats and going inside the buildings. When it rains, they open their umbrellas but keep walking.

Stanza 5

People in tall buildings
And in stores below;
Riding elevators
Up and down they go.

Word-Meaning *Elevators - Lifts*

Exp. There are people in huge buildings and even in the stores below them. The speaker watches them as they go up and down in elevators.

Stanza 6

People walking singly,
People in a crowd;
People saying nothing,
People talking loud.

Exp. There are all kinds of people in the city. Some people walk alone while some people walk in groups. Some of them talk loudly with each other and others stay quiet.

Stanza 7

People laughing, smiling,
Grumpy people too;
People who just hurry
And never look at you!

Word-Meaning *Grumpy - Easily annoyed or complaining*

Exp. In these lines, the speaker describes people's expressions. Some can be seen laughing or smiling while some people have a grumpy (annoyed) look on their faces. Some people can be seen passing hurriedly. They do not look at anyone as they are too busy.

Stanza 8

Sing a song of people
Who like to come and go;
Sing of city people
You see but never know!

Exp. In this last stanza, the poet asks the readers to sing a song of city people who will keep coming and going. It says that we see them, but we will never know them as everyone is in a hurry.

NCERT FOLDER

Reading is Fun (NCERT Page 146)

Q.1 Which modes of transport do the people use to move around in the city?

Ans. People use buses, autos, taxis, cars, scooters, cycles, etc. to travel in the city.

Q.2 What are the things that the people carry with them, while moving around?

Ans. While moving around, people carry hats, bags, wallets, water bottles and umbrellas with them.

Q.3 Where all do you find these very busy people?

Ans. I find very busy people on roads, streets, in lifts, stores, in the subways, at the bus stops, in tall buildings and at the airports.

Q.4 Where have you seen crowds of people?

Ans. I have seen crowds of people in and around public places like railway stations, bus stops, hospitals, cinema halls and shopping malls.

Q.5 Why do you think all these people are in a hurry?

Ans. I think all these people are in a hurry to reach their destinations on time and to finish their work.

Language Use (NCERT Page 146)

Let's write the opposites of the following words.

slow	________	up	________
back	________	tall	________
below	________	crowd	________
loud	________	go	________

Ans.

slow - fast		up - down	
back - front		tall - short	
below - above		crowd - alone	
loud - mild		go - come	

Let's Listen (NCERT Page 147)

Read and listen to these two poems with your partner and find out what are the things that the village child and the city child like.

The Village Child	The City Child
My home is a house Near a wood I'd live in a street If I could! I do wish someone Lived near. There's no one to play with At all. The trees are so high And so tall: And I should be lonely For hours. Were it not for the birds And the flowers.	I live in a city In a street; It is crowded with traffic And feet; There are buses and motors And trams. I wish there were meadows And lambs. The houses all wait In a row There is smoke everywhere That I go. I don't like the noises I hear I wish there were woods Very near.

Ans. Do it yourself.

Let's Talk (NCERT Page 147)

The people who live in cities often wish they could live in quiet towns. Do you like the place you live in?

Tell your partner two things you like and don't like about the place you live in.

Ans. I live in the main city. I like the place where I live.

Two things that I like about the place where I live are

- Clean and green environment
- Helpful neighbours

Two things I don't like

- The honking noise from the traffic.
- There are no big parks nearby.

Let's Write (NCERT Page 148)

Q.1 Did you observe that in the poem, the last words in every second and fourth line rhyme with each other? Can you write a four line poem?

Ans. In every heart, a story dwells In laughter, sorrow and whispered spells together we dance through joy and strife a tapestry woven, the fabric of life.

Q.2 Find out how many people are there in our country. Do we have enough land for all people on this Earth? Is there enough food and water for all people?

Ans. There are about 1.428 billion people in our country. I don't think we have enough land for all the people on this Earth. No, there is not enough food and water for all people.

Q.3 Find out the following from ten families living in your neighbourhood.

Count the number of	F1*	F2	F3	F4	F5	F6	F7	F8	F9	F10	Total
children below 5 years of age											
children from 5-14 years											
grown up children from 15-20											
elders from 21-50 years											
old people who are above 50 years											
total number of people in the family											

*F =Family

(i) How many members are educated in each family?

Ans. Do it yourself with the help of your teacher.

(ii) From amongst the ten families, how many are educated?

Ans. Do it yourself.

Now talk to your partner and then write a report about your neighbourhood.

Hints : How to write a report

- **Title** A heading for the report.
- **Introduction** Write about the purpose of the report.
- **Body** It covers the facts and details about the particular event.
- **Conclusion** End by giving a concluding statement.

Let's Interview (NCERT Page 149)

Q.1 Interview your teacher and get her responses for the following questions.

(i) Why did you become a teacher?

Ans. Because I love to teach.

(ii) How do you come to school everyday?

Ans. I came to school by auto-rickshaw.

(iii) Do you have any pets?

Ans. No, I don't have pets.

(iv) What kinds of books do you like to read?

Ans. I like to read novels and thriller books.

(v) What are your hobbies?

Ans. Painting and Reading.

Q.2 Now write a paragraph about your teacher with the information you have gathered.

My Teacher

My teacher says she became a teacher because

____

____

____

____

Ans. My teacher says that she became a teacher because she loves to teach and help people become better individuals. She comes to school everyday on a rickshaw after working at her home. She doesn't have any pets and likes to read novels and thriller books. Her hobbies include painting and reading.

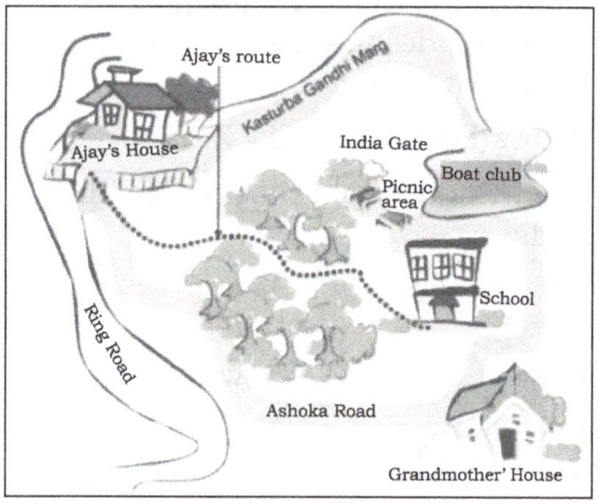

Use the above map to answer the questions.

1. What does the dotted line on the map show?
2. What road would Ajay take to get to the boat club?
3. What building is next to the picnic area?
4. What road passes by Ajay's house?
5. What other way could Ajay use to get from his house to his grandmother's house?

Now write : Use verbs like: go, turn, cross

Use prepositions like: across, between, in front of, beside, near, behind and write how you get home from school.

Ans. 1. The dotted line on the map shows the route from Ajay's house to the school.

2. In order to get to the boat club, Ajay would take Kasturba Gandhi Marg.
3. India gate is next to the picnic area.
4. The road which passes by Ajay's house is 'Ring Road'.

5. Ajay can go to his grandmother's house by Ashoka Road from his house.

Ajay can also go through the Kasturba Gandhi Marg to reach the Boat Club. Then, he could go across the picnic area. From the picnic area, he could turn right, walk a few steps further and reach his grandmother's house.

Let's Listen (NCERT Page 151)

Do you like to float paper boats?

Listen to the poem given below.

Day by Day I Float My Paper Boats

Day by day I float my paper boats one by one down the running stream. In big black letters I write my name on them and the name of the village where I live.

I hope that someone in some strange land will find them and know who I am.

I load my little boats with shiuli flowers from our garden, And hope that these blooms of the dawn will be carried safely to land in the night.

Rabindranath Tagore

(i) Discuss with your partner how you would send a similar message to someone.

(ii) Also find out how people sent messages in olden days and how they send them nowadays.

Ans. (i) I would write a message on a piece of paper, make a paper plane and fly it from my balcony.

(ii) In the olden days, people used to send messages through messengers and pigeons.

Nowadays, people send messages through post, telephones, mobiles, and e-mails.

Let's Write (NCERT Page 152 and 153)

Q.1 See the picture Travel Time below. Answer the questions that follow.

(i) Where did you go for an excursion/holiday?

(ii) With whom did you go?

(iii) What did you take with you?

(iv) What was the first thing you saw when you reached your destination?

(v) What did you like best about the place?

(vi) How long did you stay there?

(vii) What did you miss about home?

Ans. (i) I went to Himachal Pradesh.

(ii) I went with my parents.

(iii) I took my winter clothes to keep myself warm. A camera to capture the beautiful moments.

(iv) I saw mountains covered with snow.

(v) The best thing I liked there was street food.

(vi) I stayed there for a week.

(vii) I missed my pet dog, Kiwi.

Q.2 Make sentences using any two new words which you have learnt in the lesson.

(i) ______________________

(ii) ______________________

Ans. (i) I reached the seventh floor using the elevators.

(ii) To reach my school, my parents sometimes take me through the subway.

Q.3 Which do you think would be more fun — travelling by aeroplane or sailing on a ship? Write why you think so.

Ans. Travelling by aeroplane would be more fun as it is faster and offers a great view.

We can look out of the windows and enjoy watching the fluffy clouds.

Q.4 Look at the following words. They are group names.

- troop of soldiers
- swarm of bees
- team of players
- litter of puppies
- fleet of ships
- library of books

Fill in the blanks choosing group words from the box.

clump cluster choir bunch flock band

(i) The travellers rested under the ______ of trees.

(ii) The ______ sang beautifully.

(iii) The ______ of flowers was lying on the table.

(iv) The girl looked up at the ______ of stars.

(v) The ______ of robbers escaped.

(vi) The hunter shot at the ______ of birds

Ans. (i) clump (ii) choir

(iii) bunch (iv) cluster

(v) band (vi) flock

Q.5 Some words describe actions. Many of them end in -ly.

The girl danced **beautifully**.

Fill in the blanks by changing the word in the brackets suitably.

(i) The girl slept ______. [sound]

(ii) The children finished their work ______. [quick]

(iii) The old man shouted ______. [loud]

(iv) The boys played ______. [quiet]

(v) Do your work ______. [neat]

(vi) I can do the sum ______. [easy]

Ans. (i) soundly (ii) quickly (iii) loudly

(iv) quietly (v) neatly (vi) easily

Fun Time (NCERT Page 154)

Q.1 Which country would you like to visit when you grow up?

Make a project by drawing or pasting.

(i) a map of that country, its national flag

(ii) stamps of the country, its currency

(iii) some famous monuments or landmarks

Ans. Do it yourself.

Q.2 Do you know that there are seven wonders in the world? Can you tell the name of the one which is in India? Find out and write the names of all the seven wonders and the countries they are located in.

Wonders of the world	Countries
(i) The Taj Mahal	______
(ii) The Great Wall of China	______
(iii) ______	______
(iv) ______	______
(v) ______	
(vi) ______	
(vii) ______	

Ans. (i) The Taj Mahal, India

(ii) The Great Wall of China, China

(iii) Christ the redeemer statue, Brazil

(iv) Machu Picchu, Peru

(v) Chichen Itza, Mexico

(vi) The Roman Colosseum, Italy

(vii) Petra, Jordan

Fun With Sounds (NCERT Page 155)

When an 'e' is added to some words, the words change along with their sounds and meanings.

cap	mat	pin	not
cape	mate	pine	note
kit	sit	fin	hat
kite	site	fine	hate
cut	bit	quit	din
cute	bite	quite	dine

A Little Bit Of Nonsense

There was an old Man with a beard
Who said, "It is just as I feared!
Two Owls and a Hen,
Four Larks and a Wren,
Have all built their nests in my beard!

PRACTICE QUESTIONS

Multiple Choice Questions

1. How is the life of people who live in cities?
   (a) Busy (b) Free
   (c) Boring (d) None of these
2. Which mode of transport do the people use to move around in the city?
   (a) Tractor (b) Taxis
   (c) Bullock cart (d) Ship
3. Where do you find busy people?
   (a) City
   (b) Village
   (c) Town
   (d) None of the above
4. Who lives in tall buildings?
   (a) People living in village
   (b) People living in cities
   (c) People living in towns
   (d) None of the above
5. Choose the correct meaning for 'underneath'.
   (a) Above (b) Below
   (c) Lift (d) Around

Ans. 1. (a), 2. (b), 3. (a), 4. (b), 5. (b)

Fill in the Blanks

1. People in the city are ________ on the go.
2. Some people smile and laugh but some are ________.
3. People of the city ride the ________ up and down.
4. Walking fast or slow, people in the city are always in a ________.

Ans. 1. always, 2. grumpy, 3. elevators, 4. hurry

True or False

1. People in the city are always in a hurry.
2. People in the city are always happy and smiling.
3. People in the city use buses, taxis, or subways to go from one place to another.
4. There are no tall buildings in the city.

Ans. 1. True, 2. False, 3. True, 4. False

Answer the Following Questions

1. Why are people in the city always in a hurry?

Ans. The people in the city are always in a hurry to reach their destinations and complete their work.

2. What are some of the different types of people you can see in the city?

Ans. We can see many different type of people in the city. Some people have friends while some don't. Some talk a lot while others don't.

CHAPTER 1 MALU BHALU

Summary of the Poem This poem is about a little polar bear named Malu Bhalu. Malu Bhalu lives in an icy lair (cave) with her parents. She is clever and curious. She likes to learn new things from her parents. The poem covers how Malu Bhalu learns to swim.

Stanza-wise Explanation

Stanza 1

High up in an icy lair
Lived a little polar bear
Snow white, snow bright was her mane,
Malu Bhalu was her name.

Word-Meaning *Lair - A cave or a den; Mane - Long hair on neck of an animal.*

Exp. The poem begins with Malu Bhalu's introduction. She is a little polar bear who lives in an icy lair with her parents. Her fur is bright white in colour.

Stanza 2

Very soon our Malu Bhalu
Learnt the things her parents knew.
Fish to catch, big and small...
Malu was a clever girl.

Exp. Malu Bhalu begins to learn new things from her parents very soon. She learned to catch big as well as small fish and she was a clever bear.

Stanza 3

Malu said to her mother one day:
Ma, I'm going far out to play.
I want to see the things that lie
There beyond the big blue sky.
A little patience, child, said Mum,
In the summer when next it comes.
Summer?... Patience?... What a test!
Malu simply could not rest.

Word-Meaning *Patience - The quality of being able to stay calm.*

Exp. One day, Malu tells her mother that she wishes to go out to play. She told her that she wanted to see the things on the other side of the blue sky. Seeing her curiosity, her mother asks her to have patience. Her mother advises her that she could go out when she learns to swim the next summer. Malu wants to wait until summer to learn to swim, but she thinks it will be hard. She knows it will test her patience because it's a long time away.

Stanza 4

First things first! Malu's mum
Clasped Malu tight within her arms.
Then she said — her voice was firm
Now my dear you'll have to swim.

Word-Meaning *Clasped - To hold closely*

Exp. In these lines, Malu's mother prepares her for her first swimming lesson. She holds her in her arms and tells her in a firm tone that she must learn to swim.

Stanza 5

But Ma! said Malu, what do I know?
How will I? I've never swum before!
Don't worry dear, said Malu's mother,
Do as I do, that's all, she advised her.

Exp. Malu gets scared as she has never swum before. So, her mother comforts her and advises her to follow what she does.

Stanza 6

She had no choice, no other way,
Malu had to swim that day.
Tight she gripped her mother's hand,
Into the water splash! to land.

Exp. Malu understood that she would need to learn to swim that day. She had no other choice. So, she held her mother's hand tightly and jumped into the water.

Stanza 7

Brave mother's brave young daughter!
Doubt and fear she left behind her.
Malu swam with all her might,
It didn't matter wrong or right.

Word-Meaning *Might - great strength or power*

Exp. Malu was brave like her mother so she put all her focus into swimming. She used all her power and tried to swim.

Stanza 8

But swimming came so naturally,
Her mother knew this and all could see.
Fearless was Malu, this she knew,
Not just brave, but special too.

Exp. Malu was naturally a good swimmer. Her mother knew that she could do it. She was confident that Malu was not only brave, but fearless too. She also believed that Malu was very special.

NCERT FOLDER

Reading is Fun (NCERT Page 163)

Q.1 Where did the polar bear live with her family?

Ans. The polar bear lived in an icy lair with her family.

Q.2 What did Malu learn to do from her parents?

Ans. Malu learnt swimming and fishing from her parents.

Q.3 Where did Malu want to travel?

Ans. Malu wanted to travel beyond the big blue sky.

Q.4 What was it that Malu's parents wanted her to learn?

Ans. Malu's parents wanted her to learn swimming.

Q.5 Was Malu scared to swim? Did she learn it easily?

Ans. Yes, she was scared to learn how to swim, but she learnt it easily.

Q.6 Read the last two stanzas of the poem. Whom does 'she' stand for in both?

Ans. In the first stanza, 'she' stands for Malu Bhalu and in the next stanza, 'she' refers to her mother.

Q.7 See the picture shown below and talk about it.

Ans. Do it yourself.

Use A Chart (Page No 160)

Malu Bhalu	True or False	Character Sketch
	1. Malu's hair was white.	brave, strong, hardworking, eager to learn more, smart, caring, impatient, female, affectionate, bold, playful, white, adventurous, clever, young, fearless
	2. Malu knew how to swim.	
	3. Malu was playing with the penguins.	
	4. Malu was good at catching fish.	1. ________ 2. ________
	5. Malu was a brave bhalu.	3. ________
	6. Malu did not lover her mother.	4. ________ 5. ________
	7. Malu's mother was firm.	6. ________

Ans.

True or False	Character Sketch
1. False	1. Malu Bhalu was brave.
2. False	2. She was strong and hard working.
3. False	3. She was very smart.
4. True	4. She was eager to learn.
5. True	5. She was bold, fearless and adventurous.
6. False	6. She was affectionate.
7. True	

Character Sketch of Malu Bhalu

Malu Bhalu is a curious and an intelligent young polar bear. She is clever and smart as she is always ready to learn new things from her parents. She is also eager to explore the world beyond her home. She is a little impatient but very loving towards her mother. Despite her fear, she is brave and determined to learn to swim. This shows that she is bold and adventurous.

Let's Talk (NCERT Page 161)

Read the following passage carefully.

One day Meena plucks a mango and brings it home. Her grandmother gives the larger piece to Raju because he is a boy. Meena protests. After all, she brought the mango and she is the elder of the two. She insists she has a greater right over her share. Her father comes to her help and divides the mango equally.

Now answer the questions.

(i) Who brought the mango home?

(ii) Why did Meena's grandmother give a larger piece to Raju?

(iii) Who do you think should have got the larger piece?

Ans. (i) Meena brought the mango at home.

(ii) Meena's grandmother gave a larger piece to Raju because he was a boy.

(iii) I think that Meena should have got the larger piece because she brought the mango home and decided to share it with her family.

Q.1 Using the following clues write about yourself in the space below

name, place you live in, physical features, habits, likes and dislikes etc.

Ans. My name is Akash. I live in Delhi with my parents and an elder sibling. I am fairly tall for my age and have a round face. I'm curiosity and creative, always eager to explore new ideas. I enjoy reading as well as playing video games. Friends describe me as a good listener and a supportive companion, always ready to lend a helping hand or share a laugh.

Q.2 What are the things you mother asks you to do?

Things you like to do

____

____

Things you do not like to do

____

____

Ans.

Things you like to do	Things you do not like to do
• Going to the park with my friends	• Doing homework
• Helping my father	• Eating vegetables
• Listening to my grandmother's stories	• Folding my clothes and putting them in the cupboard
• Going to the mall	• Drinking milk

Let's Write (Page No 162)

Malu lived with Malu's parents in the North Pole. Malu had great fun with seagull Malu's friends.

One day, Malu's father told Malu that the hunters had come to trap Malu and Malu's family. Malu knew how to hide very well.

Malu shut Malu's eyes and curled up like a ball of snow.

The hunters searched for Malu and Malu's family everywhere but in vain.

We can avoid repeatin the names by using certain other words in their place. Study the table below.

	Singular	Plural
person speaking	I, me	we, us
person spoken	you	You
other persons	He, him, she, her,	They, them
Places, things	it	

Now rewrite the above paragraph using words from the above table.

Ans. Malu lived with her parents in the Polar region. She had great fun with her penguin friends. One day, hunters had come to trap Malu and her family. She knew how to hide very well. She shut her eyes an curled up like a ball of snow.

The hunters searched for her and her family everywhere but they couldn't find them.

PRACTICE QUESTIONS

Multiple Choice Questions

1. What was it that Malu's parents wanted her to learn?
   (a) Flying (b) Swimming
   (c) Eating (d) Sleeping
2. Who said "I am going far out to play"?
   (a) Malu (b) Malu's mother
   (c) Malu's father (d) Poet
3. Which of the following is not the trait of "Malu"?
   (a) Clever (b) Adventurous
   (c) Shy (d) Brave
4. Which of the following is a rhyming word for "Malu"?
   (a) Snow (b) Bhalu
   (c) Bear (d) None of these
5. Choose the correct meaning for 'lair' .
   (a) Place where a wild animal lives
   (b) Encircle
   (c) Hair on the neck
   (d) Liar
6. How was Malu at catching fish?
   (a) Good (b) Bad
   (c) Average (d) Very bad

Ans. 1. (b), 2. (a), 3. (c), 4. (b), 5. (a), 6. (a)

Fill in the Blanks

1. Malu Bhalu is a little________bear.
2. Malu wants to go _________the _________.
3. Malu's mother teaches her to _________.

Ans. 1. polar, 2. beyond, blue sky, 3. swim.

True or False

1. Malu is curious and likes to learn new things from her parents.
2. Malu's mother wants her to have patience.
3. Malu is afraid to swim.
4. Malu is not brave.

Ans. 1. True, 2. True, 3. True, 4. False

Answer the Following Questions

1. Why does Malu's mother want her to learn to swim?

Ans. Malu's mother wants her to learn swimming as it is a basic life skill that she must know as a polar bear.

2. How does Malu's mother help her overcome her fear of swimming?

Ans. Malu's mother comforts her and helps her overcome her fear of swimming by asking her to copy her.

3. Write the important characteristics of "Malu Bhalu".

Ans. Malu Bhalu is a curious and a confident girl. Her most important characteristic is that she is always ready to learn new things.

CHAPTER 2

WHO WILL BE NINGTHOU?

Summary of the Chapter

This is a story from Manipur which tells us about what qualities a good ruler must have. The story is about the Ningthou (King) and Leima (Queen) of Kangleipak (a place in Manipur). They were kind and very caring towards the people in their kingdom. They were loved not only by the people but also by the animals and birds of the kingdom. They had four children, three sons and a little daughter.

One day, the Ningthou and the Leima decided to choose the future king for their kingdom and organised a horse race for the selection of a worthy king. All three of their sons participated in the race and finished it together as they all were expert riders. Therefore, the winner could not be decided. To solve this problem, Ningthou and Leima asked each one of them to do something different. To show their skills, the three sons performed different tricks by piercing a big banyan tree through their spear and uprooting it.

This made the Ningthou's daughter, Sanatombi, very sad. Seeing this, the Ningthou and Leima declared Sanatombi the future Leima (Queen) of Kangleipak. They believed that she was worthy of becoming a ruler as she was the only one who felt the pain of the tree. It showed them that she was very caring and kind towards all living beings. To sum up, this story teaches us that a good ruler is someone who is kind towards everyone and understands their pain.

WORD-MEANING

Dearly - Very much; Worthy - Deserving of, Contest - Competition; Spear - Hunter's weapon; Triumphantly - Victoriously; Majestically - In a beautiful way; Announcement - The act of telling a group of people about something important.

NCERT FOLDER

Reading Is Fun (NCERT Page 168)

Q.1 Name the place in Manipur where the Ningthou and Leima ruled.

Ans. Ningthou and Leima ruled over the land called Kangleipak in Manipur.

Q.2 Why did the people of Kangleipak love their king and queen?

Ans. The people of Kangleipak loved their king and queen because they took care of their people and wanted to see them happy.

Q.3 Why did the Ningthou want to choose a future king?

Ans. The Ningthou wanted to choose a future king because he felt it was the right time and his children were all grown up.

Q.4 How did the king want to select their future king?

Ans. The king wanted to select their future king by choosing the one who was most worthy. To do this, he organised a horse race and said that the winner will be selected as the future king.

Q.5 What kind of child was Sanatombi?

Ans. Sanatombi was a kind and lovely girl. She cared about everyone.

Q.6 Have you ever seen an animal or a bird in pain? What did you do?

Ans. Yes, once I saw a pigeon in my backyard, wounded by a kite thread. With the help of my mother I took it into the house and removed the kite thread. I gave it some water and some grains to eat.

Let's Listen And Talk (NCERT Page 168)

Q.1 Where is Manipur on the map of India?

Ans. Manipur is in the North-Eastern part of India.

Q.2 What language do the people of Manipur speak?

(i) Assamese (ii) Maithailon (iii) Mizo

Ans. (ii) Maithailon

Q.3 Who do you think should have been made the future king?

- Sanajaoba, the one who jumped through the tree.
- Sanayaima, the one who jumped over the tree.
- Sanatomba, the one who uprooted the tree.

Why do you think so?

Who was made the future queen and why?

Ans. None of the Ningthou's sons should have been made the future king. When the Ningthou asked them to do something different, they all thought of showing everyone only their power and skills. No one thought of the pain that khongnang (the banyan tree) felt. A good ruler is one who always cares for all the living beings in his kingdom. Therefore, Santombi was made the future queen. She was the only one who understood the pain that the tree must have felt.

Word Building (NCERT Page 169)

Q.1 Say aloud the following names in your mother tongue.

In Manipuri

Ningthou

Leima

Meeyam

Khongnang

Ans. Do it yourself

Q.2 Write the meanings of the following in English.

1. Tunggi Ningthou - ________________
2. Thouro ! Thouro ! - ________________
3. Phajei ! Phajei ! - ________________
4. Shagol thauba nupa! - ____________

Ans. 1. Future King
2. Bravo! Bravo!
3. Wonderful! Wonderful!
4. Such fine horsemen

Fun With Sound Words (NCERT Page 170)

Some interesting words sound like the noises for which they stand. You use a different tone of voice when you say these words. The voice becomes louder and more forceful.

For example,

Zoom! went the car.

Bang! went the door.

Pip! pop! flippety flop!

say the following and write what would make these sounds or actions.

- Click!
- Chirp!
- Whisper!
- Bravo!
- Oh!
- Ah!
- Hurrah!
- Alas!
- Wonderful!
- Hi!
- Ho!
- Hop away!

Ans.

Click!	-	camera
Chirp!	-	bird
Whisper!	-	talking in low voice
Bravo!	-	It is said when someone is doing well.
Oh!	-	It is said to express surprise and pain.
Ah!	-	It is said to express pleasure.
Hurrah!	-	It is said to express happiness and excitement.
Alas!	-	It is said to express sadness and sorrow.
Wonderful!	-	It is said to express pleasure, happiness or achievement.
Hi!	-	It is said to greet someone.
Ho!	-	It is said to attract someone's attention.
Hop away!	-	It is a sound produced at the time of jumping.

Language Use (Page no. 170)

Q.1 Read the lesson carefully and put a circle around all the action words with -ed at the end. Then write them in one column and their present form in another. One is done for you.

Action words with -ed at the end Action words in present form	
admitted	admit

Ans.

1. shouted	shout
2. Jumped	Jump
3. reached	reach

Q.2 Fill in the correct word in the blanks and complete the story.

In a forest, there ________ (live/lives/lived) a goblin named Cruel. One day, he __________ (meet/met/meets) an old man wandering in the forest. Immediately, Cruel ___________ (leap/ leaps/leapt) on to the old man's shoulders and _________ (order/ orders/ ordered) him, "Let's go. Move fast." The frightened old man _________ (obey/obeys/ obeyed) the nasty goblin and _______ (walk/ walks/walked) on. As they _______on, (move/moves /moved) he _________ (notice/ notices/ noticed) that the goblin's feet were very tender. The old man ________ (ask/asks/

asked) Cruel, " Sir, how are your feet so soft and tender?" Cruel ________, (reply/ replies/replied) "I have taken a vow that I will not touch the ground with my feet, till I wash them." They soon __________ (come/comes/ came) to a pool. The goblin _______ (instruct/ instructs/ instructed) the old man to wait for him while he __________ (enter/enters/ entered) the pool. The old man __________ (think/ thinks/ thought) to himself, "Now that the goblin has wet his feet, he does not need me. Let me run for my life or he will surely eat me up." So he ________ (run/runs/ran) off.

Ans. lived, met, leapt, ordered, obeyed, walked, moved, noticed, asked, replied, came, instructed, entered, thought, ran.

Q.3 Make a list of the action words from this story.

-ed action words		irregular action words	
live	lived	meet	met
______	______	______	______
______	______	______	______
______	______	______	______

Ans.

reach - reached	go - went
turn - turned	hold - held
happen - happened	grow - grew

Project Work (NCERT Page 172)

Q.1 Sit in groups of five. Now, each student will tell a story. Decide which story was the best and declare a Ningthou or Leima of the group.

Ans. Do it yourself.

Q.2 Find out stories about other great people's lives and their childhood and write these in your notebook. Collect at least two such stories and share them with your friends.

You could think of famous

- scientists
- religious people
- freedom fighters
- brave children
- astronauts
- artists

Ans. Do it with the help of your teacher.

PRACTICE QUESTIONS

Multiple Choice Questions

1. Choose the correct meaning for "Thouro! Thouro!"
   (a) Future king
   (b) Bravo! Bravo!
   (c) Wonderful
   (d) Such a fine horse man
2. Who said, "Everybody in Kangleipak should live in peace?
   (a) Sanajaoba
   (b) Sanayaima
   (c) Ningthou
   (d) Sanatomba
3. Which language do the people of Manipur speak?
   (a) Assamese (b) Mizo
   (c) Manipuri (d) Nepali
4. Who was crowned as future king/queen? (DIKSHA)
   (a) Sanatombi (b) Sanajaoba
   (c) Sanayaima (d) Sanatomba
5. Which is not the quality of Sanatombi?
   (a) Soft (b) Beautiful
   (c) Adorable (d) Cruel

Ans. 1. (b), 2. (c), 3. (c), 4. (a), 5. (d)

Fill in the Blanks

1. The Ningthou and Leima were _______ ______ by their people.
2. The Ningthou and Leima wanted to choose the __________, the future king.
3. ___________ was the eldest son.
4. The Ningthou and Leima declared___________the future Leima.

Ans. 1. dearly loved
2. Tunggi Ningthou
3. Sanajaoba
4. Sanatombi

True or False

1. The Ningthou and Leima were not good rulers.
2. The three sons finished the horse race at different times.
3. Sanatombi was the youngest child.
4. The Ningthou and Leima believed that a good ruler must be kind and caring.

Ans. 1. False, 2. False, 3. True, 4. True

Answer the Following Questions

1. What qualities should a good ruler have, according to the story?

Ans. A good ruler should feel the pain of the people, the animals, the birds and the tree. This would help them do better for their people. A ruler is one who doesn't hurt anybody in the kingdom.

2. Who was declared as the future ruler of Kangleipak by Ningthou and why?

Ans. Sanatombi was declared to be the future ruler of Ningthou because only she realised the pain of the tree.

3. What did the three sons do to show their skills?

Ans. The three sons rode their horses at great speeds and crossed the fallen banyan tree with expertise to show their skill.

4. Did Ningthou do the right thing by choosing Sanatombi as future Leima? Why do you think so?

Ans. Yes, I think that Ningthou did the right thing by choosing the little Sanatombi to be the future ruler of the kingdom. This is because she seems to be kind and caring to all. She cannot see anyone in pain.

Let's Write!

1. The story teaches you about a leader- the ruler of a kingdom. What do you think are the qualities of an ideal leader? Write a paragraph on it.

Ans. A good leader is someone who possesses a unique combination of characteristics. He not only inspires and motivates others but also brings out the best in their team.
A leader who is honest, trustworthy and creates a foundation of trust. He is respected among their team members.

They act in a way that aligns with their values and principles, making decisions that are fair and just. They should actively listen and be open to feedback, creating an environment where ideas and opinions are valued.

Empathy and compassion are two qualities that distinguish a good leader from a great one.

रिमझिम

(हिंदी)

अध्याय 1

राख की रस्सी

पाठ का सार

लोनपो गार तिब्बत के बत्तीसवें राजा सौनगवसैन के मंत्री थे। वे अपनी चालाकी और हाज़िरजवाबी के लिए मशहूर थे। उनका बेटा बहुत भोला था, इस कारण वे हर समय चिंतित रहा करते थे। वे चाहते थे कि उनका बेटा भी होशियार बने। एक दिन लोनपो गार ने अपने बेटे को सौ भेड़ें देते हुए कहा, ''तुम इन्हें लेकर शहर जाओ। इन्हें मारना या बेचना नहीं तथा इन्हें सौ जौ के बोरों के साथ वापस लाना वरना मैं तुम्हें घर में नहीं घुसने दूँगा।'' लोनपो गार का बेटा भेड़ें लेकर शहर पहुँच गया। वह बहुत चिंतित था, क्योंकि उसके पास सौ जौ के बोरे खरीदने के लिए रुपये नहीं थे। लोनपो गार का बेटा दु:खी होकर सड़क के किनारे बैठकर सोचने लगा। तभी एक लड़की आई और उसने उसके दु:खी होने का कारण पूछा, उसने लड़की को सारी समस्या बताई। लड़की ने भेड़ों के बाल उतारकर उन्हें बाज़ार में बेच दिया और उनसे जो रुपये मिले उनसे जौ के सौ बोरे खरीदकर लड़के को घर वापस भेज दिया। बेटे की आपबीती सुनकर लोनपो गार खुश नहीं हुए। उन्होंने दूसरे दिन अपने बेटे से कहा- ''तुम दोबारा उन्हीं भेड़ों को लेकर जाओ। उनके साथ जौ के सौ बोरे लेकर ही लौटना।''

लोनपो गार का बेटा शहर में उसी जगह पर जाकर बैठ गया, जहाँ वह पहले बैठा था। वह लड़की फिर से आई और समस्या का समाधान बताते हुए उसने भेड़ों के सींग काटकर बाज़ार में बेच दिए। उससे जो रुपये मिले, उनसे जौ के सौ बोरे खरीदकर लड़के को घर वापस भेज दिया। लड़के ने सारी आपबीती लोनपो गार को बताई। तब लोनपो गार ने कहा, ''उस लड़की से कहो कि हमें नौ हाथ लंबी राख की रस्सी बनाकर दे।'' लड़के ने पिता का संदेश लड़की को बताया, जिसे सुनकर लड़की ने भी एक शर्त रखी कि मेरे द्वारा बनाई गई रस्सी को तुम्हारे पिता को गले में पहनना होगा। लड़का शर्त को स्वीकार कर लेता है। अगले दिन लड़की ने नौ हाथ लंबी रस्सी पत्थर के सिल पर रखकर जला दीया, जिससे रस्सी जल गई तथा राख शेष बच गई। वह सिल को लोनपो गार के पास ले गई और उसे पहनने के लिए कहा। लड़की की समझदारी के सामने लोनपो गार की चालाकी धरी रह गई, क्योंकि वे जानते थे कि राख की रस्सी को गले में डालना तो दूर की बात है, उसे उठाना तक कठिन है। अत: बिना समय नष्ट किए लोनपो गार ने अपने बेटे की शादी उस लड़की से करा दी।

शब्दार्थ

मशहूर–प्रसिद्ध, हाज़िरजवाबी–जल्दी से उत्तर देना, चैन–शांति, समस्या–परेशानी, आपबीती–अपने ऊपर घटित, चकित रह जाना–हैरान होना।

NCERT फोल्डर

भोला भाला

1. तिब्बत के मंत्री अपने बेटे के भोलेपन से चिंतित रहते थे।

(क) तुम्हारे विचार से वे किन-किन बातों के बारे में सोचकर परेशान होते थे?

(ख) तुम तिब्बत के मंत्री की जगह होती तो क्या उपाय करती?

उत्तर (क) तिब्बत के मंत्री सोचते थे कि उनका बेटा बहुत भोला है तथा उसे दुनिया की समझ नहीं है, जिसके कारण कोई भी इसका फ़ायदा उठा सकता है। इसकी शादी कैसे होगी, वह मेरे बाद अपना जीवन कैसे निर्वाह करेगा आदि बातों को सोचकर वे परेशान होते थे।

(ख) मैं उसे स्वयं पढ़ाती-लिखाती, दुनियादारी की बातें सिखाती तथा समय-समय पर उसकी समझ अथवा ज्ञान की परीक्षा भी लेती।

शहर की तरफ

1. "मंत्री ने अपने बेटे को शहर की तरफ़ रवाना किया।"

(क) मंत्री ने अपने बेटे को शहर क्यों भेजा था?

(ख) उसने अपने बेटे को भेड़ों के साथ शहर में ही क्यों भेजा?

(ग) तुम्हारे घर के बड़े लोग पहले कहाँ रहते थे? घर में पता करो। आस-पड़ोस में भी किसी ऐसे व्यक्ति के बारे में पता करो जो किसी दूसरी जगह जाकर बस गया हो। उनसे बातचीत करो और जानने की कोशिश करो कि क्या वे अपने निर्णय से खुश हैं। क्यों? एक पुरुष, एक महिला और एक बच्चे से बात करो। यह भी पूछो कि उन्होंने वह जगह क्यों छोड़ दी?

उत्तर (क) मंत्री ने अपने बेटे को शहर इसलिए भेजा, ताकि वह दुनियादारी सीखे और समझदार बने।

(ख) शहर के लोग होशियार और बुद्धिमान होते हैं। ऐसे लोगों के बीच रहकर उनका बेटा भी होशियार और सूझ-बूझ वाला बन जाएगा। इसी कारण उसने अपने बेटे को भेड़ों के साथ शहर में ही भेजा।

(ग) हमारे घर के बड़े लोग पहले गाँव में रहते थे। मेरे पड़ोस में एक परिवार गाँव से यहाँ शहर में आकर अभी बसा है। वह अपने इस निर्णय से बहुत खुश हैं, क्योंकि गाँव में मूलभूत सुख-सुविधाएँ नहीं थीं। वह यहाँ अपने बच्चों को पढ़ा-लिखाकर सभी सुविधाएँ देकर अच्छा नागरिक बनाना चाहते हैं।

एक पुरुष अपनी नौकरी के स्थानांतरण होने के कारण दूसरी जगह पर जाकर बस गया। एक महिला व एक बच्चा क्रमशः अपने पति व अपने माता-पिता के साथ रहने के कारण एक जगह को छोड़कर दूसरी जगह चले गए।

2. 'जौ' एक तरह का अनाज है, जिसे कई तरह से इस्तेमाल किया जाता है। इसकी रोटी बनाई जाती है, सत्तू बनाया जाता है और सूखा भूनकर भी खाया जाता है। अपने घर में और स्कूल में बातचीत करके कुछ और अनाजों के नाम पता करो।

गेहूँ	**जौ**
....	....
....	....

उत्तर गेहूँ, जौ, मक्का, धान, बाजरा, ज्वार।

3. गेहूँ और जौ अनाज होते हैं और ये तीनों शब्द संज्ञा हैं। 'गेहूँ' और 'जौ' अलग-अलग किस्म के अनाजों के नाम हैं इसलिए ये दोनों व्यक्तिवाचक संज्ञा हैं और 'अनाज' जातिवाचक संज्ञा है। इसी प्रकार 'रिमझिम' व्यक्तिवाचक संज्ञा है। और 'पाठ्यपुस्तक' जातिवाचक संज्ञा है।

(क) नीचे दी गई संज्ञाओं का वर्गीकरण इन दो प्रकार की संज्ञाओं में करो।

लेह, धातु, शेरवानी, भोजन, ताँबा, खिचड़ी, शहर, वेशभूषा

(ख) ऊपर लिखी हर जातिवाचक संज्ञा के लिए तीन-तीन व्यक्तिवाचक संज्ञाएँ खुद सोचकर लिखो।

उत्तर (क) **व्यक्तिवाचक संज्ञा** लेह, शेरवानी, ताँबा, खिचड़ी।
जातिवाचक संज्ञा धातु, भोजन, शहर, वेशभूषा।

(ख) **धातु** लोहा, पीतल, चाँदी
भोजन चावल, दाल, रोटी
शहर दिल्ली, गुजरात, बिहार
वेशभूषा कुर्ता, सलवार, साड़ी

तुम सेर, मैं सवा सेर

1. इस लड़की का तो सभी लोहा मान गए। था न सचमुच नहले पर दहला! तुम्हें भी यही करना होगा। तुम ऐसा कोई काम ढूँढो, जिसे करने के लिए सूझबूझ की ज़रूरत हो। उसे एक कागज़ में लिखो और तुम सभी अपनी-अपनी चिट को एक डिब्बे में डाल दो। डिब्बे को बीच में रखकर उसके चारों ओर गोलाई में बैठ जाओ। अब एक-एक करके आओ, उस डिब्बे से एक चिट निकालकर पढ़ो और उसके लिए कोई उपाय सुझाओ। जिस बच्चे ने सबसे ज्यादा उपाय सुझाए वह तुम्हारी कक्षा का 'बीरबल' होगा।

उत्तर विद्यार्थी स्वयं करें।

2. मंत्री ने बेटे से कहा, "पिछली बार भेड़ों के बाल उतारकर बेचना मुझे जरा भी पसंद नहीं आया।" क्या मंत्री को सचमुच यह बात पसंद नहीं आई थी? अपने उत्तर का कारण भी बताओ।

उत्तर मंत्री को यह बात जरूर पसंद आई होगी, लेकिन इसमें उसके बेटे का कोई योगदान नहीं था। इसलिए दोबारा उन्हीं भेड़ों के साथ उसे शहर वापस भेज दिया, ताकि उसे अपनी होशियारी दिखाने व उस लड़की की बुद्धिमत्ता की परीक्षा लेने एक और अवसर मिल जाए।

सींग और जौ

पहली बार में मंत्री के बेटे ने भेड़ों के बाल बेच दिए और दूसरी बार में भेड़ों के सींग बेच डाले। जिन लोगों ने ये चीज़ें खरीदी होंगी, उन्होंने भेड़ों के बालों और सींगों का क्या किया होगा? अपनी कल्पना से बताओ।

उत्तर भेड़ों के बालों से उन्होंने ऊन बनाई होगी और ऊन से गरम कपड़े; जैसे—स्वेटर, कंबल, शॉल आदि। भेड़ों के सींगों से उन्होंने विभिन्न सजावट की चीजें बनाई होंगी।

बात को कहने के तरीके

1. नीचे कहानी से कुछ वाक्य दिए गए हैं। इन बातों को तुम किस तरह से कह सकती हो?
   (क) चैन से जिंदगी चल रही थी।
   (ख) होशियारी उसे छूकर भी नहीं गई थी।
   (ग) मैं इसका हल निकाल देती हूँ।
   (घ) उनकी अपनी चालाकी धरी रह गई।

उत्तर (क) जीवन शांतिपूर्ण कट रहा था।
(ख) वह बिलकुल भी होशियार नहीं था।
(ग) मैं इसका उपाय बताती हूँ।
(घ) उनकी अपनी चालाकी काम नहीं आई।

2. लोनपो गार का बेटा होशियार नहीं था।
   (क) 'होशियार' और 'चालाक' में क्या फ़र्क होता है? किस आधार पर किसी को तुम चालाक या होशियार कह सकती हो? इसी प्रकार 'भोला' और 'बुद्धू' के बारे में भी सोचो और कक्षा में चर्चा करो।
   (ख) लड़की को तुम 'समझदार' कहोगी या 'बुद्धिमान'। क्यों?

उत्तर (क) **होशियार** शब्द का अर्थ है—समझदार। इस शब्द का प्रयोग सकारात्मक अर्थ में होता है। 'चालाक' शब्द का अर्थ है—चतुर। इसका प्रयोग अधिकतर नकारात्मक रूप में होता है।

भोला शब्द का अर्थ होता है—सीधा-साधा। यदि कोई व्यक्ति भोला है, तो इसका अर्थ यह नहीं कि वह मूर्ख है। वह जानकार और पढ़ा-लिखा है, किंतु हृदय से सीधा है।

बुद्धू शब्द का अर्थ है—मूर्ख या बेवकूफ। इसका प्रयोग 'ना समझ' के संदर्भ में किया जाता है।

(ख) लड़की बुद्धिमान थी। उसने अपनी बुद्धि से हर समस्या का समाधान निकाल लिया था तथा लोनपो गार को इतना प्रभावित किया कि उसने अपने बेटे से उसकी शादी कर दी।

नाम दो

कहानी में लोनपो गार के बेटे और लड़की को कोई नाम नहीं दिया गया है। नीचे तिब्बत में बच्चों के नामकरण के बारे में बताया गया है। यह परिचय पढ़ो और मनपसंद नाम छाँटकर बेटे और लड़की को कोई नाम दो।

नायिमा, डावा, मिगमार, लाखपा, नुखू, फू दोरजे ये क्या हैं? कोई खाने की चीज़ या घूमने की जगहों के नाम। जी नहीं, ये हैं तिब्बती बच्चों के कुछ नाम। ये सारे नाम तिब्बत में शुभ माने जाते हैं।

'नायिमा' नाम दिया जाता है। रविवार को जन्म लेने वाले बच्चों को मानते हैं कि इससे बच्चे को उस दिन के देवता सूरज जैसी शक्ति मिलेगी और जब-जब उसका नाम पुकारा जाएगा, यह शक्ति बढ़ती जाएगी। सोमवार को जन्म लेने वाले बच्चों का नाम 'डावा' रखा जाता है। यह लड़का-लड़की दोनों का नाम हो सकता है। तिब्बती भाषा में डावा के दो मतलब होते हैं— सोमवार और चाँद। यानी डावा चाँद जैसी रोशनी फैलाएगी और अँधेरा दूर करेगी। तिब्बत में बुद्ध के स्त्री-पुरुष रूपों पर भी नामकरण करते हैं खासकर दोलमा नाम बहुत मिलता है। यह बुद्ध के स्त्री रूप तारा का ही तिब्बती नाम है।

उत्तर बेटे का नाम—मिगमार, लड़की का नाम—दोलमा।

अभ्यास प्रश्न

बहुविकल्पीय प्रश्न

1. **तिब्बत के बत्तीसवें राजा सौनगवसैन के मंत्री कौन थे?**
   (क) दोलमा (ख) लोनपो गार
   (ग) मिगमार (घ) नायिमा

2. **लोनपो गार का बेटा कैसा था?**
   (क) भोला (ख) चालाक
   (ग) होशियार (घ) बुद्धू

3. **लोनपो गार ने अपने बेटे को कहाँ भेजा था?**
   (क) शहर (ख) गाँव (ग) जंगल (घ) मंदिर

4. **लोनपो गार ने अपने बेटे को क्या देकर भेजा था?**
   (क) बकरी (ख) भेड़ें (ग) गाय (घ) मछली

उत्तर 1. (ख) लोनपो गार 2. (क) भोला
3. (क) शहर 4. (ख) भेड़ें

गद्यांश पर आधारित प्रश्न

निम्नलिखित गद्यांश को पढ़कर उस पर आधारित प्रश्नों के उत्तर दीजिए।

गद्यांश

एक दिन लोनपो गार ने अपने बेटे को सौ भेड़ें देते हुए कहा, ''तुम इन्हें लेकर शहर जाओ, लेकिन इन्हें मारना या बेचना नहीं। इन्हें वापस लाना सौ जौ के बोरों के साथ वरना मैं तुम्हें घर में नहीं घुसने दूँगा।''

इसके बाद उन्होंने बेटे को शहर की तरफ़ रवाना किया। लोनपो गार का बेटा शहर पहुँच गया, लेकिन इतने बोरे जौ खरीदने के लिए उसके पास रुपये ही कहाँ थे? वह इस समस्या पर सोचने-विचारने के लिए सड़क किनारे बैठ गया, लेकिन कोई हल उसकी समझ में ही नहीं आ रहा था। वह बहुत दु:खी था। तभी एक लड़की उसके सामने आ खड़ी हुई। ''क्या बात है तुम इतने दु:खी क्यों हो?'' लोनपो गार के बेटे ने अपना हाल कह सुनाया। ''इसमें इतना दु:खी होने की कोई बात नहीं। मैं इसका हल निकाल देती हूँ।'' इतना कहकर लड़की ने भेड़ों के बाल उतारे और उन्हें बाज़ार में बेच दिया। उससे जो रुपये मिले, उनसे जौ के सौ बोरे खरीदकर उसे घर वापस भेज दिया।

1. **लोनपो गार ने भेड़ों को किसके साथ वापस लाने के लिए कहा?**
   (क) दो सौ जौ के बोरे के साथ (ख) लड़की के साथ
   (ग) भेड़ों के बाल व सींग के साथ (घ) सौ जौ के बोरों के साथ

2. **लोनपो गार के बेटे के दु:खी होने का क्या कारण था?**
   (क) शहर में स्वयं को अकेला पाना
   (ख) किसी से मदद प्राप्त न होना
   (ग) जौ खरीदने के लिए पैसों का न होना
   (घ) अनजान लोगों से बात न कर पाना

3. **लोनपो गार ने अपने बेटे को सौ भेड़ें देते हुए क्या कहा?**

4. **लोनपो गार के बेटे की समस्या सुनकर लड़की ने क्या किया?**

उत्तर

1. (घ) सौ जौ के बोरों के साथ
2. (ग) जौ खरीदने के लिए पैसों का न होना
3. लोनपो गार ने अपने बेटे को सौ भेड़ें देते हुए कहा, ''तुम इन्हें लेकर शहर जाओ, लेकिन इन्हें मारना या बेचना नहीं। इन्हें वापस लाना सौ जौ के बोरों के साथ। वरना मैं तुम्हें घर में नहीं घुसने दूँगा।''
4. लोनपो गार के बेटे की समस्या सुनकर लड़की न उसका तुरंत हल निकाल लिया और इतना कहकर भेड़ों के बाल उतारकर बाजार में बेच दिए।

निम्नलिखित प्रश्नों के उत्तर दीजिए

1. **पाठ के आधार पर बताइए कि लड़की लोनपो गार के बेटे से बेहतर कैसे थी?**

उत्तर लड़की लोनपो गार से बेहतर इसलिए थी, क्योंकि वह समझदारी से हर बार समस्या का सही हल ढूँढ लिया करती थी।

2. **आपने 'राख की रस्सी' पाठ से क्या सीखा? अपने शब्दों में लिखिए।**

उत्तर 'राख की रस्सी' पाठ से हमनें यह सीखा कि व्यावहारिक समझदारी और चतुर सोच के कठिन-से-कठिन कार्यों को भी हल किया जा सकता है।

3. **लोनपो गार अपने पुत्र द्वारा सौ बोरे जौ लाने पर भी खुश क्यों नहीं हुए?**

उत्तर लोनपो गार अपने पुत्र द्वारा सौ बोरे जौ लाने पर इसलिए खुश नहीं हुए, क्योंकि वे उसकी समझदारी व बुद्धिमानी को जानना चाहते थे तथा अपने बेटे को होशियार बनाना चाहते थे, किंतु वह अपनी बुद्धि का प्रयोग न करके लड़की के कहे अनुसार सौ बोरे जौ लेकर आता है।

अध्याय 2 फ़सलों के त्योहार

पाठ का सार

सर्दियों का मौसम है और सूरज दस दिनों से नहीं निकला है। पूरा दिन बोरसी (अँगीठी) के आगे बैठकर हाथ तापते हुए निकल जाता है। मकर संक्रांति (खिचड़ी का त्योहार) का दिन आ गया है, लेकिन सर्दी कम नहीं हुई है, फिर भी हम सभी नहा-धोकर एक कमरे में इकट्ठे हो गए। दादा और चाचा ने सफेद धोती और कुर्ता पहना है तथा दादी खादी की सफेद साड़ी पहने हुए मचिया (चौकी) पर बैठी थी। उनके सामने केले के कुछ पत्ते कतार में रखे हैं, जिस पर तिल, गुड़, चावल आदि रखे हुए हैं। दादी ने हम सबको इन चीजों को बारी-बारी से छूने और प्रणाम करने के लिए कहा। बाद में इन सभी को दान में दे दिया गया। मकर संक्रांति के दिन चूड़ा-दही और खिचड़ी खाने का रिवाज़ है, किंतु अप्पी दिदिया को दोनों में से कोई चीज़ पसंद न होने के बाद भी खानी होगी। इस दिन तिल, गुड़ और चीनी के तिलकुट भी खाए जाते हैं।

जनवरी माह के मध्य में भारत के लगभग सभी राज्यों में फ़सलों से जुड़ा कोई-न-कोई त्योहार मनाया जाता है। उत्तर प्रदेश, बिहार, मध्य प्रदेश में **मकर संक्रांति या तिल संक्रांति,** असम में **बीहू,** केरल में **ओणम,** तमिलनाडु में **पोंगल,** पंजाब में **लोहड़ी,** झारखंड में **सरहुल** आदि सभी खेती और फ़सलों से जुड़े त्योहार हैं।

झारखंड में चार दिनों का सरहुल पर्व पूरे उत्साह के साथ मनाया जाता है। इस दिन आदिवासी प्रकृति की पूजा के साथ विशेष रूप से **साल के पेड़ की पूजा** करते हैं। संथाल लोग फरवरी-मार्च में तथा ओराँव लोग इसे मार्च-अप्रैल में मनाते हैं। इस समय से मौसम खुशनुमा हो जाता है तथा इस दिन से वसंत ऋतु की शुरुआत भी मानी जाती है। इस पर्व पर धान की पूजा करके उसे अगली फ़सल में बोया जाता है। तमिलनाडु में फसलों से जुड़ा त्योहार 'पोंगल' है। इस दिन खरीफ़ की फ़सलें— चावल, अरहर, मसूर आदि कटकर घरों में पहुँचती हैं और लोग नए धान कूटकर चावल निकालते हैं। प्रत्येक घर में मिट्टी का नया मटका लाकर उसमें नए चावल, दूध और गुड़ डालकर पकने के लिए धूप में रख देते हैं। जैसे ही दूध-चावल मटके से बाहर गिरने लगता है, तो **पोंगला-पोंगल, पोंगला-पोंगल** के स्वर सुनाई देते हैं। गुजरात में पतंग उड़ाकर आनंदपूर्वक इस पर्व को मनाया जाता है। कुमाऊँ में मकर संक्रांति को **घुघुतिया** भी कहते हैं। इस दिन आटे और गुड़ से बने पकवानों को विभिन्न प्रकार के आकार देकर माला में पिरोकर बच्चों के गले में पहनाया जाता है। इस प्रकार, मकर संक्रांति को अलग-अलग अंदाज़ में मनाया जाता है। इस दिन तिल दान करना, पानी में तिल डालकर नहाना, आग में तिल डालना, नदी में स्नान करना आदि विशेष महत्त्व रखते हैं।

शब्दार्थ

बोरसी-आग रखने का मिट्टी का बर्तन, केरा-केला, नईखे-नहीं, देह-शरीर, कनकना देना-ठंडा कर देना, गौर से-ध्यान से, फरमाइशी-इच्छानुसार, सुस्ताना-आराम करना, इजहार करते हैं-व्यक्त करते हैं, जश्न-मौज-मस्ती, प्रथा-परंपरा, सैलाब-बाढ़, तिल रखने की जगह न होना-बहुत भीड़ होना।

NCERT फोल्डर

मौसम का अंदाज

1. "खिचड़ी में अइसन जाड़ा हम पहिले कब्बो ना देखनी।" यहाँ तुम 'खिचड़ी' से क्या मतलब निकाल रही हो?

उत्तर यहाँ 'खिचड़ी' से मतलब मकर संक्रांति के त्योहार से है।

2. क्या कभी ऐसा हो सकता है कि सूरज बिल्कुल ही न निकले? अगर ऐसा हो तो ....

उत्तर नहीं, ऐसा कभी भी नहीं हो सकता, क्योंकि अगर ऐसा होगा तो चारों ओर अँधेरा छा जाएगा, ठंड बढ़ती ही जाएगी। मानव जीवन का प्रमुख स्रोत सूरज ही है। अत: सूरज न निकलने से प्रकृति में ऊर्जा की कमी आएगी और धीरे-धीरे सब जीवों का अंत हो जाएगा।

3. बाहर देखने से समय का अंदाजा क्यों नहीं हो रहा था? जिनके पास घड़ी नहीं होती वे समय का अनुमान किस तरह से लगाते हैं?

उत्तर बाहर देखने से समय का अंदाजा इसलिए नहीं हो रहा था, क्योंकि सूरज नहीं निकला था। सर्दी की चादर से सब ढका हुआ था। जिनके पास घड़ी नहीं होती, वे समय का अंदाजा सूरज की गति, ताप और उसकी चमक से लगाते हैं।

तुम्हारी जुबान

(क) "आज ई लोग के उठे के नईखे का?"

(ख) "जा भाग के देख केरा के पत्ता आइल की ना?"

इन वाक्यों को अपने घर की भाषा में लिखो।

उत्तर (क) आज ये लोग उठेंगे या नहीं?

(ख) दौड़कर जाओ और देखो कि केले का पत्ता आया कि नहीं।

भारत तेरे रंग अनेक

1. विविधता हमारे देश की पहचान है। फसलों का त्योहार हमारे देश के विविध रंग-रूपों का एक उदाहरण है। नीचे विविधता के कुछ और उदाहरण दिए गए हैं। पाँच-पाँच बच्चों का समूह एक-एक उदाहरण ले और उस पर जानकारी इकट्ठी करे। (जानकारी चित्र, फोटोग्राफ, कहानी, कविता, सूचनापरक सामग्री के रूप में हो सकती है।) हर समूह इस जानकारी को कक्षा में प्रस्तुत करे।

- भाषा
- कपड़े
- नया वर्ष
- भोजन
- लोककला
- लोक संगीत

उत्तर
- **भाषा** भारत में अनेक भाषाएँ बोली जाती हैं। उदाहरण के लिए, हिंदी, गुजराती, कश्मीरी, मराठी, पंजाबी, कन्नड़, तेलुगू आदि। हिंदी भारत की मुख्य व राष्ट्रभाषा है, क्योंकि यह अधिकतम लोगों द्वारा बोली जाती है।
- **कपड़े** भारत में अलग-अलग क्षेत्रों के लोग अलग-अलग मौसम में अलग-अलग तरह के कपड़े पहनते हैं। उत्तर भारत में महिलाएँ सलवार-कमीज़, घाघरा-चोली, साड़ी और फिरन पहनती हैं। पुरुष कुर्ता, अचकन, कमीज़, शेरवानी, धोती और चूड़ीदार सलवार पहनते हैं। भारत में सिर पर पहनावे का प्रचलन है और राजस्थान में साफों के अलग-अलग रंग और बाँधने की अलग-अलग शैली का उपयोग होता है।
- **नया वर्ष** हिंदी कैलेंडर के अनुसार चैत्र माह के शुक्ल पक्ष की प्रतिपदा से नववर्ष की शुरुआत मानी जाती है।
- **भोजन** यहाँ हर राज्य का अपना खास भोजन है; जैसे— राजस्थान में दाल-बाटी, चूरमा आदि, गुजरात में ढोकला, थेपला, खांडवी आदि, दक्षिण भारत में सांभर, डोसा, इडली आदि, महाराष्ट्र में पूरन पोली, मिसल पाव और बटाटा वड़ा आदि।
- **लोककला** कलमकारी, गोंड, चित्तर, तंजावुर, पातचित्र, पिछवई, पिथोरा चित्रकला, मधुबनी तथा वरली आदि भारत की प्रमुख लोक कलाएँ हैं।
- **लोक संगीत** गरबा, डांडिया, पहाड़ी, बिहू गीत, भटियाली, भांगड़ा और गिद्धा आदि भारत के लोक संगीत हैं।

2. तुम्हें कौन-सा त्योहार सबसे अच्छा लगता है और क्यों? इस दिन तुम्हारी दिनचर्या क्या रहती है?

उत्तर मुझे दिवाली का त्योहार सबसे प्रिय लगता है, क्योंकि इस दिन मेरे घर में चारों ओर दीप प्रज्वलित किए जाते हैं और मिठाइयों का सेवन किया जाता है। इस दिन सुबह से ही मन में बहुत उत्साह रहता है। इस दिन मेरी दिनचर्या माताजी के साथ शाम की पूजा के साथ शुरू होती है। शाम की पूजा में मुझे ढेर सारे उपहार मिलते हैं।

अन्न के बारे में

(क) फसल के त्योहार पर 'तिल' का बहुत महत्त्व होता है। तिल का किन-किन रूपों में इस्तेमाल किया जाता है? पता करो।

(ख) तुम जानती हो कि तिल से तेल बनता है और किन चीज़ों से तेल बनता है और कैसे? हो सके तो तेल की दुकान में जाकर पूछो।

उत्तर (क) तिल से लड्डू, तिलकुट, तिल की पट्टी, रेवड़ियाँ और गज्जक जैसी मिठाइयाँ बनाई जाती हैं।

(ख) तिल के अलावा मूँगफली, सरसों, सोयाबीन, सूरजमुखी आदि से तेल बनाया जाता है। इन चीजों को पीसकर (निचोड़कर) इनका तेल निकाला जाता है।

किसान और चीजों का सफर

किसान और खेती हममें से बहुत-से लोगों की जानी-पहचानी दुनिया का हिस्सा नहीं हैं। विशेष रूप से शहर के ज्यादातर लोगों को यह अहसास नहीं है कि हमारी जिंदगी किस हद तक इनसे जुड़ी हुई है। देश के कई हिस्सों में आज किसानों को जिंदा रहने के लिए बहुत मेहनत और संघर्ष करना पड़ रहा है।

अगर यह जानने की कोशिश करें कि हम दिनभर जो चीजें खाते हैं वे कहाँ से आती हैं, तो किसानों की हमारी जिंदगी में भूमिका को हम समझ पाएँगे। आलू की पकौड़ी, बर्फी और आइसक्रीम- इन तीन चीज़ों के बारे में नीचे दिए बिंदुओं को ध्यान में रखते हुए जानकारी इकट्ठी करो और 'मेरी कहानी' के रूप में उसे लिखो।

- किन चीज़ों से बनती है?
- इन चीज़ों का जन्म कहाँ होता है?
- हम तक पहुँचने का उनका सफ़र क्या है?
- किन-किन हाथों से होकर हम तक पहुँचती है?
- इस पूरे सफर में किन लोगों की कितनी मेहनत लगती है?
- इन लोगों में से किसको कितना मुनाफा मिलता है?

अगले वर्ष कक्षा छः में सामाजिक एवं राजनैतिक जीवन के बारे में पढ़ोगी, तो ऊपर लिखे सफर में शामिल लोगों की दिनचर्या पता करने का मौका भी मिलेगा।

उत्तर **आलू की पकौड़ी** मैं हूँ आलू की पकौड़ी, मैं आलू और बेसन से मिलकर बनती हूँ। किसान के द्वारा इन आलुओं को खेत में बोया जाता है। फिर इन्हें बाज़ार में भेजा जाता है। बाज़ार से आप लोग इन्हें खरीदकर अपने घर ले आते हो।

बर्फी बर्फी को दूध के खोये से बनाया जाता है। दूध का खोया बनाकर उसमें चीनी मिश्रित करके बर्फी को बनाया जाता है।

आइसक्रीम दूध में आइसक्रीम पाउडर और चीनी डालकर उसे गाढ़ा करके उबाला जाता है और ठंडा होने के लिए रख दिया जाता है उसके बाद साँचों में डालकर फ्रीज में रख दिया जाता है।

बर्फी व आइसक्रीम बनाने के लिए दूध ग्वालों द्वारा बड़ी-बड़ी कंपनियों में दे दिया जाता है। ये चीजें व्यापारियों व विक्रेताओं से हम तक पहुँचती हैं। इस पूरी प्रक्रिया में किसानों व मजदूरों का परिश्रम होता है, जिसमें किसानों को कम व व्यापारियों को अधिक मुनाफा प्राप्त होता है।

खास पकवान

1. **'गया' शहर तिलकुट के लिए भी प्रसिद्ध है। हमारे देश में छोटी-बड़ी ऐसी कई जगह हैं, जो अपने खास पकवान के लिए मशहूर हैं। अपने परिवार के लोगों से पता करके उनके बारे में बताओ।**

उत्तर
- मुंबई की पानी पुरी
- मेरठ की नानखताई
- गुजरात की घारी
- आगरा का पेठा
- मथुरा का पेड़ा
- केरल का सांभर

2. **पिछले दो वर्षों में तुमने 'काम वाले शब्दों' के बारे में जाना।**

इन शब्दों को क्रिया भी कहते हैं, क्योंकि क्रिया का संबंध कोई काम 'करने' से है। नीचे खिचड़ी बनाने की विधि दी गई है। इसमें बीच-बीच में कुछ क्रियाएँ छूट गई हैं। उचित क्रिया का प्रयोग करते हुए इसे पूरा करो।

छोंकना पीसना पकाना
धोना परोसना भूनना

बंगाली 'खिचुरी' (5 व्यक्तियों के लिए)

सामग्री	मात्रा
अदरक	20 ग्राम
लहसुन	3 फाँकें
इलायची के दाने	3 छोटी
दालचीनी	$2\frac{1}{2}$ सेमी का एक टुकड़ा
पानी	4 प्याले
मूँग दाल	$\frac{1}{2}$ प्याला
सरसों का तेल	3 बड़े चम्मच
तेज पत्ते	2
जीरा	$\frac{1}{2}$ छोटा चम्मच
प्याज बारीक कटा हुआ	1 मँझोल
चावल धुले हुए	1 प्याला

फूलगोभी बड़े-बड़े टुकड़ों में कटी हुई	200 ग्राम
आलू छीलकर चार-चार टुकड़ों में कटे हुए	2
मटर के दाने	$\frac{1}{2}$ प्याला
धनिया पिसा हुआ	1 बड़ा चम्मच
लाल मिर्च पिसी हुई	$\frac{1}{2}$ छोटा चम्मच
चीनी	1 छोटा चम्मच
घी	2 बड़े चम्मच
नमक और हल्दी	अंदाज से

विधि इलायची, दालचीनी और लौंग में थोड़ा-थोड़ा पानी (एक छोटा चम्मच) डालते हुए ······· लो। अदरक और लहसुन को इकट्ठा पीसकर पेस्ट बनाओ। दाल को कढ़ाई में डालो और मध्यम आँच पर सुनहरी भूरी होने तक ······· लो, अब दाल निकालकर ······· लो। तेल को कुकर में डालकर गर्म करो। तेल गर्म होने पर तेज पत्ते और जीरा डालो। जीरा जब चटकने लगे, तो प्याज डालकर सुनहरा भूरा होने तक भूनो। अब अदरक-लहसुन का पेस्ट डालकर कुछ मिनट तक ·······। धुली हुई दाल, चावल और सब्जी डालो और अच्छी तरह मिलाओ और शेष पानी (4 प्याले) डालकर एक बार हिलाओ। कुकर बंद करो। तेज आँच पर पूर्ण प्रेशर आने दो। अब आँच तेज करके 4 मिनट तक ·······। भाप निकल जाने पर कुकर खोलो, मसालों का पेस्ट मिलाओ। खिचड़ी घी, हींग, जीरा, साबुत लाल मिर्च से ······· कर ······· गरमागरम।

उत्तर पीस, भून, पीस, भूनो, पकाओ, छोंक, परोसो

अभ्यास प्रश्न

बहुविकल्पीय प्रश्न

1. फसलों का त्योहार किसे कहा गया है?
   (क) पोंगल को (ख) मकर संक्रांति को
   (ग) सरहुल को (घ) ये सभी

2. दादी ने कौन-से रंग की साड़ी पहनी है?
   (क) नीली (ख) पीली
   (ग) हरी (घ) सफेद

3. केले के पत्ते पर किसके ढेर पड़े हुए हैं?
   (क) गुड़ और चावल के (ख) चावल और सब्ज़ी के
   (ग) रुई के (घ) चावल और दही के

4. अप्पी दिदिया को क्या पसंद नहीं है?
   (क) तिल (ख) गुड़
   (ग) चूड़ा-दही (घ) दूध

5. झारखंड में फसलों के त्योहार का क्या नाम है?
   (क) पोंगल (ख) सरहुल
   (ग) बीहू (घ) ओणम

उत्तर

1. (घ) ये सभी 2. (घ) सफेद 3. (क) गुड़ और चावल के 4. (ग) चूड़ा-दही 5. (ख) सरहुल

गद्यांश पर आधारित प्रश्न

निम्नलिखित गद्यांश को पढ़कर उस पर आधारित प्रश्नों के उत्तर दीजिए।

गद्यांश

झारखंड में चार दिनों का सरहुल पूरे उत्साह के साथ मनाया जाता है। इस दिन आदिवासी प्रकृति की पूजा के साथ विशेष रूप से 'साल के पेड़ की पूजा' करते हैं। संथाल लोग फरवरी-मार्च में, तो ओराँव लोग इसे मार्च-अप्रैल में मनाते हैं। इस समय से मौसम बहुत खुशनुमा हो जाता है। लोग घरों को सजाकर उसके अगले दिन नृत्य करते हैं। इसी दिन से वसंत ऋतु की शुरुआत मानी जाती है। धान की भी पूजा की जाती है। पूजा किया हुआ आशीर्वादी धान अगली फ़सल में बोया जाता है।

1. झारखंड में सरहुल का त्योहार कितने दिन तक मनाया जाता है?
   (क) एक (ख) दो
   (ग) तीन (घ) चार

2. मकर संक्रांति से कौन-से मौसम की शुरुआत मानी जाती है?
   (क) गर्मी
   (ख) सर्दी
   (ग) वसंत
   (घ) बरसात
3. आदिवासी लोग किसकी पूजा करते हैं? लिखिए।
4. पूजा किया हुआ धान किस प्रयोग में लाया जाता है?

उत्तर

1. (घ) चार   2. (ग) वसंत
3. आदिवासी प्रकृति की पूजा के साथ विशेष रूप से 'साल के पेड़ की पूजा' करते हैं।
4. पूजा किया हुआ आशीर्वादी धान अगली फ़सल में बोया जाता है।

निम्नलिखित प्रश्नों के उत्तर दीजिए

1. दादी ने मेज पर रखे समान के संदर्भ में क्या कहा?

उत्तर दादी ने मेज पर रखे समान को बारी-बारी से छूने और प्रणाम करने के लिए कहा।

2. मकर संक्रांति के समय किस प्रकार का मौसम होता है? लिखिए।

उत्तर मकर संक्राति के समय सर्दी का मौसम होता है। यह त्योहार जनवरी माह के मध्य मनाया जाता है।

3. मकर संक्रांति मनाने के कारण को विस्तार से लिखिए।

उत्तर मकर संक्राति का त्योहार भारत में अलग-अलग राज्यों में भिन्न-भिन्न नाम से जाना और मनाया जाता है। इस त्योहार का मुख्य उद्देश्य सूर्य की उपासना करना व जरूरतमंद लोगों को भिन्न-भिन्न वस्तुएँ दान में देना होता है।

4. अलग-अलग राज्यों में मकर संक्रांति किन-किन नामों से मनाई जाती है?

उत्तर उत्तर प्रदेश, बिहार, मध्य प्रदेश में मकर संक्रांति या तिल संक्रांति, असम में बीहू, केरल में ओणम, तमिलनाडु में पोंगल, पंजाब में लोहड़ी, झारखंड में सरहुल के नाम से यह त्योहार मनाया जाता है।

5. गुजरात में किसके बिना मकर-संक्रांति का जश्न अधूरा माना जाता है?

उत्तर गुजरात में पतंगों के बिना मकर संक्रांति का जश्न अधूरा माना जाता है।

व्याकरण संबंधी प्रश्न

1. पाठ में खिचड़ी बनाने की विधि जानी। अब खिचड़ी से बने मुहावरे के अर्थ बताकर उनका वाक्य में प्रयोग कीजिए।
   - खिचड़ी पकाना
   - बीरबल की खिचड़ी
2. दिए गए शब्दों के विलोम शब्द लिखिए
   - मौखिक
   - विशाल
   - जीवित
   - स्वच्छ

उत्तर

1. **अर्थ** छिपकर काम करना
   वाक्य प्रयोग मोहन और सोहन के बीच अलग ही खिचड़ी पक रही थी।
   अर्थ आसान काम को मुश्किल बताना
   वाक्य प्रयोग तुमने अपना गृह कार्य करने में दो दिन लगा दिए, गृह कार्य को तुमने बीरबल की खिचड़ी बना दिया है।
2. लिखित, लघु, मृत, दूषित

लेखन संबंधी प्रश्न

1. दिए गए चित्र का वर्णन कीजिए।

उत्तर प्रस्तुत चित्र मकर संक्रांति के मौके पर पतंग उत्सव के आयोजन का है। चित्र में मैदान में बच्चे, बड़े सभी मिल-जुलकर पतंग उड़ाते हुए दिखाई दे रहे हैं। कुछ लोग कुर्सी पर बैठे हैं तो कुछ लोग पास में ही खड़े होकर बातें कर रहे हैं व पतंग उड़ा रहे हैं।

मैदान में दूर कुछ गाड़ियाँ भी खड़ी हैं। आसमान में चारों ओर रंग-बिरंगी पतंगों के उड़ने से दृश्य सुंदर लग रहा है। सभी उत्साहपूर्वक पतंग उड़ाकर मकर संक्रांति का पर्व मना रहे हैं।

अध्याय 3

खिलौनेवाला

कविता का सार

एक बालक खिलौनेवाले को देखकर अपनी माँ से कहता है कि आज खिलौनेवाला तरह-तरह के नए-नए खिलौने लेकर आया है। बालक अपनी माँ से चार पैसे लेता है और खिलौना लेने के बारे में सोचता हुआ कहता है कि वह खिलौने न लेकर तलवार और तीर-कमान लेगा। वह जंगल जाकर भगवान राम की तरह ताड़का को मारना चाहता है, किंतु इस विचार से तुरंत ही वह चिंतित हो जाता है कि माँ के बिना वह जंगल में किस प्रकार रह पाएगा?

काव्यांशों की व्याख्या

काव्यांश 1

वह देखो माँ आज
खिलौनेवाला फिर से आया है।
कई तरह से सुंदर-सुंदर
नए खिलौने लाया है।
हरा-हरा तोता पिंजड़े में
गेंद एक पैसे वाली
छोटी-सी मोटरगाड़ी है।
सर-सर-सर चलने वाली।

शब्दार्थ *पिंजड़ा-लोहे से बना पक्षी को रखने का स्थान।*

संदर्भ/प्रसंग प्रस्तुत पंक्तियाँ पाठ्यपुस्तक 'रिमझिम भाग-5' में संकलित कविता 'खिलौनेवाला' से ली गई हैं। प्रस्तुत कविता कवयित्री 'सुभद्रा कुमारी चौहान' द्वारा रचित है। इस कविता में कवयित्री ने एक खिलौने वाले को देखकर बालक के अलग-अलग तरह के खिलौने लेने के लिए उत्साहित होने का वर्णन किया है।

व्याख्या प्रस्तुत पंक्तियों में एक बालक खिलौनेवाले को देखकर बहुत उत्साहित हो जाता है। वह अपनी माँ से कहता है कि आज खिलौनेवाला तरह-तरह के खिलौने लेकर आया है। उसके पास पिंजड़े में बंद हरा-हरा तोता है, एक पैसे वाली गेंद और छोटी-सी मोटरगाड़ी है, जो सर-सर-सर करके चलती है।

काव्यांश 2

सीटी भी है कई तरह की
कई तरह के सुंदर खेल
चाभी भर देने से भक-भक
करती चलने वाली रेल।।
गुड़िया भी है बहुत भली-सी
पहिने कानों में बाली
छोटा-सा 'टी सेट' है।
छोटे-छोटे हैं लोटा-थाली।

शब्दार्थ *बाली-कानों में पहनने वाला गोल चूड़ीनुमा गहना।*

संदर्भ/प्रसंग पूर्ववत्।

व्याख्या प्रस्तुत पंक्तियों में बालक कहता है कि खिलौनेवाले के पास कई तरह की सीटियाँ और कई तरह के खेल हैं। चाभी से चलने वाली सुंदर रेल और एक गुड़िया है, जिसने कानों में बालियाँ पहनी हुई हैं। उसके पास छोटा टी-सेट और छोटे-छोटे लोटा-थाली भी रखे हुए हैं।

काव्यांश 3

छोटे-छोटे धनुष-बाण हैं।
हैं छोटी-छोटी तलवार
नए खिलौने ले लो भैया
ज़ोर ज़ोर वह रहा पुकार।
मुन्नू ने गुड़िया ले ली है।
मोहन ने मोटरगाड़ी
मचल-मचल सरला कहती है।
माँ से लेने को साड़ी
कभी खिलौनेवाला भी माँ
क्या साड़ी ले आता है।
साड़ी तो वह कपड़े वाला
कभी-कभी दे जाता है।

शब्दार्थ *जोर-जोर-तेज, पुकार-आवाज़ लगाना।*

संदर्भ/प्रसंग पूर्ववत्।

व्याख्या प्रस्तुत पंक्तियों में बालक कहता है खिलौनेवाले के पास नए-नए खिलौने हैं। उसके पास छोटे-छोटे धनुष बाण और तलवार हैं। खिलौनेवाला जोर-जोर से आवाज़ लगाकर नए खिलौने लेने के लिए कह रहा है। मुन्नू खिलौनेवाले से गुड़िया और मोहन मोटरगाड़ी खरीदता है। सरला अपनी माँ से साड़ी ख़रीदने के लिए जिद करती है। बालक अपनी माँ से पूछता है कि क्या खिलौनेवाला साड़ियाँ लेकर आता है, साड़ियाँ तो कपड़े बेचनेवाले लाते हैं, जो कभी-कभी आते हैं।

काव्यांश 4

अम्मा तुमने तो लाकर के
मुझे दे दिए पैसे चार
कौन खिलौना लेता हूँ मैं
तुम भी मन में करो विचार।
तुम सोचोगी मैं ले लूँगा।
तोता, बिल्ली, मोटर, रेल
पर माँ, यह मैं कभी न लूँगा
ये तो हैं बच्चों के खेल।
मैं तलवार खरीदूँगा माँ
या मैं लूँगा तीर-कमान
जंगल में जा, किसी ताड़का
को मारूँगा राम समान।

शब्दार्थ *अम्मा-माँ, विचार-सोचना।*

संदर्भ/प्रसंग पूर्ववत्।

व्याख्या प्रस्तुत पंक्तियों में बालक कहता है कि तुमने मुझे चार पैसे दिए हैं, तुम भी मन में सोचो कि मैं इन चार पैसों से कौन-सा खिलौना लेता हूँ। तुम सोच रही होंगी कि मैं तोता, बिल्ली, मोटर, रेल लूँगा। ये सब बच्चे के खिलौने हैं। मैं ये सारे खिलौने न लेकर तलवार और तीर कमान लेना चाहता हूँ और जंगल में जाकर भगवान राम की तरह ताड़का को मारना चाहता हूँ।

काव्यांश 5

तपसी यज्ञ करेंगे, असुरों-
को मैं मार भगाऊँगा
यों ही कुछ दिन करते-करते
रामचंद्र बन जाऊँगा।
यहीं रहूँगा कौशल्या मैं
तुमको यहीं बनाऊँगा।
तुम कह दोगी वन जाने को
हँसते-हँसते जाऊँगा।

पर माँ, बिना तुम्हारे वन में
मैं कैसे रह पाऊँगा।
दिन भर घूमूँगा जंगल में
लौट कहाँ पर आऊँगा।
किससे लूँगा पैसे, रूठूँगा।
तो कौन मना लेगा
कौन प्यार से बिठा गोद में
मनचाही चीजें देगा।

शब्दार्थ *तपसी-साधु, यज्ञ-हवन द्वारा करने वाली पूजा, असुर-राक्षस।*

संदर्भ/प्रसंग पूर्ववत्।

व्याख्या प्रस्तुत पंक्तियों में बालक कहता है कि वह असुरों को जंगल से मार भगाना चाहता है, जिससे तपस्वी अर्थात् साधु आसानी से यज्ञ कर सकेंगे। इस प्रकार एक दिन मैं, रामचंद्र और तुम कौशल्या बन जाओगी और मैं यहीं तुम्हारे साथ रहूँगा। बालक कहता है कि अगर माँ तुम मुझे वन जाने का आदेश दोगी तो खुशी-खुशी मैं वन भी चला जाऊँगा, लेकिन तभी बालक दु:खी हो जाता है और कहता है कि वह जंगल में अकेले नहीं रह पाएगा। दिनभर जंगल में घूमकर लौटकर कहाँ आऊँगा। वह कहता है कि वहाँ उसे पैसे देने वाला, मनाने वाला और गोद में बिठाकर मनचाही चीज़ें दिलाने वाला कोई नहीं होगा।

NCERT फोल्डर

कविता और तुम

1. तुम्हें किसी-न-किसी बात पर रूठने के मौके तो मिलते ही होंगे।

(क) अकसर तुम किस तरह की बातों पर रूठती हो?

(ख) माँ के अलावा घर में और कौन-कौन हैं, जो तुम्हें मनाते हैं?

उत्तर (क) जब पापा मुझे डाँटते हैं या जब मम्मी मुझे अधिक देर तक बाहर खेलने नहीं देतीं तो मैं रूठ जाती हूँ।

(ख) माँ के अलावा घर में मेरे पिताजी, दादीजी और बड़े भाई हैं, जो प्यार-दुलार देकर मुझे मनाते हैं।

2. हम ऐसे कई त्योहार मनाते हैं, जो बुराई पर अच्छाई की जीत पर बल देते हैं। ऐसे त्योहारों के बारे में और उनसे जुड़ी कहानियों के बारे में पता करके कक्षा में सुनाओ।

उत्तर ऐसे त्योहारों में दशहरा मुख्य है। इस दिन राम ने रावण का वध करके बुराई पर अच्छाई की जीत हासिल की थी।

3. तुमने रामलीला के जरिए या फिर किसी कहानी के जरिए रामचंद्र के बारे में जाना-समझा होगा। तुम्हें उनकी कौन-सी बातें अच्छी लगीं?

उत्तर रामचंद्र जी बहुत ही आज्ञाकारी पुत्र थे। वे अति बलशाली व शांत व मर्यादित स्वभाव के थे। उनका सबके प्रति प्रेम, दया, धैर्य, सहनशक्ति, वीरता व आदर की भावना आदि मन को मोहित करती हैं।

4. नीचे दिए गए भाव कविता की जिन पंक्तियों में आए हैं, उन्हें छाँटो

(क) खिलौनेवाला साड़ी नहीं बेचता है।

(ख) खिलौनेवाला बच्चों को खिलौने लेने के लिए आवाज़ें लगा रहा है।

(ग) मुझे कौन-सा खिलौना लेना चाहिए-उसमें माँ की सलाह चाहिए।

(घ) माँ के बिना कौन मनाएगा और कौन गोद में बिठाएगा।

उत्तर (क) कभी खिलौनेवाला भी माँ क्या साड़ी ले आता है।

(ख) नए खिलौने ले लो भैया ज़ोर-ज़ोर वह रहा पुकार।

(ग) कौन खिलौने लेता हूँ मैं तुम भी मन में करो विचार।

(घ) तो कौन मना लेगा कौन प्यार से बिठा गोद में मनचाही चीज़ें देगा।

5. 'मूँगफली ले लो मूँगफली!
गरम करारी टाइम पास मूँगफली!'

तुमने फेरीवालों को ऐसी आवाज़ें लगाते ज़रूर सुना होगा। तुम्हारे गली-मोहल्ले में ऐसे कौन-से फेरीवाले आते हैं और किस ढंग से आवाज़ लगाते हैं? उनका अभिनय करके दिखाओ। वे क्या बोलते हैं, उसका भी एक संग्रह तैयार करो।

उत्तर
- **कुल्फीवाला** ठंडी, मीठी, केसर, पिस्ते वाली कुल्फी लो।
- **कबाड़ीवाला** कबाड़ी .... पेपर, रद्दी, लोहा बेच ..... कबाड़ी वाला।
- **फलवाला** केला लो, सेब लो, अमरूद लो।
- **सब्जीवाला** आलू लो, प्याज लो, गोभी लो।

खेल-खिलौने

1. (क) तुम यहाँ लिखे खिलौनों में से किसे लेना पसंद करोगी क्यों?

गेंद	हवाई जहाज़	मोटरगाड़ी
रेलगाड़ी	फिरकी	गुड़िया
बर्तन सेट	धनुष-बाण	बल्ला या कुछ और

उत्तर मैं इनमें से गुड़िया लूँगी, क्योंकि मैं और मेरी बहन दोनों मिलकर गुड़ियाँ के साथ तरह-तरह के खेल खेलेंगे।

(ख) तुम अपने साथियों के साथ कौन-कौन से खेल खेलती हो?

उत्तर मैं अपने साथियों के साथ छुपन-छुपाई, पकड़म-पकड़ाई, खो-खो, बैडमिंटन आदि खेल खेलती हूँ।

2. खिलौनेवाला शब्द संज्ञा में 'वाला' जोड़ने से बना है। नीचे लिखे वाक्यों में रेखांकित हिस्सों को ध्यान से देखो और संज्ञा, क्रिया आदि पहचानो।

- पानवाले की दुकान आज बंद है।
- मेरी दिल्लीवाली मौसी बस कंडक्टर हैं।
- महमूद पाँच बजे वाली बस से आएगा।
- नंदू को बोलने वाली गुड़िया चाहिए।
- दाढ़ीवाला आदमी कहाँ है?
- इस सामान को ऊपर वाले कमरे में रख दो।
- मैं रात वाली गाड़ी से जम्मू जाऊँगी।

उत्तर • पान — संज्ञा
• पाँच — विशेषण
• दाढ़ी — विशेषण
• रात — विशेषण
• दिल्ली — संज्ञा
• बोलना — क्रिया
• ऊपर — क्रिया-विशेषण

तुम्हारी रामलीला

क्या तुमने रामलीला देखी है? रामलीला की किसी एक लघु-कहानी को चुनकर कक्षा में अपनी रामलीला प्रस्तुत करो।

उत्तर छात्र स्वयं करें।

कविता में कथा

इस कविता में तीन नाम- राम, कौशल्या और ताड़का आए हैं।

(क) ये तीनों नाम किस प्रसिद्ध कथा के पात्र हैं?

(ख) यहीं रहूँगा कौशल्या मैं तुमको यहीं बनाऊँगा।
इन पंक्तियों का कथा से क्या संबंध है?

(ग) इस कथा के कुछ संदर्भों की बात कविता में हुई है। अपने आस-पास पूछकर इनका पता लगाओ।
• तपसी यज्ञ करेंगे, असुरों को मैं मार भगाऊँगा।
• तुम कह दोगी वन जाने को हँसते-हँसते जाऊँगा।

उत्तर (क) राम, कौशल्या और ताड़का-ये तीनों नाम प्रसिद्ध रामायण कथा के पात्र हैं।

(ख) बालक स्वयं को राम और अपनी माँ को कौशल्या के रूप में देखता है, लेकिन वह राम की तरह वन जाने को तैयार नहीं है, बल्कि माँ कौशल्या के पास घर में रहना चाहता है।

(ग) • ऋषि-मुनि जब यज्ञ करते थे, तो राक्षस उनका यज्ञ भंग करते थे। श्रीराम ने उनका राक्षसों का वध करके ऋषि-मुनियों को निश्चिंत होकर यज्ञ करने में सहायता की।
• बालक अपनी माँ से कहता है कि यदि तुम मुझे जाने को कहोगी, तो मैं भी श्रीराम की तरह 14 वर्ष के वनवास पर चला जाऊँगा

अभ्यास प्रश्न

बहुविकल्पीय प्रश्न

1. पिंजड़े में कौन-सा पक्षी (खिलौना) बंद था?
(क) चिड़िया (ख) मोर
(ग) तोता (घ) कबूतर

2. खिलौनेवाले के पास कौन-से खिलौने का सेट था?
(क) कमरे का सेट (ख) टी-सेट
(ग) किचन-सेट (घ) गुड्डे-गुड़िया का सेट

3. बालक अपनी माँ से कितने पैसे लेता है?
(क) एक पैसा (ख) दो पैसा
(ग) तीन पैसे (घ) चार पैसे

4. बालक जंगल से किसको मार भगाना चाहता है?
(क) असुरों को (ख) ऋषियों को
(ग) पक्षियों को (घ) पशुओं को

5. खिलौनेवाले के पास क्या नहीं होती?
(क) रेलगाड़ी (ख) गुड़िया (ग) साड़ी (घ) बाण

उत्तर 1. (ग) तोता 2. (ख) टी-सेट
3. (घ) चार पैसे 4. (क) असुरों को
5. (ग) साड़ी

रिक्त स्थान भरें

नीचे दिए गए वाक्यों में रिक्त स्थान की पूर्ति उचित शब्द से कीजिए।

1. बालक जंगल जाकर भगवान राम की तरह ………… को मारना चाहता है।
2. साड़ियाँ तो ………… बेचनेवाले रखते हैं।
3. मुन्नू ने खिलौनेवाले से ……… और मोहन ने……… खरीदी।
4. सरला माँ से ………. लेने की जिद करती है।
5. बालक खुद को ………… और अपनी माँ को ………… बनाना चाहता है।

उत्तर 1. ताड़का 2. कपड़े 3. गुड़िया, मोटरगाड़ी
4. साड़ी 5. रामचंद्र, कौशल्या

सत्य–असत्य

नीचे दिए गए वाक्यों में से सत्य या असत्य कथन की पहचान कीजिए।

1. खिलौनेवाले के खिलौने सुंदर नहीं थे। (सत्य/असत्य)
2. खिलौनेवाले के पास छोटे-छोटे धनुष-बाण थे। (सत्य/असत्य)

3. बालक तीर-कमान लेना चाहता है। (सत्य/असत्य)
4. माँ ने बालक को वन भेज दिया। (सत्य/असत्य)
5. बालक बिना माँ के जंगल में रहने के लिए तैयार है। (सत्य/असत्य)

उत्तर 1. असत्य 2. सत्य 3. सत्य 4. असत्य 5. असत्य

काव्यांश पर आधारित प्रश्न

निम्नलिखित काव्यांश को पढ़कर उस पर आधारित प्रश्नों के उत्तर दीजिए।

तपसी यज्ञ करेंगे, असुरों–
को मैं मार भगाऊँगा
यों ही कुछ दिन करते-करते
रामचंद्र बन जाऊँगा।

यहीं रहूँगा कौशल्या मैं
तुमको यहीं बनाऊँगा।
तुम कह दोगी वन जाने को
हँसते-हँसते जाऊँगा।

1. तपसी क्या करेंगे?
(क) हवन (ख) यज्ञ (ग) पूजा (घ) आरती
2. बालक क्या बन जाएगा?
(क) तपसी (ख) रामचंद्र (ग) असुर (घ) तोता
3. बालक हँसते हुए कहाँ जाना चाहता है?
4. किन लोगों को तपसी कहा जाता है?

उत्तर

1. (ख) यज्ञ 2. (ख) रामचंद्र
3. बालक हँसते हुए वन जाना चाहता है।
4. वन में तपस्या करने वाले साधु को तपसी कहा गया है।

निम्नलिखित प्रश्नों के उत्तर दीजिए

1. कविता में आए बच्चों के नाम लिखिए।

उत्तर कविता में बच्चों के मुन्नू, मोहन, सरला नाम आए हैं।

2. खिलौनेवाले के पास चाभी से चलने वाला कौन-सा खिलौना है?

उत्तर खिलौने वाले के पास चाभी से चलने वाली सुंदर रेल है।

3. खिलौनेवाले के सभी खिलौने के नाम लिखिए।

उत्तर खिलौने वाले के पास, हरा तोता, गेंद, मोटरगाड़ी, रेलगाड़ी, गुड़िया, टी-सेट, लोटा-थाली, धनुष-बाण, तलवार खिलौने हैं।

4. बालक रामचंद्र क्यों बनना चाहता है? कारण सोचकर लिखिए।

उत्तर बालक रामचंद्र बनकर ताड़का को मारना चाहता है और असुरों को जंगलों से भगाना चाहता है।

व्याकरण संबंधी प्रश्न

1. प्रस्तुत काव्यांश में आए सर्वनाम शब्दों को रेखांकित कीजिए।

यहीं रहूँगा कौशल्या मैं
तुमको यहीं बनाऊँगा।
तुम कह दोगी वन जाने को
हँसते-हँसते जाऊँगा।
पर माँ, बिना तुम्हारे वन में
मैं कैसे रह पाऊँगा।
दिन भर घूमूँगा जंगल में
लौट कहाँ पर आऊँगा।
किससे लूँगा पैसे, रूठूँगा
तो कौन मना लेगा
कौन प्यार से बिठा गोद में
मनचाही चीज़ें देगा।

उत्तर मैं, तुमको, तुम, तुम्हारे, किससे, कौन

लेखन संबंधी प्रश्न

1. 'रामचंद्र जी' पर अनुच्छेद लिखिए।

उत्तर भगवान रामचंद्र जी को विष्णु का अवतार माना जाता है। भगवान विष्णु ने धरती पर असुरों के संहार के लिए त्रेता युग में श्रीराम के रूप में सातवें मानव अवतार के रूप में जन्म लिया था।

भगवान राम को मर्यादा पुरुषोत्तम कहा जाता है, क्योंकि उन्होंने अपने जीवनकाल में अनेक कष्टों को सहते हुए मर्यादित जीवन का सर्वश्रेष्ठ उदाहरण हमारे सामने रखा। विपरीत परिस्थितियों में उन्होंने अपने आदर्शों को नहीं त्यागा, इसलिए हिंदू धर्म में रामचंद्रजी को आस्था व निष्ठा के साथ पूजा जाता है।

अध्याय 4

नन्हा फ़नकार

पाठ का सार

दस साल का केशव अपने पिता की तरह पत्थर पर नक्काशी करने का काम सीख रहा था। पिता के बताने पर वह सीधी लकीरों वाले और घुमावदार डिजाइन तो बना लेता था, लेकिन उसे डिजाइन में सबसे ज्यादा कठिन काम घंटियाँ बनाना लगता था। उसे पूरा यकीन था कि एक दिन वह सब कुछ पत्थर पर उकेरने में सफल हो पाएगा।

केशव के माता-पिता उसके जन्म से पहले ही गुजरात से आगरा आकर बस गए थे। बादशाह अकबर उस समय आगरा का किला बनवा रहे थे और केशव के पिता को यहीं काम मिल गया था। एक दिन केशव को नक्काशी का काम करते हुए सुनाई दिया "माशा अल्लाह! ये घंटियाँ कितनी सुंदर हैं। ये तुमने खुद बनाई हैं?" केशव ने पीछे मुड़कर देखा, तो उसके पास एक आदमी (बादशाह अकबर) खड़ा था। केशव ने कहा– "क्या आपको मैं नक्काशी करता नज़र नहीं आ रहा?" वह आदमी केशव के पास पड़े पत्थर पर बैठ गया। वह आदमी मँझोले कद का था। उसने सफेद अंगरखा, पजामा तथा लाल रंग की पगड़ी पहन रखी थी। उसने गले में माला और उँगलियों में अँगूठियाँ भी पहनी हुई थीं। केशव उसके व्यक्तित्व का अंदाजा लगा ही रहा था कि तभी एक पहरेदार ने आकर केशव को सावधान किया।

केशव डर गया और उसके हाथ से छैनी छूटकर गिर गई। अकबर को यह दखलंदाज़ी अच्छी नहीं लगी और उन्होंने पहरेदार को इशारा करते हुए वहाँ से चले जाने के लिए कहा। अकबर ने नरम आवाज में केशव से नक्काशी सिखाने का प्रस्ताव रखा। केशव ने तुरंत सर हिलाया और भागकर अपने पिता से छैनी-हथौड़ा लेकर आ गया। अकबर केशव के पास जमीन पर बैठ गए, केशव ने उन्हें कोयले के टुकड़े से पत्थर पर लकीरें खींचकर दीं और गंभीरता से लकीरों को तराशने के लिए कहा। लकीरें काटते समय अकबर से कटाव ज्यादा गहरा होने पर, केशव ने तुरंत गलती पकड़ी और हल्के हाथ से वार करने के लिए कहा। केशव के काम करने के तरीके को देखकर अकबर ने कहा, "एक दिन तुम बड़े फ़नकार बनोगे, हो सकता है कि एक दिन तुम मेरे कारखाने में काम करो।" केशव ने मुस्कुराते हुए स्वीकार किया। रात को केशव ने अपने पिताजी से बादशाह का सीकरी में शहर बनवाने का कारण पूछा। पिताजी ने बताया कि जब बादशाह की कोई संतान नहीं थी, तब वह ख्वाजा सलीम चिश्ती के पास सीकरी आए थे। उन्होंने ही बताया था कि बादशाह के तीन संतानें होंगी। बादशाह ने ख्वाजा सलीम चिश्ती के सम्मान में सीकरी में नगर बसाने का फैसला किया था। केशव यह सुनते-सुनते सो गया।

शब्दार्थ

नन्हा-छोटा, फनकार-कलाकार, बुदबुदाना-धीरे से बोलना, नक्काशी-पत्थर पर चित्र उकेरना, किरचें-पत्थर के टुकड़े, उकेरना-उतारना, संगतराश-साथ में नक्काशी करने वाले, पुश्तैनी-खानदानी, आहट-आवाज, तल्खी से-खीझकर, जुर्रत-हिम्मत, साहस, बदहवासी-घबराहट, असमंजस-दुविधा, कुछ समझ में न आना, इत्मीनान-तसल्ली से, त्यौरियाँ चढ़ जाना-गुस्सा आ जाना।

NCERT फोल्डर

केशव की घंटियाँ

1. "माशा अल्लाह! ये घंटियाँ कितनी सुंदर हैं! तुमने खुद बनाई हैं?"
बादशाह अकबर ने यह बात किसलिए कही होगी?
(क) केशव के काम की तारीफ़ में।
(ख) यह जानने के लिए कि घंटियाँ कितनी सुंदर हैं।
(ग) केशव से बातचीत शुरू करने के लिए।
(घ) घंटियाँ किसने बनाईं, यह जानने के लिए।
(ङ) क्योंकि उन्हें यकीन नहीं था कि 10 साल का बच्चा केशव इतनी सुंदर घंटियाँ बना सकता है।
(च) कोई और कारण जो तुम्हें ठीक लगता हो।

उत्तर (ङ) क्योंकि उन्हें यकीन नहीं था कि 10 साल का बच्चा केशव इतनी सुंदर घंटियाँ बना सकता है।

2. केशव पत्थर पर घंटियाँ तथा कड़ियाँ तराश रहा था। उसके द्वारा तराशी जा रही घंटियों और कड़ियों का चित्र अपनी कॉपी में बनाओ। तुम्हें क्या कोई खास इमारत याद आ रही है, जिसमें नक्काशी की गई हो। संभव हो तो उसकी तस्वीर चिपकाओ।

उत्तर छात्र स्वयं करें।

आना-जाना

केशव के पिता गुजरात से आगरा आकर बस गए थे। हो सकता है तुम या तुम्हारे कुछ साथियों के माता-पिता भी कहीं और से यहाँ आकर बस गए हों। बातचीत करके पता लगाओ कि ऐसा करने के क्या कारण होते हैं?

उत्तर मेरी सहपाठी व मित्र स्नेहा के माता-पिता भी मध्य प्रदेश से दिल्ली आकर बस गए हैं। स्नेहा का अपने माता-पिता के साथ दिल्ली आकर बसने का कारण रोजगार की प्राप्ति था। वे अपने बच्चों को बेहतर शिक्षा दिलवाना चाहते थे। इसके अतिरिक्त एक स्थान से दूसरे स्थान पर बसने के अन्य कारण भी होते हैं; जैसे—स्थानांतरण की स्थिति, स्वास्थ्य सेवाओं की उपलब्धता, आधुनिक जीवन-शैली आदि।

कहानी से

3. अकबर को पहरेदार की दखलंदाजी अच्छी क्यों नहीं लगी?

उत्तर अकबर को साधारण व्यक्ति बनकर केशव से बात करने में आनंद आ रहा था, इसलिए उनको पहरेदार की दखलंदाज़ी अच्छी नहीं लगी।

4. 'लगता है कोई बहुत बड़ा आदमी है,' यहाँ पर 'बड़े आदमी' से केशव का क्या मतलब है?

उत्तर यहाँ पर 'बड़े आदमी' से केशव का मतलब किसी धनी, प्रतिष्ठित और प्रभावशाली आदमी से है।

5. 'खरगोश की-सी कातर आँखें' पशु-पक्षियों से तुलना करते हुए और भी बहुत-सी बातें कही जाती हैं; जैसे-'हिरन जैसी चाल।' ऐसे ही कुछ उदाहरण तुम भी बताओ।

उत्तर
- कोयल जैसी मीठी आवाज़
- शेर जैसी दहाड़
- गाय जैसा सीधापन
- घोड़े जैसा जिद्दीपन
- हाथी जैसी मस्त चाल

6. अकबर ने जब नक्काशी सीखना चाहा, तो केशव ने उन्हें संदेहभरी नज़रों से क्यों देखा?

उत्तर अकबर ने जब नक्काशी सीखने के लिए कहा, तो केशव को संदेह इसलिए हो रहा था, क्योंकि उसके हिसाब से एक बादशाह के पास नक्काशी का काम सीखने के अतिरिक्त अन्य अधिक महत्त्वपूर्ण कार्य होते हैं।

7. केशव दस साल का है। क्या उसकी उम्र के बच्चों का इस तरह के काम से जुड़ना ठीक है? अपने उत्तर का कारण जरूर बताओ।

उत्तर इस उम्र के बच्चों का इस तरह के काम से जुड़ना ठीक नहीं है। यह उम्र बच्चों की शिक्षा प्राप्त करने की होती है। इतनी कम उम्र में काम पर लग जाने के कारण बच्चों का मानसिक और शारीरिक विकास अवरुद्ध हो जाता है। अत: उसकी उम्र के बच्चों को पढ़ने का समुचित अवसर अवश्य मिलना चाहिए।

8. 'केशव बार-बार सबको सुनाता।'
केशव सबसे क्या कहता होगा? कल्पना करके केशव के शब्दों में लिखो।

उत्तर केशव सबसे यही कहता होगा "आज बादशाह अकबर मेरे पास आए थे। उन्होंने मेरे काम की बहुत तारीफ़ करते हुए मुझसे नक्काशी का काम सिखाने को कहा। मैंने उन्हें बहुत अच्छे से नक्काशी का काम भी सिखाया। सीखने के दौरान उन्होंने मुझे 'जी हुजूर' भी कहा। वे मुझसे बड़े प्रभावित थे।"

शब्दों की निराली दुनिया

1. (क) नक्काशी जैसे किसी एक काम को चुनो (बढ़ईगिरि, मिस्त्री इत्यादि), जिसमें औज़ारों का इस्तेमाल होता है। उन खास औज़ारों के नाम और काम पता करके लिखो।

(ख) छेनी, हथौड़ा, तराशना, किरचें-ये सब पत्थर के काम से जुड़े हुए शब्द हैं। लकड़ी के दुकानदार और बढ़ई से बात करके लकड़ी के काम से जुड़े शब्द इकट्ठे करो और कक्षा में उन पर सामूहिक रूप से बातचीत करो। कुछ शब्द हम यहाँ दे रहे हैं।

आरी, रंदा, बुरादा, प्लाई, सूत ....

(ग) हो सकता है कि तुम्हारे इलाके में इन चीज़ों और कामों के लिए कुछ अलग किस्म के शब्द इस्तेमाल होते हों। उन पर भी बातचीत करो।

उत्तर (क) बढ़ईगिरि में प्रयुक्त होने वाले औज़ारों के नाम हैं

- **इंच टेप** लंबाई नापने के लिए।
- **पेंचकस** पेंच कसने या निकालने के लिए।
- **हथौड़ी** लकड़ी/दीवार में कील ठोकने के लिए।
- **आरी** लकड़ी काटने के लिए।
- **रंदा** लकड़ी की घिसाई करने के लिए।

(ख) लकड़ी के काम से जुड़े कुछ अन्य शब्द हैं—पेंच, कुंडी, कीलें, सनमाइका, हैंडिल, हथौड़ी, छेनी आदि।

(ग) छात्र स्वयं करें।

2. 'कटाव' शब्द 'कट' क्रिया से पैदा हुआ है। नीचे लिखी संज्ञाएँ किन क्रियाओं से बनी हैं?
इन संज्ञाओं का अर्थ समझो और वाक्य में प्रयोग करो।

चुनाव, पड़ाव, बहाव, लगाव

उत्तर

संज्ञा	क्रिया	वाक्य
चुनाव	चुनना	इस मुश्किल काम के लिए मोना का चुनाव किया गया है।
पड़ाव	पड़ना	अगले पड़ाव पर मोहन ने डिब्बा बदल लिया।
बहाव	बहना	इस नदी का बहाव बहुत तेज़ है।
लगाव	लगना	बच्चों को बिल्ली से बहुत लगाव है।

3. 'लड़के ने जल्दी-जल्दी कोई प्रार्थना बुदबुदाई।' रेखांकित शब्द और नीचे लिखे शब्दों में क्या अंतर है? वाक्य बनाकर अंतर स्पष्ट करो।

फुसफुसाना, बड़बड़ाना, भुनभुनाना

उत्तर **बुदबुदाई** इतना धीरे बोलना कोई भी सुन न पाए।

- **फुसफुसाना** बहुत धीरे बोलना
  वाक्य उसने मेरे कान में अपनी गलती के बारे में फुसफुसाकर बताया।
- **बड़बड़ाना** गुस्से में कुछ-कुछ बोलना
  वाक्य नौकर से गलती होने पर दादाजी बड़बड़ाने लगते हैं।
- **भुनभुनाना** जली-कटी सुनाना
  वाक्य जो भी बोलना है, वह स्पष्ट बोलो, भुनभुनाओ नहीं।

4. "बेवकूफ, खड़ा हो। हुजूरे आला के सामने बैठने की जुर्रत कैसे की तूने! झुककर इन्हें सलाम कर।"

महल के पहरेदार ने केशव से यह इसलिए कहा, क्योंकि-

(क) बादशाह के सामने बैठे रहना उनका अपमान करने जैसा है।

(ख) पहरेदार यह कहकर अपनी वफ़ादारी दिखाना चाहता था।

(ग) पहरेदार को बादशाह के आने का पता नहीं चला, इसीलिए वह घबरा गया था।

(घ) बादशाह का केशव से बात करना पहरेदार को अच्छा नहीं लगा।

उत्तर (क) बादशाह के सामने बैठे रहना उनका अपमान करने जैसा है।

अभ्यास प्रश्न

बहुविकल्पीय प्रश्न

1. केशव की उम्र कितनी थी?

(क) दस वर्ष (ख) आठ वर्ष
(ग) सात वर्ष (घ) नौ वर्ष

2. केशव कौन-सा काम सीख रहा था?

(क) चित्रकारी का
(ख) रंगाई का
(ग) नक्काशी का
(घ) बुनकर का

3. केशव के पास नक्काशी सीखने कौन आया?

(क) बच्चे (ख) अकबर
(ग) लड़की (घ) पहरेदार

4. केशव के पिताजी किस राज्य से आकर आगरा बस गए थे?

(क) दिल्ली से (ख) बिहार से
(ग) गुजरात से (घ) महाराष्ट्र से

उत्तर 1. (क) दस वर्ष 2. (ग) नक्काशी का
3. (ख) अकबर 4. (ग) गुजरात से

गद्यांश पर आधारित प्रश्न

निम्नलिखित गद्यांश को पढ़कर उस पर आधारित प्रश्नों के उत्तर दीजिए।

गद्यांश

अकबर ने धीमे स्वर में कहा, ''केशव देखना एक दिन तुम बड़े फ़नकार बनोगे, हो सकता है कि एक दिन तुम मेरे कारखाने में काम करो जब मैं यहाँ कारखाना बनवाऊँगा, तो यहाँ पर सबसे बढ़िया फ़नकार और शिल्पकार, चित्रकार, बुनकर, संगतराश सभी शिल्पकार काम करेंगे।'' केशव मुस्कुराते हुए बोला, ''मैं वहाँ ज़रूर काम करना चाहूँगा।'' रात हो चली, केशव अपने पिताजी के बिस्तर में घुसते हुए पूछता है कि ''बादशाह का सीकरी में शहर बनवाने का क्या कारण है?'' पिताजी ने बताया कि ''जब बादशाह की कोई संतान नहीं थी, तब वह ख्वाजा सलीम चिश्ती के पास सीकरी आए थे। उन्होंने ही बताया था की इन्हें तीन संतानें होंगी।'' केशव यह सुनते-सुनते सो गया।

1. बादशाह अकबर ने केशव से कहा, तुम बड़े होकर .... बनोगे।

(क) चित्रकार (ख) फनकार
(ग) शिल्पकार (घ) संगतराश

2. बादशाह अकबर सीकरी में किसके पास गए थे?

(क) चित्रकार के पास (ख) ख्वाजा सलीम चिश्ती के पास
(ग) शिल्पकार के पास (घ) राजा के पास

3. बादशाह क्या बनवाना चाहता था?

4. कारखाने में कौन-कौन काम करेंगे?

उत्तर 1. (ख) फनकार
2. (ख) ख्वाजा सलीम चिश्ती के पास
3. बादशाह कारखाना बनवाना चाहता था।
4. कारखाने में फनकार, शिल्पकार, चित्रकार, बुनकर और संगतराश काम करेंगे।

निम्नलिखित प्रश्नों के उत्तर दीजिए

1. केशव के पिताजी क्या काम करते थे?

उत्तर केशव के पिताजी पत्थर पर नक्काशी करने का काम करते थे।

2. केशव क्या काम सीख रहा था?

उत्तर केशव अपने पिताजी से नक्काशी का काम सीख रहा था, जिसमें उसे पत्थर पर घंटियाँ उकेरने का काम कठिन लगता था।

3. बादशाह अकबर ने केशव से क्या कहा?

उत्तर बादशाह अकबर ने केशव से कहा कि ''एक दिन तुम बड़े फनकार बनोगे। हो सकता है कि एक दिन तुम मेरे कारखाने में काम करो।

4. केशव की त्यौरियाँ क्यों चढ़ जाती थीं?

उत्तर अकबर जब लकीरों को उकेर रहे होते हैं, तो उनसे जरा-सी भी चूक हो जाने पर केशव की त्यौरियाँ चढ़ जाती थीं।

अध्याय 5

जहाँ चाह वहाँ राह

पाठ का सार

इला सचानी छब्बीस साल की दिव्यांग महिला हैं, जो गुजरात के सूरत जिले में रहती हैं। इनके हाथ काम नहीं करते हैं। इस कमी को इन्होंने दिल से स्वीकार करते हुए अपने पैरों से काम करना सीखा। इन्होंने दाल-भात खाना, दूसरों के बाल बनाना, फर्श बुहारना, कपड़े धोना, तरकारी (सब्जी) काटना, तख्ती पर लिखना जैसे काम पैरों से करने सीखे। इला बच्चों के साथ खेल में भाग तो लेती थीं, पर खेल को पूरा नहीं कर पाती थीं। इला का खेलने को तो बहुत मन करता था पर हार मानकर एक तरफ़ बैठ जाती थीं। इला ने जब स्कूल में दाखिला ले लिया तो सभी को उनकी सुरक्षा व काम की गति की चिंता रहती थी, लेकिन जिस फुर्ती से इला कोई काम करती थीं, उसे देखकर सभी हैरान रह जाते थे। छोटी-छोटी परेशानी जरूर आती थी, लेकिन इला इन परेशानियों के आगे झुकने वाली नहीं थी।

इन्होंने दसवीं कक्षा तक पढ़ाई की, परंतु दसवीं की परीक्षा पास नहीं कर पाईं, क्योंकि वे निश्चित समय में लिखने का काम पूरा नहीं कर पाईं। यदि उन्हें यह मालूम हो जाता कि उन्हें ऐसे व्यक्ति की सुविधा मिल सकती थी, जो परीक्षा में उनके लिए लिखने का काम कर सके, तो शायद वह परीक्षा में असफल नहीं होतीं। इस बात का उन्हें अत्यधिक दु:ख है। इला की माँ और दादी कशीदाकारी करती थीं। वह उन्हें सुई में रेशम पिरोने से लेकर बूटियाँ उकेरते हुए देखती थीं। एक दिन इला ने भी अपने पैरों से कशीदाकारी करने की सोची। दोनों अँगूठों से सूई पकड़कर उसमें कच्चा रेशम पिरोना आसान कार्य नहीं था, लेकिन इला ने अपने धैर्य और विश्वास से इस काम को पूर्ण किया। पंद्रह-सोलह साल की होते-होते इला काठियावाड़ी कशीदाकारी में माहिर हो चुकी थीं। किस वस्त्र पर किस तरह के नमूने बनाए जाएँ, कौन-से रंगों से नमूना खिल उठेगा और टाँके कौन-से लगेंगे, यह सब वह अच्छी तरह समझ गई थीं और उनके द्वारा काढ़े गए परिधानों की प्रदर्शनी लगी। इन परिधानों में काठियावाड़ के साथ-साथ लखनऊ और बंगाल की कशीदाकारी की भी झलक दिख रही थी। उन्होंने पत्तियों को चिकनकारी से सजाया था तथा डंडियों को कांथा से उभारा था। प्रदर्शनी में आए लोगों ने उनकी कला की काफी प्रशंसा की। इस प्रकार, इला 'जहाँ चाह वहाँ राह' उक्ति पर खरी उतरती हैं। इला की कहानी यह बताती है कि परिस्थितियों के अनुसार ढलना और नए कौशल सीखना सफलता के लिए ज़रूरी है।

शब्दार्थ

टाँका-हाथ की सिलाई, अनूठी-बेमिसाल, अद्भुत, मिसाल-उदाहरण, घुटने टेकना-झुकना, कुदरत-प्रकृति, माहिर-निपुण, अव्वल, परिधान-पहनने का कपड़ा, प्रदर्शनी-नुमाइश, पारंपरिक-जिसका रिवाज काफी समय से चला आ रहा हो।

NCERT फोल्डर

जहाँ चाह वहाँ राह

1. इला या इला जैसी कोई लड़की यदि तुम्हारी कक्षा में दाखिला लेती तो तुम्हारे मन में कौन-कौन से प्रश्न उठते?

उत्तर यदि इला के समान कोई लड़की मेरी कक्षा में दाखिला लेती तो मेरे मन में तरह-तरह के प्रश्न उठते; जैसे— वह कपड़े कैसे पहनती होगी?, वह खाना कैसे खाती होगी? वह अपना गृहकार्य कैसे करती होगी?, वह अपने बाल कैसे बनाती होगी?

2. इस लेख को पढ़ने के बाद क्या तुम्हारी सोच में कुछ बदलाव आए?

उत्तर पहले मैं सोचती थी कि दिव्यांग व्यक्ति शारीरिक रूप के साथ मानसिक रूप से भी कमजोर होते हैं। उन्हें सहारे और सहानुभूति की जरूरत होती है।

वे खुद से कोई काम नहीं कर सकते, लेकिन अब मेरी सोच बिल्कुल बदल गई है। अब मैं उन्हें आत्मविश्वास और साहस से भरा पाती हूँ। वे हर कार्य में हमारी तरह ही सक्षम होते हैं और अपना कार्य कुशलतापूर्वक पूर्ण करते हैं।

मैं कुछ भी कर सकती हूँ

1. यदि इला तुम्हारे विद्यालय में आए तो उसे किन-किन कामों में परेशानी आएगी?

उत्तर उसे अपना बस्ता उठाकर आने-जाने में, किताबों के पन्ने पलटने में, अपनी कक्षा के साथियों के साथ झूला झूलने, खेलने आदि में परेशानी आएगी।

2. उसे यह परेशानी न हो इसके लिए अपने विद्यालय में क्या तुम कुछ बदलाव सुझा सकती हो?

उत्तर उसकी मदद के लिए बच्चे तैयार रहेंगे। उनके लिए लिखने का कार्य आदि में उसके सहपाठी मदद करेंगे। साथ ही विद्यालय में एक सहायक कर्मचारी नियुक्त किया जा सकता है, जो इला जैसे बच्चों के कार्यों में मदद करे।

प्यारी इला....

इला के बारे में पढ़कर जैसे भाव तुम्हारे मन में उठ रहे हैं उन्हें इला को चिट्ठी लिखकर बताओ। चिट्ठी की रूपरेखा नीचे दी गई है।

उत्तर

प्रीत विहार,

नई दिल्ली।

दिनांक 5 मार्च, 20XX

प्रिय इला,

तुम्हारी दृढ़ इच्छाशक्ति के लिए मुझे तुम पर गर्व होता है। तुम आत्मविश्वास से पूर्ण हो। तुम्हारी दृढ़ इच्छाशक्ति ने अपंगता को कभी अपने ऊपर हावी नहीं होने दिया। हाथों में जान न होने के बावजूद भी तुमने कशीदाकारी जैसी मुश्किल कला में निपुणता हासिल कर ली है। यह वास्तव में बेमिसाल है। तुम मेरे लिए प्रेरणा की स्रोत हो। भगवान तुम्हारे आत्मविश्वास और दृढ़ इच्छाशक्ति को बनाए रखें। जीवन में सदैव प्रसन्न रहना।

तुम्हारी

सुरभि

सवाल हमारे, जवाब तुम्हारे

1. इला को लेकर स्कूल वाले चिंतित क्यों थे? उनका चिंता करना सही था या नहीं? अपने उत्तर का कारण लिखो।

उत्तर स्कूल वाले उसकी सुरक्षा और उसकी अपंगता को लेकर चिंतित थे। उनका चिंता करना कुछ हद तक सही था। इला अपने सभी काम करने में समर्थ थीं, लेकिन स्कूल में उनके हिसाब से सुविधा का होना आवश्यक था। असुविधा ही चिंता का मुख्य कारण है।

2. इला की कशीदाकारी में खास बात क्या थी?

उत्तर इला अपनी कशीदाकारी में काठियावाड़ के साथ-साथ लखनऊ और बंगाल की झलक भी डालती थी। पत्तियों को चिकनकारी से सजाना, डंडियों को कांथा से उभारना, ज्यामितीय आकृतियों को कसूती और जंजीर से उठाना आदि। इला की कशीदाकारी में खास बातें थीं।

3. सही के आगे (✔) का निशान लगाओ।
इला दसवीं की परीक्षा पास नहीं कर सकी, क्योंकि

- परीक्षा के लिए उसने अच्छी तरह तैयारी नहीं की थी।
- वह परीक्षा पास करना नहीं चाहती थी।
- लिखने की गति धीमी होने के कारण वह प्रश्न-पत्र पूरे नहीं कर पाती थी।
- उसको पढ़ाई करना कभी अच्छा लगा ही नहीं।

उत्तर लिखने की गति धीमी होने के कारण वह प्रश्न-पत्र पूरे नहीं कर पाती थी।

4. क्या इला अपने पैर के अँगूठे से कुछ भी करना सीख पाती, यदि उसके आस-पास के लोग उसके लिए सभी काम स्वयं कर देते और उसको कुछ करने का मौका नहीं देते?

उत्तर यदि इला के आस-पास के लोग उसके लिए सभी काम स्वयं कर देते और उसको कुछ करने का मौका नहीं देते, तो वह अपने पैर के अँगूठे से कुछ भी करना सीख नहीं पाती।

कशीदाकारी

(क) इस पाठ में सिलाई-कढ़ाई से संबंधित कई शब्द आए हैं। उनकी सूची बनाओ। अब देखो कि इस पाठ को पढ़कर तुमने कितने नए शब्द सीखे।

उत्तर (क) कशीदाकारी, चिकनकारी, कांथा, जंजीर, कसूती, भरवाँ टाँका, बेल-बूटे

(ख) नीचे दी गई सूची में से किन्हीं दो से संबंधित शब्द (संज्ञा और क्रिया दोनों ही) इकट्ठा करो।

फुटबॉल, बुनाई (ऊन), बागबानी, पतंगबाजी

उत्तर (ख) **बागबानी** पौधे, खाद देना, पानी डालना, खुरपी

पतंगबाजी पतंग, मांझा, चरखी पकड़ना, पतंग उड़ाना

2. एक सादा रूमाल लो या कपड़ा काटकर बनाओ। उस पर नीचे दिए गए टाँकों में से किसी एक टाँके का इस्तेमाल करते हुए बड़ों की मदद से कढ़ाई करो।

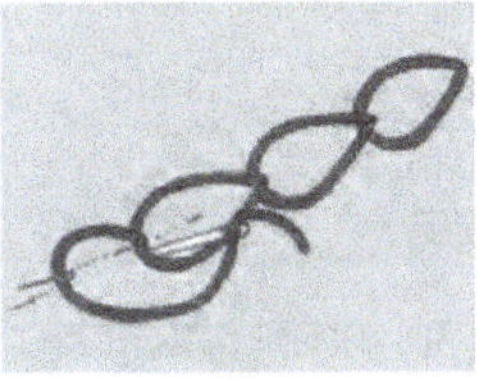
जंजीर

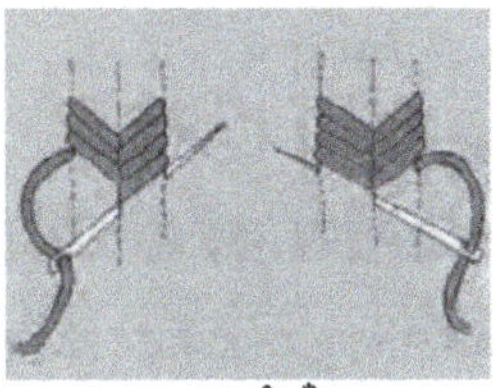
मछली टाँका

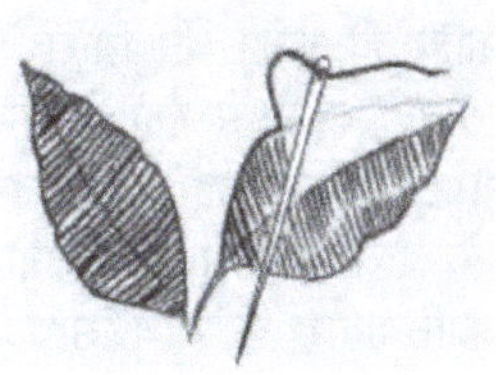
भरवाँ टाँका

उल्टी बखिया

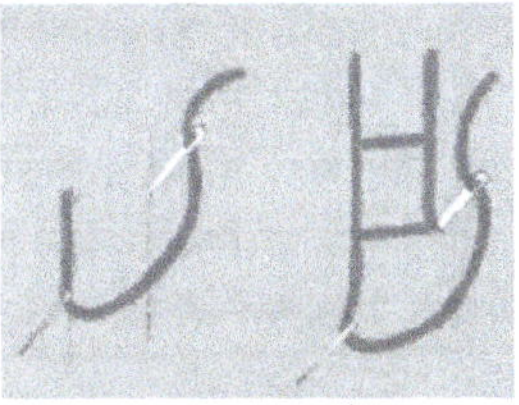
खुला हुआ जंजीर टाँका

ये काम कक्षा के लड़के-लड़कियाँ सब करें।

उत्तर छात्र स्वयं करें।

अभ्यास प्रश्न

बहुविकल्पीय प्रश्न

1. इला सचानी किस कारण से दसवीं कक्षा पास नहीं कर पाईं?

(क) लिखने की गति धीमी होने के कारण
(ख) परीक्षा न देने के कारण
(ग) रोल नंबर खो जाने के कारण
(घ) उपरोक्त में से कोई नहीं

2. इला सचानी अपने काम पैरों से क्यों करती थीं?

(क) क्योंकि उनके हाथ खराब थे
(ख) क्योंकि उनके पैरों में अधिक क्षमता थी
(ग) उन्हें पैरों से काम करना पसंद था
(घ) उपरोक्त में से कोई नहीं

3. इला कौन-से राज्य से हैं?

(क) दिल्ली
(ख) बिहार
(ग) गुजरात
(घ) राजस्थान

4. क्या कभी इला सचानी के काम की प्रदर्शनी लगी है?

(क) हाँ (ख) नहीं
(ग) शायद (घ) इनमें से कोई नहीं

5. इला के विश्वास और धैर्य को किसने झुठला दिया?

(क) सहपाठियों ने
(ख) मित्रों ने
(ग) परिवारजनों ने
(घ) कुदरत ने

उत्तर

1. (क) लिखने की गति धीमी होने के कारण
2. (क) क्योंकि उनके हाथ खराब थे
3. (ग) गुजरात
4. (क) हाँ ने
5. (घ) कुदरत ने

गद्यांश पर आधारित प्रश्न

निम्नलिखित गद्यांश को पढ़कर उस पर आधारित प्रश्नों के उत्तर दीजिए।

इला काठियावाड़ी कशीदाकारी में माहिर हो चुकी थीं। किस वस्त्र पर किस तरह के नमूने बनाए जाएँ, कौन-से रंगों से नमूना खिल उठेगा और टाँके कौन-से लगेंगे, यह सब वह अच्छी तरह समझ गई थी और बहुत जल्दी उसके द्वारा काढ़े गए परिधानों की प्रदर्शनी लगी। इन परिधानों में काठियावाड़ के साथ-साथ लखनऊ और बंगाल की भी झलक थी। उसने पत्तियों को चिकनकारी से सजाया था। डंडियों को कांथा से उभारा था। प्रदर्शनी में आए लोगों ने उसकी कला को काफी सराहा। इस प्रकार इला 'जहाँ चाह वहाँ राह' पंक्ति पर खरी उतरती है। इला की कहानी यह बताती है कि परिस्थितियों के मुताबिक ढलना और नए कौशल सीखना सफलता के लिए ज़रूरी है।

1. इला किस काम में माहिर हो चुकी हैं?

(क) काठियावाड़ी (ख) कशीदाकारी
(ग) चिकनकारी (घ) ये सभी

2. इला के बनाए परिधानों में काठियावाड़ के साथ-साथ किन राज्यों की झलक थी?

(क) लखनऊ और दिल्ली की (ख) पंजाब और बंगाल की
(ग) लखनऊ और बंगाल की (घ) महाराष्ट्र और बंगाल की

3. इला ने पत्तियों को किससे सजाया था?

4. इला की कहानी से क्या सीख मिलती है?

उत्तर

1. (घ) ये सभी
2. (ग) लखनऊ और बंगाल की
3. इला ने पत्तियों को चिकनकारी से सजाया था।
4. इला की कहानी से हमें यह सीख मिलती है कि जहाँ चाह होती है, वही राह होती है।

निम्नलिखित प्रश्नों के उत्तर दीजिए

1. इला सचानी अपने पैरों से घर के कौन-कौन से काम कर लेती हैं?

उत्तर इला सयानी अपने पैरों से घर के काम; जैसे—फर्श साफ करना, कपड़े धोना, तरकारी (सब्ज़ी) काटना आदि काम कर लेती थीं।

2. इला सचानी के दसवीं कक्षा पास न करने का क्या कारण था?

उत्तर इला सचानी दसवीं कक्षा की परीक्षा में दिए गए समय में लिखने का काम पूरा नहीं कर पाई थीं, इसी कारण वे परीक्षा पास नहीं कर पाईं।

3. इला की माँ और दादी क्या काम करती थीं?

उत्तर इला की माँ और दादी कशीदाकारी का काम करती थीं।

4. इला काठियावाड़ी कशीदाकारी में किस प्रकार माहिर हो चुकी थीं? लिखिए।

उत्तर इला ने धैर्य और विश्वास के साथ कच्चा रेशम पिरोने जैसा कठिन कार्य करना शुरू किया, जिसमें इला 15-16 साल की होते-होते काठियावाड़ी कशीदाकारी में माहिर हो चुकी थीं।

लेखन संबंधी प्रश्न

1. इला सचानी जैसे छात्र-छात्रा की मदद करने का विचार करते हुए दो सहपाठियों में हुई बातचीत को संवाद लेखन के रूप में लिखिए।

उत्तर

रीना कैसी हो नेहा?

नेहा मैं ठीक हूँ! तुम कैसी हो?

रीना मैं भी ठीक हूँ। क्या तुमने इला की परेशानियों को देखा?

नेहा हाँ, मुझे उसे देखकर दु:ख होता है, क्योंकि कई बार वह अपने काम स्वयं न कर पाने पर बेबस दिखाई देती है।

रीना हाँ, मुझे भी! तो क्यों न विद्यालय में हम एक समूह बनाएँ, जिसमें हर समय इला की सहायता के लिए एक छात्र उसके पास रहे।

नेहा तुम ठीक कहती हो, हमें उसकी हर तरह से मदद करनी चाहिए।

रीना तो चलो, सभी सहपाठियों से इस विषय पर बात करते हैं।

नेहा हाँ चलो।

अध्याय 6

चिट्ठी का सफ़र

पाठ का सार

संदेश को एक स्थान से दूसरे स्थान तक पहुँचाने के लिए हम पत्र का प्रयोग करते हैं। पत्र हमारे जीवन में महत्त्वपूर्ण भूमिका निभाते हैं। पत्र लिखने की परंपरा बहुत पुरानी है। इसके लिए कई बातों को ध्यान में रखना पड़ता है। पत्र जिसके लिए लिखा जा रहा है उस तक निश्चित समय पर पहुँच जाए, इसके लिए हम पत्र पर पता लिखकर डाक टिकट लगाते हैं। पते में सबसे छोटी भौगोलिक इकाई अर्थात् घर के नंबर के बाद गली-मोहल्ले का नाम, फिर गाँव, कस्बे, शहर के जिस हिस्से में है उसका नाम, फिर गाँव या शहर का नाम लिखते। शहर के नाम के बाद पिनकोड लिखा जाता है।

पिनकोड लिखने से स्थान का पता लगाने में डाक कर्मचारियों को मदद मिलती है, जिससे पत्र जल्दी बाँटे जा सकते हैं। पिनकोड की शुरुआत 15 अगस्त, 1972 को डाक तार विभाग ने पोस्टल नंबर योजना (Postal Index Number) अर्थात् 'पिन' शब्द के नाम से की थी। किसी भी स्थान का पिनकोड 6 अंकों का होता है। उदाहरण के लिए, पिनकोड 110016 में पहले स्थान पर दिया गया अंक अर्थात् 1 यह बताता है कि यह पिनकोड दिल्ली, हरियाणा, हिमाचल प्रदेश, पंजाब या जम्मू-कश्मीर का है। अगले दो अंक अर्थात् 10 यह बताते हैं कि यह दिल्ली (राष्ट्रीय राजधानी क्षेत्र) के उपक्षेत्र दिल्ली का कोड है। अगले तीन अंक अर्थात् 016 दिल्ली उपक्षेत्र के ऐसे डाकघर का कोड, जहाँ से डाक बाँटी जाती है।

प्राचीन समय में कबूतरों के द्वारा संदेश भेजे जाते थे। उस समय संचार और परिवहन के साधन बेहद सीमित थे। हरकारे पैदल चलकर आम आदमी तक चिट्ठी-पत्री पहुँचाते थे। राजा-महाराजा अपने संदेशों को भेजने के लिए घुड़सवार हरकारों का प्रयोग करते थे। आज भी भारतीय डाकसेवा जम्मू-कश्मीर के लद्दाख खंड में पद्म (जास्कर) जैसे अनेक स्थानों पर डाक पहुँचाने के लिए हरकारों पर निर्भर है। समय के साथ डाक सेवाओं में निरंतर बदलाव और विकास होता रहा है। आजकल संदेश भेजने के हवाई जहाज़, पानी के जहाज़ आदि नए और तेज़ साधन उपलब्ध हैं। डाक विभाग भी पत्र, मनीऑर्डर, ई-मेल, बधाई कार्ड आदि लोगों तक पहुँचा रहा है। यह सोचकर आश्चर्य होता है कि कबूतर जैसा पक्षी संदेशवाहक का काम कैसे करता होगा? केवल गिरहबाज या हूमर नामक प्रजाति को ही प्रशिक्षित करके डाक संदेश भेजने के काम में लाया जा सकता है। उड़ीसा पुलिस आज भी हूमर कबूतरों का प्रयोग राज्य के कई दुर्गम इलाकों में संदेश पहुँचाने के लिए कर रही है। कबूतरों की संदेश सेवा बहुत सस्ती है और उन पर खास खर्च नहीं आता है। इन कबूतरों का जीवन 15-20 साल होता है और ये 8-10 साल तक वे बहुत अच्छा काम करते हैं।

शब्दार्थ

गौर-ध्यान, भौगोलिक-भूगोल (स्थान) से संबंधित, संदेश-समाचार, गंतव्य-पहुँचने का स्थान, संग्रह-एकत्र या इकट्ठा करना, संदेशवाहक-समाचार ले जाने वाला, निरंतर-लगातार, जाहिर-स्पष्ट, हरकारे-पैदल चलकर एक स्थान से दूसरे स्थान पर समाचार ले जाने वाले लोग, दुर्गम-कठिन, प्रवासी-बाहर जाकर रहने वाले।

NCERT फोल्डर

चिट्ठी–पत्री

1. गाँधीजी को सिर्फ़ उनके नाम और देश के नाम के सहारे पत्र कैसे पहुँच गया होगा?

उत्तर गांधीजी देश-विदेश में प्रसिद्ध थे। वे किस समय में किस स्थान पर हैं, यह सभी को पता होता था। इस कारण उनको सिर्फ़ उनके नाम और देश के नाम के सहारे पत्र मिल जाता था।

2. अगर एक पत्र में पते के साथ किसी का नाम हो तो क्या पत्र ठीक जगह पर पहुँच जाएगा?

उत्तर हाँ, बिल्कुल पत्र ठीक जगह पर पहुँच जाएगा, क्योंकि नाम के साथ उसका पता भी लिखा जाता है।

3. नाम न होने से क्या समस्याएँ आती हैं?

उत्तर नाम न होने से पत्र किसका है, यह स्पष्ट रूप से पता नहीं चलता। यह भी संदेह रहता है कि उस आदमी की जगह किसी और के पास पत्र न पहुँच जाए।

4. पैदल हरकारों को किस-किस तरह की दिक्कतों का सामना करना पड़ता होगा?

उत्तर पैदल हरकारों को मुश्किल जगहों पर पहुँचना होता था। उन्हें डाक की रक्षा भी करनी होती थी। डाकू, लुटेरों या जंगली जानवरों की चपेट में आने जैसी दिक्कतों का सामना करना पड़ता होगा।

5. अगर तुम किसी को चिट्ठी लिख रहे हो तो पते में यह जानकारी किस क्रम में लिखोगे? गली/मोहल्ले का नाम, घर का नंबर, राज्य का नाम, खंड का नाम, कस्बे/शहर/गाँव का नाम, जनपद का नाम नीचे दी गई जगह में लिखो।

....

....

....

....

....

तुमने इस क्रम में ही क्यों लिखा?

उत्तर घर का नंबर

गली/मोहल्ले का नाम

खंड का नाम

कस्बे/शहर/गाँव का नाम

जनपद का नाम

राज्य का नाम

हमने पता इस क्रम में इसलिए लिखा, क्योंकि पता लिखते समय छोटी भौगोलिक इकाई से शुरू करके बड़ी की ओर बढ़ा जाता है।

6. अपने घर पर कोई पुराना (या नया) पत्र ढूँढो। उसे देखकर नीचे लिखे प्रश्नों का जवाब लिखो।

(क) पत्र किसने लिखा?

(ख) किसे लिखा?

(ग) किस तारीख को लिखा?

(घ) यह पत्र किस डाकखाने में तथा किस तारीख को पहुँचा?

(ङ) यह उत्तर तुम्हें कैसे पता चला?

उत्तर (क) यह पत्र दादाजी ने लिखा।

(ख) यह पत्र पिताजी को लिखा।

(ग) यह पत्र 15 जुलाई, 1992 को लिखा।

(घ) यह पत्र कश्मीरी गेट डाकखाने में 20 जुलाई , 1992 को पहुँचा।

(ङ) यह उत्तर मुझे पत्र पर लगी मोहर को देखकर पता चला।

7. चिट्ठी भेजने के लिए आमतौर पर पोस्टकार्ड, अंतर्देशीय पत्र या लिफ़ाफ़ा प्रयोग किया जाता है। डाकघर जाकर इनका मूल्य पता करके लिखो।

पोस्टकार्ड ....

अंतर्देशीय पत्र ....

लिफाफा ....

उत्तर **पोस्टकार्ड** एक रुपये
अंतर्देशीय पत्र पाँच रुपये
लिफाफा पाँच रुपये

8. डाक टिकट इकट्ठा करो। एक रुपये से लेकर दस रुपये तक के डाक टिकटों को क्रम में लगाकर कॉपी पर चिपकाओ। इकट्ठा किए गए डाक टिकटों पर अपने साथियों के साथ चर्चा करो।

उत्तर छात्र स्वयं करें।

शब्दकोश

नीचे शब्दकोश का एक अंश दिया गया है, जिसमें 'संचार' शब्द का अर्थ भी दिया गया है।

संगीतज्ञ संगीत जानने वाला, संगीत की कला में निपुण। **संग्रह** पु. 1. जमा करना, इकट्ठा करना, एकत्र करना, संचय। प्र. दीपक आजकल पक्षियों के पंखों का संग्रह करने में लगा है। 2. इकट्ठी की हुई चीजों का समूह या ढेर, संकलन; जैसे—टिकट संग्रह, निबंध संग्रह।	**संचार** पु. 1. किसी संदेश को दूर तक या बहुत-से लोगों तक पहुँचाने की क्रिया या प्रणाली, कम्युनिकेशन। उ. टेलीफ़ोन, टेलीविज़न, सेटेलाइट आदि संचार के माध्यमों से दुनिया आज छोटी हो गई है। 2. किसी चीज़ का प्रवाह, चलना, फैलना; जैसे—शरीर में रक्त क संचार, विद्युत का संचार।

(क) बताओ कि कौन-सा अर्थ पाठ के संदर्भ में ठीक है?

उत्तर किसी संदेश को दूर तक या बहुत-से लोगों तक पहुँचाने की क्रिया या प्रणाली, कम्युनिकेशन।

(ख) इस पन्ने को ध्यान से देखो और बताओ कि शब्दकोश में दिए गए शब्दों के साथ क्या-क्या जानकारी दी गई होती है?

उत्तर शब्दकोश में शब्द के साथ उसके भिन्न-भिन्न अर्थ, लिंग, वचन, पुरुष आदि जानकारियाँ दी गई होती हैं।

अभ्यास प्रश्न

बहुविकल्पीय प्रश्न

1. 'पिन' का पूरा नाम चुनिए।
   (क) पोस्ट इंडियन नंबर (ख) पोस्टल इंडेक्स नंबर
   (ग) पोस्ट इंडेक्स नंबर (घ) पोस्टल इंडियन नंबर
2. पिनकोड की शुरुआत कब हुई?
   (क) 11 अगस्त, 1972 को (ख) 15 अगस्त, 1972 को
   (ग) 26 अगस्त, 1972 को (घ) 15 अगस्त, 1970 को
3. कौन-सा पक्षी संदेशवाहक का काम करता है?
   (क) कौआ (ख) चील (ग) तोता (घ) कबूतर
4. कौन-सी प्रजाति के कबूतर का प्रयोग संदेशवाहक के रूप में किया जाता है?
   (क) गिरहबाज प्रजाति (ख) हूमर प्रजाति
   (ग) 'क' और 'ख' दोनों (घ) इनमें से कोई नहीं

उत्तर 1. (ख) पोस्टल इंडेक्स नंबर 2. (ख) 15 अगस्त, 1972 को 3. (घ) कबूतर 4. (ग) 'क' और 'ख' दोनों

सत्य-असत्य

नीचे दिए गए वाक्यों में से सत्य या असत्य कथन की पहचान कीजिए।

1. शहर के नाम के बाद पिनकोड लिखा जाता है। (सत्य/असत्य)
2. कबूतर पक्षी संदेशवाहक का काम नहीं करता है। (सत्य/असत्य)
3. समय के साथ डाक सेवाओं में निरंतर बदलाव और विकास होता रहा है। (सत्य/असत्य)
4. हरकारों को डाक की रक्षा नहीं करनी होती थी। (सत्य/असत्य)

उत्तर 1. सत्य 2. असत्य 3. सत्य 4. असत्य

रिक्त स्थान

नीचे दिए गए वाक्यों में रिक्त स्थान की पूर्ति उचित शब्द से कीजिए।

(छोटी, बड़ी, 6, डाक-घर, हरकारों)

1. पिनकोड .... अंकों का होता है।
2. पते में सबसे .... भौगोलिक इकाई लिखते हुए .... भौगोलिक इकाई की ओर बढ़ते हैं।
3. राजा-महाराजा अपने संदेशों को भेजने के लिए घुड़सवार .... का प्रयोग करते थे।
4. पिन कोड की जानकारी ...... से प्राप्त की जा सकती है।

उत्तर 1. 6 2. छोटी, बड़ी 3. हरकारों 4. डाक-घर

गद्यांश पर आधारित प्रश्न

निम्नलिखित गद्यांश को पढ़कर उस पर आधारित प्रश्नों के उत्तर दीजिए

गद्यांश

जब संचार और परिवहन के साधन बेहद सीमित थे, तब हरकारे पैदल चलकर आम आदमी तक चिट्ठी-पत्री पहुँचाते थे। आज भी भारतीय डाक सेवा जम्मू-कश्मीर के लद्दाख खंड में डाक पहुँचाने के लिए हरकारों पर निर्भर है। समय के साथ डाक सेवाओं में निरंतर बदलाव और विकास होता रहा है। आजकल संदेश भेजने के हवाई जहाज़, पानी के जहाज़ आदि नए और तेज़ साधन उपलब्ध हैं। बड़ी हैरानी की बात है कबूतर जैसा पक्षी संदेशवाहक का काम कैसे करता होगा। उड़ीसा पुलिस आज भी हूमर कबूतरों का प्रयोग राज्य के कई दुर्गम इलाकों में संदेश पहुँचाने के लिए कर रही है। कबूतरों की संदेश सेवा बहुत सस्ती है और उन पर खास खर्च नहीं आता है। इन कबूतरों का जीवन 15-20 साल होता है और ये 8-10 साल तक अच्छा काम कर लेते हैं।

1. भारत के किस स्थान पर आज भी डाक सेवा हरकारों पर निर्भर है?
   (क) जम्मू-कश्मीर के लद्दाख खंड में
   (ख) बिहार में
   (ग) उत्तराखंड में
   (घ) दिल्ली में
2. गद्यांश के अनुसार कौन-सी संदेश सेवा सस्ती है?
   (क) कबूतर द्वारा (ख) कौए द्वारा
   (ग) जंगली जानवरों द्वारा (घ) डाकघर द्वारा
3. उड़ीसा पुलिस आज भी किन कबूतरों का इस्तेमाल राज्य के कई दुर्गम इलाकों में संदेश पहुँचाने के लिए कर रही है?
4. आजकल संदेश भेजने के कौन-कौन से नए साधन उपलब्ध हैं?

उत्तर

1. (क) जम्मू-कश्मीर के लद्दाख खंड में
2. (क) कबूतर द्वारा
3. उड़ीसा पुलिस आज भी हूमर कबूतरों का इस्तेमाल राज्य के कई दुर्गम इलाकों में संदेश पहुँचाने के लिए कर रही है।
4. आजकल संदेश भेजने के हवाई जहाज़, पानी के जहाज़ आदि नए और तेज़ साधन उपलब्ध हैं।

निम्नलिखित प्रश्नों के उत्तर दीजिए

1. राजा-महाराजा अपने संदेश किस प्रकार पहुँचाते थे?

उत्तर राजा-महाराजा अपने संदेश घुड़सवार हरकारों के माध्यम से पहुँचाते थे।

2. भारतीय डाक सेवा आज भी दुर्गम व पहाड़ी इलाकों तक डाक पहुँचाने के लिए किस पर निर्भर है?

उत्तर भारतीय डाक सेवा आज भी दुर्गम व पहाड़ी इलाकों तक डाक पहुँचाने के लिए हरकारों पर निर्भर है।

3. क्या आधुनिक युग में पत्रों का महत्त्व कम हो गया है? सोच-विचारकर लिखिए।

उत्तर आधुनिक युग में पत्रों का स्थान ई-मेल, मैसेज, फैक्स आदि ने ले लिया है, किंतु पत्रों का महत्त्व कम नहीं हुआ। आज भी पत्रों को संदेश भेजने का सर्वोत्तम साधन माना जाता है।

4. पत्र के लिए पता क्यों ज़रूरी है?

उत्तर पत्र में पत्ते का होना व सही लिखा होना बहुत ज़रूरी है। इससे पत्र सही व्यक्ति के पास समय पर पहुँच जाता है तथा डाक बाँटने वाले कर्मचारियों को भी मदद मिलती है।

व्याकरण संबंधी प्रश्न

1. नीचे दिए शब्दों में से स्थानवाचक संज्ञा का चुनाव कीजिए।

कबूतर, संदेश, राजा-महाराजा, घुड़सवार, हरकारों, डाकू, लुटेरों, जंगल, संचार, परिवहन, जम्मू-कश्मीर, लद्दाख, हवाई जहाज़, पानी के जहाज़

उत्तर

1. जंगल, जम्मू-कश्मीर, लद्दाख

लेखन संबंधी प्रश्न

1. 'पत्रों के लाभ' विषय पर अनुच्छेद लिखिए।

उत्तर पत्र संचार का एक सुगम माध्यम है। पत्र के द्वारा कोई भी व्यक्ति अपनी बात को आसानी से लिखकर दूसरे व्यक्ति तक भेज सकता है। पत्रों को लंबे समय तक आसानी से सुरक्षित रखा जा सकता है। पत्र को कहीं भी व कभी भी पढ़ा जा सकता है। पत्र में निजता का भाव सुरक्षित रहता है। दूर स्थानों में जहाँ जाना संभव नहीं हो पाता, पत्रों के माध्यम से वहाँ अपनी उपस्थिति को स्थापित किया जा सकता है।

अध्याय 7

डाकिए की कहानी, कँवरसिंह की जुबानी

पाठ का सार

प्रस्तुत पाठ लेखिका 'प्रतिमा शर्मा' और डाकिए 'कँवरसिंह' के साथ की गई बातचीत के आधार पर लिखा गया है। शिमला के माल रोड पर स्थित जनरल पोस्ट ऑफिस में सुबह 11:30 बजे एक कमरे में डाक छाँटने का काम चल रहा था। यह काम दो पैकर और तीन महिला डाकिया कर रहे थे। वहीं पर सरकार से पुरस्कृत डाकिया कँवरसिंह जी भी थे। लेखिका कँवरसिंह से बातचीत करते हुए उनके व्यक्तिगत और पारिवारिक जीवन से संबंधित प्रश्न पूछती है। कँवरसिंह जी बताते हैं कि वह हिमाचल प्रदेश के शिमला जिले के नेरवा गाँव के रहने वाले हैं। उनकी उम्र पैंतालीस वर्ष है।

उनके चार बच्चे हैं, जिनमें तीन लड़कियाँ और एक लड़का है। एक लड़का और भी था, जो पहाड़ी से लकड़ी लाते समय गिरकर मर गया था। कँवरसिंह पहले भारतीय डाक सेवा में ग्रामीण डाक सेवक थे, लेकिन अभी वे पैकर के पद पर कार्यरत हैं। वे चिट्ठियाँ, रजिस्टरी पत्र, पार्सल, बिल, बूढ़े लोगों की पेंशन आदि बाँटने के लिए गाँव-गाँव जाते हैं। कँवरसिंह ने तीन साल लाहौल स्पीति जिले के किब्बर गाँव में, पाँच साल तक काज़ा में और पाँच साल तक किन्नौर जिले में नौकरी की थी। हिमाचल में एक गाँव से दूसरे गाँव की दूरी लगभग चार या पाँच किलोमीटर तक होती है। उन्हें डाक पहुँचाने के लिए लगभग 26 किलोमीटर रोज़ाना चलना पड़ता था। लेखिका ने जब कँवरसिंह से काम के दौरान हुई किसी खास बात का जिक्र करने को कहा तो उन्होंने बताया कि वर्ष 1998 में उनका तबादला शिमला के जनरल पोस्ट ऑफिस में हो गया था। एक दिन उन्हें रात के समय गेस्ट हाउस और पोस्ट ऑफिस की चौकीदारी का काम सौंपा गया। उसी रात 10:30 बजे किसी ने दरवाज़ा खटखटाया। दरवाज़ा खोलते ही पाँच-छः लोग अंदर घुस गए और उन्हें मारना-पीटना शुरू कर दिया, जिससे उनका सिर फट गया और वह बेहोश हो गए। यह घटना 29 जनवरी, 1998 की है। घटना के दौरान चिल्लाने की आवाज़ सुनकर आए उनके बेटे और अन्य लोगों ने उन्हें शिमला के इंदिरा गाँधी मेडिकल कॉलेज के अस्पताल में भर्ती कराया। इस हादसे के कारण उनकी एक आँख की रोशनी भी चली गई। उनकी इस बहादुरी के लिए सरकार ने उन्हें वर्ष 2004 में डाक की चीज़ें बचाने के लिए 'बेस्ट पोस्टमैन' का इनाम दिया। इस इनाम में ₹ 500 और प्रशस्ति-पत्र दिया गया। कँवरसिंह जी को इस बात का गर्व है कि वे 'बेस्ट पोस्टमैन' हैं।

शब्दार्थ

पुरस्कृत-जिसे पुरस्कार मिला हो, ग्रामीण-गाँव का/की, मुख्यालय-मुख्य कार्यालय, प्रशस्ति-पत्र-असाधारण उपलब्धियों के लिए मान्यता प्राप्त सम्मान।

अभ्यास प्रश्न

बहुविकल्पीय प्रश्न

1. कँवरसिंह जी के कितने बच्चे हैं?
   (क) एक (ख) दो (ग) तीन (घ) चार
2. कँवरसिंह जी कहाँ के रहने वाले हैं?
   (क) दिल्ली के (ख) हिमाचल प्रदेश के
   (ग) मध्य प्रदेश के (घ) बिहार के
3. कँवरसिंह जी का एक बेटा किस कारण मर गया था?
   (क) बीमारी के कारण
   (ख) लड़ाई के कारण
   (ग) पहाड़ी से लकड़ियाँ लाते समय गिरने के कारण
   (घ) तनाव के कारण
4. कँवरसिंह जी को इनाम में कितने रुपये मिले थे?
   (क) ₹ 400 (ख) ₹ 500
   (ग) ₹ 600 (घ) ₹ 700
5. कँवरसिंह ने किस घटना का होना असाधारण नहीं माना?
   (क) स्कूल का कई किलोमीटर दूर होना
   (ख) गाँव जाकर संदेश पहुँचाना
   (ग) तिरछी ढलानों से घास काटते हुए नीचे गिरकर मर जाना
   (घ) डाक सेवा का कार्य करना

उत्तर

1. (घ) चार
2. (ख) हिमाचल प्रदेश के
3. (ग) पहाड़ी से लकड़ियाँ लाते समय गिरने के कारण
4. (ख) ₹ 500
5. (ग) तिरछी ढलानों से घास काटते हुए नीचे गिरकर मर जाना

सत्य–असत्य

नीचे दिए गए वाक्यों में से सत्य या असत्य कथन की पहचान कीजिए।

1. कँवरसिंह जी सरकार से पुरस्कृत डाकिया हैं। (सत्य/असत्य)
2. 29 जनवरी, 1998 की घटना के दौरान कँवरसिंह जी की दोनों आँखों की रोशनी चली गई। (सत्य/असत्य)
3. कँवरसिंह जी को वर्ष 2004 में डाक की चीजें बचाने के लिए 'बेस्ट पोस्टमैन' का इनाम दिया गया। (सत्य/असत्य)
4. गाँव में डाकिया का लोग बहुत आदर-सम्मान करते हैं। (सत्य/असत्य)
5. कँवरसिंह जी को डाक का काम करना पसंद नहीं है। (सत्य/असत्य)

उत्तर 1. सत्य 2. असत्य 3. सत्य 4. सत्य 5. असत्य

रिक्त स्थान

नीचे दिए गए वाक्यों में रिक्त स्थान की पूर्ति उचित शब्द से कीजिए।
(ठंडे, ऊँचे, रोशनी, बेस्ट पोस्टमैन, खुशी, बस)

1. मनीऑर्डर पहुँचाने, नियुक्ति-पत्र का रजिस्टरी-पत्र पहुँचाने और पेंशन पहुँचाने पर लोगों का ………… भरा चेहरा देखकर उनको बहुत खुशी मिलती है।
2. किन्नौर और लाहौल स्पीति, हिमाचल प्रदेश के बहुत ………… तथा ………… जिले हैं।
3. हादसे के कारण उनकी एक आँख की ………… भी चली गई।
4. हमारे गाँव में अभी तक ………… नहीं पहुँच पाती है।
5. कँवरसिंह जी को गर्व है कि वे ………… हैं।

उत्तर 1. खुशी 2. ठंडे, ऊँचे 3. रोशनी 4. बस 5. बेस्ट पोस्टमैन

गद्यांश पर आधारित प्रश्न

निम्नलिखित गद्यांश को पढ़कर उस पर आधारित प्रश्नों के उत्तर दीजिए।

गद्यांश

एक दिन उन्हें रात के समय चौकीदारी का काम सौंपा गया। उसी दिन रात के 10:30 बजे किसी ने दरवाज़ा खटखटाया। दरवाज़ा खोलते ही पाँच-छः लोगों ने अंदर घुसते ही उन्हें मारना-पीटना शुरू कर दिया। इसके कारण उनका सिर फट गया और वह बेहोश हो गए। यह घटना 29 जनवरी, 1998 की है।

घटना के दौरान चिल्लाने की आवाज़ सुनकर आए उनके बेटे और अन्य लोगों ने उन्हें शिमला के इंदिरा गाँधी मेडिकल कॉलेज के अस्पताल में भर्ती कराया। इस हादसे के कारण उनकी एक आँख की रोशनी भी चली गई। उनकी इस बहादुरी के लिए सरकार ने उन्हें वर्ष 2004 में डाक की चीज़ें बचाने के लिए 'बेस्ट पोस्टमैन' का इनाम दिया। इस इनाम में ₹ 500 और प्रशस्ति-पत्र दिया गया। कँवरसिंह जी को गर्व है कि वे 'बेस्ट पोस्टमैन' हैं।

1. **दरवाज़ा खुलते ही कितने लोग अंदर घुस गए?**
   (क) दो-तीन
   (ख) चार-पाँच
   (ग) पाँच-छ:
   (घ) छ:-सात
2. **हादसे के बाद उन्हें कौन-से अस्पताल में भर्ती कराया गया?**
   (क) शिमला के इंदिरा गाँधी मेडिकल कॉलेज में
   (ख) दिल्ली के इंदिरा गाँधी मेडिकल कॉलेज में
   (ग) उत्तराखंड के इंदिरा गाँधी मेडिकल कॉलेज में
   (घ) उनका इलाज़ घर में हुआ
3. **सरकार ने उन्हें कौन-से साल में डाक की चीजें बचाने के लिए 'बेस्ट पोस्टमैन' का इनाम दिया?**
4. **कँवरसिंह जी के साथ मारपीट की घटना किस दिन हुई थी?**

उत्तर

1. (ग) पाँच-छ:
2. (क) शिमला के इंदिरा गाँधी मेडिकल कॉलेज में
3. सरकार ने उन्हें वर्ष 2004 में डाक की चीजें बचाने के लिए 'बेस्ट पोस्टमैन' का इनाम दिया।
4. कँवरसिंह जी के साथ मार-पीट की घटना 29 जनवरी, 1998 को की गई थी।

निम्नलिखित प्रश्नों के उत्तर दीजिए

1. **पाठ के आधार पर सोच-विचारकर लिखिए कि एक डाकिए का कार्य कैसा होता है?**

उत्तर डाकिए का कार्य बहुत कठिन होता है। उसे डाक पहुँचाने के लिए रोज कई किलोमीटर चलना पड़ता है। सर्दी, गर्मी, धूप की चिंता न कर उसे अपना कार्य पूरा करना होता है तथा उसका वेतन भी कम होता है।

2. **यदि घटना के बाद कँवरसिंह जी को किसी ने अस्पताल में भर्ती नहीं कराया होता, तो क्या हो सकता था?**

उत्तर यदि घटना के बाद कँवरसिंह जी को किसी ने अस्पताल में भर्ती नहीं कराया होता, तो शायद उनकी जान भी जा सकती थी।

3. **सरकारी डाक की चीजों को बचाने के लिए सरकार ने क्या किया?**

उत्तर उन्हें जान पर खेलकर सरकारी डाक की चीज़े बचाने के लिए 'बेस्ट पोस्टमैन' का इनाम दिया।

4. **गाँव में डाकिए का आदर व सम्मान क्यों हैं?**

उत्तर संचार के नवीन साधन आ जाने के बाद भी गाँव में आज भी संदेश पहुँचाने का सबसे बड़ा जरिया डाक ही है इसलिए गाँव में लोक डाकिए का बड़ा आदर व सम्मान करते हैं।

व्याकरण संबंधी प्रश्न

1. **'तबादला' शब्द का अर्थ लिखकर वाक्य बनाइए।**
2. **'मैं बेस्ट पोस्टमैन' हूँ।' इस वाक्य का पूर्ण हिंदी में अनुवाद कीजिए।**

उत्तर

1. 'तबादला' का अर्थ है— एक स्थान से दूसरे स्थान पर भेजना (स्थान बदलना)।
   वाक्य रोहन के पिताजी का दिल्ली में तबादला हो गया है।
2. मैं सबसे अच्छा डाकिया हूँ।

लेखन संबंधी प्रश्न

1. **महात्मा गाँधी सार्वजनिक पुस्तकालय, मेरठ के पुस्तकालय अध्यक्ष की ओर से एक सूचना जारी कीजिए कि जनता की माँग पर पुस्तकालय रविवार को पूर्वाह्न 11 बजे से अपराह्न 4 बजे तक खुला रहेगा।**

उत्तर

महात्मा गाँधी सार्वजनिक पुस्तकालय, मेरठ

सूचना

दिनांक 23 सितंबर, 20XX

पुस्तकालय के समय में बदलाव से संबंधित

समस्त जनसामान्य को सूचित किया जाता है कि आगामी गाँधी जयंती 2 अक्टूबर, 20XX से लोगों की माँग पर पुस्तकालय हर रविवार को पूर्वाह्न 11 बजे से अपराह्न 4 बजे तक खोला जाएगा।

रविकांत त्यागी
(पुस्तकालय अध्यक्ष)

अध्याय ४
वे दिन भी क्या दिन थे

पाठ का सार

प्रस्तुत कहानी भविष्य में होने वाले शिक्षा के तकनीकी बदलावों पर आधारित है। कहानी में कुम्मी और रोहित नाम के दो बच्चे हैं। कुम्मी अपनी डायरी में 17 मई, 2155 की रात को लिखती है कि रोहित को आज एक बहुत पुरानी पुस्तक मिली है। कुम्मी के दादा ने बताया था कि उनके समय में कहानियाँ कागज़ पर छपती थीं और पढ़ी जाती थीं। पुस्तक में पेज़ हुआ करते थे, जिन्हें पलटकर अगले पेज़ पर जाते थे।

रोहित ने कहा कि तब तो टेलीविज़न ही अच्छा है, जिसमें पुस्तक नई की नई रहती है। कुम्मी के पुस्तक के विषय में पूछने पर रोहित ने बताया कि उसे यह घर में रखे एक पुराने डिब्बे से मिली है। उस पुस्तक में स्कूल के बारे में लिखा था, लेकिन अब इस समय हर विद्यार्थी के घर में एक मशीन होती है। बच्चे इस मशीन के सामने बैठकर अपना पाठ याद करते हैं। गृहकार्य पूरा करके उसी मशीन में डाल देते हैं। उसी मशीन द्वारा बच्चों की परीक्षा भी होती है।

कुम्मी ने रोहित को मशीन से जुड़ी एक घटना के बारे में बताया। जब एक बार उससे भूगोल में गलतियाँ होने लगी थीं, तब एक आदमी ने आकर मशीन की गति को कुछ धीमी कर दिया था, जिससे कुम्मी से गलतियाँ होनी बंद हो गई थीं। रोहित ने कुम्मी को बताया कि पहले के ज़माने में मशीन की जगह अध्यापक होते थे, जो एक ही उम्र के बच्चों को पढ़ाते थे। जो बच्चों को सारे विषय समझाते, गृहकार्य देते और प्रश्न पूछते थे। सभी बच्चे पढ़ने के लिए एक खास भवन में जाते थे। यह सुनकर कुम्मी और उत्सुक हो गई। कुम्मी और अधिक जानना चाहती थी, लेकिन उसकी माँ ने उसे बुला लिया और दोनों अपने-अपने घर की ओर चले गए।

कुम्मी जैसे ही घर पहुँची, अंदर मशीन आगे की पढ़ाई कराने को तैयार थी। मशीन से आवाज़ आती है— आज तुम्हें सबसे पहले गणित सीखना है और कल का होमवर्क मशीन के छेद में डालो। कुम्मी सोचती है कि काश वो पुराने समय के स्कूल में जाती जहाँ सभी बच्चे हँसते-खेलते-पढ़ते हैं। ऐसे स्कूल में सभी बच्चे खुश रहते होंगे।

शब्दार्थ

पृष्ठ-पन्ना, पश्चात्-बाद, गृहकार्य-घर का कार्य, आरंभ-शुरू, भिन्न- अलग, उबाऊ-बोर करने वाला, रफ्तार-गति, उत्सुकता-जानने की इच्छा, सबक-पाठ, सिलसिला-क्रम।

NCERT फोल्डर

सोचो

1. कुम्मी के हाथ जो किताब आई थी वह कब छपी होगी?

उत्तर कुम्मी के हाथ जो किताब आई थी वह सदियों पहले छपी होगी।

2. रोहित ने कहा था, 'कितनी पुस्तकें बेकार जाती होंगी। एक बार पढ़ी और फिर बेकार हो गईं।' क्या सचमुच में ऐसा होता है?

उत्तर यदि पुस्तकों को पढ़कर उनको सँभालकर रख दिया जाए तो वे कभी बेकार नहीं होतीं, बल्कि पीढ़ी-दर-पीढ़ी पढ़ी जाती हैं। वहीं पुस्तकें बेकार होती हैं, जिनकी हम देखभाल न करके रद्दी वालों को दे देते हैं।

3. कागज के पन्नों की किताब और टेलीविजन के पर्दे पर चलने वाली किताब तुम इनमें से किसको पसंद करोगे? क्यों?

उत्तर मैं कागज़ के पन्नों की किताब को पसंद करूँगा, क्योंकि कागज़ के पन्नों की किताब को कभी भी कहीं भी पढ़ा जा सकता है। समय न होने पर या जरूरी काम आ जाने पर हम कागज़ के पन्नों को अपने अनुसार कभी भी पढ़ सकते हैं।

4. तुम कागज़ पर छपी किताबों से पढ़ते हो, पता करो कि कागज़ से पहले की छपाई किस-किस चीज़ पर हुआ करती थी?

उत्तर कागज़ से पहले की छपाई पत्तों, ताम्रपत्रों और लकड़ी पर हुआ करती थी और उससे भी पहले पत्तों, ताम्रपत्रों और लकड़ी पर स्वयं कलम द्वारा लिखा जाता था।

5. तुम मशीन की मदद से पढ़ना चाहोगे या अध्यापक की मदद से? दोनों के पढ़ाने में किस-किस तरह की आसानियाँ और मुश्किलें हैं?

उत्तर मैं कक्षा में अध्यापक की मदद से पढ़ना चाहूँगा, क्योंकि हम उनसे तुरंत प्रश्न करके उत्तर जान सकते हैं। मशीन द्वारा उत्तर प्राप्त होने से शायद मुझे संतोष न मिले, कार्य के बीच में बिजली चली जाए या अन्य किसी असुविधा के होने से उत्तर प्राप्त न हो पाए। साथ ही अकेले पढ़ने में आनंद भी नहीं आएगा।

'वे दिन भी क्या दिन थे'

बीते दिनों की प्रशंसा में कही जाने वाली यह बात तुमने कभी किसी से सुनी है? अपने बीते हुए दिनों के बारे में सोचो और बताओ कि उनमें से किस समय के बारे में तुम 'वे दिन भी क्या दिन थे!' कहना चाहोगे?

उत्तर छात्र स्वयं करें।

कल, आज और कल

1. वर्ष 1967 में हिंदी में छपी इस कहानी में कल्पना की गई है कि सालों बाद स्कूल की जगह मशीनें ले लेंगी। तुम भी कल्पना करो कि बहुत सालों बाद ये चीज़ें कैसी होंगी?
   - पेन
   - घड़ी
   - टेलीफोन/मोबाइल
   - टेलीविज़न
   - कोई और चीज़, जिसके बारे में तुम सोचना चाहो....

उत्तर छात्र अपनी कल्पना के आधार पर स्वयं करें।

2. नीचे कुछ वस्तुओं के नाम दिए गए हैं। बड़ों से पूछकर पता करें कि बीस साल पहले इनकी क्या कीमत थी और अब इनका कितना दाम है?

आलू, लड्डू, शक्कर, दाल, चावल, दूध

उत्तर

वस्तुओं के नाम	बीस साल पहले इनकी कीमत	आज के समय में इनकी कीमत
आलू	50-70 पैसे प्रति किग्रा	40-50 रुपये प्रति किग्रा
लड्डू	10-20 रुपये प्रति किग्रा	150-200 रुपये प्रति किग्रा
शक्कर	3-4 रुपये प्रति किग्रा	40-50 रुपये प्रति किग्रा
दाल	4-5 रुपये प्रति किग्रा	120-147 रुपये प्रति किग्रा
चावल	5-10 रुपये प्रति किग्रा	100-150 रुपये प्रति किग्रा
दूध	4-5 रुपये प्रति किलो लीटर	57-65 रुपये प्रति किलो लीटर

3. आज हमारे कई काम कंप्यूटर की मदद से होते हैं। सोचो और लिखो कि अपने व्यक्तिगत और सार्वजनिक जीवन में हम कंप्यूटर का इस्तेमाल किन-किन उद्देश्यों के लिए करते हैं?

उत्तर व्यक्तिगत

- मनोरंजन के लिए।
- रेल टिकट कटाने के लिए।
- संदेश भेजने के लिए।
- जानकारियाँ प्राप्त करने के लिए।

सार्वजनिक

- किसी भी सार्वजनिक कार्य के लिए; जैसे–गली-मुहल्ले की सफ़ाई हेतु सरकार को सूचना देना।
- किसी भी सार्वजनिक सूचना को जानने के लिए आदि।

जानकारी देने या लेने के लिए कई तरीके अपनाए जाते हैं। हम जो कुछ सोचते या महसूस करते हैं उसे अभिव्यक्त करने या बताने के भी कई ढंग हो सकते हैं। बॉक्स में ऐसे कुछ साधन दिए गए हैं, उनका वर्गीकरण करके नीचे दी गई तालिका में लिखो।

संदेश	अभिनय	रेडियो	नृत्य के हाव-भाव
फोन	विज्ञापन	नोटिस	संकेत-भाषा
चित्र	मोबाइल	टी.वी.	मोबाइल संदेश
फैक्स	इंटरनेट	तार	इश्तहार

ऊपर लिखी चीज़ें इकतरफ़ा भी हो सकती हैं और दो तरफ़ा भी। जिन चीज़ों के ज़रिए इकतरफा संप्रेषण होता है, उनके आगे (→) का निशान लगाओ। दो तरफ़ा संवाद की चीज़ों के आगे (↔) का निशान लगाओ।

उत्तर

जानकारी	भावनाएँ
संदेश, रेडियो, विज्ञापन, नोटिस, फोन, मोबाइल टी.वी., फैक्स, इंटरनेट, इश्तहार।	अभिनय, रेडियो, नृत्य के हाव-भाव, संकेत-भाषा, चित्र, मोबाइल संदेश, तार।

इकतरफा संप्रेषण (→)	दो तरफा संप्रेषण (↔)
चित्र, संकेत-भाषा, अभिनय, इश्तहार, विज्ञापन, रेडियो, नोटिस, टी.वी., तार, नृत्य के हाव-भाव	संदेश, फोन, फैक्स, मोबाइल, इंटरनेट, मोबाइल संदेश

तुम्हारी डायरी

- डायरी लिखना एक निजी काम या शौक है। तुम अपनी डायरी किसी और को पढ़ने को देते हो या नहीं यह तुम्हारी अपनी मर्जी है।
- कई व्यक्तियों ने अपनी डायरियाँ छपवाई भी हैं, ताकि अन्य लोग उन्हें पढ़ सकें। ऐसी ही कोई डायरी खोजकर पढ़ो और उसका कोई अंश कक्षा में सुनाओ।
- अपनी डायरी बनाओ और उसमें खुद से जुड़ी महत्त्वपूर्ण बातें लिखो।
- डायरी में तुम अपने स्कूल के बारे में क्या लिखना चाहोगे?

उत्तर मैं अपनी डायरी में अपने विद्यालय के वातावरण के विषय में लिखूँगा। विद्यालय में शिक्षक-शिक्षिकाएँ कैसे पढ़ाते हैं, दोस्तों का व्यवहार कैसा है, विद्यालय में कौन-कौन-सी सुविधाएँ उपलब्ध हैं। ये सभी बातें मैं अपनी डायरी में लिखूँगा।

तुम भी कल्पना करो

दोस्तों के साथ बात करके अंदाजा लगाओ कि 50 साल बाद इनमें क्या-क्या बदल जाएगा?

- फिल्मों में ....
- गाँव की हालत में ....
- तुम्हारी परिचित किसी नदी में ....
- स्कूल में ....

उत्तर
- फिल्मों में .... सिनेमा हाल की शायद ज़रूरत न पड़े, क्योंकि संभव है, किसी विशेष स्थान पर या सीधे मशीन पर देख सकें।
- गाँव की हालत में .... गाँव पहले से अधिक विकसित होंगे। गाँव में एक-से-एक नई तकनीक द्वारा खेती होगी।
- तुम्हारी परिचित किसी नदी में .... हो सकता है, यमुना नदी गायब हो जाए या उस नदी का जल स्वच्छ व निर्मल हो जाए।
- स्कूल में .... संभव है, स्कूल ऑनलाइन ही हो जाए। केवल खेल के दिन ही जाना पड़े।

था, है, होगा

1. असीमोव की कहानी 2155 यानी भविष्य में आने वाले समय के बारे में है। फिर भी कहानी में 'थे' का इस्तेमाल हुआ है, जो बीते समय के बारे में बताता है। ऐसा क्यों है?

उत्तर कहानी में 'थे' का इस्तेमाल इसलिए हुआ है, क्योंकि भूतकाल की घटना के लिए 'थे' का प्रयोग किया जाता है।

2. (क) 'जब मुझे बहुत डर लगा था ………… ' मैं जब छोटा था….' इस शीर्षक से जुड़े किसी अनुभव का वर्णन करो।

(ख) तुम्हें 'मैं' शीर्षक से एक अनुच्छेद लिखना है। अपने स्वभाव, अच्छाइयों, कमियों, पसंद-नापसंद के बारे में सोचो और लिखो। या किसी मैच का आँखों देखा हाल ऐसे लिखो मानो वह अभी तुम्हारी आँखों के सामने हो रहा है।

(ग) अगली छुट्टियों में तुम्हें नानी के पास जाना है। वहाँ तुम क्या-क्या करोगे, कैसे वक्त बिताओगे? इस पर एक अनुच्छेद लिखो।

तुमने जो तीन अनुच्छेद लिखे, उनमें से पहले का संबंध उससे है, जो बीत चुका है। दूसरे में अभी की बात है और तीसरे में बाद में घटने वाली घटनाओं का वर्णन है। इन अनुच्छेदों में इस्तेमाल की गई क्रियाओं को ध्यान से देखो। ये बीते हुए, अभी के और बाद के समय के बारे में बताती हैं।

उत्तर (क) मैं जब छोटा था तो एक बार सोया हुआ था। एक बार मम्मी को किसी ज़रूरी काम से पड़ोस में जाना पड़ा। गिलास गिरने की आवाज़ पर देखा तो सामने एक बड़ा बंदर बैठा था। मैं डर के मारे कुछ बोल नहीं पा रहा था, लेकिन वह बंदर दो मिनट बाद खुद ही चला गया। मैंने जल्दी से जाकर दरवाज़ा बंद कर दिया। मम्मी के आने तक मैं ज़ोर-ज़ोर से रोता रहा।

(ख) मेरा नाम वर्षा है। मैं अपने माता-पिता और एक छोटे भाई के साथ रहती हूँ। मैं स्वभाव से बहुत भावुक हूँ। किसी को दु:खी व परेशान देखकर उनकी सहायता करने में विश्वास रखती हूँ। मेरे इस स्वभाव के कारण स्कूल में सभी मुझे प्यार करते हैं। मुझे अकेले रहना अच्छा नहीं लगता। मुझे पेड़-पौधों से भी बहुत प्यार है।

(ग) अगली छुट्टियों में मैं अपनी मम्मी के साथ नानी के घर जाऊँगा। वहाँ पूरी छुट्टी रहूँगा। नानी का घर बहुत बड़ा और सुंदर है। नानी के घर में एक नीम का पेड़ है, जिस पर हम सब बच्चे मिलकर झूला झूलेंगे। कभी-कभी नानाजी के साथ सब्ज़ी खरीदने बाजार जाऊँगा और वहाँ से खाने की चीजें लाऊँगा। मेरी नानी मुझे अपने साथ मंदिर लेकर जाया करेंगी।

अभ्यास प्रश्न

1. प्रस्तुत पाठ में कुम्मी अपनी डायरी किस दिन लिखती है?
(क) 17 मई, 2025 (ख) 17 मई, 2155
(ग) 17 मई, 2024 (घ) 10 मई, 2155

2. रोहित को पुराने डिब्बे में क्या मिला?
(क) पुस्तक (ख) माचिस (ग) पेंसिल (घ) अखबार

3. कुम्मी और रोहित किससे पढ़ते हैं?
(क) पुस्तकों से (ख) मशीन से
(ग) नहीं पढ़ते हैं (घ) अध्यापक से

4. कुम्मी की मशीन को किसने ठीक किया?
(क) रोहित ने (ख) माताजी ने
(ग) अध्यक्ष ने (घ) आदमी ने

उत्तर 1. (ख) 17 मई, 2155 2. (क) पुस्तक 3. (ख) मशीन से 4. (घ) आदमी ने

सत्य-असत्य

नीचे दिए गए वाक्यों में से सत्य या असत्य कथन की पहचान कीजिए।

1. मशीन पर टेलीविज़न की तरह एक पर्दा होता था। (सत्य/असत्य)
2. रोहित को एक बहुत पुरानी पुस्तक मिली थी। (सत्य/असत्य)
3. पाठ के अनुसार 2155 में हर विद्यार्थी के घर में एक मशीन होती है। (सत्य/असत्य)
4. 'वे भी क्या दिन थे' कहानी सच्ची घटना पर आधारित है। (सत्य/असत्य)

उत्तर 1. सत्य 2. सत्य 3. असत्य 4. असत्य

रिक्त स्थान

नीचे दिए गए वाक्यों में रिक्त स्थान की पूर्ति उचित शब्द से कीजिए।
(अध्यापक, कागज़, बच्चे, मशीन)

1. कुम्मी और रोहित नाम के दो …………… हैं।
2. कुम्मी के दादा को उनके दादा ने बताया था कि उनके समय में कहानियाँ …………… पर छपती थीं।
3. गृहकार्य पूरा करके उसी ……… में डाल दिया जाता है।

4. रोहित ने कुम्मी को बताया कि पहले के जमाने में मशीन की जगह .... होते थे।

उत्तर 1. बच्चे 2. कागज़ 3. मशीन 4. अध्यापक

गद्यांश पर आधारित प्रश्न

निम्नलिखित गद्यांश को पढ़कर उस पर आधारित प्रश्नों के उत्तर दीजिए

गद्यांश

कुम्मी ने रोहित को मशीन से जुड़ी एक घटना के बारे में बताया, जब एक बार उससे भूगोल में गलतियाँ होने लगी थीं, तब एक आदमी ने आकर मशीन की गति को कुछ धीमी कर दिया था, जिससे कुम्मी से गलतियाँ होना बंद हो गई थीं। रोहित ने कुम्मी को बताया कि पहले के ज़माने में मशीन की जगह अध्यापक होते थे, जो एक ही उम्र के बच्चों को पढ़ाते थे, जो बच्चों को सारे विषय समझाते, गृहकार्य देते और प्रश्न पूछते थे। सभी बच्चे पढ़ने के लिए एक खास भवन में जाते थे। यह सुनकर कुम्मी और उत्सुक हो गई। कुम्मी और अधिक जानना चाहती थी, लेकिन उसकी माँ ने उसे बुला लिया और दोनों अपने-अपने घर की ओर चले गए।

1. **कुम्मी से कौन-से विषय में गलती होने लगी थी ?**
(क) हिंदी (ख) विज्ञान (ग) भूगोल (घ) गणित
2. **पहले के ज़माने में अध्यापक किन बच्चों को पढ़ाते थे?**
(क) एक ही आयु के बच्चों को
(ख) अलग-अलग आयु के बच्चों को
(ग) मेधावी बच्चों को
(घ) उपरोक्त में से कोई नहीं
3. **पुराने समय में सभी बच्चों को पढ़ाने के लिए क्या होते थे?**
4. **कुम्मी और रोहित की बातों को आप कितना समझे?**

उत्तर

1. (ग) भूगोल
2. (क) एक ही आयु के बच्चों को
3. पुराने समय में सभी बच्चों को पढ़ाने के लिए अध्यापक होते थे।
4. कुम्मी और रोहित भविष्य में रहते हुए पुराने समय की शिक्षा प्रणाली के बारे में बातें कर रहे हैं। उनको बड़ा ही आनंद आ रहा है ये सब बातें करते हुए।

निम्नलिखित प्रश्नों के उत्तर दीजिए

1. **कुम्मी और रोहित पुराने समय की शिक्षा से इतना प्रभावित क्यों हो रहे हैं?**

उत्तर कुम्मी और रोहित पुराने समय की शिक्षा से इसलिए प्रभावित हो रहे थे, क्योंकि उस समय कहानियाँ कागज पर छपती थीं और पढ़ी जाती थीं।

2. **कुम्मी की उत्सुकता का कारण क्या था?**

उत्तर कुम्मी की उत्सुकता का कारण भवन अर्थात् स्कूल था। उसे ज्ञात हुआ कि सभी बच्चे पढ़ने के लिए एक खास भवन में जाते थे। कुम्मी पुस्तक पढ़कर स्कूल के बारे में बातें जानकर उत्सुक हो रही थी।

3. **क्या आप कुम्मी और रोहित की तरह घर पर मशीन से पढ़ना चाहते हो?**

उत्तर नहीं, मैं कुम्मी और रोहित की तरह घर पर मशीन से नहीं पढ़ना चाहता, क्योंकि मुझे स्कूल जाकर अध्यापकों व अपने सहपाठियों के साथ पढ़ने में आनंद आता है।

4. **पुस्तकें नई-की-नई कब और कहाँ रहती हैं?**

उत्तर टेलीविज़न पर पुस्तकें नई-की-नई रहती हैं। टेलीविजन के पर्दे पर पुस्तकों की सामग्री आ जाती है। इसी कारण वह नई रहती हैं

व्याकरण संबंधी प्रश्न

1. **श्रुतिसम भिन्नार्थक शब्दों के अर्थ लिखिए।**

- उतर
- उत्तर
- मेला
- मैला

उत्तर
उतर — उतरना
उत्तर — जवाब
मेला — उत्सव
मैला — गंदगी

लेखन संबंधी प्रश्न

1. **आप अपने मित्र को पत्र लिखकर पूछिए कि उसे किस प्रकार से पढ़ाई करना पसंद है?**

उत्तर परीक्षा भवन,
दिल्ली।
दिनांक 25 अक्टूबर, 20XX

प्रिय मित्र,

सप्रेम नमस्कार।

आशा है तुम ठीक होंगे। मित्र मैंने एक कहानी पढ़ी, जिसमें मैंने मशीन से पढ़ाई करने के विषय में जाना। मुझे तो विद्यालय में पढ़ाई करना पसंद है। विघालय में सभी मिल-जुलकर पढ़ाई करते हैं व खेलते-कूदते हैं, साथ ही अन्य महत्त्वपूर्ण बातों को भी सीखते हैं। मशीन द्वारा की गई पढ़ाई ज्यादा प्रभावित नहीं होती। मित्र तुम्हारे विचार से शिक्षा किस प्रकार की होनी चाहिए? अपने विचार मुझे अवश्य अगले पत्र में लिखकर बताना। शेष अगले पत्र में।

तुम्हारा मित्र
क.ख.ग.

अध्याय ९

एक माँ की बेबसी

कविता का सार

प्रस्तुत कविता कुँवर नारायण द्वारा रचित है। इस कविता में एक ऐसे बच्चे की चर्चा की गई है, जो बोल नहीं सकता। उस बच्चे का नाम रतन है और देखने में वह अन्य सामान्य बच्चों की तरह ही लगता है। वह रोज बच्चों के साथ खेलने आया करता था। रतन जब खेलता था, तो उसकी माँ उसके आस-पास बैठी रहती थी, उसकी नज़र हमेशा रतन पर होती। वह रतन की सुरक्षा को लेकर परेशान रहती थी। कवि कुँवर नारायण को रतन की माँ का वह बेबस चेहरा भी याद आ रहा है। वे कहते हैं कि रतन से भी ज्यादा परेशान और चिंतित उसकी माँ रहती थीं।

काव्यांशों की व्याख्या

काव्यांश 1

न जाने किस अदृश्य पड़ोस से
निकलकर आता था वह
खेलने हमारे साथ
रतन, जो बोल नहीं सकता था
खेलता था हमारे साथ
एक टूटे खिलौने की तरह
देखने में हम बच्चों की ही तरह
था वह भी एक बच्चा।
लेकिन हम बच्चों के लिए अजूबा था
क्योंकि हमसे भिन्न था।

शब्दार्थ *अदृश्य–जो दिखाई न दे, अजूबा–विचित्र, भिन्न–अलग।*

संदर्भ/प्रसंग प्रस्तुत पंक्तियाँ हमारी पाठ्यपुस्तक 'रिमझिम भाग-5' में संकलित कविता 'एक माँ की बेबसी' से ली गई हैं। इन कविता को कुँवर नारायण द्वारा लिखा गया है। प्रस्तुत पंक्तियों में कवि द्वारा एक गूँगे बच्चे के विषय में बताया गया है।

व्याख्या कवि कहते हैं कि हमारे पड़ोस में रतन नाम का एक बच्चा रहता था, जो बोल नहीं सकता था। वह एक टूटे खिलौने की तरह हमारे साथ खेलता था। वह देखने में बिल्कुल हमारे जैसा लगता था, लेकिन फिर भी वह हमसे अलग था, इसीलिए हम बच्चों के लिए वह एक अजूबे जैसा था।

काव्यांश 2

थोड़ा घबराते भी थे हम उससे
क्योंकि समझ नहीं पाते थे।
उसकी घबराहटों को,
न इशारों में कही उसकी बातों को,
न उसकी भयभीत आँखों में
हर समय दिखती
उसके अंदर की छटपटाहटों को।

शब्दार्थ *इशारों-संकेतों, भयभीत-डरा हुआ, छटपटाहटों-बेचैनी।*

प्रसंग प्रस्तुत पंक्तियों में बच्चों का रतन से घबराने व उनकी छटपटाहट का वर्णन किया गया है।

व्याख्या हम सभी बच्चे रतन से थोड़ा घबराते भी थे, क्योंकि हम उसकी घबराहटों को कभी समझ नहीं पाते थे। वह इशारों में बहुत बातें कह देता था, पर हम उन्हें समझ नहीं पाते थे। रतन की आँखों में हमेशा एक भय व छटपटाहट का भाव रहता था। हम उसे भी समझ नहीं पाते थे।

काव्यांश 3

जितनी देर वह रहता
पास बैठी उसकी माँ
निहारती रहती उसका खेलना।
अब जैसे-जैसे
कुछ बेहतर समझने लगा हूँ
उनकी भाषा जो बोल नहीं पाते हैं।
याद आती
रतन से अधिक
उसकी माँ की आँखों में
झलकती उसकी बेबसी।

शब्दार्थ *निहारती रहती-देखती रहती, बेहतर-और अच्छा, झलकती-दिखती, बेबसी-लाचारी।*

प्रसंग प्रस्तुत पंक्तियों में कवि द्वारा गूँगे बच्चे रतन की माँ की बेबसी का वर्णन किया गया है।

व्याख्या कवि कहता है कि रतन, जो कि बोल नहीं सकता है, वह जितनी देर बच्चों के साथ खेलने आया करता है, उतनी देर उसकी माँ उसके पास बैठी रहती है। उसकी नज़र हमेशा खेलते हुए रतन पर होती थी। कवि कहता है कि तब वह छोटा बच्चा था और बहुत कुछ समझ नहीं पाता था। अब बड़ा हो गया है और समझदार भी। अब उसे रतन की भाषा समझ में आने लगी है। यह भी याद आने लगा है कि कैसे उसकी माँ बेबस आँखों से अपने गूँगे बच्चे को निहारती थी। रतन से भी ज्यादा बेबस तो उसकी माँ थी। बड़ा होकर कवि एक गूँगे बच्चे की माँ की पीड़ा को महसूस करने लगा है।

NCERT फोल्डर

कविता से

1. यह बच्चा कवि के पड़ोस में रहता था, फिर भी कविता 'अदृश्य पड़ोस' से शुरू होती है। इसके कई अर्थ हो सकते हैं; जैसे-

(क) कवि को मालूम नहीं था कि यह बच्चा ठीक-ठीक किस घर में रहता था।

(ख) पड़ोस में रहने वाले बाकी बच्चे एक-दूसरे से बातें करते थे, पर यह बच्चा बोल नहीं पाता था, इसलिए पड़ोसी होने के बावजूद वह दूसरे बच्चों के लिए अनजाना था।

इन दो में से कौन-सा अर्थ तुम्हें ज़्यादा सही लगता है? क्या कोई और अर्थ भी हो सकता है?

उत्तर (क) कवि को मालूम नहीं था कि यह बच्चा ठीक-ठीक किस घर में रहता था।

2. 'अंदर की छटपटाहट' उसकी आँखों में किस रूप में प्रकट होती थी?

(क) चमक के रूप में (ख) डर के रूप में
(ग) जल्दी घर लौटने की इच्छा के रूप में

उत्तर (ख) डर के रूप में

तरह-तरह की भावनाएँ

1. नीचे लिखी भावनाएँ कब या कहाँ महसूस होती हैं?

(क) छटपटाहट

- **अधीरता** कहीं जाने की जल्दी हो और जाना संभव न हो; जैसे-स्कूल की छुट्टी में अभी काफ़ी देर हो, पर घर पर ऐसा कोई मेहमान आने वाला हो, जिसे तुम बहुत पसंद करते हो।
- **इच्छा** किसी चीज़ को पाने की इच्छा हो, पर वह तुरंत न मिल सकती हो; जैसे-भूख लगी हो, पर खाना तैयार न हो।

- **संदेश** हम कोई संदेश देना चाह रहे हों, पर दूसरे समझ न पा रहे हों; जैसे-शिक्षक से कहना हो कि घंटी बज गई है, अब पढ़ाना बंद करें, पर उन्हें घंटी सुनाई न दी हो।

इनमें से कौन-सा अर्थ या संदर्भ इस बच्चे पर लागू होता है?

उत्तर 'छटपटाहट' के संदर्भ में 'संदेश' वाला अर्थ बच्चे पर लागू होता है। रतन अन्य बच्चों तक इशारों में अपनी बात पहुँचाना चाहता है, परंतु बच्चे उसके इशारों को नहीं समझ पाते हैं, जिसके कारण वह छटपटाहट महसूस करता है।

(ख) **घबराहट**

हमें जब किसी बात की आशंका हो तो घबराहट महसूस होती है; जैसे–

(क) अँधेरा होने वाला हो और हम घर से काफ़ी दूर हों या अकेले हों।

(ख) समय कम हो और हमें कोई काम पूरा कर लेना हो; जैसे– परीक्षा में देखा जाता है।

(ग) यह डर हो कि दूसरे के मन में क्या चल रहा है। जैसे–पापा को मालूम चल गया हो कि काँच का गिलास तुमसे टूटा है।

उत्तर घबराहट तब महसूस होती है, जब हम अकेले हों, किसी काम को पूरा करने के लिए समय कम हो या हमसे कोई गलती हुई हो।

2. **जो बच्चा बोल नहीं सकता, वह किस-किस बात की आशंका से 'घबराहट' महसूस कर सकता है?**

उत्तर जो बच्चा बोल नहीं सकता उसके इशारे को न समझते हुए उसे डाँटें या चिढ़ाने लगें तथा जब कोई उसी की उम्र का बच्चा उसे उसे चिढ़ाने लगे तब वह घबराहट महसूस कर सकता है।

3. **"थोड़ा घबराते भी थे हम उससे, क्योंकि समझ नहीं पाते थे उसकी घबराहटों को"**
   - रतन क्या सोचकर घबराता होगा?
   - अपने दोस्तों से पूछकर पता करो, कौन क्या सोचकर और किस काम को करने में घबराता है? कारण भी पता करो।

उत्तर रतन यह सोचकर घबराता होगा कि लोग मेरी बात को समझ पा रहे हैं या नहीं।

दोस्त/सहेली का नाम	किस बात से घबराता है?	घबराने का कारण
अमन	भीड़ से	कहीं भीड़ में खो न जाए।
रूपा	ऊँचाई से	ऊँचाई देखते ही चक्कर आते हैं।
मोहित	डॉक्टर से	कहीं डॉक्टर कड़वी दवा के साथ सुई न लगा दे।

भाषा के रंग

1. **कवि ने इस बच्चे को 'टूटे खिलौने' की तरह बताया है। जब कोई खिलौना टूट जाता है तो वह उस तरह से काम नहीं कर पाता जिस तरह से पहले करता था। संदर्भ के अनुसार खाली स्थान भरो।**

उत्तर

खिलौना	टूटने का कारण	नतीजा
गाड़ी	पहिया निकल जाने पर	चल नहीं पाती
गुड़िया	सीटी निकल जाने पर	बज नहीं पाती
गेंद	हवा निकल जाने पर	उछल नहीं पाती
जोकर	चाबी निकल जाने पर	नाच नहीं पाता

2. **'बेबस' शब्द 'बे' और 'वश' को जोड़कर बना है। यहाँ बे का अर्थ 'बिना' है। नीचे दिए शब्दों में यही 'बे' छिपा है। इस सूची में तुम और कितने शब्द जोड़ सकती हो?**

   बेजान बेचैन ....
   बेसहारा बेहिसाब ....

उत्तर बेजान बेचैन बेकार बेहोश
बेसहारा बेहिसाब बेईमान बेअसर

देखने के तरीके

1. **इस कविता में देखने से संबंधित कई शब्द आए हैं। ऐसे छः शब्द छाँटकर लिखो।**

उत्तर अदृश्य, देखने में, इशारे, निहारती, आँखों में, झलकती।

2. **'माँ की आँखों में झलकती उसकी बेबसी'**

   आँखें बहुत कुछ कहती हैं। वे तरह-तरह के भाव लिए हुए होती हैं। नीचे ऐसी कुछ आँखों का वर्णन है। इनमें से कौन-सी नज़रें तुम पहचानते हो?
   - सहमी नज़रें
   - प्यार भरी नज़रें
   - क्रोध भरी आँखें
   - उनींदी आँखें
   - शरारती आँखें
   - डरावनी आँखें।

उत्तर मैं इन नज़रों को पहचानता हूँ– प्यार भरी नज़रें, क्रोध भरी आँखें, उनींदी आँखें, शरारती आँखें।

3. **नीचे आँखों से जुड़े कुछ मुहावरे दिए गए हैं। तुम इनका प्रयोग किन संदर्भों में करोगे?**
   - आँख दिखाना
   - नज़र चुराना
   - आँख का तारा
   - नज़रें फेर लेना
   - आँख पर पर्दा पड़ना

उत्तर • **आँख दिखाना** गुस्सा दिखाना
पिताजी ने जैसे ही आँखें दिखाईं सोनू डर गया।
• **नज़र चुराना** सामने जाने से बचना
अध्यापक को देखते ही कुछ बच्चे नज़र चुराने लगते हैं।
• **आँख का तारा** प्यारा होना
रतन अपनी माँ की आँखों का तारा था।
• **नज़रें फेर लेना** अनदेखा करना
मतलब पूरा होते ही मोतीराम ने नज़रें फेर लीं।
• **आँख पर पर्दा पड़ना** सच नहीं जानना
मंजू की आँखों पर पर्दा पड़ गया है, उसे विनय का झूठ नहीं दिखता।

माँ

'याद आती रतन से अधिक उसकी माँ की आँखों में झलकती उसकी बेबसी'

1. **रतन की माँ की आँखों में किस तरह की बेबसी झलकती होगी?**

उत्तर अपने बेटे को बोल सकने में असमर्थ देखकर।

2. **अपनी माँ के बारे में सोचते हुए नीचे लिखे वाक्यों को पूरा करो**

(क) मेरी माँ बहुत खुश होती हैं, जब
(ख) माँ मुझे इसलिए डाँटती हैं, क्योंकि
(ग) मेरी माँ चाहती हैं कि मैं
(घ) माँ उस समय बहुत बेबस हो जाती हैं, जब
(ङ) मैं चाहती/ता हूँ कि मेरी माँ

उत्तर (क) **मेरी माँ बहुत खुश होती हैं, जब** मैं अच्छे अंकों से पास होता हूँ।
(ख) **माँ मुझे इसलिए डाँटती हैं, क्योंकि** मैं वही गलती बार-बार करता हूँ।
(ग) **मेरी माँ चाहती हैं कि मैं** समझदार इंसान बन जाऊँ।
(घ) **माँ उस समय बहुत बेबस हो जाती हैं जब** मैं बीमार पड़ जाता हूँ।
(ङ) **मैं चाहती/ता हूँ कि मेरी माँ** हमेशा मेरे साथ रहे।

अभ्यास प्रश्न

बहुविकल्पीय प्रश्न

1. **रतन किस काम में असमर्थ था?**
(क) चलने में (ख) पढ़ने में (ग) बोलने में (घ) रोने में

2. **प्रस्तुत कविता 'एक माँ की बेबसी' किस कवि द्वारा रचित है?**
(क) महादेवी द्वारा (ख) प्रेमचंद द्वारा
(ग) कुँवर नारायण द्वारा (घ) जयशंकर द्वारा

3. **कवि को रतन की माँ की आँखों में क्या दिखता/दिखती है?**
(क) प्यार (ख) दुलार (ग) बेबसी (घ) गुस्सा

4. **रतन दूसरे बच्चों के लिए अजूबा क्यों था?**
(क) क्योंकि वे उसकी छटपटाहट समझ नहीं पाते थे
(ख) क्योंकि रतन कारीगर था
(ग) क्योंकि रतन जादूगर था
(घ) उपरोक्त में से कोई नहीं

5. **रतन के बोल न पाने से वह अन्य बच्चों के लिए क्या था?**
(क) बेबस (ख) अजूबा
(ग) लाचार (घ) आत्म-विश्वास

उत्तर 1. (ग) बोलने में
2. (ग) कुँवर नारायण द्वारा
3. (ग) बेबसी
4. (क) क्योंकि वे उसकी छटपटाहट समझ नहीं पाते थे
5. (ख) अजूबा

काव्यांश पर आधारित प्रश्न

निम्नलिखित काव्यांश को पढ़कर उस पर आधारित प्रश्नों के उत्तर दीजिए।

काव्यांश

जितनी देर वह रहता
पास बैठी उसकी माँ
निहारती रहती उसका खेलना।
अब जैसे-जैसे
कुछ बेहतर समझने लगा हूँ
उनकी भाषा जो बोल नहीं पाते हैं।
याद आती
रतन से अधिक
उसकी माँ की आँखों में
झलकती उसकी बेबसी।

1. **जितनी देर रतन खेलता उसे कौन निहारता रहता था?**

(क) रतन की माँ (ख) पड़ोस के बच्चे

(ग) कवि (घ) इनमें से कोई नहीं

2. **रतन से ज्यादा बेबस कौन है?**

(क) रतन की माँ

(ख) कवि

(ग) अन्य बच्चे

(घ) उपरोक्त में से कोई नहीं

3. **कवि क्या और क्यों समझने लगा है?**

4. **रतन जितनी देर खेलता उसकी माँ उसके आस-पास ही बैठी रहती। क्यों?**

उत्तर 1. (क) रतन की माँ

2. (क) रतन की माँ

3. कवि रतन की माँ की बेबसी समझने लगा है, क्योंकि अभी कवि बड़ा हो गया है।

4. रतन की माँ उसके आस-पास ही बैठी रहती थीं, क्योंकि उनको रतन की सुरक्षा की चिंता थी।

निम्नलिखित प्रश्नों के उत्तर दीजिए

1. **यदि आपके आस-पास रतन जैसा बच्चा हो तो आप क्या करेंगे?**

उत्तर यदि हमारे आस-पास रतन जैसा बच्चा होगा तो हम उसकी सुविधा के लिए उसे साधन उपलब्ध कराएँगे, उसके साथ खेलेंगे, हम उसे असुरक्षित व असहाय महसूस नहीं होने देंगे।

2. **रतन की माँ रतन की बातों को किस प्रकार से समझती होंगी?**

उत्तर रतन की माँ रतन की बातों को इशारों से समझती होंगी।

3. **रतन की आँखों में भय किस कारण था?**

उत्तर रतन की आँखों में भय इसलिए था, क्योंकि वह सामान्य बच्चों से अलग था। वह बोल नहीं सकता था, जिससे बच्चे उससे डरते थे व उसकी बातों को समझ नहीं सकते थे।

4. **देखने में रतन कैसा था?**

उत्तर देखने में रतन बिल्कुल सामान्य बच्चों की तरह था।

लेखन संबंधी प्रश्न

1. **दिए गए चित्र को ध्यानपूर्वक देखकर अपनी भाषा में चित्र वर्णन कीजिए**

उत्तर प्रस्तुत चित्र समुद्र किनारे का एक दृश्य है। समुद्र का जल स्वच्छ एवं शांत है। छोटी-छोटी लहरें किनारे से टकरा रही हैं। समुद्र का किनारा अत्यंत स्वच्छ है। आसमान में बादल छाए हैं। दो पक्षी वहाँ उड़ रहे हैं। समुद्र के किनारे दो बच्चे खेल रहे हैं। बच्चों के पास बाल्टी व मिट्टी उठाने का औजार है। बच्चा समुद्र के किनारे की मिट्टी से किला बना रहा है तथा बच्ची किले पर झंडा लगा रही है। बच्चे के पास एक बॉल रखी है।

अध्याय 10

एक दिन की बादशाहत

पाठ का सार

आरिफ़ और सलीम दोनों बच्चे अपने घरवालों की पाबंदियों से बहुत परेशान हैं। एक दिन दोनों बच्चों को एक तरकीब सूझी। उन्होंने अपने अब्बा के सामने दरखास्त पेश की कि उन्हें एक दिन के लिए बड़ों के अधिकार दे दिए जाएँ और सब छोटे बन जाएँ। अब्बा अच्छे मूड में थे, इसलिए उन्होंने बच्चों को बड़ों के अधिकार दे दिए। सुबह होने में थोड़ा समय था, आरिफ़ ने अम्मी को झिंझोड़ डाला, 'अम्मी, जल्दी उठिए, नाश्ता तैयार कीजिए!' अम्मी को गुस्सा तो बहुत आया, लेकिन उस दिन के लिए उनके सारे अधिकार छीने जा चुके थे। अब दादी की बारी थी। जैसे ही उन्होंने बादाम का हरीरा पीना शुरू किया, आरिफ़ ने उन्हें रोका, "दादी! कितना हरीरा पिएँगी आप ...... पेट फट जाएगा!" इसी प्रकार आरिफ़ ने खानसामे को आदेश देकर अपने सामने अंडे और मक्खन रखवाया और घर के बाकी सदस्यों को दलिया और दूध-बिस्कुट देने को कहा। खाने के समय सलीम ने अम्मी को पान के गंदे दाँतों के लिए टोका।

सलीम अब्बा की तरफ़ मुड़कर बोला, "···· बाल बढ़े हुए, शेव की नहीं, कल कपड़े पहने थे और आज इतने मैले कर डाले!" यह सुनकर अब्बा को हँसी आ गई, क्योंकि दोनों बच्चे बड़ों की सही नकल उतार रहे थे। दस बजते ही आरिफ़ चिल्लाने लगा, 'अब्बा, जल्दी ऑफिस जाइए।' थोड़ी देर बाद खानसामा बेगम से खाना बनाने के विषय में पूछने आए, तो उन्होंने खानसामे को आदेश देना शुरू कर दिया, "आलू, गोश्त ······· तभी सलीम तुरंत आगे बढ़कर अम्मी की नकल उतारते हुए बोला, आज ये चीजें नहीं पकेंगी! आज गुलाब जामुन, गाजर का हलवा और मीठे चावल पकाओ!" इसी समय दादी के किसी से तू-तू, मैं-मैं करने पर उन्होंने रोक दिया।

कॉलेज का समय हो जाने पर भाईजान के शाम को देर से आने व दोस्तों के साथ फिल्म देखने जाने का कहने पर उन्हें धमकाया। तभी बच्चों की नज़र आपा पर पड़ गई। सलीम उनका गौर से मुआयना करके बोला, "इतनी भारी साड़ी क्यों पहनी? शाम तक गारत हो आएगी।····· आज वह सफ़ेद वॉयल की साड़ी पहनना।" आपा ने कहा, 'हमारे कॉलेज में आज फंक्शन है।" "हुआ करे ... मैं क्या कह रहा हूँ ····· सुना नहीं ····· ?" अपनी इतनी अच्छी नकल देखकर आपा शर्मिंदा हो गईं।

अगले दिन सुबह सलीम की आँख खुली तो आपा नाश्ते की मेज सज़ाए उन दोनों के उठने का इंतज़ार कर रही थी। अम्मी ने खानसामे को हर खाने के साथ एक मीठी चीज़ बनाने का आदेश दे दिया। अब्बा का भी रुख अब बदल गया था। अब्बा सलीम से कह रहे थे। स्कूल जाते एक चवन्नी जेब में डाल लिया करो क्या हर्ज़ है......।

शब्दार्थ

पाबंदी-रोक, तकरार-झगड़ा, तरकीबें-उपाय, खिदमत में-सेवा में, दरखास्त-अर्जी, ऊधम मचाना-शोर मचाना, झापड़ रसीद करना-थप्पड़ मारना, गुसलखाना-स्नानघर, गत-दशा, तुनककर-गुस्सा कर, खून का घूँट पीकर रह जाना-गुस्सा दबा लेना, निहायत-बिल्कुल, हुक्म-आदेश, हर्ज-नुकसान।

NCERT फोल्डर

कहानी की बात

1. अब्बा ने क्या सोचकर आरिफ़ की बात मान ली?

उत्तर अब्बा ने सोचा होगा कि कभी-कभी बच्चों की बात भी मान लेनी चाहिए। वे देखना चाहते थे कि बच्चे किस प्रकार घर को सँभालते हैं।

2. वह एक दिन बहुत अनोखा था जब बच्चों को बड़ों के अधिकार मिल गए थे। वह दिन बीत जाने पर इन्होंने क्या सोचा होगा?
   - आरिफ़ ने
   - अम्मी ने
   - दादी ने

उत्तर
- आरिफ़ ने सोचा होगा कि कितना अच्छा होता यदि कभी-कभी उनको भी घर के बड़ों जैसे अधिकार मिलते रहे।
- अम्मी ने सोचा होगा कि बच्चों की मर्ज़ी भी सुननी चाहिए।
- दादी ने सोचा होगा कि अच्छा हुआ वह एक दिन बीत गया नहीं तो ये बच्चे नाक में दम कर देते।

तुम्हारी बात

1. अगर तुम्हें घर में एक दिन के लिए सारे अधिकार दे दिए जाएँ तो तुम क्या-क्या करोगी?

उत्तर यदि मुझे घर में एक दिन के लिए सारे अधिकार दिए जाएँ तो निम्न कार्य करूँगी
- बहुत देर तक दोस्तों के साथ खेलूँगी।
- मम्मी से अपने सभी मनपसंद खाना बनवाऊँगी।
- उस दिन पढ़ाई बिल्कुल नहीं करूँगी।

2. कहानी में ऐसे कई काम बताए गए हैं, जो बड़े लोग आरिफ़ और सलीम से करने के लिए कहते थे। तुम्हारे विचार से उनमें से कौन-कौन से काम उन्हें बिना शिकायत किए कर लेने चाहिए थे और कौन-कौन से कामों के लिए मना कर देना चाहिए था?

उत्तर मेरे विचार से आरिफ और सलीम को ये सभी काम बिना शिकायत किए कर लेने चाहिए थे
- रात को जल्दी सोने और सुबह जल्दी उठने का काम
- घर में शांति से रहने का काम
- दोस्तों के साथ गप्पे नहीं मारने का काम
- कम जेब खर्च में ही संतुष्ट रहने का काम

मेरे विचार से उन्हें इन सभी कामों के लिए मना कर देना चाहिए
- बेकार के कपड़े पहनने से
- मिर्ची के सालन खाने से

तरकीब

"दोनों घंटों बैठकर इन पाबंदियों से बच निकलने की तरकीबें सोचा करते थे।"

1. तुम्हारे विचार से वे कौन-कौन-सी तरकीबें सोचते होंगे?
2. कौन-सी तरकीब से उनकी इच्छा पूरी हो गई थी?
3. क्या तुम उन दोनों को इस तरकीब से भी अच्छी तरकीब सुझा सकती हो?

उत्तर
1. वे सोचते होंगे कि घर के बड़े लोग उन पर रोक-टोक न लगाएँ, उनकी बात को भी सुनें और समझें।
2. अब्बा से दरखास्त पेश की तरकीब कि एक दिन उन्हें बड़ों के सारे अधिकार दे दिए जाएँ और सब बड़े छोटे बन जाएँ।
3. उन दोनों ने जो तरकीब अपनाई, वह सबसे अच्छी है। इस तरकीब ने बड़ों को इस बात का अहसास करा दिया कि बच्चे हर बात पर गलत नहीं होते। सिर्फ हुक्म देते रहना ठीक नहीं है।

अधिकारों की बात

"...आज तो उनके सारे अधिकार छीने जा चुके हैं।"

1. अम्मी के अधिकार किसने छीन लिए थे?
2. क्या उन्हें अम्मी के अधिकार छीनने चाहिए थे?
3. उन्होंने अम्मी के कौन-कौन से अधिकार छीने होंगे?

उत्तर
1. आरिफ़ और सलीम ने अम्मी के अधिकार छीन लिए थे।
2. वैसे तो अम्मी के अधिकार नहीं छीनने चाहिए थे, लेकिन कोई उनकी बात समझने को तैयार नहीं था, इसलिए ऐसा करना ज़रूरी था।
3. उन्होंने अम्मी के बिन कारण डाँटने का अधिकार, अम्मी के पसंद का भोजन बनवाने का अधिकार, पाबंदियाँ लगाने का अधिकार छीने होंगे।

बादशाहत

1. 'बादशाहत' क्या होती है? चर्चा करो।

उत्तर बादशाह द्वारा अपने राज्य में अपनी मर्जी के अनुसार हुकूमत चलाना ही बादशाहत है।

2. **तुम्हारे विचार से इस कहानी का नाम 'एक दिन की बादशाहत' क्यों रखा गया है? तुम भी अपने मन से सोचकर कहानी को कोई शीर्षक दो।**

उत्तर ऐसा शीर्षक इसलिए रखा गया है, क्योकि आरिफ और सलीम ने एक दिन के लिए बादशाह की तरह अपनी मर्जी से घर पर शासन किया। वे घर के सभी सदस्यों को आदेश देते कि कौन-सा काम किस तरह होना है? इस कहानी का दूसरा शीर्षक हो सकता है— 'एक दिन का राजा।'

3. **कहानी में उस दिन बच्चों को सारे बड़ों वाले काम करने पड़े थे। ऐसे में कौन एक दिन का असली 'बादशाह' बन गया था?**

उत्तर आरिफ एक दिन का असली 'बादशाह' बन गया था।

तर माल

"रोज़ की तरह आज वह तर माल अपने लिए न रख सकती थी।"

1. कहानी में किन-किन चीज़ों को तर माल कहा गया है?
2. इन चीज़ों के अलावा और किन-किन चीज़ों को 'तर माल' कहा जा सकता है?
3. कुछ ऐसी चीज़ों के नाम भी बताओ, जो तुम्हें 'तर माल' नहीं लगतीं।
4. इन चीज़ों को तुम क्या नाम देना चाहोगी? सुझाओ।

उत्तर

1. अंडे और मक्खन को तर माल कहा गया है।
2. हलवा, पूरी, मालपुआ आदि को 'तर माल' कहा जा सकता है।
3. दाल, चावल, रोटी आदि तर माल नहीं लगतीं।
4. छात्र स्वयं करें।

मनपसंद कपड़े

"बिल्कुल इसी तरह तो वह आरिफ़ और सलीम से उनकी मनपसंद कमीज़ उतरवाकर निहायत बेकार कपड़े पहनने का हुक्म लगाया करती हैं।"

1. **तुम्हें भी अपना कोई खास कपड़ा सबसे अच्छा लगता होगा। उस कपड़े के बारे में बताओ। वह तुम्हें सबसे अच्छा क्यों लगता है?**

उत्तर छात्र स्वयं करें।

2. **कौन-कौन सी चीज़ें तुम्हें बिल्कुल बेकार लगती हैं?**

(क) पहनने की चीजें (ख) खाने-पीने की चीजें

(ग) करने के काम (घ) खेल

उत्तर (क) पहनने की चीजें — ज्यादा ढीले व बड़े कपड़े।

(ख) खाने-पीने की चीजें — दलिया, लौकी की सब्ज़ी, सेब का रस।

(ग) करने के काम — अलमारी साफ़ करना, फ्रीज़ में पानी की बोतल भरकर रखना।

(घ) खेल — फुटबॉल, शतरंज।

हल्का–भारी

(क) "इतनी भारी साड़ी क्यों पहनी?"

यहाँ पर 'भारी साड़ी' से क्या मतलब है?

- साड़ी का वज़न ज्यादा था।
- साड़ी पर बड़े-बड़े नमूने बने हुए थे।
- साड़ी पर बेल-बूटों की कढ़ाई थी।

उत्तर • साड़ी पर बेल-बूटों की कढ़ाई थी।

(ख) • भारी साड़ी • भारी अटैची

• भारी काम • भारी बारिश।

ऊपर 'भारी' विशेषण का चार अलग-अलग संज्ञाओं के साथ इस्तेमाल किया गया है।

इन चारों में 'भारी' का अर्थ एक-सा नहीं है। इनमें क्या अंतर है?

उत्तर

- **भारी साड़ी** साड़ी पर बेल-बूटों की कढ़ाई होने पर यह भारी लगने लगती है। यहाँ 'भारी' का अर्थ महँगी और अत्यधिक कढ़ाईदार होने से है।
- **भारी अटैची** अटैची में सामान है, जिससे वह भारी हो गई है। अत: यहाँ 'भारी' का अर्थ है— वज़नदार।
- **भारी काम** कोई काम जब बहुत बड़ा, मुश्किल और पेचीदा होता है, तब उसके पहले 'भारी' विशेषण का प्रयोग किया जाता है। अत: यहाँ 'भारी' का अर्थ काम के बड़े, मुश्किल और पेचीदा होने से है।
- **भारी बारिश** वर्षा जब बहुत अधिक होती है, तो उसके पहले प्रायः हम भारी विशेषण लगाते हैं। अत: यहाँ 'भारी' का अर्थ 'अधिक' से है।

(ग) भारी की तरह 'हल्का' का भी अलग-अलग अर्थों में इस्तेमाल करो।

उत्तर

- **हल्का बदन या शरीर** कम खाना खाने से शरीर भी हल्का लगता है।
- **हल्की बात** मेरे सामने इतनी हल्की बात मत करो।
- **हल्का काम** ये काम जो तुम कर रहे हो बहुत ही हल्का काम है, इसे तो कोई भी कर लेगा।
- **हल्का खाना** मैं हमेशा हल्का खाना खाती हूँ।

अभ्यास प्रश्न

बहुविकल्पीय प्रश्न

1. **क्या आरिफ़ और सलीम अपने घरवालों की रोका-टोकी से परेशान थे?**

(क) नहीं (ख) हाँ
(ग) हो सकता है (घ) इनमें में से कोई नहीं

2. **अम्मी ने चाहा कि वे आरिफ़ को एक झापड़ रसीद कर दें, लेकिन कर न सकीं। क्यों?**

(क) क्योंकि उनके अधिकार छिन चुके थे
(ख) क्योंकि वे आरिफ़ को बहुत प्रेम करती थीं
(ग) अब्बा ने मना किया था
(घ) आपा ने मना किया था

3. **कौन रोज़ की तरह आज तर माल नहीं खा सकती थीं?**

(क) दादी (ख) आपा
(ग) अम्मी (घ) इनमें से कोई नहीं

4. **खून का घूँट पीकर कौन रह गया?**

(क) आरिफ़ (ख) सलीम (ग) दादी (घ) आपा

उत्तर 1. (ख) हाँ
2. (क) क्योंकि उनके अधिकार छिन चुके थे
3. (ख) आपा
4. (ग) दादी

गद्यांश पर आधारित प्रश्न

निम्नलिखित गद्यांश को पढ़कर उस पर आधारित प्रश्नों के उत्तर दीजिए।

गद्यांश

आरिफ़ और सलीम दोनों बच्चे अपने घरवालों की पाबंदियों से बहुत परेशान हैं। घर के बाहर जाते हैं अम्मी बोल पड़ती बाहर क्यों जा रहे हो? घर में रहते हैं, तो दादी बोल पड़ती हैं बाहर जाओ, शोर मत करो, ये मत करो, वो मत करो, हर समय बस यही चलता रहता है। उनकी मर्ज़ी तो कभी चलती नहीं है।

एक दिन दोनों बच्चों को एक तरकीब आई। वे अपने अब्बा के सामने दरखास्त पेश करते हैं कि उन्हें एक दिन के लिए बड़ों के अधिकार दे दिए जाएँ और सब छोटे बन जाएँ। अब्बा अच्छे मूड में थे, उन्होंने बच्चों को बड़ों के अधिकार दे दिए। सुबह होने में थोड़ा समय था आरिफ़ ने अम्मी को झिंझोड़ डाला, "अम्मी, जल्दी उठिए, नाश्ता तैयार कीजिए!" अम्मी को गुस्सा तो बहुत आया, लेकिन उस दिन के लिए उनके सारे अधिकार छीने जा चुके थे। अब दादी की बारी थी। जैसे ही उन्होंने बादाम का हरीरा पीना शुरू किया, आरिफ़ ने उन्हें रोका, "दादी! कितना हरीरा पिएँगी आप... पेट फट जाएगा!" इसी प्रकार आरिफ़ ने खानसामे को आदेश देकर अपने सामने अंडे और मक्खन रखवाया और घर के बाकी सदस्यों को दलिया और दूध-बिस्कुट देने को कहा। आपा भी बेबस थीं उस दिन।

1. **घर में किसके अधिकार छिन चुके थे?**

(क) अब्बा के
(ख) अब्बा, अम्मी, दादी, आपा, भाईजान के
(ग) अब्बा, अम्मी, भाईजान के
(घ) अब्बा, अम्मी, दादी, आपा के

2. **आरिफ और सलीम ने अब्बा के सामने क्या पेश किया?**

(क) अखबार (ख) दरखास्त (ग) पुस्तक (घ) कलम

3. **बादाम का हरीरा कौन पी रहा था?**

4. **आरिफ ने खानसामे को क्या आदेश दिया?**

उत्तर

1. (ख) अब्बा, अम्मी, दादी, आपा, भाई जान
2. (ख) दरखास्त
3. बादाम का हरीरा दादी पी रही थीं।
4. आरिफ ने खानसामे को आदेश दिया कि अपने सामने अंडे और मक्खन रखें और घर के बाकी सदस्यों को दलिया और दूध-बिस्कुट दें।

निम्नलिखित प्रश्नों के उत्तर दीजिए

1. **क्या आपको आरिफ और सलीम की तरह घर के अधिकार मिले हैं?**

उत्तर नहीं, मुझे कभी भी आरिफ और सलीम की तरह घर के अधिकार नहीं मिले हैं।

2. **क्या कारण होगा कि अब्बा के साथ घर के अन्य सभी लोगों ने अपने अधिकार सलीम और आरिफ़ को दे दिया?**

उत्तर अब्बा के साथ घर के अन्य सभी लोगों ने अपने अधिकार सलीम और आरिफ को इसलिए दे दिए, क्योंकि अब्बा घर के बड़े थे। उन्होंने सभी को अधिकार देने का आदेश दिया था।

अध्याय 11

चावल की रोटियाँ

पाठ का सार

'चावल की रोटियाँ' एकांकी में आठ साल का एक बर्मी लड़का कोको है, जिसके तीन दोस्त नीनी, तिन सू और मिमि हैं। उ बा तुन जनता की दुकान का प्रबंधक है। कोको के माता-पिता धान लगाने खेत पर चले जाते हैं। माँ की अनुपस्थिति में उसे घर की देखभाल करनी होती है। माँ उसके लिए चार चावल की रोटियाँ बनाकर अलमारी में रख देती हैं। कोको को चावल की रोटियाँ बेहद पसंद हैं। उन्हें खाने के लिए वह झट से बैठता ही है कि तभी दरवाज़े पर नीनी दस्तक देता है। उसे भी चावल की रोटियाँ बहुत पसंद हैं। वह दरवाज़ा खोलने से पहले उन रोटियों को छिपा देता है। नीनी कोको से दरवाज़ा खोलने में देरी का कारण पूछता है, तो कोको झूठ बोलता है कि वह नाश्ता करके मुँह धोने लगा था। नीनी उसके पास रेडियो पर परीक्षा संबंधी सूचना के बारे में जानकारी लेने आता है। कोको रेडियो खराब होने का बहाना बना देता है। नीनी को खबर ज़रूरी सुननी है। अत: वह फौरन तिन सू के घर चला जाता है।

कोको राहत की साँस लेते हुए चावल की रोटियाँ लेकर खाने बैठता ही है कि दरवाज़े पर मिमि की दस्तक होती है। कोको फिर रोटियाँ छिपाकर दरवाज़ा देरी से खोलता है। मिमि बताती है कि अभी तुम्हारी माँ ने बताया कि तुम्हारे लिए चावल की कुछ रोटियाँ रखी हैं। कोको तपाक से बोलता है कि रोटियाँ तो थीं, परंतु मैंने सब खा लीं। मिमि कहती है कि अकेले-अकेले खाना बुरी बात होती है। मेरी माँ ने मुझे चार केले के पापड़ दिए, दो तुम्हारे लिए और दो मेरे लिए। चावल की रोटियों के साथ केले के पापड़ का नाश्ता बड़ा अच्छा होता है। कोको मन-ही-मन पछताने लगता है। मिमि एक पापड़ उठाकर कोको से चाय माँगती है। कोको चाय लाकर मिमि को देता है।

उसी समय कोको का पेट गुड़गुड़ करने लगता है। मिमि के पूछने पर कोको बताता है कि उसके घर में चूहा घुस आया है। वही यह आवाज़ कर रहा है। दरवाज़े पर फिर तिन सू की दस्तक होती है। वह गेंदे के फूलों का गुच्छा लाता है। मिमि उसे केले का पापड़ और एक कप चाय देती है। तिन सू फूलदान में फूल लगाने के लिए बढ़ता है तभी कोको उसे रोक देता है, क्योंकि वहीं पर उसने रोटियाँ छिपाई हैं। दरवाज़े पर फिर उ बा तुन (दुकान का प्रबंधक) की दस्तक होती है। वह कोको से कहता है कि तुम्हारी माँ हमारी दुकान से एक गुलाबी फूलदान लाई थी। उन्हें नीला फूलदान चाहिए था इसलिए मैं उसे बदलने के लिए आया हूँ। इतना कहकर उ बा तुन गुलाबी फूलदान उठाकर उसकी जगह नीला फूलदान रख देता है। फूलदान के साथ कोको की चावल की रोटियाँ भी चली गईं। वह सभी (चारों) रोटियाँ खाने के चक्कर में एक भी रोटी नहीं खा पाता है और दु:खी होता है। अंत में कोको उ बा तुन को गुड बाय चाचा और गुड बाय मेरे चावल की रोटियाँ कहता है।

शब्दार्थ

दस्तक-खटखटाना, भुक्खड़-बहुत भूखा, तलाशी-खोजबीन, इर्द-गिर्द-आसपास, बदकिस्मती-दुर्भाग्य, नेकी-भलाई, खुशकिस्मती-सौभाग्य, जिस्म-शरीर, यकीन-विश्वास, प्रबंधक-व्यवस्था करने वाला।

NCERT फोल्डर

मंच और मंचन

एक सादा कमरा, दीवारों पर बाँस की चटाइयाँ। एक दीवार के सहारे रखी अलमारी। अलमारी के ऊपर एक रेडियो, चाय की केतली, कुछ कप और खाली गुलाबी फूलदान रखा है। कमरे के बीच फर्श पर एक चटाई बिछी है, जिसके ऊपर कम ऊँचाई वाली गोल मेज रखी है। दो दरवाज़े। एक दरवाजा पीछे की ओर खुलता है और दूसरा एक किनारे की ओर। पंछियों के चहचहाने के साथ-साथ पर्दा उठता है। दूर कहीं मुर्गा बाँग देता है। कुत्ता भौंकता है। कहीं प्रार्थना की घंटियाँ बजती हैं। कोको आता है, जम्हाई लेकर अपने को सीधा करता है। ऊपर लिखी पंक्तियों में कोको के घर के एक कमरे का वर्णन किया गया है। दरअसल नाटक के लिए मंच सज्जा कैसी हो, यह निर्देश उसके लिए है। तुम इस वर्णन को पढ़कर उस मंच का एक चित्र बनाओ जो ठीक वैसा ही होना चाहिए जैसा कि बताया गया है।

उत्तर छात्र स्वयं करें।

नाटक की बात

1. **नाटक में हिस्सा लेने वालों को पात्र कहते हैं। जिन पात्रों की भूमिका महत्त्वपूर्ण होती है, उन्हें मुख्य पात्र और जिनकी भूमिका ज्यादा महत्त्वपूर्ण नहीं होती है, उन्हें 'गौण पात्र' कहते हैं। बताओ इस नाटक में कौन-कौन मुख्य और गौण पात्र कौन हैं?**

उत्तर इस नाटक के मुख्य पात्र कोको है व नीनी, मिमि, तिन सू और उ बा तुन गौण पात्र हैं।

2. **पात्रों को जो बात बोलनी होती है उसे संवाद कहते हैं। क्या तुम किसी एक परिस्थिति के लिए संवाद लिख सकती हो? (इसके लिए तुम टोलियों में भी काम कर सकती हो।) उदाहरण के लिए, खो-खो या कबड्डी जैसा कोई खेल खेलते समय दूसरे दल के खिलाड़ियों से बहस।**

उत्तर खिलाड़ी 1 (पहले दल का) – तुम्हारा खिलाड़ी आउट है।

खिलाड़ी 2 (दूसरे दल का) – नहीं वह आउट होते-होते बच गया है, वह आउट नहीं है।

खिलाड़ी 1 – मैंने इसे पाले में आने से पहले ही आउट कर दिया था।

खिलाड़ी 2 – नहीं उसका पैर पाले में आ चुका था जब तुमने आउट करने का प्रयास किया था।

खिलाड़ी 1 – तुम हर खेल में ऐसे ही झूठ बोलते हो।

खिलाड़ी 2 – झूठ तुम बोलते हुए, इसलिए बहस न करके खेल शुरू करो।

3. **क्या आपने कभी कोई चीज़ या बात दूसरों से छिपाई है या छिपाने की कोशिश की है, उस समय क्या-क्या हुआ था?**

उत्तर एक बार मेरा दोस्त मेरी साइकिल माँगने आया था, पर मैंने बहाना बनाकर उसे साइकिल नहीं दी, क्योंकि वह बहुत लापरवाह है और मुझे मेरी साइकिल प्यारी है। वह मुझे मेरे जन्मदिन पर उपहार में मिली थी। मेरे मना करने पर भी वह बार-बार मुझसे साइकिल माँग रहा था, जिससे हम दोनों में थोड़ी बहस भी हो गई थी।

4. **कहते हैं, एक झूठ छिपाने के लिए सौ झूठ बोलने पड़ते हैं। क्या तुम्हें कहानी पढ़कर ऐसा लगता है? कहानी की मदद से इस बात को समझाओ।**

उत्तर हाँ, यह बात बिल्कुल सही है कि एक झूठ छिपाने के लिए सौ झूठ बोलने पड़ जाते हैं। कोको चावल की चारों रोटियाँ स्वयं खाना चाहता है, लेकिन संयोग ऐसा होता है कि जब-जब वह रोटियाँ खाने बैठता है, उसका कोई-न-कोई दोस्त आ जाता है। वह रोटियाँ उनके साथ बाँटकर नहीं खाना चाहता है और उन्हें छिपाने की कोशिश में बार-बार झूठ बोलता है।

एक चावल कई-कई रूप

1. **कोको की माँ ने उसके लिए चावल की रोटियाँ बनाकर रखी थीं। भारत के विभिन्न प्रान्तों में चावल अलग-अलग तरीके से इस्तेमाल किया जाता है-भोजन के हिस्से के रूप में भी और नमकीन और मीठे पकवान के रूप में भी। तुम्हारे प्रांत में चावल का इस्तेमाल कैसे होता है? घर में बातचीत करके पता करो और एक तालिका बनाओ। कक्षा में अपने दोस्तों की तालिका के साथ मिलान करो तो पाओगी कि भाषा, कपड़ों और रहन-सहन के साथ-साथ खान-पान की दृष्टि से भी भारत अनूठा है।**

उत्तर हमारे प्रांत हैदराबाद में चावल का इस्तेमाल निम्नलिखित चीजें बनाने में होता है; जैसे—सादा सफेद चावल, नमकीन पुलाव, मीठे चावल, खीर, इडली, डोसा।

2. **अपनी तालिका में से चावल से बनी कोई एक खाने की चीज़ बनाने की विधि पता करो और उसे नीचे दिए गए बिंदुओं के हिसाब से लिखो।**

- **सामग्री**

उत्तर **चावल का नमकीन पुलाव बनाने की विधि**

सामग्री चावल, गोभी, मटर, गाजर, आलू, धनिया पत्ता।

तैयारी सबसे पहले सभी सब्जियों (धनिया पत्ता नहीं) को अच्छी तरह धोकर काट लो और चावल को भी अच्छी तरह धो लो।

विधि चावल को धोकर हल्का सुखा लो। फिर उसे घी में भूनकर निकाल लो। अब कटी सब्जियों को घी में भूनो। भूनते समय उसमें नमक, मिर्च पाउडर, हल्दी पाउडर व इलायची डालो। जब उनका रंग सुनहरा हो जाए, तो उसमें चावल को डालकर थोड़ी देर फिर भूनो। अब प्रेशर कुकर में चावल के अंदाजे से पानी चढ़ाओ। जब पानी गर्म हो जाए, तो उसमें कड़ाही की सामग्री डाल दो। फिर उसे बंद कर दो। एक सीटी के बाद उतार लो। थोड़ी देर बाद गर्मागरम परोसो। चाहो तो ऊपर में धनिया पत्ता बारीक-बारीक काटकर पुलाव पर फैला दो।

3. **"कोको के माता-पिता धान लगाने के लिए खेतों में गए।" कोको की माँ ने उसके लिए चावल की रोटियाँ बनाईं। एक ही चीज़ के विभिन्न रूपों के अलग-अलग नाम हो सकते हैं। नीचे ऐसे कुछ शब्द दिए गए हैं। उनमें अंतर बताओ।**

चावल, धान, भात, मुरमुरा, चिउड़ा
साबुत दाल, धुली दाल, छिलका दाल
गेहूँ, दलिया, आटा, मैदा, सूजी

उत्तर
- **चावल** धान से निकला दाना चावल कहलाता है।
- **धान** छिलका लगा चावल धान कहलाता है।
- **भात** पका हुआ चावल भात कहलाता है।
- **मुरमुरा** चावल या धान का भुना हुआ रूप मुरमुरा कहलाता है।
- **चिउड़ा** धान को भिगोकर या उबालकर कूटने से चिउड़ा तैयार होता है।
- **साबुत दाल** छिलके वाली दाल, जो टुकड़ों में नहीं है।
- **धुली दाल** टूटी हुई बिना छिलके वाली दाल।
- **छिलका दाल** टूटी हुई छिलके वाली दाल।
- **गेहूँ** गेहूँ साबुत दाना होता है।
- **दलिया** गेहूँ के दानों को दलकर दलिया बनाया जाता है।
- **आटा** गेहूँ के दानों को पीसकर आटा बनाया जाता है।
- **मैदा** गेहूँ के दानों को बहुत अधिक बारीक पीसकर मैदा बनाया जाता है।
- **सूजी** जौ आदि अनाज से बना आटा सूजी कहलाता है।

के, में, ने, को, से

"कोको की माँ ने कल दुकान से एक फूलदान खरीदा था।"

ऊपर लिखे वाक्य में जिन शब्दों के नीचे रेखा खिंची है, वे वाक्य में शब्दों का आपस में संबंध बताते हैं। नीचे एक मजेदार किताब 'अनारको के आठ दिन' का एक अंश दिया गया है। उसके खाली स्थानों में इस प्रकार के सही शब्द लिखो।

अनारको एक लड़की है। घर ...... लोग उसे अन्नो कहते हैं। अन्नो नाम छोटा जो है, सो उस ...... हुक्म चलाना आसान होता है। अन्नो, पानी ले आ, अन्नो धूप ...... मत जाना, अन्नो बाहर अँधेरा है-कहीं मत जा, बारिश ...... भीगना मत, अन्नो! और कोई बाहर ...... घर में आए, तो घर वाले कहेंगे-ये हमारी अनारको है, प्यार ...... हम इसे अन्नो कहते हैं। प्यार ...... हुँ-ह-ह!

आज अनारको सुबह सोकर उठी तो हाँफ रही थी। रात सपने ...... बहुत बारिश हुई। अनारको ...... याद किया और उसे लगा, आज ...... सपने में जितनी बारिश हुई उतनी तो पहले के सपनों ...... कभी नहीं हुई। कभी नहीं। जमके बारिश हुई थी आज ...... सपने ...... और जमकर उसमें भीगी थी अनारको। खूब उछली थी, कूदी थी, चारों तरफ पानी छिटकाया था और खूब-खूब भीगी थीं।

उत्तर के, से, में, में, से, से, से, में, ने, के, में, के, में

अभ्यास प्रश्न

बहुविकल्पीय प्रश्न

1. कोको कितने साल का लड़का है?
   (क) सात (ख) आठ
   (ग) नौ (घ) दस
2. कोको के माता-पिता कहाँ गए थे?
   (क) खेत में (ख) शहर में
   (ग) दुकान में (घ) दोस्तों के घर में
3. कोको को सबसे ज्यादा क्या पसंद है?
   (क) बाजरे की रोटियाँ (ख) आटे की रोटियाँ
   (ग) गेहूँ की रोटियाँ (घ) चावल की रोटियाँ
4. कोको ने चावल की रोटियाँ कौन-से फूलदान में छिपाई थीं?
   (क) नीले फूलदान में (ख) पीले फूलदान में
   (ग) गुलाबी फूलदान में (घ) हरे फूलदान में
5. सबसे पहले दरवाज़े पर कौन दस्तक देता है?
   (क) मिमी (ख) नीनी
   (ग) कोको (घ) दुकान का प्रबंधक

उत्तर 1. (ख) आठ 2. (क) खेत में
3. (घ) चावल की रोटियाँ
4. (ग) गुलाबी फूलदान में
5. (ख) नीनी

गद्यांश पर आधारित प्रश्न

निम्नलिखित गद्यांश को पढ़कर उस पर आधारित प्रश्नों के उत्तर दीजिए।

गद्यांश

मिमि के पूछने पर कोको बताता है कि उसके घर में चूहा घुस आया है। वही यह आवाज़ कर रहा है। दरवाज़े पर फिर दस्तक होती है। इस बार तिन सू होता है। वह गेंदे के फूलों का गुच्छा लाता है। मिमि उसे केले का पापड़ देती है और एक कप चाय। तिन सू फूलदान में फूल लगाने के लिए बढ़ता है। कोको उसे रोक देता है, क्योंकि वहीं पर उसने रोटियाँ छिपाई हैं। दरवाज़े पर फिर दस्तक होती है। कोको दरवाज़ा खोलता है तो सामने उ बा तुन (दुकान का प्रबंधक) को पाता है। वह कोको से कहता है कि तुम्हारी माँ हमारी दुकान से एक गुलाबी फूलदान लाई थी। वे नीला फूलदान चाहती थीं, लेकिन उस समय वह मेरे पास नहीं था। मेरे पास अब नीला फूलदान आ गया है। मैं उसे बदलने के लिए आया हूँ।

1. उ बा तुन (दुकान के प्रबंधक) कौन-सी वस्तु बदलने के लिए कोको के घर आए?
   (क) चायपत्ती (ख) चीनी (ग) फूलदान (घ) फल
2. कोको तिन सू को फूलदान में फूल लगाने से क्यों रोकता है?
   (क) फूलदान के टूटे होने के कारण
   (ख) उसमें रोटियाँ छिपाने के कारण
   (ग) फूल अच्छे न लगने के कारण
   (घ) उपरोक्त सभी
3. कोको की माँ कौन-से रंग का फूलदान लेना चाहती थीं?
4. पेट की गुड़गुड़ की आवाज़ को कोको किसकी आवाज़ बता रहा था?

उत्तर

1. (ग) फूलदान
2. (ख) उसमें रोटियाँ छिपाने के कारण
3. कोको की माँ नीले रंग का फूलदान लेना चाहती थीं।
4. पेट की गुड़गुड़ की आवाज़ को कोको चूहे की आवाज़ बता रहा था।

निम्नलिखित प्रश्नों के उत्तर दीजिए

1. आपने चावल से बनी कौन-कौन सी खाद्य सामग्री खाई है? सोचकर लिखिए।

उत्तर मैंने चावल से बनी रोटियाँ, इडली, खीर आदि खाई हैं।

2. कोको के चावल की रोटियों के पीछे लालच का क्या कारण होगा? सोचकर लिखिए।

उत्तर कोको को चावल की रोटियाँ बेहद पसंद थीं, इसलिए वह किसी को उसे नहीं देना चाहता होगा।

3. मिमि के पास केले के कितने पापड़ थे। चाहे तो मिमि भी सारे पापड़ स्वयं खा सकती थी, पर उसने ऐसा नहीं किया, क्या कारण होगा?

उत्तर मिमि के पास केले के चार पापड़ थे। वह चारों पापड़ को स्वयं भी खा सकती थी, किंतु वह आपस में बाँटकर खाने में विश्वास रखती है, इसलिए उसने चारों पापड़ खुद नहीं खाए।

अध्याय 12

गुरु और चेला

कविता का सार

एक दिन गुरु और उनका चेला बिना पैसे के घूमने के लिए निकल पड़े और अँधेर नगरी पहुँच गए। यहाँ का राजा बिल्कुल मूर्ख है। गुरुजी ने सोचा ऐसी नगरी में रहना ठीक नहीं है। गुरुजी वहाँ से चले गए, परंतु चेला उसी नगरी में रुक गया। एक दिन चेला बाज़ार में गया। वहाँ उसने देखा कि सभी चीज़ें टके सेर मिल रही हैं। चेले को सब कुछ अजीब लग रहा था। उसी साल बहुत वर्षा हुई जिसके कारण राज्य की एक दीवार गिर गई। राजा ने संतरी को तुरंत बुलाया और उससे दीवार गिरने का कारण पूछा। संतरी ने कारीगर को दोषी ठहराया, फिर कारीगर को बुलाया गया तो उसने भिश्ती को दोषी ठहराया, क्योंकि उसने गारा गीला कर दिया था। भिश्ती ने मशकवाले पर दोष मढ़ा, जिसने ज्यादा पानी की मशक बना दी थी। मशकवाले ने मंत्री को दोषी बताया, क्योंकि उसी ने बड़े जानवर का चमड़ा दिलवाया था। फिर मंत्री को बुलाया गया। वह अपने बचाव में कुछ न कह सका।

राजा ने उसे फाँसी पर चढ़ाने का आदेश दिया। अत: जल्लाद उसे फाँसी पर चढ़ाने चला था, लेकिन मंत्री इतना दुबला था कि उसकी गर्दन में फाँसी का फंदा आया ही नहीं। राजा ने आदेश दिया कि कोई मोटी गर्दन वाले को पकड़ लाओ और उसे फाँसी पर चढ़ा दो। चेले की गर्दन मोटी थी। मंत्री ने चेले को पकड़कर राजा के सामने प्रस्तुत किया। राजा ने उसे फाँसी पर चढ़ा देने का आदेश दे दिया।

चेला चालाक था। उसने कहा कि फाँसी पर चढ़ाने से पहले मुझे मेरे गुरुजी के दर्शन कराओ। गुरुजी ने चेले के कान में कुछ मंत्र गुनगुनाया। उसके बाद दोनों आपस में झगड़ने लगे। गुरु कहता, मैं फाँसी पर चढ़ूँगा और चेला कहता कि मैं फाँसी पर चढ़ूँगा। राजा ने कुछ देर तक उनका झगड़ा देखा और उन दोनों को अपने पास बुलाया और झगड़े का कारण पूछा तो गुरु ने बताया कि यह बहुत ही शुभ मुहूर्त है। इस मुहूर्त में जो फाँसी पर चढ़ेगा वह राजा नहीं, बल्कि चक्रवर्ती बनेगा। पूरे संसार का छत्र उसके सिर चढ़ेगा। मूर्ख राजा बोल पड़ा यदि ऐसी बात है, तो मैं फाँसी पर चढ़ूँगा। राजा को फाँसी पर चढ़ा दिया गया। इधर प्रजा में खुशी की लहर दौड़ गई। आखिरकार उन्हें मूर्ख राजा से मुक्ति मिल गई।

काव्यांशों की व्याख्या

काव्यांश 1

गुरु एक थे और था एक चेला,
चले घूमने पास में था न धेला
चले चलते-चलते मिली एक नगरी,
चमाचम थी सड़कें चमाचम थी डगरी।
मिली एक ग्वालिन धरे शीश गगरी,
गुरु ने कहा तेज़ ग्वालिन न भग री।
बता कौन नगरी, बता कौन राजा,
कि जिसके सुयश का यहाँ बजता बाजा।

शब्दार्थ चेला-शिष्य, धेला-पैसा, डगरी-रास्ता, शीश-सिर, मस्तक, सुयश-प्रसिद्धि।

संदर्भ/प्रसंग प्रस्तुत पंक्तियाँ हमारी पाठ्यपुस्तक 'रिमझिम भाग-5' में संकलित कविता 'गुरु और चेला' से ली गई हैं। इसके रचयिता 'सोहनलाल द्विवेदी' हैं। प्रस्तुत कविता में कवि ने गुरु चेले के द्वारा घूमते हुए अँधेर नगरी पहुँचने और वहाँ के राजा का वर्णन किया है।

व्याख्या एक गुरु और एक चेला बिना पैसों के घूमने निकले थे। चलते-चलते वे एक ऐसी नगरी में पहुँचे, जहाँ की डगर और सड़क चमक रही थी। एक ग्वालिन के सर पर गगरी थी गुरुजी ने उसी से पूछा ये कौन-सा नगर है? यहाँ का राजा कौन है? यहाँ किसका सुयश है?

काव्यांश 2

कहा बढ़के ग्वालिन ने महाराज पंडित,
पधारे भले हो यहाँ आज पंडित।
यह अँधेर नगरी है अनबूझ राजा,
टके सेर भाजी, टके सेर खाजा।
गुरु ने कहा-जान देना नहीं है,
मुसीबत मुझे मोल लेना नहीं है।
न जाने की अँधेर हो कौन छन में?
यहाँ ठीक रहना समझता न मन में।

शब्दार्थ पधारे-आए, भाजी-सब्जी, मुसीबत-समस्या।

प्रसंग पूर्ववत्।

व्याख्या गुरु के पूछने पर ग्वालिन ने बढ़कर कहा, महाराज पंडित, भले ही आप यहाँ आए हैं, लेकिन यह अँधेर नगरी है। यहाँ का राजा निरा मूर्ख है। यहाँ सब कुछ टके सेर मिलता है, चाहे वह भाजी हो या खाजा। सुनकर गुरु का माथा ठनका। उन्होंने सोचा कि यहाँ रहना उचित नहीं, क्योंकि किसी भी पल कुछ भी अनर्थ हो सकता है।

काव्यांश 3

गुरु ने कहा किंतु चेला न माना,
गुरु को विवश हो पड़ा लौट जाना।
गुरुजी गए, रह गया किंतु चेला,
यही सोचता हूँगा मोटा अकेला।
चला हाट को देखने आज चेला,
तो देखा वहाँ पर अजब रेल-पेला।
टके सेर हल्दी, टके सेर जीरा,
टके सेर ककड़ी, टके सेर खीरा।

शब्दार्थ विवश-मजबूर, हाट-बाज़ार।

प्रसंग पूर्ववत्।

व्याख्या यह जानने पर कि यह अँधेर नगरी है, गुरु ने तुरंत उस जगह को छोड़ने का निर्णय ले लिया। उसने चेले से चलने के लिए कहा, परंतु वह नहीं माना। गुरुजी अकेले ही चले गए और चेला वहीं रह गया। एक दिन वह उस नगरी का बाज़ार देखने निकला। वह हैरान रह गया यह जानकर कि वहाँ सब कुछ टके सेर बिक रहा था चाहे वह खीरा हो या ककड़ी, हल्दी हो या जीरा।

काव्यांश 4

टके सेर मिलती है रबड़ी मलाई,
बहुत रोज़ उसने मलाई उड़ाई।
सुनो और आगे का फिर हाल ताज़ा।
थी अँधेर नगरी, था अनबूझ राजा।।
बरसता था पानी, चमकती थी बिजली,
थी बरसात आई, दमकती थी बिजली।
गरजते थे बादल, झमकती थी बिजली,
थी बरसात गहरी, धमकती थी बिजली।

शब्दार्थ अनबूझ-मूर्ख।

प्रसंग पूर्ववत्।

व्याख्या उस अँधेर नगरी में सब कुछ टके सेर मिलता था। चेले ने बहुत समय तक खूब रबड़ी मलाई खाई। कवि कहता है कि अब आप आगे का ताजा हाल सुनिए। मूर्ख राजा की अँधेर नगरी में उस साल वहाँ खूब बरसात हुई। खूब पानी बरसता था, खूब बिजली चमकती थी और खूब बादल गरजते थे।

काव्यांश 5

गिरी राज्य की एक दीवार भारी,
जहाँ राजा पहुँचे तुरंत ले सवारी।
झपट संतरी को डपटकर बुलाया,
गिरी क्यों यह दीवार, किसने गिराया?
कहा संतरी ने–महाराज साहब,
न इसमें खता मेरी, ना मेरा करतब!
यह दीवार कमज़ोर पहले बनी थी,
इसी से गिरी, यह न मोटी घनी थी।

शब्दार्थ *खता–गलती।*

प्रसंग पूर्ववत्।

व्याख्या भारी बरसात के कारण अँधेर नगरी राज्य की एक दीवार गिर गई। राजा तुरंत वहाँ पहुँच गया। उसने संतरी को बुलाया और उससे दीवार गिरने का कारण पूछा। संतरी ने झट जवाब दिया कि दीवार गिरने में उसकी कोई गलती नहीं है। दरअसल दीवार कमज़ोर बनी थी, मोटी और घनी नहीं है, इसीलिए गिर गई।

काव्यांश 6

खता कारीगर की महाराज साहब,
न इसमें खता मेरी, या मेरा करतब!
बुलाया गया, कारीगर झट वहाँ पर,
बिठाया गया, कारीगर झट वहाँ पर।
कहा राजा ने कारीगर को सजा दो,
खता इसकी है आज इसको सजा दो।
कहा कारीगर ने, ज़रा की न देरी,
महाराज! इसमें खता कुछ न मेरी।

शब्दार्थ *करतब–कारनामा।*

प्रसंग पूर्ववत्।

व्याख्या संतरी ने महाराज से कहा, इसमें उसकी कोई गलती या कारनामा नहीं है। तब कारीगर को फ़ौरन बुलाया गया। राजा ने आदेश दे दिया कि कारीगर को सज़ा दो। इसकी गलती से दीवार गिरी है। अत: इसे मौत दो। कारीगर बिना एक पल गँवाए बोल पड़ा, महाराज! इसमें मेरी कोई गलती नहीं है।

काव्यांश 7

यह भिश्ती की गलती यह उसकी शरारत,
किया गारा गीला उसी की यह गफलत।
कहा राजा ने जल्द भिश्ती बुलाओ।
पकड़कर उसे जल्द फाँसी चढ़ाओ।
चला आया भिश्ती, हुई कुछ न देरी,
कहा उसने–इसमें खता कुछ न मेरी।
यह गलती है जिसने मैशक को बनाया,
कि ज्यादा ही उसमें था पानी समाया।

शब्दार्थ *भिश्ती–पानी भरने वाला, शरारत–गलती, गफलत–भूल।*

प्रसंग पूर्ववत्।

व्याख्या कारीगर ने तुरंत अपना बचाव करते हुए भिश्ती को दोषी करार दिया। उसने राजा से कहा, भिश्ती की गलती से दीवार गिरी है, क्योंकि उसी ने गारा गीला कर दिया था। राजा के आदेश पर भिश्ती को बुलाया गया। भिश्ती को देखते ही राजा ने उसे फाँसी पर चढ़ाने का आदेश दे दिया। भिश्ती ने कहा, इसमें मेरी गलती नहीं है, बल्कि मशक बनाने वाले की गलती है। उसी ने इतनी बड़ी मशक बना दी कि उसमें पानी ज्यादा समा गया, जिसके कारण दीवार कमज़ोर हो गई और गिर गई।

काव्यांश 8

मशक वाला आया, हुई कुछ न देरी,
कहा उसने इसमें खता कुछ न मेरी।
यह मंत्री की गलती, है मंत्री की ग़फ़लत,
उन्हीं की शरारत, उन्हीं की है हिकमत।
बड़े जानवर का था चमड़ा दिलाया,
चुराया न चमड़ा मशक को बनाया।
बड़ी है मशक खूब भरता है पानी,
ये गलती न मेरी, यह गलती बिरानी।

प्रसंग पूर्ववत्।

व्याख्या भिश्ती के कहने पर मशक वाले को बुलाया गया। उसने भी चतुरता से कहा कि दीवार गिरने में मेरी नहीं, बल्कि मंत्री की गलती है। यह उन्हीं की भूल और उन्हीं की लापरवाही है। उन्होंने ही मुझे बड़े जानवर का चमड़ा दिलवा दिया। मैंने चमड़ा चुराया नहीं और एक बड़ी मशक बना दिया। इस मशक में पानी ज्यादा भरता है। इस प्रकार यह गलती मेरी नहीं, बल्कि किसी और की है।

काव्यांश 9

है मंत्री की गलती तो मंत्री को लाओ,
हुआ हुक्म मंत्री को फाँसी चढ़ाओ।
चले मंत्री को लेके जल्लाद फौरन,
चढ़ाने को फाँसी उसी दम उसी क्षण।
मगर मंत्री था इतना दुबला दिखाता,
न गर्दन में फाँसी का फंदा था आता।
कहा राजा ने जिसकी मोटी हो गर्दन,
पकड़कर उसे फाँसी दो तुम इसी क्षण।

शब्दार्थ *हुक्म–आदेश, जल्लाद– फाँसी पर चढ़ाने वाला आदमी।*

प्रसंग पूर्ववत्।

व्याख्या जब राजा ने बोला कि मंत्री की वजह से दीवार गिरी है, तो मंत्री को हाजिर करो। मंत्री आया तो राजा ने उसे फाँसी पर चढ़ा देने को कहा। जल्लाद तुरंत आ गया और मंत्री को उसी समय फाँसी पर चढ़ाने के लिए लेकर चला, किंतु मंत्री काफ़ी दुबला था।

उसकी गर्दन इतनी पतली थी कि फाँसी के फंदे में नहीं आ रही थी। राजा ने कहा उसकी जगह किसी मोटी गर्दन वाले को पकड़कर लाओ और उसे फाँसी पर चढ़ाओ।

काव्यांश 10

चले संतरी ढूँढने मोटी गर्दन,
मिला चेला खाता था हलुआ दनादन।
कहा संतरी ने चलें आप फ़ौरन,
महाराज ने भेजा न्यौता इसी क्षण।
बहुत मन में खुश हो चला आज चेला,
कहा आज न्यौता छकुँगा अकेला!!
मगर आके पहुँचा तो देखा झमेला,
वहाँ तो जुड़ा था अजब एक मेला।।

शब्दार्थ *दनादन–जल्दी-जल्दी, फौरन–तुरंत।*

प्रसंग पूर्ववत्।

व्याख्या संतरी मोटी गर्दन वाले व्यक्ति की खोज में निकल पड़े। उन्हें नगर में चेला हलुआ खाते हुए मिल गया। उन्होंने चेले से कहा कि महाराज ने आपको न्यौता दिया है। आप इसी क्षण चलिए। चेला यह सोचकर मन-ही-मन खुश था कि राजा के दरबार में खूब छककर खाऊँगा, लेकिन आकर देखा तो वहाँ एक नया झमेला खड़ा था। चारों तरफ़ लोगों की भीड़ उमड़ी थी।

काव्यांश 11

यह मोटी है गर्दन, इसे तुम बढ़ाओ,
कहा राजा ने इसको फाँसी चढ़ाओ!
कहा चेले ने–कुछ खता तो बताओ,
कहा राजा ने–'चुप' न बकबक मचाओ।
मगर था न बुद्धू–था चालाक चेला,
मचाया बड़ा ही वहीं पर झमेला!!
कहा पहले गुरुजी के दर्शन कराओ,
मुझे बाद में चाहे फाँसी चढ़ाओ।

शब्दार्थ *बकबक–बकवास बातें।*

प्रसंग पूर्ववत्।

व्याख्या चेले की मोटी गर्दन देखकर राजा ने तुरंत उसे फाँसी पर चढ़ाने का आदेश दे दिया। चेले ने राजा से पूछा कि आखिर मेरी गलती क्या है? कम-से-कम मेरी गलती तो बताएँ। राजा ने फ़ौरन यह कहकर उसे चुप करा दिया कि ज्यादा बकबक मत करो, लेकिन चेला बुद्धू नहीं, चालाक था। उसने वहीं पर एक बड़ा झमेला खड़ा कर दिया। कहा मुझे मेरे गुरु के दर्शन कराओ बाद में फाँसी चढ़ाओ।

काव्यांश 12

गुरुजी बुलाए गए झट वहाँ पर,
कि रोता था चेला खड़ा था जहाँ पर।
गुरु जी ने चेले को आकर बुलाया,
तुरत कान में मंत्र कुछ गुनगुनाया।
झगड़ने लगे फिर गुरु और चेला,
मचा उनमें धक्का बड़ा रेल-पेला।
गुरु ने कहा–फाँसी पर मैं चढ़ूँगा,
कहा चेले ने–फाँसी पर मैं मरूँगा।

शब्दार्थ *गुनगुनाया–बुदबुदाया।*

प्रसंग पूर्ववत्।

व्याख्या चेले के कहने पर गुरुजी को बुलाया गया। चेले को रोते देख उन्होंने उसे अपने पास बुलाया और कान में कुछ मंत्र गुनगुनाया। फिर दोनों की आपस में लड़ाई शुरू हो गई। दोनों जमकर लड़ने लगे। गुरु कहता था–मैं फाँसी पर चढ़ूँगा। दोनों जिद पर अड़े थे।

काव्यांश 13

हटाए न हटते अड़े ऐसे दोनों,
छुटाए न छुटते लड़े ऐसे दोनों।
बढ़े राजा फ़ौरन कहा बात क्या है?
गुरु ने बताया करामात क्या है?
चढ़ेगा जो फाँसी महूरत है ऐसा,
न ऐसी महूरत बनी बढ़िया जैसी।
वह राजा नहीं, चक्रवर्ती बनेगा,
यह संसार का छत्र उस पर तनेगा।

शब्दार्थ करामात–चमत्कार।

संदर्भ पूर्ववत्।

व्याख्या फाँसी पर चढ़ने के लिए गुरु और चेले हटाने से भी नहीं हटते थे। राजा ने बढ़कर पूछा कि आखिर बात क्या है? इस पर गुरु ने बताया कि शुभ मुहूर्त है फाँसी पर चढ़ने का। इस मुहूर्त में जो फाँसी पर चढ़ेगा वह राजा नहीं चक्रवर्ती बनेगा। पूरे संसार का ताज उसके सिर पर होगा।

काव्यांश 14

कहा राजा ने बात सच गर यही
गुरु का कथन, झूठ होता नहीं है।
कहा राजा ने फाँसी पर मैं चढ़ूँगा
इसी दम फाँसी पर मैं ही टँगूँगा।
चढ़ा फाँसी राजा बजा खूब बाजा
प्रजा खुश हुई जब मरा मूर्ख राजा
बजा खूब घर-घर बधाई का बाजा
थी अँधेर नगरी, था अनबूझ राजा।।

शब्दार्थ दम–क्षण, अनबूझ–मूर्ख।

संदर्भ पूर्ववत्।

व्याख्या राजा ने कहा यदि गुरु की बात सच है, तो मैं स्वयं इसी क्षण फाँसी पर चढ़ूँगा। गुरु का वचन झूठा नहीं होता। इस प्रकार राजा फाँसी पर चढ़ गया। प्रजा में खुशी की लहर दौड़ गई। मूर्ख राजा के मरते ही घर-घर में बधाई का बाजा बजने लगा। अब तक यह अँधेर नगरी थी और इसका राजा मूर्ख था।

NCERT फोल्डर

टके की बात

1. टका पुराने जमाने का सिक्का था। अगर आजकल सब चीज़ें एक रुपया किलो मिलने लगें तो उससे किस तरह के फायदे और नुकसान होंगे?

उत्तर यदि आजकल सब चीज़ें एक रुपया किलो में मिलने लगें, तो इससे गरीब लोगों को फ़ायदा होगा, क्योंकि उन्हें चीज़ें एक रुपया किलो में मिलने लगेंगी, लेकिन सभी वस्तु को बनाने की क्रिया अलग-अलग होती है, क्योंकि किसी वस्तु को बनाने में बहुत मेहनत और साधन लगते हैं, तो कोई वस्तु कम मेहनत में बन जाती है। इससे काम करने वाले लोगों को उनकी मेहनत का सही मूल्य नहीं मिलेगा। यह एक बड़ा नुकसान होगा।

2. भारत में कोई चीज़ खरीदने-बेचने के लिए 'रुपये' का इस्तेमाल होता है और बांग्लादेश में 'टके' का। 'रुपया' और 'टका' क्रमशः भारत और बांग्लादेश की मुद्राएँ हैं। नीचे लिखे देशों की मुद्राएँ कौन-सी हैं?

सऊदी अरब, जापान, फ्रांस, इटली, इंग्लैंड

उत्तर

सऊदी अरब	रियाल
जापान	येन
फ्रांस	यूरो
इटली	यूरो
इंग्लैंड	पौंड/स्टर्लिंग

कविता की कहानी

1. इस कविता की कहानी अपने शब्दों में लिखो।

उत्तर इस प्रश्न के उत्तर के लिए कविता का सार देखें।

2. क्या तुमने कोई और ऐसी कहानी या कविता पढ़ी है, जिसमें सूझबूझ से बिगड़ा काम बना हो, उसे अपनी कक्षा में सुनाओ।

उत्तर छात्र स्वयं करें।

3. कविता को ध्यान से पढ़कर 'अंधेर नगरी' के बारे में कुछ वाक्य लिखो। (सड़कें, बाजार, राजा का राजकाज)

उत्तर अँधेर नगरी के बारे में कुछ वाक्य

(क) अँधेरी नगरी की सड़कें चमकदार थीं।
(ख) अँधेर नगरी में बाज़ार में सभी चीज़ें टके सेर भाव में मिलती थीं।
(ग) अँधेर नगरी में कोई नियम नहीं था।
(घ) अँधेर नगरी में राजा को न्याय करना नहीं आता था।

4. क्या ऐसे देश को 'अँधेर नगरी' कहना ठीक है? अपने उत्तर का कारण भी बताओ।

उत्तर हाँ, बिल्कुल ऐसे देश को 'अँधेर नगरी' कहना ठीक है, क्योंकि यहाँ मूर्ख राजा का शासन है, जिसे कोई ज्ञान नहीं है।

कविता की कहानी

1. "प्रजा खुश हुई जब मरा मूर्ख राजा।"

(क) अँधेर नगरी की प्रजा राजा के मरने पर खुश क्यों हुई?

उत्तर अँधेर नगरी की प्रजा राजा के मरने पर इसलिए खुश हुई, क्योंकि राजा की मूर्खता के कारण लोग परेशान थे।

(ख) यदि वे राजा से परेशान थे, तो उन्होंने उसे खुद क्यों नहीं हटाया? आपस में चर्चा करो।

उत्तर प्रजा ने राजा को खुद इसलिए नहीं हटाया, क्योंकि राजा के खिलाफ़ जाना आसान नहीं होता है। वह अपने धन के बल पर अधिक शक्तिशाली होता है। इसलिए ऐसे राजा से कोई बुद्धिमान व्यक्ति ही अपनी बुद्धि का प्रयोग करके उस राजा के शासन से प्रजा को आज़ाद करवा सकता है।

2. "गुरु का कथन झूठ होता नहीं है।"

(क) गुरु जी ने क्या बात कही थी?

उत्तर गुरुजी ने कहा था कि यह मुहुर्त फाँसी पर चढ़ने के लिए शुभ है।

(ख) राजा यह बात सुनकर फाँसी पर लटक गया। तुम्हारे विचार से गुरुजी ने जो बात कही, क्या वह सच थी?

उत्तर राजा गुरुजी की बात सुनकर फाँसी पर लटक गया, लेकिन गुरुजी ने जो बात कही थी, वह सच नहीं थी।

3. गुरुजी ने यह बात कहकर सही किया या गलत? आपस में चर्चा करो।

उत्तर गुरुजी ने यह बात कहकर सही किया, क्योंकि इस झूठ से उन्होंने अपने बेगुनाह चेले की जान बचाई थी।

अलग तरह से

अगर कविता ऐसे शुरू हो तो आगे किस तरह बढ़ेगी?
थी बिजली और उसकी सहेली थी बदली

उत्तर फिर से एक बार कविता पढ़ो और इस प्रश्न को स्वयं करो।

क्या होता यदि

1. मंत्री की गर्दन फंदे के बराबर की होती?

उत्तर मंत्री की गर्दन फंदे के बराबर की होती तो मंत्री को फाँसी पर चढ़ा दिया जाता।

2. राजा गुरुजी की बातों में न आता?

उत्तर राजा गुरुजी की बातों में न आता तो चेले को फाँसी पर चढ़ा दिया जाता।

3. अगर संतरी कहता कि "दीवार इसलिए गिरी, क्योंकि पोली थी" तो महाराज किस-किस को बुलाते? आगे क्या होता?

उत्तर अगर संतरी कहता कि दीवार इसलिए गिरी, क्योंकि पोली थी, तो महाराज कारीगर, भिश्ती और मशकवाले को बुलाते। फिर शायद वह इन सबको फाँसी की सजा देने की आज्ञा दे देते।

शब्दों की छानबीन

1. नीचे लिखे वाक्य पढ़ो जिन शब्दों के नीचे रेखा खिंची है, उन्हें आजकल कैसे लिखते हैं? यह भी बताओ।

(क) न जाने की अँधेर हो कौन छन में!
(ख) गुरुजी ने खा तेज़ ग्वालिन न भग री!
(ग) इसी से गिरी, यह न मोती घनी थी!
(घ) ये गलती न मेरी, यह गलती बिरानी!
(ङ) न ऐसी महूरत बनी बढ़िया जैसी

उत्तर

(क) छन	क्षण	(ख) भग	भाग
(ग) घनी	गहरी	(घ) बिरानी	पराई
(ङ) महूरत	मुहूर्त		

2. 'चमाचम थी सड़कें'········ इस पंक्ति में 'चमाचम' शब्द आया है। नीचे लिखे शब्दों को पढ़ो और दिए गए वाक्यों में ये शब्द भरो

पटापट चकाचक फटाफट चटाचट झकाझक खटाखट चटपट

- आँधी के कारण पेड़ से ············ फल गिर रहे हैं।
- हँसा अपना सारा काम ············ कर लेती है।
- आज रहमान ने ············ सारे लड्डू खा डाले।
- उस भुक्खड़ ने ············ सारे लड्डू खा डाले।
- सारे बर्तन धुलकर ········· हो गए।

उत्तर
- आँधी के कारण पेड़ से **पटापट** फल गिर रहे हैं।
- हँसा अपना सारा काम **फटाफट** कर लेती है।
- आज रहमान ने **झकाझक** सारे लड्डू खा डाले।
- उस भुक्खड़ ने **चटपट** सारे लड्डू खा डाले।
- सारे बर्तन धुलकर **चकाचक** हो गए।

अभ्यास प्रश्न

बहुविकल्पीय प्रश्न

1. गुरु और चेला किसके बिना निकल पड़ते हैं?
   (क) पैसे के (ख) खाने के
   (ग) पानी के (घ) कपड़ों के
2. चलते-चलते गुरु और चेला किस नगरी में पहुँच जाते हैं?
   (क) उजाला नगरी (ख) अँधेर नगरी
   (ग) हरी नगरी (घ) रोशनी नगरी
3. अँधेर नगरी में सभी चीज़ों का दाम कितना है?
   (क) एक टका (ख) दो टका
   (ग) तीन टका (घ) चार टका
4. अँधेर नगरी का राजा कैसा था?
   (क) समझदार (ख) मूर्ख
   (ग) बहादुर (घ) बुद्धिमान
5. संतरी ने दीवार के विषय में क्या बताया?
   (क) दीवार कमजोर बनी थी (ख) दीवार मोटी नहीं थी
   (ग) दीवार घनी नहीं थी (घ) ये सभी

उत्तर 1. (क) पैसे के 2. (ख) अँधेर नगरी
3. (क) एक टका 4. (ख) मूर्ख
5. (घ) ये सभी

काव्यांश पर आधारित प्रश्न

निम्नलिखित काव्यांश को पढ़कर उस पर आधारित प्रश्नों के उत्तर दीजिए।

काव्यांश

वह राजा नहीं, चक्रवर्ती बनेगा,
यह संसार का छत्र उस पर तनेगा।
कहा राजा ने बात सच गर यही
गुरु का कथन, झूठ होता नहीं है।
कहा राजा ने फाँसी पर मैं चढ़ूँगा
इसी दम फाँसी पर मैं ही टँगूँगा।
चढ़ा फाँसी राजा बजा खूब बाजा
प्रजा खुश हुई जब मरा मूर्ख राजा
बजा खूब घर-घर बधाई का बाजा
थी अँधेर नगरी, था अनबूझ राजा।।

1. गुरु के अनुसार कौन-सा राजा चक्रवर्ती बनेगा?
   (क) जो संसार की रक्षा करेगा
   (ख) जो सच बोलेगा
   (ग) जो महूरत में फाँसी पर चढ़ेगा
   (घ) उपरोक्त में से कोई नहीं
2. राजा फाँसी पर क्यों चढ़ा?
   (क) क्योंकि गुरु की बात सही होती है
   (ख) क्योंकि राजा का मन कर रहा था
   (ग) क्योंकि फाँसी राजा के नाप की थी
   (घ) क्योंकि राजा की गर्दन मोटी थी
3. प्रजा खुश क्यों हुई?
4. गुरु और चेला आपस में क्यों लड़ रहे थे?

उत्तर 1. (ग) जो महूरत में फाँसी पर चढ़ेगा
2. (क) क्योंकि गुरु की बात सही होती हैं
3. प्रजा इसलिए खुश हुई, क्योंकि मूर्ख राजा मर गया था।
4. गुरु और चेला लड़ने का नाटक कर रहे थे, ताकि राजा को उनकी बात पर विश्वास हो जाए।

निम्नलिखित प्रश्नों के उत्तर दीजिए

1. चेले ने गुरु की बात क्यों नहीं मानी? कारण सोच-समझकर लिखिए।

उत्तर चेला लालची था, वह अँधेर नगरी की बातों को सुनकर गुरु की बात नहीं मानता और उसी नगरी में रह जाता है।

2. चेला नगरी को देखकर प्रसन्न क्यों हुआ?

उत्तर चेला नगरी को देखकर इसलिए प्रसन्न हुआ, क्योंकि वहाँ हर चीज का दाम एक टका था।

3. यदि आपके घर के पास सभी सामान एक रुपये में मिलें तो आप क्या खरीदेंगे?

उत्तर यदि मेरे घर के पास सभी सामान एक रुपये में मिले, तो मैं तब भी केवल अपनी जरूरत के सामान को ही खरीदूँगा।

4. आपके विचार से दीवार गिरने का क्या कारण होगा?

उत्तर मेरे विचार से दीवार को बनाने में घटिया सामान का उपयोग किया गया होगा, जिसके कारण दीवार कमजोर बन गई होगी व गिर गई होगी।

अध्याय 13

स्वामी की दादी

पाठ का सार

स्वामीनाथन की दादी एक बंद-सी कोठरी में अपने सामान के साथ रहती थीं। स्वामीनाथन अपनी दादी के पास सुरक्षित महसूस करता था। उसने पहले राजम और मणि की दुश्मनी और फिर दोस्ती की कहानी दादी को कह सुनाई। स्वामीनाथन ने दादी को बताया कि राजम के पास सचमुच की पुलिस की वर्दी है। उसके पिता पुलिस अधीक्षक हैं अर्थात् पुलिस के सबसे बड़े अफसर। इन बातों ने दादी को बहुत प्रभावित किया। दादी को अपने पुराने दिन याद आते हैं, जब स्वामीनाथन के दादा रौबदार सब-मजिस्ट्रेट थे और जिनके दफ्तर में पुलिस वाले काँपते हुए खड़े रहते थे।

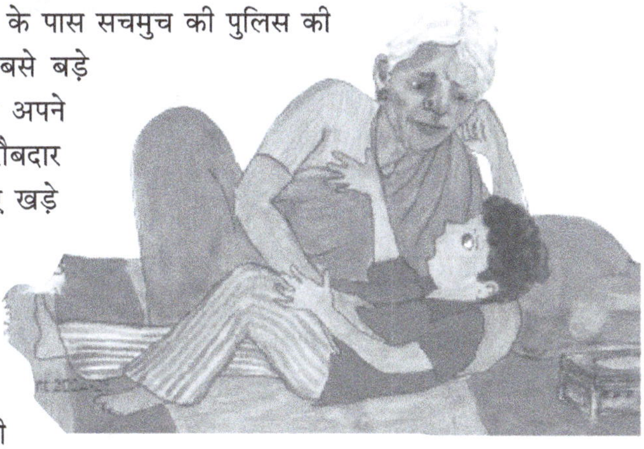

खूँखार डाकू डरकर भाग जाते थे। स्वामीनाथन दादी की कहानी से ऊब जाता है और दादी को रोककर राजम के बारे में बताने लगता है। राजम को गणित में 100 में से 90 अंक मिलने की बात पर दादी उसे भी अच्छे अंक लाने की सलाह देती है। वह बताती है कि उसके दादाजी कम समय में सवालों का जवाब दे देते थे, जिससे अध्यापक भी हैरान हो जाते थे। उन्हें एम. ए. पास करने पर बड़ा मैडल मिला था। कई वर्षों तक उस मैडल को मैं गले में पहनती रही, फिर उसे तुम्हारी बुआ को दे दिया, जो इतनी बेवकूफ निकली कि उसे गलवाकर मामूली-सी चूड़ियाँ बनवा लीं।

स्वामीनाथन ने दादी को फिर से कहा बेकार की बातें मत करो, राजम के बारे में सुनना नहीं चाहती हो क्या? दादी ने झट कहा हाँ-हाँ बोलो। वह बताता है कि राजम के पिता एक जंगल में डेरा डाले हुए थे तो अचानक दो शेर उन पर झपटे और एक ने पीछे से हमला करके उसके पिता को गिरा दिया। दूसरे ने राजम का पीछा किया। राजम ने एक झाड़ी में छिपकर शेर को गोली से मार गिराया। कहानी खत्म होते ही वह दादी से पूछता है बताओ कितने शेर थे? दादी के गलत जवाब से स्वामीनाथन उनसे चिढ़ जाता है और कहता है कि तुम इसीलिए ऐसा कर रही हो, क्योंकि तुम राजम को पसंद नहीं करतीं, लेकिन दादी के विश्वास दिलाने पर कि राजम सचमुच बहुत प्यारा लड़का है, तो स्वामीनाथन फिर खुश हो जाता है। उसके बाद दादी उसे हरिश्चंद्र की कहानी सुनाने लगती हैं, लेकिन बीच में ही स्वामीनाथन सो जाता है और खर्राटे भरने लगता है। दादी भी रुक-रुककर कहानी बोलती हुई सो जाती हैं।

शब्दार्थ

कक्ष-कमरा, खूँखार-डरावना, खतरनाक, दफ्तर-ऑफिस, अधीर-बेचैन, परीक्षक-जो परीक्षा की कॉपी जाँचते हैं, चकित कर देना-हैरान कर देना, ऊलजलूल-बेकार।

NCERT फोल्डर

कहानी से

1. **"सच? राजम बड़ा बहादुर लड़का है।" स्वामी को क्यों लगा कि दादी ने यह बात उसे खुश करने के लिए कही?**

उत्तर स्वामी अच्छी तरह जानता था कि उसकी दादी राजम को पसंद नहीं करती हैं। इसलिए उनके मुँह से राजम की बड़ाई सुनकर उसे लगा कि वे उसे खुश करने के लिए ऐसा कर रही हैं।

2. **मैडल से चूड़ियाँ बनवा लेने पर दादी ने बुआ को महामूर्ख क्यों माना?**

उत्तर मैडल आसानी से प्राप्त नहीं होता है। उसे हासिल करने के लिए कड़ी मेहनत करनी पड़ती है। मैडल प्रेरणा देता है। बुआ ने उसका महत्त्व नहीं समझा और उससे चूड़ियाँ बनवा लीं। इसीलिए दादी ने उसे महामूर्ख कहा।

3. **पाठ के आधार पर दादी या स्वामी के स्वभाव, आदतों आदि के बारे में तुम्हें क्या पता चलता है? किसी एक के बारे में दस-बारह वाक्य लिखो।**

उत्तर स्वामी कम उम्र का लड़का था, जो अपनी दादी के साथ उनकी कोठरी में रहता था। उसे दादी से बहुत लगाव था। वह दादी की गोद में जब सिर रखकर लेटता था तो स्वयं को बहुत सुरक्षित महसूस करता था। उसे दादी की पुरानी बातें बिल्कुल भी पसंद नहीं थीं। वह हमेशा यही चाहता था कि दादी उसकी सारी बात सुनें और उनका जवाब भी दें। कभी-कभी वह दादी से चिढ़ भी जाता था, लेकिन तब भी उसके मन में दादी ही समाई रहतीं।

तुम्हारी समझ से

1. **स्वामी ने राजम को 'ऊँची चीज़' माना। क्या तुम स्वामी की राय से सहमत हो? अपने उत्तर के कारण लिखो।**

उत्तर हाँ, मैं स्वामी की राय से सहमत हूँ। स्वामी राजम से बहुत प्रभावित था, क्योंकि राजम पढ़ने में तेज़ था। उसके गणित में अच्छे नंबर आते थे। वह बहादुर भी था। उसने बचपन में एक शेर को मारा था और तो और उसके पिताजी पुलिस के सबसे बड़े अफसर थे। उसके पास पुलिस की वर्दी थी।

2. **स्वामी का अपनी दादी के साथ कैसा रिश्ता था? तीन-चार वाक्यों में लिखो।**

उत्तर स्वामी को अपनी दादी से बहुत प्रेम था। वह उनकी गोद में सिर रखकर सुरक्षित महसूस करता था। वह उनसे चिढ़कर भी बहुत प्यार करता था। रोज़ रात में उनके साथ सोता था। दादी के साथ से वह बेहद खुश था।

कहानी और तुम

1. **(क) "स्वामीनाथन के दादा रौबदार सब मजिस्ट्रेट थे।" किसी व्यक्ति का रौब किन बातों से पता चलता है?**

(ख) क्या तुम्हारे आसपास कोई रौबदार व्यक्ति है? शब्दों के जरिए उसका खाका खींचो।

उत्तर

(क) किसी व्यक्ति का रौब उसके पद और पद के साथ उसकी ईमानदारी व सामाजिक व्यवहार से पता चलता है। एक अच्छे प्रभावशाली व्यक्तित्व की सब इज्जत करते हैं।

(ख) छात्र स्वयं करें।

2. **"स्वामीनाथन दादी के पास ········ बहुत प्रसन्न और सुरक्षित महसूस कर रहा था।" तुम कब असुरक्षित महसूस करती हो?**

उत्तर जब मेरे माता-पिता कहीं जाते हैं और मैं घर में अकेली होती हूँ, तब मैं असुरक्षित महसूस करती हूँ। अपने परिवार के साथ रहने पर मुझे असुरक्षा का भाव नहीं होता।

3. **तुम इन हालात में कैसा महसूस करती हो?**

(क) दोस्त के घर में।

(ख) जब तुम पहली बार किसी के घर जाती हो।

(ग) रेलगाड़ी या बस में किसी सफ़र पर।

(घ) जब तुम मुख्याध्यापक के कमरे में जाती हो।

उत्तर

(क) दोस्त के घर में अच्छा महसूस करती हूँ।

(ख) जब पहली बार किसी के घर जाती हूँ तो पहले थोड़ा संकोच और डर महसूस होता है, लेकिन कुछ देर बातचीत करने पर ठीक हो जाती हूँ।

(ग) रेलगाड़ी या बस में सफ़र करते समय मैं बेहद खुशी का अनुभव करती हूँ और मम्मी के साथ ही रहना पसंद करती हूँ।

(घ) जब मैं मुख्याध्यापक के कमरे में जाती हूँ, तो थोड़ी घबराहट होती है।

पता करो

1. सब-मजिस्ट्रेट कौन होता है? क्या वह पुलिस विभाग में होता है?

उत्तर सब-मजिस्ट्रेट एक न्यायाधीश (जज) होता है। वह पुलिस विभाग से संबंधित नहीं होता।

2. तुम्हारा घर या स्कूल किस थाने में आता है? थाने में कौन-कौन से पद होते हैं? उन व्यक्तियों के नाम भी पता करो जो इन पदों पर हैं। नीचे दी गई तालिका में इकट्ठा की गई जानकारी को दर्ज करो।

थाने का नाम	....
पद	व्यक्ति का नाम
....	....
....	....
....	....

उत्तर थाने में जो पद होते हैं, उनका नाम क्रमानुसार

एस. एच. ओ.

सब-इंस्पेक्टर

हवलदार

सिपाही

नोट विद्यार्थी अपने थाने का नाम पता करें और उपर्युक्त पदों पर जो व्यक्ति आसीन हैं, उनका नाम भी लिखें।

दादी का बक्सा

"उसका (दादी) सामान था-पाँच दरियाँ, तीन चादरें .... लकड़ी का एक छोटा बक्सा, जिसमें ताँबे के सिक्के, इलायची, लौंग और सुपारी पड़े रहते थे।"

1. दादी अपने बक्से में इलायची, लौंग और सुपारी क्यों रखती होंगी?
2. क्या तुम्हारे घर में इनका इस्तेमाल होता है? किस-किस तरह से होता है?
3. ताँबे के सिक्के बनाने के लिए किस-किस धातु का इस्तेमाल होता है?
4. सिक्के कौन-कौन सी धातु के बने हो सकते हैं?

उत्तर

1. खाना खाने के बाद उसे पचाने के लिए।
2. हाँ, मेरे घर में भी इन चीज़ों का इस्तेमाल होता है। इलायची और लौंग का प्रयोग चाय और सब्ज़ियों को बनाने में होता है। सुपारी का प्रयोग पूजा में होता है।
3. ताँबे और लोहे जैसी दो धातुओं से ताँबे के सिक्के बनाए जाते हैं।
4. सिक्के ताँबा, सोना, चाँदी, लोहा आदि के बने होते हैं।

शब्दों की बात

1. नीचे पहले स्तंभ के रेखांकित विशेषणों और दूसरे स्तंभ के शब्दों का वाक्य में प्रयोग करो। तुम एक से अधिक वाक्यों का सहारा भी ले सकती हो।

<u>ऊलजलूल</u> कल्पना	चेतावनी
<u>रूखा</u> स्वर	मिठास
<u>खूँखार</u> डाकू	समर्थन

उत्तर **ऊलजलूल** दादी की **ऊलजलूल** बातों से स्वामी ऊब गया था।

रूखा हमें **रूखा** व्यवहार करने से बचना चाहिए।

खूँखार **खूँखार** जंगली जानवर अब सड़कों पर देखने को मिल जाते हैं।

चेतावनी नेहा ने अपने भाई को उसका सामान न लेने की **चेतावनी** दी है।

मिठास छोटे बच्चों की बोली में बड़ी **मिठास** होती है।

समर्थन हम सब पेड़ बचाने के **समर्थन** में हाज़िर हैं।

2. नीचे कहानी से कुछ वाक्यों के अंश दिए गए हैं। इनमें जिन शब्दों के नीचे रेखा खिंची है, उनका लिंग पहचानो और लिखो।

पुलिस की <u>वर्दी</u>	काफी बड़ा <u>दफ्तर</u>
ताँबे के <u>सिक्के</u>	अपने सारे <u>सामान</u>
दसवाँ <u>हिस्सा</u>	उस जैसा <u>महामूर्ख</u>

उत्तर

शब्द	लिंग
वर्दी	स्त्रीलिंग
सिक्के	पुल्लिंग
हिस्सा	पुल्लिंग
दफ्तर	पुल्लिंग
सामान	पुल्लिंग
महामूर्ख	पुल्लिंग

अभ्यास प्रश्न

बहुविकल्पीय प्रश्न

1. स्वामीनाथन किसके साथ अपने को सुरक्षित महसूस करता है?

(क) राजम के साथ (ख) बुआ के साथ
(ग) दादी के साथ (घ) दोस्त के साथ

2. किसने शेर को मारा था?

(क) राजम ने (ख) बुआ ने
(ग) दादी ने (घ) स्वामीनाथन ने

3. बुआ ने मैडल पिघलवाकर क्या बनवा लिया?

(क) घर (ख) चूड़ियाँ (ग) पायल (घ) हार

4. राजम को गणित में कितने अंक मिले?

(क) पचास (ख) साठ (ग) अस्सी (घ) नब्बे

उत्तर 1. (ग) दादी के साथ 2. (क) राजम ने
3. (ख) चूड़ियाँ 4. (घ) नब्बे

गद्यांश पर आधारित प्रश्न

निम्नलिखित गद्यांश को पढ़कर उस पर आधारित प्रश्नों के उत्तर दीजिए।

गद्यांश

स्वामीनाथन की दादी एक बंद-सी कोठरी में अपने सामान के साथ रहती थीं। स्वामीनाथन दादी के पास सुरक्षित महसूस करता था। उसने पहले राजम और मणि की दुश्मनी और फिर दोस्ती की कहानी दादी को कह सुनाई।

स्वामीनाथन ने दादी को यह भी बताया कि राजम के पास सचमुच की पुलिस की वर्दी है। उसके पिता पुलिस अधीक्षक हैं। उन्होंने स्वामीनाथन को यह भी बताया कि दादाजी से डरकर खूँखार डाकू तक भाग जाते थे। स्वामीनाथन दादी की कहानी से ऊब रहा था। वह अधीर होकर दादी की गढ़ी हुई बातों को खत्म होने का इंतज़ार कर रहा था। उसने दादी को रोका और राजम के बारे में बताने लगा। राजम को गणित में 100 में से 90 अंक मिलते हैं। इस पर दादी ने उसे सलाह दी कि तुम्हें भी इतने अच्छे अंक लाने चाहिए।

1. किसके पास सचमुच की पुलिस की वर्दी थी?

(क) राजम (ख) दादी (ग) मणि (घ) बुआ

2. किसके पिता पुलिस अधीक्षक हैं?

(क) दादी (ख) मणि (ग) बुआ (घ) राजम

3. स्वामीनाथन दादी की बातों से क्यों ऊब रहा था?

4. राजम के अंक सुनकर दादी ने स्वामीनाथन को क्या सलाह दी?

उत्तर

1. (क) राजम 2. (घ) राजम
3. स्वामीनाथन दादी की बातों से इसलिए ऊब रहा था, क्योंकि उसे दादी की बातों में कोई रुचि नहीं थी।
4. राजम के अंक सुनकर दादी ने स्वामीनाथन को उतने ही अच्छे अंक लाने की सलाह दी।

निम्नलिखित प्रश्नों के उत्तर दीजिए

1. स्वामीनाथन बार-बार राजम की बातें क्यों करता था?

उत्तर स्वामीनाथन बार-बार राजम की बातें इसलिए करता था, क्योंकि राजम स्वामीनाथन का दोस्त था।

2. स्वामीनाथन को अंत में दादी की किस बात से खुशी हुई?

उत्तर अंत में जब दादी ने विश्वास दिलाया कि राजम सचमुच बहुत प्यारा लड़का है, तब यह सुनकर स्वामीनाथन को बहुत खुशी हुई।

3. स्वामीनाथन के चिढ़ने का कारण क्या था?

उत्तर राजम की बहादुरी भरी कहानी पर जब दादी की ओर से कोई प्रतिक्रिया नहीं आई और वह सो गई, इस बात पर स्वामीनाथन चिढ़ गया था।

लेखन संबंधी प्रश्न

1. आप अपने दादा-दादी से दूर रहते हो, उन्हें याद करते हुए उनकी कुशलता पूछने हेतु एक पत्र लिखिए।

उत्तर परीक्षा भवन,
दिल्ली।

दिनांक 26 अक्टूबर, 20XX

आदरणीय दादा-दादी जी,

नमस्कार
आशा है आप सब वहाँ ठीक होंगे। मैं भी यहाँ ठीक हूँ। दादीजी आज मैंने एक कहानी पढ़ी जिसे पढ़कर मुझे आपकी बहुत याद आ गई और तुरंत ही मैं आपको पत्र लिखने बैठ गया।

मैं आपके द्वारा बताई गई प्रेरणास्प्रद बातों व शिक्षा को ध्यान में रखता हूँ और जीवन में उच्च मूल्यों को अपनाता हूँ और आपके दिखाए जीवन के आदर्शों का पालन करता हूँ। आप दोनों अपना ध्यान रखिए और जल्द ही हम सब आपसे मिलने आएँगे।

आपका प्यारा पोता

क. ख. ग.

अध्याय 14

बाघ आया उस रात

कविता का सार

प्रस्तुत कविता में दो बच्चे बाघ के बारे में अपने बाबा से बातचीत करते हैं। एक बच्चा अपने बाबा से कहता है, बाघ इधर से निकला था और उधर चला गया था। वह रात के समय आया था। हो सकता है वह फिर आ जाए। अत: आप रात के समय बाहर मत निकलना। बच्चा आगे बताता है—बाघ झरने के पास रहता है। मैं जब दिन के समय वहाँ गया था, तो उसे देखा था और उसे ही नहीं, उसके दो बच्चे और बाघिन को भी देखा था। बाघिन पूरा दिन पहरा देती रहती है। बाघ या तो सोता है या अपने बच्चों के साथ खेलता है। इस पर दूसरा बच्चा कहता है, बाबा बाघ कोई काम नहीं करता है। वह न तो ऑफिस जाता है और न कॉलेज। वह स्कूल में भी नहीं जाता है। पाँच वर्ष के बेटू ने एक बार फिर अपने बाबा को मना किया रात में बाहर होकर बाथरूम जाने के लिए।

काव्यांशों की व्याख्या

काव्यांश 1

"वो इधर से निकला।
उधर चला गया"
वो आँखें फैलाकर
बतला रहा था–
"हाँ बाबा, बाघ आया उस रात,
आप रात को बाहर न निकलो!
जाने कब बाघ फिर से आ जाए।"
"हाँ, वो ही! वो ही जो
उस झरने के पास रहता है।
वहाँ अपन दिन के वक्त
गए थे न एक रोज़?
बाघ उधर ही तो रहता है।
बाबा, उसके दो बच्चे हैं।
बाघिन सारा दिन पहरा देती है।
बाघ या तो सोता है।
या बच्चों से खेलता है....."

शब्दार्थ वक्त–समय, पहरा–निगरानी।

संदर्भ/प्रसंग प्रस्तुत पंक्तियाँ हमारी पाठ्यपुस्तक 'रिमझिम भाग-5' में संकलित कविता 'बाघ आया उस रात' से ली गई हैं। इस कविता के रचयिता "नागार्जुन" हैं। इन पंक्तियों में कवि ने एक रात बाघ के आने का वर्णन किया है।

व्याख्या एक बच्चा आँखें फैलाते हुए दूसरे बच्चे को बताता है कि बाघ इधर से निकला था और उधर चला गया था। वह अपने बाबा से कहता है कि हाँ बाबा, बाघ उस रात को आया था। आप बाहर नहीं निकलना। वह किसी भी समय कभी भी आ सकता है। वह बाघ झरने के पास रहता है। जब मैं दिन के समय वहाँ गया था, तो बाघ को उधर ही देखा था। उसके दो बच्चे हैं। बाघिन पूरा पहरा देती है। बाघ या तो सोता है या बच्चों के साथ खेलता है।

काव्यांश 2

दूसरा बालक बोला
"बाघ कहीं काम नहीं करता
न किसी दफ्तर में
न कॉलेज में ऽऽ"
छोटू बोला-
"स्कूल में भी नहीं... "
पाँच-साला बेटू ने
हमें फिर से आगाह किया
"अब रात को बाहर होकर बाथरूम न जाना!"

शब्दार्थ *दफ़्तर-काम करने का स्थान, आगाह-सावधान।*

प्रसंग इन पंक्तियों में कवि ने बाघ द्वारा कोई काम न किए जाने का वर्णन किया है।

व्याख्या दूसरा बालक भी कहता है, बाघ कोई काम नहीं करता। वह न ऑफिस जाता है और न किसी स्कूल-कॉलेज में जाता है। पाँच वर्ष का बेटू फिर हमें सावधान करते हुए कहता है, आप रात को बाहर होकर बाथरूम मत जाना बाघ के आने का खतरा है।

NCERT फोल्डर

बात-बात में

1. "वो इधर से निकला, उधर चला गया"
(क) यह बात कौन-किसे बता रहा होगा?
(ख) तुम्हें यह उत्तर कविता की किन पंक्तियों से पता चला?

उत्तर (क) यह बात बेटू-छोटू को बता रहा होगा।

(ख) छोटू बोला
"स्कूल में भी नहीं..."
पाँच-साला बेटू ने
हमें फिर से आगाह किया
"अब रात को बाहर होकर बाथरूम न जाना!"

खबर तेंदुए की

(क) कक्षा-2 की रिमझिम में अखबार में छपा एक समाचार दिया गया है। साथ में उस समाचार के आधार पर लिखी एक कहानी भी दी गई है। उसे एक बार फिर से पढ़ो।

(ख) अब 'बाघ आया उस रात' कविता के आधार पर एक 'समाचार' लिखो।

(ग) तेंदुए और बाघ में क्या अंतर है? पता करो। इस काम के लिए तुम बड़ों से बातचीत भी कर सकते हो।

उत्तर (क) छात्र स्वयं करें।

(ख) **रात को बाघ ने गाँव में मचाया कोहराम** कल रात के अँधेरे में एक बाघ गाँव में घुस आया। बाघ के आने पर चारों ओर उथल-पुथल मच गई। लोग अपनी जान बचाकर भागने लगे। चारों तरफ हलचल मच गई व भय का वातावरण छा गया। सभी लोग अपने बच्चों को घर के अंदर ले गए। इस बाघ को लोगों ने दो दिन पहले जंगल के किनारे देखा था। वह अपने बच्चों के साथ खेल रहा था और बाघिन पहरा दे रही थी। गाँव के सभी लोग बाघ के आ जाने से भयभीत हैं।

(ग) तेंदुए बाघ से थोड़े छोटे होते हैं। इनके दौड़ने की गति भी एक समान नहीं होती। तेंदुए पर गोल धब्बे जैसे निशान होते हैं, जबकि बाघ के शरीर पर धारियाँ होती हैं।

उस रात

इस कविता में एक ऐसी रात की बात की गई है, जिस रात को कुछ अनोखी घटना घटी थी।

(क) उस रात को कौन-सी अनूठी बात हुई थी?
(ख) तुम्हारे विचार से क्या सचमुच यह बात अनूठी है? क्यों?
(ग) उस रात को और क्या-क्या हुआ होगा? अपने साथियों से बातचीत करके लिखो।

उत्तर (क) उस रात को गाँव में बाघ आ गया था।

(ख) हाँ, यह बात सचमुच अनूठी है, क्योंकि बाघ हिंसक होते हैं। उनका घर जंगल होता है। किसी भी कारण से जब वे मानव बस्ती में आ जाते हैं, तो दहशत मचा देते हैं।

(ग) उस रात को बाघ के आ जाने से लोगों में खलबली मच गई होगी। सभी लोग डर से घरों में छिप गए होंगे।

बाघ के काम

"बाघ कहीं काम नहीं करता, न किसी दफ्तर में, न कॉलेज में"

बाघ दिन भर क्या-क्या करता होगा? कहाँ-कहाँ जाता होगा? अपने साथियों के साथ मिलकर जानकारी एकत्रित करो। फिर

चर्चा करके उस पर एक चित्रात्मक पुस्तक तैयार करो। इसे तुम अपने पुस्तकालय में भी रख सकते हो।

उत्तर बाघ अपने भोजन की तलाश में इधर-उधर भटकता होगा, वह अपने बच्चों के साथ खेलता होगा। उनकी रक्षा करता होगा तथा नदियों, झरनों तालाबों में जाता होगा।

नोट चित्रात्मक पुस्तक विद्यार्थी स्वयं तैयार करें।

आँखें फैलाकर

वो इधर से निकला उधर चला गया।
वो आँखें फैलाकर बतला रहा था।

नीचे आँख से जुड़े कुछ और मुहावरे दिए गए हैं, वाक्यों में इनका इस्तेमाल करो।

आँख लगना - आँख दिखाना
आँख मूँदना - आँख बचाना
आँखें भर आना - सिर-आँखों पर बैठाना

उत्तर **आँख लगना** टी.वी. देखते-देखते मेरी **आँख लग** गई।

आँख मूँदना बीमारी के कारण उन्होंने कम उम्र में अपनी **आँखें मूँद** लीं।

आँखें भर आना उस गरीब बालक को देखकर मेरी **आँख भर** आई।

आँख दिखाना सीमा ने रीमा को **आँखें दिखाकर** डरा दिया।

आँख बचाना-आज पूजा ने गृहकार्य नहीं किया देखो कैसे अध्यापक से **आँखें बचाकर** बैठी है।

सिर-आँखों पर बैठाना अरे! उसने तो अपने पालतू पशु को **सर पर बिठाकर** रखा है।

शब्दों की दुनिया

(क) **पाँच साला बेटू ने हमें फिर से आगाह किया। 'आगाह किया' का मतलब क्या हो सकता है?**

(i) सचेत किया
(ii) मनोरंजन किया
(iii) बताया
(iv) समझाया

उत्तर (i) सचेत किया

(ख) **कविता में इनमें से कौन-सा भाव झलकता है?**

उत्तर डर का भाव

(ग) **किन-किन पंक्तियों/शब्दों से ये भाव व्यक्त हो रहे हैं?**

- आश्चर्य
- डर
- अविश्वास

उत्तर
- **आश्चर्य** "वो इधर से निकला उधर चला गया ऽऽ"
- **डर** "अब रात को बाहर होकर बाथरूम न जाना।"
- **अविश्वास** "जाने कब बाघ फिर से आ जाए?"

(घ) **जब हम कविता के ज़रिए कोई बात कहते हैं, तो आमतौर पर शब्दों के क्रम को बदल देते हैं।**

- जैसे कविता का शीर्षक "बाघ आया उस रात" गद्य में "उस रात बाघ आया" होगा। ऐसा क्यों किया जाता होगा?
- इस किताब की दूसरी कविताएँ भी पढ़ो और शब्दों के क्रम में आए बदलाव पर गौर करो। ऐसे ही कुछ वाक्यों की सूची भी बनाओ।
- क्या शब्दों के क्रम में बदलाव अख़बार की खबरों में भी आता है? नीचे बने कोलाज को देखो और बताओ।

उत्तर
- कविता में लय बनाने के लिए आमतौर पर शब्दों के क्रम को बदल दिया जाता है।
- **दूसरी कविताओं में शब्दों के क्रम में आए बदलाव**
  -गुरु एक थे और था एक चेला।।
  -यह मोटी है गर्दन, इसे तुम बढ़ाओ'
  -था वह भी एक बच्चा
- हाँ, खबरों में भी शब्दों के क्रम में बदलाव आता है; जैसे—
  -जहरीली हवा की चपेट में आ रही है राजधानी दिल्ली
  -आसमान से जमीन पर गिरी सब्जियाँ
  -स्वीपर कर रहे हैं डॉक्टर का काम
  -इस बार कठिन होगा बच्चों को रिझाना

अभ्यास प्रश्न

बहुविकल्पीय प्रश्न

1. कविता में बच्चे किसके बारे में बात कर रहे हैं?
(क) शेर (ख) चीता (ग) बाघ (घ) हिरन

2. कविता में कितने बच्चे हैं?
(क) एक (ख) दो (ग) तीन (घ) चार

3. कविता में बच्चे किसे सावधान कर रहे हैं?
(क) बाबा को (ख) माँ को
(ग) अध्यापक को (घ) दोस्त को

4. बेटू कितने साल का है?
(क) एक (ख) दो (ग) तीन (घ) पाँच

5. बाघ कहाँ रहता है?
(क) घर में (ख) गाँव में
(ग) झरने के पास (घ) तालाब में

उत्तर 1. (ग) बाघ 2. (ख) दो
3. (क) बाबा को 4. (घ) पाँच
5. (ग) झरने के पास

काव्यांश पर आधारित प्रश्न

निम्नलिखित काव्यांश को पढ़कर उस पर आधारित प्रश्नों के उत्तर दीजिए।

काव्यांश

दूसरा बालक बोला
"बाघ कहीं काम नहीं करता
न किसी दफ्तर में
न कॉलेज में ऽऽ"
छोटू बोला–
"स्कूल में भी नहीं...."
पाँच-साला बेटू ने
हमें फिर से आगाह किया
"अब रात को बाहर होकर बाथरूम न जाना!"

1. "बाघ कहीं काम नहीं करता, न किसी दफ्तर में, न कॉलेज में ऽऽ" किसने कहा?
(क) छोटू (ख) बेटू (ग) बाबा (घ) दीदी

2. बेटू किसे आगाह कर रहा था?
(क) छोटू को (ख) दीदी को
(ग) दादी को (घ) बाबा को

3. बेटू रात को बाबा को क्या करने के लिए मना कर रहा है?

4. क्या बेटू भी बाघ से डरा हुआ है?

उत्तर
1. (क) छोटू 2. (घ) बाबा को
3. बेटू रात को बाबा को बाथरूम जाने के लिए मना कर रहा है।
4. हाँ, बेटू भी बाघ से डरा हुआ है।

निम्नलिखित प्रश्नों के उत्तर दीजिए

1. क्या बाघ या अन्य जानवरों को चिड़ियाघर में रखना ज़रूरी है? हाँ और ना का कारण बताएँ।

उत्तर हाँ, बाघ या अन्य जानवरों को चिड़ियाघर में रखना जरूरी है, क्योंकि ये जानवर लोगों को क्षति पहुँचा सकते हैं।

2. क्या छोटू और बेटू के अतिरिक्त भी अन्य लोग परेशान होंगे?

उत्तर हाँ, जंगल में बाघ के आ जाने के कारण छोटू और बेटू के अतिरिक्त वहाँ रहने वाले अन्य लोग भी परेशान होंगे।

3. 'अब रात को बाहर होकर बाथरूम न जाना' पंक्ति का आशय स्पष्ट कीजिए।

उत्तर प्रस्तुत पंक्ति का आशय है कि बच्चे अपने बाबा को रात को बाहर बाथरूम जाने से मना करते हैं, क्योंकि न जाने कब और कहाँ से बाघ आ जाए।

लेखन संबंधी प्रश्न

1. यदि आपको अचानक बाघ दिख जाएँ तो आप क्या करेंगे? लगभग 50 शब्दों में अपने विचार व्यक्त करें।

उत्तर यदि मुझे अचानक बाघ दिख जाए, तो मैं बाघ को देखकर पहले तो भयभीत हो जाऊँगा और मदद के लिए किसी को पुकार लगाऊँगा। आस-पास कहीं छुपने की जगह की खोज करूँगा। मैं बाघ पर निगरानी रखूँगा और वहाँ से कोई अन्य व्यक्ति आ रहा होगा तो उसे भी सचेत करूँगा, साथ ही वहाँ से बाघ को हटाने का उपाय करूँगा जिससे मैं वहाँ से सुरक्षित अपने घर चला जाऊँ।

अध्याय 15

बिशन की दिलेरी

पाठ का सार

दस वर्ष का बालक बिशन रोज़ की तरह प्रात:काल घर से कर्नल दत्ता के फ़ार्म हाउस जाने के लिए निकल पड़ा। वह कर्नल दत्ता की पत्नी के पास पढ़ता है। अचानक उसे गोली चलने की आवाज़ सुनाई दी। बिशन डर गया और पेड़ों की आड़ में छिप गया। अभी वह सोच ही रहा था कि गोली किसने और क्यों चलाई होगी कि तभी उसे एक और गोली के चलने की आवाज़ आई। बिशन गोली चलने का कारण समझ गया कि शिकारी गेहूँ के खेतों में दाना चुगते तीतरों को मारने के लिए उन पर गोली चला रहा होगा।

वह पेड़ों के बीच से निकलकर खेतों के किनारे चलने लगा। उसने शिकारियों को सबक सिखाने का निर्णय ले लिया। तभी उसकी नज़र एक घायल तीतर पर पड़ गई। उसने स्वेटर उतारकर तीतर पर डाल दिया और अपने सीने से चिपकाकर तेजी से पहाड़ी की ओर दौड़ पड़ा, ताकि किसी शिकारी की नज़र उस पर न पड़े। बिशन का दिल तेजी से धड़कने लगा, पर वह रुका नहीं। अचानक शिकारी उसके काफी नजदीक आ गया।

वह गुस्से में चिल्ला रहा था, ''मैं तुझे देख लूँगा, तू मेरा शिकार चुराकर नहीं ले जा सकता।'' बिशन धमकी की परवाह न करते हुए काँटेदार झाड़ियों से होकर छोटे रास्तों से निकला और किसी तरह कर्नल दत्ता के फार्म हाउस पहुँच गया और तीतर को सुरक्षित स्थान पर छिपाकर बाहर निकल गया और शिकारियों की नजर से बचने के लिए खपरैल की ढलावदार छत पर चिमनी के पीछे छिपकर बैठ गया। यहाँ से वह देख रहा था कि शिकारी कर्नल साहब के नजदीक पहुँचकर मेरे व तीतर के बारे में पूछे रहे हैं। कर्नल साहब ने आप से बाहर होकर उन्हें खूब डाँटा और वहाँ से भगा दिया। शिकारियों के जाते ही वह घायल तीतर को लेकर कर्नल दत्ता की पत्नी के पास पहुँच गया। कर्नल साहब भी वहाँ पहुँच गए। फिर दोनों ने मिलकर तीतर का उपचार किया। कर्नल साहब की पत्नी ने उसे दलिया खिलाया। फिर बिशन उसे लेकर अपने घर चला गया।

शब्दार्थ

फार्म हाउस–खेत में बना घर, पगडंडी–खेत के किनारे बना पतला लंबा रास्ता, अल्सेशियन–कुत्ते की नस्ल, लाइसेंस–सरकार द्वारा किसी वस्तु को रखने की अनुमति।

NCERT फोल्डर

कहानी से

1. "जी हाँ, हमारे पास लाइसेंस वाली बंदूकें हैं। सरपंच माधोसिंह भी हमें जानता है।" शिकारियों ने कर्नल साहब से क्या सोचकर ऐसा कहा होगा?

उत्तर शिकारियों ने कर्नल साहब से ऐसा इसलिए कहा होगा, ताकि कर्नल साहब यह समझ जाएँ कि वे अवैध रूप से शिकार नहीं कर रहे हैं, बल्कि उन्हें सरकार से लाइसेंस वाली बंदूकें मिली हैं। वह कर्नल को यह भी बताता है कि सरपंच माधोसिंह अच्छी तरह जानता है।

2. बिशन घायल तीतर को क्यों बचाना चाहता था?

उत्तर घायल तीतर को देखकर बिशन भावुक हो गया। बिशन जानता था कि अगर तीतर को उसके हाल पर छोड़ दिया तो वह मर जाएगा। इसलिए उसने तीतर को बचाना सही समझा।

3. घायल तीतर को बचाने के लिए उसे किस तरह की परेशानियाँ हुईं?

उत्तर घायल तीतर को बचाने के लिए बिशन ने कई तरह की परेशानियाँ सहीं; जैसे—कँटीले तारों की बाड़ में से होकर गुजरना, घुटने के बल चलना, हाथ-पाँव पर काँटों की बहुत-सी खरोंचें लगना, कमीज की एक आस्तीन भी फट जाना आदि।

4. घायल तीतर अगर तुम्हें मिला होता, तो क्या तुम उसे पालते या अच्छा होने पर छोड़ देते? क्यों?

उत्तर यदि घायल तीतर मुझे मिला होता तो मैं भी उसे स्वस्थ होने तक अपने पास रखता। उसका अच्छे से इलाज करवाता और जब वह ठीक हो जाता, तो उसे खुले आसमान में आजाद कर देता, जिससे वह अपना जीवन स्वतन्त्रता से अपनी इच्छानुसार व्यतीत कर सके।

भाषा की बात

1. इन वाक्यों को अपने शब्दों में लिखो।
   - सुबह की हल्की धूप में खेत सुनहरे दिखाई दे रहे थे।
   - वह इतना तेज़ चल रहा था मानो उसके पंख लग गए हों।

उत्तर
- सुबह की हल्की धूप में खेत सोने जैसा चमक रहा था।
- उसकी चाल इतनी तेज़ थी मानो पैर में पंख लगे हों।

2. "तीतर स्वेटर में फँस गया तो बिशन ने उसे पकड़ लिया और अपने सीने से चिपका लिया।" ऊपर लिखे वाक्य में 'उसे' शब्द का इस्तेमाल 'तीतर' के लिए किया गया है। एक ही संज्ञा का बार-बार इस्तेमाल करने की बजाय उसकी जगह पर कुछ खास शब्दों का प्रयोग किया जाता है। ऐसे शब्दों को सर्वनाम कहते हैं। नीचे लिखे वाक्यों में सर्वनाम का ठीक रूप छाँटकर लिखो।

   (क) मास्टर साहब ने अप्पाराव को ...... पास बुलाकर कहा ...... कल .... घर आना। (मैं, अपना, तुम)

   (ख) सेंटीला ...... घर नागालैंड के किस शहर में है? (तुम)

   (ग) सुधा ने ...... बुआ से पूछा, पापा ...... कितने बड़े हैं? (आप)

   (घ) मोहन को समझ में नहीं आ रहा कि ...... क्या करना चाहिए? (वह)

   (ङ) विमल ने ...... अफ़सर को याद दिलाया कि ...... चार बजे बैठक में जाना है। (आप, वह)

उत्तर (क) अपने, तुम, मेरे (ख) तुम्हारा (ग) अपनी, आपसे (घ) उसे (ङ) अपने, उन्हें

3. इन वाक्यों को पूरा करो

   (क) वह इतना धीरे चल रहा था, मानो ....

   (ख) रात में चमकते तारे ऐसे दिख रहे थे, मानो ....

   (ग) तुम तो मंगल ग्रह के बारे में ऐसे बता रहे हो, मानो ....

   (घ) बिल्ली चूहे को ऐसी ललचाई नज़रों से देख रही थी, मानो ....

उत्तर (क) वह इतना धीरे चल रहा था, मानो **कछुवा चल रहा हो।**

(ख) रात में चमकते तारे ऐसे दिख रहे थे, मानो **हीरे चमक रहे हों।**

(ग) तुम तो मंगल ग्रह के बारे में ऐसे बता रहे हो, मानो **तुम वहीं रहते हो।**

(घ) बिल्ली चूहे को ऐसी ललचाई नज़रों से देख रही थी, मानो **अभी खा ही जाएगी।**

फसलों के इर्द-गिर्द

1. इस कहानी में सेबों के खेत और सीढ़ीनुमा खेत का ज़िक्र आया है। अनुमान लगाकर बताओ कि यह कहानी भारत के किस भौगोलिक क्षेत्र की होगी और वहाँ सीढ़ीनुमा खेती क्यों की जाती होगी?

उत्तर यह कहानी भारत के पहाड़ी इलाके की होगी। पहाड़ों में ऊँची-नीची जमीन होने के कारण ही वहाँ सीढ़ीनुमा खेती की जाती होगी।

2. "सेबों के बाग में कीटनाशक दवा का छिड़काव हो रहा था।" यों तो कीटनाशक दवाएँ फलों, सब्जियों और अनाज की फसलों को कीड़ा लगने से बचाती हैं, पर

(क) ये कीटनाशक दवाएँ कीड़ों को नष्ट करती हैं। इनसे इनका सेवन करने से क्या हमें भी नुकसान होता होगा? पता करो और कक्षा में बातचीत करो।

(ख) ऐसे में फलों और सब्जियों का इस्तेमाल करने से पहले किन बातों को ध्यान में रखना जरूरी होगा?

उत्तर (क) कीटनाशक दवाएँ फलों, सब्जियों और अनाज की फसलों को कीड़ों से बचाती हैं, लेकिन जब हम इन्हें खाते हैं, तो ये हमें भी नुकसान पहुँचाती हैं। हमारा पाचन तंत्र गड़बड़ हो जाता है।

(ख) फलों और सब्जियों को इस्तेमाल करने से पहले अच्छी तरह धोकर पोंछ लेना चाहिए। जहाँ तक संभव हो उनके छिलके को उतार लेना चाहिए।

तुम्हारे आस-पास

1. कर्नल दत्ता ने घायल तीतर को गेंदे की पत्तियों का रस पिलाने के लिए कहा। पत्तों का इस्तेमाल कई कामों के लिए होता है। नीचे लिखी पत्तियों का इस्तेमाल किसलिए होता है?

तुलसी	नीम	मीठानीम	आम
अमरूद	तेजपत्ता	केला	सागवान

उत्तर **तुलसी** तुलसी के पत्तों का इस्तेमाल पूजा-पाठ और दवाइयों के रूप में किया जाता है।

नीम नीम की पत्तियों को पानी में उबालकर उस पानी से नहाया जाता है, पत्तियों को पीसकर घाव पर उसका लेप भी चढ़ाया जाता है।

मीठा नीम सब्जियों तथा दाल को अधिक जायकेदार बनाने में मीठे नीम की पत्तियों का इस्तेमाल होता है।

आम आम की पत्तियों का उपयोग पूजा-पाठ में होता है।

अमरूद अमरूद के पत्तों का उपयोग दवा बनाने में होता है।

तेजपत्ता सब्जियों को जायकेदार बनाने में तेजपत्ता का प्रयोग होता है।

केला केले के पत्ते का प्रयोग पूजा-पाठ में होता है।

सागवान इनके पत्तों से पत्तल तथा दोने बनाए जाते हैं।

2. कर्नल साहब के कहने पर बिशन दौड़कर दवाइयों का बक्सा ले आया। इसे तुम प्राथमिक चिकित्सा बॉक्स/फर्स्ट एड बॉक्स के नाम से जानते होंगे।

(क) इस बॉक्स में क्या-क्या चीजें होती हैं?

(ख) इसका इस्तेमाल कब-कब किया जाता है?

उत्तर (क) प्राथमिक चिकित्सा बॉक्स में रूई, डिटॉल, क्रेप बैंडेड, छोटी कैंची, घाव पर लगाने के लिए मरहम, पट्टी आदि चीजें होती हैं।

(ख) जब किसी को मामूली चोट लग जाती है या शरीर के किसी अंग से खून निकलने लगता है तब इनका उपयोग किया जाता है।

3. तुमने पर्यावरण अध्ययन में पढ़ा होगा कि पहाड़ी क्षेत्रों में आमतौर पर छतें ढलावदार बनाई जाती हैं। सोचकर बताओ ऐसा क्यों किया जाता है?

उत्तर क्योंकि ढलावदार छत से बारिश का पानी व बर्फ से पिघला पानी रुकता नहीं है बह जाता है।

पहाड़ी इलाका

इस कहानी में पहाड़ी, घाटी शब्दों का इस्तेमाल हुआ है। पहाड़ी इलाके से जुड़े हुए और शब्द सोचकर लिखो; जैसे-ढलान, चट्टान आदि।

उत्तर पथरीला, चोटी, सीढ़ीनुमा, झाड़ीदार, टेढ़ा-मेढ़ा, पहाड़ी, नदी, बर्फीला पहाड़, सँकरा, जंगली फल-फूल आदि।

तीतर

1. पहेली तीतर के दो आगे तीतर
तीतर के दो पीछे तीतर
बोलो कितने तीतर

उत्तर तीन तीतर

2. यहाँ तीतर का फोटो दिया गया है। गौर से देखो और उसका वर्णन करो। चौथी कक्षा में तुम यह कर चुके हो।

उत्तर तीतर कम ऊँचाई तक उड़ान भरने वाला एक छोटा पक्षी है। इसके पंख छोटे-छोटे होते हैं तथा यह देखने में सुंदर प्रतीत होता है। यह ज्यादातर झुंड में रहना पसंद करता है।

3. तीतर के बारे में और जानकारी इकट्ठा करो; जैसे-तीतर का घोंसला, वह क्या खाता है? आदि।

उत्तर तीतर को पेड़ से गिरने का डर होता है, इसलिए वह अपना घोंसला पेड़ पर व अधिक ऊँचाई पर नहीं बनाता। वह दलिया, गेहूँ के दाने, फल-फूल व कीड़े-मकोड़े आदि खाता है।

अभ्यास प्रश्न

बहुविकल्पीय प्रश्न

1. **बिशन कितने वर्ष का है?**
(क) नौ (ख) दस (ग) आठ (घ) सात

2. **फार्म में लगे सेबों के बाग में क्या हो रहा था?**
(क) पेड़ों की कटाई
(ख) कीटनाशक दवा का छिड़काव
(ग) पेड़ों की कटाई
(घ) सेबों को अलग करने का काम

3. **जब फ़सल पक जाती है, तो गेहूँ के खेत में कौन-से पक्षी दाना चुगने आते हैं?**
(क) कौए (ख) तोते (ग) मोर (घ) तीतर

4. **शिकारी किसे मारने चले आते हैं?**
(क) तीतर को (ख) मोर को
(ग) बिशन को (घ) कुत्ते को

5. **क्या बिशन तीतर की जान बचाने में सफल रहा?**
(क) नहीं (ख) हाँ
(ग) तीतर पहले से ही मरा हुआ था
(घ) उपरोक्त में से कोई नहीं

उत्तर 1. (ख) दस 2. (ख) कीटनाशक दवा का छिड़काव
3. (घ) तीतर 4. (क) तीतर को
5. (ख) हाँ

गद्यांश पर आधारित प्रश्न

निम्नलिखित गद्यांश को पढ़कर उस पर आधारित प्रश्नों के उत्तर दीजिए।

गद्यांश

बिशन दु:खी हो गया। वह समझ गया कि शिकारी ही तीतरों पर गोलियाँ चला रहे हैं। फिर तो वह पेड़ों के बीच से निकलकर खेतों के किनारे-किनारे चलने लगा। चलते-चलते उसने शिकारियों को सबक सिखाने का निर्णय ले लिया, तभी उसकी नज़र एक घायल तीतर पर पड़ गई। उसने स्वेटर उतारकर उस पर (तीतर पर) डाल दिया और जब वह स्वेटर में फँस गया तो उसे पकड़ लिया। उसने उसे सीने से चिपका लिया और तेजी से पहाड़ी की ओर दौड़ पड़ा, ताकि किसी शिकारी की नज़र उस पर न पड़े, लेकिन जिस बात का उसे डर था वही हुआ। वह कुछ ही दूर गया होगा कि पीछे से किसी की भारी आवाज़ सुनाई दी, "लड़के, रुक जा, नहीं तो मैं गोली मार दूँगा।" बिशन का दिल तेजी से धड़कने लगा। डर के बावजूद उसने आगे बढ़ना जारी रखा। अचानक शिकारी उसके काफी नजदीक आ गया। वह गुस्से में चिल्ला रहा था, "मैं तुझे देख लूँगा, तू मेरा शिकार चुराकर नहीं ले जा सकता।" बिशन के लिए आगे निकल भागने का रास्ता नहीं था। अत: उसने खेतों के छोटे रास्ते, जो काँटेदार झाड़ियों से भरे थे, से जाना निश्चित किया।

1. **बिशन ने शिकारियों के लिए क्या निर्णय लिया?**
(क) सबक सिखाने का (ख) डराने का
(ग) हमला करने का (घ) शिकायत करने का

2. **बिशन तीतर को लेकर तेज़ी से क्यों दौड़ने लगा?**
(क) ताकि किसी शिकारी की नज़र उस पर न पड़े
(ख) ताकि किसी जानवर की नज़र उस पर न पड़े
(ग) ताकि किसी सिपाही की नज़र उस पर न पड़े
(घ) उपरोक्त में से कोई नहीं

3. **बिशन ने किसे सीने से चिपका लिया था?**

4. **क्या बिशन को शिकारियों से डर नहीं लगा?**

उत्तर
1. (क) सबक सिखाने का
2. (क) ताकि किसी शिकारी की नज़र उस पर न पड़े
3. बिशन ने तीतर को सीने से चिपका लिया था।
4. बिशन को शिकारियों से डर लगा होगा, लेकिन उसका उद्देश्य तीतर की जान बचाना था।

निम्नलिखित प्रश्नों के उत्तर दीजिए

1. **बिशन ने तीतर को क्यों बचाया होगा?**

उत्तर बिशन को पक्षियों से प्रेम होगा। अत: शिकारी के शिकार से उसकी रक्षा करने हेतु तीतर को बचाया होगा।

2. **क्या आपने कभी किसी घायल पशु-पक्षी की जान बचाई है किस प्रकार? लिखिए। यदि नहीं लेकिन मौका मिलेगा तो क्या जान बचाएँगे?**

उत्तर नहीं, मुझे किसी घायल पशु-पक्षी की जान बचाने का मौका नहीं मिला, यदि मौका मिलेगा तो उसके बचाव के लिए मैं उसका अच्छे से उपचार करूँगा तथा पशु-पक्षियों के डॉक्टर या वैद्य के पास शीघ्र ही लेकर जाऊँगा।

3. **बिशन ने तीतर के जल्दी स्वस्थ होने के विषय में क्या उपाय बताया?**

उत्तर बिशन ने कहा कि तीतर को गेंदे के पत्तों का रस दो-तीन बार दिन में पिलाएँ, ताकि वह जल्दी स्वस्थ हो जाए।

अध्याय 16 पानी रे पानी

पाठ का सार

पानी का प्रयोग विश्व के सभी मानव व जीव-जंतु करते हैं, लेकिन शायद ही कोई इसके बारे में सोचता होगा कि पानी कहाँ से आता है? कहाँ चला जाता है? भूगोल की किताब में जलचक्र के बारे में बताया जाता है। समुद्र से उठी भाप बादल बनकर पानी में बदलती है और फिर वर्षा होती है। वर्षा का जल समुद्र में वापस मिलकर जलचक्र की प्रक्रिया पूरी करता है।

आज के समय में हर जगह नलों के माध्यम से पानी आता है। नलों में भी अब पूरे समय पानी नहीं आता। पानी की आवश्यकता के कारण लोग नींद की परवाह किए बिना सुबह-सुबह बाल्टियाँ, बर्तन, घड़े आदि लेकर नलों पर इकट्ठे हो जाते हैं, जहाँ लोगों में आपस में बहस भी हो जाती है। पानी वाले झगड़ों से बचने के लिए कई घरों में लोग पाइप में मोटर लगवा लेते हैं। इससे कई घरों का पानी खिंचकर एक ही घर में आ जाता है और आसपास के घरों के हक छिन जाते हैं। पानी की दिक्कत से बचने के लिए अब ज्यादातर घर यही करने लगे हैं। परिणामस्वरूप पानी की कमी बढ़ गई है। देश के बड़े-बड़े शहरों में भी लोग पानी की कमी के कारण कष्ट का सामना कर रहे हैं। देश के कई हिस्सों में तो गर्मी में अकाल जैसी स्थिति बन जाती है और बरसात में कई इलाके बाढ़ में डूब जाते हैं। यह बाढ़ न गाँवों को छोड़ती है और न मुम्बई जैसे बड़े शहरों को। अकाल और बाढ़ एक ही सिक्के के दो पहलू हैं। इन्हें समझना जरूरी है।

जिस तरह हम गुल्लक में पैसा जमा करते हैं कि इन्हें ज़रूरत पड़ने पर इनका उपयोग कर सकें। ठीक उसी प्रकार हम पानी को धरती की गुल्लक में जमा कर सकते हैं। हमारे गाँव एवं शहर में जो छोटे-बड़े तालाब, झील आदि हैं, वे धरती की गुल्लक में पानी भरने का काम करते हैं। इनमें जमा पानी ज़मीन के नीचे छिपे जल के भंडार में धीरे-धीरे रिसकर, छनकर जा मिलता है। इससे हमारा भूजल भंडार समृद्ध होता जाता है।

पानी का यह खजाना हमें दिखता नहीं, लेकिन इसी खजाने का हम बरसात का मौसम बीत जाने के बाद पूरे साल भर तक उपयोग कर सकते हैं। लेकिन ज़मीन के लालच में हमने अपने तालाबों व झीलों को कचरे से पाटकर (भरकर) समतल बना दिया है, ताकि उस पर मकान, बाज़ार, स्टेडियम आदि खड़े कर सकें। इसी लालच के कारण हमें पानी की दिक्कत का सामना करना पड़ रहा है। गर्मी के दिनों में नल सूखे मिलते हैं और बरसात में बस्तियाँ डूबी। यदि हमें इन समस्याओं से बचना है, तो अपने आसपास के जल स्रोतों की, तालाबों की और नदियों आदि की रखवाली अच्छे ढंग से करनी पड़ेगी। हमें जरूरत है जलचक्र ठीक से समझने की, बरसात में उसे थामने की, अपने भूजल भंडार को सुरक्षित रखने की और अपनी गुल्लक भरते रहने की। तभी हम पानी की समस्या से उबर पाएँगे।

शब्दार्थ

बेवक्त-असमय, तू-तू मैं-मैं-झगड़ा, तकरार, हक-अधिकार, थम जाना-रुक जाना, विशाल-बहुत बड़ा, समृद्ध-धनी।

NCERT फोल्डर

तुम्हारे आस–पास

अपने आस-पास के बड़ों से पूछकर पता लगाओ

1. तुम्हारे घर में पानी कहाँ से आता है?
2. तुम्हारे घर का मैला पानी बहकर कहाँ जाता है?
3. (क) तुम्हारे इलाके में धरती के अंदर का पानी कितने फीट या कितने हाथ नीचे है?
   (ख) आज से पंद्रह वर्ष पहले यह पानी कितने नीचे था?

उत्तर 1. हमारे घर में पानी जल बोर्ड की सप्लाई से आता है।

2. हमारे घर का मैला पानी बहकर नालों एवं सीवर में चला जाता है।

3. (क) हमारे इलाके में धरती के अंदर का पानी लगभग 75-95 फीट नीचे है।
   (ख) आज से पंद्रह वर्ष पहले यह पानी लगभग 25-30 फीट नीचे था।

अनुमान लगाओ

पाठ के आधार पर बताओ

1. अपने घर के नल के पाइप में मोटर लगवाना दूसरों का हक छीनने के बराबर है। लेखक ऐसा क्यों मानते हैं?
2. बड़ी संख्या में इमारतें बनने से बाढ़ और अकाल का खतरा कैसे पैदा होता है?
3. धरती की गुल्लक किन-किन साधनों से भरती है?

उत्तर 1. मोटर लगवाने वाले को पर्याप्त पानी मिल जाता है, जबकि जिनके घर मोटर नहीं लगी है, यह उनका हक छीनने के बराबर है।

2. बड़ी संख्या में इमारतें बनने से खाली भूमि कम पड़ती जाती है। ढकी भूमि जल नहीं सोख पाती है, जिससे धरती की गुल्लक भर नहीं पाती। इससे गर्मी में अकाल और बरसात में बाढ़ की स्थिति पैदा हो जाती है। लोग बारिश के पानी को जमा भी नहीं करते हैं।

3. हमारे गाँव एवं शहर में जो छोटे-बड़े तालाब, झील आदि हैं, वे धरती की गुल्लक भरने का काम करते हैं।

यदि हाँ तो ....

1. क्या तुम्हारे इलाके में कभी बाढ़ आई है? यदि हाँ, तो उसके बारे में लिखो।
2. क्या तुम्हारे घर में पानी कुछ ही घंटों के लिए आता है? यदि हाँ, तो बताओ कि कैसे तुम्हारे परिवार की दिनचर्या नल में पानी आने के साथ बँधी होती है?
3. क्या तुम्हारे मोहल्ले में रोज़मर्रा की ज़रूरतें पूरी करने के लिए लोगों को पानी खरीदना पड़ता है? यदि हाँ, तो बताओ कि तुम्हारे घर में रोज़ औसतन कितने लीटर पानी खरीदा जाता है? इस पर कितना खर्चा होता है?

उत्तर 1. हमारे इलाके में बाढ़ तब आई थी, तब सरकार ने हमें पहले ही इसके विषय में चेतावनी दे दी थी। इस दौरान हमारे घर को काफी नुकसान हुआ, लेकिन सरकार से समय पर जानकारी मिलने से हम सुरक्षित थे। वे दिन बहुत उदास भरे थे।

2. हाँ, मेरे घर में पानी कुछ ही घंटों के लिए आता है, इसलिए सबको जल्दी नहाना पड़ता है। घर के पानी वाले काम सबको मिलकर करने होते हैं; जैसे—कपड़े धोना, बर्तन धोना, पौधों में पानी देना आदि। ऐसा करने से हम पानी की बचत करते हैं व हमारी पानी की टंकी भी भर जाती है।

3. हाँ, मेरे मोहल्ले में रोज़मर्रा की ज़रूरतें पूरी करने के लिए लोगों को पानी खरीदना पड़ता है। मेरे घर में भी 30 लीटर पानी रोजाना खरीदा जाता है, जिस पर रोज औसतन 40-50 रुपये खर्च होते हैं।

संकट क्यों?

1. पाठ में पानी के संकट के किस प्रमुख कारण की बात की गई है?
2. पानी के संकट का एक और मुख्य कारण पानी की फिजूलखर्ची भी है। कक्षा में पाँच-पाँच के समूह में बातचीत करो और बताओ कि अपनी रोज़मर्रा की जिंदगी में पानी की बचत करने के लिए तुम क्या-क्या उपाय कर सकते हो?
3. जितना उपलब्ध है, उससे कहीं ज्यादा खर्च करने से पानी का संकट उत्पन्न होता है। क्या यही बात हम बिजली के संकट के बारे में भी कह सकते हैं?

उत्तर 1. नदी-नालों तथा तालाबों को कचरे से पाटकर (भरकर) समतल बना देना पानी के संकट का प्रमुख कारण है।

2. हम पानी की बचत के लिए निम्न उपाय कर सकते हैं

- नहाने के लिए आवश्यकतानुसार पानी का इस्तेमाल करना।
- गाड़ी साफ़ करने के लिए पाइप से धोने के स्थान पर बाल्टी से पानी डालना।
- नल के पानी को व्यर्थ न करना, उसे कसकर बंद करना।
- कपड़े व बर्तन धोने के लिए आवश्यकतानुसार पानी का उपयोग करना।

3. हाँ, यही बात हम बिजली के संकट के बारे में भी कह सकते हैं। हमें बिजली को सावधानीपूर्वक खर्च करना चाहिए। यदि खर्च उपलब्धता से अधिक होगा तो जाहिर है कि संकट पैदा होगा ही।

पानी का चक्कर–भाषा का चक्कर

1. पानी की समस्या या बचत से संबंधित पोस्टर और नारे तैयार करो। यह काम तुम चार-चार के समूह में कर सकते हो।

2. "पानी की बर्बादी, सबकी बर्बादी" इस नारे में 'बर्बादी' शब्द का एक अर्थ है या दो अलग अर्थ हैं? सोचो।

3. पानी हमारी जिंदगी में महत्त्वपूर्ण तो है ही, मुहावरों की दुनिया में भी उसकी खास जगह है। पानी से संबंधित कुछ मुहावरे इकट्ठे करो और उनका उचित संदर्भ में प्रयोग करो।

उत्तर 1. जल है तो कल है।

- पानी बचाओ, जीवन बचाओ
- बूँद-बूँद से घड़ा भरता है।
- जल ही जीवन है।
- यदि जीवन से करते हो प्यार, तो पानी को न करो बर्बाद।

2. 'पानी की बर्बादी' में 'बर्बादी' का अर्थ है—पानी को बर्बाद करना। 'सबकी बर्बादी' में 'बर्बादी' का अर्थ है— पानी की कमी से होने वाली परेशानियाँ।

3. पानी से संबंधित कुछ मुहावरे और उनका वाक्य प्रयोग

- **मुँह में पानी आना** मिठाइयाँ देखते ही मोहित के मुँह में पानी आ गया।
- **आँखों में पानी भर आना** सुरेश की कहानी सुनकर मेरी माँ की आँखों में पानी भर आया।
- **पानी-पानी होना** अपनी गलती के कारण भरी सभा में रवि पानी पानी हो गया।
- **गई भैंस पानी में** बारिश न होने पर किसान बोलने लगे 'गई भैंस पानी में'।

अभ्यास प्रश्न

बहुविकल्पीय प्रश्न

1. भूगोल की किताब में किस बारे में पढ़ाया जाता है?

(क) खाने के बारे में (ख) स्कूल के बारे में
(ग) जलचक्र के बारे में (घ) इनमें से कोई नहीं

2. घरों के पाइप में मोटर लगवाने का क्या कारण है?

(क) ताकि पानी तेज़ गति से आए
(ख) मोटर सस्ती होती है इसलिए
(ग) पानी जल्दी भर जाता है
(घ) उपरोक्त में से कोई नहीं

3. शहरों में कई चीज़ों की तरह और क्या बिकने लगा है?

(क) हवा
(ख) पानी
(ग) पाइप
(घ) मोटर

4. पानी की कमी किन स्थिति में डाल देती है?

(क) अकाल जैसी स्थिति में
(ख) बाढ़ जैसी स्थिति में
(ग) भुखमरी जैसी स्थिति में
(घ) बेहोशी जैसी स्थिति में

5. बाढ़ आने का क्या परिणाम होता है?

(क) कुछ दिनों के लिए सब थम जाता है
(ख) सब कुछ बह जाता है
(ग) देश के कई भाग डूब जाते हैं
(घ) उपरोक्त सभी

उत्तर 1. (ग) जलचक्र के बारे में
2. (क) ताकि पानी तेज़ गति से आए
3. (ख) पानी
4. (क) अकाल जैसी स्थिति में
5. (घ) उपरोक्त सभी

गद्यांश पर आधारित प्रश्न

निम्नलिखित गद्यांश को पढ़कर उस पर आधारित प्रश्नों के उत्तर दीजिए।

गद्यांश

अकाल और बाढ़ एक ही सिक्के के दो पहलू हैं। इन्हें ठीक से समझना ज़रूरी है। तभी हम इन समस्याओं से छुटकारा पा सकते हैं। हम गुल्लक में पैसा जमा करते हैं, ताकि इन्हें ज़रूरत पड़ने पर उपयोग में ला सकें। ठीक उसी प्रकार हम पानी को धरती की गुल्लक में जमा कर सकते हैं। हमारे गाँव एवं शहर में जो छोटे-बड़े तालाब, झील आदि हैं, वे धरती की गुल्लक में पानी भरने का काम करते हैं। इनमें जमा पानी ज़मीन के नीचे छिपे जल के भंडार में धीरे-धीरे रिसकर, छनकर जा मिलता है। इससे हमारा भूजल भंडार समृद्ध होता जाता है। पानी का यह खजाना हमें दिखता नहीं, लेकिन ज़मीन के लालच में हम अपने तालाबों को कचरे से पाटकर (भरकर) समतल बना देते हैं, ताकि उस पर मकान, बाज़ार, स्टेडियम आदि खड़े हो सकें। इसी लालच के कारण हमें पानी की दिक्कत का सामना करना पड़ रहा है।

1. **पानी की कमी का कारण क्या है?**
   (क) बारिश का पानी जमा नहीं करना
   (ख) ज्यादा पानी पीना
   (ग) पानी को अधिक खर्च करना
   (घ) उपरोक्त में से कोई नहीं

2. **पानी की गुल्लक किसे कहा गया है?**
   (क) पानी की टंकी को (ख) नदियों को
   (ग) छोटे-बड़े तालाब व झीलों को (घ) इनमें से कोई नहीं

3. **जमीन के लालच में हम क्या गलती करते हैं?**

4. **अकाल और बाढ़ एक ही सिक्के के दो पहलू कैसे हैं?**

उत्तर

1. (क) बारिश का पानी जमा नहीं करना
2. (ग) छोटे-बड़े तालाब व झीलों को
3. जमीन के लालच में हम अपने तालाबों को कचरे से पाटकर (भरकर) समतल बना देते हैं।
4. अकाल और बाढ़ दोनों ही समस्याओं का सामना करना कष्टदायक है। दोनों ही पानी की कमी व अति से संबंधित हैं।

निम्नलिखित प्रश्नों के उत्तर दीजिए

1. **आज के समय में पानी कैसे आता है?**

उत्तर आज के समय में हर जगह (स्कूल, दफ्तर, कारखाने आदि) पानी नलों के माध्यम से आता है।

2. **धरती को गुल्लक कहने से क्या आशय है?**

उत्तर धरती को गुल्लक कहने से आशय है कि हम पानी को तालाब, झीलों आदि में जमा करके रख लेते हैं और जरूरत पड़ने पर उसका इस्तेमाल करते हैं।

3. **यदि एक दिन के लिए आपको पानी न मिले तो आपकी हालत कैसी होगी? विचार करके लिखिए।**

उत्तर यदि एक दिन के लिए हमें पानी न मिले तो हमारे सभी काम रुक जाएँगे। हम पानी के बिना जीवित नहीं रह सकते हैं, इसलिए पानी हमारे जीवन का महत्त्वपूर्ण आधार है।

4. **पानी का खज़ाना क्या है? स्पष्ट कीजिए।**

उत्तर जमीन के नीचे छिपे जल के भंडार अथवा भूजल भंडार के समृद्ध साधनों को पानी का खजाना कहा गया है।

लेखन संबंधी प्रश्न

1. **'जल ही जीवन है' उक्ति के आधार पर जल की उपयोगिता व लाभ बताते हुए लगभग 80 शब्दों में एक लेख लिखिए।**

उत्तर जहाँ पानी होता है वहीं जीवन होता है। जल हमें प्रकृति द्वारा दिया गया उपहार है। हमें इसे व्यर्थ बर्बाद न करके इसका सम्मान करना चाहिए। जल के बिना हमारा जीवन संभव नहीं है। यह पीने सभ्यता के विकास, संयंत्रों के संचालन और वनस्पतियों के विकास के लिए आवश्यक है।

जल हमारी रोजमर्रा की जिंदगी का एक महत्त्वपूर्ण भाग है। हमारे शरीर की संरचना का 70% भाग जल का है। पृथ्वी पर महासागर, नदियाँ, झील, भूमिगत जल और वर्षा जल के मुख्य और सबसे बड़े स्रोत हैं। जल के बिना हम जीवन की कल्पना भी नहीं कर सकते। अत: हम सभी का कर्त्तव्य है कि हमें पानी को बचाकर रखना चाहिए।

अध्याय 17

छोटी-सी हमारी नदी

कविता का सार

''रवींद्रनाथ'' ठाकुर द्वारा रचित प्रस्तुत कविता में बताया गया है कि हमारी एक छोटी नदी है, जिसकी धार टेढ़ी-मेढ़ी है। गर्मियों में नदी में कम पानी के कारण उसे पार करना आसान होता है। इस नदी के किनारे ऊँचे हैं और पाट ढालू हैं। इसके तल में बालू कीचड़ का नामोनिशान नहीं है। इसके दूसरे किनारे पर ताड़ के वन हैं, जिनकी छाँहों में ब्राह्मणों का टोला बसा है। वे नदी में नहाते हैं और उसके बाद अगर समय बचा तो मछली भी मारते हैं। उनके घर की स्त्रियाँ बालू से बर्तन साफ़ करती हैं। फिर कपड़े धोती हैं, लेकिन जैसे ही आषाढ़ के महीने में यह नदी पानी से भर जाती है, तब इसकी धार बहुत तेज़ हो जाती है। इसकी कलकल की आवाज़ से चारों तरफ़ कोलाहल मच जाता है। बरसात के दौरान नदी में भँवरे भी देखने को मिलती हैं। लोग झुंड में वर्षा का उत्सव मनाते हैं।

काव्यांशों की व्याख्या

काव्यांश 1

छोटी-सी हमारी नदी टेढ़ी-मेढ़ी धार,
गर्मियों में घुटने भर भिगो कर जाते पार।
पार जाते ढोर-डंगर, बैलगाड़ी चालू,
ऊँचे हैं किनारे इसके, पाट इसका ढालू।
पेटे में झकाझक बालू कीचड़ का न नाम,
काँस फूले एक पार उजले जैसे घाम।।
दिन भर किचपिच-किचपिच करती मैना डार-डार,
रातों को हुआँ-हुआँ कर उठते सियार।

शब्दार्थ *ढोर-डंगर-जानवर, किचपिच-किचपिच-मैना की आवाज़।*

संदर्भ/प्रसंग प्रस्तुत पंक्तियाँ हमारी पाठ्यपुस्तक 'रिमझिम भाग-5' में संकलित कविता 'छोटी-सी हमारी नदी' से ली गई हैं। इसके रचयिता ''श्री रवींद्रनाथ ठाकुर'' हैं। प्रस्तुत कविता में कवि ने नदी का सुंदर वर्णन किया है।

व्याख्या कवि कहता है कि छोटी-सी हमारी नदी है और इसकी धार टेढ़ी-मेढ़ी है। गर्मी के दिनों में इसमें घुटने भर तक पानी होता है। इसे पार करना सबके लिए आसान होता है। चाहे वह आदमी हो या जानवर या बैलगाड़ी। इस नदी के किनारे ऊँचे हैं और इसके पाट ढालू हैं, किंतु इसकी तली में बालू कीचड़ का नामोनिशान नहीं है। काँस के फूल खिलने पर धूप जैसे सफ़ेद दिखते हैं। इसकी डालियों पर मैना दिनभर किचपिच-किचपिच करती रहती हैं। रात के समय सियार हुआँ-हुआँ करते हैं।

काव्यांश 2

अमराई दूजे किनारे और ताड़-वन,
छाँहों-छाँहों बाम्हन टोला बसा है सघन।
कच्चे-बच्चे धार-कछारों पर उछल नहा लें,
गमछों-गमछों पानी भर-भर अंग-अंग पर ढालें।
कभी-कभी वे साँझ-सकारे निबटा कर नहाना
छोटी-छोटी मछली मारें आँचल का कर छाना।
बहुएँ लोटे-थाल माँजती रगड़-रगड़ कर रेती,
कपड़े धोतीं, घर के कामों के लिए चल देतीं।।

शब्दार्थ *छाँहों-छाया में, सघन-घना, सकारे-सवेरे, रेती-बालू।*

प्रसंग पूर्ववत्।

व्याख्या कवि आगे कहते हैं कि इस नदी के दूसरे किनारे पर आम और ताड़ के पेड़ हैं। उन्हीं की छाँह में ब्राह्मण का टोला बसा है। उनके छोटे-छोटे बच्चे किनारों पर उछल-उछलकर नहाते हैं। वे गमछों में पानी भरकर अपने शरीर पर उड़ेलते हैं। कभी-कभी जब वे नहाकर जल्दी निबट जाते हैं तो नदी में मछलियाँ पकड़ते हैं। उनके घर की औरतें नदी से बालू लेकर बर्तन माँजकर कपड़े धोने के बाद घर के काम करने के लिए चल देती हैं।

काव्यांश 3

जैसे ही आषाढ़ बरसता, भर नदिया उतराती,
मतवाली-सी छूटी चलती तेज़ धार दन्नाती।
वेग और कलकल के मारे उठता है कोलाहल,
गँदले जल में घिरनी-भँवरी भँवराती है चंचल।
दोनों पारों के वन-वन में मच जाता है रोला,
वर्षा के उत्सव में सारा जग उठता है टोला।

शब्दार्थ *आषाढ़-बरसात का एक महीना, दन्नाती-तेज़ी से, कोलाहल-शोर, गँदले-गंदा, जग-संसार।*

प्रसंग पूर्ववत्।

व्याख्या कवि कहता है कि आषाढ़ के महीने में जब खूब वर्षा होती है तब यह नदी पानी से भर जाती है। तब इसकी धार काफी तेज़ हो जाती है। इसकी तेज़ चाल से इतनी कलकल की आवाज़ से चारों ओर शोर मच जाता है।

इसका पानी गंदा हो जाता है। गंदे पानी में पानी की घिरनी भँवरी की तरह चलती है। नदी के दोनों तरफ के वनों में खूब कोलाहल मचा रहता है। वर्षा के दौरान उत्सव जैसा माहौल हो जाता है। सारा संसार जाग उठता है उत्सव मनाने के लिए।

NCERT फोल्डर

तुम्हारी नदी

1. तुम्हारी देखी हुई नदी भी ऐसी ही है या कुछ अलग है? अपनी परिचित नदी के बारे में छूटी हुई जगहों पर लिखो।

   .... सी हमारी नदी .... धार

   गर्मियों में ...., ... जाते ...... पार

उत्तर **चंचल** सी हमारी नदी **तेज़ इसकी** धार

गर्मियों में **हम बच्चे**, **मिलकर** जाते **नाव से** पार

2. कविता में दी गई इन बातों के आधार पर अपनी परिचित नदी के बारे में बताओ।
   - धार
   - पाट
   - बालू
   - कीचड़
   - किनारे
   - बरसात में नदी

उत्तर
- **धार** मेरी परिचित नदी की धार बहुत तेज़ है।
- **पाट** नदी के पाट ढालदार हैं।
- **बालू** नदी के तल में बालू रहता है।
- **कीचड़** बरसात के समय नदी में बहुत कीचड़ हो जाता है।
- **किनारे** इस नदी के किनारों पर नारियल के पेड़ हैं।
- **बरसात में नदी** बरसात में नदी का स्तर बढ़ जाता है।

3. तुम्हारी परिचित नदी के किनारे क्या-क्या होता है?

उत्तर मेरी परिचित नदी के किनारे बड़ी-बड़ी सीढ़ियाँ हैं, जहाँ श्रद्धालु गण बैठकर नदी को देखने का सुख प्राप्त करते हैं। कुछ लोग नदी में नहाकर नदी की पूजा करते हैं। नदी में बहुत-सी नावें भी हैं, जो लोगों को इस पार से उस पार ले जाती हैं।

4. तुम जहाँ रहते हो, उसके आस-पास कौन-कौन सी नदियाँ हैं? वे कहाँ से निकलती हैं और कहाँ तक जाती हैं? पता करो।

उत्तर छात्र स्वयं करें।

कविता के बाहर

1. इसी किताब में नदी का ज़िक्र और किस पाठ में हुआ है? नदी के बारे में क्या लिखा है?

उत्तर ठीक इस पाठ से पहले नदी का सफ़र नाम से लेख दिया गया है, जिसमें नदी कहाँ से आती हैं और कहाँ जाती हैं इसके बारे में बताया गया है।

2. नदी पर कोई और कविता खोजकर पढ़ो और कक्षा में सुनाओ।

उत्तर छात्र स्वयं करें।

3. नदी में नहाने के तुम्हारे क्या अनुभव हैं?

उत्तर नदी में नहाने का मेरा एक बहुत सुखद अनुभव है। गर्मियों की छुट्टियों में हम नानी के घर गए। वहाँ नदी का पानी ठंडा व साफ होता है। हम सभी बच्चे मिलकर उसमें खूब नहाते हैं। बार-बार बुलाने पर भी हमारा नदी से बाहर आने का मन नहीं करता। नदी में इस प्रकार नहाना हमें शांति व प्रसन्नता का भाव प्रदान करता है।

4. क्या तुमने कभी मछली पकड़ी है? अपने अनुभव साथियों के साथ बाँटो।

उत्तर छात्र स्वयं करें।

ये किसकी तरह लगते हैं?

1. नदी की टेढ़ी-मेढ़ी धार?
2. किचपिच-किचपिच करती मैना?
3. उछल-उछल के नदी में नहाते कच्चे-बच्चे?

उत्तर 1. साँप की तरह

2. कभी सुरीली और कभी तीखी आवाज़ वाला पक्षी।

3. ऐसे लगते हैं, जैसे मछलियाँ एकसाथ उछल-कूद कर रही हों।

कविता और चित्र

कविता के पहले पद को दोबारा पढ़ो। वर्णन पर ध्यान दो। इसे पढ़कर जो चित्र तुम्हारे मन में उभरा उसे बनाओ। बताओ चित्र में तुमने क्या-क्या दर्शाया?

उत्तर छात्र स्वयं करें।

कविता से

1. इस कविता के पद में कौन-कौन से शब्द तुकांत हैं? उन्हें छाँटो।

उत्तर तुकांत शब्दों की सूची

- धार-पार
- चालू-ढालू
- नाम-धाम
- डार-सियार
- वन-सघन
- नहा लें-ढालें
- नहाना-छाना
- रेती-देती
- उतराती-दलाती
- कोलाहल-चंचल
- रोला-टोला

2. किस शब्द से पता चलता है कि नदी के किनारे जानवर भी जाते थे?

उत्तर ढोर-डंगर।

3. इस नदी के तट की क्या खासियत थी?

उत्तर तट ऊँचे थे और पाट ढालू।

4. अमराई दूजे किनारे .... चल देतीं।

कविता की ये पंक्तियाँ नदी किनारे का जीता-जागता वर्णन करती हैं। तुम भी निम्नलिखित में से किसी एक का वर्णन अपने शब्दों में करो

- हफ्ते में एक बार लगने वाला हाट।
- तुम्हारे शहर या गाँव की सबसे ज्यादा चहल-पहल वाली जगह।
- तुम्हारे घर की खिड़की या दरवाज़े से दिखाई देने वाला बाहर का दृश्य।
- ऐसी जगह का दृश्य, जहाँ कोई बड़ी इमारत बन रही हो।

उत्तर **प्रकृति का सुंदर दृश्य** मेरे घर की खिड़की या दरवाज़े से दिखाई देने वाला बाहर का दृश्य बहुत ही सुंदर है। प्रकृति की हरियाली मन को मोह लेती है। खुला आसमान, मैदान, पैड़-पौधों की सुंदरता, पक्षियों का कलरव, मन में स्फूर्ति, आनंद को भर देता है। प्रात:काल उठते ही स्वच्छ वायु शरीर में ताज़गी भर देती है। मैं प्रात: उठते ही अपने घर की खिड़की-दरवाजे खोलकर बाहर के प्राकृतिक दृश्य का खूब आनंद लेता हूँ।

5. तेज़ गति शोर मोहल्ला धूप किनारा घना

ऊपर लिखे शब्दों के लिए कविता में कुछ खास शब्दों का इस्तेमाल किया गया है। उन शब्दों को नीचे दिए गए अक्षरजाल में ढूँढो।

धा	म		वे	
			ग	
		टो		
	रो	ला		पा
स	घ	न		ट

उत्तर तेज़ गति — वेग   शोर — रोला   मोहल्ला — टोला

धूप — धाम   किनारा — पाट   घना — सघन

अभ्यास प्रश्न

बहुविकल्पीय प्रश्न

1. 'छोटी-सी हमारी नदी' कविता किस कवि द्वारा रचित है?
   (क) महादेवी वर्मा द्वारा (ख) राकेश शर्मा द्वारा
   (ग) निराला द्वारा (घ) रवींद्रनाथ ठाकुर द्वारा
2. गर्मियों में नदी पार करना किस कारण आसान होता है?
   (क) भीड़ कम होने के कारण
   (ख) नदी में पानी कम होने के कारण
   (ग) नाव के कारण
   (घ) दोस्तों के कारण
3. नदी के किनारे कैसे हैं?
   (क) ऊँचे (ख) समतल (ग) लंबे (ग) मोटे
4. कौन-से महीने में खूब बारिश होती है?
   (क) आषाढ़ (ख) चैत्र
   (ग) माघ (घ) इनमें से कोई नहीं
5. वर्षा के दौरान कैसा माहौल होता है?
   (क) गंदा (ख) कीचड़
   (ग) उत्सव (घ) उदासी

उत्तर 1. (घ) रवींद्रनाथ ठाकुर द्वारा
2. (ख) नदी में पानी कम होने के कारण
3. (क) ऊँचे
4. (क) आषाढ़
5. (ग) उत्सव

काव्यांश पर आधारित प्रश्न

निम्नलिखित काव्यांश को पढ़कर उस पर आधारित प्रश्नों के उत्तर दीजिए।

काव्यांश

अमराई दूजे किनारे और ताड़-वन,
छाँहों-छाँहों बाम्हन टोला बसा है सघन।
कच्चे-बच्चे धार-कछारों पर उछल नहा लें,
गमछों-गमछों पानी भर-भर अंग-अंग पर ढालें।
कभी-कभी वे साँझ-सकारे निबटा कर नहाना
छोटी-छोटी मछली मारें आँचल का कर छाना।
बहुएँ लोटे-थाल माँजती रगड़-रगड़ कर रेती,
कपड़े धोतीं, घर के कामों के लिए चल देतीं।।

1. नदी के दूसरे किनारे किसके पेड़ हैं?
   (क) आम और ताड़ के (ख) नीम और आम के
   (ग) नीम और पीपल के (घ) पीपल और जामुन के
2. नदी के दूसरे किनारे पर पेड़ों के नीचे किसका टोला बसा है?
   (क) महिलाओं का
   (ख) युवाओं का
   (ग) बुजुर्ग लोगों का
   (घ) ब्राह्मणों का
3. औरतें नदी से बालू लेकर कौन-सा काम करती हैं?
4. नदी में मछली कौन पकड़ते हैं?

उत्तर
1. (क) आम और ताड़ के
2. (घ) ब्राह्मणों का
3. औरतें नदी से बालू लेकर बर्तन धोती हैं।
4. नदी में मछली ब्राह्मणों के बच्चे पकड़ते हैं।

निम्नलिखित प्रश्नों के उत्तर दीजिए

1. गर्मियों में नदी को पार करना आसान क्यों होता है?

उत्तर गर्मियों में नदी में कम पानी होने के कारण उसे पार करना आसान होता है।

2. नदी पानी से कब भर जाती है?

उत्तर आषाढ़ का महीना आने पर नदी पानी से भर जाती है।

3. बरसात के दौरान नदी में क्या देखने को मिलता है?

उत्तर बरसात के दौरान नदी का पानी गंदा हो जाता है। उस समय पानी की घिरनी भँवरी की तरह चलती है।

4. वर्षा के दौरान कैसा माहौल होता है?

उत्तर वर्षा के दौरान उत्सव जैसा माहौल हो जाता है।

अध्याय 14

चुनौती हिमालय की

पाठ का सार

जवाहरलाल नेहरू अपने चचेरे भाई के साथ कश्मीर घूमने निकले थे। दोनों जोज़ीला से होकर लद्दाखी इलाके की ओर चले आए थे, उन्हें अमरनाथ जाना था। किशन गड़ेरिया ने उन्हें रास्ते की मुश्किलों के बारे में बताया। मुश्किलों के बारे में सुनकर सफ़र के लिए वे और भी उत्सुक हो गए। उनके साथ कुली तो था ही, किशन और उसकी बेटी भी उसके साथ जाने को तैयार हो गए। अगले दिन सुबह-सुबह जवाहरलाल नेहरू तैयार होकर बाहर आ गए। तिब्बती पठार का दृश्य निराला था। दूर-दूर तक वनस्पति रहित उजाड़ चट्टानी इलाका दिखाई दे रहा था। सर्द हवा के झोंके की ठंडक हड्डियों तक पहुँच रही थी। जवाहरलाल जी ने अपनी हथेलियाँ आपस में रगड़कर गरम कीं और कमर में रस्सी लपेटकर चलने को तैयार हो गए। हिमालय की दुर्गम पर्वतमाला एक बड़ी चुनौती थी। उन्होंने इसे सहर्ष स्वीकार किया।

किशन गड़ेरिया उनका गाइड बन गया। जवाहरलाल ने आठ मील की चढ़ाई चढ़नी शुरू कर दी। रास्ता सुनसान था। चारों तरफ़ बस पथरीली चट्टानें और सफ़ेद बर्फ दिख रही थी। हरियाली तो दूर-दूर तक नहीं दिखती थी। जवाहरलाल ज्यों-ज्यों ऊपर चढ़ते गए, त्यों-त्यों साँस लेने में दिक्कत होने लगी। कुली की नाक से खून बहने लगा। जल्दी से जवाहरलाल ने उसका उपचार किया। थोड़ी देर में बर्फ पड़ने लगी और फिसलन बढ़ गई। सुबह चार बजे से चढ़ाई करते-करते दिन के बारह बजे तक वे लगभग सोलह हज़ार फ़ीट की ऊँचाई पर आ गए, किंतु अभी भी अमरनाथ की गुफा का कुछ पता नहीं चल पा रहा था।

कुली ने उन्हें वापस कैंप में चलने की सलाह दी, किंतु उन्होंने नहीं मानी, तभी किशन ने बताया कि अमरनाथ की गुफा तो दूर बर्फ के मैदान के पार है। यह सुनकर जवाहरलाल में और भी जोश आ गया। वे फुर्ती से बढ़ने लगे। अचानक उन्हें एक बड़ी गहरी खाई दिखी। इसके पहले कि वे अपने को सँभालते, लड़खड़ाकर खाई में गिर पड़े। रस्सी से बँधे वे हवा में लटकने लगे। लोगों ने रस्सी खींचकर उन्हें बाहर निकालने की बात सोची, लेकिन जवाहरलाल ने उन्हें ऐसा नहीं करने दिया और खाई की दीवार से उभरी चट्टान को मज़बूती से पकड़ लिया एवं पथरीले धरातल पर पैर जमा लिए व किसी तरह ऊपर पहुँच गए। कपड़े झाड़कर वे फिर चलने को तैयार हो गए। खाइयाँ पार करने का उचित सामान भी किसी के पास न था। इस कारण जवाहरलाल को अमरनाथ तक का सफर अधूरा छोड़कर वापस लौटना पड़ा।

शब्दार्थ

गाइड-रास्ता बताने वाला, दूभर-मुश्किल, वीरान-सुनसान, सुकून-अच्छा एहसास, स्फूर्ती-तेजी, उपचार-इलाज, हिम-बर्फ, शिखर-चोटी, मुकुट-ताज, ओझल-आँखों से दूर हो जाना, दुर्गम-कठिन, ढल जाएगा-बीत जाएगा, हिदायत-चेतावनी, तादाद-संख्या।

NCERT फोल्डर

कहाँ क्या है?

1. (क) लद्दाख जम्मू-कश्मीर राज्य में है। ऊपर दिए भारत के नक्शे (NCERT पेज नं. 144) में ढूँढो कि लद्दाख कहाँ है और तुम्हारा घर कहाँ है?

(ख) अनुमान लगाओ कि तुम जहाँ रहते हो, वहाँ से लद्दाख पहुँचने में कितने दिन लग सकते हैं और वहाँ किन-किन ज़रियों से पहुँचा जा सकता है?

(ग) किताब के शुरू में तुमने तिब्बती लोककथा 'राख की रस्सी' पढ़ी थी। नक्शे में तिब्बत को ढूँढो।

उत्तर छात्र मानचित्र की सहायता से इन प्रश्नों को स्वयं करें।

वाद-विवाद

1. (क) बर्फ से ढके चट्टानी पहाड़ों के उदास और फीके लगने की क्या वजह हो सकती थी?

उत्तर बर्फ से ढके चट्टानी पहाड़ों के उदास और फीके लगने का कारण यहाँ हरे-भरे पेड़-पौधे व आबादी का न होना था।

(ख) बताओ, ये जगहें कब उदास और फीकी लगती हैं और यहाँ कब रौनक होती है?

घर बाज़ार स्कूल खेत

उत्तर

जगह	कब उदास और फीकी लगती है?	कब यहाँ रौनक होती है?
घर	जब घर के लोग बाहर गए होते हैं।	जब घर के सभी लोग घर में होते हैं और आपस में प्यार से बोलते-बतियाते हैं।
बाज़ार	दोपहर के समय	शाम के समय, त्योहारों के अवसर पर
स्कूल	जब स्कूल में बच्चों की छुट्टी होती है।	जब तक स्कूल में बच्चे रहते हैं, वहाँ रौनक ही रौनक होती है।
खेत	जब फसल कट जाती है।	जब खेत में फसल लहलहाती है।

2. जवाहरलाल को इस कठिन यात्रा के लिए तैयार नहीं होना चाहिए। तुम इससे सहमत हो तो भी तर्क दो, नहीं हो तो भी तर्क दो। अपने तर्कों को तुम कक्षा के सामने प्रस्तुत भी कर सकते हो।

उत्तर मैं इससे सहमत नहीं हूँ। रास्ते की कठिनाइयों का अंदाजा लगाकर काम को शुरू न करना ये तो कोई अच्छी बात नहीं है। अपनी इच्छाशक्ति से हम प्रत्येक कठिनाई का सामना कर सकते हैं। कठिन कार्य को चुनौती समझकर करना चाहिए, जैसा नेहरू जी ने किया था।

कोलाज

'कोलाज' उस तस्वीर को कहते हैं, जो कई तस्वीरों को छोटे-छोटे टुकड़ों में काटकर एक कागज़ पर चिपकाकर बनाई जाती है।

1. तुम मिलकर पहाड़ों का एक कोलाज बनाओ। इसके लिए पहाड़ों से जुड़ी विभिन्न तस्वीरें इकट्ठा करो-पर्वतारोहण, चट्टान, पहाड़ों के अलग-अलग नज़ारे, चोटी, अलग-अलग किस्म के पहाड़। अब इन्हें एक बड़े से कागज़ पर पहाड़ के आकार में ही चिपकाओ। यदि चाहो तो ये कोलाज तुम अपनी कक्षा की एक दीवार पर भी बना सकते हो।

2. अब इन चित्रों पर आधारित शब्दों का एक कोलाज बनाओ। कोलाज में ऐसे शब्द हों, जो इन चित्रों का वर्णन कर पा रहे हों या मन में उठने वाली भावनाओं को बता रहे हों।

अब इन दोनों कोलाजों को कक्षा में प्रदर्शित करो।

उत्तर इन प्रश्नों के उत्तर छात्र स्वयं करें।

तुम्हारी समझ से

1. इस वृत्तांत को पढ़ते-पढ़ते तुम्हें भी अपनी कोई छोटी या लंबी यात्रा याद आ रही हो तो उसके बारे में लिखो।

उत्तर छात्र स्वयं करें।

2. जवाहरलाल को अमरनाथ तक का सर अधूरा क्यों छोड़ना पड़ा?

उत्तर जवाहरलाल को अमरनाथ तक का सफर अधूरा इसलिए छोड़ना पड़ा, क्योंकि आगे का रास्ता अनेकों गहरी और चौड़ी खाइयों से भरा पड़ा था। खाइयाँ पार करने का उचित सामान भी उनके पास नहीं था।

3. जवाहरलाल, किशन और कुली सभी रस्सी से क्यों बँधे थे?

उत्तर जवाहरलाल, किशन और कुली सभी रस्सी से इसलिए बँधे थे, ताकि पैर फिसलने के कारण या किसी और कारण से वे पहाड़ से गिर जाएँ तो रस्सी के सहारे लटककर अपनी जान बचा सकें।

4. (क) पाठ में नेहरू जी ने हिमालय से चुनौती महसूस की। कुछ लोग पर्वतारोहण क्यों करना चाहते हैं?

उत्तर कुछ लोगों को पर्वतारोहण बेहद रोमांचक और चुनौतीपूर्ण लगता है। उनके अंदर कुछ असाधारण काम करने की लालसा होती है।

(ख) ऐसे कौन-से चुनौती भरे कार्य हैं, जो तुम करना पसंद करोगे?

उत्तर कक्षा में प्रथम आना या किसी विशेष प्रतियोगिता में विजय प्राप्त करना ये एक प्रकार के चुनौती वाले कार्य ही हैं।

बोलते पहाड़

1. उदास फीके बर्फ से ढके चट्टानी पहाड़
हिमालय की दुर्गम पर्वतमाला मुँह उठाए चुनौती दे रही थी।
'उदास होना' और 'चुनौती देना' मनुष्य के स्वभाव हैं। यहाँ निर्जीव पहाड़ ऐसा कर रहे हैं। ऐसे और भी वाक्य हैं; जैसे–
- बिजली चली गई।
- चाँद ने शरमाकर अपना मुँह बादलों के पीछे कर लिया।

इस किताब के दूसरे पाठों में भी ऐसे वाक्य ढूँढो।

उत्तर ऐसे कुछ वाक्य नीचे दिए जा रहे हैं
- नल आधे समय सूखा ही रहता है।
- फसल तैयार खड़ी है।
- सुबह की हल्की धूप में खेत सोने जैसे चमक रहे हैं।
- सामने वाली गुफा मुँह फाड़े निगलने को तैयार बैठी है।

एक वर्णन ऐसा भी

पाठ में तुमने जवाहरलाल नेहरू की पहाड़ी यात्रा के बारे में पढ़ा। नीचे एक और पहाड़ी इलाके का वर्णन किया गया है, जो प्रसिद्ध कहानीकार निर्मल वर्मा की किताब 'चीड़ों पर चाँदनी' से लिया गया है। इसे पढ़ो और नीचे लिखे प्रश्नों के उत्तर दो।

क्या यह शिमला है-हमारा अपना शहर-या हम भूल से कहीं और चले आए हैं? हम नहीं जानते कि पिछली रात जब हम बेखबर सो रहे थे, बर्फ चुपचाप गिर रही थी। खिड़की के सामने पुराना, चिर-परिचित देवदार का वृक्ष था, जिसकी नंगी शाखों पर रूई के मोटे-मोटे गालों-सी बर्फ चिपक गई थी। लगता था जैसे वह सांता क्लॉज हो, एक रात में ही जिसके बाल सन-से सफेद हो गए हैं.......। कुछ देर बाद धूप निकल आती है-नीले चमचमाते आकाश के नीचे बर्फ से ढकी पहाड़ियाँ धूप सेंकने के लिए अपना चेहरा बादलों के बाहर निकाल लेती हैं।

(क) ऊपर दिए पहाड़ के वर्णन और पाठ में दिए वर्णन में क्या अंतर है?

उत्तर ऊपर दिए पहाड़ के वर्णन में वृक्ष (देवदार) का वर्णन है। पाठ में उजाड़ चट्टानों का वर्णन है।

(ख) कई बार निर्जीव चीज़ों के लिए मनुष्यों से जुड़ी क्रियाओं, विशेषण आदि का इस्तेमाल होता है; जैसे-पाठ में आए दो उदाहरण "उदास फीके, बर्फ से ढके चट्टानी पहाड़" या "सामने एक गहरी खाई मुँह फाड़े निगलने के लिए तैयार थी।" ऊपर लिखे शिमला के वर्णन में ऐसे उदाहरण ढूँढो।

उत्तर
- बर्फ़ चुपचाप गिर रही थी।
- जिसकी नंगी शाखा पर रूई के मोटे-मोटे गालों-सी बर्फ चिपक गई थी।
- कुछ देर बाद धूप निकल आती है।
- नीले चमचमाते आकाश के नीचे बर्फ से ढकी पहाड़ियाँ धूप सेंकने के लिए अपना चेहरा बादलों के बाहर निकाल लेती हैं।

अभ्यास प्रश्न

◘ बहुविकल्पीय प्रश्न

1. जवाहरलाल ने अपने चचेरे भाई पर कैसी दृष्टि डाली?
   (क) बुरी (ख) गहरी
   (ग) प्रश्नसूचक (घ) उदासी

2. जवाहरलाल नेहरू किसके साथ कश्मीर घूमने निकले थे?
   (क) पिताजी के साथ (ख) माताजी के साथ
   (ग) बहन के साथ (घ) चचेरे भाई के साथ

3. जवाहरलाल नेहरू को कहाँ जाना था?
   (क) दिल्ली (ख) अमरनाथ (ग) बनारस (घ) मथुरा

4. जवाहरलाल नेहरू के लिए हिमालय की दुर्गम पर्वतमाला क्या थी?
   (क) एक बड़ी चुनौती (ख) एक आसान काम
   (ग) एक बेकार काम (घ) इनमें से कोई नहीं

5. जवाहरलाल नेहरू ने कितने बजे से चढ़ाई शुरू की थी?
   (क) सुबह चार बजे से (ख) सुबह दस बजे से
   (ग) दोपहर एक बजे से (घ) शाम चार बजे से

उत्तर

1. (ग) प्रश्नसूचक 2. (घ) चचेरे भाई के साथ
3. (ख) अमरनाथ 4. (क) एक बड़ी चुनौती
5. (क) सुबह चार बजे से

◘ गद्यांश पर आधारित प्रश्न

निम्नलिखित गद्यांश को पढ़कर उस पर आधारित प्रश्नों के उत्तर दीजिए।

गद्यांश

हिमालय की दुर्गम पर्वतमाला एक बड़ी चुनौती थी, उन्होंने इसे सहर्ष स्वीकार किया। किशन गड़ेरिया उनका गाइड बन गया। जवाहरलाल ने आठ मील की चढ़ाई चढ़नी शुरू कर दी। आठ मील की दूरी कोई बहुत नहीं होती, लेकिन इन पहाड़ी रास्तों पर आठ कदम चलना मुश्किल लगने लगा। रास्ता सुनसान था। चारों ओर बस पथरीली चट्टानें और सफेद बर्फ दिख रहे थे। हरियाली तो दूर-दूर तक नहीं दिखती थी। जवाहरलाल बढ़ते जा रहे थे। ज्यों-ज्यों ऊपर चढ़ते गए, त्यों-त्यों साँस लेने में दिक्कत होने लगी। कुली की नाक से खून बहने लगा। जल्दी से जवाहरलाल ने उसका उपचार किया। थोड़ी देर में बर्फ पड़ने लगी और फिसलन बढ़ गई। चलना कठिन होने लगा।

1. नेहरू जी कहाँ जाने के लिए उत्सुक थे?
   (क) अमरनाथ (ख) केदारनाथ
   (ग) बद्रीनाथ (घ) वैष्णोदेवी

2. जवाहरलाल ने कितने मील की चढ़ाई चढ़नी शुरू कर दी?
   (क) आठ मील (ख) सात मील
   (ग) चार मील (घ) दस मील

3. नेहरू जी के सफ़र का रास्ता कैसा था?

4. नेहरू जी का चलना कठिन क्यों हो गया?

उत्तर

1. (क) अमरनाथ
2. (क) आठ मील
3. रास्ता सुनसान था। चारों तरफ़ बस पथरीली चट्टानें और सफेद बर्फ दिख रहे थे। हरियाली तो दूर-दूर तक नहीं दिखती थी।
4. बर्फ पड़ने लगी और फिसलन बढ़ गई, जिससे नेहरू जी का चलना कठिन होने लगा।

◘ निम्नलिखित प्रश्नों के उत्तर दीजिए

1. नेहरू जी को पहाड़ पर चढ़ने पर कैसा लगा होगा?

उत्तर नेहरू जी को दुर्गम पर्वतमाला पर चढ़ना चुनौतीपूर्ण लगा, पर उन्होंने इसे सहर्ष स्वीकार किया।

2. पहाड़ों पर हरियाली क्यों नहीं होती होगी?

उत्तर पहाड़ों पर हरियाली इसलिए नहीं होती, क्योंकि वहाँ पथरीली चट्टानें होती हैं तथा सभी ओर बर्फ होने के कारण वहाँ हरियाली नहीं होती।

3. जवाहरलाल नेहरू जी को जोश कैसे आया था?

उत्तर जहवाहरलाल नेहरू ने जब सुना कि अमरनाथ की गुफा बर्फ के पार है, तो वे फुर्ती से बढ़ने लगे उनमें जोश आ गया था।

Looking Around (EVS)

CHAPTER 1

SUPER SENSES

About the Chapter

This chapter is about the unique senses of different animals. Different animals have special senses that help them in different ways. Some can see far, some can hear well and others have a strong sense of smell. For example, ants, dogs, mosquitoes and tigers can smell things really well. Birds like eagles, vultures and kites can see things from far away.

Animals also make sounds to warn others of danger. Animals like snakes and tigers have good hearing power. Some animals, like lizards, hide and sleep in winter. Sloth is a very lazy animal which sleeps for 17 hours a day. Many animals are hunted for their tusks, horns or skin, which are sold for money. To protect animals, the government has made national parks where they can live safely.

GLOSSARY

Sense To understand or feel something.

Faint Sounds which cannot be heard easily.

Prey When an animal kills another animal for food.

Tsunami A large wave in the sea which causes a disaster and destroys everything when it comes on land.

Whiskers Long stiff hairs that grow near the mouth of the animals and help them to communicate.

Warning Call A sound or signal made by an animal to alert others of a potential threat or danger.

NCERT FOLDER

Think and Tell (Page 2-3)

Q.1 How did the ant know that the other ants were not from its group?

Ans. The ant knew that the other ants were not from its group because of its special senses. Ants follow each other's smell. Through their antennas known as feelers, they can recognise their group members.

Q.2 How did the guard ant recognise this ant?

Ans. The guard ant had a keen sense of smell by which it recognised this ant and let it in the hole.

Try This and Write (Page 2)

Drop some sugar, jaggery or anything sweet on the ground. Wait until the ants come there.

Q.1 How long did it take for the ants to come?

Ans. It took 10-15 minutes for ants to come. This is because ants have a keen sense of smell.

Q.2 Did one ant come first or a group of ants came together?

Ans. One ant came first, followed by a group of ants.

Q.3 What did the ants do with the food?

Ans. Ants broke the food into small pieces and carried their food into their hole for storage.

Q.4 Where do they go from there?

Ans. They carry the food to their hole.

Q.5 Do they move in a line?

Ans. Ants always move in a line.

Now carefully, without harming the ants, block their path for a while with a pencil.

Q.6 Now observe, how do the ants move?

Ans. Ants still move in a line. They climb up the pencil placed in front of them.

Q.7 Now can you guess why the ants behaved like that when you blocked their path?

Ans. Ants were still moving in line when I blocked their path. This is because they follow each other's smell to recognise their path. So, the ants followed the smell of the first ant and climbed up the pencil.

Q.8 Have you ever been troubled by mosquitoes? Just think, how do they know where you are?

Ans. Yes, I get troubled by mosquitoes. They can find us by using their sense of smell. They can smell the sole of our feet and recognise us by the heat of our body.

Q.9 Have you ever seen a dog sniffing here and there? What do you think it is trying to smell?

Ans. Yes, I have seen a dog sniffing here and there. Dogs mark their own area and they can smell if other dogs have come to their area through the smell of its urine. Dogs smell here and there to identify his area.

Write (Page 4)

Q.1 In what ways do human beings make use of this special sense of smell of dogs?

Ans. The special sense of smell of dogs is used by human beings in many ways.
Some examples are

- To catch the thieves
- To detect stolen things
- To detect bombs
- To detect danger

Q.2 When do you find your sense of smell helpful to you? List some examples.

Like to know by its smell that food has gone bad or that something is burning.

Ans. I find my sense of smell helpful in many ways apart from smelling bad food or burning.
Some ways are

- To identify leakage of gas in the house
- To smell good food
- To recognise the smell of perfume
- To identify flowers and fruits

Q.3 Name the animals that you would be able to recognise only by their smell, without seeing them?

Ans. We can identify animals like dogs, cows, buffaloes, horses, fish, etc. by their smell.

Q.4 Write the names of five things whose smell you like and five things whose smell you do not like.

I like the smell of	I do not like the smell of

Ans.

I like the smell of	I do not like the smell of
Perfumes	Garbage
Flowers	Dead animals
Freshly cooked food	Rotten food
Fresh air	Urinal smell
Hand wash soap	Burnt milk

Q.5 Do you and your friend have similar answers?

Ans. Yes, I and my friend mostly have similar answers.

Discuss (Page 5)

Q.1 Do the clothes of any of your family members smell? Whose?

Ans. Clothes often smell of sweat. It could be t-shirt, socks, pants, etc.

My father's clothes often smell of sweat when he comes back from work.

Q.2 Did you ever come across any smell in a crowded place such as a fair, bus, train etc?

Ans. Yes, I have come across both good and bad smells in crowded places. I have smelt fresh flowers and food at fair. I have also smelt sweat in buses and trains.

Think and Discuss (Page 5)

Q.1 Sushila covered her nose when she cleaned Deepak's nappy, but not when she cleaned her daughter. Why do you think she did this?

Ans. Sushila covered her nose when she cleaned Deepak's nappy because she was not used to this smell. She thought that Deepak's nappy might be dirty. She did not cover her nose when she cleaned her daughter because she was used to that smell.

Q.2 How do you feel when you walk near a heap of garbage? Think of the children who spend the whole day picking things from such garbage.

Ans. I feel very sick and bad when I walk near a heap of garbage. I often cover my nose because of the bad smell. Children who pick up things from the garbage get used to that smell and do not feel bad when they do it daily.

Q.3 Is a smell 'good' or 'bad' for everyone in the same way? Or does it depend on how each one feels about it?

Ans. 'Good' and 'bad' smell depends on how a person thinks about a certain smell. Some smells can be good for a group of people and bad for another group of people.

Let's See (Page 6)

Q.1 Write the name of a bird which has eyes in front of its head (like in humans).

Ans. Owl has eyes in front of its head like human beings.

Q.2 Write the names of some birds which have eyes on either side of the head. What is the size of their eyes as compared to the size of their head?

Ans. Some birds which have eyes on either side of their head are eagles, pigeons, sparrows, parrots, etc. They have very small eyes as compared to their face.

Looking with one or both eyes (Page 6-7)

Close your right eye or cover it with your hand. Tell your friend to stand to your right, at some distance, and ask him to do some action (wave hand, shake head, etc.)

Q.1 Could you see your friend's action, without moving your neck?

Ans. I could not see my friend's action without moving my neck.

Q.2 Now try to look at your friend's action with both your eyes open but without moving your neck.

Ans. Yes, I could see my friend's actions now.

Q.3 What was the difference on looking with one or both eyes?

Ans. I can see better and wider with both eyes.

Q.4 Now toss a small ball or a coin, and try to catch it. Try this with both your eyes open. Then, close one eye and try to catch it. When was it easier to catch?

Ans. It was easier to catch with both eyes open.

Q.5 Imagine how it would be to have your eyes in place of your ears? What would you be able to do then, which you cannot do now?

Ans. If I had eyes in place of my ears, I could see left and right without moving my head. I could also observe two things at one time.

Q.6 Now can you guess from what distance can an eagle in the sky can see a *roti* on the ground?

Ans. An eagle can see the roti on the ground from a distance of almost two kilometres.

Write (Page 8)

Q.1 The names of ten animals whose ears can be seen.

Ans. Ten animals whose ears can be seen are dog, cat, elephant, zebra, rabbit, lion, mouse, cow, horse and donkey.

Q.2 The names of some animals whose ears are bigger than our ears.

Ans. Some animals whose ears are bigger than our ears are elephants, rabbits, cows, dogs, etc.

Think (Page 8)

Q.1 Is there some link between the size of animals' ears and their hearing?

Ans. Yes, animals with bigger ears can hear better and clearer, while animals with smaller ears have less sense of hearing.

Try this (Page 8)

Q.1 For this activity find a quiet place in your school. Tell one of your friends to stand at a short distance and ask him to say something softly. The rest of you should listen carefully. Then, all of you put your hands behind your ears, as shown in the picture. Let the same child say something again as softly as before.

(a) In which case was the sound sharper? Ask your friends too.

Ans. The sound was sharper when I put my hands behind the ears.

(b) Put your hands over your ears and say something. Can you hear your own voice?

Ans. Yes, I can hear my own voice when I put my hands over my ears and say something.

Q.2 Sit near a desk. Tap the desk once with your hand. Listen carefully. Now put your ear on the desk as shown in the picture. Tap on the desk once again with your hand. Listen again. Was there any difference in the sound of the tap?

Ans. Yes, I could hear a sharper sound when I put my ear on the desk.

Write (Page 10)

Q.1 Can you understand the sounds of some animals? Which animals?

Ans. Yes, I can understand the sounds of some animals. They are dogs, cats, cows, horses, etc.

Q.2 Do some animals understand your language? Which ones?

Ans. Yes, some animals like dogs, cows, cats, parrots, etc. understand human language.

Say it with Sounds (Page 10)

Q.1 Just like birds and dolphins you can also make your own language of sounds for giving messages. Remember you have to talk to your friends with only sounds and no words. How and when will you need to give an alarm call? For example, when the teacher is coming to the classroom!

Ans. We can produce sounds like babble or YAHOO! to alarm our classmates when the teacher is coming to the classroom.

Page 10-13

Q.1 Have you noticed that during the cold season you cannot see any lizard in the house? Where do you think they have gone?

Ans. Yes, I have noticed that I cannot see any lizards during the cold season. They hide themselves somewhere safe to take protection from the cold.

Q.2 Given here is the sleeping time of some animals. Write below each picture for how many hours a day that animal sleeps.

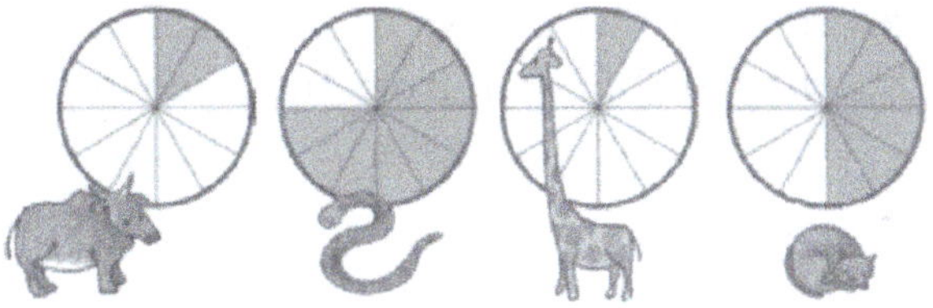

Cow______ Python______ Giraffe______ Cat______

Ans. Cow- 4 hours; Python - 18 hours; Giraffe - 2 hours; Cat - 12 hours

Q.3 When you see different animals, do you have any questions about them? Make a list of ten such questions.

Ans. Yes, I have many questions about them. Some of them are

- Can they understand our language?
- Can they talk to each other?
- Can they see during the night?
- How do they know about any danger?
- How do they identify their food?
- Do they have friends?
- How do they save themselves in bad weather?
- Can they see colours?
- What do they do when they get injured?
- How do they know what time of the day it is?

Q.4 What do you think are some of the dangers to tigers in the jungle?

Ans. Hunters and poachers are the biggest danger to tigers as they kill the tigers for their skin. Tigers can also be harmed by other strong animals like lions.

Q.5 Can human beings also be a threat to animals? How?

Ans. Yes, human beings can also be a threat to animals. Human beings kill animals for their body parts.For example,Snakes are killed for their skins, elephants for their tusks, etc.

Find Out (Page 13)

Q.1 Where are other such National Parks?

Ans. There are many National Parks. Some of them are

- Kanha National Park (Madhya Pradesh)
- Gir National Park (Gujarat)
- Kaziranga National Park (Assam)
- Ranthambore National Park (Rajasthan)

Q.2 Collect information on these and write a report.

Ans. The Indian government has made many National Parks for the protection and safety of animals. It is necessary to protect our animals and plants. Some animals get special status in some parks. For example, Kaziranga National Park gives protection to rhinos while Jim Corbett National Park is for tigers.

What have we Learnt (Page 13)

Q.1 Have you noticed that sometimes singers put their hand on their ear when they sing? Why do you think they may be doing this?

Ans. Yes, I have noticed that sometimes singers put their hands on their ears when they sing. They do it to hear their voice more clearly and to minimise the noise around them.

Q.2 Give examples of animals that may have a very strong sense of sight, hearing or smell.

Ans. Some animals that have strong sense of sight, hearing or smell are

- An eagle has a keen sense of sight - it can see its prey from very far.
- A police dog-it can smell explosives and any other harmful items.
- A mosquito-it can smell sole of our feet

CHAPTER 2 A SNAKE CHARMER'S STORY

About the Chapter

This chapter is about the relationship between snake charmers and their snakes. It tells us about the life of a snake charmer. Aryanath is a young Kalbeliya boy who knows how to play the *been*, a special instrument. Kalbeliyas are snake charmers who pass down this skill in their families. Aryanath's grandfather, Roshan Nath, learned this skill from his ancestors.

Snake charmers would carry snakes in bamboo baskets and travel from village to village. They entertained people and gave them medicines made from plants. They could recognise poisonous snakes, cure snake bites and safely remove a snake's poisonous fangs. Some people think snake charmers harm the snakes, but they actually take good care of them and even gift them to their families. Now, there is a law that stops people from catching wild animals so the art of snake charmers is disappearing.

GLOSSARY

Cultural Something that belongs to a particular group of people.
Traditional Something that belongs to the old times and can be passed on next generation.
Saperas Snake-charmers
Skill Ability
Fangs Poisonous teeth of snakes.
Livelihood Way of earning money for survival.
Been A musical instrument made out of dried bottle gourd, used by snake charmers.

NCERT FOLDER

Think and Tell (Page 17)

Q.1 Have you ever seen anyone playing a *been*? Where?

Ans. Yes, I have seen snake-charmers playing a *been*, usually in fairs or traditional melas.

Q.2 Have you ever seen a snake? Where?

Ans. Yes, I have seen a snake. I have seen them with snake-charmers and in the zoo.

Q.3 Were you scared by it? Why?

Ans. Yes, I was scared by the snakes because I have heard that they are poisonous.

Q.4 Do you think all snakes are poisonous?

Ans. No, I do not think all snakes are poisonous. Some snakes are not poisonous.

Q.5 In chapter 1 you read that snakes do not have ears which you can see. Can the snake hear the been or does it dance when the *been* moves? What do you think?

Ans. Snakes do not have ears so they cannot hear the *been*. They dance when the *been* moves. They follow the *been's* movement.

Write (Page 19)

Q.1 Have you ever seen animals being used for entertainment of people? (For example, in a circus, on the road, or in a park)

Ans. Yes, I have seen animals being used for entertainment of people.

Q.2 When and where did you see this?

Ans. I have seen this in a circus near my house.

Q.3 Which animal show did you see?

Ans. I saw a circus show which had lions, tigers, monkeys and dogs.

Q.4 How did people behave with the animals in the show?

Ans. People behaved friendly with the animals. They did not tease or harm them.

Q.5 Was anyone teasing the animals? How?

Ans. Noone was teasing animals in the circus but I saw some boys throwing water on dogs in the street.

Q.6 What kind of questions came to your mind after seeing the animal show?

Ans. Many questions came to my mind after seeing the animal show. Some of them are

- How were these animals found and caught?
- Were they harmed during training?
- Is it fair to harm animals for the entertainment of people?
- Does the circus staff take care of these animals?
- Are they given proper food to eat?
- Would it not be better if those animals were free and lived with their other friends?

Q.7 Imagine that you are an animal in a cage. Think how you would feel. Complete the following sentences.

(i) I am afraid when __________

(ii) I wish I __________

(iii) I am sad when __________

(iv) If I had a chance I would __________

(v) I do not like at all when __________

Ans. (i) my trainer beats me for any mistake.

(ii) was also free and enjoyed like others.

(iii) I remember how I played with my friends in the jungle.

(iv) escape the cage and go to the jungle.

(v) children tease me and make fun of me.

Write (Page 20-21)

Q.1 Like snake-charmers, which other people depend on animals for their livelihood?

Ans. Apart from snake-charmers, many people depend on animals for their livelihood. They are milkmen, poultry farmers, ranchers, fishers, tongawala, etc.

Survey - People who keep animals

Talk to some people in your neighbourhood who keep one or more animals for their livelihood-for example, a horse for a tonga, hens for eggs, etc.

Q.2 Name the animal they keep.

Ans. There is a milkman, Ramji Singh, in my neighbourhood. He has buffaloes, cows and goats.

Q.3 How many animals are there?

Ans. Ramji Singh has 3 buffaloes, 5 cows and 2 goats.

Q.4 Is there a separate place for the animals?

Ans. Yes, there is a separate place for the animals. He keeps them in a big shed that he has constructed for them.

Q.5 Who looks after them?

Ans. Ramji Singh and his wife look after them.

Q.6 What do the animals eat?

Ans. Cows, buffaloes and goats eat grass and animal fodder.

Q.7 Do the animals ever fall ill? What does the keeper do then?

Ans. Yes, sometimes the animals fall ill. When it happens, Ramji Singh takes them to a nearby veterinary hospital for proper treatment. He takes good care of their health and gives them proper medicines.

Q.8 Make some more questions and discuss.

Ans. Some more questions can be

- Do the animals like to play?
- Do you think the animals understand you?
- How do the animals show their love to each other?

Q.9 Make a report on your project and read it out in the class.

Ans. Ramji Singh is a milkman in my neighbourhood. He has 3 buffaloes, 5 cows and 2 goats who he keeps in a proper shed. These animals eat grass and other animal fodder. Ramji takes proper care of his animals with his wife. He also takes them to the veterinary hospital when they get sick. They are Ramji's source of livelihood as he earns money by selling milk.

What have we Learnt? (Page 21)

Q.1 The government has made a law that no one can catch and keep snakes. What do you think about this law? Give reasons for your answer and write in your own words.

Ans. Animals are harmed and misused by people. They are caught and their skins and body parts are sold for earning money. Hunters kill the animals. They are also harmed for the entertainment for people. This law, which prevents everyone from catching and keeping snakes and other animals, is a good law. It will keep the animals safe.

CHAPTER 3 FROM TASTING TO DIGESTING

About the Chapter

This chapter is about how different foods are digested, their tastes, smells and how long digestion takes. Different foods have different tastes like sweet, sour, salty and bitter, and our tongue can recognise these tastes. Some foods, like onions, have a strong smell. Chewing food properly is important because it helps with digestion.

Our body gives us signs when it needs food and sometimes we get angry when hungry. When we are sick, our body can't digest food well and we might need glucose drips for energy. In 1822, Dr. Beaumont did an experiment on a soldier's stomach to see how long foods take to digest. Eating good food is important for the body's growth and every child has the right to proper food.

GLOSSARY

Digestion The process of breaking down food into smaller parts, so that the body can absorb it and provide energy.

Glucose A type of sugar that gives instant energy to our body.

Digestive Juice A juice released in the stomach which helps in breaking down the food for digestion.

Pungent smell A strong, sharp smell which is bad and unpleasant.

Acidic Something that has a high quantity of acid and is often very sour in taste.

NCERT FOLDER

Discuss and Write (Page 23-24)

Q.1 Jhoolan's mouth started watering when she heard the word *imli*. When does your mouth water? List five things you like to eat and describe their taste.

Ans. My mouth waters when I see my favourite food. I like to eat sweet things.

Five things I like to eat are

(i) Cake - Sweet

(ii) Biryani - Salty

(iii) Mangoes - Sweet

(iv) *Imli* - Sour

(v) Potato Chips - Salty

Q.2 Do you like only one kind of taste or different ones? Why?

Ans. I like different kind of tastes like sweet, sour and salty. Eating only one taste of foods is boring.

Q.3 Jhoolan put a few drops of lemon juice in Jhumpa's mouth. Do you think we can make out the taste with just a few drops?

Ans. Yes, sour things like lemon juice can be recognised with a few drops.

Q.4 If someone were to put a few seeds of saunf (aniseed) on your tongue, would you be able to tell with your eyes closed? How?

Ans. Yes, if someone puts a few seeds of saunf on my tongue, I will be able to tell with my eyes closed. I can taste the saunf and smell its fragrance

Q.5 How did Jhumpa make out the fried fish? Can you guess the names of certain things only by their smell, without seeing or tasting them? What are these things?

Ans. Jhumpa can make out the fried fish by its smell.

Yes, I can guess many things by their smell. For example, I can smell omelette, pakodas, fish, kheer, etc.

Q.6 Has anyone ever told you to hold your nose before taking medicine? Why do you think they tell you to do this?

Ans. Yes, my mom tells me to hold my nose. She tells me to do so because medicines taste bitter. Closing the nose when taking a medicine helps to hide the taste of medicine and reduces the bad smell.

Close your Eyes and Tell (Page 24)

Collect a few food items having different kinds of taste. Play a game with your friends like Jhumpa and Jhoolan did. Tell your friend to taste the food and ask

Q.1 How did it taste? What was the food item?

Ans. The food item was a cooked bitter gourd. It tasted bitter.

Q.2 On which part of the tongue could you get the most taste? In front, at the back, on the left or right side of the tongue?

Ans. I could get the most taste at the back of the tongue.

Q.3 Which taste could be made out on which part of the tongue? Mark these parts on the picture given below

Ans.

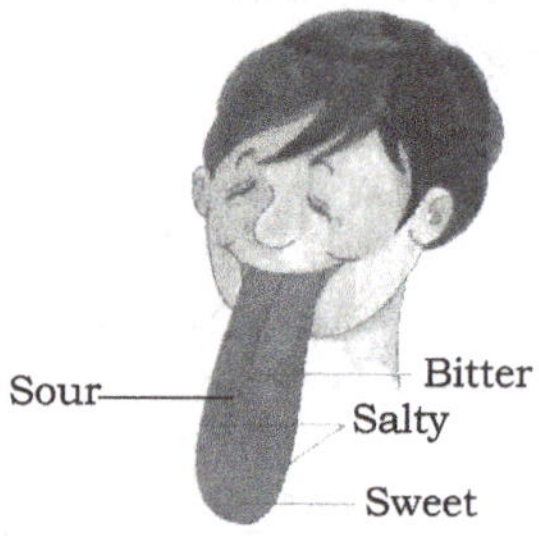

Q.4 One at a time put some things to eat in other parts of your mouth– under the tongue, on the lips, on the roof of the mouth. Did you get any taste there?

Ans. No, I could not get any taste when I put some things to eat in other parts of my mouth.

Page 25

Q.1 Use a clean cloth to wipe the front part of your tongue so that it is dry. Put some sugar or jaggery there. Could you taste anything? Why did this happen?

Ans. No, I could not taste anything because my tongue did not have any saliva.

Q.2 Stand in front of a mirror and look closely at your tongue. How does the surface look? Can you see any tiny bumps on the surface?

Ans. The surface looks very rough. Yes, there are tiny bumps on the surface.

Tell (Page 25-26)

Q.1 If someone asks you to describe the taste of amla or cucumber, you might find it difficult to explain. How would you describe the taste of these – tomato, onion, saunf, garlic. Think of words that you know or make up your own words to describe the taste.

Ans.

Food	Taste
Tomato	Sweet, sour, juicy
Onion	Pungent
Saunf	Sweet
Garlic	Bitter and pungent

Q.2 When Jhumpa tasted some of the things, she said "Sssee, sssee, sssee ...."□ What do you think she may have eaten?

Ans. She may have eaten a spicy thing like red or green chillies.

Q.3 Why don't you make sounds that describe some tastes? From your expressions and sounds ask your friends to guess what you might have eaten?

Ans. I make the following sounds that describe different tastes.

Expressions and sounds	Food items
Mmmmm .... (Yum-Yum)	Chocolates
Tch-Tch	Pickles
Suuuurr (Slurp)	Noodles

Try this together in class:

- Each of you take a piece of bread or *roti* or some cooked rice.
- Put it in your mouth, chew three to four times and swallow it.

Q.4 Did the taste change as you chewed it?

Ans. The taste did not change much as I chewed it. It was almost the same.

Q.5 Now take another piece or some rice and chew it thirty to thirty-two times. Was there any change in the taste after chewing so many times?

Ans. Yes, there was a change in the taste after chewing many times. The food tasted sweet.

Discuss (Page 26)

Q.1 Has anyone at home told you to eat slowly and to chew well so that the food digests properly? Why do you think they say this?

Ans. Yes, my parents tell me to eat slowly and chew well. They say this because chewing the food properly helps in its digestion.

Q.2 Imagine you are eating something hard like a green guava. What kinds of changes take place in it? From the time you bite a piece and put it in your mouth to when you swallow it?

Ans. When I bite a piece of green guava, it is hard at first and tastes somewhat bitter. After chewing a little, it becomes softer and sweeter. The saliva mixes with the guava and helps to break it down into pieces.

Q.3 Think what does the saliva in our mouth do?

Ans. Saliva mixes with the food and makes it soft. Soft food is easy to digest. So, saliva helps in the process of digestion.

Page 27

Q.1 Where do you think the food must be going after you put it in your mouth and swallow it? In the picture given here, draw the path of the food through your body. Share your picture with your friends. Do all of you have similar pictures?

Ans. I think the food goes into my stomach after I swallow it. Yes, my friends and I have similar pictures.

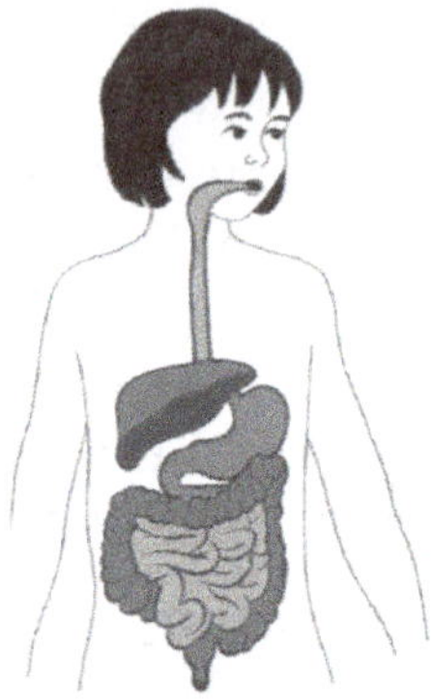

Discuss (Page 27)

Q.1 How do you feel when you are very hungry? How would you describe it? For example, sometimes we jokingly say, 'I am so hungry I could eat an elephant!'

Ans. When I am hungry, I feel tired and my stomach starts to make sounds. I could eat anything at that time. I say 'I have butterflies in my stomach. I can eat anything.'

Q.2 How do you come to know that you are hungry?

Ans. I start getting a headache and I have a strong urge to eat something. This is a signal that shows that I am hungry.

Q.3 Think what would happen if you do not eat anything for two days?

Ans. If I do not eat anything for two days, I will become very weak and will fall sick.

Q.4 Would you be able to manage without drinking water for two days? Where do you think the water that we drink goes?

Ans. I don't think I will be able to manage without drinking water for two days. I think water is used up by our body for various functions. Any excess water is removed from the body by urine and sweat.

Talk and Discuss (Page 28-29)

Q.1 Do you remember that in Class IV you made a solution of sugar and salt? Nitu's father also made this and gave her. Why do you think this is given to someone who has vomiting and loose motions?

Ans. In case of vomiting and loose motions, the water, glucose and salt amount decreases in the body. It can be a dangerous situation. So, a sugar and salt solution is given to give energy to the body.

Q.2 Have you heard the word 'glucose', or seen it written anywhere? Where?

Ans. Yes, I have heard the word glucose and seen it written on the packs of glucose powder available in the market. I have seen many TV advertisements of glucose and glucose biscuits.

Q.3 Have you ever tasted glucose? How does it taste? Tell your friends.

Ans. Yes, I have tasted glucose. It tastes very sweet.

Q.4 Have you or anyone in your family been given a glucose drip? When and why? Tell the class about it.

Ans. Yes, my grandmother was given a glucose drip. She had cholera and could not digest any food. She was very weak so she was admitted in the hospital and a glucose drip was given to her.

Q.5 Nitu's teacher used to tell the girls to have glucose while playing hockey. Why do you think she did this?

Ans. Nitu's teacher used to tell the girls to have glucose while playing hockey because when we play outdoor games, we sweat a lot. As a result, we lose water, sugar and salts from the body very quickly. We feel tired and weak. Glucose can help in maintaining the level of sugar and salt in the body and give us instant energy.

Q.6 Look at Nitu's picture and describe what is happening. How is the glucose drip being given?

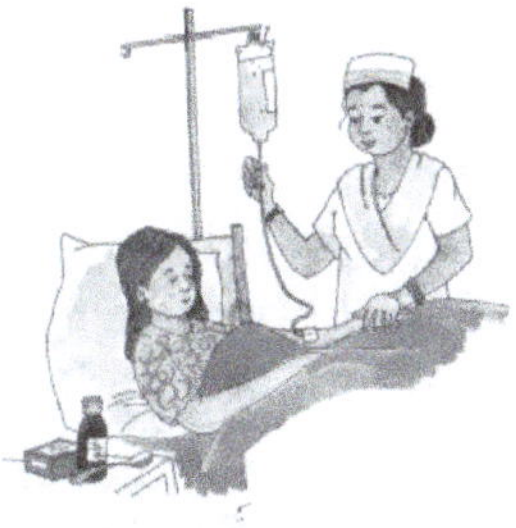

Ans. The picture shows a glucose drip being given to Nitu in the hospital. There is some glucose solution in the bottle and it is being supplied to the body by a needle.

Think and Discuss (Page 31)

Q.1 Imagine if you had been in place of Dr. Beaumont, what experiments would you have done to find out the secrets of our stomach? Write about your experiments.

Ans. If I were in place of Dr. Beaumont, I would have done the experiments with boiled rice, cooked dal and paratha. I would have taken out the digestive juices from the body and kept all the food items in three different glass bowls. I would have observed the time it took to digest the food in the stomach and the glasses.

Discuss (Page 33)

Q.1 Why do you think Rashmi could eat only one *roti* in the whole day?

Ans. Rashmi could eat only one *roti* in the whole day because she was not able to afford a proper meal. She was very poor.

Q.2 Do you think Kailash would like games and sports?

Ans. Kailash would not like games and sports because he is not very active. He is fat and flabby which shows that he does not like physical activities.

Q.3 What do you understand by 'proper' food?

Ans. 'Proper' food means adequate and nutritious food according to one's body requirement.

Q.4 Why do you think that the food of Rashmi and Kailash was not proper?

Ans. Rashmi is not eating the right amount of food that her body needs. On the other hand, Kailash is eating too much food and he is not eating good food. He is only eating junk food. That is why Rashmi and Kailash both are not eating 'proper' food.

Find Out (Page 33)

Q.1 Talk with your grandparents or elderly people and find out what they ate and what work they did when they were of your age. Now think about yourself– your daily activities and daily diet–Are these similar or different from what your grandparents did and ate?

Ans. My grandparents used to a very healthy diet which included rice, dal, green vegetables, milk, fruits, etc. They were very active and used to do a lot of physical activities. They went to school by walking and played games which involved running, jumping, etc. Now, it is different. We eat healthy food like rice, dal, vegetables but we have also added a lot of junk food like burgers, pizza, etc. to our diet. We also do less physical activities. I go to school by bus unlike my grandparents and I spend my time sitting on the sofa or bed, playing video games.

Think and Discuss (Page 34)

Q.1 Do you know any child who does not get enough to eat in the whole day? What are the reasons?

Ans. Yes, I know some children who do not get enough food to eat in the whole day because they are poor people who do not have money to eat a proper meal.

Q.2 Why do you think people suffer from starvation?

Ans. Starvation means not having enough food to eat. There are many reasons for it. Some of them are

- Poverty - When people are poor, they cannot afford proper food.
- Natural disasters - In case of disasters like earthquake, floods, etc. it is difficult for people to get proper food.
- Diseases and Improper health - Some body diseases make it impossible to get a proper diet.

Q.3 What kind of health problems occur when we do not get enough food for a very long time?

Ans. When we do not get enough food for a very long time, our body feels weak and it is not able to recover well. Lack of proper food also slows down our growth. Not eating enough food can make us sick.

Q.4 Where do the grains from the field go after reaching the mandis?

Ans. The grains can go to different places after reaching mandis. They can go to processing houses for grinding or can be stored in storage houses. After being grinded into flour, they are sold in the market.

Q.5 Have you come across any news related to huge spoilage in mandis or godowns? Collect some news of food spoilage or wastage on a large scale in mandis or godowns.

Ans. Yes, I have heard about huge spoilage in mandis and godowns. Students can look in the newspapers and cut out the news related to food spoilage in mandis.

Q.6 Read the news and find out the reasons of spoilage of grains. How can such incidents be checked?

Ans. There are many reasons for spoilage of grains. For example, improper storage temperature, bad conditions and pests like rats and cockroaches spoil the grains.

These incidents can be checked by making proper arrangements for storage of grains. Pest control is also important.

CHAPTER 4 MANGOES ROUND THE YEAR

About the Chapter

This chapter is about preparation and preservation of different foods we eat. Spoilt food is bad food, which gives us many health problems. Foods can get spoiled because of temperature, weather and fungus. It is important to preserve food properly to prevent it from spoilage. For example, milk can be boiled, pickles and chutneys can be put in glass jars, some foods can be dried, and salt or sugar can be mixed in some food items. In the chapter, Chittababu and Chinnababu's mother makes *mamidi tandra* (aam papad) with ripe mango pulp to enjoy them all round the year.

GLOSSARY

Spoilt Something has been damaged or gone bad, especially food items like milk, bread, etc.
Preserve To keep something safe from getting bad or spoilt.
Mamidi Tandra It is a type of *aam papad* made with mango pulp.

NCERT FOLDER

Discuss (Page 35)

Q.1 How did Aman know that the potato *sabzi* had got spoilt?

Ans. Aman knew that the potato *sabzi* had got spoilt by the bad smell coming from it.

Q.2 Have you ever seen some food that has got spoilt? How did you know that it was spoiled?

Ans. Yes, I have seen some foods that have gone spoilt. I could recognise the spoiled food from its bad smell and different look.

Q.3 Preeti told Nitu not to eat the potato *sabzi*. What would have happened if she had eaten it?

Ans. If Nitu had eaten the potato *sabzi* that was spoilt, she might have fallen ill with a bad stomach ache.

Write (Page 36)

Q.1 Look in your kitchen and write down names of food items that
(a) can get spoilt in 2-3 days
(b) can be kept for a week
(c) would not spoil till one month

Ans. (a) milk, cooked dal, paneer, bread, etc.
(b) potato, banana, tomato, onion, etc.
(c) ghee, uncooked pasta, raw rice, pickles, etc.

Q.2 Look at your friend's list and discuss in the class.

Ans. Your friend's list will be similar to yours.

Q.3 Will your list be same in all the seasons? What would change?

Ans. No, the list will change according to the season. In the summer season, foods get spoiled faster than in the winter season. In the rainy season, due to more moisture in the air, the food gets spoiled easily.

Q.4 When food gets spoilt in your house, what do you do with it?

Ans. When food gets spoilt, we throw it in the dustbin because we cannot keep it.

Page 36

Q.1 Look at the picture of the bread packet here and guess why Biji returned it?

Ans. Biji may have seen that the expiry date of the bread is past and the bread is expired.

Q.2 How did she find that the bread had got spoilt?

Ans. She may have seen green grey spots on the bread which indicates the presence of fungus.

Find Out (Page 36)

Look carefully at two-three packets of food items:

Q.1 What can we know from what is written on the packet?

Ans. We can get following information from the food packet

- Price
- Date of manufacturing
- Weight
- Ingredients
- Date of expiry
- Nutrition value

Q.2 When you buy anything from the market, what do you look for on the packet?

Ans. When I buy anything from the market, I look for the manufacturing date and expiry date. I also look for the price.

Page 37-38

Q.1 Fill up the chart everyday after discussing the changes seen.

	Changes in the bread or *roti*			
Day	**By touch**	**By smell**	**By looking through hand lens**	**By colour**
1.				
2.				
3.				
4.				
5.				
6.				

Ans.

	Changes in the bread or roti			
Day	**By touch**	**By smell**	**By looking though hand lens**	**By colour**
1.	Soft	Light smell	Normal	Normal
2.	Soft	Light stinking smell	Velvet like white layer	Normal
3.	Soft and moist	Stinking smell	Velvet like white layer	Slightly white
4.	Soft and moist	Stinking smell	Greenish-white layer	Greenish white
5.	Soft and moist	Stinking smell	Greenish layer with grass like structures	Greenish
6.	Soft and moist	Stinking smell	Greenish black layer with grass-like structures	Greenish black

Q.2 Find out the reason for these changes. From where did the fungus come on the bread?

Ans. These changes happened due to spoiling of the bread. Fungus is present in the air. It came on the bread because of moisture on the bread surface.

Q.3 Different kinds of food items spoil due to different reasons. Some foods spoil soon, some stay good for long. List some seasons and conditions in which food spoils quickly.

Ans. In summers, the food gets spoilt faster than in winter. In rainy season, the food absorbs a lot of moisture and gets spoilt.

Conditions in which food spoils quickly are

- If milk is not boiled properly.
- If cooked food is kept outside the fridge for too long.
- If raw vegetables are kept in hot and humid places.
- If the uncooked food is not kept safe from moisture.

Page 38

Q.4 Given below are some food items and some simple methods by which these could be kept fresh for 1-2 days. Match the correct pairs.

Food Items	Methods
Milk	Put in a bowl and keep the bowl in a container with some water.
Cooked rice	Wrap in a damp cloth.
Green coriander (*Dhania*)	Boil it.
Onion, garlic	Keep it in a dry open place.

Ans.

Food Items	Methods
Milk	Boil it.
Cooked rice	Put in a bowl and keep the bowl in a container with some water.
Green coriander (*Dhania*)	Wrap in a damp cloth.
Onion, garlic	Keep it in a dry open place.

Write (Page 40)

Q.1 Why was sugar and jaggery mixed into the mango pulp and dried in the Sun?

Ans. Sugar and jaggery were mixed into the mango pulp and dried in the Sun to make *mamidi tandra* (*aam papad*).

Q.2 Why did *Appa* first choose the most ripe mangoes to be used for making the *mamidi tandra*?

Ans. Appa chose the most ripe mangoes because they have more juice and less fibre.

Q.3 How did the brothers make the *mamidi tandra*? Write down step-by-step what they did for this.

Ans. The brothers followed these steps to make *mamidi tandra*

- They bought a mat woven from the palm tree leaves, poles of casuarina tree, string made of coconut husk, some jaggery and sugar.
- Then, they made a high platform using the poles and the mat.
- They took out the mango pulp from the ripe mangoes.
- Then they filtered the mango juice using a muslin cloth.
- They added the crushed jaggery and sugar in the pulp.

- Now, they left a thin layer of the prepared mango pulp on the mat to dry.
- In the evening, they covered the mat with a clean saree to keep it safe from dust.
- They spread many layers over it for the next four weeks.
- After four weeks, a thick golden layered cake of *mamidi tandra* was ready to be cut into pieces.

Q.4 What things are made in your house from ripe and unripe mangoes?

Ans. Many things are made with mangoes. With unripe mangoes, we make chutneys, pickles and aam panna. With ripe mangoes, we make mango shakes, aam papad and mango ice-cream.

Q.5 Make a list of all the different types of pickles that you know about and share with your friends.

Ans. Some types of pickles are mango, chilli, lime, amla, carrot, potato, radish, turnip, garlic, etc.

Find Out and Discuss (Page 41)

Q.1 Is there any kind of pickle made in your house? What kind of pickle is it? Who makes it? From whom did they learn to make the pickle?

Ans. Yes, there are many kinds of pickles made in my house. They are made from mango, chillies, lemon, amla, etc. My mother makes these pickles. She learnt it from my grandmother.

Q.2 What all things are needed to make any one type of pickle in your house? How is the pickle made? Find out and write the recipe.

Ans. Let us take an example of lemon pickle. My mother needs the following things for salty lemon pickle:

Lemons and lemon scraps, salt, oil, mustard seeds, kalaunji, aniseed, methi, red chilli powder, lemon juice, whole dried red chillies and garlic cloves.

Process

- Lemons are cut into small pieces and dried in the Sun for one day to remove the moisture.
- Then, these pieces are added into a glass jar with some lemon juice, salt and turmeric powder.
- The jar is covered and kept aside for one day. Now, a tempering is prepared. In a pan placed on the stove, mustard oil is heated.
- Then, mustard seeds, kalaunji, aniseed, garlic cloves and red chillies are added. The oil mixture is cooled for a bit and poured on the lemons.
- The glass jar is kept in the Sun for a week. The pickle is ready to be enjoyed.

Q.3 How are these things made in your house? Papad - Chutney - Badiyan - Sauce

Ans.
- **Papad** Papad is made from different dals and potatoes. My mom makes urad dal papad. She grinds the urad dal with salt, chilli powder, baking powder and other spices. Then, she makes a dough out of it. She rolls out thin papads and leaves them in the Sun to dry.
- **Chutney** Chutney is made from many ingredients like dhania, mirchi, mangoes, etc. In my house, dhania and raw mango chutney is prepared. My mom adds the dhania, mango pieces, green chillies, salt and some dry mango powder to a mixer jar and grinds it into a paste. The chutney is ready.
- **Badiyan** Badiyan are made with urad dal. Urad dal is soaked in the water for the whole night and then, ground into a coarse paste. Salt and some spices are added to the mixture. Then, small lumps are made out of the mixture and left out to dry in the Sun.
- **Sauce** Sauce is made using ripe tomatoes. The tomatoes are ground into a fine paste. Then, salt, sugar and other spices are added to the tomato paste. This paste is boiled and made thick. Then, the mixture is cooled down to room temperature. The sauce is ready.

Q.4 It is a two-day journey by train from Pune to Kolkata. If you were to go on this trip, what food items would you carry with you? How would you pack them? Make a list on the blackboard of all the packed food. What food would you eat first?

Ans. I will carry the food items that do not spoil easily. I will pack them in dry containers and zip-lock bags to keep them safe.

Some things that I will carry are chiwda, murmure (rice puffs), makhanas, sattu, curd, dry fruits, biscuits, dry sweets, puri, dry aloo sabzi, etc.

What have we Learnt (Page 41)

Q.1 Glass jars and bottles are dried well in the Sun before filling them with pickles. Why is this done? Do you remember what happened to the bread in the experiment?

Ans. Glass jars and bottles are dried well in the Sun before filling them with pickles to remove any excess moisture from them.

In the experiment, the bread got spoiled due to the moisture and fungus started growing on it.

Q.2 To eat mangoes round the year, we make different items like pickles, *aam papad, chutney, chikki,* etc. List some other food with which we make different things, so that we can enjoy it throughout the year.

Ans. Following are the examples of food that can be enjoyed throughout the year

- Pickles made from many things like chillies and amla.
- Murrabas made with mango and amla.
- Sun dried vegetables like tomato and cauliflower.
- Sweets made with milk like pedas, ladoos, etc.
- Potato and banana chips.
- Papads from potatoes and dals.

CHAPTER 5 SEEDS AND SEEDS

About the Chapter

This chapter is about different types of seeds, their shapes, sizes and colours. Seeds are small parts of plants that grow into new plants. Different seeds have different colours, shapes and textures. We also eat seeds like lentils, chana and rajma. Some seeds are soaked or sprouted before cooking. Some plants, called trap plants, can catch and eat insects.

Seeds can travel from one place to another by air, water, animals and humans. In 1948, George Mestral studied seeds and invented velcro, a material used to stick many things. We learn that some foods grow in India like mangoes and bananas but others like tomatoes, green chilies and coffee beans come from different countries.

GLOSSARY

Soaking When you put something in water for a long time.
Sprouting The process of making sprouts from the seeds is called sprouting.
Sprouts These are germinated seeds with growing stems and roots often eaten by us.
Pitcher A pitcher is a container with a handle and a mouth, used for pouring liquids.
Split To split means cut anything in half or divide anything into two parts.
Trap To catch something with grip so that it cannot leave.

NCERT FOLDER

Discuss (Page 42)

Q.1 What things are soaked before cooking in your house? Why?

Ans. Things soaked before cooking are *chana*, moong, dry peas, rajma, soyabean, pulses like *urad dal*, rice, etc. These things become soft after soaking. This makes it easier to grind or cook them.

Q.2 What things do you eat after sprouting? How are they sprouted? How much time does it take?

Ans. We eat chana, moong, chickpeas, etc after sprouting.

They are sprouted using a simple process. They are soaked in water overnight and then, the water is drained out. After that, they are tied in a damp cloth and hung for a few days.

Chana usually takes two-three days to sprout, moong takes one- two days and other pulses take different time.

Q.3 Has the doctor or someone you know ever told you to eat sprouts? Why?

Ans. Yes, my family doctor has advised me to eat sprouts because they are good for health and provide nutrition to the body.

Do this and Find Out (Page 43)

Q.1 Do you remember that in Class IV you did an activity with seeds? Now try another one.

- Take some *chana* and three bowls.
- Put five *chana* in the first bowl and fill it up with water.
- Put a damp piece of cloth or some cotton wool in the second bowl. Now keep the same number of *chanas* in it. Make sure that the cotton wool or cloth remains wet.
- Put the same number of *chanas* in the third bowl. Do not put anything else in it. Cover all the three bowls.

Observe after two days and note the changes in the bowls.

	Bowl 1	Bowl 2	Bowl 3
Are the seeds getting air?	No	Yes	Yes
Are the seeds getting water?			
What changes did you see?			
Have the seeds sprouted?			

Ans.

	Bowl 1	Bowl 2	Bowl 3
Are the seeds getting air?	No	Yes	Yes
Are the seeds getting water?	Yes	Yes	No
What changes did you see?	*Chanas* have soaked water and swelled up	*Chanas* have sprouted	No change
Have the seeds sprouted?	No	Yes	No

Tell and Write (Page 43)

Q.1 In which bowl did the seeds sprout? What difference did you see between this bowl and the other bowls?

Ans. Seeds sprouted in bowl 2 only. For sprouting of seeds, we need both air and water. In bowl 2, the seeds got both water and air, so they could sprout easily. In bowl 1, seeds only got water, so they didn't sprout. In bowl 3, both air and water were not there, so the seeds did not change.

Q.2 Why did Gopal's mother tie the *chana* in a damp cloth?

Ans. Gopa's mother tied the *chana* in a damp cloth so that the seeds could get both air and water. This will help them sprout easily.

Page 44

Q.1 When you split the whole *masoor*, you get me -*masoor dal.* But then you cannot sprout me! Can you think why?

Ans. When a seed is split into two, it cannot be sprouted because it loses its ability to sprout.

Draw (Page 44)

Q.2 Look carefully at your sprouted *chana* and make its drawing.

Ans.

Note : This image show how a sprouted chana looks. Students can see this to make their drawing.

Project: Plant your Seeds (Page 44)

Q.1 Take a clay pot or a tin can with a wide mouth. Make a small hole at the bottom of the can. Fill your can with soil. Put four or five seeds of the same kind in the soil and press them gently. Different groups can plant different kinds of seeds, such as mustard (*sarson*), fenugreek (*methi*), sesame (*til*) or coriander (*dhania*).

Ans. Do it yourself

Write (Page 44)

Q.1 (a) Name of the seed: ___________

(b) The date on which you planted them: ___________

(c) The day you observe something coming out of the soil, start filling the table

Date	Height of the plant (in cm)	Number of leaves seen	Any other change

Ans. (a) Mustard

(b) 28th September, 2024

(c)

Date	Height of the plant (in cm)	Number of leaves seen	Any other change
4th October	1 cm	2	No
5th October	1.5 cm	3	No
6th October	3 cm	5	Stem became thicker, leaves became greener
7th October	4 cm	6	Stem started becoming stiff and stable

For measuring the height of a plant, use a thread and measure it on a scale.

Find Out (Page 45)

Q.1 How long did it take for the plant to come out from the soil?

Ans. It took about 6 to 7 days for the plant to come out from the soil.

Q.2 What was the difference in the height of the plant on the first and second day?

Ans. The height on the second day was half a centimetre more than the first day.

Q.3 On which day the height of the plant increase the most?

Ans. The height of the plant increased the most on the third day.

Q.4 Did new leaves come out of the plant every day?

Ans. Yes, new leaves came out of the plant every day.

Q.5 Was there any change in the stem of the plant?

Ans. The stem of the plant grew thicker day-by-day. It also became more stiff and stable.

Discuss (Page 45)

Q.1 Which seeds took the most number of days for the stem to come out of the soil?

Ans. Seeds of sesame (*til*) took the most number of days for the stem to come out of the soil.

Q.2 Which seeds took the least number of days to come out?

Ans. Mustard seeds (*sarson*) took the least number of days to come out.

Q.3 Which seeds did not grow at all? Why?

Ans. All the seeds grew because there was water and air. If there was no water or air, the seeds would not grow.

Q.4 Did anyone's plant dry up or turn yellow? Why did this happen?

Ans. Yes, my friend's plant dried up and turned yellow because he did not give enough water to the plant.

Q.5 What would happen if the plants do not get water?

Ans. If the plants do not get water, they will start turning yellow and will dry up.

Straight from your Heart (Page 45)

Q.1 What is inside the seed?

Ans. There are two parts inside the seed-cotyledons and embryo. Cotyledon is the outer covering of the seed and embryo is the inner part of the seed.

Q.2 How does a big plant grow from the tiny seed?

Ans. A tiny seed can grow into a big plant through a process called germination. In germination, the seed is given water and air and it produces a seedling. A seedling further absorbs water and nutrients from the soil, and grows into a big plant day-by-day.

Think and Imagine (Page 46)

Q.1 What would happen if plants could walk? Draw a picture.

Ans.

Find Out (Page 46)

Q.1 Do some plants grow without seeds?

Ans. Yes, some plants grow without seeds. For example, roses and money plant.

So many Seeds (Page 46-47)

How many types of seeds can you collect? Where will you find them? Each of you should try to collect as many different types of seeds as you can. After that, put all the seed collections together. Now observe these seeds carefully-their shapes, sizes, colours, textures (smooth or rough). Make a seed chart to put up in the class. You can start with a table like this.

Name of the seed	Colour	Shape (draw)	Texture
Rajma	Reddish brown		Smooth

Ans.

Name of the seed	Colour	Shape (draw)	Texture
Rajma	Reddish brown		Smooth
Moong	Green		Soft
Mango	Whitish Yellow		Rough
Papaya	Black		Rough
Cumin	Brown		Soft
Aniseed	Green		Soft

Think (Page 47)

Q.1 Did you keep aniseed (*saunf*) and cumin (*jeera*) in your list?

Ans. Yes, I kept both of them in my list.

Q.2 Which was the smallest seed and which was the biggest seed in your collection?

Ans. In my collection, the smallest seed was cumin and the biggest was mango.

Makes lists of (Page 47)

Q.1 Seeds that are used as spices in your home.

Ans. Cumin, mustard, aniseed, *kalonji*, etc.

Q.2 Seeds of vegetables.

Ans. Cucumber, tomato, pumpkin, ladyfinger, brinjal, etc.

Q.3 Seeds of fruits.

Ans. Mango, papaya, apple, guava, orange, etc.

Q.4 Light seeds (check by blowing them).

Ans. Coriander (dhaniya), aniseed (*saunf*).

Q.5 Seeds which are flat.

Ans. Apple, cumin, sesame, etc.

Q.6 Make more groups. How many groups of seeds did you make?

Ans. Seeds can be grouped as

- Edible seeds
- Seeds which give oil
- Heavy seeds

I made three groups.

Q.7 Do you know any game that you can play with seeds? Discuss with your friends?

Ans. Yes, there are many games that we can play with seeds. Mango seeds are used to make flutes. We can also play 'Touch and Guess' with different types of seeds.

Page 48

Q.1 Have you ever seen any seed that can fly?

Ans. Yes, I have seen such seeds. It has small white hair attached to it. When you blow, it flies.

Q.2 What is it called in your area?

Ans. It is called *budhiya ke baal* in my area.

Q.3 Look at your seed collection. Guess how many of them could have travelled by flying?

Ans. I think some of the seeds like cumin and aniseed can travel by flying.

Q.4 Did you get any new idea from these seeds?

Ans. Yes, when I was looking at seeds, I thought that they could be used for decorating something.

Page 49

Q.1 Look at the pictures given below and guess how the seeds travel and reach different places.

Ans. The first picture shows a squirrel carrying the seed.

The second picture shows that a bird is carrying the seed. So, seeds can travel with the help of animals and birds.

Third picture shows a coconut floating on the water. So, seeds can travel with the help of water too.

Q.2 Some plants spread their seeds over long distances. When the soyabean pods are ripe, they burst and the seeds are thrown out. Have you ever heard their sound?

Ans. No, I have not heard their sound.

Q.3 Think what would happen, if seeds did not spread and remained at one place.

Ans. If seeds did not spread and remained at once place only, they will not grow properly. They will not get enough water, sunlight and air which will prevent germination of the seeds.

Q.4 Make a list of the different ways by which seeds are spread.

Ans. Seeds are spread by the following ways

- Through animals and birds
- Through humans
- By water
- By air

Page 50

Q.1 What all was grown in India long ago? Were mangoes and bananas grown here? What came from other countries? Imagine food without potatoes or tomatoes!

Ans. Many crops like mango, tea, orange, radish, *methi*, spinach, banana, etc were grown in India long ago.

Yes, mangoes and bananas were grown here. Tomatoes, green chillies, coffee, *bhindi*, etc. have come from other countries. Potatoes and tomatoes are used in most of the dishes. Many dishes would be incomplete without them.

What we have Learnt (Page 50)

Q.1 Reena has drawn this picture of the seed sprouted by her. What do you think the seeds need for sprouting? Write in your own words. How would Reena's seeds look if they did not get the things needed. Show by drawing a picture.

Ans. For sprouting, water and air are needed. The seeds would not sprout or show any change if they did not get water and air.

Draw a picture of seeds which did not sprout.

Q.2 How do seeds spread to far off places? Write in your own words.

Ans. Seeds spread to far off places in the following ways

- Seeds are spread by birds, animals, air and water. Many animals eat the fruit but throw the seeds somewhere. This helps in spreading the seeds.
- Sometimes, seeds get stuck to the fur of animals or clothes of human beings. This way, they travel to other places.
- Some seeds float on water and go to far off places.

CHAPTER 6 EVERY DROP COUNTS

About the Chapter

This chapter is about the importance of water and how we can save it. It also tells us about water scarcity. Ghadsisar was a lake in Jaisalmer that everyone used. Rainwater was also collected here. But now, it's not used as houses have been built around it. A traveller named Al-Biruni came to India many years ago and wrote about the ponds here. In Rajasthan, where it rains very little, people know how important water is. They collect water through johads and rainwater harvesting. Stepwells are also used to collect water.

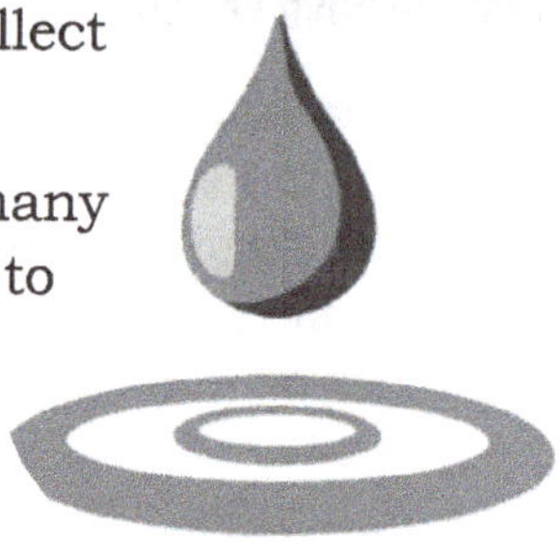

Many festivals and customs are related to water. Water is supplied in many ways like taps, tankers, hand pumps and borewells. Some people work to help communities get enough water by building or fixing lakes. For example, a woman named Darki Mai from Rajasthan was helped by the group Tarun Bharat Sangh to get water for her area.

GLOSSARY

Sar The word sar means a lake.

Ghats It is the bank of a river. It also has steps leading down to a river or body of water.

Stepwell Stepwells are deep wells with a series of steps leading down to the water level.

NCERT FOLDER

Observe and Find Out (Page 52)

Q.1 Look at the area around your school. Are there any fields, farms, pucca roads, drains, etc. Is the area sloping, rocky or flat? Think, what will happen here when it rains? Where will the rainwater go-into the drains, pipes or pits? Is some water also getting soaked into the soil?

Ans. Yes, there are fields. Farms, pucca roads and drains near my school. The area is somewhat flat. When it rains, the rainwater goes into drains and then, into a nearby lake connected to the drains.

Page 53

Q.1 How do you think the rainwater that falls on the roof will reach the underground tank? Draw the path.

Ans. The rainwater that falls on the roof will go from the roof into the pipes. These pipes carry the water to an underground tank made for its storage.

Page 54

Q.1 Have you ever faced a shortage of water in your area? If yes, then what was the reason for it?

Ans. Yes, we have faced a shortage of water in our area. The reason behind this was irregular supply of water from the Jal Board.

Q.2 Talk to your grandmother or any elderly person. Find out, when they were of your age:

From where did they get water for the house? Has there been a change now?

Ans. They got the water from the rivers, hand pumps and wells near their house.

Yes, the situation has changed now. We get water from pipelines of 'Jal Boards'. We have better facilities now.

Q.3 What kind of water arrangements were made for travellers- for example piau, mashak (leather bag) or any other? Now what do people do about water when they travel?

Ans. Earlier, the kings used to get *piau* made for travellers. Free water was available to everyone at these *piaus*. People also used to carry mashak when they were travelling.

Nowadays, people carry bottled water in different sizes.

Find Out (Page 55)

Is there a lake, well or stepwell near your house or school? Visit it and find out more about it.

Q.1 How old is it? Who got it built?

Ans. Yes, there is a lake near my house. It is almost a hundred years old. A rich king of that time got it built.

Q.2 What kinds of buildings are around it?

Ans. There are some houses and a small market around it. There are also some ruins of an old palace.

Q.3 Is the water clean? Is it cleaned regularly?

Ans. The water is not very clean. It is not cleaned regularly.

Q.4 Who all use the water?

Ans. The water is used by some washermen to wash the clothes. Some cattle herders also bring their cows for a bath in the lake.

Q.5 Is there any festival celebrated at this place?

Ans. Yes, an annual boating festival and two fairs are celebrated at this place.

Q.6 Is there any water today, or is it dry?

Ans. There is some water in the lake.

Discuss (Page 56)

Q.1 There are two old wells in the area where Punita lives. Her grandmother says that about fifteen - twenty years ago there was water in these wells. The wells could have dried up because

- Water is being pumped up from under the ground, with the help of electric motors.
- The lakes in which rain water used to collect are no longer there.
- The soil around trees and parks is now covered with cement.

Is there some other reason for this? Explain.

Ans. Apart from the reasons given above, there can be some other reasons too. The well is not being maintained properly. Also, the trees, which help in storing water, around it have been cut and destroyed.

Page 56

Q.2 Let us see the different ways in which people manage water today. See page 57 and discuss. Do you get water in your house by any of these ways? Put a tick (✓) on that. If you get water by some other way, write in your notebook.

Ans. We get water by the following ways

- We get water from Jal Board pipelines fitted in our houses. We have a motor connected with the supply line which helps us fill the tank on the rooftop.
- The village area near my house gets water from the well that is made in their locality. In case of shortage of water, Jal Board tanker comes once a day.

Discuss (Page 58)

Q.1 Everyone has the right to live. Yet, is everybody getting enough water to live or even water to drink? Why is it that some people have to buy drinking water? Should it be like this? Water on this earth is for one and all. Some people draw out water from the ground by deep bore wells. How far is it correct? Have you ever seen this? Why do some people put a pump directly in the Jal Board pipeline? What problems would other people face due to this? Do you have any such experience?

Ans. Do it yourself

Look at this bill and tell (Page 58)

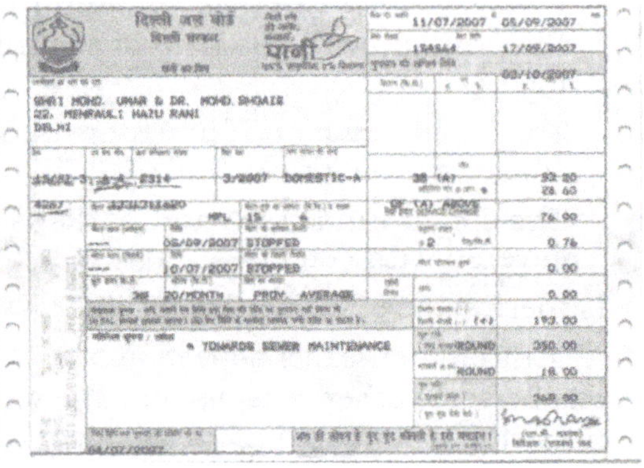
दिल्ली जल बोर्ड
दिल्ली सरकार
पानी
11/07/2007 05/09/2007
17/09/2007
03/10/2007
SHRI MOHD. UMAR & DR. MOHD. SHOAIB
22, MEHRAULI HAUZ RANI
DELHI
3/2007 DOMESTIC-A
05/09/2007 STOPPED
10/07/2007 STOPPED
20/MONTH PROV. AVERAGE
* TOWARDS SEWER MAINTENANCE
76.00
0.76
0.00
0.00
193.00
350.00
18.00
368.00
04/07/2007

Q.1 From which office has this bill come?

Ans. The bill has come from the Delhi Jal Board Office.

Q.2 Do you get a water bill at home? Find out from where it is sent?

Ans. Yes, we get a water bill at home. It is sent by the Department of Water Supply.

Q.3 Why do you think Dilli Sarkar (Government of Delhi) is written under Delhi Jal Board?

Ans. Dilli Sarkar is written under Delhi Jal Board because Delhi Jal Board is a department under the Government of Delhi.

Q.4 In whose name is the bill? How much money do they have to pay for each month?

Ans. The bill is in the name of Shri Mohd Umar and Dr. Mohd Shoaib. The bill for two months is ₹ 350. So, they have to pay ₹ 175 per month.

If they do not pay within the time, they have to pay a surcharge of ₹ 18, making the total ₹ 368, which means ₹ 183 per month.

Q.5 Do you have to pay for water? How much? Is the rate of water different in different colonies? Ask your elders.

Ans. Yes, we have to pay for water. We pay around ₹ 750 for drinking water. The rate of water is the same in different colonies.

What we have Learnt (Page 59)

Q.1 Make a poster : Do you remember the slogan 'Water on Earth is for one and all.' Think of some other such slogans. Draw pictures and make a nice poster.

Ans.

Some other slogans are

- Water is life
- Water is a necessity, not a luxury.
- Water: Use it or lose it
- Just another drop to fill the cup

Q.2 Bring a water bill, look at it and tell

- This bill is from__________date to_________date.
- How much money is to be paid for this bill?
- What else can you see in the bill, like the money spent on repair, maintenance, etc.?

Ans.
- 1st August, 2024 to 31st October, 2024.
- ₹ 450 is to be paid for this bill.
- I can see that ₹ 50 is charged for maintenance and repair.

CHAPTER 7 EXPERIMENTS WITH WATER

About the Chapter

This chapter teaches us about water by doing different experiments. Ayesha noticed that when her mother made puris, they first sank in the oil, then floated after puffing up. She tried putting a ball of dough in water and it sank. Some things, like soap cases, float in water but others, like soap, sink. Adding salt to water can help things float. Ayesha saw this when she added too much salt while boiling eggs and the eggs floated. The Dead Sea is also very salty and people can't drown in it.

Some things dissolve quickly in water, but others take time. For example, sugar takes time to dissolve. Some liquids flow easily but others do not. Water turns into gas when it boils. Salt is made by collecting seawater in shallow beds. In 1930, Gandhiji led the Dandi March to protest against British salt laws.

GLOSSARY

Floating It means staying on the surface of a liquid, such as water.
Sinking It means going down to the bottom or going under the surface of a liquid.
Dissolved It means to mix up something with water so that it cannot be seen separately.
Seashore It is the area along the coast of a sea or ocean. It is where the land meets the water.
Drown To die by suffocating in liquid, especially water.

NCERT FOLDER

Think What would Happen If (Page 60)

Q.1 Ayesha put a puffed puri in a bowl of water. Would it sink or float?

Ans. A puffed puri will float on the water.

Q.2 You put a steel plate on water. Would it sink or float? What would happen to a spoon?

Ans. The steel plate will sink on the water. The spoon will sink in the water.

Q.3 Would the cap of a plastic bottle sink or float on water?

Ans. The cap of a plastic bottle will float on the water.

Do this and Find Out (Page 61-62)

Do this experiment in groups of four friends. Each group will need a big pot filled with water and the things listed in the table. Put each thing one-by-one in water and observe.

Q.1 Mark (✓) for the things that float. Mark (✗) for those that sink.

Ans.

Things to be put in water	I guessed before I did it	I saw, when I did it
(a) Empty bowl (*katori*)	✗	✗
(b) After putting in 6-7 small pebbles, one-by-one	✗	✗
Iron nail or pin	✗	✗
Matchstick	✓	✓
(a) Empty plastic bottle with its lid closed	✓	✓
(c) Bottle half-filled with water	✓	✓
(c) Bottle full of water	✗	✗
Aluminium foil (from medicine packing)		
(a) Open and spread out	✓	✓
(b) Pressed tightly into a ball	✗	✗
(c) In a cup-like shape	✓	✓
(a) Soap cake	✗	✗
(b) Soap cake on a small plastic plate	✓	✓
A piece of ice	✓	✓

Q.2 Find out from the other groups which things floated and which sank in the water.

Ans. A ball, a soap case and a bottle cap floated on water. Aluminium foil ball, a key and a needle sank in water.

After doing the experiment, fill in the blanks.

1. The iron nail ______ in water but the katori ______. I think this happened because ____________________ .
2. The empty plastic bottle ______ on water. The bottle filled with water ______ because ____________________ .
3. The aluminium foil ______ when it was spread out. When pressed tightly into a ball it ________. This may have happened because ________________ .

Ans. 1. Sank; floated; an iron nail could displace less amount of water but the katori displaced more water.

2. Floats; sinks; less amount of water was displaced by the bottle filled with water.
3. Floated; sank; spread out foil displaced more amount of water than the ball of foil.

Page 63

Q.1 Take some water in a glass. Put a lemon in it. Now keep putting salt in the water, half-a-spoon at a time. Were you able to float your lemon in water?

Ans. Yes, the lemon started to float on water after adding salt.

Q.2 What do you think, the lemon floated in salty water, because.....

Ans. The lemon floated in salty water because the water becomes thick after adding salt to it.

Q.3 Suggest some ways to Hamid for quickly dissolving sugar.

Ans. For quickly dissolving the sugar, Hamid could

- Heat the mixture on stove
- Stir the mixture thoroughly
- Use powdered sugar

Do this Experiment (Page 64)

Make groups of four friends. For the experiment, you will need 4-5 glasses or bowls, spoons, water and the things listed in the table. Take some water in each glass. Now try to dissolve one thing in one glass. Observe what happens and note in the table.

Ans.

Things	Did it dissolve or not?	What happened after keeping for 2 minutes?
Salt	Yes	Salt and water mixed together. Water remained transparent.
Soil	No	Soil sank to the bottom and settled down. The water became muddy.

Things	Did it dissolve or not?	What happened after keeping for 2 minutes?
Chalk powder	No	Chalk powder sat at the bottom. The water became a little white.
1 spoon milk	Yes	Milk and water mixed together. Water changed colour to white.
Oil	No	Oil floats on surface of water.

Tell (Page 64)

Q.1 Could you see the salt after it dissolved in water? If no, why?

Ans. No, I could not see the salt after it dissolved in water. This happened because salt is completely soluble in water.

Q.2 Does that mean that now the water does not have salt? If it has, then where is the salt?

Ans. Water has salt in it. The salt got dissolved in the water.

Q.3 What difference did you see-in the water with salt, and the water with chalk powder-after keeping for sometime?

Ans. The difference was that salt mixed with water completely, but chalk powder settled at the bottom and did not mix.

Q.4 Which of the two would you be able to separate from the water by straining with a cloth-salt or chalk powder?

Ans. We would be able to separate chalk powder from the water by straining it with a cloth.

Page 65

Q.1 Do you think the oil got dissolved in the water? Why do you think so?

Ans. No, the oil did not dissolve in the water. Yellow drops of oil floating on the water made me think so.

Q.2 You also try to do the same and then tell-which drop went ahead? Why did it slide faster?

Ans. Drops of water slide first, then drops of sugar solution and at last, drops of oil. Drops of water slide faster and oil was the slowest. This is because water is non-sticky and light in weight.

Where did the Water go? (Page 65)

Q.1 Think where did the water go?

Ans. The water turned into gas and disappeared. This means that the water evaporated.

Q.2 Why did Chittibabu and Chinnababu keep their mango jelly in the Sun?

Ans. They kept the mango jelly in the Sun because they wanted the water in the jelly to evaporate quickly.

Q.3 At your house, what things are made by drying in the Sun?

Ans. Chips, *papads*, badiyan, pickles, etc. are made by drying in the Sun.

What have we Learnt? (Page 66)

Q.1 You have washed your handkerchief and you want to dry it quickly. What all can you do?

Ans. To dry my handkerchief quickly, I will squeeze out the water first.

Then, I will spread it out on the clothesline to dry naturally in the Sun. I can also use a hot iron to dry it quickly.

Q.2 What things do you put in water to make tea? Which of those things dissolves in water?

Ans. For making tea, I put tea leaves, sugar and milk in the water. Sugar and milk dissolve in the water.

Q.3 You have been given some mishri pieces (lumps of sugar). Suggest some ways to dissolve them quickly.

Ans. To dissolve the *mishri* pieces quickly, follow these steps

(i) First, crush the *mishri* pieces into fine powder.

(ii) Put the *mishri* powder in the water and mix it thoroughly.

(iii) The mixture can also be warmed on the stove to dissolve the *mishri* quickly.

CHAPTER 8

A TREAT FOR MOSQUITOES

About the Chapter

This chapter is about how mosquitoes spread diseases like malaria and dengue. We can find out about these diseases by doing a blood test. Malaria is spread by female mosquitoes called Anopheles and it can be treated with medicine made from the bark of Cinchona trees. Houseflies also spread diseases, especially those that make our stomachs sick. Baby mosquitoes are called larvae.

To stop mosquitoes, we should keep our surroundings clean, use mosquito nets and sprays, and not let water collect around us. Scientist Ronald Ross discovered how mosquitoes spread diseases. Anaemia is a condition wherein our body has low iron. We can fix Anaemia by eating iron-rich foods.

GLOSSARY

Disease It is a problem in the body caused due to various reasons like mosquito bites, flies, etc.

Malarial parasite They are tiny organisms that infect the bloodstream and cause the disease malaria.

Haemoglobin Part of blood by which blood gets red colour.

Microscope It is a device which makes things look bigger than the original size.

Breeding It means the process of producing young ones.

Repellant It is something that keeps away insects or other animals. It comes in many forms like coils, lotions, sprays, etc.

Vein It is thin tube like structure which carries blood from one part of the body to another.

NCERT FOLDER

Find Out (Page 68)

Q.1 Do you know anyone who has had malaria?

Ans. Yes, my mother had malaria once.

Q.2 How did they find out that they had malaria?

Ans. They found out that they had malaria by a blood test.

Q.3 What problems did they have on having malaria?

Ans. My mother had many problems. She had a high fever. The fever kept on increasing and her body was shivering. She became very weak.

Q.4 What other diseases can be caused by mosquito bites?

Ans. Other diseases caused by mosquito bites are dengue, chikungunya and viral fever.

Q.5 In which season is malaria more common? Why do you think this happens?

Ans. Malaria is more common in the rainy season.

This happens because mosquitoes get a suitable environment to breed due to rains and standing water.

Q.6 What do you do in your house to protect yourself from mosquitoes? Also find out from your friends about what they do.

Ans. To protect ourselves from mosquitoes, we used mosquito repellent spray in our house. My friends use the following things

- Mosquito repellent coils
- Mosquito repellent creams on their body
- Mosquito nets

Page 69

Q.1 Look at the report of the blood test given here. Which words in the report help us to know that the person has malaria?

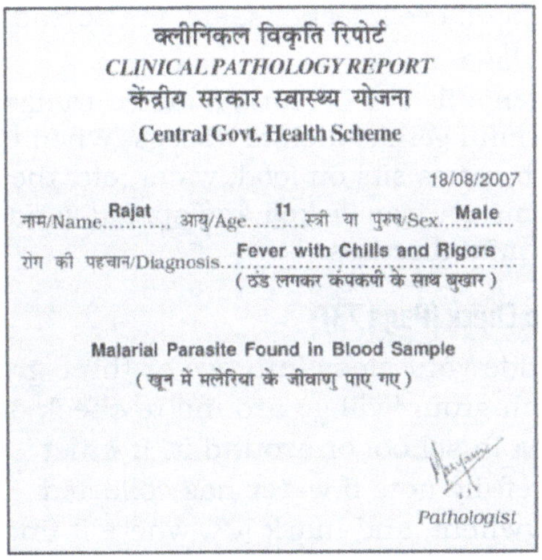

क्लीनिकल विकृति रिपोर्ट
CLINICAL PATHOLOGY REPORT
केंद्रीय सरकार स्वास्थ्य योजना
Central Govt. Health Scheme

18/08/2007

नाम/Name Rajat आयु/Age 11 स्त्री या पुरुष/Sex Male

रोग की पहचान/Diagnosis Fever with Chills and Rigors
(ठंड लगकर कंपकपी के साथ बुखार)

Malarial Parasite Found in Blood Sample
(खून में मलेरिया के जीवाणु पाए गए)

Pathologist

Ans. In the report, the words 'Malaria Parasite Found in Blood Sample' help us to know that the person has malaria.

Tell (Page 70)

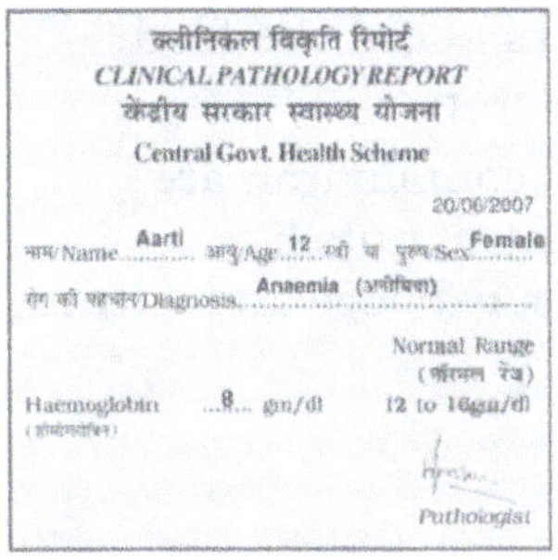

क्लीनिकल विकृति रिपोर्ट
CLINICAL PATHOLOGY REPORT
केंद्रीय सरकार स्वास्थ्य योजना
Central Govt. Health Scheme

20/06/2007

नाम/Name Aarti आयु/Age 12 स्त्री या पुरुष/Sex Female

रोग की पहचान/Diagnosis Anaemia (अनीमिया)

Normal Range (नॉरमल रेंज)

Haemoglobin (हीमोग्लोबिन) 8 gm/dl 12 to 16gm/dl

Pathologist

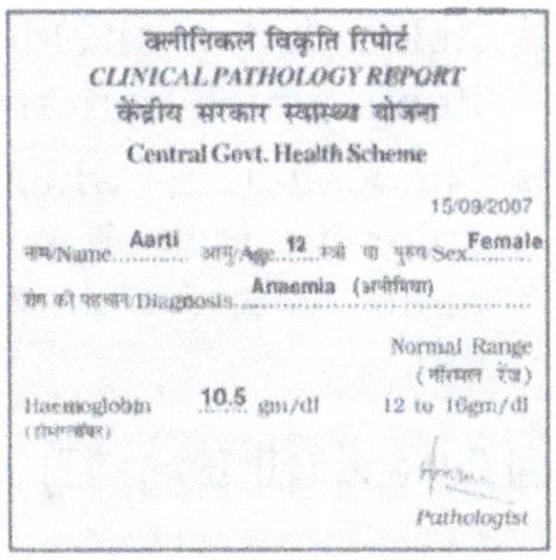

क्लीनिकल विकृति रिपोर्ट
CLINICAL PATHOLOGY REPORT
केंद्रीय सरकार स्वास्थ्य योजना
Central Govt. Health Scheme

15/09/2007

नाम/Name Aarti आयु/Age 12 स्त्री या पुरुष/Sex Female

रोग की पहचान/Diagnosis Anaemia (अनीमिया)

Normal Range (नॉरमल रेंज)

Haemoglobin (हीमोग्लोबिन) 10.5 gm/dl 12 to 16gm/dl

Pathologist

Q.1 Look at Aarti's blood report and find out the minimum required haemoglobin

Ans. The minimum required haemoglobin is 12 gm/dl.

Q.2 How much did Aarti's haemoglobin go up and how long did it take for that?

Ans. Aarti's haemoglobin increased by 2.5 gm/dl, which is around 30% increase. It took almost three months.

Q.3 What does the newspaper report say about the problems caused by anaemia?

Ans. The newspaper report says that anaemia affects both mental and physical health of children. They do not grow properly due to anaemia. It affects their ability to study as well.

Q.4 Have you or anyone in your family ever needed to get a blood test? When and why?

Ans. Yes, my little brother had to get a blood test done because he was suffering from a high fever along with vomiting.

Q.5 What was found out by the blood test?

Ans. It was found out that he was suffering from dengue.

Q.6 Have you ever had a health check-up in your school? What did the doctor tell you?

Ans. Yes, my school had a health check-up camp around six months ago. They organise it every year.

The doctor told me that I am fit and fine, and I should eat healthy food like green vegetables.

Find Out (Page 71)

Q.1 Ask a doctor or elders about the food items which contain iron.

Ans. The food items which contain iron are spinach, dark chocolates, nuts like almonds and walnuts, cabbage and lettuce, etc.

Find Out and Tell (Page 72)

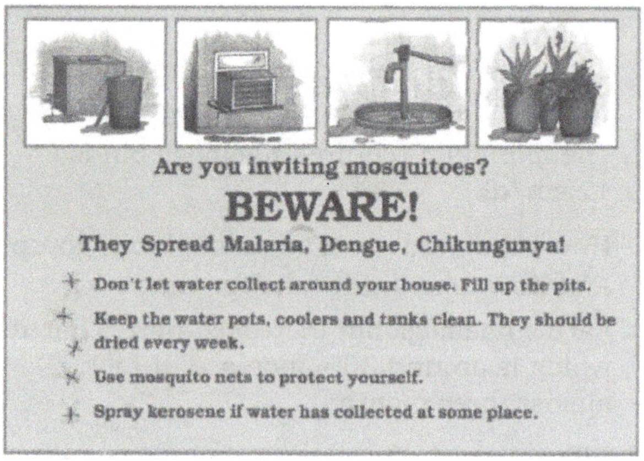

Q.1 Have you seen any poster like this put up anywhere?

Ans. Yes, I have seen posters like these near my school and in my neighbourhood.

Q.2 Who do you think puts up such posters, or gives ads in the newspapers?

Ans. I think the government puts up such posters or gives ads in the newspapers to make people aware.

Q.3 What are some of the important points given in the poster?

Ans. Some important points given in the poster are as follows

- Beware of mosquitoes because they cause diseases like malaria, dengue and chikungunya.
- Do not let water collect near your house and fill up the pits.
- Water pots, coolers and tanks should be cleaned and dried every week.
- Use mosquito nets for prevention against mosquito bites.
- Kerosene oil should be sprayed in the areas where water is collected.

Q.4 Why do you think pictures of a tank, cooler and pits are shown in the poster?

Ans. Pictures of tanks, coolers and pits are given to make us aware that these are the places where water can collect and stagnate. Mosquitoes get a breeding ground here.

Think (Page 72)

Q.1 Why do you think it talks about putting fish in the tank? What do you think the fish eats?

Ans. It talks about putting fish in the tank because the fish eats larvae of mosquitoes which can breed in the tanks.

Q.2 What will happen when the oil is spread on water?

Ans. When the oil is spread on water, it will cut the oxygen supply and prevent larvae from breathing. This way larvae will be killed.

Find Out (Page 73)

Q.1 Which diseases are spread by flies and how?

Ans. Many diseases like cholera, dysentery, typhoid, eye infections, etc. are spread by the flies.

When a fly sits on contaminated things, harmful germs stick to its legs. When the fly with germs sits on food, water, etc. the germs get transferred and spread various harmful diseases.

Mosquito Check (Page 73)

Q.1 Divide your class into two or three groups. Each group will go around to check one area in school or around it. It must carefully note if water has collected anywhere, and mark (✓). where it finds stagnant water.

Pot [ ] Cooler [ ] Tank [ ] Any open space in the school ground [ ] Gutter [ ] Any other place ________.

Ans. Pot [✓] Cooler [✓] Tank [✓] Any open space in the school ground [✓] Gutter [✓] Any other place <u>No</u>.

Q.2 Since how many days has water collected there?

Ans. The water has been collected there for 8-10 days.

Q.3 Who is responsible for keeping these places clean?

Ans. School authorities are responsible for keeping the places inside the school clean. Municipal authorities are responsible for places outside the school.

Q.4 Who is responsible to get the gutters and drains repaired?

Ans. Municipal authorities of the city are responsible for getting the gutters and drains repaired.

Q.5 Can any larvae be seen in the collected water?

Ans. Yes, many tiny larvae could be seen in the collected water.

Q.6 Has it caused any problem in the area? Write.

Ans. Yes, it has caused many problems in the area. The area is always dirty. Mosquitoes and flies keep swarming around, causing a lot of problems for the people.

Make a Poster (Page 73)

Q.1 In your group, make a poster with a message to keep the cooler, tank, drains and the area clean (wherever water collects). Put up your poster in and around your school.

Ans.

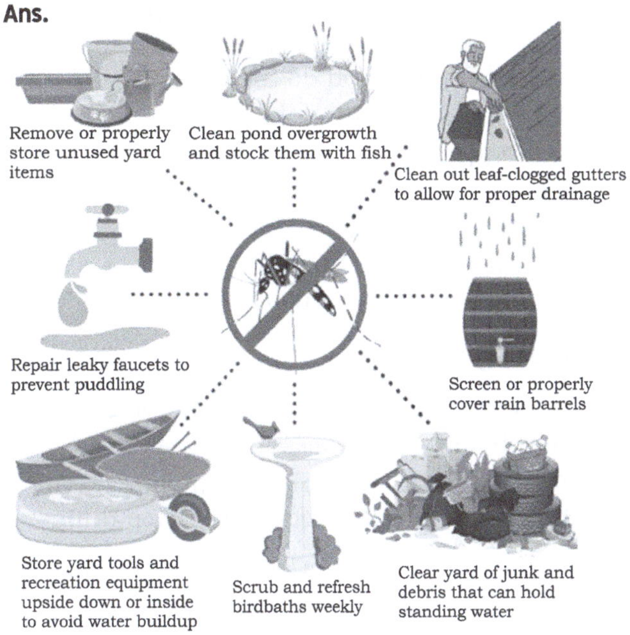

Q.2 Find out who is responsible for keeping the area around your school clean. Write a letter from your class, reporting your findings and suggestions. Find out to whom the letter should be written and to which office it should be sent.

Ans. The municipality is responsible for keeping the area around our school clean. The letter should be written to the ward councillor under which my school comes and it should be sent to the Municipal Corporation Office.

The Ward Councillor
Ward Number 15
Ganpatnagar

Subject Request for maintenance of cleanliness around Shardashram Vidyamandir, Senior Secondary School

Sir/Ma'am

This is to request you to maintain the cleanliness in ward number 15. We have made a survey around our school and found lack of cleanliness. We found stagnant water at several places which are perfect breeding grounds for mosquitoes. These ditches have the potential for spreading serious diseases.You are requested to look into the matter and do the needful.

For this, we shall ever be grateful to you.

Thanking You
Yours sincerely

Students of Class V
Shardashram Vidyamandir
Senior Secondary School, Dadar

Tell (Page 74)

Q.1 Is there a pond or river around your house or school?

Ans. Yes, there is a pond around my house. Go and look around and observe these things:

Q.2 Can you see algae in or around the water?

Ans. Yes, I can see algae in the water.

Q.3 Where else have you seen algae?

Ans. I have seen algae on some damp walls.

Q4. Are there plants growing on the side or in water? Find out their names. Draw some of these in your notebook.

Ans. Yes, some plants like mosses, liverworts, duckweeds are growing on the side and in the water.

Q5. Do you think these were planted by someone or did they grow on their own?

Ans. These plants were not planted by someone. They grow on their own.

Q6. What else can you see in water? Make a list.

Ans. I can see fish, prawns, larvae, crabs and alligators in the water.

What have we Learnt (Page 75)

Q.1 What can you do so that mosquitoes do not breed in your house, school and neighbourhood?

Ans. We can take the following actions to prevent the breeding of mosquitoes

(i) Do not let the water collect in and around your house.

(ii) Clean the tanks and coolers on a regular basis.

(iii) Spray kerosene oil, DDT, mosquito repellent wherever needed.

(iv) Use mosquito repellent coils and creams on a regular basis.

(v) Cultivate fish in nearby ponds to kill larvae.

Q.2 How can you find out if someone has malaria?

Ans. We can find out if someone has malaria by getting a blood test. If the blood test report shows the presence of malaria parasite, it is confirmed that the person has malaria.

CHAPTER 9

UP YOU GO!

About the Chapter

This chapter is about mountaineering and its challenges. In 1984, the Nehru Institute of Mountaineering took a group to a mountaineering camp. Through Sangeeta's story, we learn the importance of teamwork, discipline and mental strength. Sangeeta became the leader of Group 7 which was a big responsibility.

Mountaineering camps include tough activities like crossing rivers and rock climbing, which require special equipment such as ropes, hooks and climbing shoes. Confidence is essential for facing these challenges. The group camps in the mountains, sets up tents and cooks food on a chulha. They also meet Bachhendri Pal, the first Indian woman to climb Mount Everest. Sangeeta wins the 'Best Performance Award'.

GLOSSARY

Mountaineering An adventure where people use special tools and skills to reach the top of tall mountains.

Rucksack A special type of bag for carrying necessary things. It can be hung upon the back.

Pitons Metal spikes or pillar like structures that are hammered into rocks to provide support for climbers.

Rock climbing A sport in which people use their hands, feet and various techniques to climb up big rocks.

NCERT FOLDER

Tell (Page 77)

Q.1 Have you ever seen the mountains? Have you also climbed a mountain? When and where?

Ans. Yes, I have seen mountains on my trip to Shimla. I also got a chance to climb the mountains during our trip.

Q.2 How far have you walked at one time? How far can you walk?

Ans. I have walked about 2 kms at one time. I think I can walk up to 10 km.

Imagine (Page 77)

Q.1 What do you think about the paths on the mountains? Draw a picture.

Ans. The paths on the mountains have sharp curves and rough surface.

Tell (Page 78)

Q.1 What do you think about the responsibilities of a group leader?

Ans. There can be many responsibilities of a group leader. Some can include

- Taking care of all the group members.
- Taking care of what your group members need.
- Making good decisions.

Q.2 How would you feel if you were made a leader in such a camp?

Ans. I would feel very proud of getting such an opportunity but I would also be very nervous.

Q.3 What does a monitor in your class have to do?

Ans. The monitor in our class does the following things

- Arrange necessary things like duster, chalk, dustbin, etc.
- Tell the problems faced by students to the teachers.
- Maintain discipline of the class in the absence of the teacher.
- Help other students of the class

Q.4 Would you like to be the class monitor? Why?

Ans. Yes, I would like to be a class monitor because this is a challenging task and it can teach me good lessons.

Find Out and Write (Page 80)

Q.1 What kinds of tools are needed for climbing mountains?

Ans. For climbing mountains, we need a thick rope, pegs, stick, axe, etc. We also need things like food packets, water bottles, plastic sheets, sleeping bags, diary, torch, first aid kit, oxygen tank, etc.

Q.2 Have you ever seen a hook and rope being used for anything else? Where?

Ans. Yes, I have seen a hook and rope being used. I saw it being used to rescue people and to draw water from a well.

Q.3 What else can we use if we want to cross a river in the mountains?

Ans. We can use thick ropes, pitons and hooks for crossing a river in the mountains.

Q.4 Why do we need extra energy on the mountains?

Ans. On the mountains, there is less oxygen and we walk in the opposite direction to gravity. The surface is also very rough. That is why we need extra energy on the mountains.

Q.5 Have you ever heard of anyone who has done something adventurous? What?

Ans. Yes, my elder brother is very adventurous. He has done adventures like river rafting and scuba diving.

Q.6 Have you ever done anything adventurous? If yes, tell your class. Write about it in your own words.

Ans. Do it yourself.

Tell (Page 81-82)

Q.1 Have you ever climbed a tree? How did you feel? Were you scared? Did you ever fall?

Ans. Yes, I have climbed a tree. I climbed a mango tree in my grandparents's home in the village. It was adventurous and thrilling. I was feeling scared but I did not fall.

Q.2 Have you ever seen someone climb a small wall? What do you think is the difference between climbing a wall and climbing a high rock?

Ans. Yes, I have seen a person who lives near my house climb a small wall.

I think there is no difference between climbing a wall and climbing a high rock.

Q.3 Is there anyone in your class whose language you do not understand, or who does not understand yours? What do you do in such a case?

Ans. Do it yourself.

Q.4 Have you ever lost your way? What did you do then?

Ans. Yes, I have lost my way once. I kept calm and asked around for directions. Then, I called my father to inform him about my location. I stayed there till my father came to pick me up.

Q.5 Why do you think Khondonbi would have sung loudly?

Ans. Khondonbi would have sung loudly so that she could send signals to her group members. Singing a song is a good way to do so.

Q.6 Have you ever seen someone doing something special to get over their fear? What and when?

Ans. Yes, I have seen my brother closing his eyes during a ride on the pendulum.

Try (Page 82)

Q.1 Ask your friend for a book without speaking. Try to explain something to the class in the same way.

Ans. Do it yourself.

Discuss (Page 84)

Q.1 Why do you think a drain was dug around the tent?

Ans. The drain was dug out to keep away insects and animals like snakes. It was also dug so that water could slope into it from the roof of the tents in case of rain.

Q.1 Besides mountaineering, what are other activities that can be called adventurous? Why?

Ans. Besides mountaineering, other activities like river rafting, scuba diving, skydiving, hang gliding, parachuting, etc. can be called adventurous. It is because we feel thrilled when we do them.

Imagine and Write (Page 85)

Q.1 You are on a mountain. How do you feel there? What can you see? What do you feel like doing there?

Ans. I feel very excited when I am on a mountain. It feels like a dream come true. I can see a vast blue sky and white snow all around me. I feel like sitting peacefully, eating something warm and enjoying the view.

Think (Page 86)

Q.1 Why did Bachhendri Pal put up the Indian flag on the peak?

Ans. Bachhendri Pal put up the Indian flag on the peak as a sign of achieving something. It was to honour our country.

Q.2 When have you seen our national flag being hoisted? Collect information of our national flag.

Ans. Do it yourself.

Q.3 Make groups of 6-8 children. Design a flag for your group. Explain why you chose that design.

Ans. Do it yourself.

Q.4 Have you seen the flag of any other country? Where?

Ans. Yes, I have seen flags of different countries in books, television, mobile phones, etc.

What we have Learnt (Page 86)

Q.1 Explain why it can be adventerous and challenging to climb a mountain. How would you prepare if you were to climb a mountain? What would you take with you? Write in your own words.

Ans. Climbing a mountain can be adventurous and challenging because many difficulties are involved in it. The rough path, high altitude and less oxygen can make it more challenging. Problems such as crossing a river safely or climbing the rocky slopes can be difficult.

I would practise before the actual climb. I will also prepare myself with necessary things like food packets, rope, water bottles, oxygen cylinder, medicines, etc. and take a backpack with me.

CHAPTER 10 WALLS TELL STORIES

About the Chapter

This chapter is about old forts and palaces, especially Golconda Fort. Shailja, Shridhar and Kalyani visit the fort with Didi, who studies history. The fort, built a long time ago around 1200 A.D, is very big. It has thick walls, a big gate and 87 bastions to protect it. Many rulers lived there and there were palaces, gardens, fields and factories inside it.

The children see a cannon used by Aurangzeb to attack the fort. They learn how the fort was made safe and secure to keep enemies out. There was a proper system to collect water. After visiting the fort, they go to a museum in Hyderabad where they see old items and artefacts to learn more about the old times.

GLOSSARY

Bastion A round shaped structure on the fort used for the security purpose.
Carving The art or craft of cutting or shaping wood, stone or other materials into decorative objects.
Ruins The remains of something that has been destroyed or is in a state of decay.
Cannons Large gun-like structures used as a weapon in attacks and wars.
Echo A sound which you can hear back or which is reflected back from a surface.
Flattery The act of praising someone.
Mehrab A semi-circular arch usually found in forts and mosques.
Museum A place where antique items having historical significance are kept.
Artefacts Things from an earlier time period that give information about past culture, beliefs or technologies.

NCERT FOLDER

Think (Page 88)

Q.1 Why were bastions made in the fort wall?

Ans. Bastions were made in the fort wall to ensure the safety of the fort.

Q.2 Why were big holes made in them?

Ans. Big holes were made in the bastions for soldiers so that they could see at a distance and keep a watch on the enemies coming towards them.

Q.3 What difference would be there if you were to look from a straight flat wall or a bastion at a height? How would the soldiers find peeping from the holes in the bastions useful while attacking?

Ans. Bastions made at a height ensured safety of soldiers. They also provided a better point to look at a larger area. This would not have been possible from a flat wall.

Soldiers were at a better position to look at the enemy from the holes in the bastions and they could plan their attack from there easily.

Think and Discuss (Page 89)

Q.1 How would the fountains have worked?

Ans. The fountains would have worked by getting water supply from a large reservoir.

Q.2 What arrangements would have been made in the building for air and light?

Ans. Door, big windows and ventilators would have been there in the building to allow natural sunlight. These would have also allowed the fresh air to come in.

Q.3

Look carefully at the picture of the beautiful carving on the wall. What kind of tools would have been used for such fine carving?

Ans. Hammer and Chisel made of iron would have been used for such a fine carving.

Q.4 We still do not have any electricity at many places in our country. Even at places which do have electricity, imagine what would happen if there was no electricity for one week. What are the things that would be difficult to manage without it?

Ans. If there was no electricity for a week, it would have been difficult to manage everyday things like cooking, cleaning, studying, etc. Everything like the refrigerator, fans, tubelights, washing machine, television, etc. cannot function without electricity.

Page 90

Q.1 At the place you are, where does the Sun rise? Where does it set? Where you are standing, find out what all is there to your East. What all is there to your West? Also find out what places are to your North and South?

Ans. The Sun rises in the East and sets in the West. I am standing in my balcony from where I see a tall building in the East. I can see a beautiful park to my West.

To my North, there is a road that connects with the main street. I cannot see clearly towards my South.

Tell and Write (Page 90)

Look carefully at the map of Golconda. On the map, arrows show all the four directions.

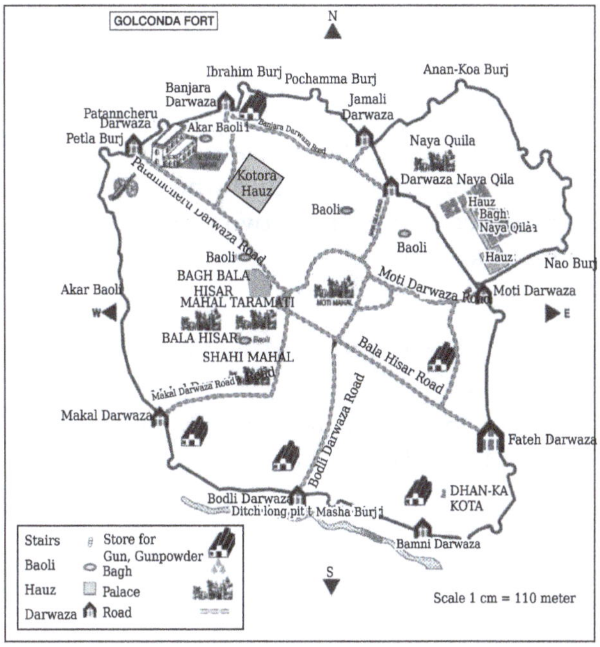

(a) If you are peeping inside from Bodli Darwaza, in which direction from you is Katora Hauz?

Ans. Katora Hauz is in the North direction.

(b) If someone is entering from Banjara Darwaza, in which direction from here is Katora Hauz?

Ans. In the South direction.

(c) In which direction will you walk from Bala Hisar to reach Moti Mahal?

Ans. We will walk in the East direction.

(d) How many gates can you see on the outer walls of the Fort?

Ans. There are nine gates on the outer walls of the Fort.

(e) Count how many palaces are there in the fort?

Ans. There are three palaces in the fort.

(f) What arrangements for water can you see inside the fort? For example, wells, tanks, stepwells.

Ans. There are five baolis and three hauz in the fort for water.

On the map, 1 cm distance is equal to a distance of 110 metres on the ground. Now tell :

Q.1 On the map, the distance between Bala Hisar and Fateh Darwaja is _____ cm. On the ground, the distance between the two would be _____ metres.

Ans. 8;880

Q.2 How far is Makai Darwaza from Fateh Darwaza?

Ans. Makai darwaza is approx. 100 metres far from Fateh Darwaza.

Discuss (Page 93)

Q.1 Have you recently read or heard about any country attacking or going to war with another country?

Ans. Yes, I have heard about it. Russia recently attacked Ukraine for a war.

Q.2 Find out what was the reason for this war.

Ans. The reason for this war was that Russia had political issues with Ukraine's government.

Q.3 What kind of weapons were used in this war?

Ans. Tanks, fighter planes, helicopters, machine guns and missiles were some weapons used in this war.

Q.4 What kind of destruction was caused because of this?

Ans. The attack caused a lot of destruction. There was huge loss to life and property. Many people were killed and a lot of buildings were damaged.

Find Out (Page 93)

The big gun that Shreedhar saw was made of bronze.

Q.1 Have you seen anything made of bronze? What?

Ans. Yes, I have seen some things like diyas, statues and utensils made of bronze

Q.2 Find out from your elders about some of the things made from bronze that were or are still used in your house. From its colour try to identify which one of them is made from copper, which from brass, and which from bronze.

Ans. Items made from copper- tumbler, lota. Items made from brass - water pot, puja thali.
Items made from bronze - statues in my mandir, diya.

Page 94

Q.1 The picture shown below is made after seeing a very old painting of those times. Can you think why bullocks have been used here?

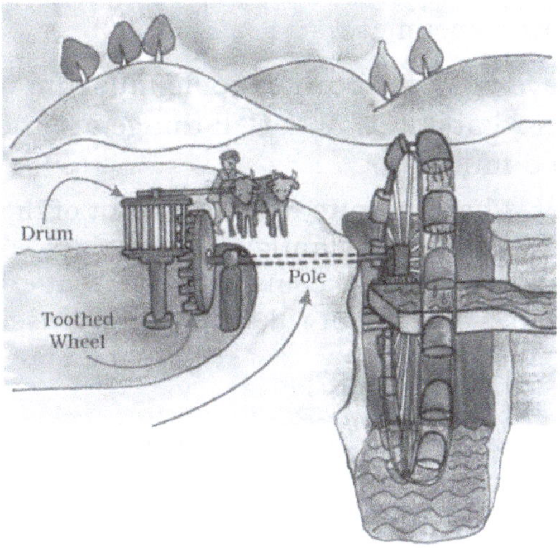

Ans. The bullocks have been used to move the wheel and draw water.

Q.2 Use your hand movement to show in which direction the drum attached to the rod moves when the bullocks move.

Ans. The drum attached to the rod would move anti-clockwise when the bullocks moved.

Q.3 In which direction would the 'toothed wheel' move?

Ans. The toothed wheel's would move in the clockwise direction.

The pole shown under the ground joins with another wheel which has a number of pots on it.

Q.4 Now imagine, how would this garland of pots lift water from the well?

Ans. The garland of pots is attached with the 'toothed wheel'□and it can move. When a pot gets filled with water, it moves upwards carrying water along with it. When the pot reaches the level of the canal, water is emptied into the canal.

Q.5 Do you now get some idea about how the tanks could have been filled by lifting water from the wells?

Ans. The bullocks would have been used to move the garland of pots. The pots would have moved to the level of the tanks and water is emptied into it.

Q.6 Where else have you seen such wheels attached to each other? For example, in the gear of a cycle or somewhere else?

Ans. I have seen such wheels attached to each other in mechanical watches, electronic toy car machines, clocks and sewing machines.

Q.7 Look around and find out how water is pumped up from the ground to higher places?

Ans. There are many ways to pump water from the ground to higher places. Nowadays, electric motor pumps are used. In villages, bullocks are still used for this purpose.

Q.8 How is water pumped up using electricity? How is water lifted without electricity?

Ans. Water is pumped up by an electric motor. The motor runs the water pump that sucks the water from the ground or the tank. Without electricity, the water is lifted using hand pumps or pulleys.

Page 95

Q.1 What is the Sultan doing in the palace? What kind of clothes is he wearing? What dishes are being offered to him? But why does he seem so worried? And in what language is he talking?

Ans. The Sultan is having a meeting with his various ministers on important matters. He is wearing a traditional chola dress with lots of gold jewellery. Different types of fruits, mughlai dishes, drinks and sweet dishes like kheer are being offered to him.

He is worried because an enemy kingdom is probably planning an attack on his kingdom. He is talking in Persian.

Page 96

Q.1 Imagine the rooms in the palace–the beautiful carpets and curtains, the fountains on the terrace .... and the sweet smell of roses and chameli–where is this coming from?

Ans. The rooms in the palace are huge and they are decorated beautifully. They look grand with persian carpets spread across the floor.

The curtains have mughlai patterns and they are embroidered with gold thread.

The fountains are beautifully designed. There is a big garden on the terrace from where the sweet smell of roses and *chameli* is coming.

Q.2 What are the different kinds of factories you can see? How many people are working there? What are they doing? What are they wearing? How long do you think they work?

Ans. I can see many different types of factories where things like clothes, toys, utensils, papers, arms, artefacts and gold coins are being made. Around 25-30 people are working in a factory.

They are doing different things like checking the electric current, packing things, making designs, etc. They are working with their tools, mostly made of iron. They are wearing cotton dhotis of different colours.

I think they work for very long hours like from early morning to late evening.

Q.3 Look there! See how finely those craftsmen are carving the stones using a chisel and hammer? Can you see the stone dust in the air? Do you think this stone dust would harm them in some way?

Ans. Yes, I can see the stone dust in the air. The stone dust can be harmful. It can cause many health problems like allergies.

Write (Page 97)

Q.1 What kinds of pots have you seen around you?

Ans. I have seen pots made of different metals like steel, iron, aluminium, brass, copper, plastic and glass.

Q.2 Try to find out from your grandparents about the other kinds of pots and pans they used in their time?

Ans. During my grandparents time, most of the pots were made of brass and they were very heavy. They also used clay pots and copper pots sometimes.

Q.3 Have you ever been to some museum or heard about it? What all things are there in a museum?

Ans. Yes, I have been to museums a lot of times. We see artefacts, antique designs, manuscripts and coins from different eras, clothes of different rulers, etc. in a museum.

Survey and Write (Page 97)

Q.1 Is there any old building or monument near your house which people come to see? If yes, name it.

Ans. Yes, my house is on Lodhi Road and Safdarjung Tomb is near my house. Many people come to see it.

Q.2 Have you ever gone to see an old monument? Which was that? Did you feel it told you a story? What could you know about those times from it?

Ans. Yes, I have gone to see Red Fort in Delhi. I felt that the building told me a story about the Mughal Empire. I could know how the Mughal kings used to live and also, the architectural design of that time.

Q.3 How old was it? How did you know?

Ans. It is about 400-450 years old. I have read about it in my EVS book.

Q.4 What was it made of?

Ans. The Red Fort is made of red-coloured sandstone.

Q.5 What colour was it?

Ans. It is red in colour.

Q.6 Were there any special kind of designs on the old building? Draw them in your notebook.

Ans. Yes, there are geometrical and floral designs on the building.

Hint: Look at some pictures of the Red Fort and observe the design. Draw them in your notebook.

Q.7 Who used to live there in the olden days?

Ans. In olden days, the Mughal Kings from Bahadur Shah Zafar to Shah Jahan used to live there.

Q.8 What kinds of activities took place there?

Ans. Activities like day to day meetings, bazaars and martial exercises took place there.

Q.9 Do some people still live there?

Ans. No, nobody lives there. It is an empty fort.

Page 98

This painting is 500 years old. It shows Agra Fort being constructed.

Q.1 What kinds of work are people doing? How many men and women are working?

Ans. People are doing construction work. Some people are carrying the bricks while others are fixing them. Some people are finishing the wall. 30 men and 20 women are working.

Q.2 See, how they are taking the huge pillar up along the slope. Is it easier to lift a heavy thing straight up or along a slope?

Ans. Yes, it is easier to lift a heavy thing along a slope.

Q.3 Are you able to see the man carrying water in a mashak (leather bag)?

Ans. Yes, I am able to see the man carrying the water in a mashak (leather bag).

What have we Learnt (Page 98)

Q.1 Sangeeta thinks it is useless to keep old things in a museum. How would you convince her that it is important to have a museum?

Ans. I will convince Sangeeta by telling that the various old things kept in a museum are not useless. They tell us a lot about the olden times. These things represent the people and culture of our ancestors and we can understand a lot from them. Thus, things kept in the museum are important and useful.

Q.2 Why do you think the chapter is named, 'Walls Tell Stories'?

Ans. The chapter is about historical structures, people, art, craft, culture and traditions of olden times. It tells about forts and historical buildings which used to be homes of the kings. Thus, it is named 'Walls Tell Stories'.

CHAPTER 11 SUNITA IN SPACE

About the Chapter

This chapter is about Earth, space, gravity, the globe and the phases of the Moon. Uzaira and Shahmir play with a globe and talk about space. They learn that Earth is round and that a globe is a model of the Earth. They are excited to meet Sunita Williams, an American astronaut of Indian origin, who shares her fun and difficult experiences of living in space. She explains that everything floats in space because there is no gravity.

On Earth, gravity pulls things down when we throw them up. From space, we can only see land and sea, not the different countries. Uzaira and Shahmir observe the night sky and learn that the Moon has different phases and it rises and sets at different times each day.

GLOSSARY

Globe A spherical model of the Earth. It's like a small Earth that you can hold in your hand.
Space The big, empty place outside of Earth where there are stars, planets and galaxies.
Spaceship A special type of vehicle used for going to space.
Blob A small, round mass of something, often thick or sticky.
Full Moon When the Moon appears as a full circle in the sky.

NCERT FOLDER

Straight from the Heart (Page 99)

Q.1 What do you think the Earth looks like? Make a drawing of the Earth in your notebook. On your drawing show where you are. Take a look at your friends' drawings too.

Ans. The Earth looks like a sphere or a ball.

What do you Think? (Page 100)

Q.1 If the Earth is round like a globe, how is it that we do not fall off?

Ans. There is a gravitational force on the Earth which attracts everything towards itself. So, we do not fall off even if the Earth is round.

Q.2 Do the people in Argentina stand upside down?

Ans. No, they do not stand upside down. They stand 'up' like everyone else in the world.

Look at the Photographs and Write (Page 101)

Q.1 Can you think why Sunita's hair is standing?

Ans. On Earth, our hair remains down due to gravitational force. But in space, there is no gravity and our hair does not hold down. Sunita was in space. So her hair is standing.

Q.2

Look at Sunita's photographs and the dates written on each of them. Write what all is happening and when?

Ans. The events that happened are

Date	Event
09-12-2006	The astronauts are taking off in spacecraft.
11-12-2006	Astronauts are floating inside the spacecraft.
11-12-2006	The astronauts are eating food that is flying.
13-12-2006	Sunita Williams is working. Her hair is standing.
16-12-2006	Sunita is outside the spacecraft, roaming in space.

Classroom becomes a Spaceship (Page 103)

Q.1 Close your eyes. Imagine that your class is a spaceship. Zooo...m – in 10 minutes you have entered in space. Your spaceship is now going around the Earth. Now say–

(a) Are you able to sit at one place?

Ans. No, I am floating in the air.

(b) What about your hair?

Ans. My hair are standing up.

(c) Oh look ...... where are your bags and books going?

Ans. My bags and books are flying and floating in the air.

(d) And what is your teacher doing? Where is her chalk?

Ans. My teacher is trying to catch the chalk. Both my teacher and the chalk are floating.

(e) How did you eat your food during the break? How did you drink water? What happened to the ball that you threw up?

Ans. We caught the food flying in the air. The water floated in the air as blobs and we had to suck them. The ball started floating in the air when I threw it up.

Q.2 Act out or draw the scene.

Ans. Do it yourself.

Page 103

Q.1 Can you now say why Sunita's hair kept standing?

Ans. Yes, Sunita's hair kept standing because there was zero gravity in space.

Q.2 Think why water flows downwards on any slope. On mountains too water flows downwards, not upwards.

Ans. The water flows downwards on any slope because the Earth attracts everything towards itself. It has a force of gravity.

Page 104

Magic 1. A Tiny Paper Races a Coin

Take a 5 rupee coin and a small piece of paper. The paper should be about one-fourth the size of the coin.

Q.1 Hold the coin in one hand and the paper in the other. Drop them at the same time. What happened?

Ans. When a coin and the paper are dropped at the same time, the coin falls more quickly than the piece of paper.

Q.2 Now place the tiny paper on the coin and drop them. What happened this time? Surprised!

Ans. A tiny paper and the coin fell down at the same time.

Magic 2. A Mouse Lifts an Elephant!

To play this you will need a small stone, a bigger stone (lemon-sized), a thick roll of paper (which can be made with layers of papers), mouse and an elephant made of paper.

- Take a string about 2 feet long.
- At one end of the string tie the small stone. Stick or tie the mouse to the stone.
- Put the string into the roll of paper.
- At the other end of the string tie the bigger stone and stick the elephant.
- Hold the roll of paper and move your hand to rotate the small stone.

Q.3 Who is pulling whom? You will be surprised! The mouse lifts the elephant! How did this magic happen?

Ans. This happens when the small stone starts rotating, it creates a force due to which the bigger stone is pulled up. That is why the mouse lifts the elephant.

Look at this Photograph and Tell (Page 105)

Q.1 Can you see India?

Ans. Yes, I can see India.

Q.2 Can you recognise any other place?

Ans. Yes, I can recognise other places like Sri Lanka and Europe.

Q.3 Where is the sea?

Ans. The blue part in the picture shows the sea.

Q.4 Do you find anything similar between the globe and this picture of the Earth? In what ways are they different?

Ans. Yes, I can find similarities. The similarity is that the land and the sea can be distinguished. However, the difference is that in this picture, it is difficult to recognise any country but in the globe different countries are marked.

Q.5 Do you think Sunita could make out Pakistan, Nepal and Burma separately, when she saw the Earth from space?

Ans. No, I don't think that Sunita could make out the mentioned countries separately when she saw the Earth from space.

Look at a Globe in your School and Tell (Page 105)

Q.1 Can you find India?

Ans. Yes, I can very easily find India.

Q.2 Where all do you find the sea?

Ans. On the globe, the sea is shown by blue colour.

Q.3 Which countries can you see?

Ans. I can see all the countries. Some of them are the USA, UK, Canada, France, Italy, Africa, etc.

Q.4 Can you see some of the countries with which India plays cricket matches? For example, England, Australia, Pakistan, Bangladesh and South Africa.

Ans. Yes, I can easily see these countries.

Q.5 What else can you see on the globe?

Ans. I can see mountains, islands, sea, etc. on the globe.

Look at the Map of your Country and Tell (Page 106)

Q.1 Can you find the state in which you live? Write its name on the map.

Ans. Yes, I can easily find the state in which I live. It is Uttar Pradesh.

Q.2 Which are the states next to the state you live in?

Ans. The states next to the state I live in are Uttarakhand, Bihar, Haryana, Punjab and Jharkhand.

Q.3 Have you been to any other state?

Ans. Yes, I have been to many states such as Kerala, Bihar, Rajasthan and Madhya Pradesh.

Q.4 Shahmir thinks that there are lines drawn on the ground between the states. What do you think?

Ans. I think that these lines are drawn only on the maps and not on the ground between the states.

Page 106

Q.1 Why don't you try to do the same with a coin? How many centimetres away from the eye did you keep the coin to hide the Moon?

Ans. When I tried to do it, the same thing happened. I kept the coin at 30 cm from my eye and the Moon completely disappeared.

Think (Page 106)

Q.1 Do you think the moon is flat like a coin or round like a ball?

Ans. No, I don't think that the Moon is flat like a coin. I think that the Moon is round like a ball.

Page 107

Q.1 Look at the moon tonight and draw what it looks like. Look and draw again after one week and then after 15 days.

Today's Date	Date after a week	Date after 15 days

Ans.

Today's Date	Date after a week	Date after 15 days

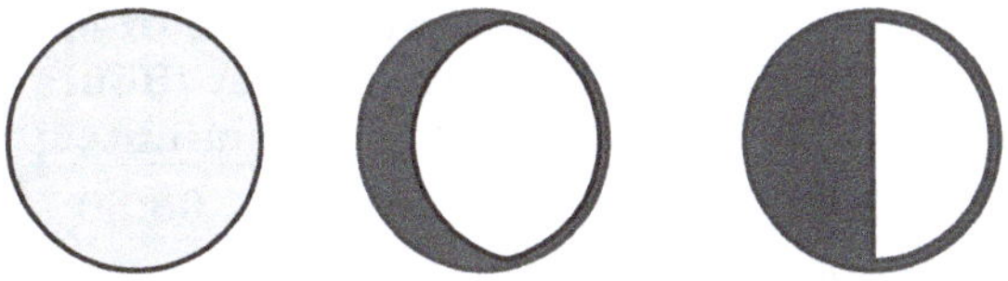

Find Out (Page 107)

Q.1 When is the next full Moon? At what time will the Moon rise on this day? What does the Moon look like on this day? Draw it.

Ans. The next full Moon is on the 17th of this month. The Moon will rise in the evening just after sunset.

Q.2 What are the festivals related to the Moon?

Ans. There are many festivals related to the Moon, like Holi, Eid, Karwa Chauth, Chaturdashi, Ganesh Chaturthi, etc.

Q.3 At night look at the sky carefully for 5 minutes

- What could you see?

Ans. I could see the Moon and the twinkling stars.

- Did you see anything moving in the sky? What do you think it could be? A star or a shooting star or a satellite (satellites are used for the TV, telephones and for weather reports). Find out more about this.

Ans. Yes, I saw some things moving in the sky. The thing that crosses the sky very quickly is a shooting star. I could also see a satellite which appeared like a dot.

Look at the Table and Tell (Page 107-108)

Given below are the times at which the Moon rises and sets in Delhi (on the given days).

Date	Time of Moon rise (Hours : minutes)	Time of Moon set (Hours : minutes)
28.10.2007	19:16	08:50
29.10.2007	20:17	10:03
30.10.2007	21:22	11:08
31.10.2007	22:29	12:03

Q.1 On 28 October the Moon came out at ___ minutes past ___ o'clock.

Ans. 16 minutes past 7 o'clock

Q.2 On 29 October the Moon came out at ___ minutes past ___ o'clock.

Ans. 17 minutes past 8 o'clock

Q.3 On 29 October there was a difference of __ hours and __ minutes in the time of the Moon rise (as compared to 28 October).

Ans. 1 hour and 1 minute

Q.4 If you saw the Moon rising at 7 pm today, would you see it at the same time tomorrow?

Ans. No, I would not see the Moon rising at the same time tomorrow.

Q.5 On 31 October the time of setting of the Moon is given as 12:03. Have you ever seen the Moon at 12 in the afternoon? Why don't we easily see the Moon or stars during the day?

Ans. No, I have never seen the Moon at 12 in the afternoon. During the day, we are not able to see the Moon and stars due to excessive sunlight.

An Interesting Photograph (Page 108)

Q.1 See how the Earth is looking. Can you see the surface of the Moon? Do you have some questions after looking at this picture? Write down those questions and discuss them in the class.

Ans. I can see the surface of the Moon very clearly. Some questions that came to my mind are:

(i) Who clicked the picture?

(ii) What does the surface of the Moon look like in real life?

(iii) Are there people on the Moon?

What we have Learnt (Page 109)

Q.1 Why do children always slide down the slide and not slide up? If this slide were there in Sunita's spacecraft, would children slide like this? Why?

Ans. The children always slide down the slide and not slide up because of the force of gravity of the Earth. It pulls everything towards itself.

If this slide was there in Sunita's spacecraft, she would not be able to slide like this. There is no gravity in the spacecraft.

Q.2 Why do we see stars mostly at night?

Ans. We see stars mostly at night because there is no sunlight during the night. The light from the stars is hidden by the excessive sunlight during the day.

Q.3 Looking at Earth from the space, Sunita said, "Different countries cannot be seen as separate from here. These lines are on paper. They are made by us". What do you understand by this?

Ans. Nature has made a single Earth with no lines between countries. Boundaries are made by human beings to separate different places. We should remember that all of us are the same members of one Earth.

CHAPTER 12 WHAT IF IT FINISHES...?

About the Chapter

This chapter is about the importance of saving natural resources like petroleum and CNG. It starts with a group of school children on a trip to Adalaj stepwell. They count different vehicles on the road and notice that there are not many bicycles. At a petrol pump, they see a poster that says we should save petrol for future generations. They learn that petrol comes from oil found deep underground and takes millions of years to form. The CNG comes from the Earth and that some vehicles can run on CNG and electricity.

The oil is found under the Earth and it is refined to get petrol, diesel and other things. It has many uses, like fuel for cars, cooking and making plastic. Many people in India use wood and other fuels like LPG and kerosene for cooking. Overall, the chapter teaches us to save our natural resources for the future.

GLOSSARY

CNG Compressed Natural Gas (CNG) is a pollution free natural gas used as a fuel.
LPG Liquified Petroleum Gas (LPG) is a type of gas used in the kitchen as fuel. It is filled in cylinders and used for cooking.
Refinery A large industrial unit where raw materials like crude oil are processed.
Chulha A traditional Indian stove made out of clay used for cooking.
Uple Cow dung cakes used to cook and to keep the food warm.
Twigs A thin, short branch of a tree that does not usually have leaves.
Treasures Valuable things in any form like precious metals, oils, money, etc.

NCERT FOLDER

Tell (Page 111)

Q.1 Do you ride a bicycle? If yes, where all do you go on it?

Ans. Yes, I ride a bicycle. I use it to go to school, playground, market and dance classes.

Q.2 How do you come to school?

Ans. I come to school by bicycle.

Q.3 How do your family members go to work from home?

Ans. My father goes to the office by car and my mother takes the metro. My uncle goes by his scooter

Q.4 What problems can we have from smoke coming out of vehicles?

Ans. Some problems caused by smoke coming out of vehicles is coughing, nausea, headache and breathing problems.

Q.5 What kind of problems can we face from noise of vehicles (honking)?

Ans. Noise of vehicles (honking) can cause hearing problems like loss of hearing power or deafness.

Look at the Picture and Write (Page 111)

Q.1 What are the different kinds of vehicles that you can see?

Ans. I can see many vehicles like car, bus, scooter, motor-cycle, autorickshaw, bicycles, cycle-rickshaw, etc.

Q.2 What do you think they need petrol and diesel as fuel?

Ans. Cars, motorcycles, scooters, buses, auto-rickshaws need petrol and diesel as fuel but bicycles do not need it.

Q.3 Which of the vehicles do you think give off smoke? Put a red mark on those.

Ans. Put a red circle on cars, buses, motorcycles, auto-rickshaws and scooters.

Q.4 Which are the vehicles run without petrol and diesel?

Ans. Bicycles, cycle rickshaws and CNG vehicles run without petrol and diesel.

Q.5 What problems do we face from the speeding vehicles?

Ans. Speeding vehicles are the main reason behind road accidents. Many vehicles crash because of high speed.

Find Out and Discuss (Page 113)

Q.1 Which States of India have oil fields?

Ans. Assam, Maharashtra, Gujarat and Andhra Pradesh have oil fields.

Q.2 Besides oil, what else is found deep inside the Earth?

Ans. Besides oil, many types of minerals such as iron, copper, gold, silver, bauxite, coal, etc. are found deep inside the Earth.

Q.3 Find out the traffic rules and discuss them in class.

Ans. Do it yourself.

Q.4 We should use petrol and diesel judiciously. Think why?

Ans. Petrol and diesel are available to us naturally but they are limited in quantity. They take lakhs of years to be formed.

Further, they also cause a lot of pollution and global warming. Thus, judicious use of petrol will help us save fuel and the environment.

Write (Page 114)

Q.1 What all can vehicles run on?

Ans. Vehicles can run on different fuels like petrol, diesel, CNG, battery and solar energy.

Q.2 What kinds of problems will we face, if the number of vehicles keep on increasing? For example, more traffic on the road. Talk to your elders and write about it.

Ans. If the number of vehicles keep increasing day by day, it will cause many problems like increased traffic on the road, noise pollution, air pollution, frequent accidents, etc.

Q.3 Manju said, "Why doesn't everyone use a bus"? What do you think, why don't people travel by buses?

Ans. People do not travel by buses because buses are usually crowded.

Q.4 Suggest some ways to deal with the problems arising out of the growing number of vehicles.

Ans. Some ways to deal with the problems arising out of the growing number of vehicles are;

- People should travel by public transport like buses, metros, local and inter-state trains, etc.
- Carpooling, i.e. sharing a car with a friend, colleague or somebody you know, is a good way.

Q.5 What are the benefits, if we switch off the engine of the vehicles at the red light on the road?

Ans. If we switch off the engine of the vehicles at the red light on the road, it will reduce our petrol usage. This will also stop the unnecessary smoke emitted out of cars while standing at a signal.

Find Out and Write (Page 115)

How much oil?	Scooter	Car	Tractor
How much petrol/diesel can be filled at a time?	10 litres	40-55 litres	40-50 litres
How far can it go on one litre of petrol/diesel?			

Ans.

How much oil?	Scooter	Car	Tractor
How much petrol/diesel can be filled at a time?	10 litres	40-55 litres	40-50 litres
How far can it go on one litre of petrol/diesel?	40 kms	50kms	18-20 kms

The rates of petrol are different in each city. The rates of petrol and diesel in Delhi are given here. Look at the table and answer the questions.

Oil	Petrol	Diesel
Rate of one litre in 2002 (Oct)	₹ 29.91	₹ 18.91
Rate of one litre in 2007 (Oct)	₹ 43.52	₹ 30.48
Rate of one litre in 2014 (Oct)	₹ 67.86	₹ 58.97
Rate of one litre in 2017 (Oct)	₹ 64.91	₹ 54.70

Q.1 In 2014, as compared to 2007 the rate of petrol went up by ____________ rupees. The rate of diesel increased by __________ rupees.

Ans. 24.34; 28.49

Q.2 What was the difference in the rates of petrol and diesel from 2002 to 2007, 2007 to 2014 and 2014 to 2017?

Ans. The difference in rates of petrol and diesel from 2002 to 2007 is ₹13.61 and ₹11.57 respectively. From 2007 to 2014, the difference in rates of petrol was ₹ 24.34 and diesel was ₹ 28.49. From 2014 to 2017, the price of petrol decreased by ₹ 2.95 and price of diesel reduced by ₹ 4.27.

Q.3 What is the change in prices of diesel and petrol from 2007 to 2014?

Ans. The prices of diesel increased by ₹ 28.49 from 2007 to 2014.

Find Out (Page 115)

Q.1 How much did the price of petrol and diesel change from 2014 to 2017?

Ans. From 2014 to 2017, the price of petrol decreased by ₹ 2.95 and price of diesel reduced by ₹ 4.27.

Q.2 What is the price of petrol and diesel in your area?

Ans. Petrol is priced at ₹ 94.95 and diesel is ₹ 87.83 in my area.

Q.3 Why are the prices of petrol and diesel going up?

Ans. The prices of petrol and diesel are going up because the demand is increasing day by day but the resources are available in limited quantities.

Q.4 In one month, how much petrol and diesel is used in your home? What is it used for?

Ans. In my home, about 50 litres of petrol and 5 litres of diesel is used. Petrol is used for car and scooters, and diesel is used for generators.

Page 116

Q.1 One poster is given here.

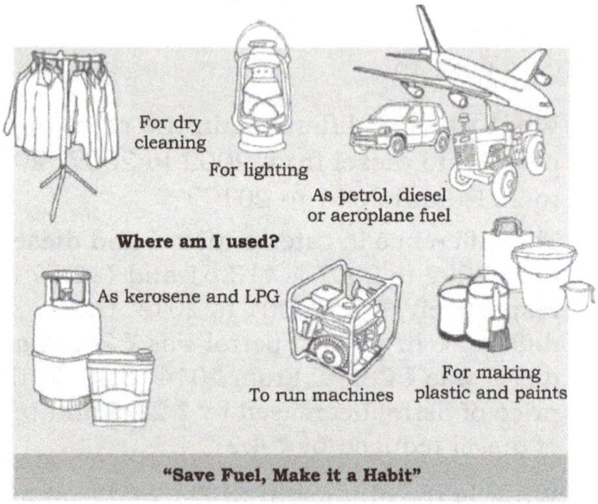

See the Poster and Write

Q.1 Where is the oil used?

Ans. Oil is used for various things like dry cleaning, lighting, as fuel in cars and aeroplanes, for making plastic and paints, as kerosene and LPG, and to run machines.

Q.2 Where is diesel used? Find out.

Ans. Diesel is used as a fuel for some automobiles like buses, cars, auto-rickshaws, trains, trucks, etc. It is also used in generators.

Think and Discuss (Page 117)

Q.1 What would happen if you don't get petrol or diesel for a week in your village or town?

Ans. Do it yourself.

Q.2 Suggest some ways to save oil.

Ans. Some ways to save oil are

- Use public transport instead of private vehicles.
- Prefer walking or taking a bicycle if you want to go nearby.
- Switch of the car engine at the signal.
- Use solar energy.
- Check your vehicles and maintain them regularly.

Discuss (Page 117-118)

Q.1 Have you ever collected dry wood or made cow dung cakes? How are they made?

Ans. Yes, I have collected dry wood to make a bonfire during winters. I have never made cow dung cakes but I have seen some people making them in my grandmother's village.

They are made by mixing dry hay with cow dung and then, the mixture is given the shape of a cake. It is dried in the Sun to make cakes.

Q.2 Do you know anyone who collects dry wood or leaves to be used for lighting a chulha?

Ans. I have seen some people collecting dry wood and leaves to light a chulha in my grandparents' village.

Q.3 Who cooks food in your family? What about other families in your area?

Ans. My mother and my grandmother cook the food in my family.

In other families, the ladies of the house cook food. In some houses, there are servants to cook food.

Q.4 If they cook food using wood or upla (cow dung cakes), what difficulties do they face due to smoke?

Ans. If the food is cooked using wood or upla, they face many difficulties like coughing, nausea, headache and lung diseases.

Q.5 Can Durga use anything else instead of wood? Why not?

Ans. Durga can use cow dung cakes instead of wood but she cannot use anything else. She is too poor to buy fuel like LPG.

Page 118-119

Kancha had seen a bar chart in a book. The chart shows the number of houses out of 100 that use each type of fuel. It also shows the use of which fuel has increased and which fuel has decreased over the past twenty years.

Change in fuel use over twenty years

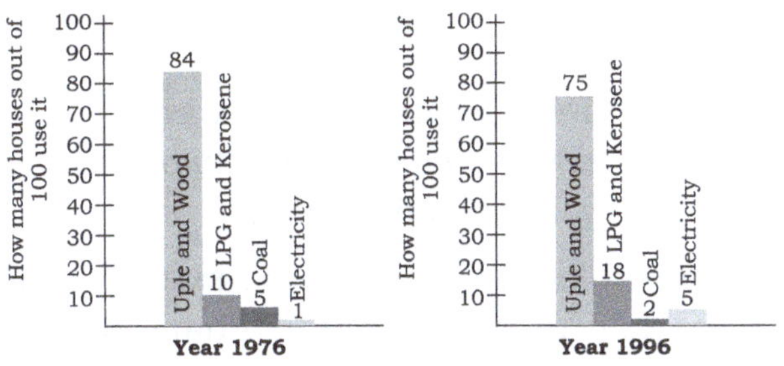

Q.1 In year 1976, out of 100, how many houses used uple and wood?

Ans. 84 houses.

Q.2 Which was the fuel used the least in 1976?

Ans. Electricity

Q.3 In 1976, LPG and kerosene were used in______houses and in 1996 this increased to______. This means that in twenty years their use increased by________

Ans. 10; 18; 80%

Q.4 Out of 100, how many houses were using electricity in 1996?

Ans. Five

Q.5 Which fuel was used the least in 1996? What percentage of houses used it in the year 1976?

Ans. Coal was used the least in 1996. In 1976, it was being used by 5% of houses.

Find Out from your Elders (Page 119)

Q.1 When they were young what was then used to cook food at home?

Ans. When they were young, they used coal to cook food. They also used firewood and cow dung cakes.

Q.2 In the past 10 years use of which cooking fuel has increased in your area? Use of which fuel has decreased?

Ans. In the past 10 years the use of LPG and electricity have increased in my area. The use of coal and cow dung cakes has decreased.

Q.3 Guess the use of which fuel would increase and which would decrease in the next 10 years.

Ans. In the next ten years, the use of electricity will increase more and the use of coal, wood and uple will reduce to a minimum.

What we have Learnt (Page 119)

Q.1 Imagine that a company has given you a chance to design a new vehicle like a mini bus. What kind of vehicle would you design? Write about it. Draw a picture and colour it.

Ans. Do it yourself.

Q.2 While making the design, what did you plan to take care of

- old people
- children
- those who cannot see?

Ans. While making the design, I took care of the following things

- Old people: Low floor, seat belts and comfortable seats.
- Children: Low floor, child lock and grills on windows.
- Those who cannot see: Sensors at the gate, grab handles and ramp accessibility.

Q.3 Look out for news reports on oil. Cut these and make a collage. Put up a chart in your classroom. Also write your own views on these news reports.

Ans. Do it yourself.

Q.4 Make a poster with a message on saving fuel. Write a slogan too. Where would you like to put up this poster?

Ans. Do it yourself.

CHAPTER 13 A SHELTER SO HIGH!

About the Chapter

In this chapter, Gaurav Jani shares his motorcycle journey from Mumbai to Ladakh, discussing various shelters and lifestyles in different regions. Gaurav starts his two-month adventure on the highest roads of India through his motorcycle named 'Loner'.

He packs essentials like a tent, sleeping bag, warm clothes, food, a camera and extra petrol. He begins his trip from Mumbai, passing through Maharashtra, Gujarat, Rajasthan and Delhi. Then, he reaches the high roads in Jammu and Kashmir to get to Leh in Ladakh.

In Leh, Gaurav sees a cold desert and beautiful white houses. He meets Tashi in Ladakh who shows him a home designed for the local weather. Gaurav then, travels to the rocky plains of Changthang, where he meets the Changpa tribe, known for weaving warm Pashmina shawls. They live in temporary tents called Rebos.

Finally, he visits Srinagar and sees many different houses like houseboats, dongas and old houses. On his way back in Jammu, he sees cement houses.

GLOSSARY

Cold deserts Deserts at high elevations, which can experience significant temperature variations and can receive snow.

Nylon An artificial fibre which is strong and lightweight.

Hay Grass that has been cut and dried for use as animal food.

Stacks To arrange objects like paper, stones, etc., one over the other.

Courtyard An open area which is enclosed by walls and buildings.

NCERT FOLDER

Find Out (Page 121)

Q.1 Check in your map. Which States would one pass through while travelling from Mumbai to Kashmir?

Ans. One would pass through Maharashtra, Gujarat, Rajasthan, Haryana, Punjab, Himachal Pradesh, Jammu and Kashmir while travelling from Mumbai to Kashmir.

Q.2 Gaurav Jani passed through several States while going from Mumbai to Delhi. Find the capital cities of these States. Was there any other big town on his way?

Ans. Gaurav Jani passed through many States. The States and their capitals are given below

Maharashtra: Mumbai
Gujarat: Gandhinagar
Rajasthan: Jaipur
Haryana: Chandigarh

Q.3 Is Manali a plain or a hilly area? In which State is it?

Ans. Manali is a hilly area. It is in Himachal Pradesh.

Tell (Page 122)

Q.1 Have you ever stayed in a tent? Where? What was it like?

Ans. Yes, I have stayed in a tent while camping with my family in Kullu. It was an adventurous experience.

Q.2 Imagine that you were to stay alone in a small tent for two days and could take with you only ten things. Make a list of those ten things.

Ans. If I were to stay alone in a small tent for two days, I would take clothes, jacket, blanket, torch, food packets, water bottles, mosquito repellant, toothbrush and toothpaste, shoes and a camera with me.

Q.3 What are the different types of houses that you have seen? Tell your friends about it. Make drawings too.

Ans. I have seen different types of houses like Pucca houses- made from bricks, cement, wood, etc.

Kuchcha houses - made of mud and dry leaves.

Stilt houses- made of bamboo.

Wood houses - made of wood.

Kuchcha House

Pucca House

Stilt House

Wood House

Write (Page 123)

Q.1 During winters, Tashi and his family live on the ground floor. Why would they be doing so?

Ans. Tashi and his family live on the ground floor during winters because there are no windows. This keeps the room warm.

Q.2 What is the roof of your house like? What all is the roof used for?

Ans. The roof of my house is made of bricks and is flat. It is cemented and whitewashed.

My mother dries clothes, and food items like papad, achaar, etc., on the roof. We also sleep on the roof-top sometimes during summers.

Find Out (Page 124)

Q.1 At what height is the place where you live?

Ans. I live in Noida, Uttar Pradesh. It is situated at a height of 220 metres above the sea level.

Q.2 Why did Gaurav Jani say - "place is so high that it is difficult to breathe normally?"

Ans. When we go to places which have higher altitude or height, the air becomes thinner and there is less oxygen. It gets difficult to breathe there. That is why Guarav Jani said so.

Q.3 Have you ever been to a hilly place? Where?

Ans. Yes, I have been to a hilly place. I went to Sikkim with my family for my summer holidays.

Q.4 At what height was it? Did you have any difficulty in breathing there?

Ans. Sikkim is about 3000-3500 metres above sea level.

Yes, I had difficulty in breathing there.

Q.5 Which is the highest place you have been to?

Ans. I have been to Zero Point in Lachung, Sikkim. It is about 5100 metres from sea level.

Page 127

Q.1 For the Changpas, their animals are a very important part of their life. Is any animal part of your life? For example, as a pet, or as helpers in farming.

Ans. Yes, I have a pet dog who is an important part of my life.

Q.2 List five ways in which different animals are a part of your life.

Ans. Five ways in which different animals are a part of our lives is as follows

- Dogs – Dogs protect our house and they are man's best friends.
- Cows and Buffaloes – They give us milk.
- Hen – We get products like eggs from hen.
- Horse – horses are used for pulling carts.

Q.3 Do goat and sheep need their own fur and wool? Discuss.

Ans. Yes, goat and sheep need their own fur and wool to stay warm and safe. It's like their own jacket that protects them from cold weather and rain.

Find Out (Page 127)

Q.1 You read that in Changthang the temperature drops below 0°C. Look at newspapers on the TV to find cities in India or abroad where the temperature drops below 0°C. In which months do you expect to see this?

Ans. There are many cities in India where the temperature drops below 0°C. Some of them are Shimla, Manali, Munnar, Leh, Ladakh.

There are many places like Ottawa, Winnipeg, etc., where the temperature drops below 0°C.

We can see this during the months of December and January.

Tell (Page 129-130)

Q.1 The houses in different parts of Jammu and Kashmir are made to suit the climate and the needs of the people there. Are there different types of houses in the place where you live? If yes, think about the reasons.

Ans. Yes, there are different types of houses in the place I live.

In my city, there are flats in multi-storeyed buildings for middle class people. The rich live in bungalows and *kothis*. There are kutchcha houses in the slum area made of tin or wood where poor people live.

Q.2 Think of your own house. Is there something special in it like a sloping roof as it rains a lot, or a courtyard where you can sleep when it is hot or where things are kept in the Sun (for drying, etc.)? Make a drawing.

Ans. Yes, my house has a big terrace and multiple balconies. We sit on the terrace and enjoy ourselves during different seasons. We also fly kites on Basant Panchami. Multiple balconies give proper fresh air in the house. We also dry clothes and foods like papad, achars in the balconies. My mom and dad enjoy their morning tea in the balcony attached to their room.

Students can draw their house according to their description.

Q.3 What are the materials used for making your house? Is it mud, brick, stone, wood or cement?

Ans. The materials used for making my house are brick, stone, cement, iron and glass.

Discuss and Write (Page 130)

Look at this picture. Can you see any houses in the picture? These houses are made of stone and mud. Nobody lives here in winter. In summer, the Bakarwal people live here when they bring their goats to higher lands for grazing.

Q.1 Can you guess the similarities and differences in the life of Bakarwal people and the life of the Changpas.

Ans. The similarities between the life of Bakarwal people and the life of Changpas are

- Both of them live in the mountains of Jammu and Kashmir at a high altitude.
- They move from one place to another and have no permanent shelter.
- They are dependent on their animals for their livelihood and sell their wool.

The differences between the life of Bakarwal people and Changpas are

- Bakarwals stay at both higher and lower altitudes but Changapas stay only at higher altitudes.
- The houses of Bakarwals are made of stone but Changapa' houses are made of yak's skin.
- Bakarwals graze any type of goats but Changapas graze special types of goats.

What we have learnt!

You read about different kinds of shelters in Jammu and Kashmir– Some on high mountains, some on water, some with beautiful designs in wood and stone and some mobile shelters that can even be packed and carried to another place.

Q.2 Describe how these shelters suit the needs of the people who live there.

Ans. Houses in Jammu and Kashmir are made to suit the needs of the people. Houseboat and dongas are complete houses on boats. They are made using stone and wood which provide warmth during cold weather. Changapas use tent houses made from Yak skin which keeps them warm. They are also good for people with wandering lifestyles. The wood houses made on mountains with sloping roofs are the best for people living on high altitudes.

Q.3 How are these different from the house you live in?

Ans. Our houses are usually pucca houses made using bricks, stones, cement, glass and iron. They have flat slopes. Our houses cannot move, unlike Changapas' tents. These are permanent and strong houses.

CHAPTER 14

WHEN THE EARTH SHOOK!

About the Chapter

This chapter is about earthquakes, the problems they cause and what to do during an earthquake. Jasma, who lives in the Kutch area of Gujarat, experienced a big earthquake when she was eleven. The earthquake damaged everything, including homes, hospitals and food supplies and many people were hurt. Doctors and villagers worked together to help the people who were injured. People from cities brought food, medicine and clothes, and some helped set up tents for those in need. The village was rebuilt safely.

During an earthquake,we should leave the house and go to an open area. If it is not possible to leave, we should lie down and hide under something strong, like a table and hold on until the shaking stops.

GLOSSARY

Earthquake A natural calamity where the surface of the Earth starts shaking suddenly due to some movement inside the Earth.

Sarpanch The elected head of a Gram Panchayat, which is a local government body in rural India.

Engineer Someone who helps in maintaining and designing the buildings, machines or any other technical equipment.

Whitewashed To paint the wall with a white liquid paint.

Thatched roof A type of roof made with straw or dried plant material.

Architect Someone who specialises in designing the buildings according to one's need.

NCERT FOLDER

Discuss and Write (Page 132)

Q.1 Have you or anyone that you know ever faced such difficulty?

Ans. Yes, my uncle and aunt live in Assam. They have experienced earthquakes multiple times.

Q.2 Who all helped at such time? Make a list.

Ans. People who help at such time are neighbours, local natives, political leaders, NGOs, social help groups, doctors and nurses, etc.

Discuss (Page 134)

Q.1 A lot of people from other places came to Jasma's village. Who were these people? In what ways would they have helped the villagers?

Ans. Many people came from other places to Jasma's village. Some of them were from NGOs, some were scientists, engineers and architects. Some of them may have been doctors and nurses.

Q.2 People in Jasma's village rebuilt their houses with suggestions from the engineers.

Will these houses be safer than before in case there is an earthquake again? Why?

Ans. Yes, these houses will be safer than before in case there is an earthquake because engineers suggested the people to build the houses in such a way that there would be least damage in case of earthquakes.

Q.3 Think, if there were an earthquake where you live, would your house be in danger?

Ans. In case of an earthquake, my house would be in danger. The walls can crack and tear down. The household items will also be damaged.

Q.4 What will you do to save pet animals during natural disaster?

Ans. During natural disaster, I will keep my pet safely with me in an open ground or under a safe space. I will make sure that my pet does not panic. I will prepare an emergency bag and carry it with me. I will try to contact a pet shelter and send my pet there for proper care.

Write (Page 134)

Q.1 Compare your house with that of Jasma. List in your notebook what materials were used in making both houses.

Jasma's House	Your House

Ans.

Jasma's House	Your House
Clay, mud, cow dung, mirror, etc.	Bricks, cement, water, iron, etc.

Page 135

Q.1 Have you been told in your school or anywhere else about what to do in case of an earthquake?

Ans. Yes, there was a workshop in our school where they taught us what to do in case of an earthquake. We were taught that we should immediately go to an open area like a playground. If someone cannot go into an open space, they were taught to hide under a solid thing like a table and hold on tightly.

Q.2 Why do you think one should go under a table during an earthquake?

Ans. The table can save someone from damage as it can take the blow during an earthquake. Hiding under the table will protect you from any injury.

Write (Page 135-136)

Q.1 According to the TV report, thousands of people were injured and some died in Gujarat. If the buildings had been made in a way that they would not fall in the earthquake, would the damage have been different? How?

Ans. Yes, if the buildings were made in a way that they would not fall in the earthquake, the damage would have been different. Such buildings would not have collapsed and there would have been less loss of life and property.

Q.2 At times like this, when people have lost their homes and all their belongings, what kind of help would they need?

Ans. People would need medical help along with things like clothes, food, shelter, water and medicines.

Q.3 In such situations whose help would be needed and for what? Write in your notebook as shown here.

Whose help will be needed	How will they help
Dog	To smell out where people are lying trapped
Doctors	

Ans.

Whose help will be needed	How will they help
Dog	To smell out where people are lying trapped.
Doctors	To examine patients and help the injured people.
Labourers	To help in removing the rubble and construct new buildings.
Government organisations	To provide support and relief measures.

Discuss (Page 136)

Q.1 Have you ever seen people in your area helping each other? When?

Ans. Yes, I have seen people help each other in my area. Once, there was an earthquake in my area. During that time, people shouted to make others aware of the danger. They also helped in rescue operations and provided food and medical aid to others.

Q.2 Why do people live together in a neighbourhood?

Ans. People live together in a neighbourhood so that they can help each other in times of need. They also live together so that they can share their joys with each other.

Q.3 Imagine living in a place where there were no other houses or people around. How would it be? For example, whom would you play with? With whom would you celebrate festivals and special days? Would you be scared?

Ans. I will be scared. It would be difficult to seek help if there are no other houses. It will also be boring to be alone on festivals and special days.

Q.4 People face a lot of difficulties when they lose people from their family or their houses and belongings. In newspapers of the last one month, look for news related to such disasters– earthquakes, floods, fire, cyclones, etc., in different parts of the world. Collect these news reports and paste them in your notebook.

Ans. Do it yourself.

Your News Report (Page 137)

Q.1 Make your own report which mentions the following

- Cause of the disaster, date and time.
- What kind of damage did it cause–to lives, belongings, livelihoods?
- Which people came forward to help? Which government offices or other groups?

Ans. Assam

A massive earthquake hit this hilly State during the afternoon. Many houses collapsed and many lives were lost. There were many fires because of short circuits. There were reports of gas leaks too. As per the latest data,10 people have died and 25 are injured severely. Most of the people have lost their homes and are at the mercy of relief agencies. Army Jawans from nearby cantonments have been called to help the people. Many NGOs have also been informed and have reached. Some national political leaders have announced a relief package for the place.

Q.2 Have people in your area ever got affected by famine or drought? Find such reports of different countries from newspapers. Make your own report.

Ans. Yes, people in my area got affected by drought once.

Madhya Pradesh

A severe drought is sweeping across the State, causing widespread hardship for farmers and communities alike. The lack of rainfall has led to slow water supplies, parched fields and declining agricultural yields. Farmers are struggling to maintain their crops and livestock as water sources dry up. Many have resorted to using limited groundwater reserves or purchasing expensive water supplies. More than 1000 villages have been affected. Government officials are closely monitoring the situation and implementing measures to mitigate the drought's impact .

Q.3 You may need some help from these in case of an accident or emergency. Find out and write their addresses and phone numbers. Add more names to this list.

	Address	Phone Number
Fire Station		
Nearby Hospital		
Ambulance		
Police Station		

Ans.

	Address	Phone Number
Fire Station	Karol Bagh, Delhi	101
Nearby Hospital	BLK Super Speciality Hospital, Karol Bagh	011-23236000
Ambulance	Karol Bagh, New Delhi	102
Police Station	Karol Bagh, New Delhi	011-23433090

Difficult Times (Page 137-138)

Q.1 Write a report with the help of the following words: floods, river water, injured people, food packets, rescue work, camps, dead bodies, dead animals floating in water, houses, under water, aerial survey (to see the scene of disaster from a plane), sad people, diseases spread by dirty water, homeless people, trapped people.

Ans. A flood has struck the region in the district of Purnea, leaving a trail of destruction. Rains have caused rivers to overflow, destroying entire villages and towns. The floodwaters have swept away houses, roads and bridges, leaving many people homeless and injured.

Rescue teams have been working to help trapped individuals and provide relief to those affected. Many people remain stranded in flooded areas, lacking access to basic necessities like food packets, water and medical care. It has been advised by the Chief Minister to take an aerial survey of the damage. The situation is made worse by the presence of dead animals floating in the water, posing a significant health risk. The dirty water has led to the spread of diseases, including waterborne illnesses like cholera and typhoid.

What we have Learnt (Page 138)

Q.1 What type of difficulties are faced by people during floods? Look at the picture, what kind of a school have the children come to after the flood? Write down what people had to do to make their life normal again after the flood.

Ans. Following difficulties are faced by people during floods

- Many people lose their relatives, friends and near ones.
- Some people get injured severely.
- There is a loss of property and life.
- There is a shortage of things like food, water, medicines, etc.
- Roads and rail networks are badly affected.
- Water is dirty so diseases spread in the affected area.

After the flood, people had to do following things for their survival

- People had to restart and rebuild their life to normal.
- Children were forced to study in a makeshift school.
- They had to arrange for drinking water which is clean and fresh.
- People had to rebuild their houses.

CHAPTER 15 BLOW HOT, BLOW COLD

About the Chapter

This chapter is about blowing air from our mouths and how it can be hot or cold. One cold day, a woodcutter was cutting wood and his fingers became numb, so he blew warm air on them to warm them up. Mian Balishitye saw this and asked him why he was blowing on his hands. The woodcutter explained that he was trying to keep his hands warm. Later, he blew on a fire to help it burn and then, on a hot potato to cool it down.

Mian Balishitye got confused about how the woodcutter could blow both hot and cold air. We can blow warm air to cool warm things and cold air to warm up cool things. Some musical instruments can also be played by blowing air in them. If you put a finger under your nose, you can feel your breath. When we exercise, we breathe faster.

GLOSSARY

Woodcutter A person who cuts down wood from the trees to learn his living.
Numb It means not being able to feel anything in a part of the body.
Whistle A high-pitched sound produced by blowing air through a small opening.

NCERT FOLDER

Do this (Page 141)

Mian Balishtiye was confused when he saw the woodcutter blowing on his cold hands to make them warm and on the hot potatoes to cool them.

Q.1 Have you warmed your hands in winter by blowing on them when they are cold? How does it feel?

Ans. Yes, I have warmed my hands in winter by blowing on them when they are cold. It feels warm and comfortable.

Q.2 Blow hard from your mouth onto your hands. How did you find the air from your mouth as compared to the air around? Was it hotter, or cooler?

Ans. The air from my mouth felt hotter than the air around me when I blew hard from my mouth onto my hands.

Q.3 Now put your hands at some distance from your mouth, and blow again. Does the air from your mouth feel warm? Why?

Ans. When I put my hands at some distance, the air does not feel much warm.

This could happen because air travels some distance and gets mixed up with the air around. This reduces its warmth.

Think and Tell (Page 142)

Q.1 Can you think of any other way in which you use the warmth from your breath?

Ans. Yes, I can think of another way. When somebody gets hurt or there is redness in the eye, a part of handkerchief is warmed by blowing over it. The warm handkerchief is then used to provide warmth to the affected area.

Q.2 Fold a piece of cloth 3-4 times. Now bring it close to your mouth and blow hard on it. Did the cloth become warm?

Ans. Yes, the cloth became warm.

Q.3 Balishtiye saw that the woodcutter was trying to cool the hot potatoes by blowing on them. What would have happened if he had eaten the potatoes without cooling them?

Ans. If the woodcutter had eaten the potatoes without cooling them, his mouth would have burnt.

Q.4 Have you ever burnt your tongue when you ate or drank something that was too hot? How do you cool some food when it is too hot?

Ans. Yes, I have burnt my tongue many times when I was having soup. I keep the food under a fan for sometimes or I blow over it to cool the soup.

Q.5 If you were to cool these three hot things– *dal, roti,* rice– in which ways would you do so?

Ans. These hot things *dal, roti,* rice can be cooled either by blowing over them or keeping them under the fan for a while. They should be put in wide containers so that they cool down easily.

Q.6 **Picture 1**

Mini tried to cool her tea by blowing on it. Which do you think will be hotter– Mini's tea or the air she blew from her mouth?

Ans. I think Mini's tea would be hotter than the air she blew from her mouth.

Picture 2

Sonu was feeling very cold. He kept blowing on to his hands. Now think and write, which will be cooler– Sonu's hands or his breath?

Ans. Sonu's hands will be cooler than his breath.

Q.7 For what other things do you blow air from your mouth?

Ans. I blow air from my mouth for the following activities

- Whistling
- Removing dust from something
- Cleaning the spectacles
- Blowing bubbles
- Filling air in the balloons

Blow in Different Ways (Page 143)

Q.1 Make whistles of the things given below. Write in a sequence – from the loudest to the softest whistle.

- Wrapper of a toffee
- A leaf
- A balloon
- The cap of a pen
- Any other thing

Ans. Do it yourself.

Page 144

Q.1 Have you seen people playing different musical instruments like *flute*, *dholak*, *been* ...., *guitar*, *mridang*, etc. Can you recognise their sounds with your eyes closed? Find out more about these musical instruments. Collect their pictures too.

Ans. Yes, I can recognise the sounds of some instruments like *flute*, *dholak*, *been*, *guitar*, *mridang*, etc. with my eyes closed.

Some of the instruments are discussed below

- **Flute** It is a type of wind instrument made from bamboo. It is played by blowing air in it.
- **Dholak** Dholak is made of wood and membrane of leather. It is played by beating on the membrane with sticks.
- **Been** It is a type of wind instrument made by dried pumpkin.
- **Guitar** It is made of metal strings and wood.

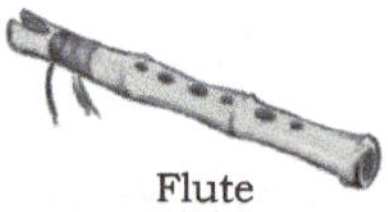
Flute

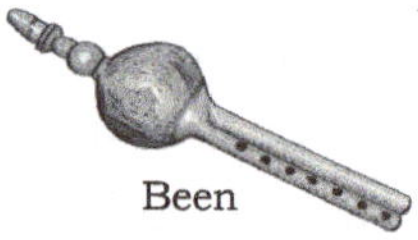
Been

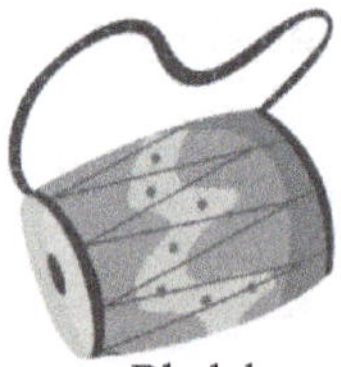
Dholak

Guitar

Write (Page 144)

Q.1 Can you name some things which produce melodious or pleasing sounds when we blow into them.

Ans. Some wind instruments like saxophone, mouth organ, flute, *shehnai*, etc. *produce* pleasing sounds when we blow into them.

Do this and Discuss (Page 144)

Q.1 Have you seen someone blowing on their spectacles to wipe them clean? How does the air from the mouth help in cleaning the spectacles?

Ans. Yes, I have seen my grandfather blowing on his spectacles to wipe them clean. The air that is blown from the mouth is hotter than the surface of the glass. When the air touches the cold glass, it turns into fine water droplets because there is moisture in the air. These droplets help in cleaning the spectacles.

Q.2 Take a glass. Bring it near your mouth and blow hard on it. Do this two or three times. Does the glass look hazy?

Ans. Yes, the glass looks hazy after blowing on it two to three times.

Q.3 Put your hand on your chest. When you breathe in, does your chest come out or go in.

Ans. My chest comes out when I breathe in.

Q.4 Measure your chest

- Take a deep breath in
- Ask your friend to measure your chest with a thread. Measurement___________
- Now breathe out. Again ask your friend to measure your chest. Measurement_____
- Was there any difference in the two measurements of your chest?

Ans. Do it yourself.

How many Breaths in One Minute? (Page 145)

Q.1 Put your finger under your nose. Can you feel any air when you breathe out from your nose?

Ans. Yes, I can feel the air when I breathe out from my nose.

Q.2 Count how many times in one minute do you breathe in and breathe out.

Ans. In one minute, I breathe in and out about 20-25 times.

Q.3 Jump 30 times. Did you feel breathless?

Ans. Yes, I felt breathless on jumping 30 times.

Q.4 Now again count how many times in one minute you breathed in and out.

Ans. I breathed in and out about 30 times now.

Q.5 What was the difference in your count before and after jumping?

Ans. I breathed in and out around 10 times more after jumping than what I normally did. Jumping increased my rate of breathing.

The Clock Inside You (Page 145)

Q.1 You have all heard the 'tick tick' of the clock. Have you seen a doctor using a stethoscope to listen to our chest? What do you think she hears? Where is the sound coming from? Is there a clock inside your chest that keeps ticking away?

Ans. Yes, I have seen doctors using a stethoscope to listen to our chest. I think the doctor hears the heartbeat. The sound is coming from our heart.

No, there is not any clock. Heart is not a clock. It is an organ on the left side of chest that pumps blood.

Q.2 Do you want to listen to your heartbeat? Take a rubber tube as long as the distance from your shoulder to your elbow. At one end of the tube fix a funnel. Place the funnel on the left side of your chest. Put the other end of the tube to your ear. Listen carefully. Did you hear a *dhak dhak* sound?

Ans. Yes, I heard a *dhak dhak* sound.

Snake Tells the Flow of Air (Page 146)

Q.1 For this take a round paper 10-15 cm wide. Cut this paper in a spiral shape (as shown in picture (1). To hold this snake, tie a thread on both sides.

Tie a knot or a button to make it hang. Now the snake is ready to move.

Hang this snake near a hot thing. For this you can take hot tea, water or a burning candle. Now see from the top, in which direction the snake moves. Whenever the air flows upwards it will move in a clockwise direction. When the air flows downwards the snake will move in the opposite direction. Stand with this snake below a fan. Look in which direction it moves. Take this paper snake to different places and observe its movement.

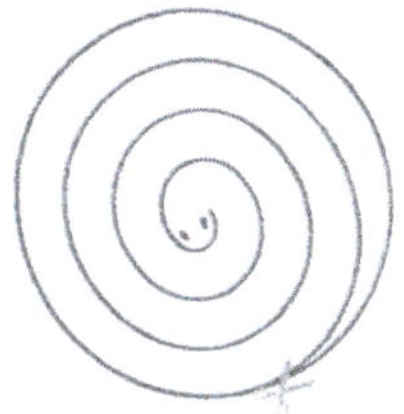

Picture 1

Ans. When the snake is kept below the fan, it moves in an anti-clockwise direction. This happens because the air is moving in downward direction.

Q.2 Can you understand from the movement of the snake - if the air is moving upwards or downwards?

Ans. When the snake is moving in a clockwise direction, it means the air is moving upwards. When the snake is moving anti-clockwise, the air is moving downwards.

What we have Learnt (Page 146)

Q.1 While playing, Amit hit a wall. His forehead was swollen. *Didi* immediately folded a scarf (4-5 times), blew on it and kept it on Amit's forehead. Why do you think *didi* did this?

Ans. When the air is blown on scarf, it becomes warm. Pressing the affected area i.e Amit's forehead with the warm scarf will give some warmth and relief to Amit. That's why *didi* did this.

Q.2 We blow to cool hot things as well as to warm them. Give examples of each.

Ans. We blow to cool hot things like tea, coffee, hot food items, etc. We blow to warm the cool things like our hands in winter, part of the handkerchief, scarf, etc.

CHAPTER 16 WHO WILL DO THIS WORK?

About the Chapter

It tells the stories of Gandhiji and Dr. Babasaheb Ambedkar, who fought against untouchability. In society, certain jobs, like cleaning, are often done by people from specific communities known as 'untouchables', who face poverty and discrimination.

Gandhiji believed in the value of all work and required everyone in his ashram to participate in all tasks, including cleaning the toilets. He emphasised that no work is too small.

Dr. Ambedkar faced discrimination himself when a barber refused to cut his hair but he would cut a cow's hair. This experience inspired him to fight for justice for untouchables. He later played a key role in drafting the Indian Constitution after Independence, advocating for equality and rights for all.

GLOSSARY

Ashram A place where old people or saints live a very simple life and do everything themselves.

Community A group of people living in the same place or having a particular characteristic in common.

Untouchability An old practice in which touching a person from backward caste was considered bad.

Justice Quality of being fair and treating people equally.

Constitution A set of laws made to provide the basic rules to run the state or country.

NCERT FOLDER

Page 147

Q.1 Have you ever seen such scenes around you?

Ans. Yes, I have seen such scenes around me.

Q.2 Have you ever thought of people who do this work? What is our responsibility to keep the place clean?

Ans. Yes. Sometimes, I think of the people who do this work.

We also have a responsibility towards keeping the places clean. We can help by throwing our garbage in bins and not throwing it here and there

Q.3 Why do you think people need to do this kind of work?

Ans. People need to do this kind of work due to poverty.

Write (Page 148)

Talk with people who do the cleaning job around your house and school.

Q.1 Since when have they been doing this work?

Ans. They have been doing this work for 15-20 years.

Q.2 How much have they studied?

Ans. Most of them have studied till Class 5 or 8. Some of them have not studied at all.

Q.3 Have they tried to look for some other work?

Ans. No, they have not tried to look for some other work.

Q.4 Did the elders in their family also do this work?

Ans. Yes, the elders in their family also did this work.

Q.5 What kind of difficulties do they face in doing this work?

Ans. They face many health-related difficulties by doing this work. The garbage has mosquitoes and flies on it which makes them sick.

Page 149

Q.1 What are the different kinds of work being done in this drawing? List any five of these.

Ans. Five different kinds of work being done in the drawing are

- Milking a cow
- Sweeping the road
- Teaching the students
- Driving a bus
- Rag picking

Q.2 If you were asked to do any five jobs shown in this picture, which would you choose? Why?

Ans. I would choose the following five jobs

- Teacher
- Doctor
- Shopkeeper
- Scientist
- Artist

I want to take up a job which I enjoy and where I can earn good money. I need to make my parents proud by getting a respectable job.

Q.3 Which five jobs would you not choose? Why?

Ans. I would not choose the following jobs

- Sweeper
- Labourer
- Hawker
- Construction worker
- Gatekeeper

I want to do a respectable job so that I can earn good money and respect, and make my parents proud.

Discuss (Page 150)

Q.1 What kinds of work or jobs do people not want to do? Why?

Ans. People do not want to do jobs which require hard work and physical labour like cleaning, sweeping, guarding a door, etc. This is because they want to take up jobs which require mental ability and are well-paying.

Q.2 So, who does this kind of work? Why do people do this kind of work that others do not want to do?

Ans. People who are poor and are not able to study in their life do this kind of work. They cannot study because of poverty. Lack of education makes them unsuitable for other jobs.

Imagine (Page 150)

Q.1 What would happen if nobody did this work? If nobody cleared the garbage lying outside your school or your house for one week, then what would happen?

Ans. If nobody did this work, it would create problems for everyone.

If nobody picked up the rash, the garbage would get collected outside our school and houses. It will start rotting and give off a foul smell. It will also attract insects like mosquitoes and flies, which will spread diseases. The place will look very ugly.

Tell (Page 151-152)

Q.1 Why did Gandhiji and his team start doing the job of cleaning? What do you think about this?

Ans. Gandhiji and his team started doing the job of cleaning to bring a change in the mindset of people about this kind of work. He respected all kinds of jobs and wanted people to do the same. He wanted people to understand that a particular job is not meant only for a particular person, caste or community.

Q.2 Do you know any such people in your area who try to help others in solving their problems? Find out and discuss in the class.

Ans. Yes, my neighbour always helps other people in solving their problems. He always gives books to poor children who cannot afford them.

Q.3 Guests at Gandhiji's Ashram had to learn this work also. If you were one of these guests, what would you do?

Ans. If I was one of these guests, I would happily learn the work and do it everyday.

Q.4 What are the toilet arrangements in your house? Where is the toilet? Inside the house, or outside? Who cleans the toilet?

Ans. Do it yourself.

Q.5 How did the man who was returning from the toilet behave with Mahadevbhai? Why did he behave like this?

Ans. The man who was returning from the toilet behaved in a very insulting way with Mahadevbhai.

He behaved like this because he thought that cleaning the toilets was dirty work and a menial job. He considered people who do these jobs as 'untouchables'.

Q.6 How do people generally behave with those people who clean toilets and drains? Write.

Ans. People generally behave very rudely and insultingly with the people who clean toilets and drains. People consider them as untouchables and do not talk to them.

Q.7 Narayan and Gandhiji discussed all this many years ago. Have things changed now?

Ans. Yes, things have changed a lot nowadays. Untouchability has almost finished from society and people have started respecting every type of work. Every person is equal as awareness among people has increased.

Tell (Page 153)

Q.1 Who does the cleaning in your school? What all has to be cleaned?

Ans. There are special people like sweepers employed who do the cleaning in my school. Classrooms, playground, terrace and toilets have to be cleaned.

Q.2 Do all children like you help in this? If yes, how?

Ans. Yes, most of the children help in this by keeping their classroom and other surroundings clean.

They throw the waste in the dustbin and do not litter around.

Q.3 If all do not help, why not?

Ans. Some children who do not help think that the work of cleaning is dirty and not good.

Q.4 Do all children do all kinds of work?

Ans. No, all children do not do all kinds of work because they consider some work as bad and menial.

Q.5 Do they sometimes have to miss classes to do this work?

Ans. No, they do not have to miss classes to do this work because it takes 5-10 minutes per day to do it.

Q.6 Do the girls and boys do the same kinds of work?

Ans. Yes, both girls and boys do the same kinds of work.

Q.7 What all work do you do at home?

Ans. Do it yourself.

Q.8 Is the work done by boys and girls, men and women the same?

Ans. No, the work done by boys and girls, men and women is not the same. Some work like cooking, sewing, washing, ironing, etc are supposed to be done by girls and women.

Other works like repairing faults, repairing the car, lifting heavy things, etc are supposed to be done by men and boys.

Q.9 Would you like to bring some change? What kind?

Ans. Yes, I would like to bring some changes.

Men/boys should also do the work that is supposed to be done by girls/women. Women should also do men's work. There should be equality in division of work.

Discuss (Page 153)

Q.1 Do people look at different kinds of work in the same way? If not, why is this so? Why is it important to bring change?

Ans. No, people do not look at different kinds of work in the same way.

They consider some works like cleaning, sweeping, etc as dirty and menial.

It is important to bring change because every work is equal and important for society. No job is useless. People should learn to respect each other's work and treat them equally.

Q.2 Gandhiji's favourite song (*bhajan*) is given here. This *bhajan* is in Gujarati. Try to understand the meaning of these lines with the help of your elders.

Think about these lines.

वैष्णव जन तो तेणे कहिए जे पीड़ पराई जाणे रे,
पर दुःखे अपमान सहे जे मन अभिमान ना आणे रे

Ans. The meaning of these lines is An ideal person is someone who understands the pain of others. He is willing to insult and take away suffering from other people's lives. An ideal person should have any ego in his mind.

What we have Learnt (Page 153)

Q.1 Gandhiji used to say that every person should do every kind of work. What do you feel about this? If everyone followed this, what are the things that would change? What are some changes that will happen in your own house?

Ans. Do it yourself.

CHAPTER 17 ACROSS THE WALL

About the Chapter

This chapter is about gender inequality and how girls face different challenges compared to boys. It tells the story of the Nagpada Basketball Team in Maharashtra, which includes girls like Afsana, Zarin, Khushnoor and Afreen. These girls worked hard to play basketball and had to convince their parents to let them join the team.

They were the first girls' team in their area and people used to watch them play with curiosity. Their coach, Noor Khan, helped them learn the game and stay motivated. Unity and cooperation is important for playing in a team. Now, they play for the Maharashtra State team. Even though they have made progress, girls still face challenges, like having to go home right after the game and help with household work, while boys don't have to do the same.

GLOSSARY

Association A group of people who come together for a common purpose or goal.
Equipment Tools or objects that are used for a particular purpose.
Coach Someone who teaches and helps others to improve their skills in a game.
Dodge To avoid something quickly by using a trick or a sudden movement.
United It means joined together or combined as one for a common purpose or a common man.
Cooperation It means working together with others to achieve a common goal.

NCERT FOLDER

Find Out (Page 155)

Q.1 Is there any place to play near your house?

Ans. Yes, there is a ground near my house where children play.

Q.2 What do people play there? Who plays there?

Ans. People play all sorts of games there like cricket, badminton, football, basketball, kho-kho, etc. Mostly, children of all ages play there.

Q.3 Do the children of your age also get a chance to play there?

Ans. Yes, the children of my age also get to play there.

Q.4 What other things happen at this place?

Ans. Many activities happen at this place. Some adults come here for jogging, walking, yoga. Many people just sit under the sheds and enjoy fresh air.

Tell (Page 156)

Q.1 Has anyone ever stopped you from playing some games? Which games?

Ans. Yes, I have been stopped from playing games like cricket and football.

Q.2 Who stopped you and why? What did you do then?

Ans. My grandparents stopped me. They wanted me to focus on studies and not waste my time playing games.

I convinced them and told them that I can do both.

Q.3 Did anyone help you and encourage you to play?

Ans. Yes, my parents and my brother help me and encourage me to play.

Discuss (Page 158)

Q.1 Do girls and boys play different types of games in your school or neighbourhood? If yes, then which games do the boys play and which do the girls play?

Ans. Yes, girls and boys play different types of games.

Boys play games like cricket, football, hockey and basketball and girls play games like badminton, table tennis, kho-kho, etc.

Q.2 Do you think that there is any difference between the games and the way they are played by boys and girls?

Ans. Yes, there is some difference between the games that are played by boys and games that are played by girls.

Boys play games that need more physical strength while girls play games that need less physical strength. Girls prefer easy and simple games.

Q.3 Should the games for boys and the girls be different? What do you think?

Ans. No, the games for boys and girls should not be different.

I think that everyone should be allowed to play all the games. There should not be any difference in the games that the girls and boys choose to play.

Write (Page 159)

Q.1 Have you ever played as part of a team of your class, school or neighbourhood? Whom did you play with? What game did you play?

Ans. Yes, I have played as a part of a team in my class. I played with my friends and classmates. We played volleyball.

Q.2 What is the difference between playing for yourself and for the team?

Ans. Playing for yourself means playing selfishly only for yourself. Playing for the team means that you play as a part of the team for a common goal.

Q.3 While playing in a team would you like to play for yourself or for the team? Why?

Ans. I would like to play for the team while playing in a team. This is because the team has to win and it can only do so with the efforts of all the people in the team.

Q.4 Is your team like the team Afsana played with at Sholapur or like the Nagpada team? How?

Ans. Our team is like the Nagpada team. The girls in the Nagpada team support and respect each other. They do not insult the members of the team.

In our team, we cooperate with each other and play together. We help and motivate each other. So, our team is like the Nagpada team.

Discuss (Page 160)

Q.1 Have you ever taken part in some game or competition from your school or area? How did you feel?

Ans. Yes, I have taken part in a game. I felt very happy and excited because I was playing for my school team in an inter-school competition.

Q.2 Did you go to some other place to play? What was that place like? How did you like going to that place?

Ans. Yes, I along with my team went to another school in Lucknow. It was a very beautiful place with big open buildings. I enjoyed going there, especially Bhul Bhulaiya in Lucknow.

Q.3 Have you seen matches being played between India and other countries? Which ones?

Ans. Yes, I have seen many cricket matches being played between India and other countries.

Page 161

Q.4 We all know about the cricketers of India, and we all like them. Do people also know and like the Indian players who play some other games? (Yes or No). What do you feel about it? Do you know the players of the Indian football or kabaddi team?

Ans. Yes, we know some other players who play other games. They are very popular and very good players.

Yes, I know the players of the Indian football and kabaddi team. Footbal team players are Sunil Chhetri, Mehtab Hossain, Karanjit Singh, etc. Kabaddi team players are Rakesh Kumar, Anup Kumar, etc.

Discuss (Page 162)

Q.1 What would happen if girls are not allowed to play games, to study or do some other work of their choice?

Ans. It will not be good for the girls if they are not allowed to play games, to study or do some other work of their choice. This will not be fair to them. They will not be able to use their full talent. This will also restrict their physical activity.

Q.2 How would you feel if you were not allowed to take part in some game or drama?

Ans. If I was not allowed to take part in some game or drama, I would be very sad. I would feel demotivated .

Q.3 Have you heard of any women players? Name them and the games they play.

Ans. Yes, I have heard of many women players. Some of them are

- PV Sindhu (Badminton)
- Saina Nehwal (Badminton)
- PT Usha (Athletics)
- Sania Mirza (Tennis)
- Manu Bhaker (Shooting)
- Mary Kom (Boxing)

Q.4 In which areas other than sports have you heard of women getting recognition.

Ans. Women have got recognition in many fields like

- Indira Gandhi - First Woman Prime Minister of India
- Pratibha Patil - First Woman President of India
- Kiran Bedi- First Woman IPS officer
- Bacchendri Pal - First Indian woman to climb Mount Everest

Q.5 Are these women less known than men? Why?

Ans. No, these women are not less known than men. They are equally popular as men. This is so because they have done something that no one expected them to do. They showed that women and men are equal.

Q.6 How would you find the world to be, if girls never got a chance to take part in games, drama or dance? How would you feel if such a thing happened to boys?

Ans. If girls never got a chance to take part in games, drama or dance, it would be an uneven and unfair world where only boys get the opportunities. Similarly, if such a thing happened to boys, it would be a difficult problem.

Q.7 Do you know of any woman or girl who you would want to be like when you grow up? (Think of names other than a film actor or a model).

Ans. Yes, I want to be like Manu Bhaker when I grow up.

Think and Write (Page 164)

Q.1 The newspaper report said, "Afsana has jumped over the wall. The gender wall that her mother had put up for her". Think and write in your own words, what was this wall? What do you understand about 'gender bias'?

Ans. Gender bias means different treatment for boys and girls. Gender wall refers to the restrictions placed on Afsana because of her gender.

In India, girls are not allowed to study, play or opt a career of their choice. They are forced to do only household work. Afsana has suffered from gender bias. Her mother treated her differently from her brother. She wanted Afsana to do only house work. By managing to be a star of the basketball team, she has broken the wall of gender bias which was put by her mother.

What we have Learnt (Page 164)

Q.1 Should games for boys and girls be different? Think and write what you feel.

Ans. Games for boys and girls should not be different. Both should be allowed to play all the games. Physical activity is equally important for both girls and boys. By playing games, a child develops both mentally and physically. Overall growth and development is important for both boys and girls. That's why they should play similar types of games.

Q.2 If you are made the leader of a team, how will you prepare your team?

Ans. If I am made the leader of my team, I will do the following things

- I will encourage the team members to play with hard work.
- I will promote the value of cooperation.
- I will ask the team to support each other.
- I will tell them the value of team spirit.

CHAPTER 18 NO PLACE FOR US ?

About the Chapter

This chapter is about a family that had to leave their village because a dam was built nearby. It shows how development can change the lives of people in rural areas and the problems they face. Jatryabhai was born in Khedi village, where his family had lived for many years. Life in Khedi was simple; people farmed and collected wild fruits, roots and wood to use and sell. When the dam was built on a nearby river, Jatrya's family had to move to Sinduri village.

Sinduri was very different from Khedi. The roads were made of coal tar and everything was expensive. The houses were small and even though there were hospitals and schools, they didn't have good facilities. After some time in Sinduri, Jatrya moved his family to Mumbai, where life was even harder. They had to pay for water and Jatrya's young son, Sidya also had to work to help the family. Jatrya was worried that they would have to move from Mumbai because they didn't have a proper place to stay in such a big city.

GLOSSARY

Gurgle A sound that is made by flowing water like a river.
Murmur A low, continuous sound.
Dam A structure built across a river or stream to control the flow of water.
Imitating The act of copying someone or something.

NCERT FOLDER

Think and Tell (Page 166)

Q.1 Jatrya felt alone, even in a crowd of people. Have you ever felt like this?

Ans. Yes, I have felt alone in a crowd of people. When I moved to a new school due to my father's transfer, I felt alone even in a crowd of people. I did not know anyone there.

Q.2 Imagine how it feels to leave one's own place and go far away to live in a new place?

Ans. It must be very hard to leave one's own place and go far away to live in a new place.

Everything is unknown and new. You know nobody in the new place. The people and the place will look very strange.

Q.3 Why do you think families like that of Jatrya's are coming to big cities?

Ans. Families like that of Jatrya are coming to big cities because there are very few opportunities and facilities in villages. People want to earn more which they can in cities.

Q.4 Have you seen any children (in your school or neighbourhood) who also go to work?

Ans. Yes, I have seen many children who also go to work.

Q.5 What kind of work do they do? Why do they have to work?

Ans. They do different types of work such as cleaning the car, rag picking, etc. Many children sell different items at traffic signals. Some also work at tea stalls.

They have to work because they have to support their families by earning more money.

Tell (Page 167)

Q.1 In Khedi village what all did children learn?

Ans. In Khedi village, children learnt many things while working with their elders like dancing, playing flute and *dhol*, making pots of clay and bamboo, recognising birds and imitating their sounds.

Q.2 What do you learn from your elders?

Ans. We learn many things from our elders like

- respecting others
- being disciplined
- helping everyone
- maintaining good relation with everyone

Q.3 Jatrya learnt so many things in Khedi. How many of those would be useful for him in Mumbai?

Ans. Some of the skills that Jatrya learnt in Khedi would be useful for him in Mumbai for earning money. For example, fish catching, selling goods in the market, playing instruments like dhol and flute, etc.

Q.4 Do you hear the sounds of birds everyday? Which ones?

Ans. Yes, I hear the sounds of some birds everyday.

They are sparrows, crow, cuckoo bird, etc.

Q.5 Can you imitate the sound of any bird? Show how.

Ans. Yes, I can imitate the sound of cuckoo and crow.

Q.6 What are some of the sounds that you hear everyday, but the people of Khedi may not be hearing?

Ans. The sounds that I hear everyday which the people of Khedi may not have heard are honking of vehicles, sounds of ambulances, sound of trains, etc.

Q.7 Have you experienced silence? When and where?

Ans. I do experience silence when I go to a temple or church.

Discuss and Tell (Page 169)

Q.1 Many people in Jatrya's village did not agree to move away from their land and forest. Why? They had to leave even though they didn't want to. Why?

Ans. The land and forest in the village were full of memories for people living there. Their families had been living there for a long time. They were connected to the place.

They had to leave because government officials and police forced them to leave the place.

They promised the villagers that they would be sent to a new place with better facilities.

Q.2 In Khedi, how many people were there in Jatrya's family? When he thought about his family who all came to his mind?

Ans. There were three people in Jatrya's family: his mother, his father and himself.

When he thought about his family, his future wife and children also came to his mind.

Q.3 Who all come to your mind when you think about your family?

Ans. When I think about my family, my grandparents, parents, uncles and aunts, brother and sister, and cousins come to my mind.

Q.4 Have you heard of people who don't want to be moved from their old place? Talk about them.

Ans. Yes, my grandparents do not want to be moved from their old house in the village. They want to live in their old place because they enjoy the open and fresh air there. They do not feel comfortable in cities.

Q.5 Do you know some people who have never been to school? Do you also know of any place where there is no school?

Ans. Yes, the helper in our house has never been to school. There is no school in some small villages in my area.

Imagine (Page 169)

Q.1 Think of the kinds of difficulties people have to face where a dam is being built.

Ans. People living in the area where the dam is being built have to face many difficulties.

Some of them are

- Many houses and villages get destroyed.
- Many people are forced to leave their place and shift to a new place where there are less facilities.
- They have to start their life again and face many new challenges.

Q.2 Draw a picture of Khedi village and a picture of Jatrya's dream village. Discuss the differences between them. Also look at the pictures your friends have drawn.

Ans. Difference between Khedi village and Jatrya's dream village are

Khedi village	Jatrya's dream village
Houses are made of bamboo, mud and grass.	Houses are made of brick and cement.
There is no electricity.	There is electricity supply and good poles with street lights.
There is very little drinking water.	There is a proper water supply.
There is no school or hospital.	There is a primary school and a primary health centre.

Write (Page 171)

Q.1 Was Sinduri like the village of Jatrya's dreams?

Ans. Sinduri was not like the village of Jatrya's dreams.

Q.2 What difference did he find between Sinduri and his dream village?

Ans. There was a lot of difference between Sinduri and his dream village. The houses in Sinduri were made of tin sheets. They were very weak. There was electricity only for some time in the day. The hospitals had no doctors. The teachers in the school did not care for children. Jatrya had to burn an old tyre as fuel to cook food. There was no open space. But in his dream village, everything was perfect.

Q.3 Have you ever been to anyone's house as an 'unwanted guest'? How did you feel?

Ans. Yes, once I went to my new friend's house to do a group project. Nobody in his family welcomed me. I felt very strange, like an 'unwanted guest'.

Q.4 What all does your family do, when you have guests at home for a few days?

Ans. When we have guests at home for a few days, we make sure that they are comfortable.

We take good care of them, give them respect and treat them with love. My mother makes special food for them. My parents take them to visit popular places in the city. My family members spend time with them so that they enjoy their stay.

Think (Page 172)

Q.1 What had Jatryabhai thought while moving to Mumbai? Did he find Mumbai as he had imagined?

Ans. Jatryabhai felt like an 'unwanted guest' in Sinduri village. He thought if he had to feel like that in Sinduri, he might as well leave the village and move to the city. He did not find Mumbai as he had imagined. It was very difficult to live in Mumbai.

Q.2 What kind of school do you think Jatrya's children would be going to in Mumbai?

Ans. I think Jatrya's children would be going to a government aided school in Mumbai.

Find Out and Write (Page 173)

Q.1 Do you know of any family that has come to your town after having moved out of their place? Talk to them and find out:

Ans. Yes, the maidservant who comes to our house has come from a small village in Bangladesh.

(a) From where have they come? Why did they have to come here?

Ans. She and her family has come from a small village in Bangladesh. They came to Delhi as refugees.

(b) What kind of place did they live in there? How do they find this new place compared to the old one?

Ans. They used to live in a *kuchcha* house in the village. In the new place, they are living in a small room made of tin in a slum area. The area is very unhygienic as there is a drain near it.

(c) Is their language and way of living any different from that of the people here? In what ways?

Ans. Yes, they mostly speak Bengali so they are uncomfortable in speaking Hindi.
They are managing to communicate with people in broken Hindi.

(d) Learn some words from their language and write them in your notebook.

Ans. Some words which people from Bengal use in their language are

- *Aami* - I myself
- *Macch* - Fish
- *Bhat* - Rice
- *Bondhu* - Friend

(e) Do they know how to make some things that you cannot make? What?

Ans. Yes, they make beautiful toys using dry palm leaves. I do not know how to make them.

Q.2 Have you ever read or heard of a city slum being removed? How do you feel about this?

Ans. I have read about a city slum being removed from near Yamuna river due to some construction work.

I feel this is very unfair to poor people who live in slums. For them, finding a shelter is very difficult. I feel very bad hearing this type of news.

Q.3 People also shift from one place to another when they get transferred in their jobs? How do they feel then?

Ans. Transfers from one place to another are a part of many jobs. It is always difficult to leave one place and start a new life at a new place. It involves a lot of stress like packing, shifting, finding a place, etc. A child has to move to a new school where he knows no one. It is very challenging.

Debate (Page 173)

Q.1 Some people say that– "The city people do not create garbage. Cities are dirty because of the slums." How do you feel about this? Discuss and debate between yourselves.

Ans. It is unfair to put all blame on slum dwellers. City people also produce a lot of garbage and do not manage it well. Many people throw garbage on roads and litter at other places. Businesses in cities also generate a lot of waste.

What we have Learnt (Page 173)

Q.1 Like Jatrya's family, thousands of families come to stay in big cities for many different reasons. Do you think their life may be better in a big city from what it was before? Imagine how they feel in a big city.

Ans. Many people move to big cities due to many reasons. Their life is different from the village life and it is very challenging for them to survive. Cities may have many opportunities but people have to compromise with very less space in the cities. Poor people who cannot afford proper places are forced to leave unhygienically. They may be earning more in the big cities but they cannot save money because everything is very costly. There is also a difference in language and lifestyle. They feel very strange in a big city.

CHAPTER 19

A SEED TELLS A FARMER'S STORY

About the Chapter

This chapter is about how farming has changed from old ways to modern methods and the importance of different seeds and crops. Damjibhai was a farmer in Vangaam, Gujarat, who grew grains like bajra and vegetables during different seasons. He made a wooden box to store seeds so they could be passed down through generations. The villagers helped each other with farming and enjoyed a special dish called *undhiya* together in the winter.

Over time, many things changed. Canals brought water from a dam and electricity was introduced. Farmers started to grow crops that sold for better prices, like wheat and cotton, and bought new seeds instead of using stored ones. Damjibhai's son, Hasmukh, began using modern machines like tractors instead of bullocks and switched from cow dung to expensive fertilisers. They also had to spray medicines on crops to keep insects away and used hand pumps to get water. To pay for these things, farmers took loans from banks.

The soil got worse from growing the same crops and using chemicals, making it hard to make a living from farming. Hasmukh's son, Paresh, didn't want to be a farmer and the wooden seed box was now used to store screws and tools for the truck.

GLOSSARY

Compartments Separate sections or divisions within a larger space used to organise, store or protect things.

Harvest To collect or gather crops from the field especially for food.

Canal Small artificial rivers or waterways made by human beings which are used for irrigation.

Generation It is all the people in a group or country who are of a similar age.

Fertiliser Something added to soil to help plants grow better which provides essential nutrients that plants need for their growth.

Compost A natural fertiliser made by mixing things like food leftovers and peels, leaves.

NCERT FOLDER

Tell (Page 175)

Q.1 Are *rotis* made in your home? From which grains are they made?

Ans. Yes, *rotis* are made in my home. Mostly, they are made of wheat but sometimes maize is also used.

Q.2 Have you eaten *roti* made from *bajra* or *jowar*? Did you like these?

Ans. Yes, I have eaten *roti* made from *bajra* or *jowar*. I liked them.

Find Out and Write (Page 175)

Q.1 In your house what is done to protect grains and pulses from insects?

Ans. In my house, grains and pulses are kept in airtight jars and containers. My mother also dries them in the Sun to protect them against the insects.

Q.2 Which are the different festivals related to farming, celebrated in different seasons? Find out more about any one such festival and write in your notebook – The name of the festival, in which season is it celebrated, in which states of India, what special foods are made, is it celebrated only at home with the family, or together with many people.

Ans. Several festivals are related to farming such as Lohri, Baisakhi, Pongal, etc. They are celebrated in different states at different times of the year.

Baisakhi is celebrated in Punjab in the month of April. It is celebrated on 14th April every year. It marks the harvest season of Punjab. People make *Kadha prashad* and celebrate with folk dances like *Giddha* and *Bhangra*. It is celebrated as Bihu in Assam. Special dishes like *pitha* are made using *sesame* and *gud* in almost all states.

Q.2 Talk to the elders in your family and find out if there were some special foods cooked earlier that are not cooked any more?

Ans. My grandmother told me that *ladoos* of *sesame* seeds and jaggery were made at home.

Rice puff ladoos were also made at home. Now we buy *murmura ladoo* and *gajak* from the market.

Q.3 Find out about the crops– cereals, vegetables, pulses– that are grown in your area. Of those, is there anything that is famous across the country?

Ans. Many types of grains like rice, wheat, maize, potatoes, mangoes, litchi, bananas are grown in my area. Of these, wheat and mango are famous across the country.

Q.4 Can you recognise these grains?

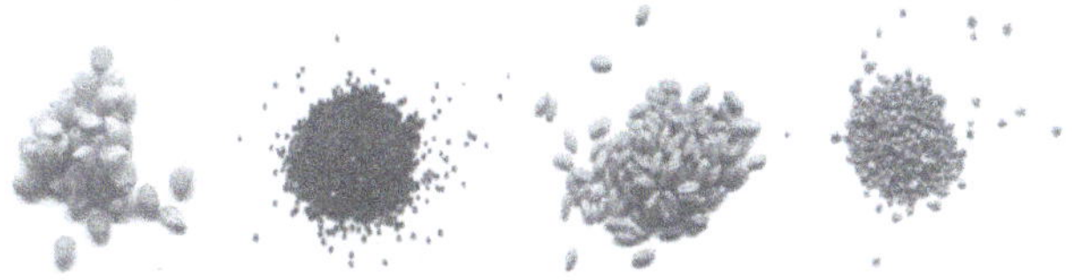

(i) (ii) (iii) (iv)

Ans. (i) Maize (ii) Mustard (iii) Wheat (iv) Bajra

Discuss (Page 177)

Q.1 The *bajra* seed saw differences in the way Damjibhai and Hasmukh did farming (for example, in irrigation, ploughing, etc). What were these differences?

Ans. Damijibhai and Hasmukh farmed in different ways

- Damijibhai used old methods like bullocks to plough the fields. He stored the grains and reused them in the next season.
- Hasmukh used modern techniques like tractors and electric motor pumps. He bought seeds from the market instead of storing them. He used expensive fertilisers for farming.

Q.2 Hasmukh said, "With profits from our fields, we can progress". What is your understanding of 'progress' ?

Ans. Progress means a better and comfortable lifestyle. People get better houses to live in. They get more nutritious food, good clothes to wear and good education. People will have all types of facilities like vehicles, air conditioners, etc.

Write (Page 177)

Q.1 What kind of progress would you like to see in your area?

Ans. I would like to see an overall progress in my area such as

- better roads
- cleanliness everywhere with no overflowing drains
- good public transport system
- big parks

Discuss and Think (Page 177-178)

Q.1 What can happen to Hasmukh's farm after some years?

Ans. Hasmukh's farm will lose soil fertility after some years because of chemical fertilisers. He can also lose money and fall in debt as he has taken loans to buy new equipment and tractors. He will not be able to work properly on his farm.

Q.2 Damjibhai's son Hasmukh chose to become a farmer like his father. Hasmukh's son Paresh is not a farmer, but a truck driver. Why would he have done so?

Ans. Paresh could see that his father was not doing well. Farming was not enough to earn a living. There was little or no profit in it. So, Paresh would have thought of not becoming a farmer.

Q.3 The seeds were not sure that what Hasmukh was talking about was really progress. What do you feel?

Ans. I think the seeds were right because this progress seen in agriculture can overexploit the soil. This leads to loss of fertility. It also depletes the groundwater and leaves little water for the future. A machine can do the work of many people but it leaves many people unemployed. It may seem like progress but it is not real progress.

Q.4 Have there been any changes near your area, which may be difficult to call 'progress' ? What changes are these? What are the different opinions about them?

Ans. Do it yourself.

Project Work (Page 179)

Q.1 What questions come to your mind about farmers and farming? Write some questions in your group and ask a farmer. For example, how many crops do they grow in a year? Which crop needs how much water?

Ans. Do it yourself.

Q.2 Visit a farm near your area. Observe and talk to the people there. Write a report.

Ans. Some people from my area visited a farm in the outskirts of the city. The farm primarily cultivated vegetables such as tomatoes, brinjal and *okra*. Traditional methods were employed, including manual labour and the use of organic fertilisers. There was a house on one edge of the farm where 5 people who take care of the farm live. It presented a beautiful colourful landscape. There are many packets of fertilisers kept in the farmhouse.

Journey of a bajra seed– from a field to a plate (Page 180-181)

Q.1 What can you see in each picture given above?

In picture 2 you can see the *bajra* cobs in the mortar (*okhli*, used for crushing). The cobs are crushed with a pestle (*moosli*) and the seeds are separated from the cob. You can see the separated seeds in picture 3. Now this work is also done by big machines, like threshers. We call both these as different 'technologies' using our hands or big machines–to crush the seeds.

Ans. Picture 1: A woman in the fields is separating and taking out the cobs from *bajra* crops.

Picture 2: The *bajra* cobs are kept in the mortar. They will be beaten using a pestle to separate grains.

Picture 3: *Bajra* seeds are kept on a plate.

Picture 4: A woman is grinding *bajra* seeds to make flour. She is utilising *chakki* for it.

Picture 5: Bajra flour is ready.

Picture 6: Dough has been made from *bajra* flour.

Picture 7: Chapattis are being prepared.

Picture 8: Chapati is being cooked on tawa.

Picture 9: Ready chapatis are served on a plate.

Q.2 What technology could have been used to cut the stem in picture 1?

Ans. The stem is cut with the sickle.

Q.3 What do you think is being done in the grinder (*chakki*) in picture 4?

Ans. The grinder is used for making flour out of seeds.

Q.4 What ways (technologies) would have been used to do the work shown in picture 5 and 6?

Ans. *Bajra* flour is being made in picture 5. It is usually made by grinding the seeds.

In picture six, dough is made by mixing water with the flour.

Q.5 You can see that the dough is ready in picture 6. When do you think a sieve (*chhalni*) would have been used?

Ans. A sieve would have been used while sieving the flour so that the husk would get separated from the flour.

Q.6 Discuss each step in detail, in any language you wish to use.

Ans. The steps are as follows

(i) Ripe *bajra* cobs are harvested manually with a sickle.

(ii) The cobs are beaten to separate the *bajra* grains out of it.

(iii) The *bajra* grains are cleaned and sieved to separate the dust particles.

(iv) A grinder (chakki) is used to make flour out of *bajra* grains.

(v) The flour obtained is sieved to remove the husk and the other unwanted particles out of it.

(vi) A dough is prepared from the flour by mixing water in it.

(vii) Small *rotis* are made from the dough.

(viii) The *rotis* are baked on a *tawa* with the help of heat.

(ix) The baked *rotis* are ready to eat.

What we have Learnt (Page 181)

Q.1 There have been many changes over time in our food. What can this mean? Use the seed story and what you know from your elders to explain.

Ans. Do it yourself.

Q.2 What would happen if all the farmers were to use only one kind of seed and grow only one kind of crop?

Ans. Do it yourself.

CHAPTER 20 WHOSE FORESTS ?

About the Chapter

This chapter is about forest people called Adivasis and how important forests are for everyone. It tells the true story of Suryamani, a girl who loved the forest since she was little. Every Sunday, she takes children from her community to teach them about the forests. Suryamani's family had a small field that couldn't support them anymore. Her uncle, Maniya, helped her go to a school in Bishanpur, where she didn't have to pay for fees, uniforms or books. She worked very hard and became the first girl in her village to finish her B.A. with a scholarship.

In college, Suryamani met a journalist named Vasavi didi and worked on the Jharkhand Jungle Bachao Andolan, a movement to save the forests. When she was 21, Suryamani and her husband, Bijoy, opened a centre called 'Torang,' where people could sing, enjoy music, and learn about forests and Kuduk traditions. Suryamani fights for everyone's rights. The government has also made a law called the Right to Forest Act in 2007 to protect the rights of people who live in forests.

GLOSSARY

Contractor Someone who takes the job to provide materials and people for any labour work.
Community A group of people who live in the same area or share common interests, beliefs or experiences.
Scholarship Some amount of money which is awarded to extraordinary students for financial help during their study.
Journalist Someone who writes and collects stories for newspapers, magazines or TV channels.
Weeds Wild unwanted plants which grow with crops or on an empty piece of land.

NCERT FOLDER

Discuss (Page 183)

Q.1 What do you think is a forest?

Ans. Forest is a vast area covered thickly with trees of different varieties. It is a home for many animals, birds and insects.

Q.2 If someone grew lots of trees close to each other, would this become a forest?

Ans. No, if someone grew lots of trees to each other, this would not become a forest. Forest is thicker than a green cover and it has a vast area.

Find Out and Write (Page 183)

Q.1 Other than trees what all is there in a forest?

Ans. There are small plants, weeds, birds, animals and other insects in the forest.

Q.2 Do all forests have similar types of trees? How many trees can you identify?

Ans. No, all forests do not have similar types of trees. Different forests have different trees. I can identify a few trees like mango, banyan, *neem*, *peepal*, etc.

Q.3 Suryamani says, "If the forests are not there, we too will not remain". Why so?

Ans. Forests are important for human beings. They help in maintaining the balance in the environment. We get a lot of products like wood, herbs and raw materials from the forests. Many tribal people like *adivasis* depend on the forest. It is also home for many birds and animals. That's why Suryamani is right when she says this.

Think and Write (Page 184)

Q.1 Do you know anyone who loves the forest?

Ans. Yes, my younger sister loves the forest.

Q.2 The contractor did not allow Suryamani's people to go into the forest. Why?

Ans. The contractor did not allow Suryamani's people to go into the forest and use it because he might be cutting the trees to sell in the market. He did not want local people to use the forest resources so that he could earn maximum profit.

Q.3 Is there any place around your area which you feel should be open to everyone, but where people are not allowed to go?

Ans. Yes, there is a lake garden in my area where people are not allowed to go. This is because of some security reasons. I think it should be open to everyone.

Discuss (Page 184)

Q.1 Who do you think the forest belongs to?

Ans. Forest belongs to everyone. It is a 'collective bank'.

Q.2 Bhudhiyamai said – "Forest is our 'collective bank' – not yours or mine alone." Are there other things which are our collective wealth? So if someone uses more, everyone would suffer?

Ans. Yes, there are some things like natural resources which are our collective wealth. For example, groundwater, minerals, rivers and seas, fossil fuels, etc. If someone uses more, the future generations will suffer.

Think and Write (Page 185)

Q.1 Do you have a friend with whom you can share everything?

Ans. Yes, I have my best friend with whom I share everything.

Q.2 Some people have moved so far away from the forest, that they can't understand the lives of forest people. Some even call them 'jungli'. Why is it not correct to say this?

Ans. The word 'jungli' is a negative word to refer to someone who is recognised as uncivilised. Forest people have their own culture, songs, dance and language. Their culture is different and unique. They are living in a way which is distinct from ours. So, calling them jungli is wrong.

Q.3 What do you know about how adivasis live? Write and draw a picture.

Ans. Adivasis live in a very simple way. They are simple people who live in jungles, wear simple clothes. They also wear costumes made of leaves and flowers during their festivals. They depend on the forest and its products for their survival.

They leave their animals in the forest for grazing and they also collect leaves to make different things with them.

Q.4 Do you have an adivasi friend? What have you learnt about the forest from her?

Ans. Yes, I have an adivasi friend. She lives in my colony. She is a very clever and intelligent girl.

I have learnt many things about the forest from her. She helped me in identifying different trees and plants. I also learnt about making medicines from herbs. She told me that many beautiful items can be made from fallen leaves.

Think (Page 187)

Q.1 Do you know of any one who works to save forests?

Ans. Yes, in my neighbourhood, a group of people run an NGO for the protection of forests.

Q.2 What is your dream? What will you do to make your dream come true?

Ans. I want to work for the society and environment by making it clean and helping to protect it. I will work hard and open an NGO one day.

Q.3 Collect reports about forests from newspapers. Did you find any news about how the cutting down of forests affects the weather? How?

Ans. Yes, I found many reports about cutting down forests and how it affects the weather.

I learnt that less forests leads to less rainfall in an area. This leads to a summer which lasts longer.

Q.4 In 'Torang' Suryamani does a lot to keep the Kuduk music, dance and traditions alive. Would you like to do something like this for your community? What would you like to keep alive?

Ans. Yes, I want to do something like this for my community. I want to preserve the traditional food and painting style of my community.

Read and Tell (Page 187)

Sikhya, a Class X girl in Odisha, wrote a letter to the Chief Minister. Read a part of the letter.

A forest is everything for us adivasis. We can't live away from the forests even for a day. Government has started many projects in the name of development–dams and factories are being built. Forests, which are ours, are being taken away from us. Because of the these projects, we need to think where the forest people will go and what will happen to their livelihood? Where will the lakhs of animals living in the forests go? If there are no forests, and we dig out our lands for minerals like aluminium, what will be left? Only polluted air, water and miles and miles of barren land ... .

Q.1 Is there any factory or some construction work going on in and around your area? What type of work?

Ans. Yes, a new flyover is under construction in my area and the roads are being repaired.

Q.2 Due to the factory is there any effect on the trees and land? Have the people in that area raised this issue?

Ans. Yes, in my area, there is a factory. A lot of smoke and dust comes out from that factory which causes pollution. People also face difficulty in breathing. Most of the trees and plants have died. People have started raising concerns on this issue.

Look at the Map and Write (Page 188-189)

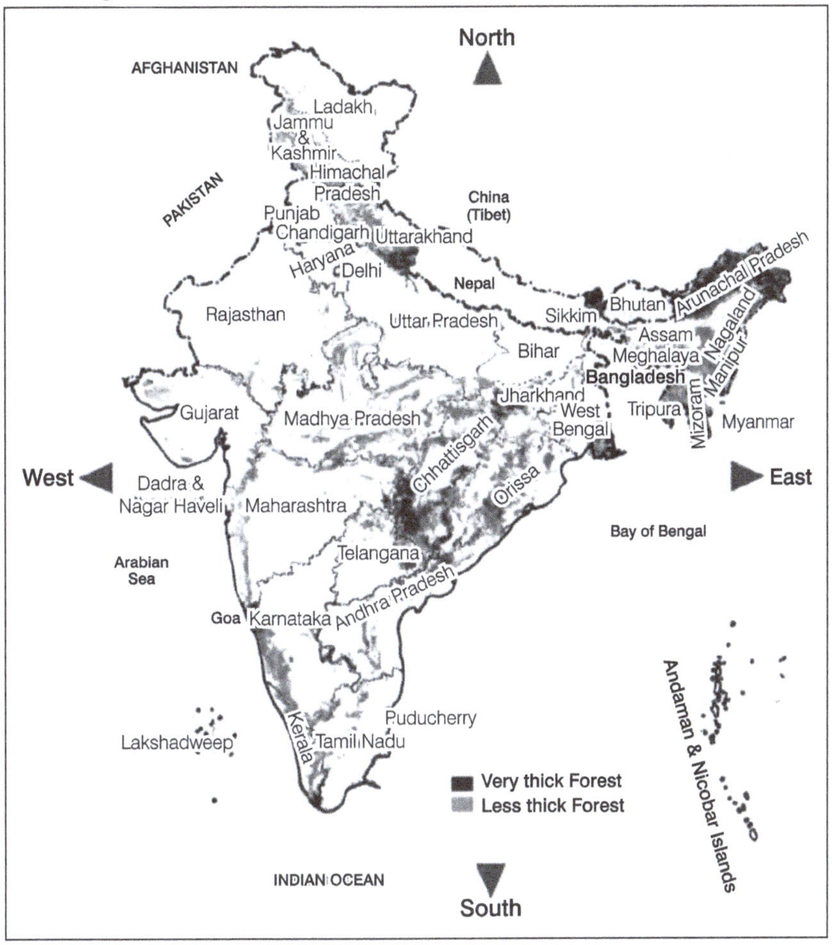

Note : See NCERT page no. 188-189 for coloured Map.

Q.1 What all is shown in the map?

Ans. Areas with very thick forests and less thick forests are shown on this map of India.

Q.2 You have read Sikhya's letter. Look for Orissa in the map.

Ans. Orissa in the South-Eastern coastal part of India. It is situated near West Bengal.

Q.3 Is there a sea close to Orissa? How did you find out?

Ans. Yes, the Bay of Bengal is close to Orissa. I could see it on the map.

Q.4 Which are the states which have the sea on one side?

Ans. West Bengal, Orissa, Andhra Pradesh, Tamil Nadu, Kerala, Goa, Maharashtra and Gujarat are the states which have the sea on one side.

Q.5 Where is Suryamani's state Jharkhand on the map?

Ans. Jharkhand is located at the North of Orissa and South of Bihar.

Q.6 Where are forests on the map? How will you find these?

Ans. Forests are there in all states in India. Some states have more forest area, others have less. They are shown by green colour in the map.

Q.7 How can you find out which states have very thick forests and which have less thick forests?

Ans. Dark green colour shows the states which have very thick forests. Light green shows the states with less thick forests.

Q.8 For someone in Madhya Pradesh, in which direction would the country's thickest forests be? Name those states.

Ans. For someone in Madhya Pradesh, the country's thickest forests would be in the North and the East direction. The states are Arunachal Pradesh, Uttarakhand, Jharkhand and Chhattisgarh.

Find Out (Page 190)

Q.1 Which are the states around Mizoram?

Ans. The states around Mizoram are Assam, Tripura and Manipur.

Q.2 Chamui said they measure land using tin. Which are the other ways of measuring land?

Ans. Land can be measured in *bigha*, yards, square metres, etc.

Q.3 Returning from school, children drank water in a bamboo cup. Who do you think would have made this cup and kept it in the forest? Why?

Ans. Forest people (*adivasis*) would have made this cup. They would have made the cups to help the people passing from the forests.

Q.4 What could be done to save forests?

Ans. Following steps could be taken to save forests

- Regulating the cutting and planting of trees
- Controlling the forest fires
- Afforestation measures
- Proper utilisation of forests and its products

Page 191

Q.1 Find out more about the 'cheraw' dance. Do it in your class. But be careful and don't hurt yourself.

Ans. Cheraw is one of the traditional and oldest dances of Mizoram. It is performed by an individual or family in most of their festivals and big occasions. It is also performed on marriage occasions.

In this dance, four people sit face to face on the ground, and tap and beat long pairs of bamboo sticks in a rhythmic beat. Girls in colourful Mizo costumes dance in and out between the bamboo sticks. Gongs and drums are used for music.

What we have Learnt (Page 191)

Q.1 What is similar and what is different between Jhoom farming and Bhaskerbhai's way of farming?

Ans. Both Bhaskerbhai and Jhoom farming used organic manures such as weeds and dried leaves.

The difference is that the weeds are burnt in Jhoom farming and ashes are mixed with the soil. In Bhakserbhai's method, he uses plant waste to prepare manure. Bhaskerbhai ploughs the land but in Jhoom farming, the land is lightly dug up.

Q.2 Explain in your own words why forests are important for the people living in forests.

Ans. Forests are a source of livelihood for people living in forests. They get firewood from the forests to cook food. They make many products from forest leaves to sell in the market and earn money. The life of adivasis is dependent on forests.

Q.3 Did you find something interesting in Jhoom farming? What is it?

Ans. Some of the things I found interesting in Jhoom farming are

- Mixing the ash with the soil acts as a natural fertiliser.
- Mixed crops are grown together in Jhoom farming.

CHAPTER 21 LIKE FATHER, LIKE DAUGHTER

About the Chapter

This chapter is about how we share some traits with our parents and relatives, and it gives us information about twins. We can get some qualities from our parents like Ashima sneezes like her father. We can also look like our distant relatives, like Nilima, whose hair is similar to her cousin Kiran's.

Twins are two children born on the same day from the same mother. They often look alike but can be different in some ways. For example, Saroj and Suvasini are twin sisters who are similar but also different in many ways. Some diseases, like polio, do not pass from parents to their children. So if a parent has polio, it won't affect their kids. A scientist named Gregor Mendel studied pea plants and found that their seeds and colours are often like their parent plants.

GLOSSARY

Limp Hair that is lacking volume and bounce and appear flat.
Distant Someone not closely related to you.
Monk A man who is a spiritual leader of a religious group.

NCERT FOLDER

Fill in the Table (Page 192)

Q.1 Ashima sneezed just like her father. Do you have any such habit or trait which is similar to that of someone in your family? What is it? Whom is it similar to?

Your special habit or trait	Whom is it similar to?

Ans.

Your special habit or trait	Whom is it similar to?
Walking	Father
Voice	Mother
Sneezing	Brother

Tell (Page 193)

Q.1 Does your face or anything else look similar to that of someone else in your family? What is it?

Ans. Yes, some parts of my face look similar to that of someone else in my family. They are:

- My nose is sharp and pointed like my father.
- My eye colour matches with my mother.
- The shape of my ears is like my grandmother.

Q.2 Did someone tell you this or did you find it out yourself?

Ans. Many of my friends and relatives have told me about this.

Q.3 How do you feel when people compare you with someone else in your family? Why do you feel so?

Ans. I feel very happy and good when people compare me with someone else in my family. I feel that I am a part of a great family.

Q.4 Who laughs the loudest in your family? Laugh like that person.

Ans. My *mama* (mother's brother) laughs the loudest in my family.

Page 193

Q.1 Make a list of all the family members from Nilima's *nani* to little Samir. How are they all related to Nilima? Write.

Ans. The list of Nilima's family members is as follows

- **Nani** Nilima's grandmother (mother's mother)
- **Eldest Nani** Nilima's nani's sister
- **Elder son of Nani** Nilima's mama (mother's brother)
- **Kiran** Nilima's cousin (Mama's daughter)
- **Samir** Nilima's nephew (Kiran's son)

Find Out (Page 193)

Q.1 In your family are there any such examples of uncle–nephews or brother-sisters, where there is a big difference in the age? Find out from your elders.

Ans. Yes, two of my *mamas* (mother's cousin brothers) are of same age as me. My real mama is older. My own nephew is of my age.

Find Out and Write (Page 194)

Does Nilima have curly hair like her *nani's*? Now you look for some special trait in your sister or brother (could also be cousins). Like the colour of eyes, dimples in cheeks, height, broad or sharp nose, voice, etc. See if this trait comes from the father's side or the mother's side. Make this table in your notebook and fill it. An example is given.

Special trait	Whom does it resemble	From whose side?	
		Mother's	Father's
Nilima's curly hair	her *nani* (grandmother)		

Ans.

Special trait	Whom does it resemble	From whose side?	
		Mother's	Father's
Nilima's curly hair	her *nani* (grandmother	✓	
My brother's eyes	his *mama*	✓	
My brother's ears	his *bua*		✓
My brother's voice	his *chacha*		✓

Q.1 Have you seen a very young child in your (or any other) family? Whom does the child's eyes, nose, hair or fingers look like in the family? Write their names.

Ans. Yes, my cousin's daughter has some traits like her family members. For example, her eyes - resembles her father; her dimples- resembles her grandfather; her nose - resembles her mother.

Q.2 Nimila's hair is like her *nani's* — thick and curly. Nilima's mother has straight, brown and limp hair? What type of hair do you have – black or brown, oily or dry?

Ans. I have oily and brown hair.

Q.3 What is the colour of your hair? Measure and write the length of your hair.

Ans. The colour of my hair is brown. My hair are 35 cm long.

Q.4 Is your hair like that of anyone else in your family? If yes, then name the person.

Ans. Yes, my hair is like my mother's.

Q.5 Measure the hair of other members of your family.

Ans. Do it yourself.

Q.6 Who has the longest hair in your family?

Ans. My *mausi* has the longest hair in my family.

Q.7 How many people do you know whose hair is longer than one metre? Does having long hair run in their family?

Ans. My friend's mother has hair longer than one metre. Yes, having long hair runs in their family.

Q.8 Do you know how to measure your height? Measure yourself from head to toe and write how tall you are.

Ans. Yes, I know how to measure my height. It can be measured using a measuring tape. My height is about 115 cm.

Q.9 How tall do you think you will be when you grow up? Is anyone else in your family of the same height?

Ans. I think I will be about 6 feet in height when I grow up. My father is 6 feet tall.

Q.10 Measure the height of your family members and write it down.

Ans. Do it yourself.

Discuss (Page 196)

Q.1 What is similar between Saroja and Suvasini? What is different between them?

Ans. Both Saroja and Suvasini look so similar that they are almost like mirror images. They are twin sisters.

The difference between them is the language they speak. Saroja can speak both Marathi and Tamil but Suvasini can only speak Tamil.

Q.2 Do you know any twins? What is similar in them? How are they different?

Ans. Yes, there are two twin brothers in my swimming class. They look very similar and have the same features.

They are different as one of the twins wears spectacles while the other does not.

Q.4 Do you know of twins who don't look the same?

Ans. Yes, there are twin sister and brother in my neighbourhood. They look different from each other.

Page 198

Q.1 Have you read or heard anything about polio? Where?

Ans. Yes, I have read about polio in books, newspapers and hoardings.

Q.2 Have you read or heard any news about 'pulse polio'? What?

Ans. Yes, I have read about pulse polio in the newspaper. It is a programme run by the government to eliminate polio from the country. Under this programme, vaccination camps are organised every month where every child under the age of five years is given polio drops for free.

Q.3 Do you know of anyone who has polio?

Ans. Yes, one of my friends has polio.

Page 199

Q.1 Are there people in your house who talk loudly? Is it their habit, or they cannot also hear very well?

Ans. My *mama* and my grandfather talk very loudly. My *mama* does it out of habit. My grandfather cannot hear very well.

Q.2 Are there times when you do not talk loudly in front of some people? When? With whom? Why? When can you speak loudly?

Ans. Yes, there are times when I do not talk loudly. I talk softly in front of my parents, uncle and aunt and my brother. I respect my elders and I do not raise my voice. I have to speak loudly in front of my grandparents because they cannot hear properly.

Q.3 Some people use a machine in their ear to help them hear better. Some use a stick or spectacles to help them in other ways. Do you know someone who does so?

Ans. Yes, my *bua* and grandfather use a machine in her ear to help her hear better. My *mausi* uses spectacles.

Q.4 Talk to people who cannot hear very well. Find out if they had this problem from birth. When did they start to have a problem with hearing? What difficulties do they face?

Ans. My grandfather cannot hear properly. The problem started around eight years ago. It is due to his old age.

Due to hearing problems, he cannot enjoy watching television and he cannot talk well on the phone. It is also difficult for him to walk on the road because he cannot hear the sound of vehicles.

What we have Learnt (Page 199)

Q.1 What do you think–what all is a part of you that you got from your mother's side?

Ans. I have got the following features from my mother's eyes.

- The colour of eyes is the same as my mother's eyes.
- My hair is like my *mausi's* hair.
- My nose is like my *mama*.

CHAPTER 22

ON THE MOVE AGAIN

About the Chapter

This chapter is about some people and their families who had to migrate to work in sugarcane fields and the challenges they face. Dhanu lives in a village where his family celebrates festivals together. They work on big farmers' land until Dussehra. After that, for six months, they borrow money from Mukadam, an agent for sugarcane factories, to help them find work. During this time, the children leave school to help their families near the sugarcane fields and factories, while older and sick family members stay back.

The families work hard every day, collecting sugarcane and getting receipts for their work. The agent checks these receipts to settle the loan. He also gives them money for food and other needs for the next week. Dhanu's uncle and aunt want him to study hard so he can get a good job in the future.

GLOSSARY

Puranpoli A sweet *roti* made by filling it with bengal gram (*chana dal*) and jaggery (dark brown sugar).

Loan It is the money taken or given in advance.

Caravan A group of people travelling from one place to another.

Receipt A written proof of something that you or sell.

NCERT FOLDER

Tell (Page 201)

Q.1 Did all the farmers in Dhanu's village have their own land?

Ans. No, only some farmers in Dhanu's village have their own land. Others work on the lands of big farmers.

Q.2 During what time of the year did Dhanu's family get work in the village? During what time did they not have work?

Ans. Dhanu's family got work in the village before the rainy season till Dussehra. The remaining six months, when there was no rain, they did not have work.

Q.3 Do you know of any families like Dhanu's, who have to leave their villages for months in search of work?

Ans. Yes, I know many families who have left their villages for months in search of work.

Think and Find Out (Page 201)

Q.1 If people in Dhanu's village did not leave the village in search of work, what difficulties would they face in their own village?

Ans. If people did not leave the village in search of work, they would face many difficulties. They would not be able to earn money for their needs like food, clothes, shelter, etc. Their children will not be able to go to school.

Q.2 In Dhanu's village, there can be no farming when there is no rain. Do you think farming can be done even without rain water? How?

Ans. Yes, farming can be done without rainwater. There are new methods of supplying water to the farms like canals, tubewells, etc.

Think (Page 202)

Q.1 Dhanu's family and many others from the village go far away for work but some people stay back in the village. Why does this happen?

Ans. Some people stay back in the village to take care of the houses and the cattle. Some elderly people, who are sick, and small children also stay back because they cannot travel and work.

Q.2 When Dhanu and other children leave the village for six months, what happens in the village school?

Ans. The students of big farmers study in the village school when Dhanu and other children leave the village.

Q.3 What arrangements are made at your home for old and unwell family members when everyone goes for work?

Ans. In my home, we have a caretaker who takes care of the old and unwell family members when everyone goes for work.

Think and Tell (Page 204)

Q.1 Why does *mami* wish that Dhanu should go to school for the whole year and study?

Ans. Mami wishes that Dhanu should go to school to study well so that he can get a good job.

She wishes for Dhanu to get rich and earn respect in the society. She does not want him to face problems that their family faces.

Q.2 What happens when you are not able to go to school for a long time?

Ans. When I do not go to school for a long time, I find it tough to understand difficult lessons.

Discuss and Write (Page 204)

Q.1 Dhanu has to go with his village people to other places. Can there be some arrangements during that time so that Dhanu continues his studies? What kind?

Ans. Yes, Dhanu can get enrolled in a distance education school. He can also go to school at the new place where he moves to.

He can continue his studies in an evening school also. It could be a government school.

Q.2 Do you know of any jobs/work for which people have to stay away from their families for many months? Look for examples from this book and write.

Ans. Yes, there are many jobs for which people have to stay away from their families for many months. Some of them are

- Jobs in the military and armed forces. Overseas jobs
- Studying or teaching in boarding school

Q.3 What are the similarities and differences in the lives of different kinds of farmers?

Ans. Similarities

- All farmers are dependent on farming for earning money.
- The family members are engaged in farming.
- They do not study much so they are illiterate.
- They depend on rainfall for irrigation.

Differences

- Some farmers have their own land.
- Some of them use modern techniques of irritation.
- Some are educated.

What we have Learnt (Page 204)

Q.1 You have read about many kinds of farmers in different lessons in this book. Fill the table.

Name of the farmer	Owns land (✓ or ✗)	What do they grow	What difficulties they face	Anything else
1. Damijibhai (Lesson ....)				
2. Hasmukh (Lesson ....)				

Ans.

Name of the farmer	Owns land (✓ or ✗)	What do they grow	What difficulties they face	Anything else
1. Damijibhai (Lesson 19)	✓	Foodgrains, like wheat, bajra, rice, jowar, etc.	Not much	He could easily get food for home.
2. Hasmukh (Lesson 19)	✓	Items like wheat and cotton which give profit	He has to face the high cost of seeds and fertilisers. The soil is not fertile due to overuse. Loans become too high.	Hasmukh is always irritated. Hasmukh's son has left farming and is driving a truck.